The Van Dongen Nobody Knows

Early and Fauvist Drawings 1895-1912

Boijmans Van Beuningen Museum, Rotterdam
November 2, 1996 - January 5, 1997

Musée des Beaux-Arts, Lyons
January 23 - April 6, 1997

Institut Néerlandais, Paris
April 17, 1997 - June 8, 1997

The Van Dongen Nobody Knows

Early and Fauvist Drawings 1895-1912

Anita Hopmans

Patron
Madame Marie-Claire van Dongen

Organizing committee
Boijmans Van Beuningen Museum Rotterdam
Chris Dercon, director
Manfred Sellink, printroom curator
Anita Hopmans, guest curator

Musée des Beaux-Arts de Lyon
Philippe Durey, director
Christian Briend, curator

Institut Néerlandais Paris
Mària van Berge-Gerbaud, director Fondation Custodia

Contents

Foreword

This catalogue and exhibition, dedicated to Kees van Dongen's early work on paper, raises an obvious question: why, after the successful retrospective of Van Dongen's work held in Rotterdam in 1989, and Paris in 1990, should we once again consider this artist's work?

These monographic shows convincingly demonstrated that Van Dongen's early work possesses an individual strength and originality which amply justify his ranking among the most important artists of his day. However, they also revealed an exceptional number of gaps in our knowledge of Van Dongen's early artistic views, and the early work he produced in Rotterdam and Paris. These exhibitions also raised questions about Van Dongen's place within Fauvism, and his relation to the work of artists such as Matisse, Picasso or even Vincent van Gogh. The most serious lacuna proved to be our lack of information about his drawings. This was a side to Van Dongen that nobody knew.

Prompted by these considerations, art historian Anita Hopmans suggested that a separate exhibition should be devoted to this aspect of Kees van Dongen's oeuvre, at the same time focusing attention on the artistic milieu in which the artist worked. It is thanks to her diligence and detective work that we have been able to produce this exhibition and catalogue. An ambitious project which is based on the outstanding importance of the drawings on display, and the wealth of information assembled by Anita Hopmans.

The catalogue provides us with an entirely new picture of the first twenty years in Van Dongen's artistic career, thereby shedding new light on the development of his oeuvre. Hopmans comes to the surprising yet persuasive conclusion that Kees van Dongen actually began his career as a pure draughtsman: his later drawings were produced in fascinating interaction with his celebrated, pioneering Fauvist paintings, which they sometimes even anticipated. A large number of previously unknown, unpublished drawings surfaced during the long period of preparation for this exhibition, thereby offering fresh proof of Kees van Dongen's unique artistry.

There are obvious grounds for showing Kees van Dongen's drawings in Boijmans Van Beuningen Museum. The museum has always had a good relationship with the Rotterdam-born artist; its Printroom is lucky enough to possess the largest group of Van Dongen drawings held in a public collection anywhere in the world: a wealth largely acquired through Van Dongen's own gift to the museum. After Rotterdam the exhibition will transfer to the Musée des Beaux-Arts in Lyons, one of the first museums in France to acquire drawings by Van Dongen. The show will then go to the Institut Néerlandais in Paris, which provided a kind of home base for Van Dongen, who was so influenced by the artistic traditions of both the Netherlands and France. Interestingly, Frits Lugt's famous drawing collection which is housed in the Institut Néerlandais, contains an important group of letters from Kees van Dongen.

Clearly an ambitious project such as *The Van Dongen Nobody Knows* can only be realized through the enormous efforts of a large number of people. We would like to express our gratitude to the many collectors throughout the world, often private individuals, for generously loaning us their valuable works of art; we are particularly indebted to those collectors who have loaned us a large number of works. We are also extremely grateful to Madame Marie-Claire van Dongen – the artist's widow – for agreeing to act as patron of the exhibition; we much appreciate her cooperation during preparation of both the show and this catalogue. The Stichting VSB Fonds and Zilveren Kruis Ziekenfondsen provided vital support. Their generous contributions enabled us to present this exhibition – and the catalogue, splendidly designed by Gracia Lebbink – to the public in a manner befitting Kees van Dongen the artist. We are also indebted to the Mondrian Foundation, a Dutch fund for the promotion of art, design and museum activities, for their support of this project.

Finally, our gratitude goes to Anita Hopmans whose unflagging enthusiasm has provided the inspiration for this project. It is thanks to her dedication that this important chapter in the life of Kees van Dongen, and thus the history of Fauvism, has been radically rewritten.

Chris Dercon
Director of the Boijmans Van Beuningen Museum

Philippe Durey
Director of the Musée des Beaux-Arts de Lyon

Lionel Veer
Director of the Institut Néerlandais

Acknowledgments

'Little is known about the early work of Kees van Dongen,' were the opening words of my request for a research subsidy which I submitted in 1990. I planned to study the early ambitions of Kees van Dongen as a draughtsman and to show the link between this and his contribution to Fauvist painting. I am most grateful to the Netherlands Organization for Scientific Research (NWO) for the grant that made it possible to carry out this work and ultimately to present the exhibition *The Van Dongen Nobody Knows*.

At Rotterdam's Boijmans Van Beuningen Museum the two curators of the Printroom, Bram Meij and Manfred Sellink, reacted positively to the project. Thanks to them, and with support from the NWO, I was appointed guest curator for the Van Dongen project which was able to grow into an undertaking of international stature. It was due to the efforts of Chris Dercon, director of the Boijmans Van Beuningen Museum, Johan R. ter Molen, former acting director of Boijmans, Philippe Durey, director of the Musée des Beaux-Arts de Lyon, and Mària van Berge-Gerbaud, director of the Fondation Custodia, that exhibition and catalogue gained their final splendid form. I hope that a great many people will enjoy them to the full.

With enormous involvement, the artist's widow, Madame Marie-Claire van Dongen, has assisted us in our preparations. It was thanks to her exceptional cooperation that I was able to trace a number of important works by Van Dongen. I am extremely grateful to her. I take this opportunity to thank the many who have so generously assisted me during the preparation of this work. I gained greatly from the wisdom of Professor Evert van Uitert of the University of Amsterdam. At the Boijmans Van Beuningen Museum I was assisted by the unfailing enthusiasm of Maartje de Haan, deputy curator of the Printroom, who together with her assistants helped me with the stupendous task of the correspondence involved in this project, with organizing the loans of the works, and with internal organization in the museum. I also experienced great support from Christian Briend, curator at the Musée des Beaux-Arts de Lyon, who helped to organize the exhibition to be held in France. In preparing the catalogue I had the good fortune to have Gracia Lebbink as designer, while for the English translation Wendie Shaffer and her team combined to produce a truly admirable book. I cannot conclude without mentioning the sterling assistance from Rudi Ekkart and Jan Teeuwisse, Hans Buijs, Guy-Patrice and Michel Dauberville, Ronald Dorn, Quentin Laurens, Marie-Cécile Commerre, and in particular Jacqueline Boucher and Ellen Melas Kyriazi, and finally the staff of the many museums, libraries, archives, auction rooms and art dealers' who at countless moments and in countless ways have contributed to the realization of this endeavour.

Anita Hopmans
Guest curator

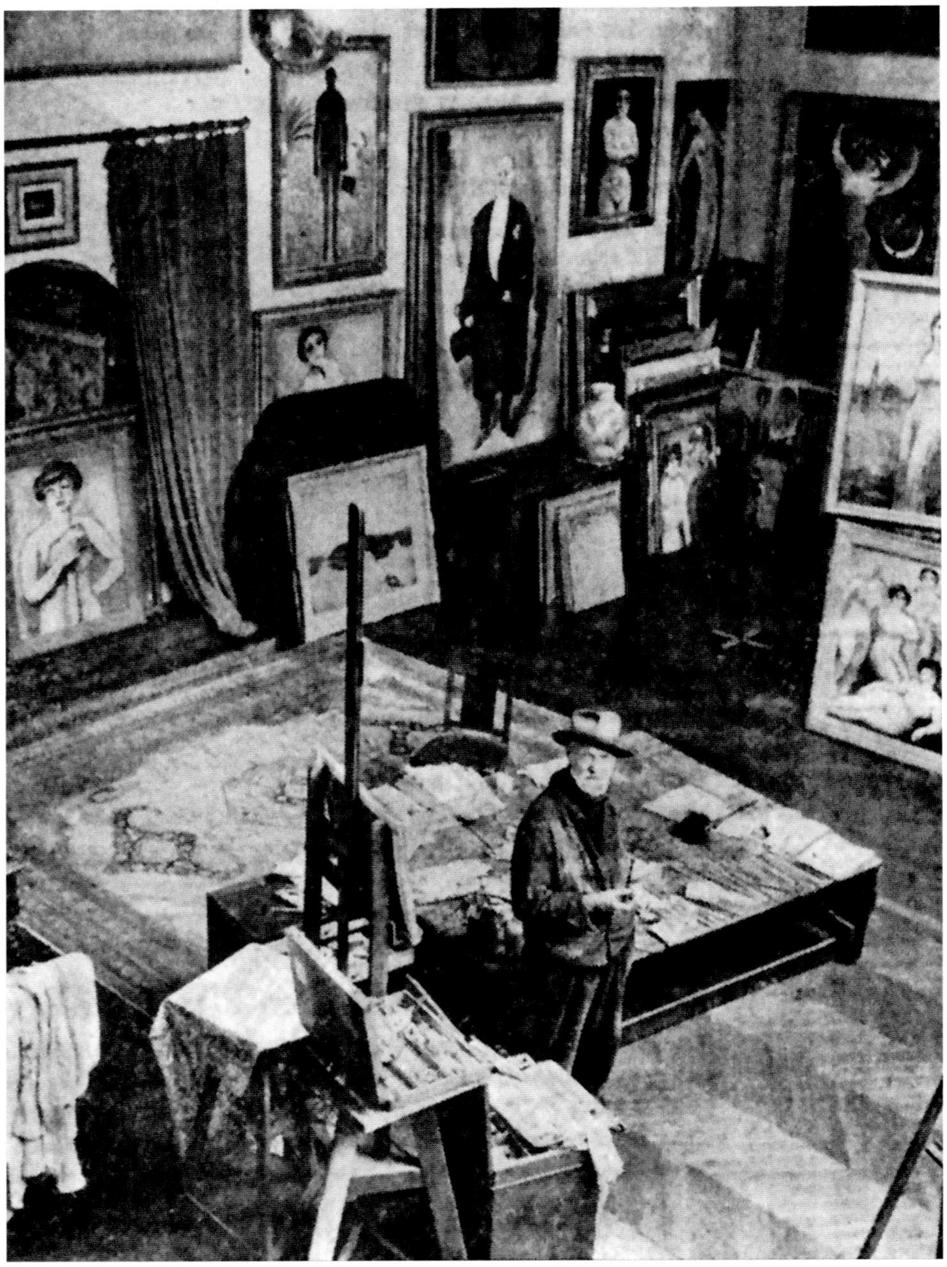

1.
Van Dongen in his studio, 1952
75, rue de Courcelles, Paris

The Van Dongen Nobody Knows

The artist Kees van Dongen (1877-1968) is known as being the Dutch painter who very sensibly left his native land at an early age to work in Paris, where after a somewhat difficult start he gained fame and fortune. He is known for his colourful Fauvist canvases, his portraits of international figures and the Parisian beau monde and possibly above all for his female nudes which were on occasion judged to be too outrageous, and even obscene.

For a long time his later success overshadowed his Fauvist beginnings. Not until the 1950s, when early Modern Art underwent a general reappraisal, was there a revival of interest in Van Dongen's early work.[1] This was directly influenced by exhibitions of his work in postwar Paris. In 1949 there was a retrospective of his paintings at Galerie Charpentier which was acclaimed as 'the high point of the season'. There followed an exhibition in 1952 of about twenty early works, organized by Galerie de Berri, which again described Van Dongen as a Fauvist, indeed, one who was 'avant la lettre'.[2] The ticklish question of whether or not the artist should be labelled a Fauvist was hereby answered in the affirmative for the time being, even though there was little factual evidence to support the decision.[3] The direct result of the exhibitions was that subsequently Van Dongen was represented at every international show dealing with Fauvism – which had certainly not been the case before.[4] Photographs of Van Dongen's studio from this period show the walls resplendent with Fauvist canvases. (fig.1)

However, hidden by the mist of time there is yet another period, covering Van Dongen's early years in Rotterdam and Paris. There is little information about these years. It seems that at this time, roughly between 1896/7 and 1904, Van Dongen's main production was drawings. The question arises: how did Van Dongen develop from being a draughtsman to a Fauvist painter? From the monograph of 1967 by Louis Chaumeil, which despite later emendations still remains the standard work, it emerges that in his early years Van Dongen made a great many drawings and illustrations; but Chaumeil only referred to a few of these, citing thereby a small number of references from the press.[5] He described about ten early drawings and illustrations. After the publication of this retrospective work, scarcely any complementary new research on the artist appeared. At the recent retrospective exhibitions in Rotterdam in 1989 and Paris in 1990 from which a broader understanding of Van Dongen's work could be gained than had been the case for a long time, a few drawings were displayed and the artist's draughtsmanship was mentioned, although a clear picture of this facet of his work was missing. Whatever the paucity of information about Van Dongen's contribution to Fauvism, this is as nothing compared with the entire lack of documentation about his drawings. Furthermore, it is far from clear what connection should be made between the ambitions Van Dongen had as draughtsman and those he had as painter. So far only general descriptions have been given of his development as an artist.

To a large extent Van Dongen created this situation himself. As he became successful he cultivated the image of the intuitive artist who has not attended art school and has no artistic training. In around 1914 the journalist Gustave Coquiot asked him to describe his development as an artist. Van Dongen replied with an oblique reference to nature – how does a tree grow, how does an idea grow?[6] He referred to himself as someone predestined to be a painter, and to work following the laws of nature and instinct. 'I paint what I see', without reference to theories or other artists.[7] The only artist with whom Van Dongen chose to link his name was Rembrandt, and in 1927 he published a highly personal biography of his fellow countryman. This reiterated Van Dongen's notion of the intuitive genius, following his own path unimpeded by schools or teachers.[8]

From the 1920s on Van Dongen organized exhibitions of his work in his own studio.[9] These only presented his most recent pieces. 'For him, what has been completed is already dead. He is always thinking of future work.' So concluded Des Courières the first monograph on Van Dongen, published in 1925.[10] This book, on which Van Dongen collaborated, is full of acclaim for the artist. It contains scarcely any illustrations of his early work. It acquired something of the nature of a propaganda piece and was placed in the room where Van Dongen's paintings were hanging. It was to be recommended, observed a subsequent author, Paul Fierens, not to ask Van Dongen questions requiring an additional answer. 'Above all, don't ask him to give the date of a certain portrait, or to explain a certain allegorical work.'[11]

In addition, there were the highly successful parties given by Van Dongen and his friend Jasmy (Léo Jacob) during the 1920s and 30s in the huge building on rue Juliette Lambert – leading, incidentally, on more than one occasion to a commission for a portrait. These too contributed to Van Dongen's image as a city swell, a kind of Great Gatsby from the Low Countries.[12] Reminiscences by his contemporaries appear strongly tinted by those days of roses and wine.[13] In an interview in 1953 with the writer Francis Carco, Matisse was explaining his method of working at the beginning of the century and referred in contrast to Van Dongen, who, he said, had drawn the dancing women in the Moulin de la Galette while he was walking behind them.[14] Fernande Olivier recalls that Van Dongen made such drawings in order to sell them to illustrated magazines, something that Picasso did not stoop to. This comment fits into the image forming, and is still cited to this day.[15]

Thus the image of Van Dongen as a successful but untrained and not profoundly serious artist flourished for many years. The more so because its foundations were laid at the beginning of this century. In the foreword written by Félix Fénéon for Van Dongen's debut exhibition in Paris in 1904 at Galerie Vollard, the critic stated that Van Dongen had attended art school with little enthusiasm, and he proclaimed (too) early that the chief theme of the young artist's work was the female nude. This in fact contradicted what was on show at the exhibition – largely landscapes and cityscapes. Van Dongen himself had contributed to the angle of Fénéon's essay by mentioning in a letter to the latter that he had journeyed to Paris in a 'train de plaisir', that he had lived in Rotterdam's red light district and had been rebuffed from his circle of Rotterdam friends because of a drawing he had made of a nude.[16] After mentioning a few more points Van Dongen concluded his letter by saying that otherwise he had forgotten everything 'nor do I consider it necessary to recall those days.' This gave Fénéon the opportunity to describe one of the few nudes in the exhibition, *The descent of Ishtar*, in great detail as typical of Van Dongen's work.[17] With this description Fénéon, doubtless intentionally, concluded his introduction to the catalogue.

In strident contrast is the picture that emerges from the early memories of some of the friends of Van Dongen's youth. The poet and singer Johan Hendrik (Koos) Speenhoff who knew Van Dongen in around 1900 in Rotterdam, describes him as a hard-working, quiet and sober young man, already a good friend of the woman he was to marry in 1901, Guus Preitinger.[18] Speenhoff recounts that Van Dongen was his opposite: 'a hermit, a total abstainer, a maid of Orleans', someone with strikingly little interest in the 'girls of easy virtue' who worked in the factory and with whom Speenhoff enjoyed 'a great deal of human pleasure'. Another fellow Rotterdammer in his memories of Van Dongen describes a visit he made to the artist's former studio in Delfshaven in about 1899 where he saw 'huge piles of sheets of cheap lining paper' covered with sketches, '...thousands of large sheets of paper filled with sketches of fragments such as parts of the human body. Hands, arms, legs, feet...all just line drawings.'[19] When Van Dongen leafed through these 'scribbled' sketches, which were recent drawings and clearly not anatomical studies, he described them as 'the real work', as the basis for his art. He emerges from this story as a studious artist who was interested in practising and improving his freehand drawing.

DRAWINGS

That there was a genuine appreciation for the early drawings of Van Dongen appears from the fact that in 1907 three of these were presented by an (unfortunately anonymous) donor to the drawing collection of the Berlin Nationalgalerie.[20] It is also note- cat. 54, 81, 82
worthy that as early as 1917 the Musée des Beaux-Arts in Lyon, under its director Henri Focillon, bought by means of a separate fund four early drawings by Van Dongen, making him to this day one of the few early modern masters to be represented in the museum's drawing collection.[21] The Boijmans Van Beuningen Museum owns a relatively cat. 50, 84, 85
large number of Van Dongen's drawings, in total 43. These were presented to the museum – with the exception of some sheets – in December 1936 by Van Dongen, shortly after the then director, Dirk Hannema, had visited the artist in his Paris studio. This meeting took place after the museum had acquired the portrait of Rappoport by Van Dongen.[22] The generous gift of drawings, sent 'in a little box', turned out to contain a cross-section of Van Dongen's work as a draughtsman. The drawings date from various periods, predominately that in Rotterdam. cat. 7, 10-12, 15

At his first solo exhibitions Van Dongen would always display both paintings and drawings. When asked for a sample of his work, in the early days he would show both drawings and paintings. For example, there is the sample selection he sent in 1905 to the art dealer Buffa, or the one he assembled for a prospective exhibition at the Rotterdam Kunstkring (a society of artists and art-lovers) in 1906.[23] Also in that year, the first purchase of Van Dongen's work by Félix Fénéon for the Paris art dealers Bernheim-Jeune, consisted of five paintings together with about fourteen early watercolours and drawings. Indeed, in 1906 there appears to have been a discussion about whether to hold an exhibition of his drawings in Galerie Bernheim Jeune.[24] This did not materialize, but in 1907 there was an exhibition in Amsterdam at the art dealer's C.M. van Gogh, entirely devoted to Van Dongen's drawings. It was only after his successes of 1908 that Van Dongen presented himself in public more or less solely as a painter. Not until the retrospectives held at Galerie Charpentier in 1942 and 1949 did his early drawings and watercolours once more emerge. Many of the sheets shown here can be traced back to these exhibitions. Largely through auctions and in a few cases later solo exhibitions, Van Dongen's drawings became scattered – chiefly among private collectors.

Most of the works on show here are undated. In this connection the complaint made by the critic Goujon in 1909 is frequently cited, namely that the chronology of Van Dongen's work is as difficult to piece together as is that of a Flemish Primitive. The artist, so noted the critic, in contrast to Matisse had made no documentation of his work: 'Van Dongen made not the slightest effort either to date or to catalogue his work.'[25] However, in connection with his first exhibitions he did in fact give dates to some of his early work and these dates provide something to hold on to. Also, several of his drawings that were published as illustrations in magazines can thereby be dated. However, it is no simple task to acquire an overview of either his drawings or his painted oeuvre. Like other modern artists Van Dongen would sometimes ante-date some of his paintings, and some of his early pieces were very difficult to trace because he cut the canvas into sections and sold these separately.[26] More significantly, his later fame together with the lacunae in knowledge about the dating of his work meant that from time to time work appeared on the market bearing his (false) signature, and remained in circulation as being 'real' Van Dongens.

Thus Goujon's complaint from 1909 referred to above has gained significance. However, with some additional research we can establish the general outline of how Van Dongen's work developed. The present catalogue provides a first answer to questions such as where are we to place the artist's early ambitions as a draughtsman, and what exactly was his connection with the avant-garde of his time? Against this background it is Van Dongen's concern with draughtsmanship and free expressive drawing that emerge as being of particular importance.

I. Early Years in Rotterdam: a painter's debut

'He doesn't tell me about any teacher, any patron, or anyone who encouraged or inspired him.'[27] This was the comment of the writer Paul Guth in 1949 and sums up the state of affairs concerning information about Van Dongen's early years. Guth visited the artist in his studio in connection with the retrospective held in the spring of that year at Galerie Charpentier, in order to gain some background information for an article he was going to write. He only managed to extract fragments of memories from the artist, who told him a little about the place Delfshaven where he was born on 27 January 1877. Van Dongen also spoke of his parents and then talked about details of his wanderings through the streets of Paris, small jobs he had on the side, his early drawings and exhibitions. The interview is one of the most informative there is among the many later ones and newspaper articles about Van Dongen. This report by Guth proved a great success and went into several reprints.

Van Dongen clearly lacks a biographer of his early years in the way that Marcelle Marquet was for her husband Albert Marquet, or Fernande Olivier was for Picasso in their years together at the Bateau Lavoir when she kept a diary from which she later published extracts. We have no memoirs from Van Dongen's subsequent wives and mistresses. His daughter Dolly, born in 1905, provided useful source material concerning her father's work, but most of it relates to his later years. She reported that her father, once he had settled definitively in Paris, destroyed a large part of his early work and writings.[28] The few sources for this early period consist of the letter Van Dongen sent to Fénéon in 1904 in connection with the introduction the latter was writing for the catalogue accompanying the exhibition of Van Dongen's work by Vollard, together with a few recollections by contemporaries, a handful of letters to friends in Rotterdam or Paris, and a meagre correspondence between Van Dongen and his wife Guus Preitinger. In addition, Louis Chaumeil noted some particulars about Van Dongen's youth and early years.

THE FIRST YEARS

Van Dongen's birthplace Delfshaven was a harbour town. The Van Dongen family, two sons and two daughters, lived at 96 Voorhaven, in a house that, according to Kees van Dongen, was built in 1602.[29] In the buildings next door, numbers 98 to 100, was the malting belonging to Jan van Dongen, Kees' father.[30] The house where the family lived lay between two harbours, so there was water on both sides. Recalling his youth, Van Dongen described the effect of the water, the ships that passed by or came to moor at the quayside and load or unload their goods, the exceptional quality of the light. 'It was half a small village, half a city. At the back of the house there was water. In front there was a small pavement and then the water. The ships passed by in front of the windows. Everything was full of light, full of colour.'[31] In an early self-portrait of Van Dongen from 1895 (fig. 2) painted in the studio of his father's malting, there is a glimpse through the window of the masts of ships at anchor in the harbour. This was where his roots

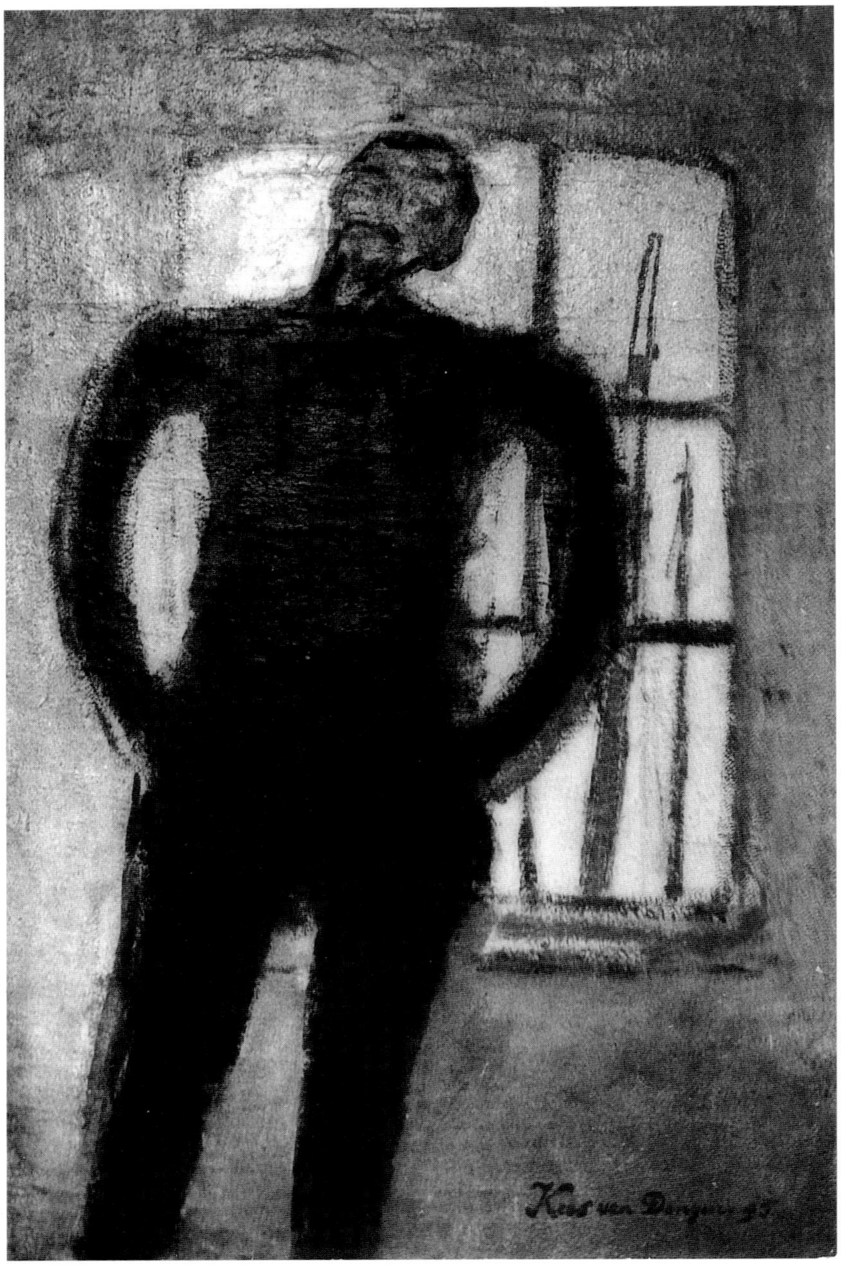

2.
Zelfportret (Self-portrait), 1895
Oil on canvas (original state)
92 x 60 cm
Musée National d'Art Moderne, Paris

were.[32] A fellow citizen of Delfshaven, Tom Schilperoort, who was to come across Van Dongen again later in his Paris days, also recalls the importance of water in the harbour town. For Schilperoort a favourite memory of the town, as he wrote in 1909, was 'as it still is sometimes on a Sunday morning when the sun is shining across the quayside lighting up a few blades of grass growing between the paving stones and making them gleam white in its rays.' He describes the 'heavy shadow of the tall chestnut trees' along the shore 'the...wall that reaches down deep into the water' and the 'narrow houses on the other side, stretching as far as the water, with their wooden extensions, and the old wooden jetties.'[33] Here, among these wooden constructions, the jetties, the quayside, the boats, the old farmhouses in the polderland behind Delfshaven, the young Van Dongen found his earliest subject matter.

From an early age Van Dongen made a great many drawings, and he recalls filling his school exercise books with sketches. He later said that 'however far back I try to remember my childhood, I always see myself drawing.'[34] Van Dongen, who was the oldest child in his family, told Fénéon in 1904: 'I was always alone and I made all the more sketches because I didn't play games. I went into the fields and made drawings of horses who looked a bit sad like I was.' His parents wanted him to train as a technical draughtsman. 'They planned for me to become an engineer or something of that sort and my mother in particular thought it would be far more suitable if I learnt to draw machines, boilers, steamboats and so forth...' But, confided Van Dongen to Fénéon, 'this proved impossible.'[35] At the end of the nineteenth century Delfshaven had its own municipal drawing academy where such subjects were taught as freehand drawing, architectural and technical drawing.[36] Possibly there were plans to let Van Dongen study here and then have him train in the studio of one of the Delfshaven factories. However, this is not what happened – although some claim it did. After working for a few years in his father's malting, and drawing and painting in his spare time, when he was about 15 years old Van Dongen became a pupil at the evening school of the Rotterdam Academy for Arts and Science which at that time stood at the centre of the town.[37]

cat. 3

ART ACADEMY AND ARTISTIC DEBUT

The only mention we have of Van Dongen at the art academy is in their published annual reports. These record that Van Dongen was a pupil there during the academic years 1892-3 and 1893-4. There is no mention of his results. In May 1940 the archives of Rotterdam Art Academy were destroyed by enemy bombing. All that survived is some printed matter.[38] The annual reports do not in fact offer information about the students who had enrolled, only about the end-of-year results. We can deduce from a letter from the Academy that Van Dongen had also enrolled for the academic year 1894-5.[39] Clearly, he spent three years at the art academy, followed by further years which covered the 4th to the 6th classes. The first mention of Van Dongen as a freelance artist dates from September 1895.[40] The Rotterdam Academy for Arts and Sciences had two main streams, where the courses lasted for six years. Van Dongen studied in the art stream, while during the same period his brother Jan was a pupil in the section for architectural and machine drawing.[41] The head of the art section at that time was the painter Jan Striening, famous for his romantic-realist cityscapes.[42] He brought a more modern approach to the teaching at the academy and raised the standards so that they were on a par with national levels.[43] At the academy, Van Dongen followed the course in freehand drawing, which was a training for freelance artists; he also studied industrial art.[44] This appears to have been at the request of his parents; he said, 'my parents didn't want me to make drawings which were of no practical use.'[45] Indeed, such a combination was quite common and was chosen by pupils who also wanted to have a practical training.[46] A fellow student, Jan Krulder, who was a friend of Van Dongen's, also followed both courses at the same time as Van Dongen.

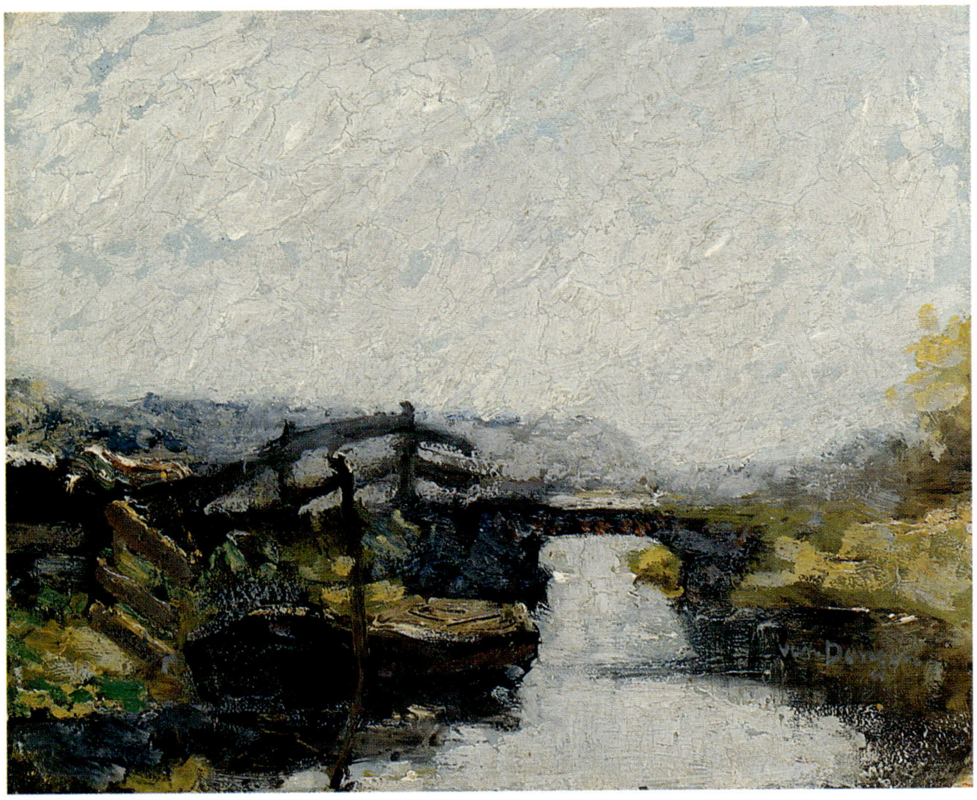

5.
Landschap bij Delfshaven
(Landscape near Delfshaven), 1895/1896
Oil on cardboard 24 x 30 cm
Private collection

For the industrial-art course, the head of department was A. Spoon, who was well-informed about the latest developments in his area. Van Dongen could specialize in such subjects as lithography and book decoration.[47] On the freehand drawing course the lessons were given by the artist Alexander van Maasdijk, who had trained in Brussels and painted according to the academic school. Although both Striening, the deputy director, and J.G. Heijberg, one of the teaching staff, have been mentioned as Van Dongen's teachers, he appears not to have studied under them.[48] It is Van Maasdijk who is regularly mentioned when friends of Van Dongen recall their student days at the Rotterdam academy, where Van Dongen was accounted 'by his mates and his truly artistically learned teachers – such as Van Maasdijk – to be a brilliant if somewhat over-confident, pupil.'[49] In fact almost all Van Dongen's artist friends from Rotterdam, were (with a very few exceptions) among the best academy students. In lower classes of the academy were such pupils as Johan Mastenbroek and Herman Schotel, there was Jan Krulder, and one year above Van Dongen was Johan Linse jr. Other painter friends had trained at the academy before Van Dongen, such as Piet de Moor, Chris Addicks and Martinus Schildt. Some of them were awarded royal scholarships after their years at the academy.[50]

Unlike the picture that Van Dongen drew of himself in later years, saying 'I was a lazy pupil at the art school,' Fénéon noted from the information he gave in 1904 that he appeared to have been an active student. Nor is this contradicted by the recollections and correspondence of friends from Rotterdam. The few works that have been preserved from Van Dongen's academy days demonstrate his keen ambition to develop as a painter, although he was also following the industrial-art course. For example, there is an early watercolour, a *View of Delfshaven* (fig. 3) which is meticulously executed according to the rules, paying careful attention to watercolour technique and perspective. The former owner received the drawing in exchange for financial support he gave Van Dongen in order to make a study trip down the river Rhine in Germany with fellow students.[51] There is a further document from this period showing that Van Dongen followed his studies with considerable diligence. He is mentioned in a letter from the head of department Striening to the board of the Rotterdam Kunstkring (artists' associa-

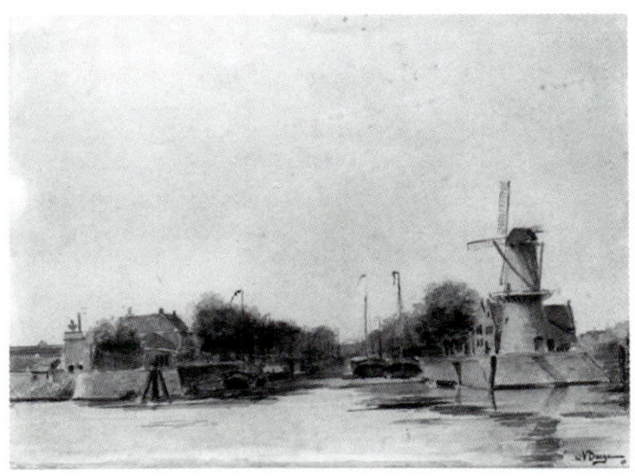

3.
Gezicht op Delfshaven, gezien vanuit de Middenkous
(View of Delfshaven, seen from the Middenkous), 1884
Watercolour

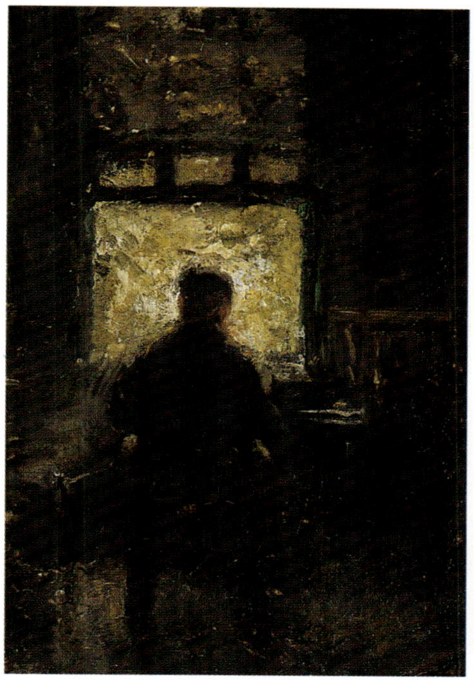

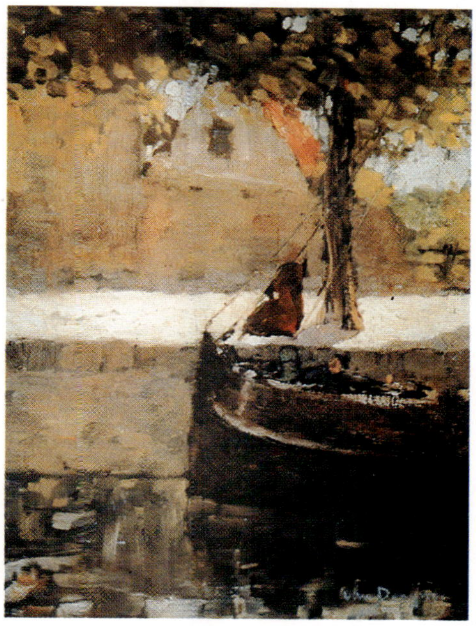

4.
Le cordonnier (The shoe mender), 1895
Oil on canvas, 55 x 38 cm
Private collection

6.
De Voorhaven (Zondag) (The harbour on Sunday), 1895/96
Oil on cardboard, 33 x 25 cm
Musée d'Art Moderne de la Ville de Paris, Paris

tion), in which the teacher requests free entrance for his pupil to the retrospective exhibition of work by Jozef Israels, held in September 1894.[52] Undoubtedly, Van Dongen would have felt a certain affinity with the work of this painter from the Hague School, called 'the Rembrandt of the 19th century.' Indeed, the atmosphere of urban poverty in Van Dongen's early work (dated as from 1895) *The shoe mender* (fig. 4) suggests immediate comparisons with Israels' interiors in the cottages of fisherfolk. The palette, the somewhat ragged technique and in particular the loose strokes of lighter colour against a dark background are very likely inspired by Israels' work. The fall of light in this piece also recalls Van Dongen's admiration for Rembrandt. Chaumeil in his monograph recorded Van Dongen's extreme admiration for his fellow countryman. With the help of illustrated books, the young Van Dongen in about 1894-5 made portraits of his family and a classmate, using a Rembrandtesque fall of light and what appear to be positions cat. 4
borrowed from Rembrandt, such as the figures seen from the side and the slightly bowed head.[53] As a young aspiring artist, Van Dongen modelled himself on this patriarchal master of Dutch art, as well as the masters in his immediate surroundings, such as Israels and Breitner. He also visited the major Dutch museums and apparently spent time copying pictures in Rotterdam's Boijmans Museum.[54]

At the Rotterdam Academy, recalled the journalist Schilperoort, 'his teachers quietly let him go his own way, half sharing his somewhat self-opinionated attitudes.'[55] This comment presumably refers to Van Dongen's final year of study, when it was common for the students to work individually. During this year and the subsequent one (about 1895-6) Van Dongen probably made the paintings of Delfshaven, with their light colours and vivid atmosphere, which he exhibited for the first time in November 1904 in Galerie Vollard, Paris. His former townsman, Schilperoort, in discussing all the critics' reviews of Van Dongen's work, paid the greatest attention to these works. They are pictures showing the quays of Delfshaven with ships moored in front of the 'low houses', filled with the feeling of a 'lazy dreaming canal anaesthetized by a Sunday stupor.' This probably refers to the canvas *Voorhaven (Zondag)* (The harbour on Sunday) (fig. 6) as well as to paintings with impressions of the canals running though the polder landscape and the farms in the hinterland, such as *Landschap bij Delfshaven* (Landscape near

Delfshaven).[56] (fig. 5) These paintings, described by another fellow Rotterdammer as 'pleasantly robust outdoor studies' are done on painters' cardboard and measure between 24 x 28 centimetres and 25 x 33 centimetres. They bear such titles as the names of the quays or the houses that lie along the river Schie near Delfshaven, clearly indicating that they were drawn in these parts.[57] Van Dongen showed about thirty such works at the exhibition at Vollard's. Not one of them bore a specific date, either on that occasion or later. In the exhibition catalogue they are presented as a group, titled 'La Hollande' with the suggestion that they were made between the years 1895/6 and 1902. On the basis of style and subject matter and the recollections and comments of contemporaries, these pieces can definitely be placed in the early Delfshaven years.[58] A painting with a similar subject, showing a ship, was submitted by Van Dongen for his debut exhibition in 1895, the presentation of Living Masters held in Amsterdam. In the catalogue accompanying the exhibition, the reference to Van Dongen gives his address as that of his parents. These paintings of city and countryside are clearly the work of a more experienced hand. The paint is applied in several layers, with both meticulous and bolder brushwork, and attention to technique. In some cases part of the paint – such as the sky and water in *Landschap bij Delfshaven* (Landscape near Delfshaven) (fig. 5) has been applied with a palette knife and then smoothed out. It would seem that Van Dongen copied this swift, free style of applying paint from the impressionist method used by Breitner in his cityscapes. Work by Breitner could be seen at various public galleries in the Netherlands, and also at the Rotterdam Academy.[59] However, unlike Breitner who was working in Amsterdam, Van Dongen did not paint the noise and bustle of the busy city – although that was nearby – but chose to present the quiet and tranquillity of the countryside which he observed so clearly. In about 1896, however, there appears to have been a watershed. The promising painterly start was interrupted, and an entirely different track was henceforth followed.

SYMBOLISM AND FREE EXPRESSIVE ART

'He set off for Rotterdam. He slept in a barn, in a stable, between the horses hooves,' reported Paul Guth from what Van Dongen told him about the year before he left for Paris in 1897.[60] The letter from Van Dongen to Fénéon also provides a point of reference: 'When I was 18 I left my parents' home and went to live on my own in Rotterdam...and then the struggle really began.' Elsewhere Van Dongen says this watershed occurred when he was 19 years old. He also told Chaumeil that during this period he changed his outlook on things and sought somewhere to live in the city. Apparently he had read some writings by the neo-Hegelian philosopher Bolland which gave rise to heated discussions in his Catholic family.[61] This is quite possible, although the topics discussed were likely to have covered other theories as well.

In early 1897 a brochure was published announcing a new Rotterdam artists' society, to be called *Vrije Kunst*, or Free Art. The brochure contained a brief manifesto signed by the actor Henri Brondgeest, the poet-singer and draughtsman Koos Speenhoff, and the architect Jacques van Gils. The leaflet had a decorative border which was drawn by Van Dongen's former classmate, Jan Krulder.[62] The new society aimed, it stated, to further 'the presence of art in everyday life', to oppose 'pretentious and worthless products' and strive for 'truth and originality'. It also announced that a series of 'artistically produced publications under the title *Vrije Kunst*' would be published. One of the signatories, Speenhoff, mentioned the existence of this society in his memoirs, but did not discuss the artistic activities of the club. He did recall that it was here he met Kees van Dongen.[63] Otherwise, there is no description of the society or its activities. There is a little information in the advertised book *Vrije Kunst I* that appeared in 1897 and the reviews in connection with it.[64]

This publication, a beautiful volume with a decorated cover and thick creamy-white paper pages, contained contributions from various Rotterdam writers such as Bernard

Canter, Arie van Veen, the critic Albert Plasschaert and the poet Theodoor Islees, as well as several musicians. The names of the two other signatories of the manifesto, Brondgeest and Van Gils, do not appear. Several of the writers are totally unknown, which suggests they were using pseudonyms.[65] All the artists were young and were therefore – somewhat ironically – greeted by the press as 'a fresh band bringing new blood', presenting themselves like a 'phalanx', a 'talented young generation.' However, this publication was not to enjoy a long life. In the introduction to the book only the ideal of 'beauty' is mentioned as a common aim. A second publication, although announced, never appeared.

The collection of texts published in *Vrije Kunst I* is clearly inspired by Symbolism. Some, indeed, by a more heroic-individualistic aspect, such as the poetry and prose of Canter and Islees in which the subject matter deals with the striving for a higher, personal and spiritual happiness. Other literary contributions have a more left-wing nature. The texts were complemented by two symbolist drawings by Piet de Moor together with several vignettes and illustrations by Krulder, Speenhoff and Kees van Dongen. The latter also illustrated two of the texts and made the drawing on the title page. (fig. 9). His name is not listed in the table of contents but lurks at the edge of the cat. 6
drawings or can be found as a monogram.

The stylistic change that Van Dongen's work underwent was enormous. The new linear type of drawing as found in *Jonker Frans* (fig. 7), the decorative, flowing lines in parallel, the visual elements such as the skull and snakes, are directly reminiscent of the symbolism of Jan Toorop, in particular such drawings as *De zangen dezer tijden* (Today's songs) (fig. 8) or *De drie bruiden* (The three brides). Evidently Van Dongen had turned his attention to contemporary art.

His admiration for Jozef Israels and Breitner placed him in the circles of established Dutch art, in such artistic milieus as that of Arti et Amicitiae, the Amsterdam society for artists established in the nineteenth century, or Pulchri Studio in The Hague. There were also the annual exhibitions of Living Masters in which Van Dongen made his debut as a painter, which were held alternately in major Dutch cities and to which any aspiring or established artist could submit his work. These exhibitions presented a cross-section of the work being produced in the Netherlands at that time, rather than the most exciting or innovative art. Symbolist artists such Toorop, Thorn Prikker and Piet de Moor protested strongly against these wishy-washy presentations.[66]

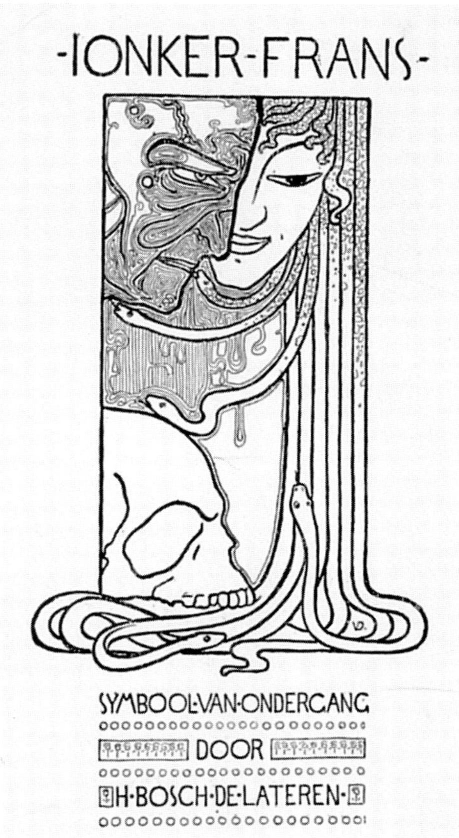

7.
Jonker Frans (Baron Frans), illustration in *Vrije Kunst*
Rotterdam 1897
Published by the 'Vrije Kunst' Association

In the Netherlands the contemporary art scene was served by clubs such as those set up respectively in 1891 in The Hague and in 1893 in Rotterdam, known as the Haagsche and Rotterdamsche Kunstkring, or art circle. What was new about these art circles was that they were not limited to only one art form but to 'multi-media' that is, the visual arts, music, literature and applied arts. As well as providing independent exhibition space for their members, these art circles offered the first platform where contemporary ideas on art and related subjects could be presented in detail.[67] At the Kunstkring in The Hague in 1892, with assistance from Jan Toorop, there were exhibitions of work by Van Gogh as well as from the two Belgian modern art circles Les XX and l'Association pour l'Art with work by such painters as Henry van Velde, Georges Seurat and Paul Signac. In 1894 there was also a retrospective in The Hague of Odilon Redon's oeuvre. In that same year Toorop held an exhibition in the art circle at which he invited the poet Emil Verhaeren to give a lecture. Previously, in 1892, the poet Paul Verlaine and the 'guru' Sar Joséphin Péladan had visited the Netherlands, and the latter had recruited artists as members of his order. What with one thing and another the ideas of Symbolism soon became familiar in the Netherlands and found a considerable following, partly combined with Neo-Impressionist ideas.[68] The opening exhibition of the Rotterdam Kunstkring in March 1893 can even be considered as a propaganda platform for Symbolism. The catalogue explained and defended this type of art and it was largely the work of Symbolist artists that was to be seen – Toorop, Thorn

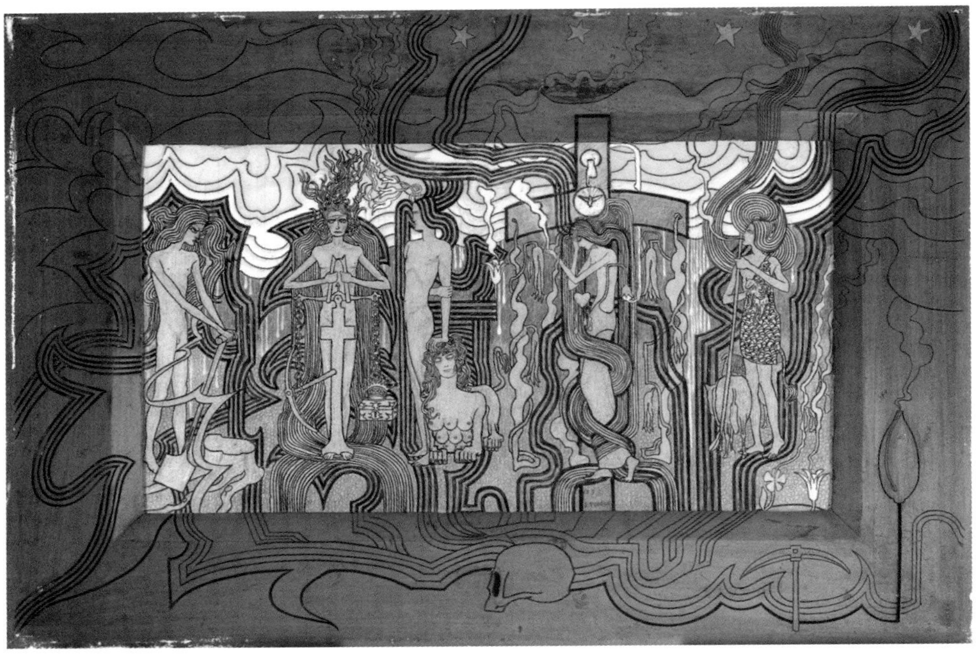

Prikker, Theo van Hoytema, Floris Verster and the 'Vrije Kunst' member already mentioned, Piet de Moor.[69] Clearly, De Moor played an important part in the organization of this show. As well as being co-founder of the Rotterdam Kunstkring he was in 1893-94 chairman of its department of Visual Art and also a member of the Hague art circle.[70]

Looking at the review of the activities carried out there in the succeeding years it emerges that in Rotterdam people were actively involved in disseminating the latest ideas – although more traditional masters were also exhibited.[71] The then director of the Boijmans Museum, Pieter Haverkorn van Rijsewijk, played a stimulating part in this respect, since he was chairman of the art circle from 1894 on. The lines laid down in the circle's first year were continued in Rotterdam with special exhibitions for modern applied art. Lectures were also held, such as that in 1894 by the Belgian August Vermeylen, editor in chief of the left-wing Symbolist magazine *Van Nu en Straks*, on connected topics, and there were various group exhibitions of Symbolist art.[72]

To begin with, all this seemed to wash over Van Dongen. The rise of Symbolism came at the same time as he started art school, when he was still completely enthralled by Rembrandt. The first change in his outlook can be noticed in 1896, when we find an
cat. 4 example of a more linear style of drawing. It was probably Piet de Moor who involved Van Dongen in work for the *Vrije Kunst* publication, not Speenhoff who only took up the artistic life in about 1897. Also, it was De Moor – who used the pseudonym H. Bosch de Lateren – who authored *Jonker Frans*, one of the texts illustrated by Van Dongen in the new linear technique.[73] At that period De Moor also worked in an elaborate, fantastical-narrative style, witness his drawings in *Vrije Kunst*. He was a great admirer of the work of Toorop and Thorn Prikker and appears to have combined in his person the Symbolist principle of the unification of the arts. For besides his already-mentioned activities could be listed his article on dance as an art form and on theatre set design. He had different pseudonyms for these different activities, one of them being 'Kets'.[75] Under this name De Moor published a light-hearted magazine in the first months of 1896 commenting on social and artistic 'hot' topics by means of cartoons and short comments. Although this publication was short-lived (only ten editions were printed) and not particularly remarkable, it does demonstrate the extent to which De Moor was au fait with the art scene of his day. He presumably passed on such knowledge to the artists he knew, such as Van Dongen. He refers in his short notes to the publication of letters by Thorn Prikker, and also lists a visit in March 1896 to the exhibition *La Libre Esthetique*, succes-

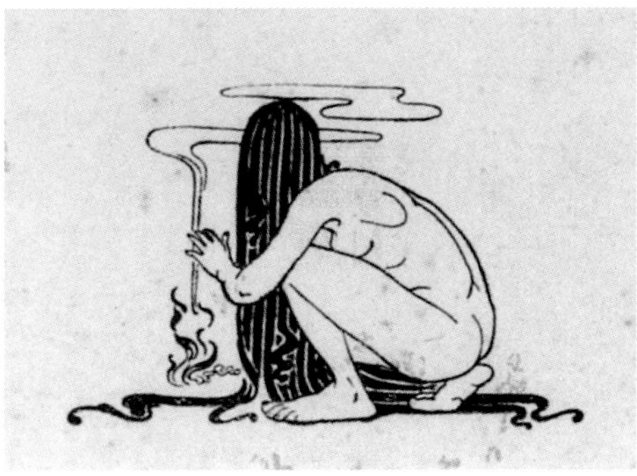

8.
Jan Toorop
De zangen dezer tijden (Today's Songs), 1893
Black and coloured chalk, pencil
320 x 585 mm
Kröller-Müller Museum, Otterlo

9.
Title page of *Vrije Kunst*, Rotterdam 1897
Published by the 'Vrije Kunst' Association

sor to *Les XX*, in Brussels, mentioning positive reviews of a poster exhibition at the Rotterdam Kunstkring and a travelling exhibition in the Netherlands of contemporary draughtsmanship.[76] It also emerges from this that De Moor knew Pol de Mont, editor in chief of the Antwerp art magazine *De Vlaamse School*. The latter is the only publication in which – presumably not without coincidence – mention is made of the setting up of the group *Vrije Kunst*.[77] This link between Rotterdam and Belgium is interesting. Through exhibitions held in Brussels and Antwerp it was possible to acquire detailed knowledge about the avant-garde of the international art world. It is worth noting here that the only trip abroad Van Dongen himself mentioned before he went to Paris, was to Belgium.[78] Finally, it is important when considering De Moor's up-to-date knowledge, as well as those artists who were involved with *Vrije Kunst*, that in 1896 two exhibitions were organized in Rotterdam in which Symbolism was extremely well represented. There can be almost no doubt that Van Dongen saw these two shows.

The first of these was a members' exhibition held in the spring and showing 11 works by Toorop which included a drawing of a sphinx and one of his preliminary studies for the picture *Le passeur d'eau*, which was inspired by the poetry of Verhaeren.[79] More important was the next presentation in September of that year, titled the *Eerste keuzetentoonstelling Hollandsche Aquarellen* (First choice exhibition of Dutch watercolours) which presented strikingly left-wing socially committed pictures by both Toorop and Thorn Prikker.[80] Jan Toorop showed, as well as a drawing of a man, the above-mentioned anarchist drawing *De zangen dezer tijden* (Today's songs) (fig. 8) and *De Zaaier* (The sower) a watercolour, supposedly representing 'the artist' sowing the seeds of truth from which 'our art and our excruciatingly stupid industrialised society' would be enabled to 'rise out of decay and destruction'. Thorn Prikker submitted his monumental drawing that had been exhibited shortly before in Brussels, titled *Fin d'une ère* (End of an era) which was also a pictorial manifesto in which he, like Toorop, expressed his hope and expectations for a coming revolution.[81] According to a letter he wrote, the drawing illustrated the precursors of this revolution, 'untamed forces [of nature]' which would eventually introduce changes into the 'utter misery' of contemporary life, which he also illustrated. The coming salvation was shown by him in a small corner as 'a woman in front of her home' watering flowers in a luxuriant natural setting and representing 'the contentment of the simple ordinary life.'[82] All this was intentionally somewhat vague – after all, it was a vision of the future. Toorop's drawing *Today's songs* was somewhat clearer in its visual language. It personified, explained Toorop, by means of the figures on the left and right of centre, material and spiritual anarchy.[83] The destructive and constructive aspects of these forces was represented by him with respectively angular and flowing lines as well as by placing the clearly recognizable figures of Cain and Abel at the sides. The personification of material anarchy appears to presage – by breaking an iron rod it disturbs the balance between labour (a pickaxe) and money and power (a strongbox and a crown) – a coming revolution.

The two literary contributions that Van Dongen illustrated in *Vrije Kunst*, titled *Jonker Frans*, and the trilogy by Koos Speenhoff, *Visioen*, *Der generatie einde* and *Geluk* appear to contain a similar revolutionary message. In the *Baron Frans, symbol of decline*, cat. 6
the violent death of the baron as a result of a dissolute life dedicated to wine and women is seen as the overthrow of the old class-ridden society. The skull in Van Dongen's drawing – also to be seen in Toorop's work – refers to this destruction. The Medusa-like woman with serpent hair represents evil. In Speenhoff's writing, illustrated by two of Van Dongen's drawings, there are female figures personifying social virtues such as Religion, Chastity and Wisdom, who are brutally murdered by Commerce represented by tradesmen, after which the murderers themselves come to a sticky end and a New Age is ushered in. This vision of the future is presented by Van Dongen in his final illustration by a woman walking through a beautiful landscape, to be compared with Thorn Prikker's representation of pure happiness.

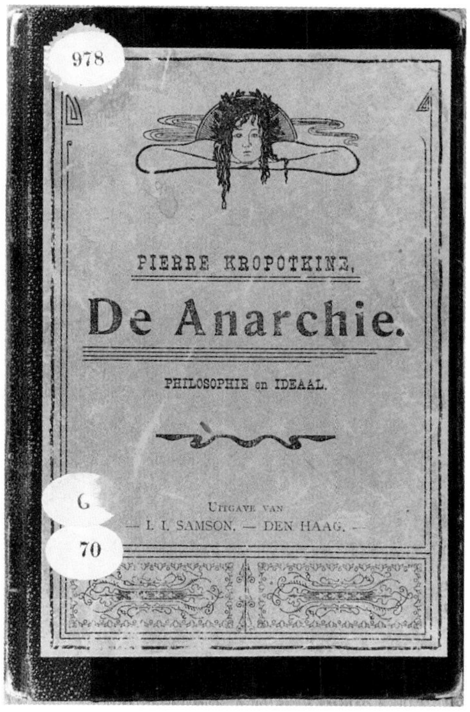

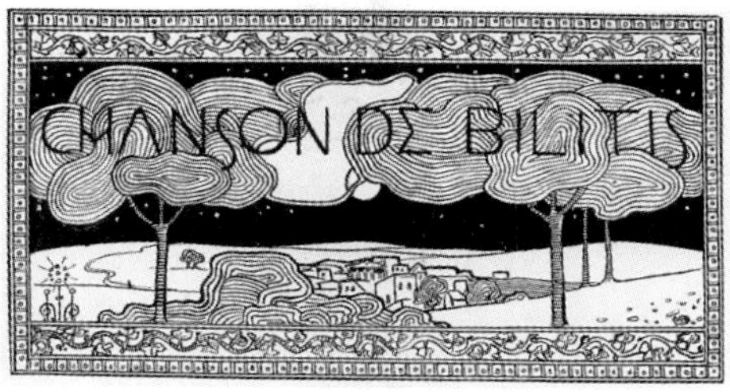

10.
Cover of Pierre Kropotkin
De Anarchie. Philosophie en Ideaal
The Hague n.d. [1897]

11.
Chanson de Bilitis (Song of Bilitis)
Illustration in *L'Image*, no. 11 (October) 1897

Although the works exhibited by Toorop and Thorn Prikker in 1896 were perhaps not immediately accessible to everyone – one reviewer wrote 'an accompanying text is essential' – the initiated knew where they could find the relevant explanation. Indeed, the just-mentioned critic, Johan de Meester, referred to this: 'having seen Thorn Prikker's large work people should go and look up the correspondence in the *Tweemaandelijksch Tijdschrift*, the Bi-monthly Magazine.' Without doubt, that is exactly what the members of the young group of artists who formed the Vrije Kunst society, did.[84]

The letters published in the above-mentioned magazine contained a statement by Thorn Prikker declaring himself to be an undisguised supporter of Anarchy. He recalled with some satisfaction the visit of the anarchist French writer Paul Verlaine to The Hague, how the latter had sung the anarchist song 'Dynamitons, anarchistes' when staying in the splendid home of the artist Philippe Zilcken.[85] And at the end of the last letter published in the *Bi-monthly Magazine* (the edition of March 1896), there was Thorn Prikker's comment on being an artist: 'If an artist understands his true mission, he should mingle with the people not as a superior, but as a fellow in the struggle; he must dedicate his powers to the Revolution.'[86] Apparently, writers and draughtsmen of Rotterdam shared these ideas sufficiently to produce their own variations on the theme. The left-wing anarchist Belgian publication *Van nu en Straks* (Today and tomorrow) to which Thorn Prikker, Toorop and the socialist politician Ferdinand Domela Nieuwenhuis would occasionally send contributions from the Netherlands, undoubtedly served as a model.[87] That Van Dongen was familiar with this magazine appears from the fact that the wavy lines he used in his vignettes closely resemble the style of Van Velde in that publication.[88] The Rotterdam club *Vrije Kunst* can undoubtedly be associated with such concepts as 'free love', 'free education' and 'free thought' which were current in anarchist circles.[89] 'They wanted to see no subjugation of any kind, not the slightest coercion from outside,' was the conclusion of the writer Frans Coenen when considering the Vrije Kunst group in an article for the Dutch socialist cultural magazine *De Kroniek*.[90]

ANARCHISM

Van Dongen's interest in the anarchist movement was not merely a quirk of youth. Around 1897 the publishing house I.I. Samson in The Hague produced a translation of a work that had appeared in a French translation the year before. It was Pierre Kropotkin's work titled *Anarchy. Philosophy and Ideal*, with an illustration by Kees van Dongen on the cover.[91] The decorative borders also appear familiar and were possibly drawn by Van Dongen's friend Jan Krulder. (fig. 10) Although the illustration is unsigned it so strongly resembles Van Dongen's work in *Vrije Kunst* it would seem most
cat. 4 improbable were it not by him. The figure of the woman in the drawing, facing the future full of hope and expectation, would even appear to be the same model used by Van Dongen in earlier work. This publication supports the thesis that even before he left for Paris Van Dongen was active in left-wing anarchist-symbolist circles in Rotterdam.

However, it is difficult to ascertain the other members of this group, apart from the already-mentioned artists from the Vrije Kunst circle.[92] Some information might be gleaned if we knew who translated the book by Kropotkin but the name is not given in the publication and this edition by Samson is not listed in the Dutch national bibliography Brinkman's Book Catalogue. Curiously, another translation of the same book (not illustrated) published in 1896 by Publicitas in Amsterdam, does appear in the national bibliography – but equally without mentioning the name of the thankless translator.[93] Earlier Kropotkin translators in the Netherlands include a Rotterdam biologist, one B.J. van der Voo, and one of the founders of the Dutch socialist party, Domela Nieuwenhuis, who began his career as a Protestant minister.[94] It appears that Van der

Voo was an ardent supporter of anarchism. During the years 1896-98 he was editor in chief of the national weekly *De An-archie*, and introduced several anarchist thinkers to his Dutch readership, via his translations – writers such as Elisée Réclus, Bakoenine and Jean Grave.[95] His publication of Grave's *La société future* (1895) had an introduction written by Domela Nieuwenhuis.[96] Also, in his weekly in April 1897 the Dutch version of Kropotkin's book *De Anarchie* was advertised – this was probably the edition with illustrations by Van Dongen.[97] It appears from the same weekly that Rotterdam had its own anarchists' society, called 'The Free Club'. However, no further information is provided about the members – names were kept secret, with a very few exceptions.[98] The only connection known for certain between the anarchist biologist and the art world is the Rotterdam painter of industrial subjects, Herman Heijenbrock. But there would seem to be no connection between him and Van Dongen.[99]

It appears, however, that at an early stage Van Dongen was familiar with the ideas of Domela Nieuwenhuis, who during this period was a staunch supporter of anarchism. In spring 1896 Domela met Kropotkin in London and was later to refer to this occasion as being the immediate cause for the following about-turn in his thinking.[100] In 1897 he quit the socialist party and founded his own anarchist newspaper, *De Vrije Socialist*.[101] According to the son of a Rotterdam wine cooper for whom Van Dongen painted a decorative mural on his shop front, both the artist and the cooper were great admirers of Domela Nieuwenhuis at that time. And it appears from various sources that Van Dongen also later – certainly throughout his Fauvist period – was a follower of Domela's ideas and in around 1900 was personally acquainted with him.[102] Pursuing various connections with Domela we come across the name of the anarchist Alexander Cohen who in the late 1880s worked as an editor for *Recht voor Allen* (Justice for All), the 'voice' of the social-democratic bond of which Domela Nieuwenhuis was the leader.[103] Threatened with imprisonment, Cohen fled to Paris in May 1888, where he became friendly with various French anarchists including Félix Fénéon, the critic with whom Van Dongen came in contact after 1900.[104] It seems most likely that Van Dongen's friendship with Cohen dates from after 1900. That is, after Cohen had spent a couple of years in exile in England and then sat out his prison sentence in the Netherlands in 1896, before returning to Paris in 1899. Possibly Domela Nieuwenhuis introduced Van Dongen to Cohen.[105]

Some publications have appeared dealing with Van Dongen's anarchist leanings during the early years in Paris. His connections with the painters Maximilien Luce and Paul Signac are well known, as are his signed entries in 1905-06 for Jean Grave's magazine *Les Temps Nouveaux*. Van Dongen's stay at the Bateau Lavoir in 1906 has also been studied, and his connections with 'la bande Picasso'.[106] On the basis of this, Van Dongen's ties with anarchism were described as arising under the influence of his Parisian acquaintances, as a kind of local deviation.[107] It would seem, however, that not only did Van Dongen's introduction to left-wing notions begin far earlier but was also of far greater significance on his development as an artist than has been thought. Furthermore, when we consider his circle of friends it is apparent that for a time Van Dongen numbered a good many left-wing and anarchist writers and artists among his close acquaintances. There were the journalists M.J. Brusse and Henri Wiessing, cat. am. 21, 22 the painters Maurice de Vlaminck, Otto van Rees and Ludovic-Rodo Pissarro.[108] The contacts are quite clearly of a left-wing nature and represent attitudes varying from socialism to anarcho-communism and Christian- or social-anarchism. Presumably this did not interfere with social relationships.[109] Indeed, anarchy was usually more of a label for a general attitude or way of life than for a programme based on one particular theory.

KROPOTKIN – DRAUGHTSMANSHIP

Artistic circles were particularly keen on the ideas of Kropotkin.[110] He placed great emphasis on the unhampered growth and development of the individual's talents and inclinations and this appealed greatly to many artists. Kropotkin's plea for the strong development of individual attitudes went hand in hand with a call for a strongly-knit society, for a kind of commune without personal property where the task of the artist was to serve the community.[111] This idea was apparently shared by Van Dongen and it is with this in mind that we should consider his early ambitions as a draughtsman. In 1901 he wrote to his friend Chris Addicks of Rotterdam Academy days: 'I have adopted the standpoint that it is better to work as much as possible for the people as a whole and not for a few conscious (or unconscious) bandits. That's why I make illustrations for papers and have given up painting – except occasionally I paint a little for my own pleasure.'[112] Painting, thus, was 'for the idle rich', working for the benefit of collectors who could afford to buy expensive pieces. In 1906 Picasso called Kees van Dongen the 'Kropotkin' of the Bateau Lavoir.[113] Two years later the art critic Guillaume Apollinaire criticized Van Dongen's entry for the Paris Salon des Indépendants of 1908 as a shameless attack on morality, with a reference to the anarchism of Domela Nieuwenhuis: 'Monsieur van Dongen crudely proclaims the most voracious appetites. He enjoys himself among the tumult...This is not the bitterness of a Multatuli [famous Dutch 19th-century writer] rather, this is the ferocity of a Domela Nieuwenhuis.'[114] Later, too, remarks are coloured by this anarchism and it appeared to be part of Van Dongen's daily life.[115] But whether or not he was deeply socially involved, it is incontestable that when Van Dongen went to Paris in 1897 he did so not on a mere whim, nor without an academic training.

WHY PARIS?

'Paris attracted me like a lighthouse' declared Van Dongen when he was explaining to Guth how he first came to the city. Elsewhere, when asked for the reason why he left Rotterdam, he explained that there was nothing to do in the harbour city, 'there were only shipowners.'[116] This remark, in view of all the activities mentioned above, seems somewhat out of place. As well as the Rotterdam Kunstkring there were exhibitions of work by painters of the Hague School or the Amsterdam School organized in various locations, while the Amsterdam art dealers Van Wisselingh presented selections from their collection from time to time.[117] The city also had a society called the Aesthetisch Genootschap which organized both tableaux-vivants and evening discussions on artistic topics.[118] But for Van Dongen – who did not choose to make his career as a painter by means of royal grants, academy prizes or members' exhibitions – this aspect of the Rotterdam art scene would scarcely have appealed. The couple of exhibitions showing foreign applied art that were organized by the Rotterdam Kunstkring in 1896 may have whetted his appetite for Paris. Early in that year the poster exhibition mentioned above was on show – presenting a selection of works by Georges de Feure, Henri Ibels, Toulouse-Lautrec and Steinlen, among others. In the autumn there was an exhibition of work by French and Belgian graphic artists, including James Ensor and Félicien Rops. It was because of these exhibitions of applied art that the draughtsman H.G. Ibels visited Rotterdam in November 1896 on the invitation of the Kunstkring, and gave a lecture on techniques of lithography.[119] This must surely have appealed to Van Dongen in those days. Having arrived in Paris, as he wrote to Fénéon in 1904, 'I went to some of the places where posters and menus are printed...the posters that are pasted up on walls.' In Rotterdam there was nothing doing in this sector. The only modern theatre company in the city in the 1890s (De Vos and Van Korlaar, whose home theatre was the Tivoli) had to close down in 1895.[120] But even in its heyday this theatre did not provide commissions for posters or decor designs. It is perhaps well-known, but this harbour city that doubled its population towards the close of the century put all its energy into building new dockyards and improving the infrastructure. The old inner city suffered as a result. 'This is what makes me feel the saddest,' wrote an ex-Rotterdammer in 1896 on his return to the city after many years in the United States, 'the enormous contrast between the splendid new buildings constructed for the shipping industry and trade, and the total lack of any modern comfort in the old inner city.' The old city, sometimes referred to as 'the polder' which had in places been pulled down, drained and filled in, now consisted almost entirely of 'narrow streets with dirty slums on either side, houses only a few metres wide, backing onto poverty-stricken inner backyards, where the Rotterdam workers lived.'[121] As was made clear by contemporaries, those who were intellectually and culturally aware in Rotterdam were limited to a small circle, despite the various activities the city boasted.[122] Not surprisingly, Van Dongen hoped that Paris would offer him more opportunities to extend his ideas and develop his skills.

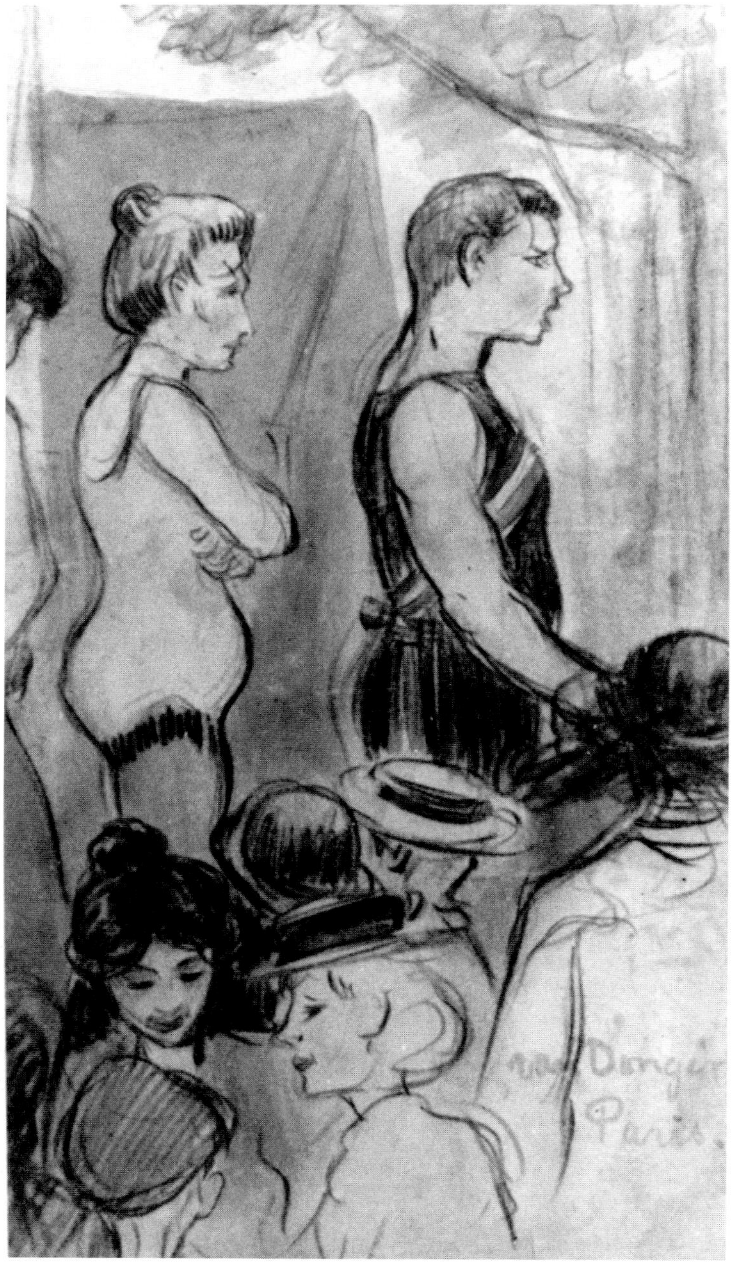

20.
Les débuts de Raoul (Raoul's Debut)
1899/1900
Black chalk, watercolour
440 x 265 mm

II. Paris, Rotterdam and Paris again. From Symbolism to Realism

The 'train de plaisir' that took Van Dongen to Paris in early July 1897 was a tourists' special offer probably in connection with the French national holiday on Bastille Day. He arrived in the capital around 12 July and recalled that 'Paris was in holiday mood, also on the 13th, the 14th and the 15th so that I began to think the festivities would never end.'[123] Apparently Van Dongen had difficulty in finding lodgings, knew not a soul, and for weeks survived on a few sous a day. At all events this is what he recounted to Fénéon, doubtless with certain dramatic additions, contrasting the festive mood of the first few days with the 'month of misery' that followed. 'I dragged myself around from place to place...'[124] Finally Van Dongen managed to gain a few commissions, 'two drawings for an illustrated magazine' and design drawings for an art-nouveau enterprise and then in late April to early May 1898 he returned to Rotterdam, 'fully determined to return to Paris as soon as possible' as he also told Fénéon in a letter. In October 1899 he once more took the train to Paris, to settle there definitively. During those years in Paris, Rotterdam and again in the French capital, Van Dongen developed from being a Symbolist to a Realist draughtsman in the style of Steinlen; 'In Paris I met some sort of journalists and took up the idea of illustrating newspapers.'[125]

PARIS: 1897-1898

Van Dongen's first stay in the city appears somewhat disastrous, but it does seem – contrary to what he suggested – that he had a couple of introductory letters with him by means of which he gained the commissions he mentioned to Fénéon. In another interview Van Dongen mentions such projects as 'designing for a firm that painted signs, and for a firm that produced posters.'[126] Some of these commissions have been traced, and place Van Dongen once more in the Symbolist camp.

Shortly after his arrival in Paris Van Dongen made several drawings for the newspaper *L'Image.* They were published in the October number. They are vignettes for titles, some in greater detail than others, and can be attributed to Van Dongen since they have his monogram in the lower right corner.[127] (fig. 11) The decorative drawings, in a style once again related to Toorop's, illustrate some verses from a prose poem, the *Chanson de Bilitis,* by Pierre Louys (Pierre Félix Louis). It is a love story inspired by Greek lyric poetry and captured public attention when Débussy composed music for it. The poem evokes an atmosphere of the ancient world, which Van Dongen represented by means of classical architecture and an expansive landscape. The lovers' embrace, described in the poem, is represented by the twisted interwoven lines of the trees and bushes. It seems most likely that this commission was organized for Van Dongen by the artist Georges de Feure, who was of Dutch extraction. De Feure illustrated both for the October number of *L'Image* and for other editions of the magazine. It was founded by the trade union for wood engravers in an effort to preserve the quality of wood carving and make advertisement for it, in the face of modern technical developments.[128] The magazine only survived for one year.

De Feure had been in Paris since autumn 1889 and enjoyed a considerable reputation as an illustrator, lithographer and designer of posters.[129] The Rotterdam artist Piet de Moor, also resident in Paris from February 1898, knew him – indeed, it was possibly through De Moor that the acquaintance with Van Dongen was made. De Moor and De Feure held a joint exhibition in May 1899 in the Théatre Antoine, in Paris.[130]

Georges de Feure is known primarily as a Symbolist and Art-Nouveau artist. His drawings, inspired by the poems of Baudelaire, showing seductive, languishing *femmes fatales*, programmatic examples of Symbolist art, and his decorative plant and flower motifs, were to be found generously strewn over magazine covers, in series of lithographs, on posters and dust covers.[131] Besides being printed in *L'Image* they appeared in several newspapers such as *Le Figaro Illustré* and *Les Maîtres de l'Affiche*. It is quite possible that De Feure is the person referred to by Van Dongen when he speaks of 'a producer of posters' – since De Feure used this description for himself – and that it was he who helped Van Dongen gain the commission for furniture design.[132] In 1897 De Feure was overwhelmed with work in this field, and designed various pieces of furniture for *L'Artisan Moderne* in that year. This was a firm dedicated to the production of modern furniture and decorative objects at as low a price as possible, to serve a wide public.[133] However, as appreciation of Art Nouveau increased – the high point for De Feure being the interior designed for Samuel Bing called the *Pavillon de l'Art Moderne* for the World Exhibition in 1900 – so did Van Dongen's interest in the style decline. He was quite explicit in his criticism of it in an illustration that appeared in *Le Sourire* in February 1902.[134] (fig. 12) In this, Van Dongen made it apparent that in his view this refined art style could easily be produced (witness the magazines lying on the floor in the illustration and the artistic ingredients in the pots on the right, as well as the lyre, symbol of poetic inspiration, on which the artist's assistant is seated) and he criticized the way in which Art Nouveau had become the prerogative of an elite. Van Dongen pictures De Feure as a dandy with his paintbrushes stuck into a top hat and objects behind him that he had designed which are more of a witness to his lack of taste than to a lofty artistic spirit. With this satire Van Dongen joined the ranks of the earliest critics of this art form, which had by now become far removed from its original ideals.[135] By now Van Dongen had long taken leave of Symbolism, but without having forsaken his left-wing involvement.

SIEBE TEN CATE, CHARLES SNABILIÉ

Two portraits have been preserved from Van Dongen's first stay in Paris that refer to other contacts he made at this time. One of them is of the Dutch painter Siebe ten Cate seated in front of his easel. (fig. 13) The portrait is captured by Van Dongen in contours and the face drawn with fine chalk lines. Ten Cate had lived in Paris since 1883 and offered a roof to his fellow artist Van Dongen at his home in the Faubourg du Temple when the latter – so the story goes – was down and out.[136] The decorative inscription on the upper left of the drawing, reminiscent of Van Dongen's earlier Symbolist work, gives the date as October 1897, suggesting that he met Ten Cate around this time. It is very likely that he already knew his work. Ten Cate often visited the Netherlands for short periods and regularly participated in exhibitions there, including some in Rotterdam.[137] He was known for his pastel drawings and harbour and cityscapes – usually scenes showing half-deserted squares or wide boulevards painted in a realistic,
cat. am. 1 semi-Impressionist manner.

The other portrait by Van Dongen from this period in Paris shows the Dutch journalist Charles Snabilié and is also dated October 1897.[138] (fig. 14) It is a lithograph, in a more realistic manner, finely capturing the writer's attitude although the left hand is slightly elongated. The lithograph print suggests that at the time Van Dongen had access to a studio and printing press. Snabilié greatly admired the work of Ten Cate and on more than one occasion made it clear that he counted the latter among his best

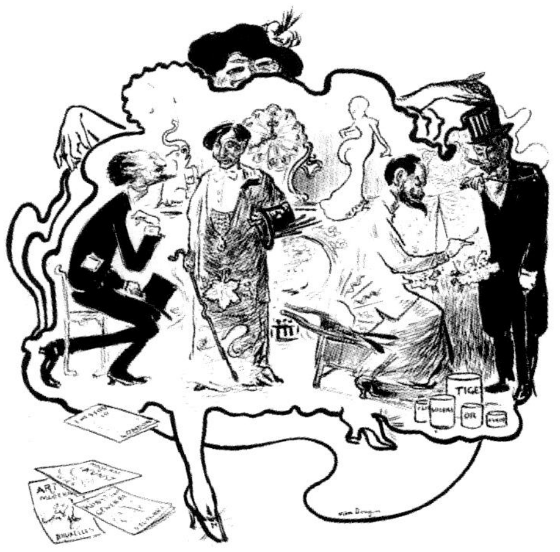

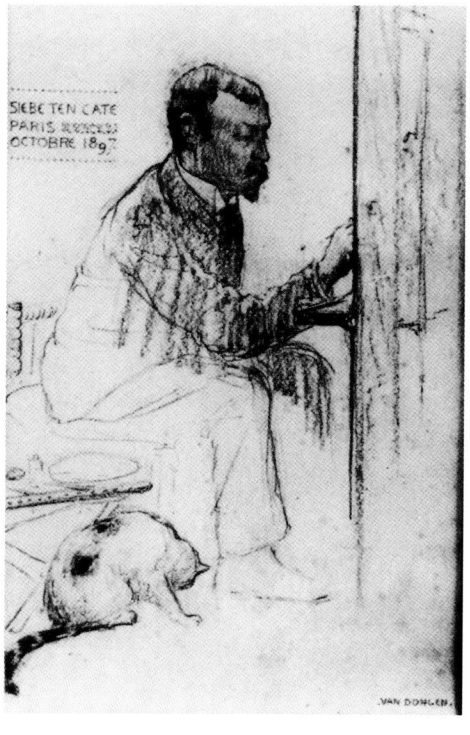

12.
Les dessous de Paris moderne (The Underbelly of Modern Paris)
Intérieur d'un atelier d'Art nouveau
Illustration in *Le Sourire*, no. 121 (15 February) 1902

13.
Portret Siebe ten Cate (Portrait of Siebe ten Cate), 1897
Black chalk
420 x 280 mm
Private collection

friends.[139] It is very likely that Snabilié, who lived in Paris from May 1895 working as foreign correspondent for various Dutch newspapers, was one of the 'sort of journalists' mentioned by Van Dongen who encouraged him to become an illustrator for magazines, newspapers and the like.[140]

His journalistic activities gave Snabilié a pivotal function in the Dutch community in Paris. He knew almost every Dutch artist, writer or journalist living in the city and would often introduce them to each other. Because of his function he was frequently involved in cultural activities such as the popular artists' banquets held to celebrate an artistic achievement. After 1900 he was secretary of the Dutch-French Society for which he organized musical evenings and performances for Dutch cultural circles.[141] He would write about these events in the newspaper under the titles *Letters from Paris* and *Letters from France*, recording a host of activities ranging from law suits to parliamentary sessions, to the night life in Montmartre. He also spoke of the exhibitions of French and Dutch artists held in Paris, including the annual Salons. It was Snabilié who wrote a review for the Dutch press of the first Paris exhibition in which Van Dongen showed his work, the *Exposition des peintres impressionistes et symbolistes* in December 1897 in the Galerie Le Barc de Bouteville. This exhibition lacked the appeal of the first in the series of annual presentations bearing this title, which was to spread the concept of Symbolism as an artistic style. This was the fifteenth exhibition and the last (organized by the successor to Le Barc after the latter's death) and presented work by a mixture of known and unknown artists such as Toulouse-Lautrec, Gauguin, Siebe ten Cate, and the Dutch debutantes Kees van Dongen and Bernard Klene, who was also in Paris at that time.[142]

The review by Snabilié appeared in March 1898, several months after the opening of the exhibition, in the Dutch weekly *De Amsterdammer*. It is interesting for being the first report of Van Dongen's stay in Paris. 'Cornelis van Dongen arrived in this city several months ago to seek his fortune in the extremely difficult world of art. He sought with determination and worked with diligence... I saw posters he had produced, portraits, illustrative drawings, scenes of Parisian life – some of them quite impressive.'[143] However, continued the article, the artist produced work of a widely differing nature and had not yet found his real niche, or 'point d'appui.' Snabilié makes it clear that he thinks he knows where this will be. He describes the two watercolours by Van Dongen as showing a scene with a few figures, disappearing into the mist 'which is dense and hangs heavy' while beside them stand rigid 'shadowy tree trunks whose tops cannot be seen'; of the other watercolour he says it has 'more light, more colour' so that figures emerge out of the mist 'visages perceived as in a late afternoon in the poor quarters of the city when the female workers are turning homewards from their factories.' And Snabilié went on to say that it was a fine artist who had inspired Van Dongen to make this work. Undoubtedly, this artist was Siebe ten Cate, whose pastel drawings the journalist had described a few lines earlier with such terms as 'the half-light of early evening' and the 'mist of autumn.'

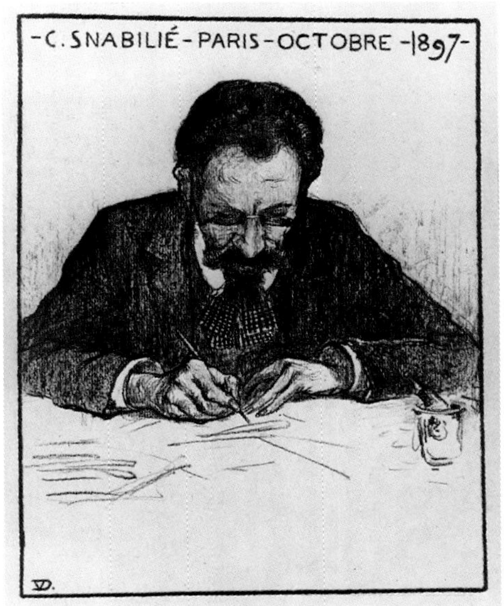

14.
Portret Charles Snabilié (Portrait of Charles Snabilié), 1897
Lithograph
386 x 264 mm
Bibliothèque Nationale, Paris

It is difficult to say exactly which works were on show. The catalogue only lists one entry, untitled, as a 'watercolour'. We know of related work by Van Dongen, such as *Paris la nuit* (fig. 21) or the night scene in the collection of the Phoenix Museum of Art. In these evening scenes Van Dongen, following the example of Ten Cate, places the passers-by like dark silhouettes against a shadowy background in an otherwise deserted city square. This type of scene with silhouettes in the dusk, thick mist or the grey sky of winter was a well-tried style that Ten Cate frequently applied.[144] Years later, in an interview in the 1950s, Van Dongen expressed his appreciation of Ten Cate. The older painter who had already made his name helped his younger colleague on the difficult path he had chosen. It seems that Ten Cate introduced Van Dongen both to the Galerie Le Barc de Bouteville as also to the art dealer Ambroise Vollard. In the latter's address books Van Dongen's name is listed under the 'C' for Cornelis – exactly as it is in the

cat. 27

exhibition catalogue of Le Barc de Bouteville – and the address given is that of Ten Cate's studio at 65 rue de Malte. Nothing is known about early acquisitions of Van Dongen's work by Vollard.[145]

During his second stay in Paris Van Dongen again contacted Ten Cate. Evidence of this is a drawing dated 22 November 1899 showing Ten Cate seated on a folding chair

cat. am. 1, 2 and sketching a passer-by, in the rue Ravignan in Montmartre. Scenes of street life, like this one Ten Cate was drawing, were made by both these artists at the time. Among these drawings are scenes showing fashionable figures – 'demimondaines' – setting off for a ball or perhaps returning from one, and drawings of a lonely figure seated wearily

cat. 19, 34-38 on a bench in a Parisian suburb. In Ten Cate's work, however, such scenes are exceptions – with him it is city and harbour views that predominate. At this time the most famous artist producing street scenes was Théophile-Alexandre Steinlen, nicknamed the 'master of the street'.[146] And although Van Dongen was extremely reticent on this topic it is quite clear that his interest in 'the street' as a subject was 'most inspired by Steinlen.' This comment was made by the journalist M.J. Brusse in connection with drawings that Van Dongen made after his first stay in Paris when he was back in Rotterdam in 1899, the year in which Brusse and the artist became friends.[147]

STEINLEN

'He saw the French *Gil Blas* in the kiosks, illustrated by Steinlen,' noted Paul Guth when he reported on his meeting with Van Dongen. Guth proffered the suggestion that Van Dongen had already seen the work of Steinlen in Rotterdam and that this was the chief reason for his going to Paris in 1897.[148] In view of Van Dongen's early preference for Symbolism, this seems unlikely. Indeed, the question arises what work by Steinlen he could have seen in the Netherlands. An 1894 publication on French draughtsmanship by Frits Lapidoth naturally contains a chapter on Steinlen, but there are few illustrations in the book.[149] There were a few poster exhibitions including the previously mentioned one in Rotterdam which showed a few works by Steinlen.[150] But we gather from various sources that the illustrated French magazines were difficult to obtain in the Netherlands.[151] Thorn Prikker, living in The Hague, wrote a letter in April 1896 offering the writer Henri Borel as an exceptional proposal several numbers of the left-wing periodical *Le Chambard Socialiste* (1893-95) – some of which contained prints by Steinlen – with the comment: 'As you know, the Chambard is banned and discontinued and all the copies have been burned by the police. It is now an extremely rare document to find second-hand!' In an earlier letter dated July 1893 we read how hard Thorn Prikker had tried to acquire for his friend a few numbers of the magazine *Gil Blas illustré*, which was not such political dynamite, containing illustrations by Steinlen.[152] The journalist M.J. Brusse, editor of home news for the daily *Nieuwe Rotterdamsche Courant* and thereby close to the pulse of the press, did not discover a copy of *Gil Blas illustré* in Rotterdam until the end of the 1890s. It was 'quite by chance,' he revealed in a lecture given in 1904 at the opening of an exhibition on topical prints in Amsterdam's Stedelijk Museum, one day when he was on his way to the newspaper offices: 'I passed a kiosk one morning in Rotterdam and was attracted by a brilliant red colour against a background of soft grey and black, with a few dabs of yellow.' He went on to describe the print – his first encounter with an illustration by Steinlen – which showed a 'dark public garden with bare, wet-black winter trees in the evening.' In the foreground was a prostitute with her arms round a fat old gentleman who was wearing a top hat with a mourning ribbon round it. In the background a couple of revolting whores. Brusse's detailed description identifies the drawing as *Vanité d'un vieillard* which adorned the cover of *Gil Blas illustré* for the edition of 9 June 1899. (fig. 15) Another admirer of Steinlen was the collector from The Hague, Cornelis Hoogendijk, who beside a core of international modern art had the largest collection of Steinlen prints and drawings ever assembled in the Netherlands. Interestingly, he began this collection only late in the nineteenth cen-

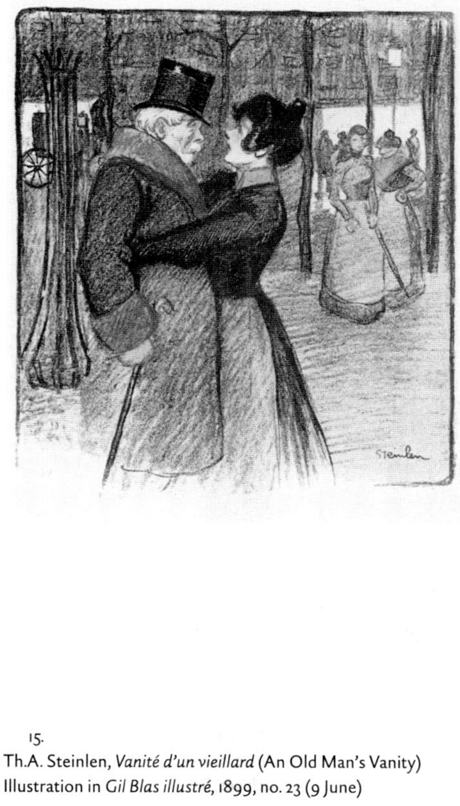

15.
Th.A. Steinlen, *Vanité d'un vieillard* (An Old Man's Vanity)
Illustration in *Gil Blas illustré*, 1899, no. 23 (9 June)

tury. His first show of part of it was held in February 1899 in The Hague.[154] Van Dongen would undoubtedly have attended the exhibition, but by that time he was already familiar with this work from his Paris days.

In Paris, it was not difficult for Van Dongen to see Steinlen's posters or prints. Steinlen's printed work was, as Brusse put it, 'everyone's property' and could be seen in all the Paris kiosks and in the small bookshops of the poorest districts. On Friday evenings the colour supplements of the newspapers were sold from piles at street corners and the Parisians could enjoy the latest numbers as they sat in their street cafes.[155] At the end of the nineteenth century any self-respecting Parisian daily would produce an illustrated supplement. What with technical advances and the end of censorship, in the course of a few decades the production of the daily press had multiplied by five and sales improved vastly if a paper were illustrated.[156] Also, several magazines such as *La Plume*, *La Revue Blanche* or *Les Temps Nouveaux* published original graphic work in separate editions by the artists associated with them, or they would print a limited number of copies of illustrations they were also publishing. This policy was also adopted by left-wing publications such as *Le Chambard Socialiste* and *La Feuille*.[157] Then there were the *kiosques à affiches* of Paris and various *cafés-artistiques* such as *Quat'z'Arts* or *Le Lapin Agile* where prints by the Montmartre artists decorated the walls, all opportunities to view this art.[158] The posters in the street provided, so wrote Fénéon in 1893 'an outdoor exhibition all year long, wherever you go...and that's art, by God, and the best kind, mixed in with life, art without any bluffing or boasting and easily accessible to the man in the street.'[159] And not only visually accessible. It was all the rage to follow the people who pasted up the posters and try to get hold of one for your collection – which Fénéon strongly recommended doing. The Dutch journalists whom Van Dongen knew in Paris, such as Snabilié and later Alexander Cohen, who took up Fénéon's suggestion, both describe how they decorated the walls of their apartments with posters as well as prints they had taken from illustrated papers.[160]

The subject matter of this graphic art was life outside the home – night life in cafes or dance halls, the hustle and bustle of the street – as so tellingly captured by Steinlen in the poster *La rue* from 1898, which shows people from different social groups.[161] This is public life, not the intimacy behind the closed front door. The theme of life in the street was something that greatly appealed to Van Dongen when he was in Paris.

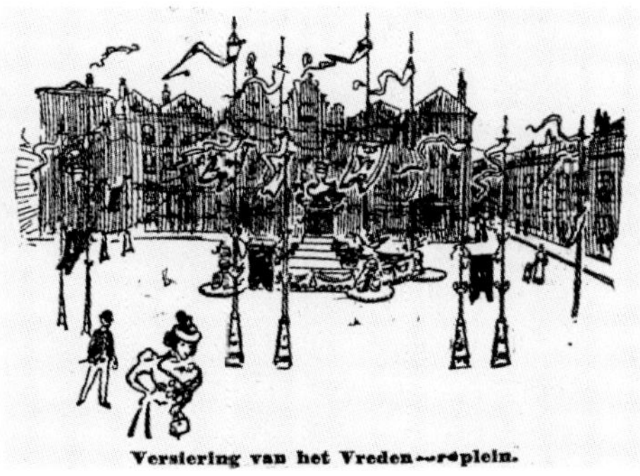

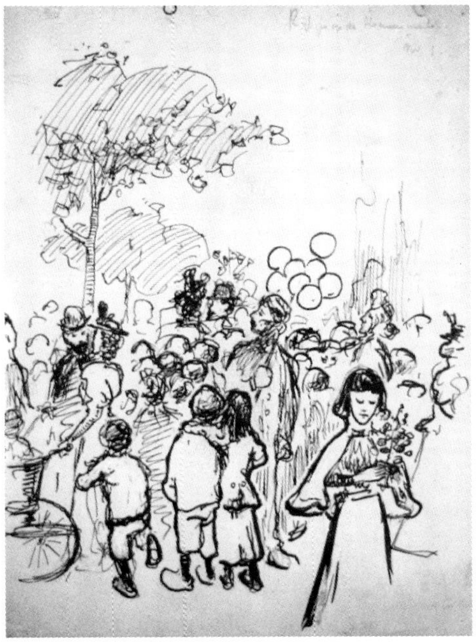

16.
Versiering van het Vredenoordplein
(Decoration of the Vredenoordplein)
Illustration in *Rotterdamsch Nieuwsblad*, 8 June 1899

17.
Kijkjes op de bloemenmarkt
(Views of the flower market), 1899
Pencil, black ink, white gouache, 322 x 245 mm
Rotterdams Nieuwsblad Archives, Rotterdam

THE STREET

The theme is in itself not a new one and can certainly be linked with many artists besides Steinlen. There is a long tradition of rendering a certain type of person in the street as representing a social class or profession. A striking example of this from the 19th century is the illustrated publication *Les Français par eux mêmes* (1840-42) which offers a complete description of the French population in word and picture.[162] This includes familiar street figures such as the tramp, street children, or the then common figure of the girl doing shopping for a household, the *trottin*. This type of iconography is also present in Steinlen's poster work. An artist from the second half of the 19th century who continued this tradition and was in his time widely admired was Jean-François Raffaelli. He invented his own term for this type of character drawing, calling it 'le caractérisme'. His work was known to Vincent van Gogh, and the artist Ten Cate appears to have been influenced by it.[163] Van Gogh studied comparable work showing national types in the English publication *The Graphic* as a young artist, and may have felt they were artistically valuable works: Raffaelli on the other hand saw them as chiefly documentary material. For him it was a kind of research and he concentrated on the lower classes because as he saw it they had been insufficiently studied so far.[164] The street as a topic had been taken up by the Impressionists and in their wake a whole stream of artists chose the Parisian boulevards as theme. Altogether they produced an illustrated city street plan.[165] For the Impressionists it was above all a contemporary subject. Encouraged by Baudelaire's essay from 1863, *Le peintre de la vie moderne*, based on the draughtsman Constantin Guys, and by the literature of the De Goncourt brothers, painters such as Manet and Monet and their followers in Holland, Breitner and Isaac Israels, recorded street life as a modern phenomenon.[166] They portrayed the city of Paris as designed by Baron Haussmann with its wide roads, its spacious street terraces, its new railway stations and bridges, or contemporary Amsterdam. Isaac Israels, who admired Van Dongen's drawings of street figures in Rotterdam's red light district, sometimes made comparable drawings but then to show how 'modern' he was.[167] For artists like Steinlen who were partly inspired by the same naturalist literature as were the Impressionists, the street as such lay somewhere else – north of the Boulevard de Clichy in Montmartre, or in one of the more outlying suburbs 'the distant suburbs with their threadbare trees.' What Steinlen saw passing before him was the life of the ordinary people, with which he identified himself. It was what the writer Anatole France described in 1903 as 'the morning stream of flesh and the sombre evening stream of the workers, the groups seated on the sidewalk, the homeless tramps of the black boulevards.'[168]

THE ART OF ILLUSTRATING: STEINLEN

In the illustrated magazines and papers of the 1890s probably the most prominent work was that of Steinlen. Around 1890 he illustrated for Aristide Bruant the songs in *Le Mirliton*, a celebration of the life in Montmartre, and he worked for several avowedly left-wing publications.[169] Examples of these are the paper referred to by Thorn Prikker, *Le Chambard Socialiste* (1893-95) whose confessed aim was to attack social inequality 'fearlessly and mercilessly', and the publications of the anarchist Jean Grave, *La Révolte* (1897-99) and *Les Temps Nouveaux* (1895-1914).[170] However, only the illustrations by Steinlen for the left-wing *La Feuille* (1897-99) published by the free anarchist Zo d'Axa (Charles Galland) appeared in the period when Van Dongen was in Paris. The poster by Steinlen announcing the first number of *La Feuille* – which shows a crowd in the street hemmed in by copies of the magazine – was pasted up in Paris in October 1897. *La Feuille*, meaning a leaf of paper, indeed consisted of one sheet; it appeared at irregular intervals and devoted several of its numbers to the Dreyfus Affair which was then a hot topic.[171] The magazine *Gil Blas illustré* was more eye-catching. It was a literary supplement that appeared with the daily *Gil Blas* and over the years 1891

to 1900 Steinlen made the illustrations for the cover almost every week, and initially also for the back page. It was through this publication that Steinlen became widely known as an illustrator and indeed gained the name for himself of being its artist.[172] Unlike the left-wing papers to which those who were interested subscribed, the successful *Gil Blas* had a wide readership and was on sale at the kiosks.[173] Probably it attracted attention because of its large size. As the theme for his full-page cover illustration Steinlen always chose a passage from the one of the accompanying literary articles appearing in the same number. These tended to be short texts usually by writers from the school of Zola or the De Goncourt brothers, such as Paul Arène or Alphonse Daudet and often described a moment in the daily life of workers, shop girls, tramps or prostitutes.[174] The scenes were regularly interposed with descriptions of the parts of the city, in the manner that Zola had used in *L'Assommoir* – allegedly the novel that brought Steinlen to Paris.[175] With their urban setting and enduring rhythm of street life, the life of the common people was presented: 'Eight o'clock. Out come the women. They flow down from Montmartre, from Belleville, from all sides…from every side street they emerge, they join the flowing movement streaming along the pavement.'[176] It was street scenes like this one that Steinlen chose for his illustrations, as can be seen in the print described by Brusse or in *Ballade d'hiver*. (fig. 15) The technique used, that of cat. 3
strong black chalk lines on rough paper, emphasizes the poverty of the scenes he portrayed. Or he adapted his approach to his purpose in some other way. In the drawing for *Ballade d'hiver* the prostitutes appear all the more forlorn because of the extreme foreshortening of the boulevard. The subjects and the style were an extension of Steinlen's cat. 14
political involvement, which was something Van Dongen understood very well. It was not the political prints, but the illustrations Steinlen made for *Gil Blas* with their general social implications that initially appealed most to Van Dongen and that he used as examples. 'The street' is certainly a major theme in his work until 1904. It is both the art and the literature that appealed to the Dutch journalists with whom Van Dongen became friends at the end of the 1890s.

Both Snabilié and Brusse mingled their journalistic observations with realistic sketches of street life, and both were inspired in their work by the pictures of contemporary illustrators. Snabilié more than once began a newspaper article with a description of traffic on the boulevards or with a drawing capturing the mood of part of the city. The same is true for Brusse who like his colleagues in Paris filled his Rotterdam office with posters and prints by contemporary artists.[177] Indeed, he referred to a poster by Steinlen as the direct inspiration for one of his most successful newspaper articles, a short story written in 1901 about the street child called Boefje, a young scamp.[178]

It shows how highly the work of Steinlen and naturalistic writing was valued. One example of the great esteem in which especially Steinlen's work was held is that after his illustrations had been published in *Gil Blas illustré* they would be returned to him and he would colour them in with chalk and sell them – 'scarcely a week after publication he had sold them all.'[179] Another example of the appreciation for illustrative art at this time is provided by the writer Charles-Louis Philippe who commented somewhat acidly upon the drawings made by Albert Marquet for his novel *Bubu de Montparnasse*: 'The first thing I thought of when I saw the illustrations by M. Albert Marquet was to run away as quickly as possible so that there would be room for them – they are so comprehensive on their own.' It should perhaps be added that these illustrations were not in the end printed in his book.[180] cat. am. 10, 11

WRITERS' CIRCLES: SNABILIÉ

The journalist and writer Charles Snabilié turns out to have had a great many connection in the circles of Parisian writers and artists. 'He really knows a lot of people,' commented Brusse on one occasion when the foreign correspondent was giving him a guided tour of Paris. In a book published in 1900 by Snabilié under the pseudonym of Bulée he offers an account of the Parisian writer's life. It is worth noting that this book, titled *Jean Lefort* and with a subtitle unquestionably modelled on Zola's 'slice of life' idea – 'a dip into the life of Paris' – bore an illustration by Kees van Dongen on its cover.[181] It is a 'drawn dip' into the Parisian life of the times. On a busy street we see two omnibuses passing each other, as well as a carriage and passers-by hurrying on their way. Van cat. 17, 18 Dongen knew the contents of the publication. He wrote in December 1900 to his Dutch friend Addicks: 'It's what you call a book about life, the author has experienced the story himself and is in fact the hero. The other characters are all based on real people – I could give you all their names.' The book, a *roman à clef*, can certainly provide more information about some of the people in Van Dongen's circle.

However, the characters in this novel are not very fully developed. Rather, the book is a guide to Paris, with all kinds of information about the city. Possibly Snabilié intended to provide a cross-section of the French writers' milieu of his day and wanted to comment on the various literary movements of the time. However, when we 'lift the tip of the veil beneath which the writer has hidden his characters' we discover that personal friends of the journalist lurk behind some of the names.[182]

Two brothers appear in the book, one a writer named Gaston Proust with 'dark eyes, a small mustache and goatee' and one an artist named Pierre Proust, described as 'the well-known artist who portrayed people from the slums, the painter of circus and street scenes.' This couple was modelled on Henri-Gabriel Ibels and his brother, the writer André Ibels.[183] At that time Henri Ibels made illustrations in a somewhat cramped style showing workers, circus figures and *café-chantant* artistes for such publications as the anarchist paper *Le Père Peinard* (1891-93) but also for *L'Echo de Paris* and *Gil Blas illustré*. He illustrated several books, including those of his brother, and in 1897 an edition of Zola's *La Terre*. His drawings were published in various collections.[185] The writer André Ibels was co-founder of the *Revue Anarchiste*, later called *Le Libertaire*, to which in around 1900 the Fauvist painter Maurice de Vlaminck contributed articles. Ibels also wrote for the left-wing newspaper *La Critique*.[185] The journalist Snabilié describes in his book how he attended several editorial meetings with André Ibels – probably of the *Mercure de France*, a newspaper for which Snabilié also occasionally wrote.[186] He visited the exhibition halls of the left-wing paper *La Plume* (both brothers published for this paper) together with Ibels as well as the exhibition hall La Bodinière, where both Ibels and Steinlen first showed their work. Clearly, the Ibels brothers moved in left-wing anarchist circles.[187]

Snabilié was a good friend of the artist Henri-Gabriel Ibels. He published a detailed article and gave a lecture to the Hague Kunstkring introducing Ibels' work to the Netherlands at an early date.[188] The lecture given by Ibels in 1896 in Rotterdam, about which Snabilié held some correspondence, has already been referred to. It seems that Van Dongen was acquainted with Henri Ibels. An early drawing by Van Dongen made at the beginning of his second period in Paris – in 1899 or 1900 – shows unmistakable p. 28 influence of Ibels' *forains* (circus types). (fig. 20) Chaumeil refers to a later cooperation between the artist and Van Dongen for the periodical *L'Assiette au Beurre*.[189] It would seem that the Ibels brothers were among those with whom Van Dongen was on easy terms.

There are other literary connections that arise in Snabilié's book such as the writer Catulle Mendès or – a good friend – René Valadon, director of *Le Figaro Illustré*, but they appear to be of less importance as far as Van Dongen is concerned.[190] However, it would seem that the writer Saint-Georges de Bouhélier was a significant figure in Van Dongen's development; he was referred to by Snabilié in the book as 'Saint Vincent de Bourgogne.'[191] Bouhélier, together with Maurice Leblond was one of the pioneers of literary naturism in 1895, a movement that arose in opposition to Symbolism. In their literary work these writers chose – following Zola – to take the common people as their subject. They described the influence of nature and the passions of life but in contrast to the naturalists they did not work in an analytical manner and they attempted to avoid trivia.[192] In 1908 both Saint-Georges de Bouhélier as well as the Leblond brothers wrote an introduction in an exhibition catalogue for Van Dongen. In artistic terms these were Van Dongen's two most important early shows in Paris, one at the art dealer's Henri Kahnweiler and the other at Galerie Bernheim Jeune. There are several records of Van Dongen's friendship with De Bouhélier at this period.[193] However, it seems probable that Van Dongen had already met Bouhélier through Snabilié. This is particularly interesting in view of the subject matter of Van Dongen's work after 1904, that largely concerns the nitty-gritty of 'life'.

The book by Snabilié sketches one of the Parisian artistic milieus – naturalist and mainly left-wing – with which Van Dongen had come into contact and gradually learnt to know. It provided him with inspiring examples of people who were illustrators-cum-draughtsmen and the recognition they received, and may well have strengthened his decision to follow this path. Finally, there are several concrete examples of Snabilié's assistance. It was for the text written by a friend of Snabilié's that Van Dongen provided the illustrations, in a Dutch handbook for the World Exhibition in Paris in 1900. It also seems probable that Van Dongen received the commission via Snabilié to cover the festivities in Amsterdam around the marriage of Queen Wilhelmina in 1901, for the monthly *Elsevier's Geillustreerd Maandschrift*. The Paris correspondent clearly takes a cat. 28-30
place of honour as one of the journalists who introduced Van Dongen into the circles of the illustrators. The great appeal that the work of Steinlen in particular held for Dutch art was recognized at an early date by the Hague critic G.H. Marius. In 1903 she concluded her work on 19th-century Dutch painting with the remark: 'In the closing years of the 19th century our young painters have again been attracted to Paris and chiefly by Steinlen the great draughtsman who appeals above all to the northern character; this latest group belongs entirely to the next century.' Undoubtedly, Kees van Dongen was one of the group.[194] When asked about the background to his early artistic ambitions his first unequivocal reply was in 1963: 'I wanted to make illustrations, not paintings, but illustrations.'[195]

ROTTERDAM: 1898-1899

Forced by necessity, it seems, Van Dongen returned to Rotterdam in April or May of 1898. He is listed in the city population register as of 3 May, living at 25 Groenendaal. A former student at the Rotterdam Art Academy, the painter Martinus Schildt, had a studio at the same address, one floor above Van Dongen. Here Van Dongen met up with old Rotterdam friends such as Chris Addicks and Johan Mastenbroek, who wrote a short passage in his biography about this period, as well as the former members of Vrije Kunst, Koos Speenhoff and Johan Krulder.[196] These two can be seen in a drawing by Van Dongen, together with Martinus Schildt, titled *Souvenir-Groenendaal. Visites à mon atelier*. The black area in this sketch is a detail that Speenhoff draws attention to in cat. 8
his recollections of the artist. Apparently the artist painted the walls of his studio black so that his work would stand out to greater advantage. In these memoirs Speenhoff also describes Van Dongen's first 'own home' in Rotterdam – opposite a tobacco factory where as he recalls 'the factory girls' would sit 'singing at their work' before the window

while in the canal that ran in front of it were barges 'laden with packages and barrels of tobacco for the factory.'[197] Not far from the house lay the oldest inner harbours of Rotterdam, the Oude and Nieuwe Haven and the Haringvliet. Speenhoff recounts that in the first months he was often at Van Dongen's and writes of their bohemian way of life. They slept in the studio on the floor 'with a Bible or a skull, wrapped in a pillowslip' and had a lot of fun. He himself did very little, 'next to nothing and sometimes even less.' Kees van Dongen, however, worked hard and according to Speenhoff produced a painting 'every day.'[198] This remark only serves to show once more how memory is influenced by later events.

ILLUSTRATIONS AND DRAWINGS

'I managed to find a job with a Rotterdam newspaper as illustrator,' wrote Van Dongen to Fénéon in 1904. The subjects he had to draw included fires in the city, openings of new buildings, festive occasions and a report of the Peace Conference held in The Hague in May 1899. He made these illustrations for the *Rotterdamsch Nieuwsblad*, a local paper which was the first in the Netherlands to illustrate its reports.[199] It seems that Van Dongen worked for this paper from the summer of 1898 until he returned to Paris in October 1899. The drawings printed in the paper are unsigned, but with the help of some of the surviving originals it proves easy to designate the work done by Van Dongen. These are mainly series of drawings made for special topics. Apparently there was a permanent illustrator for the reports of daily events.[200] The first drawings made by Van Dongen were for the festivities in connection with the inauguration of Queen Wilhelmina in August 1898. He made designs for decorative coaches, decors and street decorations, and gave a picture of the many street activities and processions. In 1899 the queen visited Rotterdam and again Van Dongen illustrated this with a series of drawings.[201] Interestingly, in most of these drawings certain elements from French street scenes can be detected. (fig. 16) Besides these and the above-mentioned subjects Van Dongen drew scenes of Rotterdam city life, including some studies of his academy and series with a linking topic such as *Langs de Schie* (Beside the Schie) and *Markten in Rotterdam* (Rotterdam Markets).[202] (fig. 17) In this way Van Dongen became skilled in making swift outdoor sketches. 'He would walk after people, drawing them in action,' recalled a contemporary, 'with a bottle of Indian ink always ready in his breast pocket.'[203] The drawings, made on shiny white paper, are quick sketches done in pen and ink with here and there a correction made in white body colour. Then they would be reduced to three or four times the original size and printed between the text in the newspaper.

Among the first drawings that Van Dongen made after his return to Rotterdam are a watercolour showing a factory girl in the street, a picture titled *Les cigarières de Rotterdam* (The girls from the cigar factory) (fig. 18) that shows three girls leaving the factory across the road from his studio, and a couple of sketches showing glass-blowers. Notes made on the sheets tell that these were drawn in a glass factory in Capelle aan de IJssel, a place near Rotterdam. The drawings are not fully worked out, but Van Dongen shows clearly the exhaustion in the girls' faces, with their white, hollow cheeks and weary dark eyes. Shortly after this, around 1899, the drawings were made showing prostitutes and their clients in Rotterdam's red light district, which is centred around
cat. 10-15 Zandstraat. These street figures, and the roughly sketched technique, are directly inspired by the work of Steinlen in his drawings for *Gil Blas illustré*. It is not clear whether naturalist literature also influenced this choice of theme. Nothing is known about Van Dongen's literary taste.

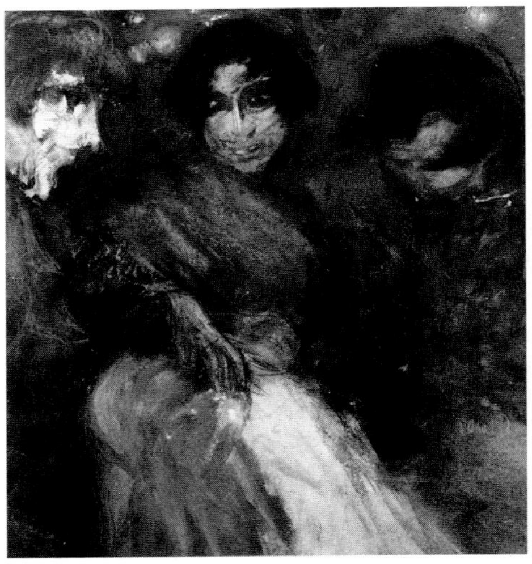

18.
Les cigarières de Rotterdam
(The girls from the cigar factory, Rotterdam), 1898
Watercolour, 320 x 290 mm

According to Brusse, he made 'hundreds of sketches in this district, drawings of types that usually have an aggressive quality to them.'[204] Apparently Van Dongen sketched the scenes on the spot and then copied them onto huge sheets of lining paper. He would give the figures 'some colour here and there with pastel or watercolour' whereby he aroused the compassion of the viewer or suggested a terrible destructive fatality. His restricted use of colour, the swiftly-drawn thick chalk lines, and the cheap rough paper are all appropriate for the wretched nature of the subjects. It would seem that Van Dongen took great care in applying this sober technique. He chose soft colours to accentuate his pictures – tones of orange-yellow or brown-red – undoubtedly influenced by Steinlen's *Gil-Blas* graphics. But more than the latter – who occasionally seems to add too much colour to the subjects of poor workers – Van Dongen consciously restrained his use of colour. He also concentrated less on the reproduction of types as on the recreation of the atmosphere in the neighbourhood. In order to become more adept at drawing, Van Dongen enrolled once again at the Rotterdam Academy.[205]

There are also a few paintings by him from this period. One is a harbour scene, *Bateaux*, another a seated nude, both canvases probably painted by Van Dongen in around 1898. (figs 22, 23) The dark scene showing Rotterdam's inner harbour is one of the strikingly few representations made by Van Dongen of this part of the city, although as subject matter it lay close by. The painting has a careful composition, set in a kind of framework, the ships in the foreground rendered with rough brushstrokes while in the second picture plane the brushstroke is finer, seeking to produce an effect of fading shapes. This style of work is markedly different from Van Dongen's earlier impressions of Delfshaven and it would seem that in this later work he was assisted by his former academy colleague Johan Mastenbroek, who was a specialist in this genre. The other canvas, showing a nude seated on a stool, somewhat resembles the harbour view in terms of its dark palette and firm brushstroke. The dating has been made partly because of this resemblance, also because the model is thought to be Van Dongen's girlfriend (and later wife) Guus Preitinger. At that time she was also having lessons at the Academy.[206] The painting is most likely the one exhibited by Van Dongen in 1904 at Vollard's, titled *Jeune Fille nue* which was then given the date of 1898. The other Rotterdam works exhibited at Vollard's were almost certainly – as was stated at the time – made before his first departure for Paris.[207] Unlike his friends Mastenbroek, Addicks and Schildt who were painting old people dozing in their chairs or realistic washerwomen or fruit sellers in the tradition of the seventeenth-century genre piece, in his second Rotterdam period Van Dongen's work chiefly consisted of drawings.[208] There is an account written in 1936 by the publisher Willy Brusse, younger brother of M.J. Brusse, telling of a visit to Van Dongen's Delfshaven studio in about 1899, which corroborates this.[209] Apparently Willy Brusse saw some nudes (paintings) and a portrait, and for the rest – drawings. This has been cited above, the 'piles of sheets of cheap lining paper, reams of the cheapest quality paper, thousands of large sheets covered with fragmentary sketches, parts of the human body, countless lines, the records of the ceaseless movement of life.' And M.J. Brusse too stressed Van Dongen's ceaseless activity as a draughtsman: 'Everywhere he went, he had a stump of charcoal or chalk in his short-fingered, red workman's hand, recording with swift accurate strokes. He worked unceasingly and with amazing speed.'

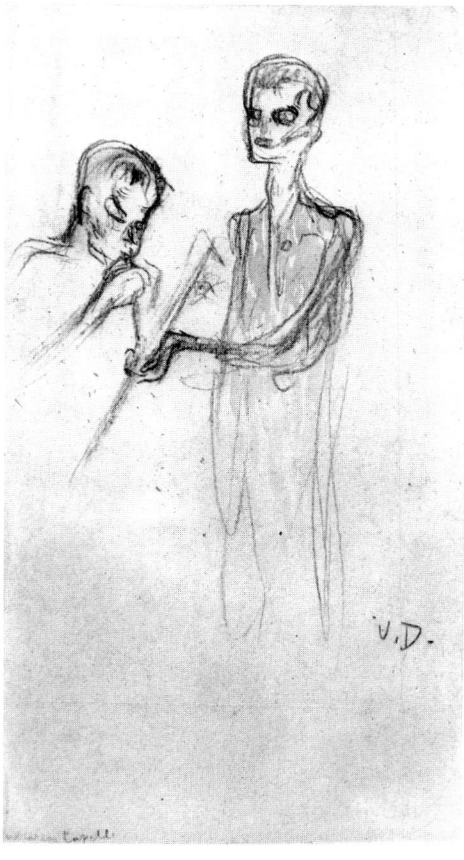

19.
Glasblazers Capelle (Capelle Glassblowers), 1898
Black chalk, watercolour
288 x 160 mm

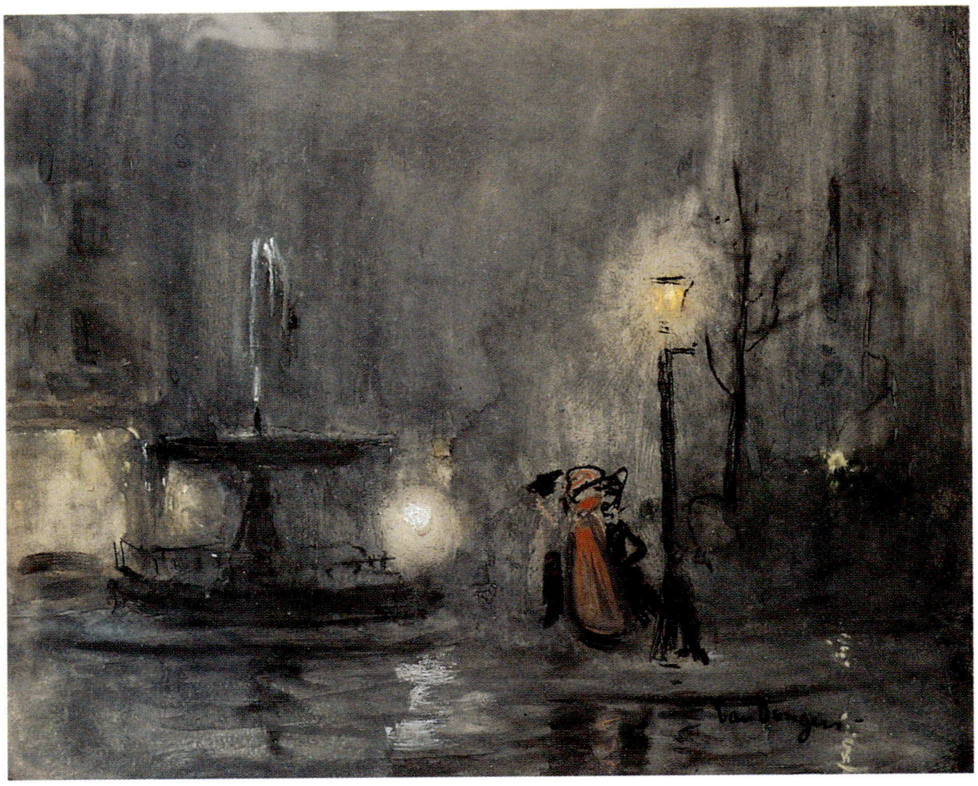

BRUSSE

The above is cited from one of the articles that M.J., also called Rie, Brusse wrote in 1927 recording his friendship with Van Dongen, on the occasion of his retrospective exhibition in Amsterdam's Stedelijk Museum.[210] Brusse was appointed editor of the newspaper *Nieuwe Rotterdamsche Courant* in 1894 and appears to have first met Van Dongen in 1899, 'after his days in Groenendaal street.' At that time the artist was living in a tiny room 'near the top floor of a miserable barracks of a house' on a 'dull, run-down street,' recalls Brusse. Van Dongen moved there, to number two on the corner of Batavierstraat and West Kruiskade, on 12 April 1899. The journalist Rie Brusse, then aged 26 and four years older than Van Dongen, was living with his mother and younger brother Willy – later to be a publisher – on Diergaardesingel close by.[211] Brusse wrote a detailed account for the newspaper of his meeting with Van Dongen. For him the contact was more than just a friendship. 'In those days – now more than thirty years ago – I used to see a young man and woman wandering together under the trees near my home, utterly engrossed in each other...and my mother, sitting beside the window, would see the young couple passing by and developed a friendly interest in them.' Once they stopped and spoke to Brusse's mother, and so the contact began. Brusse provided a detailed description of Van Dongen's appearance and character. He called him 'a good-looking, pleasant young man' who derived from the malting occupation of his ancestors his 'strength, strong wrists' and 'not-to-be-sidetracked determination' as well as an ascetic aptitude to put up with necessity's sharp pinch. His voice had something essentially soft and pleasing that leant him a gentle touch, tempering his otherwise 'ready irony, laughing cynicism and determined, almost headstrong, self-assurance.' He would often wear a pair of cotton-linen trousers and a blue sailor's pullover which gave him, together with his dashing nonchalance, a strikingly attractive appearance of artistic poverty.[212] The meeting between Brusse and Van Dongen took place at a time when the former, besides writing for the newspaper was applying himself to writing in serial form, articles that united his social and literary interests in a journalistic report. For these pieces Brusse tried to acquire material that was as genuine as possible. He would go – sometimes in disguise – to the haunts of 'the common folk' so that he could write eye-witness accounts in the style of the naturalist novels.[213]

21.
Paris la nuit (Paris at Night), c. 1900
Black chalk, watercolour, gouache, ink
490 x 630 mm

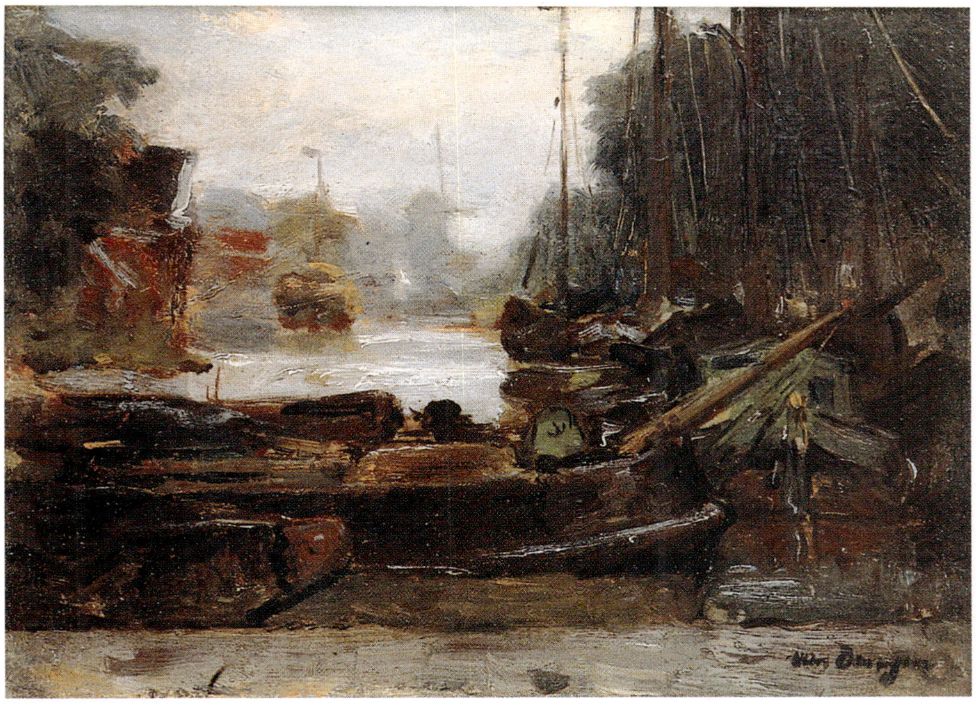

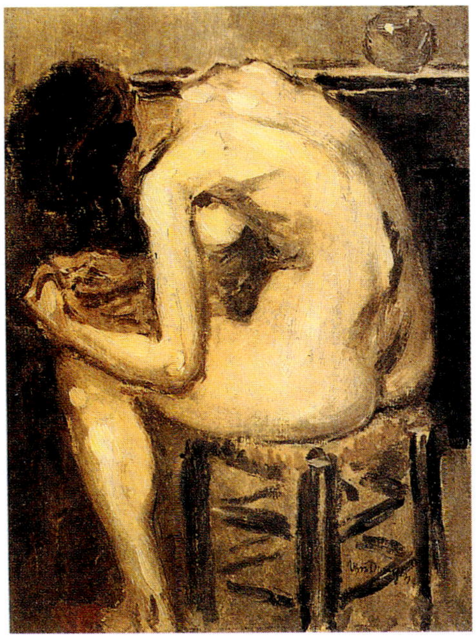

22.
Bateaux (Boats), c. 1898
Oil on paper on canvas
24 x 33 cm

23.
Femme nue (Female Nude), c. 1898
Oil on canvas
41 x 33 cm

ZANDSTRAAT

Together with Van Dongen, Brusse strolled on several occasions through the Zandstraat area, which he described as 'the old Rotterdam polder with its repressed passions.' He continued 'and we often wandered round there together, following unplanned tracks through that suspicious layered confusion of people, through the alleys and passageways between those almost coal-black hovels, narrowly opening into the night air.' For the young painter it signified 'the perpetual attraction of the pilgrimage away from the boring reality of the city.'[214] The term 'Zandstraat area' applied to the district around the Zandstraat street, covering a few streets and bordered on the north by Raamstraat and on the south by Hoogstraat – roughly speaking the area now occupied by the Rotterdam town hall and post office. This part of the city, nicknamed 'the polder', dated from the seventeenth century and consisted of dilapidated small houses, mostly one-roomed homes, on narrow streets and alleys where the daylight scarcely penetrated.[215] Lying as it did on the extension of the route across the Schiedam Dyke which led to the city centre from the river Maas and the old harbours, in the course of the 19th century this district had become a centre for the visiting sailors. Almost the whole quarter was given over to worldly pleasure! There were brothels, small shops and places to eat, cafes providing entertainment, pubs, restaurants and a good number of dance halls with imaginative names such as The Horse in the Cradle, the Seven Cent Hall and the Hopping and Skipping Shebang. Some of the places had half English names, such as the Liverpool Lichthouse and Café de Nightlamp, adapted for an international sailors' jingo. The municipal government, for whom this entertainment centre and its allied growing criminality in the city heart was an ongoing irritation, had the district pulled down in 1912.[216] Shortly before this, Brusse wrote a few final articles about it. He published this series in book form titled *Het rosse leven en sterven van de Zandstraat* (Zand Street – living and dying in a red light). The book was published in 1912, the year the district was pulled down, and included some illustrations that he owned, which had been made by Van Dongen.[217] (figs 24, 25, 26) Incidentally, these drawings should be dated 1895, not 1899, that being the year in which both of them got to know the district.

Presumably it was Van Dongen who first discovered 'the Zandstraat' as a subject –

though perhaps 'discovered' is not quite the right term, since the district lay immediately behind the art academy. To get to their drawing lessons, wrote Brusse in one of his articles, the students would walk along Raamstraat, 'a narrow column of students zigzagging through the stream of traffic, carrying their large wooden drawing boards with the set-squares attached, making their way to the Academy on Coolvest.'[218] In later years, Van Dongen enjoyed reminiscing about the neighbourhood. He wrote to Fénéon that he actually lived there: 'I often stayed in Zandstraat when I was in Rotterdam and that's why the worthy citizens of Rotterdam believe me to be crazy and impossible.'[219] In an interview he gave in 1958 he repeated these sentiments: 'That was the only district where I could survive on virtually nothing.'[220] However, it is not clear whether this is strictly based on fact. Speenhoff, who is frequently mentioned as housemate of Van Dongen at this time and was well-known as a raconteur, does not mention any lodging place in Zandstraat.[221] But clearly, the neighbourhood held a charm for Van Dongen: 'and then it is so picturesque – all the activity in this neighbourhood. The women at their large windows waiting for a client look as if they're in a showcase – sitting still, waiting,' he recalled in the interview.

The earliest descriptions by Brusse of the Zandstraat district are in his first important series, titled *Van af- tot aanmonsteren* (Sailors signing on and off for work), based on articles published in the paper in June and July 1899 – shortly after he'd got to know Van Dongen.[222] It is a well-documented report on the abuses that may be associated with the presence of sailors in a port. Brusse, writing with a strong social conscience, criticized mainly the owners of cafes and boarding houses who exploited the sailors by charging exorbitant prices for rooms and food, while at the same time trying to make a profit from the sailors' conscription.[223] In his efforts to gain accurate information Brusse disguised himself as a sailor and went round the ports in several cities, finishing up in Rotterdam. This is the point in his series of articles where he describes Zandstraat. Apparently Van Dongen was with him, and one of the illustrations owned and used by Brusse for this article in the book about the Zandstraat neighbourhood, is a picture by Van Dongen of this last expedition. (fig. 24) The drawing shows the sailors who accompanied the enterprising journalist: on the left is Toon wearing a multi-coloured scarf so characteristic of sailors (which Brusse also acquired for his disguise) and on the right, wearing a jacket, is Bakker – Brusse's guide through the sailors' haunts and the red light district.[224] The girl in front of him on the right appears in the following series of articles by Brusse on the neighbourhood: she is called Setje, and wanders slowly along the streets with a basket of paper flowers that she tries to sell to the sailors.[225]

The other drawings by Van Dongen of the Zandstraat district are mainly pictures of prostitutes. (figs 25, 26) They are seen negotiating with interested men, wandering alone down the street or peering from a door or window. 'The girls would sit re-arranging their gaudy clothes' 'their faces worn out by human passion, coloured now with rouge, their hair dry and frizzled' is how Brusse sketched the scene in 1899.[226] Elsewhere he writes of the proffered evening entertainment: 'out of the darkness a square of yellow light shining invitingly where a curtain has been pulled open' and a figure in the window 'with shiny metallic eyes squeezed into slits beneath the long fringe of sleazy hair.' One of these early sketches by Van Dongen also shows an evening scene in Zandstraat lit romantically with many-coloured oil lamps and a bright white circle in front – representing the light from a gas lamp, a new feature of the city streets at that time. This picture can also be found in Brusse's reports: 'Against the black walls of the street the dazzling lights shine in long festoons, reflecting crazily off the muddied cobblestones' where 'slender girls' are walking along towards their nightly haunts in their skimpy dresses, 'their décolletages and short colourful silk skirts hidden beneath a long dark grey raincoat.' This was how Brusse described it in his series *Religion in Zandstraat*, published in the paper in 1901.[227] With its vivid description of the atmosphere in the district, it puts a strong case for social and religious help for the women

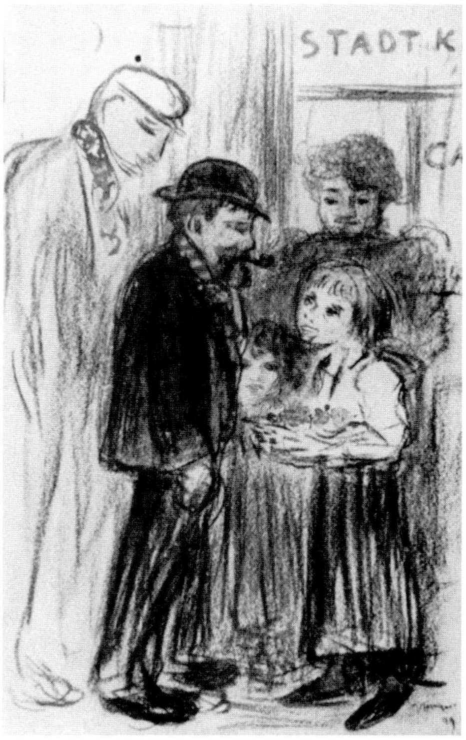

24.
Zeelui passagieren in de Zandstraat
(Sailors on Shore Leave in Zandstraat), 1899
Illustration in M.J. Brusse, *Het rosse leven en sterven van de Zandstraat* (Zandstreet – living and dying in a red light), Rotterdam 1917

earning their living as prostitutes. It was as a result of these articles that a new crisis centre was set up for the women.[228] Without doubt, Van Dongen would have been aware of Brusse's social commitment. Indeed, he presumably shared it to a large extent. And Brusse was presumably also influenced by Van Dongen's drawings when he wrote his articles.

Van Dongen made several visits to Rotterdam after 1900, and again drew scenes in this neighbourhood. There are various series of these drawings. Those from 1901-02 are more detailed and the figures are given a background setting. Some of these drawings can definitely be dated later, because of the notes written in French on them or cat. 63-67
because Van Dongen developed them as illustrations for magazines in Paris. There is a cat. 74-79
series in ink and watercolour showing the 'women of easy virtue' which can be dated 1903 because of the technique it uses. His later trips to Rotterdam are recorded in letters cat. 68, 73
and by work he made in the Netherlands. It is worth noting that although models were certainly not lacking in Paris, it seems that Van Dongen made drawings of prostitutes almost exclusively in Rotterdam.

Brusse recalls that after a time Van Dongen became an extremely familiar figure in Zandstraat. In a piece published in 1907, titled *A Painter Looking for Models*, Brusse describes a visit to the seamy side of Rotterdam together with an artist – presumably Van Dongen.[229] The artist is presented here in a brightly lit dance hall surrounded by giggling girls who 'rolled up their sleeves [to show their bare arms] and revealed their legs, bedecked in red woollen stockings, trying to outdo one another with the beauty of their shape.' Elsewhere Brusse described Van Dongen drawing in a brothel on Scharensteeg, and producing a sketch of the interior 'a rough drawing with a dash of watercolour.' This was at one time in Brusse's possession, but seems to have got lost.[230] Clearly, the writer Brusse felt a romantic attraction for this neighbourhood with its rough folk lacking in social skills.[231] He took other painters there too, such as the Amsterdam Impressionist Isaac Israels whom he met in about 1903. Israels took his sketchbook with him 'on one occasion' during a joint expedition with the writer. However, to Brusse's disappointment the artist was not entirely engrossed by the subject and soon wanted to go where he could see 'women who were well-groomed and reasonably fashionably attired.'[232] When the French Neo-Impressionist Paul Signac went to the Netherlands at Van Dongen's recommendation in 1906, Brusse also took him through this district and together they visited Nielsen's dance hall. But once again the experience was a 'grave disappointment'. Brusse's excuse was that the modern gas lamps had ruined the atmosphere entirely.[233] Quite possibly this was so, because when Van Dongen visited the city in 1907 and had started working on the painting *Liverpool light house*, he used a sketch for the impression on the left of the canvas which he had made of Zandstraat in 1899. The red light district of Rotterdam that Brusse and Van cat. 123
Dongen knew at the turn of the century, was no more.

Brusse's admiration for Van Dongen's work is preserved for us through his writings. Presumably what most intrigued him was the artistic interaction, and evidence of this can be found in a kind of painterly prose style adopted by Brusse at this time. Regretfully, we do not know what Van Dongen thought of Brusse's journalistic offerings. The correspondence between the two men is almost completely lost. The letters sent by Van Dongen – a considerable collection as the Brusse family recalled – went up in flames during the Second World War; all that survived were two drawings by Van Dongen.[234] Undoubtedly, Van Dongen would have seconded the importance of Brusse's socially committed articles. He also wrote himself at that time and in a letter cat. 67; p. 236
dated 1900 he reports that he has 'note books full of written impressions' from the Netherlands. It is not known what the subject matter of these texts was. At all events, Brusse and Van Dongen shared an interest in the work of Steinlen, and in Paris. Van Dongen went to settle for good in that city in the autumn of 1899 and very shortly after Brusse followed him 'to spend his first vacation abroad.' Back in Holland Brusse told a

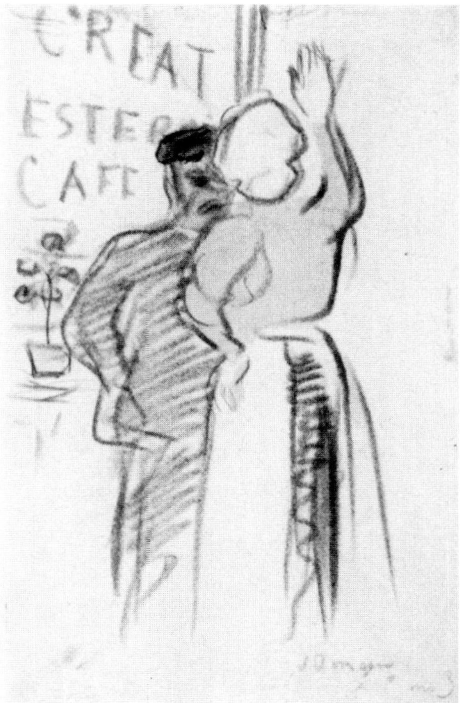

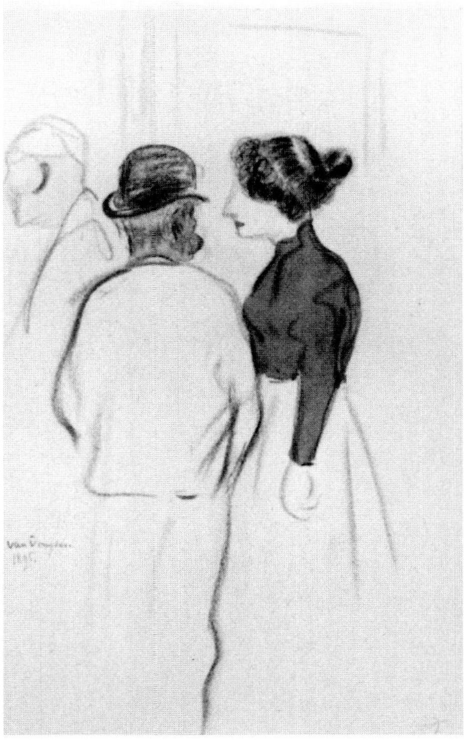

25.
Marchandeeren (Haggling), c. 1899
Illustration in M.J. Brusse,
Het rosse leven en sterven van de Zandstraat, Rotterdam 1917

26.
Zandstraattypen (Zandstraat characters), c. 1899
Illustration in M.J. Brusse,
Het rosse leven en sterven van de Zandstraat, Rotterdam 1912 (1917)

friend 'Just imagine, I spent the whole month of October in Paris with Van Dongen, a young artist from Rotterdam, who has been living there for a while. What a city! So much more open, fresher, more youthful than Holland. I really lived as a Parisian…and saw an amazing slice of the life there.'[235] We have a picture by Van Dongen of him writ-
cat. 16 ing at a table in Montmartre, a memento of their friendship.

In Rotterdam, however, there was not a great deal of enthusiasm for Van Dongen's work. Plans were made to sell his drawings and they were carefully stuck 'one by one onto white cardboard' – but, says Brusse, the sales were a complete disaster. The only person to show any interest was his newspaper colleague, the literary and cultural editor, Johan de Meester.[236] At that time there were no major periodicals in the Netherlands to which Van Dongen could regularly contribute his illustrations. There were a few satirical publications – such as *Asmodée* (1854-1911) or *Uilenspiegel* (1870-1916) – but they didn't have the right tone or level.[237] The only papers or journals which published illustrations as well as text were *Woord en Beeld*, published in Haarlem (1896-1902) and the illustrated monthly *Elsevier's Geïllustreerd Maandschrift* (1891-1940) which had a largely Amsterdam based editorial board. These two magazines published illustrations to enliven the articles which were written largely in a naturalistic style.[238] However, such openings were very limited and could hardly compete with the culture of illustration then flourishing in France. Furthermore, Van Dongen was probably strengthened in his decision to return to Paris by several exhibitions of French art shown in Holland in 1899, including the Rodin exhibition in the Rotterdam Kunstkring and the selection of contemporary French watercolours and drawings mentioned above, from the Hoogendijk Collection in The Hague. And finally, there was the World Exhibition of 1900 held in Paris – certainly an opportunity for work – which would also have influenced Van Dongen's decision to quit Holland.[239]

PARIS, OCTOBER 1899

So Van Dongen set off again for the French capital in the autumn of 1899, this time intent on a long stay.[240] In his memoirs, Brusse described this in a somewhat romantic manner – as if Van Dongen disappeared mysteriously. It seems to have been a bit different from Brusse's story. Van Dongen sent Guus Preitinger (his girlfriend) a postcard on 25 September 1899 which makes it clear that she had left for Paris a couple of days before and found somewhere to live at 95 rue Ordener in Montmartre. Van Dongen followed her shortly after this, sending some things on ahead. He wrote 'Guschie, I sent you a basket of things on Monday afternoon. So you can count on my being with you in a couple of days.'[241] The house on rue Ordener was a temporary home. After about two months it was changed for some rooms on the top floor of a building at 10 Impasse Girardon, also in Montmartre. In December 1899 Van Dongen wrote to Chris Addicks, 'I live up in the sky, very healthy, and I work hard.'[242] He lived there almost without interruption until 1906. Another letter, dated 6 December 1900, explains that during the year he rented another floor as well: 'I've furnished the attic as my studio,
cat. 17 very pleasant, but you can only stand up straight on one side. It's right under the roof.'

Altogether Van Dongen sent six letters to his friend in Rotterdam; they are now in the Fondation Custodia in Paris. The correspondence deals mainly with practical points. From time to time Van Dongen talks about his plans as an artist. The letter from December 1900 about his new studio closes with a sketch of himself painting – smoking a pipe, in stockinged feet, standing in front of a table on which there is a piece of (probably) canvas (there is no easel). This corresponds with a passage in which Van Dongen writes that in the summer he began a painting 'of a completely white house without a single window' so that he painted 'a block of white house and in the background a blue-grey sky.' The canvas was not completed when he wrote the letter, although it was the first oil painting that he worked on after arriving in Paris: 'you will observe from this I'm not a great one for painting.' The painting was probably the one exhibited in 1908 titled *La maison sans fenêtres* at Berheim-Jeune's, and dated 1902-04 in the catalogue. In September 1901 Van Dongen declared that he only made drawings and that he had allowed painting to go completely by the board. 'Though there are I don't know how many of the things [paintings] produced every year – and what is worse, sold – while the people that make them are starving hungry and thousands of others are too.' This remark comes from the letter mentioned above in connection with Kropotkin, in which Van Dongen aired his radical left-wing views.[243]

In the letter to his friend in Holland, Van Dongen mentions that he found it difficult to see being an artist as 'a goal in life' and had been forced to 'waste a great deal of time' before he could get down to work. He performed all manner of small jobs ranging from porter at the markets or lighter of coal fires to (we read in the letters he sent to Addicks) writing 'business letters' and decorating 'a party room at Aubervilliers.'[244] Van Dongen wrote 'it's not at all easy to come by these jobs here' but he was still convinced that things would work out for him in Paris, only 'it takes longer the way I'm forced to do it.' Brusse also speaks of the early difficulties, doubtless basing his remarks on his correspondence with Van Dongen in these years. According to Brusse, Van Dongen led an ascetic life in Paris, counting every centime, convinced of his 'one firm task' and 'filled with determination to force the future to conform to his plans.' Indeed, when Brusse was visiting Paris Van Dongen once accused him of being a capitalist and a careless wastrel, who would use a match to light his cigarette when about ten minutes' walk away there was a tobacco shop 'with a burning lamp hanging outside.' And Brusse recounts that a Japanese tea service he had brought to Paris as a present for Guus, was taken by Van Dongen outside into the courtyard of their house, and solemnly smashed, piece by piece, because it was an unnecessary luxury: 'The only thing that is worthwhile, is work.'[245]

DRAUGHTSMANSHIP

Despite his remark that it was sometimes difficult to settle down to regular work (even 'women are a distraction') it seems that Van Dongen produced a great many drawings during this period. Many of these were made outdoors, quick sketches of street scenes, as he wrote to Addicks, 'a scribble in chalk or ink, add a dash of colour, and it's ready.' There is a drawing of a rag- and-bone man, *Le chiffonnier* (fig. 27), an amorous couple at the Butte, or prostitutes and their hoped-for clients seated upon a bench in the evening light in a suburban Parisian street. The quick 'dash of colour' successfully enlivens the drawing. In the streets Van Dongen was attracted by the hustle and bustle of the big city, and by the solitary burdened figure, by nightworkers and circus folk, by prostitutes in their miserable loneliness, by types who, like the artist himself, lived on the fringe of society or who had succumbed through circumstances and become a tramp or beggar. There is a series showing weary work horses, *Les chevaux de Paris* dated 1900, that in its mood fits in with the street drawings. The sketchy drawings, the striking greyish washes and the rough chalk lines were intended to give the pictures a feeling of 'raw life'. The white body colour was used, not as by the artists of the Hague School, to enhance a picture with a highlight but more often to underscore the paleness of human faces in the evening light. The figures in his drawings often look as if they are being propelled: sliding, almost skating, along the street, an effect he obtained by drawing the legs and feet in one stroke. This manner of drawing suggests a difficult, heavy existence and is also found, as is the apparently crude technique, in the socially involved art of Millet, Pissarro or Van Gogh. Presumably Van Dongen saw work by all of these painters. They were being exhibited both in Paris and Rotterdam, published in illustrated magazines, or he might have seen them when visiting friends such as Snabilié.[246]

cat. 19-21, 27

cat. 22-24

One exhibition that Van Dongen undoubtedly saw was the major presentation of drawings by Van Gogh held in the Rotterdam Kunstkring until February 1901.[247] There is a postcard dated 15 February of that year, sent to Guus Preitinger, which makes it clear

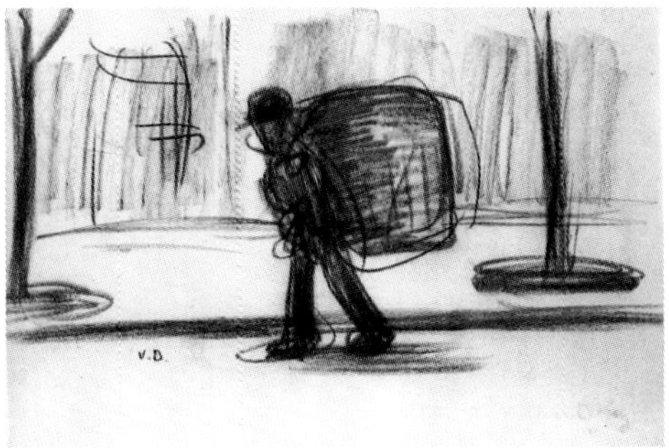

27.
Le chiffonnier (The rag-and-bone man), c. 1900
Black chalk, watercolour
190 x 295 mm
Private collection

he had already been in Holland for some time.[248] Indeed, the Van Gogh exhibition was possibly one of the reasons for Van Dongen's return to the Netherlands and he combined it with the commission mentioned earlier to make drawings for the festivities in Amsterdam connected with the wedding of Queen Wilhelmina. These celebrations took place in early March.[249] Brusse, who saw Van Dongen at that time in Rotterdam, may well have told him about the exhibition. In the same period Van Dongen worked for a few weeks in The Hague and Scheveningen in a studio with a friend of Thorn Prikker's, Sanne Bruinier, a female artist he had met in Paris.[250] On 16 March Van Dongen sent a message from which it emerges that during this stay in Holland he also visited the artist J.H. Mesdag. This painter of the Hague School owned a fine collection of French 19th-century art, part of it – including several magnificent drawings by Millet – in the Mesdag Museum.[251]

cat. 28-30

Reading the postcards that Kees sent from Holland to Guus in Paris we learn about his other activities. In Scheveningen he painted a portrait of the mother of the architect J.D. Looyen, who had been a witness at his wedding in July 1901.[252] He mentions that he is drawing a lot, along the coast, in the village of Scheveningen and later in Rotterdam. 'I have made a great number of sketches and will certainly be very busy on my return working some of these into pictures.' Also in Rotterdam Van Dongen painted an appealing portrait of his father using a colour spectrum and brushstroke reminiscent of Vuillard; there is a preliminary study of this in the Boijmans Van Beuningen Museum in Rotterdam.[253] In a final postcard sent to Guus on 16 March 1901, about a week before his return to Paris, he inquired about an entry he had presumably submitted for an exhibition: 'Has Jo [J.D. Looyen] framed all five of them and sent them in, or only 2 or 3?'[254] The question presumably refers to the drawings that he wanted to exhibit at the Paris Salon des Beaux-Arts that was to open on 22 April and where in the end only one of his drawings was shown, titled *Femme assise*. In his review of the works at the Salon, Snabilié said of the drawing: 'The talented young artist Kees van Dongen is represented by only one watercolour drawing, which is a little sombre, showing a seated woman.'[255] The entry, not surprisingly, escaped the notice of the French critics. Van Dongen's drawings of the royal wedding festivities in Amsterdam – intended for *Elsevier's* illustrated magazine – were not published. But a few months later he was to prove more successful.

cat. 31

ILLUSTRATIONS

A first notice about Van Dongen's debut in the French illustrated press appeared in the Netherlands on 1 July 1901, in a local paper and was doubtless written by a Dutch correspondent in Paris who knew the artist. 'For the past few years Paris has been the home to a young man from Rotterdam, who after a difficult beginning has now found his niche and hopes to make his way in the future. The famous draughtsman Steinlen saw his work and recommended him to the illustrated weekly *L'Assiette au Beurre*, where he immediately sold a couple of his drawings.'[256] The first drawing that was placed, showing 'a Parisian street singer' was described by the journalist as 'utterly simple in technique, totally effective in its presentation of poverty' as revealed in the expression on the singer's face. This was to become Van Dongen's specialty. 'Van Dongen, moved above all else by the misery of life, has demonstrated great skill in rendering his impressions [of street life].' When this report appeared, the drawing in question, showing a street fiddler, had already been published in *L'Assiette au Beurre*. (fig. 28) It is a sketch in black chalk with a few brushstroke contours in black ink, a common practice also used by Steinlen. Van Dongen's trademark, the looping, shapeless feet, are merged into the silhouette with one stroke.

In connection with the comment made above concerning the contact between Van Dongen and Steinlen, nothing further is known.[257] Another Dutch artist working in Paris in those years, Pieter Dupont, was a good friend of Steinlen's and also one of

Snabilié's circle.[258] Undoubtedly, Van Dongen would have known this draughtsman and graphic artist. Around 1900 Van Dongen was drawing similar subjects to Dupont, such as the series of work horses which, incidentally, were a common sight in city traffic cat. p. 108 at the turn of the century. Dupont is scarcely known internationally, but at that time made the famous portrait of Steinlen, an engraving that appeared in many Steinlen publications. Dupont knew a good deal about Steinlen's working methods and later provided Brusse with considerable information on the subject.[259] It is quite possible that he introduced Van Dongen to Steinlen. Both these draughtsmen were familiar with printing techniques and Van Dongen may well have learnt about printing practices and suchlike from them.

Another important meeting for Van Dongen, and probably the source of his following commission for illustrations, was with the anarchist writer and journalist, Alexander Cohen. In July 1899 Cohen had returned illegally to Paris and in March 1900 had been given an official resident's permit. From that date on he was able once again to publish his work in France. In 1906 he became the Paris correspondent for the Dutch paper *De Telegraaf*, and worked in the preceding years for a number of papers and journals.[260] He wrote several literary reviews and political discussions in 1900-01 for the prestigious magazine *La Revue Blanche*, of which at the time the editor in chief was his good friend, Félix Fénéon. Cohen met Van Dongen some time around 1900, about the same time as Van Dongen made a portrait of him, and it was he who will have introduced the artist to Fénéon.[261] In about the same month as Van Dongen's drawing of the street musician was printed in *L'Assiette au Beurre*, in June 1901, it appears that Fénéon had invited the artist to make several drawings for 'his' paper.

Introductions of this kind were just what was needed. Although illustrated magazines were flourishing, helped by technical developments, it was not an easy world to penetrate. Also, with the success and growing appreciation of illustrations, the number of hopeful artists for whom this represented a primary source of income, was on the increase. To mention only a few, there was Frantisek Kupka, Jacques Villon, Juan Gris and Pablo Picasso – all of whom made illustrations for magazines. The editorial boards of illustrated papers could take their pick from a fine array. Several writers and illustrators refer to this in their memoirs – there was a long queue for the beginning artists who had not yet made a name.[262]

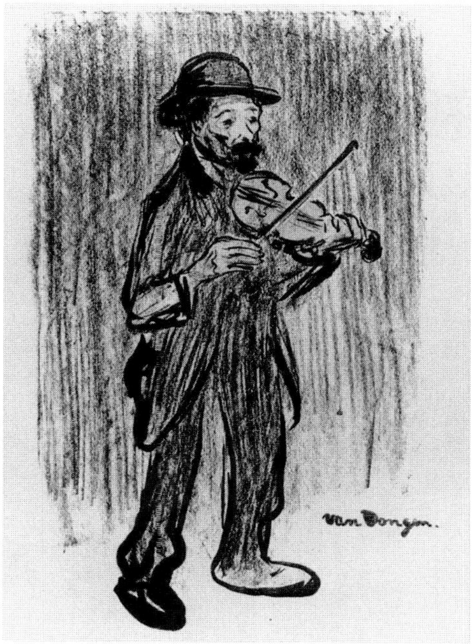

28.
J'suis ni musicien, ni chanteur...Je suis crève-faim!
(I'm neither musician nor singer...I'm down-and-out!)
Illustration in *L'Assiette au Beurre*, no. 12 (20 June) 1901

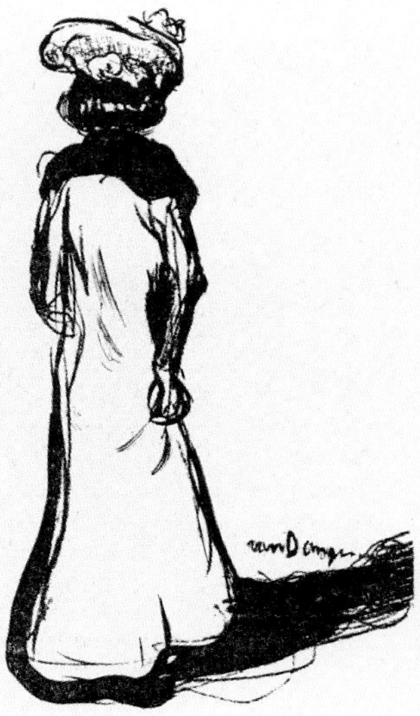

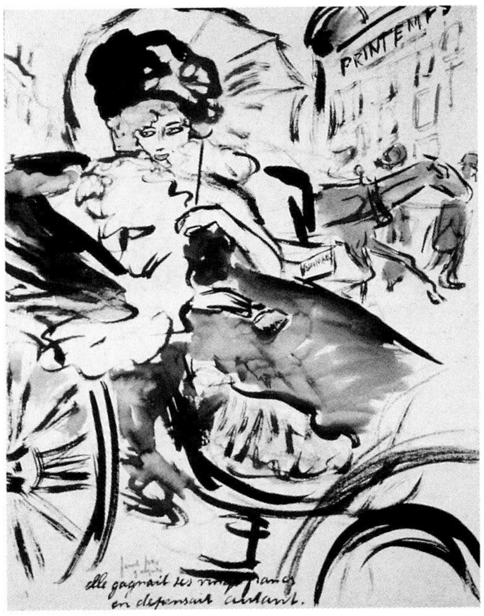

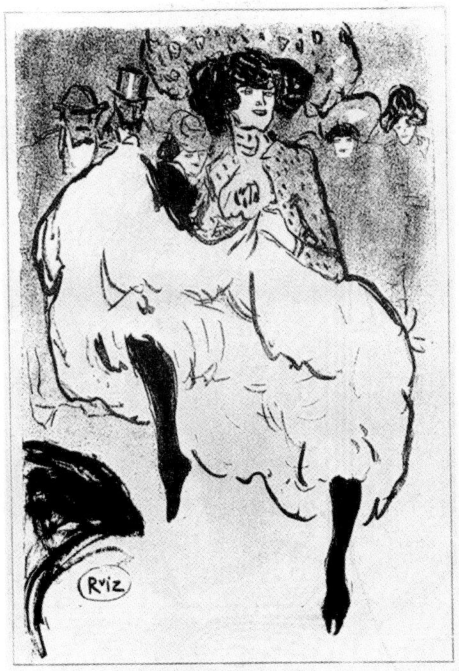

29.
Femme vue de dos (Woman seen from the back)
Illustration in *La Revue Blanche*, vol. 25 (15 August) 1901

30.
La réussite (Success), 1901
Black chalk, watercolour
580 x 470 mm

31.
P. Picasso
Appâts pour hommes (Lures for men)
Illustration in *Frou-Frou*, no. 46 (31 August) 1901

LA REVUE BLANCHE

When he started working for *La Revue Blanche* (1890-1903), a magazine with anarchist sympathies and initially leaning towards the Symbolists, run by the Natanson brothers, Van Dongen found himself in good company. Other artists working for the publication at this time included Paul Signac, Pierre Bonnard and Albert Marquet.[263] The latter two made series of ink sketches in about 1900 in a style very similar to that of Van Dongen, illustrating street life. Work by Bonnard had been previously published together with that of other painters of the Nabis group, such as Vuillard, Paul Ranson and Maurice Denis in the *Revue Blanche*, in folders containing graphic art. This gained them the reputation of being the artists of *La Revue Blanche*. Towards the end of the century, however, the symbolist tendency was taking a turn towards naturalism, reaching its peak in the years 1896 to 1900 when Léon Blum, who supported the literary opinions of the Leblond brothers, was the paper's literary critic.[264] The editor in chief Fénéon, with his well-known left-wing anarchist sympathies, worked for the paper from 1895 until it closed down. Fénéon was particularly interested in the short story as a literary form, in which an inner reality – usually dealing with the life of people in the lower classes – was described and constructed, with no contrived plot. He admired work by Charles-Louis Philippe, Paul Adam or Romain Coolus, which dealt with the passions of prostitutes and pimps, seen positively as people with an essential life force. The above writers were engaged by *La Revue Blanche* and provided the tone of sensuality for which the paper became famous.[265] It seems as if Fénéon communicated to Van Dongen his list of preferences because the artist did not draw any down-and-out labourers or work horses for *La Revue Blanche* – apart from a scene showing street musicians – but rather concentrated on scenes from the lives of demimondaine prostitutes. There are five drawings altogether, four of them placed as vignettes and with the exception of one, none of them
cat. 33-35 bears a direct relation to the text.[266] (fig. 29, 30, 31) The first of these, *L'escalier de l'Opéra*, appeared on 15 July 1901 as the closing vignette beneath a review of the debut exhibition in Paris of Pablo Picasso at Galerie Vollard. The picture shows a woman wearing a type of cloak known as the *domino*, who is attending one of the annual balls at the Opera, escorted by several gentlemen. The subject developed into a series of similar
cat. 36-38 scenes, including several attractive watercolour sheets.

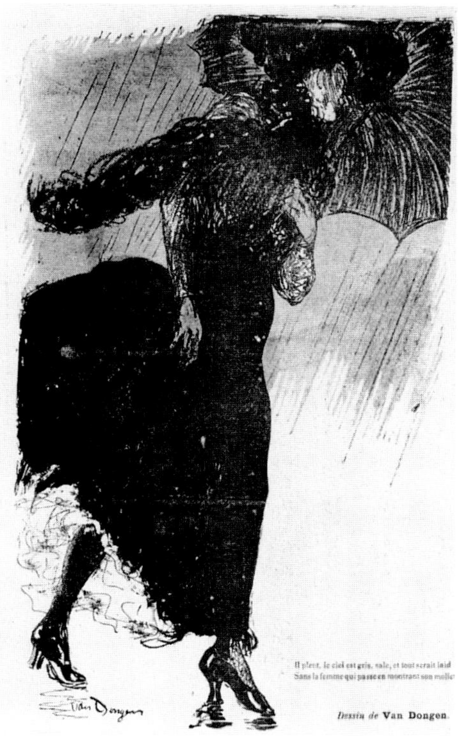

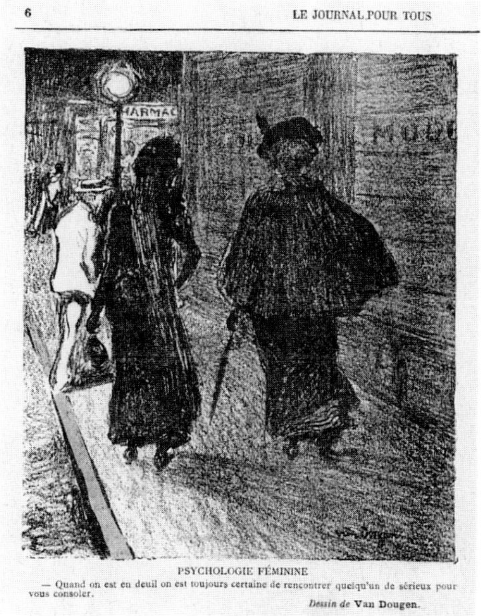

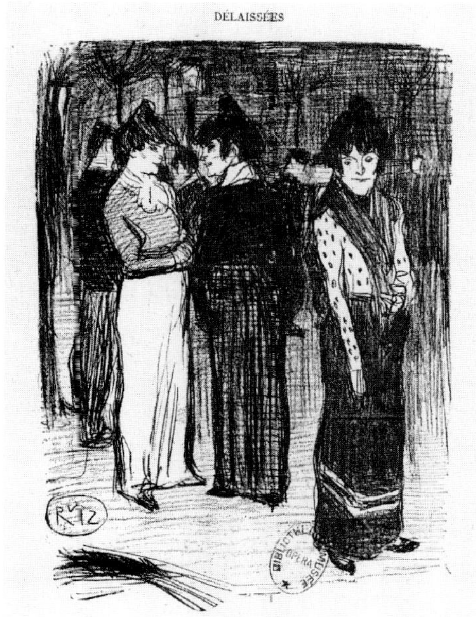

32.
Il pleut, le ciel est gris (It's raining, the sky is grey)
Illustration in *Le Journal pour tous*, no. 47 (5 December) 1901

33.
Psychologie féminine (Female psychology)
Illustration in *Le Journal pour tous*, no. 3 (16 January) 1902

34.
P. Picasso, *Délaissées* (Abandoned women)
Illustration in *Le Journal pour tous*, no. 28 (10 July) 1902

L'ASSIETTE AU BEURRE

The *Revue Blanche* appeared fortnightly, publishing work of a literary nature and usually containing two or three drawings in vignette form. Only on a few occasions did it devote an entire page to an illustration. Quite different was *L'Assiette au Beurre*, a satirical magazine that owed its popularity to its illustrations and whose only text was the captions accompanying them. In October 1901 Van Dongen was lucky enough to be able to illustrate an entire number of this weekly. This was the commission that earned him his reputation, and when people speak of his draughtsmanship it is this work they generally have in mind.[267]

The first number of *L'Assiette au Beurre* – an expression in French meaning something like 'an exceptional opportunity' – appeared in April 1901. It was initiated by the publisher S. Schwarz who owned the paper until July 1903. It continued to be published until 1912. From the very beginning Schwarz employed the best draughtsmen, people such as Steinlen, Ibels, Willette, Kupka and Villon and knew how to present his paper so that it sold well. In its time it was the only satirical paper that produced numbers illustrated by only one artist and printed the drawings full page size. A good selling point was the ironic or biting tone adopted, largely criticising social conditions and customs; as it was said 'le mauvais esprit se vendais bien à l'époque.'[268]

The number illustrated by Van Dongen was published on 26 October and contained 16 drawings. It is printed on pale grey-green paper. This seems to have been Van Dongen's own choice since he used something similar for the preliminary studies
which show the first concept for the series. (fig. 30) These preliminary studies have also cat. 40-42, 46, 48
been preserved. They are impressive sheets, measuring no less than 63 by 48.5 centime-
tres, done in black and coloured chalk, ink and watercolour. Before printing they were cat. 43, 45, 47, 49, 51, 52
reduced by about two and a half times. This too was presumably Van Dongen's idea
since there is also a drawing in the paper that is almost the same size as the preliminary
study. Using a larger size it was possible to work without bothering about details, which cat. am. 4
gave a more expressive final result. The black and white drawings were then 'etched' onto a zinc plate, using a photographic procedure, after which some sections over the entire surface, were 'eaten out' or granulated with the help of a raster. Then the plates were printed, using one to two colour stages, as the artist instructed.[269] Probably Van

Dongen was returned the preliminary studies once the paper was printed. It appears that he had coloured them in with watercolour according to the printed versions, sometimes correcting his original rendering, by making something darker, or adding colour, so that the drawing differs from the print.

In comparison with the other numbers of the magazine, the edition illustrated by Van Dongen stands out for several reasons. The pictures are drawn with a sense of space and openness, using a swift stroke. He introduced variations within the series fitting sometimes slightly caricatural elements – as in the men's expressions in *A son été* – or by producing attractive expressive pictures with few means, such as the scene
cat. p. 132 *L'hiver*, reminiscent of Steinlen. A further noteworthy consideration is that Van Dongen's contribution is not a collection of satirical caricatures on social problems – as was generally the case – but is a continuous story. The scenes follow each other chronologically, as is seen from Van Dongen's numbering and captions. They tell the story of an unmarried woman who is made pregnant by her 'lover', who then deserts her. She becomes a prostitute in order to support herself and her child. Successful to start with, she later falls ill and dies. Her daughter, caught in a vicious circle, follows the same path as her mother, with the same tragic end. This repetition makes the series of drawings more than just a statement about the miserable lot of the prostitute. After all, to gain the reader's sympathy, a once-round telling of the story would suffice. The effect of the repetition is that a firm criticism is made of a social system that offers no escape and dooms women to a dead-end existence. The street prostitute was a familiar theme in the illustrated magazines of this period – over a period of several years there are ten numbers of *L'Assiette au Beurre* alone that have this as their main topic. The prostitute came to symbolize human degradation and misery, or – in somewhat lighter vein – social evil. It would seem that Van Dongen's presentation is closer to Brusse's vision in the series *Godsdienst in de Zandstraat* (Religion in Zandstreet, 1901) than Picasso's version of the seductive and erotic aspects of prostitutes and can-can dancers. Both artists, incidentally, are influenced in their representations of prostitutes and courtesans by the work of Toulouse-Lautrec. Picasso's drawings and paintings of Parisian night-life were on show at Galerie Vollard in June and July 1901, a few months before the publication of Van Dongen's illustrations in *L'Assiette au Beurre*. Some of Picasso's drawings of theatre figures were published in the satirical paper *Frou-Frou* shortly after his exhibition.[270] (fig. 31) It is uncertain whether Van Dongen knew of this publication but he could scarcely have missed the exhibition at Vollard's. And it is most unlikely that Picasso had not seen Van Dongen's earlier illustrations in *La Revue Blanche*. The figures in the background of Picasso's drawing for *Frou-Frou*, titled *Appâts pour homme* (Lures for men), published in August of that year bear a striking resemblance to Van Dongen's pictures of such types.

Nothing is known about the background or reactions to Van Dongen's number for *L'Assiette au Beurre* which was titled 'A short story for big and little children.' Presumably the edition was a success. Differences in the printing quality suggest that several editions were published, which Schwarz only did in cases of sufficient sales. However, no second number of *L'Assiette au Beurre* illustrated entirely by Van Dongen appeared – only a few contributions to the magazine and all of them while Schwarz was editor in chief.

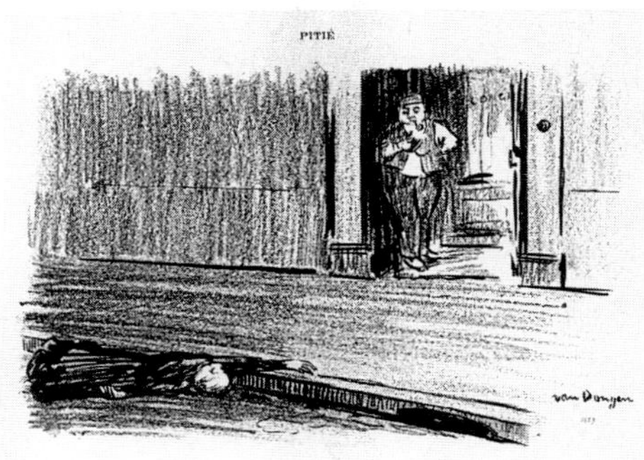

36.
Pitié (Pity)
Illustration in *L'Indiscret*, no. 58 (25 February) 1903

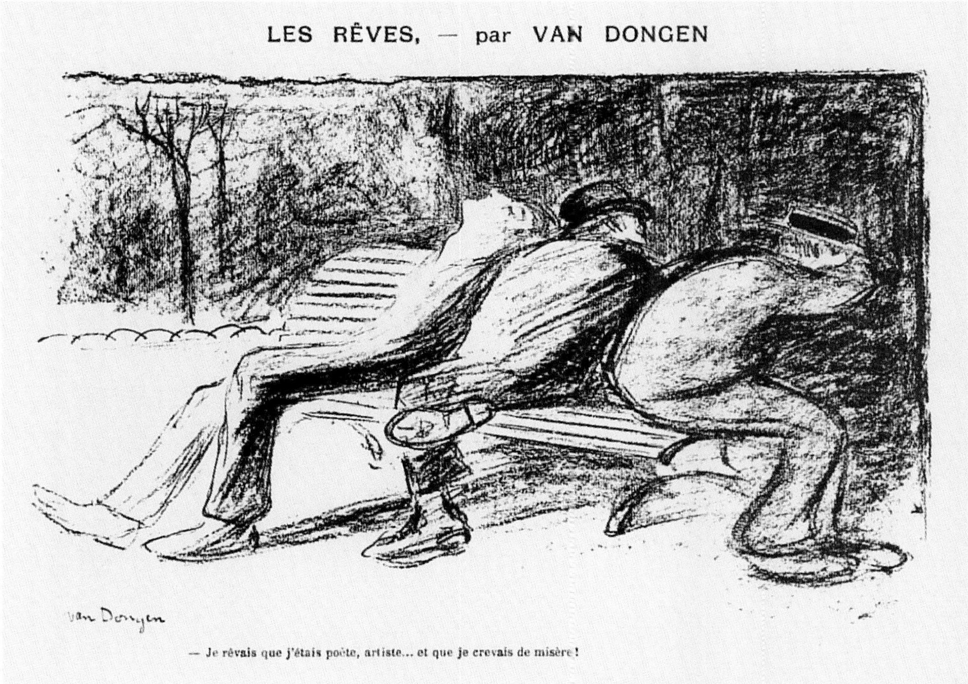

OTHER MAGAZINES

The publication in the *Assiette au Beurre* proved a fine break-through for Van Dongen. Not only was it financially rewarding, it also gave him more introductions into the world of the illustrated press.[271] However, so far we only have an incomplete and not entirely correct list of the magazines for which Van Dongen worked – such as *Gil Blas*, *Le Rab'lais*, *Frou-Frou*, *Le Rire* and *L'Indiscret*. After 1900 Van Dongen only made a few illustrations for *Gil Blas*, far too few to warrant describing him as Steinlen's successor – which some have done.[272] And although Van Dongen made a great many drawings for *L'Indiscret* he made very few for the other magazines on the list. It now seems as if other magazines, not so far associated with Van Dongen, were far more important in those years, such as *Le Journal pour Tous*, a mediocre literary supplement appearing together with *Le Journal*, left-wing papers like *La Caricature* and the more artistically-oriented *La vie en rose*. As well as *L'Indiscret* there were also magazines that were devoted to humour, such as *Le Sourire* and *La vie pour rire* (Life's a Laugh) – the title says enough about the contents. Altogether Van Dongen made about 300 illustrations up to around 1905, for magazines and periodicals.[273] This is nothing in comparison with the quantity produced by Steinlen and certainly does not qualify him to be described as an illustrator. Not all the drawings are particularly interesting or important. However, some of them – for artistic reasons, or because of their subject matter – are particularly striking.

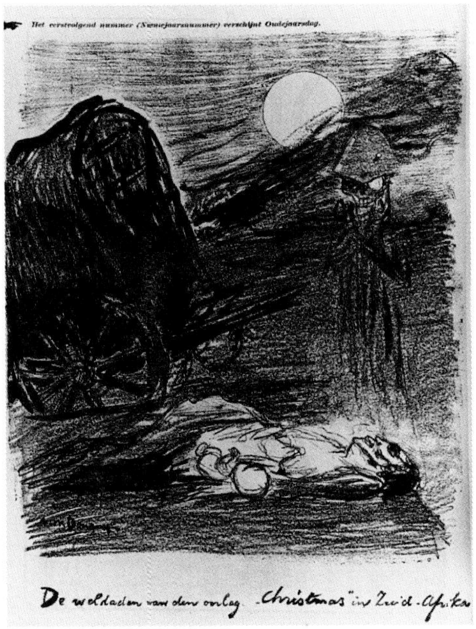

Les rêves (Dreams)
Illustration in *La Caricature*, no. 1151 (18 January) 1902

37.
De weldaden van den oorlog. 'Christmas' in Zuid-Afrika
(The blessings of war. 'Christmas' in South Africa)
Illustration in *De Ware Jacob*, no. 11 (7 December) 1901

The first drawings Van Dongen made at the end of 1901 and early 1902 for *La Caricature* and *Le journal pour Tous* are appealing. They show a woman hurrying along
through the rain, or a street scene in the dusk of evening (figs 32, 33). Once more they cat. pp. 159, 185
reveal – as also the few works of Picasso from this period for the same paper – the enormous influence of Steinlen on this type of street picture.[274] (fig. 34) The other drawings by Van Dongen for *Le Journal pour Tous* to which he contributed until 1904 are noticeably more superficial as regards subject matter. With the exception of a few drawings for *La Caricature*, *L'Indiscret* and the studies in *La vie en rose*, this judgment holds true for much of Van Dongen's post-1901 illustrations. But some of this work has a critical
nature and makes a direct comment. There is the drawing titled *Les Rêves* (fig. 35) bear- cat. pp. 96, 147, 184
ing the caption 'I dreamed I was a poet, an artist…and that I died of misery': probably a representation of the artist's bohemian life. Or the drawing titled *Pitié* (fig. 36) which is presumably offering an ironic comment on the rotund gentleman who is the porter standing in a doorway and looking towards the figure of a woman lying in the gutter

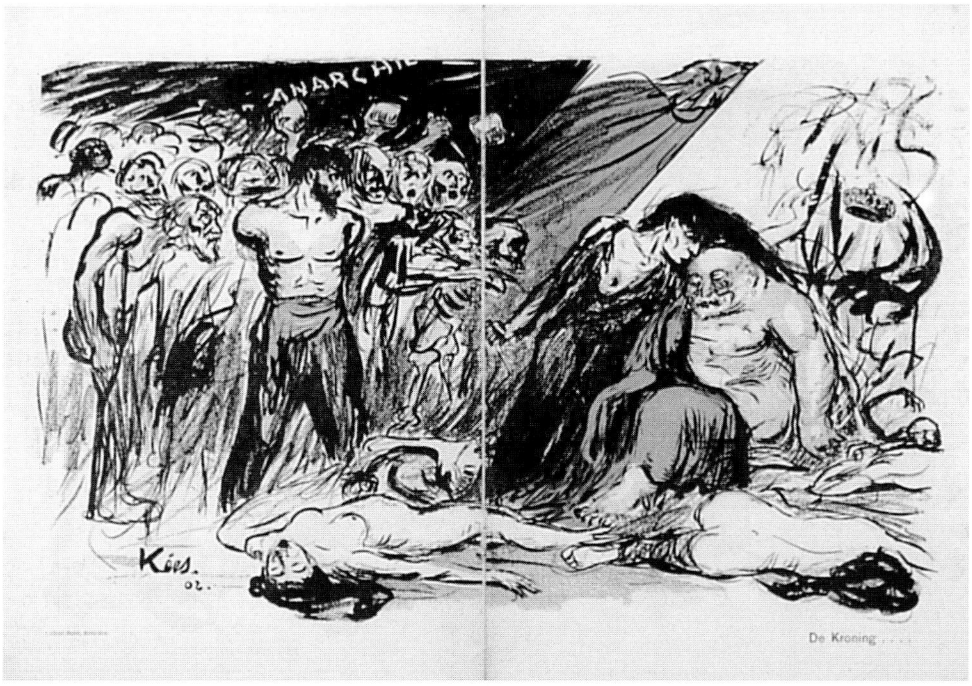

38.
De kroning... (The Coronation)
Illustration in *Vrede*, special number van de *Ware Jacob*, June 1902
Boijmans Van Beuningen Museum, Rotterdam

with the remark: 'It's astonishing – she's been lying there a quarter of an hour, and no one has cleared her away!' Other social abuses Van Dongen presented in his drawings as criticisms of society include the abuse of justice, disasters resulting from reckless investment aimed only at large profits, *Le métro-nécro*, or the laundering of Western colonial politics, as in the illustration for the anarchist *Les Temps Nouveaux*, drawn in 1905 and titled *Le péril blanc* (The white peril).[275] Such themes were not unusual in the left-wing press. However, Van Dongen's most distinct political statements appeared not in France, but 'abroad.'

DE WARE JACOB

A new satirical paper appeared in the Netherlands in October 1901, titled *De Ware Jacob* (1901-16). (Literally the title means 'The True Jacob' but this expression in Dutch also means something like 'the perfect marriage partner', or 'the one who really suits'.) This paper was the only satirical publication with a distinct artistic level, that the Netherlands produced. In its first year of production Van Dongen designed five of the covers and several illustrations, as well as producing all the illustrations for an extra number, in which he presented his social attitudes quite uncompromisingly.[276]

Van Dongen heard at an early stage of the plans to launch this publication. At the first meeting of the editorial board there was a discussion about a series of drawings by him. The paper was an initiative of some people from Rotterdam, including old friends of Van Dongen's, such as the reporter Henri Dekking who wrote for the paper *Rotterdamsch Nieuwsblad*. Van Dongen had previously made illustrations for this paper. Other friends included Koos Speenhoff and Herman Schotel, both of whom also contributed drawings to *De Ware Jacob*.[277]

The first drawing Van Dongen made for *De Ware Jacob* filled the back page of the December 1901 number. It read 'The blessings of war. Christmas in South Africa'. (fig. 37) It is powerfully drawn in black chalk, accented with brushstrokes in black ink. The areas that have been left blank claim our attention, while rendering the light from a full moon. Although the scene is stylistically related to his French drawings it is more dramatic – but then, so is the subject. The drawing refers to the second Boer War (1899-1902) in southern Africa in which the Orange Free State and Transvaal declared war on Britain. Van Dongen's drawing shows Death grinning over the dead body of a mother and child, who lie on the ground in front of him. It is a gruesome, but iconographically traditional combination, the best-known example being by Delacroix.[278] The drawing published in *De Ware Jacob* appears to refer directly to the many who died in the Transvaal concentration camps. These camps were built by the British general Kitchener, following initial successes in the war in Transvaal. The aim of the camps was to separate those who had surrendered from the rebels, who held out to the bitter end. The camps, enclosed with electrified iron-wire fences, were extremely unhygienic and accounted for more deaths – largely of women and children – than on the battlefield.

In the Netherlands, people felt extremely involved in the Boer War. The Boers of Transvaal were largely Dutch stock who had reclaimed land in this part of Africa and settled there. In the 1850s the British had recognized the Boer Republic as an independent state, but later in the century a combination of colonial expansionist policy and the discovery of the world's richest gold mines as well as diamonds in southern Africa, caused a volte-face. The Dutch public supported the Boers unanimously, as is evidenced by a flood of Dutch publications on the topic. There was also a complete translation published of the famous number in September 1901 written by Jean Véber for *L'Assiette au Beurre*. This dealt with the concentration camps, referring to them as 'camps de reconcentration' and bore a drawing on the back page that caused enormous reactions. It showed Albion, representing Britain, revealing on its backside the figure of king Edward VII.[279] This number of *L'Assiette au Beurre* sold more copies than any other, and Schwarz reprinted several editions of it.

On 31 May 1902 the Boers surrendered and the Republics became British colonies. To mark this, Van Dongen made a special number for *De Ware Jacob*, titled *Vrede* (Peace) – a publication that has gone completely unnoticed. It was published in Rotterdam in about June 1902.[280] Most striking is the fact that Van Dongen does not cat. 68
follow the Dutch tradition, presenting the Boers as victims of the power-hungry Brits; rather, he shows both groups as equal warmongerers. Both the Boers and the British are depicted as oppressors. The main illustration again makes this plain. (fig. 38) In this work Van Dongen openly supports anarchism, that rejects any shape or form of servitude. In the group seen at the left of the picture he has drawn a black inhabitant of Transvaal, representing the indigenous population that had formerly been used as slaves by the Boers, which Van Dongen also illustrates. This picture appears to be a deliberate incitement to rebel against Edward VII, who is seen on the right. Two months later, in August, he was to have his official coronation, but here a woman's figure, representing Anarchy, knocks the crown off his head.[281] The whole setting, as well as some of the individual figures, is once again reminiscent of Delacroix's scenes of war.

Around 1903 was Van Dongen's most productive period for making illustrations, and a period in which his attitudes towards social questions became explicitly defined. This can be seen in a drawing made for *Le Parvenu* (fig. 39) in June 1903, showing a fat man oozing diamonds, who is occupying three seats in a theatre, and who says to the woman further along the row, 'Yes madam, I always require three seats at the theatre, one for myself and two others for my diamonds.' A couple of months before this publication, Van Dongen had visited the Netherlands, at which time he had presumably acquired his material.[282] (fig. 40) During the same period Van Dongen produced drawings that seem to have absolutely no message, such as *Ronde du Moulin de la Galette* from July 1903 showing a group having a ball on the lookout tower of a dance hall; this appeared accompanying an equally trivial song in *Gil Blas illustré*. 'You see something on the vast rubbish heap that you think is beautiful or good or interesting or whatever – then take it,' was Van Dongen's advice at that time to a Rotterdam friend, Herman Schotel, with a reference to the drawing in *Gil Blas*.[283] Schotel, an illustrator, came under attack from Van Dongen in another passage from the same letter, on account of his socialist ideas. 'You are a fool to produce unpaid drawings for the gentlemen socialists Brusse and Spiekman; you aren't doing anything for people who live in hovels – they won't profit from it at all.' Van Dongen was referring to a publication dealing with the appalling living conditions in the old inner city of Rotterdam, brought out by W.L. and

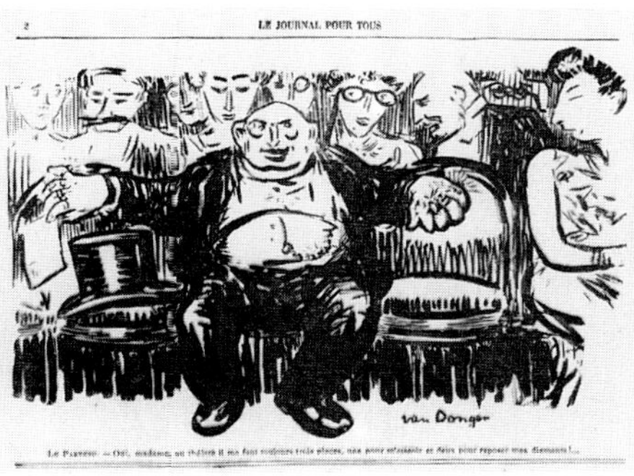

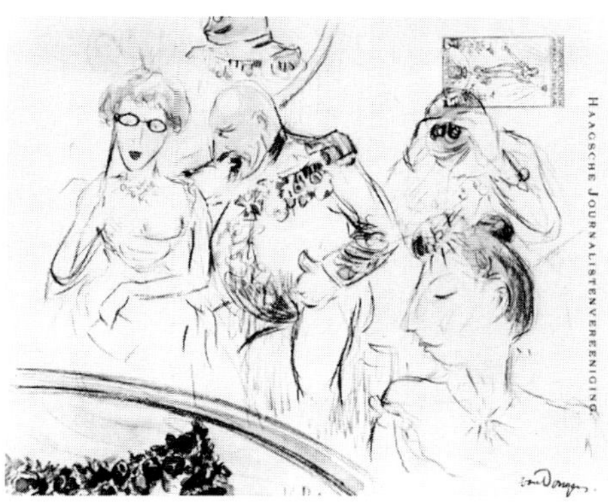

39.
Le parvenu (The parvenu)
Illustration in *Le Journal pour Tous*, no. 24 (11 June) 1903

40.
La loge (The theatre box), 1903
Black chalk, watercolour
205 x 270 mm

J. Brusse, compiled by the socialist councillor H. Spiekman and illustrated by the artist Schotel.[284] In Van Dongen's opinion it was a 'rotten book', about rotten slums and he made the comment: '"publisher" – it would be better if the word "exploiter" was used. And the less you ask for your work, the more they'll wipe the floor with you.' Van Dongen didn't mince his words.

DRAWING AS A FREE, EXPRESSIVE ART FORM

Van Dongen's drawings as an independent art form from the period also reveal the hardening in his attitude. There is an ironic picture of a park scene from 1902, showing an elegantly-dressed woman holding out her change-purse for a child to play ball with, while the poorly clothed mother looks forlornly on. (fig. 41) There are also pictures of weary workers or market sellers. An overriding preoccupation is the lonely or deserted woman, lying desperately in the street, shown as an absinthe drinker confronting death, or as a prostitute arrested by a policeman, himself having the features of Death. (fig. 42) The accompanying words are the Latin motto of the city of Paris *fluctuat nec mergitur*,
cat. 69 meaning, 'she floats, she does not go under' which go with the wooden round-bottomed boat in the city's coat of arms but are here applied to the woman of the streets who tries to keep her head above water (more figuratively than literally).[285] The subject must have appealed to Van Dongen at this time. The source for this assumption is an article about Van Dongen by Tom Schilperoort, his fellow townsman who had arrived in Paris in 1904 and wrote about the artist's early experiences in the city the following year. 'He sympathized with the life around him, the loves and the struggles – indeed, he had to struggle himself to make a living' and he had 'a double struggle, against material poverty on the one hand, and against things in himself, [on the other]...which could soon be seen in his work. ...The drawings he made during this period of financial worry and ceaseless work display in bitter clarity those relations between people [man's inhumanity to man] which in the course of time have become the heaviest and most miserable, dislocated, vicious and unholy. It is things like this that fill young people who are bright and eager and sensitive, with a hatred for their fellow men and for the world.'[286] Neither the sharpening social attitude nor the increasing bitterness were always productive from an artistic point of view. As Van Dongen gradually freed himself from the need to preach a social gospel, his drawing became freer and more expressive, and he was able ultimately to become a painter of the avant-garde.

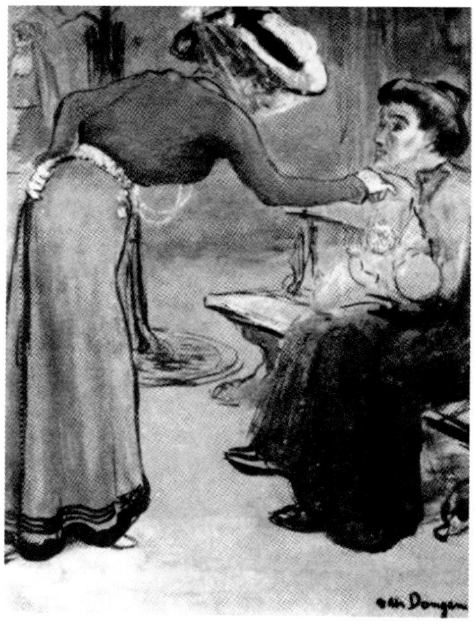

41.
Scène de rue (Street scene), c. 1902
Watercolour, gouache
460 x 360 mm

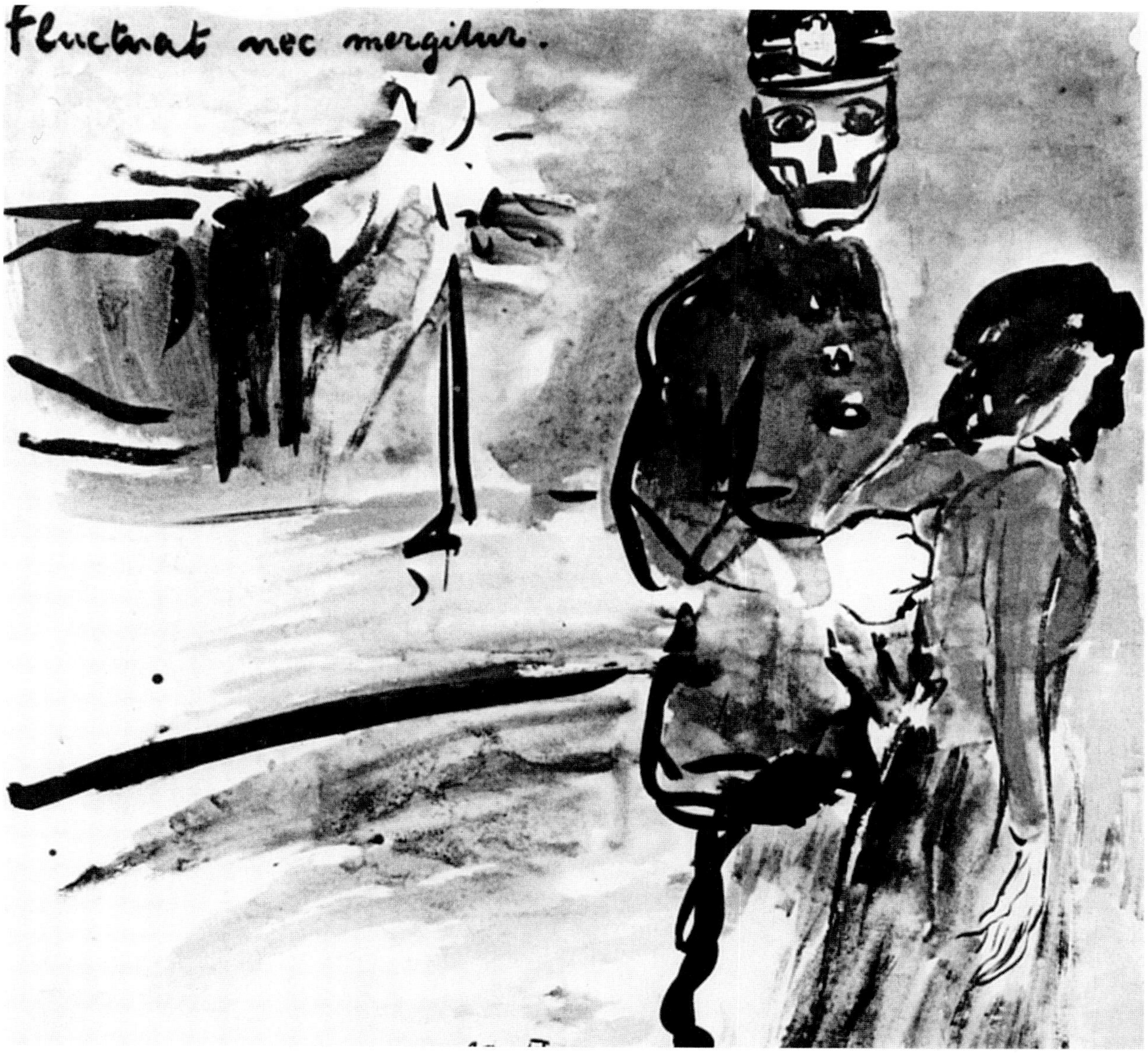

42.
Fluctuat nec mergitur, c. 1902
Ink, gouache
430 x 460 mm

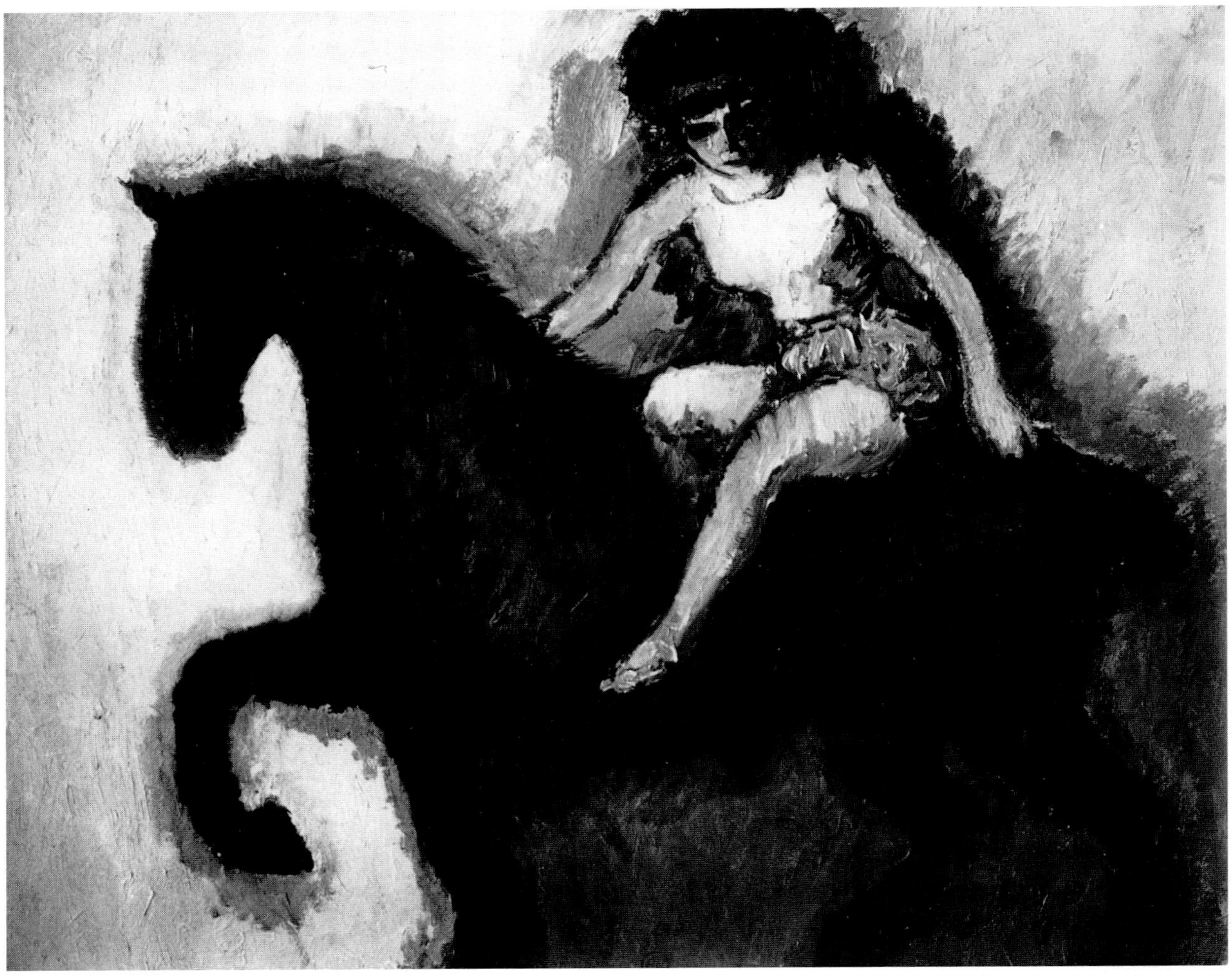

58.
L'écuyère (The horserider), 1908
Oil on canvas, 73 x 92,5 cm
Private collection

III. Drawing as a Free Expressive Art Form, and the Avant-garde

In the course of 1903 and 1904 Van Dongen made several magnificent series of drawings. They were large and emanated an impressive and comprehensive aura. These are no heavy black-chalk sketches but drawings in pen and watercolour, done in a loose and expressive manner. The ink lines are put down in a swift and flowing fashion, as if they were placed loosely on top of each other, and after that areas were filled in with watercolour or ink wash and sometimes outlined clearly with firm strokes. These are drawings that can be compared with an oil painting. Once again it is the girls of Zandstraat who are presented, sometimes seated in groups or amusing themselves in the street. (fig. 43) Also, there is an attractive, more intimate series of drawings of woman either posing naked or going about her daily tasks. (fig. 44) There are also colourful pictures of clowns, acrobats, scenes of circus entertainment and violent rides on the steam-powered roundabouts. With these Van Dongen introduced a theme that was to determine cat. 104-105
his future career. It is not known exactly why he altered his course at this point, but possibly an intensification of contacts with French artists and critics was a deciding factor.

The works are undated and are at present to be found in various, mainly private, collections. They can be arranged in series on the basis of several pieces of information. For example, M.J. Brusse refers to a visit Van Dongen made to the Netherlands in 1903 and several of the drawings and illustrations seem to reflect this. (figs 39, 40, 43) It would have been on this occasion that Van Dongen drew the scenes in Zandstraat, done in ink and watercolour. In his foreword to the Vollard exhibition of November 1904, Félix Fénéon appears to refer specifically to this series when he speaks of 'the girls of Zandstraat entertaining the sailors' and describes the drawings as done in 'Indian ink with a great variety of brightly contrasting watercolour tones or in some cases with delicate nuances.' (figs 39, 40, 43) What is particularly striking in these pieces with their cat. 74-79
wild brushstrokes are the faces and gestures of the prostitutes – a mixture of weariness and provocativeness. Unlike the previous scenes of poverty these drawings by Van Dongen suggest more of the world of sensual pleasure, then so popular among a certain public. The sheets were probably drawn on the spot in chalk and later filled in with ink and watercolour.

Following this series there is one made in Paris, portraying 'Woman' and described by Schilperoort in his 1905 article on Van Dongen as showing his 'adoration of Woman.' Fénéon described the work as follows: 'They are singularly expressive figures cat. 80-88
of women, combing their hair, washing themselves, going to bed, making love, and the artist's brush traces with an enchanting decorative touch together with an incomparable decision the line of their movement,' in this way praising above all the flowing lines that loosely followed the contours of the bodies. To judge from this description and a few illustrations a large part of this series of women can also be placed in 1903. Neither of these two series was shown at the Vollard exhibition. Presumably Fénéon saw the works before they were shown in the artist's studio.

There are three other series of drawings that were shown in the Vollard exhibition,

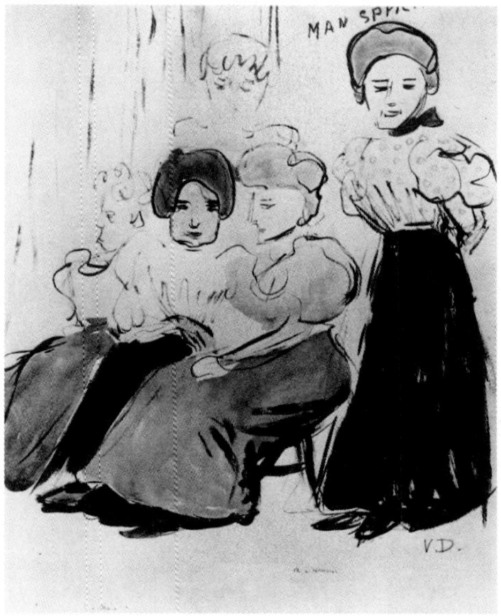

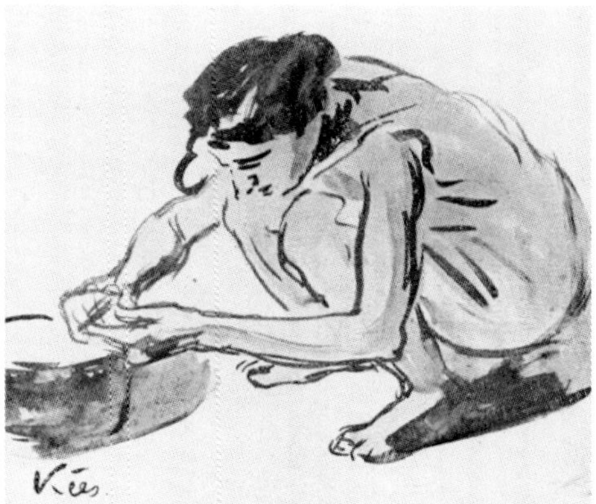

43.
Les filles de Zandstraat (The girls of Zandstraat), 1903
Ink, watercolour
670 x 540 mm

44.
Femme accroupie (Crouching woman), ca. 1903
Ink, watercolour

to wit, chalk drawings of women gathering mussels in Normandy where Van Dongen had spent the summer of 1904, a series of clowns and acrobats done in ink and watercolour titled *Les saltimbanques*, and the beginning of a new series, two drawings of
cat. 96 merry-go-rounds titled *A la fête* in the catalogue. All these drawings can be dated to 1904. The wrestlers, the clowns and the acrobats were, like the prostitutes, presented by Van Dongen not as the outcasts of society but as realistic individuals, and not as general symbols for Life, as Picasso was doing at this period. Van Dongen admired them, noted Snabilié in a review, as 'prototypes of strong and supple people' – which was how he learned to know these circus folk from nearby. At this time Van Dongen also worked – in order to supplement his earnings – as a paid stooge in the circus for the famous group 'Chez Marseille'.[287] His drawings at this time were stylistically related to the earlier pictures of Zandstraat figures, made in 1903. Van Dongen sketched the wrestlers and acrobats with powerful brushstrokes in ink and watercolour, emphasizing their vitality, as Snabilié so rightly observed, and also tying up with Fénéon's interest in such subjects. The latter did not mention the series in his Foreword but his appreciation for this work can be judged from the fact that he bought the series of clowns at the end of 1906 for the art dealer's Bernheim-Jeune, shortly after his appointment there.[288] Together with one of the scenes of the Paris Opera it comprises the few drawings by Van Dongen that ended up at Bernheim-Jeune's.

It seems that Van Dongen's contact with Fénéon increased around 1904. Indeed, Van Dongen recalls that it was Fénéon who persuaded Vollard to organize a retrospective of his work. In connection with this exhibition Van Dongen recounted his life to Fénéon in the letter that has been cited several times above. He recorded not a single fact about the years 1900 to 1904 and concluded his account with: 'I've almost forgotten all the details and I don't think it's necessary to recall them. All that's over and done with.'[289] Clearly, it was time for something new. Van Dongen now began to show far more interest than before in developments in the contemporary art scene. In this period, when he began making these series and his drawings changed both qua technique and subject matter, he turned once more to the painter's easel and palette.

The first exhibition in Paris to show paintings by Van Dongen was the 1904 Salon des Indépendants, held for the twentieth time. It opened in February of that year and Van Dongen submitted six works, earning himself a couple of mentions in the press. These were, however, extremely brief and consisted of murmurs about 'the canals of Holland' 'a particular district in Rotterdam' 'a sad tall lonely house...clothed in mauve by the rain' and say too little to be able to identify which canvases were on show.[290] It also seems certain that the first three works Van Dongen showed stemmed from his Rotterdam days and included the above-mentioned *Landscape near Delfshaven.* (fig. 5) The other three entries would have been painted in Paris in the summer and winter of 1903-4 and included *Coin de bal masqué*, a painting in which one critic said the viewer could descry 'an old gentleman' peering into 'the decolletage of a woman of no beauty.' The subject is one also found in drawings by Van Dongen of this period.[291]

The large painting *Chevaux*, a scene showing old horses in an evening street, can definitely be dated to 1904. (fig. 45) Van Dongen entered it, together with a portrait of the Dutch actress then appearing in Paris, Marie Kalff, for the second Autumn Salon of 1904. Van Dongen considered the painting of the horses, whose present location is unknown, good enough to add it – as soon as the Salon was finished – to his exhibition at Vollard's. It was then given a thorough review: 'they are work horses, standing in three rows, their eyes hidden behind the irritating blinkers...In the gathering evening light the canvas has a grey atmosphere, with a few points in the background like golden stars, which are the lights from shop windows. Passers-by are seen as black shadows adding to the sad and sombre effect of the falling evening.' Both in its tone, described as 'dull grey-blue' and in its theme this picture is related to earlier sketches on paper of Parisian work horses; but the canvas lacks the authority of Van Dongen's drawings.

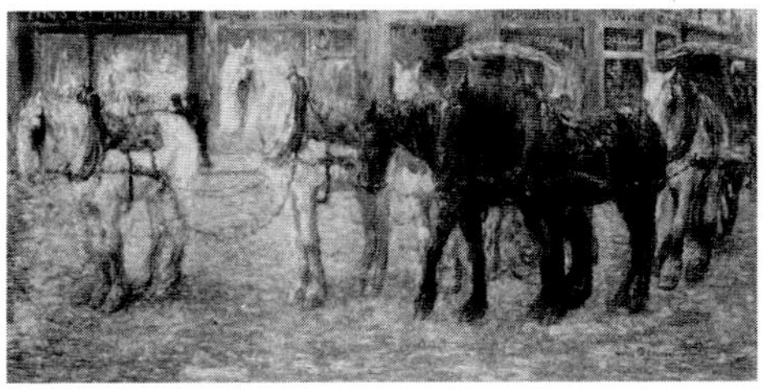

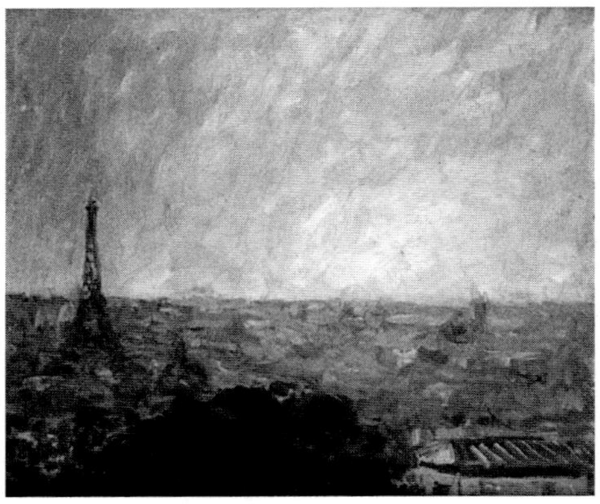

45.
Chevaux (Horses), 1904
Oil on canvas
47 x 155 cm

46.
Gezicht op Parijs (View of Paris), 1904
Oil on canvas
46 x 55,5 cm
Private collection

Possibly the somewhat stiff presentation is partly due to the models he had in mind, such as the paintings of Maximilien Luce. It is known that in those years Van Dongen and Luce were friends and as Georges Besson commented 'there was nothing so entertaining as to see [Van Dongen] walking along the boulevard in his sandals side by side with father Luce, with his rebel's face.'[293] At the time Van Dongen was helped financially by Luce, who payed the contribution for his debut exhibition at the Salon des Indépendants as well as the cost of framing his pictures. But whatever the reason, Van Dongen clearly needed a readjustment of his painting, before he could make a name for himself with that technique.

SERIES IN OILS

An important step was his production of series – first of drawings, now in oils. In this way he concentrated on methods of expression, on colour combinations and composition, and on the brushstroke. The first results of this new approach were also shown at Vollard's in 1904. It appears from Fénéon's foreword to the exhibition that Van Dongen started this method of working in the spring and summer of that year: 'Recently, this highly personal artist has undertaken and completed two series of paintings. One is of Paris seen from Montmartre; the other is of the coast of Normandy, showing only the sea, no intrusive cliff or boat, only the all-sufficient sea.'[294]

The series consist together of just over thirty canvases. Van Dongen must have worked on them non-stop. The views of Paris are seen from the heights of Montmartre and of Chaumont and present the city as a jigsaw puzzle of roofs with a few buildings rising up, such as the Eiffel Tower or Sacré-Coeur. It would seem that the series begins cat. 93-94 with the canvases showing the Eiffel Tower rising imperiously up out of the scene, and a treetop in the foreground. (fig. 46) The view could be seen from Van Dongen's studio window placed high as it was on the Impasse Girardon in Montmartre. The canvases are painted in an Impressionist manner, with reserved tones of blue, mauve, pale yellow and light green, leaving plenty of room for expression through colour and brushstroke. For a large part, this is the appeal of these canvases – there is great variety in the brushstrokes. It circles out in various directions, stroking and brushing; there are alternate open and filled-in sections as in the parts of the buildings where a palette knife is used sometimes to make the masonry appear solider or smoother.

The coastal scenes show parts of Normandy where Van Dongen stayed in the summer, and were made near Trouville and Honfleur. Their technique is similar. The waves cat. 94 replace the roof tops. In these works Van Dongen strives to achieve depth and mood chiefly with colour and brushstroke. His growing attention for the personal signature can also be seen at this time in his drawings. As he continued Van Dongen would use the two materials – paper and canvas – in greater interaction with each other, in this way adding strength to both. A fine example of this are the drawn and painted versions of the steam-powered roundabouts, illuminated by 'electric balls of white light' a theme that Van Dongen was to take up in the autumn of 1904 and that was to grow into one of his first series of 'modern' art.

Van Dongen now showed a preference for 'unspoilt' nature – for an 'unposed' woman going about her daily tasks, for an 'uncomposed' sea without anecdotal details. He concentrated on expressing what he saw by purely painterly means and this was something entirely in keeping with contemporary developments in painting. This was a time when artists were looking for a means of direct representation, both as regards subject and personal style, and expressions of primitive art were being used by the vanguard as models. This so-called Primitivism formed an important starting-point for various new movements in 20th-century art, such as Fauvism and Cubism.[295]

The year 1904 witnessed a general anticipation of new movements in art. Many artists and critics seem to have been convinced that contemporary art was at a crossroads. Most of the works shown at the Salons des Indépendants and the Salon d'Automne were denounced almost unanimously by major critics such as Charles Morice, Louis Vauxcelles or Marius Ary-Leblond for being pictorial jumble or following an exhausted formula.[296] According to these critics Impressionism, once an important movement, had succumbed to a group of artists who although possibly continuing its ideas and producing quality work, were not adding anything new. And Neo-Impressionism had come to represent a tyrannical theoretical attitude, and was even less concerned with revitalization and renewal.[297] Another group of older painters including Bonnard, Vuillard and Maurice Denis was highly respected but nothing new was expected from them. Many critics saw the work of the younger generation – such artists as Matisse, Marquet, Manguin or Camoin, pupils of the Gustave Moreau workshop – as highly promising but not revolutionary.[298] It is also significant that the Neo-Impressionist experiments shown by Matisse at the 1905 Salon des Indépendants were almost unanimously rejected as being retrogressive.

The writer Charles Morice was particularly concerned with the question of renewal. As he saw it, the new century was only at the crawling stage yet there was no question that something had come to an end (*nous sommes à la fin de quelque chose*). But where was the new beginning?[299] In order to answer this, Morice organized a questionnaire in 1905. He was art critic for the influential *Mercure de France* and addressed his inquiry to artists – including Kees van Dongen – whose replies he published in the magazine from August 1905 on.[300] He asked them to explain the meaning of the classic modernists and their own artistic ideas. But his first question was – could we really expect renewal? In an introductory word accompanying this publication Morice proposed as the possible salvation for art a *retour aux origines*, a back to basics. As he saw it this was one route somewhere along the path that had been opened up by painters like Cézanne and Gauguin. But what exactly needed to be done to find the solution, Morice was unable to make clear. In the published reactions to his questionnaire there was a suggestion for a first line of action. It was the necessity for art to be direct and natural. Not surprisingly this was the approach represented by the more established artists mentioned above.

The question was dealt with more explicitly by Maurice Denis and Maurice and Ary Leblond. In July 1904 the painter Maurice Denis published an article in the new monthly *Les Arts de la Vie* which was a defence of just such a direct and natural (unacademic) approach, called *gaucherie*. This was characteristic of primitive art from pre-history to the early Renaissance and was now presented to the younger generation of artists. In subsequent articles he mentioned contemporary exponents of this method, such as Cézanne whom he greatly admired and saw as the primitive master of still life and landscape, and Gauguin, an artist seeking inspiration in the forces of nature, who seemed to work intuitively.[301] The Leblond brothers were supporters of naturism, a development from naturalism, implying a direct reflection of nature. Both of them were on the editorial board of *Les Arts de la Vie* which published in August of that year a fascinating article on the art of 'primitive' peoples. Entitled *L'art sauvage*, it concluded with an unequivocal message for Modern art.[302] They urged the artists of their day to revive their work, through choice of colour, taking as example primitive frescoes with their colours reflecting people's deepest inner feelings and desires. However, what they stressed was that the hollow skills of the academically-trained draughtsmen would gain immeasurably from a return to the direct representation of the primitive, where the 'artist' had just sufficient knowledge to present what he saw around him in a few essential lines, and did so *gauchement*, in an unsophisticated manner.

These ideas were all to influence Van Dongen. The foreword to the catalogue for Van Dongen's exhibition at Bernheim-Jeune's in 1908 was written by the Leblond brothers (pseudonyms for Georges Athénas and Aimé Merlo). Their ideas were probably already familiar to the artist, via Fénéon or perhaps Snabilié, with whom Van Dongen was certainly in contact until 1905. Another possible link is the founder of the literary naturism, Saint-Georges de Bouhélier. A less elevated explanation for the circulation of ideas was through the articles distributed by a bureau for press clippings, and it seems that from the time of his first exhibition in Paris Van Dongen was a subscriber to this.[303]

Van Dongen's interest in unsophisticated line drawings resembled his earlier interest in this style, what he called 'the countless vibrant lines' and is also consistent with his growing appreciation of the work of Van Gogh – an artist with whom critics increasingly linked his name, from 1905 on. The Leblond brothers were also great admirers of Van Gogh because of the way in which his work was so close to 'nature' and 'life'.[304] This approach was part of the literary programme of the naturists. In his reply to Morice's questionnaire, Van Dongen stated that he did not wish to imitate the examples instanced by Morice, but to consider nature herself as his starting point, *la source même de la vie* (the very source of life). And his remarks made no attempt to disguise his admiration for the work of Cézanne and Gauguin.

It is in the light of all this that we should see Van Dongen's plan to make works in series. This aim was clearly reinforced by an exhibition held by Durand-Ruel from 9 May to 4 June 1904 showing the series of views of the river Thames painted by Monet in 1899 to 1901.[305] This exhibition added Monet's name to the list of influential Modern artists. The reaction of the press is a good indicator of the widespread interest Monet's work aroused: almost every newspaper and art journal carried a review. However, what turned the exhibition into a veritable happening was the recognition that Monet had made a palpable contribution to Impressionist art and in this way was encouraging a possible revitalization of contemporary art. Not surprisingly, it was above all the Leblond brothers who hailed the display as a 'major event.' For them, it presaged a new way forward in art. They wrote an acclamatory review in *Les Arts de la Vie* describing the importance of an entirely free manner of working, 'this absolute liberation of the hand – this indifference to all rules.'[306] Monet, working on a series of paintings rather than one masterpiece, had been entirely directed by his sensitivity and feeling for nature, his 'instinct', indifferent to all the rules of art, and had set down on the canvas what he saw, like a naive (painter) or a child. 'I paint what I see' was, according to the Leblond brothers, Monet's motto. This had already been expressed in the 19th century, but was now jointly linked with both primitive and Modern art.

The only person to point out the link between Monet's London series and Van Dongen's series of Paris was the Dutch writer Carel Scharten. He noted that 'it was the great master Monet who had the deepest influence' on Van Dongen who, he continued 'shows more impact from Monet than any other Dutch master.' This comment appears in November 1904 in Scharten's review of Van Dongen's Vollard exhibition for the Dutch paper *Algemeen Handelsblad*, for which he was then foreign correspondent in Paris.[307] It emerges from a preview he wrote of the exhibition for the same paper that Scharten had visited the artist in his studio, a 'flat in the Impasse Girardon, kind of country road on a hill in the city…a room full of light, soft colours with the walls an old-rose and light brown floor…there Van Dongen's paintings could be seen to advan-

tage.'[308] This meeting led to a friendly contact between the two as appears from a second article about Van Dongen that was published in *De Amsterdammer* of June 1905 shortly after Scharten's return to the Netherlands. Van Dongen also sent postcards and letters to Scharten in 1904 and 1905 which refer to the reviews. Later, in a lecture given to the Rotterdam Kunstkring, Scharten again referred to the contact with Van
cat. 110 Dongen.[309]

The artist had no criticism of Scharten's articles – indeed, he approved of and accepted them, saying 'we read your reviews with considerable pleasure.'[310] Most interesting in these reviews is Scharten's detailed description of Van Dongen's working methods. When Scharten objected to the disturbing appearance in a painting of the top of a tree 'beneath the window' of Van Dongen's Paris flat, the artist parried with the comment that 'the tree just happened to be there.' Such a reply, said Scharten, was typical of Van Dongen, who 'could never possibly think of inventing a composition from several sketches within the walls of his studio' and noticed that 'he sets down on paper or canvas what occurs to him – spontaneously, immediately – otherwise he can't do it, or he has the feeling that his work loses all its inner strength and truth.' Scharten went on to say that this was possibly a weakness in Van Dongen, that he felt compelled to make immediate copies of what he saw, but it was something that was absolutely essential to him. He went on to explain the artist's vision, saying 'he doesn't actually have a real technique.' Van Dongen should count himself lucky that he had no training, since 'nothing is more dangerous than to know things exactly, in an infallible and academic manner, how to achieve a certain effect, the precise way to make a certain nuance. It is in fact by experimenting oneself, and discovering things in all kinds of marvellously unexpected ways, that people acquire something strong and alive in their work.' This is the explanation for Van Dongen's series of paintings and clarifies the link with Monet.

Finally, there is a most revealing description by Scharten of how Van Dongen made the drawings of roundabouts. (fig. 50) 'Seated in the semi-dark of a mezzanine above a cafe, facing a Montmartre street fair, he would make his drawings...swiftly filling huge sheets of lining paper, one after the other, and often tearing them up because he cannot alter or adapt. He can only make lightening sketches. The artist-in-him composes the drawing unconsciously, allows the dull and misplaced moments to slip by until the point when Life itself assembles before him in all its beauty. Then he grasps it and holds tight.' Summing up, Scharten saw it as the composition of 'total, tense feeling' rather than 'sensitive thought.'[311]

MODERN SUBJECTS

As Scharten said in 1905, Van Dongen was extremely 'modern' in both his approach to art and the subjects he chose. This is also evidenced by French critics' reactions to his work. In 1905 Van Dongen submitted two paintings of merry-go-rounds for the Salon des Indépendants. One shows a roundabout in full swing, the movement suggested by a
cat. 104 slight fuzziness of the shapes. (cat. 104) The people in the foreground are portrayed as one mauvish-black mass, absorbed in their enjoyment. The criss-cross of brushstrokes above their heads – which appears to be ballooning out above them – contain the same orange, red and yellow as the roundabout they are engrossed in watching. The figures on the merry-go-round are not seated on the traditional horses, but on pink wooden pigs, and are illuminated by electric bulbs hanging above them.

'His entry for the Salon is first class' concluded the critic for the left-wing daily *L'Action*, writing under the pen name of 'le masque rouge'; 'I cannot conceive of anything that is more innovative, nor that is more personal, than his families of pigs.'[312] Clearly, this was the voice of an enthusiastic and sympathetic critic, but no less laudatory was the tone of Charles Morice, who had just begun his questionnaire. Morice was a much more serious and well-informed critic, particularly appreciative of Van Dongen's independent technique, who enthused: 'there is an extraordinary spontane-

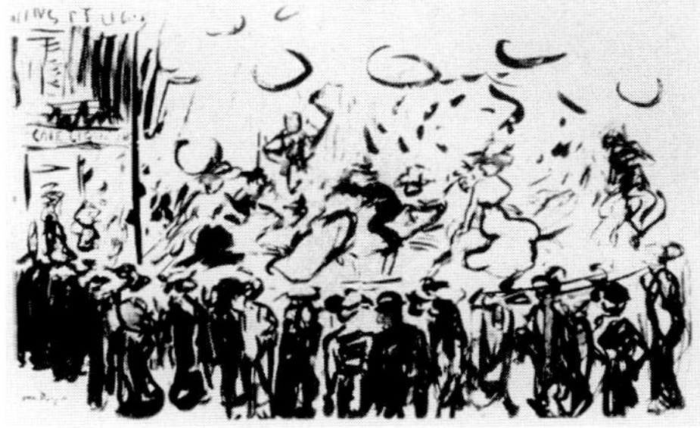

50.
Le manège des cochons (The merry-go-round of pigs), 1905
Ink, watercolour, gouache
370 x 600 mm

ity in his boisterous compositions, in his carousel of pigs…'[313] And he concluded that he would not be surprised to see Van Dongen shortly emerging as one of the new masters.

As well as the technique, the subject matter was new. This type of merry-go-round with wooden pigs lit by electric lamps was, it appears from contemporary articles and illustrations, still something of a rarity and proved a great attraction at fairs. This was as true of a 'petty-bourgeois' fair like that in Montmartre as of a more sophisticated event like the fair in Neuilly, that drew a more distinguished public.[314] The dazzling light bulbs were placed at the very centre of the canvas in Van Dongen's *Un carrousel* and their bluish-white radiance streams over the entire scene, an effect that is heightened by the accentuated diagonal lines of the roundabout's top. This subject was seen by Tom Schilperoort in 1905 as characterizing the essence of Van Dongen: 'the courage and the desire to make something out of the circling humming tops of light with their overwhelming electric balls of white light, chasing after each other like mad things, above the absurd shapes of the racing wooden pigs.'[315]

Presumably Van Dongen thought the same. In the months following this Salon success he explored the subject further, in the summer at the Neuilly fair and in the autumn at Montmartre. On 15 June 1905 he informed Scharten, in connection with the latter's article for the paper *De Amsterdammer*, that he had sent the art dealer Buffa in Amsterdam 'four paintings and four circus drawings' in the hope of finding buyers for them in the Netherlands.[316] However, the presentation was returned to him without comment. From later correspondence too, it appears that Van Dongen was still absorbed by the theme. In the summer of 1905 Van Dongen with his wife Guus and their newly-born daughter little Guus, or Dolly, went to the country village of Fleury-en-Bière, close to Barbizon. In a letter he sent to Scharten from there at the end of June, Van Dongen wrote: 'It is excellent here for the two Guuses. I like it here but I'm not crazy about it. There was a fair in Neuilly when I was last there, and now I'm sitting on the grass and keep trying to draw a merry-go-round.' Apparently the countryside cat. 110
around him did not inspire Van Dongen. From time to time he went to Paris in order to draw the merry-go-rounds from first hand, as we can read from some of the postcards he sent to Guus from the capital.[317]

Kees and Guus had gone to Fleury at the invitation of their Dutch artist friends Otto van Rees and Adya Dutilh. This couple of freethinkers had come to Paris towards the cat. am. 21
end of 1904 and lived in one of the studios in the Bateau Lavoir. In the summer months they rented an old dilapidated farmhouse in Fleury where they invited the Van Dongens and incidentally also Picasso to stay for a while.[318] Van Dongen lodged there, with some interruptions, from the beginning of June until September. After a hesitant beginning he produced an attractive series of landscape studies which he exhibited on his return to Paris in November 1905 titled *Un saison* at Druet's. At the same time he also exhibited some roundabouts: an ink drawing of this subject is illustrated in the catalogue (fig. 51); a painting with a similar theme, not mentioned in the catalogue, was placed – according to a report from the Dutch journalist Henri Wiessing – in the art dealer's shop window. It was, he said, 'the best picture Druet has that is done by Van Dongen' showing 'one of those whirligigs with its electric lights, at a Paris fair' and seated on 'pink pigs' were the courtesans, with fluttering silk ribbons in their hair.[319] (fig. 48) These pictures are more expressive, or – if you prefer – more Fauvist, than their predecessors.

This picture shows the new electric lights again in all their glory, as in the painting titled *Un carrousel. Place Pigalle* – which is most probably the canvas Druet placed in his window.[320] Like all the other works exhibited here the scene is signed with the monogram 'V.D.' and corresponds with descriptions in the press. A great deal of interest was showered on Van Dongen because of this exhibition at Druet's. Such critics as Arsène Alexandre, Charles Morice and Louis Vauxcelles who wrote for, respectively, *Le Figaro*, the *Mercure de France* and *Gil Blas*, all admired the show.[321] It was Vauxcelles who introduced Van Dongen as a specialist in the street fair genre, speaking of 'the enjoyment of

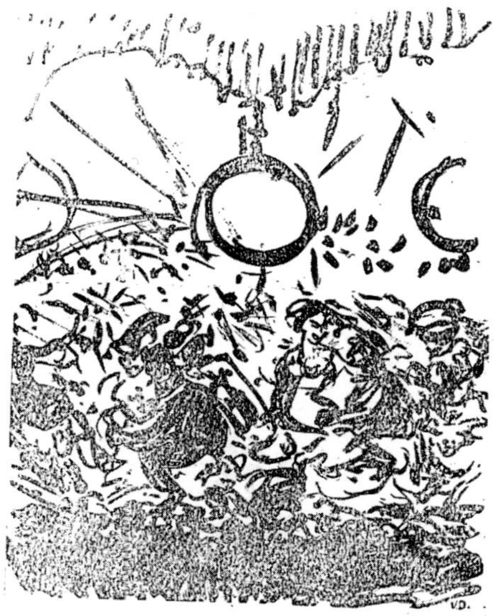

51.
Le manège des cochons (The merry-go-round of pigs), 1905
Illustration in *Kees van Dongen. Une saison*
Paris (Druet), 1905

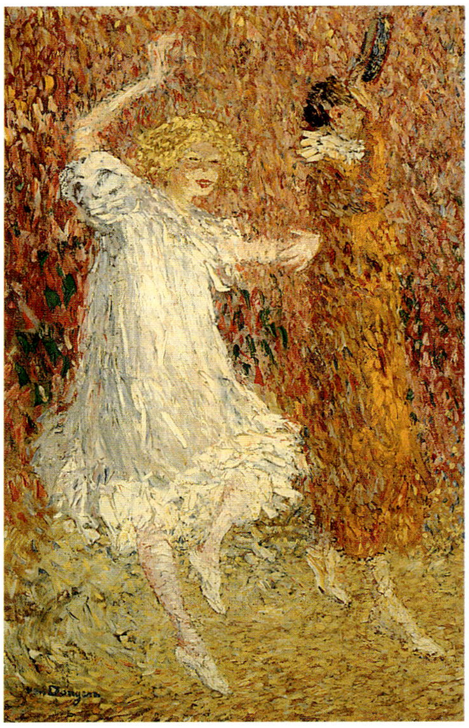

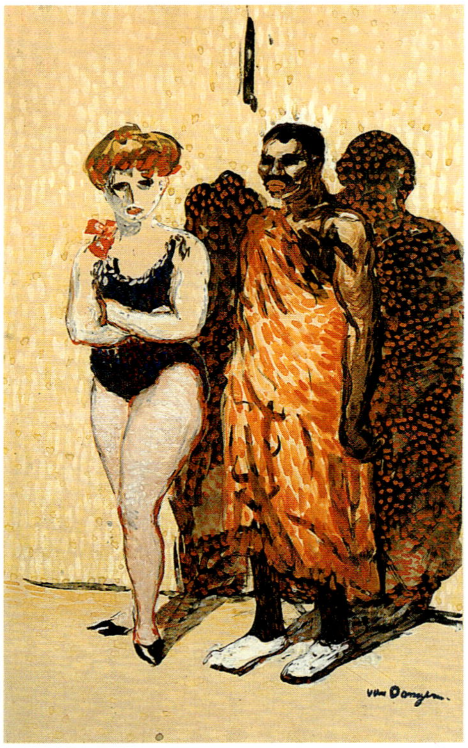

the common folk and the insanity of the Montmartre street fairs' and stressing the popular element in the subject. Arsène Alexandre labelled the exhibition as the demonstration of a new formula. Wiessing, who had succeeded Scharten as foreign correspondent for the *Algemeen Handelsblad* in Paris and had also grown to be on good terms with Van Dongen, even thought that the canvases on show at Druet's were the beginnings of 'a new direction' in art.[322] There was almost unanimous support for the opinion that Van Dongen more than fulfilled the promise shown in his work in the spring – indeed, possibly he was rushing on too fast. Morice concluded his review by indicating that he was now familiar with Van Dongen's working method, as that had been earlier described by Scharten, stating that 'the combination of challenges happily offers this artist the opportunity to achieve spectacular work.' This exhibition established Van Dongen's reputation as an up-and-coming artist.

47.
Le boniment (Sales talk), 1905
Oil on canvas
121 x 80 cm
Photograph Bernheim-Jeune, Paris

49.
Les artistes du cirque (Circus artistes), 1905
Gouache, ink
590 x 368 mm

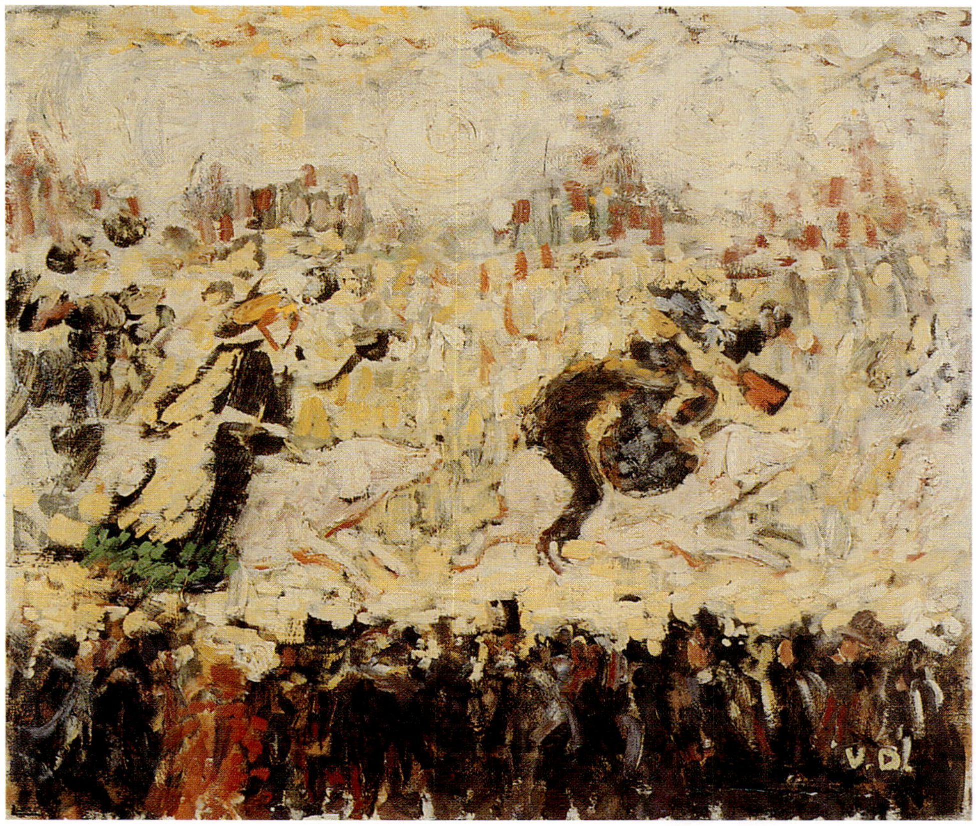

48.
Fête Place Pigalle, le manège des cochons
(Fair on Place Pigalle, the merry-go-round of pigs), 1905
Oil on canvas,
46,5 x 55 cm

THE PALETTE ALTERS

Meanwhile, Van Dongen had adopted a brighter palette. This probably took place in the winter of 1904-5. The change was observed by Kaya Batut on her return in early 1905 from a trip to (the former) French Indo-China and the Dutch East Indies (now Indonesia) with her life-partner Alexander Cohen. In a letter dated 20 February 1905 she wrote to Cohen that 'Van Dongen has worked a great deal since last year. He has changed his style, particularly his colour. Now he uses very bright, clear colours... I prefer his former sombre greys. But he himself is very pleased.'[323] This is a layman's comment, and it is not clear which canvases she was referring to. Such paintings as *Un carrousel* or *Le peignoir rose* exhibited at the Berthe Weill Gallery in January 1905 are certainly painted with swifter brushstrokes than earlier Paris cityscapes but as regards palette are fairly similar to them. Very different, however, was *Le boniment* (Sales talk), exhibited at the Salon des Indépendants in 1905, which shows a tornado of brush and palette knife strokes cataracting over the two circus figures and consisting of brilliant, clear light areas. (fig. 47) Possibly Kaya Cohen was referring to this work in her letter. The figures, a woman dressed in white and a clown in bright orange, luring the public to attend their circus by means of a parade, are placed against a bright pink background on a yellow stage. Over the background colours are contrasting bright green strokes, with purple accents on the yellow, and the blue of the tambourine contrasting with the orange of the clown's suit have the effect of strengthening each other, according to the rules of complementary shades of colour. Clearly, Van Dongen had been studying the writings of the Neo-Impressionists, such as Paul Signac's article from 1898, titled *D'Eugene Delacroix au néo-impressionisme* which appeared in the *Revue Blanche*.[324]

It would have been quite easy for Van Dongen to see examples of the type of art referred to, at the various Salon exhibitions or at solo exhibitions, such as the one organized by Galerie Druet in December 1904 showing work by Paul Signac. Possibly his interest in such ideas was stimulated by contact with the Neo-Impressionist painter Luce. It seems possible that he was introduced to Signac by Luce, and at all events by 1906 the two painters were on friendly terms with each other. Van Dongen met the painter Matisse, who was also involved with Neo-Impressionist ideas, during 1904-5. Around this time a Dutch journalist records that he met Matisse in Van Dongen's studio.[326] It was at this time that Matisse, after a period in Saint-Tropez, was experimenting with Signac's technique and studying the effects of colour according to his theories.[327] The first important result of this, titled *Luxe, calme et volupté* was shown at the Salon des Indépendants in 1905. The canvas shows a group of figures relaxing on the shore, and is painted like a mosaic, with separate strokes of colour placed side by side. Matisse's Neo-Impressionist experiment with colour was not, it is reported, appreciated and almost all the critics declared it to be a false track. Curiously, they found Van Dongen's work acceptable – such as his two clowns in the circus parade, equally Neo-Impressionist in essence, of which one writer said somewhat hilariously that the artist must be applying Pointillism with 'complete tubes of paint'; nevertheless Van Dongen's painting was hailed as 'daring' and 'startling.' It was said that Van Dongen used the Pointillist technique without being a dyed-in-the-wool Pointillist.[328] The painting *Le boniment* (Sales talk), part of the frame of which was coloured in places with the same hues as the canvas, was acquired after the Salon by Félix Fénéon.

Inspired by Neo-Impressionist ideas and methods, Van Dongen therefore embarked on a quest for colour. Two series with the same subject, both brightly coloured, followed in 1905. They are scenes on paper, showing circus figures, such as *Les artistes du cirque* (fig. 49), *Le cirque* and *La parade*, as well as the above-mentioned group of landscapes made in Fleury-en-Bière, in which Van Dongen renders the surroundings sometimes
cat. 99, 100 on paper, sometimes on canvas. The circus scenes have almost the same colour combination as *Le boniment* and were presumably made in the same period. In these pieces Van Dongen – unquestionably influenced by Matisse – applies the colour with dabs of the brush, in places working another colour according to the rules of complementary contrast, such as in the combination dark cobalt-blue and orange, or red and green, as in *Le cirque*. In these pieces watercolour has been supplemented with a layer of body colour. The scene of *Le cirque* is painted entirely in oil on paper. Presumably the reason for this was the desire for expression through colour.

FLEURY-EN-BIÈRE

The landscapes that Van Dongen drew and painted in the summer of 1905 in Fleury-en-Bière can also be seen as a series from a chronological point of view. They reflect one time of year, beginning with the ripe corn fields and ending with the harvest *La récolte*
cat. 106-114 (fig. 52) followed by mowing and threshing. With *La saison s'avance*, a painting showing a shepherd and his flock probably on their way towards the fields of stubble, the series ends. These landscapes made in Fleury are – unlike previous work – done in entirely in coloured chalk pastel. Sometimes they appear too careful, as in the *Scarecrow* or too obvious in their use of complementary contrast, but on other occasions the colour
cat. 106, 108, 109 appears more spontaneous, as in *Binding Sheaves*. (cat. 106, 108, 109). Van Dongen seems to have worked alternately on these pastel drawings and paintings; in some cases he has both drawn and painted a subject, such as *Binding Sheaves* and *Horses in a Corn Field*.

When Louis Chaumeil asked Van Dongen about the background to his method in the Fleury landscape series, the artist said that he was inspired by the Georges Seurat retrospective that he had seen at the Spring Salon in 1905.[329] However, it would seem that the paintings of Vincent van Gogh were a more likely inspiration. The Salon also organized a separate 'homage' exhibition to this Dutch painter. The connection with Van Gogh, can be found both in themes – solitary trees, golden cornfields, figures harvesting in fields – and in technique. In his painting titled *La vigne* Van Dongen has clouds painted with a twisting, restless brushstrokes, and the idea of strokes of colour in
cat. 111 the sky is unmistakably inherited from Van Gogh. (cat. 111) The painting *La récolte* (fig. 52) as described in a review recalls indisputably Van Gogh's Arles landscapes: 'This harvest scene shows a field near Barbizon with the Forest of Fontainebleau like a blue strip in the background. Between that blue distance and the somewhat stumpy grain in

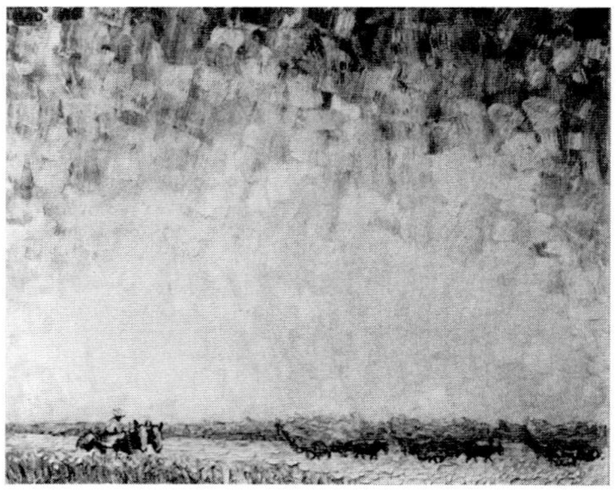

52.
La récolte (The harvest), 1905
Oil on canvas
73 × 92 cm

the foreground we see three heavily-laden carts riding across the field before us, that is completely yellow with the ripe corn. The carts, all pointing in the same direction, stand out red against a leaden grey sky...in the front at the left a farmer's lad is driving two loose-spanned cart horses. The tone and the lines have something powerfully primitive about them.'[330] The 'primitive' in Van Dongen's work was indirectly referred to by other critics of his Druet exhibition, with comparisons to medieval stained-glass windows and – in the case of the merry-go-rounds – to the simple, common qualities in his art.[331] This form of primitivism, the above-mentioned technique in which expression is achieved through colour and the violent sweeps and strokes of the brush, placed Van Dongen at the heart of the avant-garde of his time.

EXHIBITIONS, 1905

That Van Dongen occupied such an advanced position is sometimes called into question. At the 1905 Salon d'Automne his work went unnoticed. At this famous and much talked-of salon the entries from Matisse and Derain, the results of their partially-overlapping stays at Collioure, were shown in one room together with work by Camoin, Marquet and Manguin. As is commonly known, these artists became known as Les Fauves because of the wild and violent colours they used. The name caught on and also provided a kind of explanation and direction for their ideas.[332]

At this Salon Van Dongen showed two works two figures of women, one nude, the other clothed, in the catalogue referred to as *La chemise* and *Torse*. They proved difficult to trace. One critic declared emphatically that he had sought them in vain.[333] There are only a few reviews that mention them. Possibly Van Dongen sent them in too late and other paintings by him were refused. It is equally possible that Van Dongen thought his show at Druet the art dealer's – which ran almost parallel to the Salon – was more important. Apparently he referred some critics to this show.[334] At all events, Van Dongen's sparse presence in the press led to the conclusion that he should not be reckoned among the big names of Fauvism.[335] However, shortly after the Salon he did appear together with all the other Fauvist artists at the infrequently-cited exhibition at the antique dealer's Prath & Maynier on rue de Lille, held in December 1905. In an article printed about this in *Chronique des Arts* Van Dongen is mentioned in the same breath as the other 'moderns' exhibiting work in the show: 'At Prath & Maynier's there is a gathering of avant-garde painters, the masters of the intense touch and forthright colour, the champions of the Salon d'Automne' and then follow the names of Manguin, Marquet, Matisse, Camoin and Van Dongen.[336]

Towards the close of 1905 – possibly in early 1906 – Van Dongen rented a studio in the famous Bateau Lavoir building on Place Ravignan, while keeping his flat on Impasse Girardon.[337] Here, at the very heart of the avant-garde art world Van Dongen extended his contacts with the contemporary art circles. He became friendly with Picasso and it is presumably here that he also met the writers André Salmon and Roland Dorgelès as well as the artist Vlaminck.[338] Although it appears that Van Dongen was not a regular at the 'local' cafe *Le Lapin Agile* where Picasso and all his friends hung out, and also that in discussions about art – according to the above-mentioned writers – he was somewhat reserved, he undoubtedly picked up a great deal about the current ideas on art from being at the Bateau Lavoir.[339]

SALONS, 1906

The sequel of Van Dongen's development is not as well known as is often assumed. It is curious that extreme conclusions have been made about his contribution to Fauvism or his assumed second rank as an artist, without it ever being made clear exactly what work he produced in this period.[340] As already suggested, Van Dongen was himself partly responsible for this.

In 1906 the artist showed his work on two occasions: he submitted six paintings and three drawings to the Salon des Indépendants that year, had three canvases exhibited at the Salon d'Automne, and in May and June showed various recent works at an overview in the Netherlands. There are some thorough reviews of this work. They reveal that Van Dongen's work for the Salons in 1906 was placed without question in the room for the Fauvists.[341]

This could hardly be coincidence, commented one critic in connection with the exhibition at the Indépendants.[342] It was a rule of the Salon des Indépendants that the submitted work be hung in the rooms in alphabetical order, as undiscriminating as possible. However, the room where Van Dongen's pieces hung – this time beside Maurice de Vlaminck, and together with Marquet, Manguin and Jean Puy – clearly had the appearance of presenting the avant-garde, so suggested the critic Louis Vauxcelles: it was the Salon Carré of the 'young school'.[343] The only work by Matisse, the enormous painting *Le bonheur de vivre*, presently in the Barnes Foundation, showing a group of people in an Arcadian setting, was hung in a separate section – presumably because of its size.

'More of a sample of what he intends than a harmonious entity' was a comment made on Van Dongen's entries, which were variously described as a 'puzzling excess of colour', a 'violent quest' and 'frenetic scribblings.'[344] Which works were on show? The first number was *Aux Folies-Bergères* which showed 'three women viewed from the stairs at the bottom of which they are standing' (fig. 53) and can be identified as the painting by Van Dongen presently in the collection of the Royal Library in Brussels and formerly owned by the Belgian poet Emil Verhaeren.[345] The picture shows three demimondaines waiting hopefully for clients, wearing yellow, white and ochre dresses and set against a decorative blue-dotted wall. The canvas is on the original stretcher and signed on the reverse by Van Dongen as 'nº1/Aux Folies Bergères.' The second painting was of Van Dongen's small daughter Guusje, also called Dolly: 'a little girl in an elaborate dress surrounded by rich colours – overflowing with life'; the present location of this work is unknown.[346] The next entry, *La Mattchiche*, is well-known, though almost never under this name. (fig. 54) It is an outdoor scene showing dancing couples outside the Moulin de la Galette, that arrived in the Musée d'Art de Troyes Collection, by means of the Pierre Lévy donation. On the basis of various descriptions as well as the title on the reverse in Van Dongen's handwriting, the painting can be identified. It would have been painted in the summer of 1905 during one of Van Dongen's short stays in Paris. In the autumn a preliminary study of this work was shown at Druet's; the drawing is illustrated in this catalogue. (fig. 55) Once again, it is a modern subject, showing a new dance of Brazilian origin, the Maxixe, which had just reached the Old World and was being launched in the Moulin de la Galette.[347]

The canvas *A la Galette* clearly intended as a highlight, also shows guests enjoying cat. p. 225 themselves in the dance hall, this time inside the large ballroom illuminated by 'golden and colourful specks from the swinging lamps.' The scene was described by Vauxcelles as 'the scum of society having a ball, the gay girls and their Apache guys' in a brilliant electric light. He goes on to give a detailed description of the colours of the lighting, which occupies almost three quarters of the canvas: 'spheres of Neapolitan yellow, ochre and cadmium yellow, the small saffron coloured and dark-red lamps – everything is submerged beneath a fog of warmth and light.' The composition in its entirety is only known from a photograph published in a French magazine in 1906.[348] Van Dongen

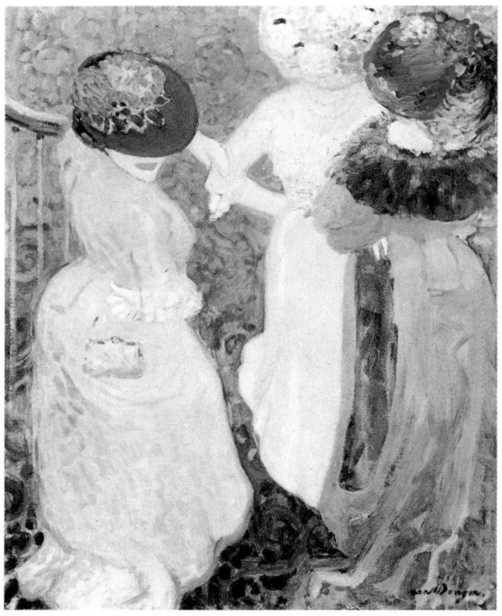

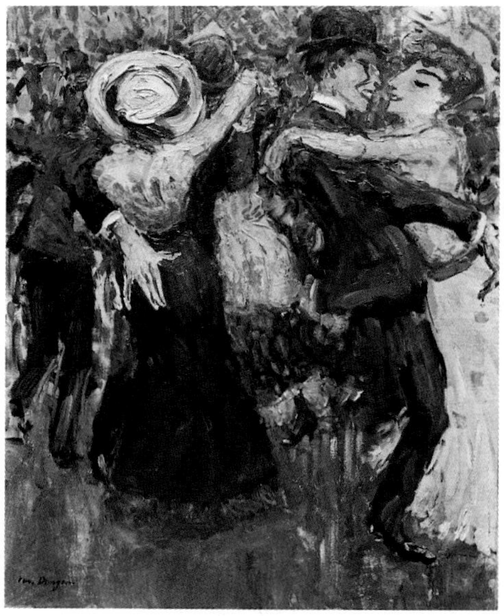

53.
Aux Folies-Bergère (At the Folies-Bergère), 1905/1906
Oil on canvas, 55 x 46,2 cm
Archives et Musée de la Littérature,
Koninklijke Bibliotheek Albert I, Brussels

54.
La mattchiche (The Maxixe Dance), 1905/1906
Oil on canvas
65 x 54 cm,
Musée d'Art Moderne, Troyes

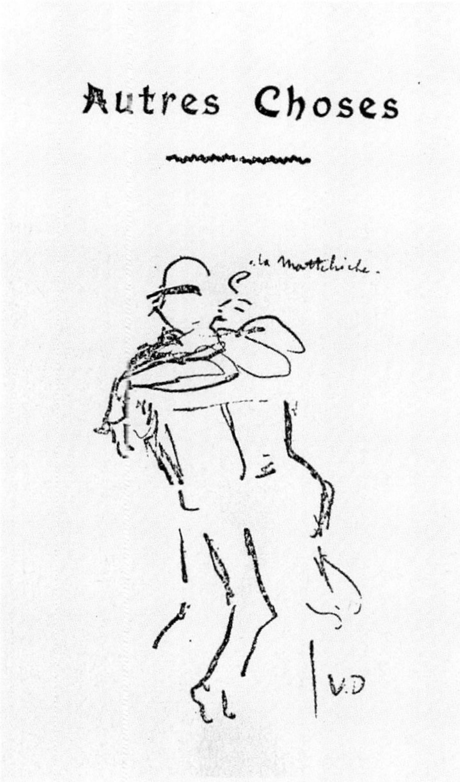

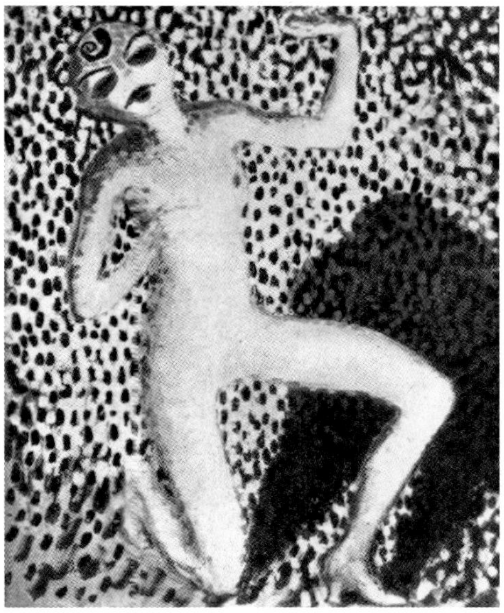

55.
La mattchiche (The Maxixe Dance), 1905
Illustration in *Kees van Dongen. Une saison*, Paris (Druet), 1905

56.
Un pierrot (Pierrot), 1906
Illustration in *Revue Théâtrale*, no. 55 (April) 1906

later had the large canvas cut into sections and sold these as separate pieces showing the interior of the Moulin de la Galette; several of these sections are known. It is calculated that the painting in its original state measured about 130 by 200 centimetres, not much smaller than Matisse's Arcadian picture *Le bonheur de vivre*, and quite possibly Van cat. p. 226
Dongen made his piece in a kind of painter's competition. A pastel drawing also submitted for the show, representing the dance hall *A la Galette*, presents the same scene cat. 115
but in a more spacious manner and more loosely sketched. Finally, there was also a picture of *Un pierrot*, a 'greenish-blue snake-like person' that has also been recorded by means of a photograph. (fig. 56) The awkwardly kneeling figure of the clown was doubtless someone Van Dongen had observed in a circus tent or music-hall entertainment, although the unusual position of the figure and the mask-like face are more reminiscent of a Javanese dancer than a Parisian circus entertainer.[349]

This sample of Van Dongen's work clearly presents a wide variety of technical styles and skills: there are realistic pieces, some are caricatural, some have passionate brushstrokes, some are more restrained and stylized. However, there are distinct resemblances in subject matter. This selection of works can be described as representative of Parisian life, especially the scenes of people enjoying themselves in *Moulin de la Galette*, the dance hall of Montmartre where the public consisted almost exclusively of the 'petty bourgeois and working class'. It was described as one of the 'most popular places for an evening out among the lower classes.'[350] These scenes showing the ordinary people enjoying themselves, kicking up their heels as it were, can be related to Van Dongen's left-wing interests. Undoubtedly, it represented a kind of quest for him. In a letter dated early April 1906 Van Dongen described his work *A la Galette* as his 'most characteristic piece', a 'ball transformed into a furious whirl of light', but shortly after this he appears to have changed styles and taken up a method similar to that used by Matisse in *Le bonheur de vivre*.[351] In this painting Matisse represents the dancing figures in the landscape by large 'flat' blocks of colour, with the shapes outlined in wide bands of colour. His 'Arcadia' was unanimously considered by Salon viewers on formal technical grounds to be too theoretical and too systematic. People asked, 'Does this portray the joy and pleasure of living? Where's the life in it?'[352] Van Dongen, however, found it exciting. He made a new painting, titled *La jarretière* (A Lady's Garter) showing a nude wearing a cat. 116
hat, against a yellow background, also executed in large blocks of colour. (cat. 116) And like Matisse, Van Dongen outlined the body with wide bands of colour – in his case, blue. The canvas was certainly painted shortly after the Salon des Indépendants exhibition of 1906, since it was painted on the stretcher of his (so far not mentioned) entry for the Salon, *Une femme en gris*. The picture *La jarretière* was bought by Fénéon in December 1906 for Galerie Bernheim-Jeune and curiously enough found its way in 1907 into the collection of Paul Signac, the same artist who had abhorred Matisse's solution in *Le bonheur de vivre* – a work which had inspired Van Dongen.[353]

This enormous painting by Matisse, the Salon's most discussed picture, is clearly of a much more theoretical nature than Van Dongen's work *La jarretière*. And although Van Dongen was evidently not in search of a more abstract style himself it appears that he greatly appreciated the canvas. This emerges from a letter he sent to Matisse in September 1906 in which he expresses his admiration for *Le bonheur de vivre* though at the same time commenting critically on another painting by the artist which was a portrait of his daughter Marguerite seated at a table reading. Van Dongen wrote: I don't greatly care for this portrait of your daughter and I have not looked carefully at the fifth canvas. Believe me. It's a bit too much of the overwhelmingly learned artist. It's one of life's small pleasures and I must say I prefer your huge pleasure of life![354] The painting referred to here is without doubt *La liseuse*, intended for the Salon d'Automne of 1906.[355] Van Dongen had probably seen it with the other entries in the Grand Palais where the Salon was to open in early October. Possibly in artistic response to Van Gogh, Matisse painted the portrait of Marguerite as a composition in complementary contrasts. The girl in her red dress is outlined with green brushstrokes, a colour combination that is repeated in her hair ribbon. Was it possibly in answer to this painting that Van Dongen submitted his picture of the ballerina winking at the viewer, *Mademoiselle Léda*, known under the title *La ballerina borgne* (The one-eyed ballerina)? (fig. 57) It is striking that this canvas is also largely painted in complementary reds and greens – but then the reverse from Matisse's work. Van Dongen's picture shows a girl in green against the background of a red 'cloud'. It looks very like a joke. It can certainly be read as a reply to Matisse.[356]

THE STORY CONTINUES

Then for a time the creative competition between the artists was interrupted. Matisse payed a short visit to Biskra in Algeria, afterwards continuing his quest in Collioure where he worked until spring 1907, producing among other works the famous blue nude. Picasso spent the summer months of 1906 in Spain. Back in Paris, influenced by Spanish sculpture and African masks, he painted *Les demoiselles d'Avignon*, the first step on the road to Cubism. Derain went to the French Mediterranean coast near l'Estaque, possibly in the footsteps of Cézanne, to return with landscapes painted in dazzling Gauguinesque colour. Each in his own way, the artists pursued the path of Primitivism.[357]

And Van Dongen? He left for the Netherlands at the beginning of 1907. Fénéon had asked him to see if he could collect work by Vincent van Gogh for an exhibition at Bernheim-Jeune's, and this seems to be the reason for his journey. A letter written by Van Dongen to Fénéon in February 1908 appears to confirm this.[358] However, it may be one of the reasons for the journey and not the main motivation. Van Dongen's visit to
cat. am. 22 his homeland lasted a good six months and for part of the time he was accompanied by the artists Maximilien Luce and Ludovic-Rodo Pissarro. In August 1907 he returned to France, armed with a considerable quantity of paintings and drawings. What can be
cat. 118-121 considered his final series of free expressive drawings were made at this time in
cat. 133, 134, 136 Holland, including views of the river Maas and several cityscapes. The work that he made on paper after this date consists almost entirely of preliminary studies or explorations of a subject. After 1907 Van Dongen turned almost exclusively to painting. It is worth noting that the works in oils that he made after his trip to Holland can be considered more painterly than his previous pieces. The large coloured areas are more flowing, the colour constructed with *passages*, or transition phases, the hues fitting better together and the broad line of contour replaced by a broken outline.

On his return to Paris Van Dongen lodged his valuable Dutch booty in a friend's studio; he had given up the studio in the Bateau Lavoir before his departure. Towards the end of August Van Dongen received a visit at the studio – it probably belonged to Rodo Pissarro – from the art dealer Daniel-Henry Kahnweiler, who had recently arrived in Paris. Incidentally, Van Dongen had arranged the visit. Would Kahnweiler perhaps be interested in seeing his latest work? This is what the art dealer recalled in the foreword to a catalogue that he wrote later. It seems that Kahnweiler saw several extremely large canvases which Van Dongen rolled out across the floor and walked over with bare feet.[359] He remembered seeing 'a horse' and a 'nude wearing a hat' and thought that he detected some influence from Picasso. Kahnweiler also took note of the changed painting technique; it was fuller, with 'a different, expansive element, an enjoyment of colour.' One of the canvases Kahnweiler saw was possibly an early work *La chimère-pie*, painted on linen.[360] This vast piece dating from Van Dongen's youth, showing a horse that seems to float against a pale grey background, had probably been brought to Paris by Van Dongen with the recent batch of work and most likely together with his early *Self-portrait*. (fig. 2)

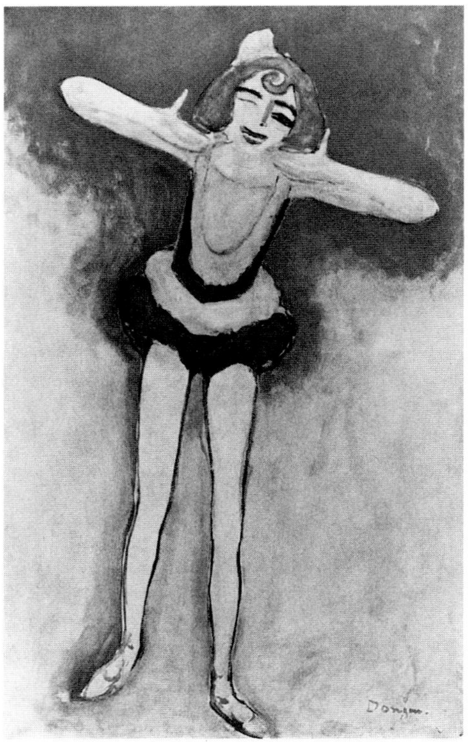

57.
Mademoiselle Léda/La ballerina borgne
(Mademoiselle Léda/The one-eyed ballerina), 1906
Oil on canvas
81 x 54 cm
Private collection

The outcome of this viewing was an exhibition in Kahnweiler's gallery, held in March 1908. It was the first important solo exhibition Van Dongen had held in Paris since those at Vollard's and Druet's in 1904 and 1905. Ten canvases were shown that Van Dongen had made during his stay in Holland, chiefly landscapes and cityscapes, some of which the art dealer acquired. Van Dongen also exhibited more recent work painted after August 1907 in his new studio in rue Lamarck into which he had moved in that month. Here, in a quiet unwonted after the Bateau-Lavoir, he produced a fine series of paintings including *L'écuyère* (fig. 58), *Le maillot blanc* and the portrait of Fernande Olivier. Quite possibly *Artistin* and *Femme à la toilette* also date from this time. Some of these pieces were exhibited in his following solo show in December 1908 at Bernheim- cat. 127, 129-131
Jeune's, together with the Rotterdam impression titled *Liverpool Light House.* cat. 123

Van Dongen's new method of working revealed a more painterly style and presented subjects such as circus and theatre figures, the female nude and landscapes. Through these, as Saint-Georges de Bouhélier put it in his foreword to the Kahnweiler exhibition, the artist presented nature and life with a kind of naive naturism – *du naturisme ingénu.* He showed the reality and tragedy of life, the passions and the grief. 'His painting *Ecuyère* (Woman on a horse) is in this respect most moving. Mounted on a heavy horse, huge and intentionally resembling one of the wooden animals on a roundabout, it is as if she is fixed for eternity, in this miserable position, forever having to turn round...All the misery of human fate is summed up in this canvas.'[361] If we consider the appreciation of the Marius-Ary Leblond brothers in the introduction to their exhibition catalogue in 1908 then we can easily connect Van Dongen's artistic vision with the literary ideas associated with naturism. He depicted 'natural' subjects, the drudgery in the everyday life of theatre people or life's moments of ecstasy, as in the painting of a nude titled *Idole.* He worked in the style of the Primitives. In this connection Kahnweiler pointed out the resemblance with Picasso. The scene presented in *L'écuyère,* a circus horse performing its act, was probably something Van Dongen had seen at the Médrano Circus, which he went to with Picasso, and certainly resembles the latter's earlier circus scenes both stylistically and iconographically.[362] Interestingly, however, the painting bears a strikingly direct and pleasing relationship to the works with which Van Dongen made his debut, such as *La chimère-pie* and the early self-portrait from 1895. (fig. 2) Possibly it was on his trip to Holland when he saw his early work again that Van Dongen perceived his way forward – in a semi-realistic variation of modern Primitivism. This new direction was what the Leblond brothers observed. They described Van Dongen's work in 1908 as 'très sauvage' and 'primitif', explaining this change by reference to the Dutch tradition in painting. It should be said, however, that this reference is somewhat facile and is a cliché that pays too little regard to the French influence.[363] It recalls Van Dongen's somewhat glib quip 'I paint what I see.' But presumably he was referring quite seriously to the naive and immediate which dominated his work.

The style that Van Dongen appropriated in 1908 signalled the end of his draughtsmanship and ushered in a new phase of superb paintings. The years before had witnessed his left-wing, anarchist attitudes, his concentration on free expressive drawing, and his experimentation with a Neo-Impressionist palette. It was from all this that his new style evolved.

1.
McMullen 1960, p. 66. For reappraisal of Modernism in the Netherlands see: Loosjes-Terpstra 1987, pp. VII-XV.

2.
Van Dongen, Paris (Galerie Charpentier), 1949. Mentioned in Chaumeil 1967, pp. 13, 242. For reception in 1949 see: A. Watt, 'Paris Commentary', *The Studio*, 138 (1949), August, p. 60, and J. Bouret, 'Le précieux diner de Kees van Dongen' (Kees van Dongen's fastidious dinner), in *Arts*, no. 342 (18 January) 1952, p. 5. In 1953: *Van Dongen, époque fauve* (Van Dongen, the Fauve period), Paris (Galerie de Berri), 15 October-15 November 1953 (20 nos). For 'Fauve avant la lettre' (Fauve before the letter) see: A. Warnod, 'Van Dongen, fauve', *Le Figaro*, 20 October 1953, p. 10; A.M. Martine, 'Van Dongen. Du maquis de Montmartre à l'avenue du Bois' (Van Dongen. From the *maquis* of Montmartre to the avenue du Bois), *Le Parisien Libéré*, 20 October 1953, p. 6. General criticism in: Clement 1994, pp. 503-504. According to Chaumeil 1967, p. 232, Van Dongen's 1942 exhibition at the Galerie Charpentier was equally successful. For negative reactions from the press see: P. Colin, 'La rétrospective Van Dongen ou le triomphe du snobisme' (The Van Dongen retrospective, or the triumph of snobbery), *Nouveau Journal*, 16 December 1942.

3.
A. Chastel, 'Van Dongen Fauve', *Le Monde*, 23 October 1953, p. 8, expresses doubt about dating.

4.
Le Fauvisme, Paris (Musée National d'Art Moderne), 1951 (9 nos.); *Les Fauves*, New York (Museum of Modern Art) etc. 1953 (5 nos.); *Triumph der Farbe: die Europäischen Fauves* (Triumph of colour: the European Fauves), Berlin (Nationalgalerie), 1959 (5 nos.). For reviews see: Clement 1994, pp. 130-131. Van Dongen not selected: *Les Fauves*, Paris (Galerie Bing), 1927. *Les Fauves. L'atelier Gustave Moreau* (The Fauves. The studio of Gustave Moreau), Paris (Galerie Beaux-Arts), 1934, included one later painting by Van Dongen.

5.
Chaumeil 1967, pp. 70-75.

6.
Coquiot 1914, p. 25, and: 'L'instinct ou le cerveau – ce qui est la même chose – peut guider à trouver les meilleures conditions. La fatalité est la toute première' (Instinct or the brain – which is the same thing – can be a guide to finding the best conditions. Fate is the very first of these); and pp. 26-27: 'Je suis une fatalité...' (I am a fated being). See also: Des Courières 1925, p. 8: 'Se riant de toute science inutile, Van Dongen se contente de peindre ce qui lui dicte son instinct prodigieux' (Laughing at every pointless science, Van Dongen is content to paint what his prodigious instinct dictates to him); and pp. 9-10, 20-24; Guth 1949, p. 140. For his unwillingness to be advertised with other artists see: M. Georges-Michel, 'Kiki, peintre mondain' (Kiki, society painter), *Le quotidien*, 7 February 1926, p. 2. Valotaire 1926, p. 83.

7.
Courières 1925, p. 42.

8.
Van Dongen 1927, esp. pp. 17-18, 24, 139. 'Intuition' described as typically Dutch in Courières, 1925, p. 20.

9.
Gsell 1925, p. 63. First exhibition in the artist's home was *Deauville 1920*, September 1920, at 29, Villa Saïd; Archives Musée National d'Art Moderne, Paris. Van Dongen's contract with Bernheim-Jeune expired in March 1916; Chaumeil 1967, p. 166-167.

10.
Des Courières 1925, p. 43; Hoog 1971, p. 97, note 1.

11.
Fierens 1927, p. 8. See also: F. Fels, 'Kees van Dongen, dernier survivant des fauves' (Kees van Dongen, last surviving Fauve), *Arts*, no. 710 (18-24 February) 1959, p. 16; J. Brusse, 'Kees van Dongen in zijn atelier' (Kees van Dongen in his studio), *De Groene Amsterdammer*, no. 19 (12 May) 1951, p. 11; M. Chapsal 1963.

12.
On Jasmy: Chaumeil 1967, pp. 168-169; and this period: pp. 171-223; esp. on success: p. 204-205, p. 218; on his *succès de scandale*: pp. 180, 186-197. P. Lazareff, 'Van Dongen a repris ses réceptions' (Van Dongen has resumed his receptions), *Paris-Midi*, 11 May 1929, p. 2.

13.
Chaumeil 1967, pp. 204-205, for De Vlaminck and Derain. Also: Georges-Michel 1954, pp. 64-75; Salmon 1945, pp. 36-40; Warnod 1955, pp. 265-268; Oberlé 1956, p. 115; Vauxcelles 1958, pp. 109-110. Exceptions are Dorgelès 1963 (1st impression 1949) and Warnod 1947.

14.
Carco 1953, p. 227: 'Il courait derrière les danseuses et les dessinait en même temps' (He would run behind the dancers, drawing them at the same time). Quoted in Chaumeil, 1967, p. 73; Schneider 1984, p. 86; Flam 1986, p. 86.

15.
Olivier 1933, p. 13. On Picasso: p. 56; Olivier 1988, pp. 202-203; Richardson 1991, p. 376.

16.
Letter from K. van Dongen, addressed to 'Cher ami' (Félix Fénéon), undated (1904); Inv. 860868 (purchased from Galerie Les Neuf Muses, Paris, 1986), Getty Center, Santa Monica. The letter contains various pieces of information which Fénéon incorporated in his foreword, the only catalogue foreword for a Van Dongen exhibition with a biographical tint. This and several pieces of information in the letter have been used to identify Fénéon as the addressee; subsequently referred to as letter K. van Dongen to Fénéon 1904.

17.
See: Diana White, *The Descent of Ishtar*, London (E. & L. Pissarro; Eragny Press), 1904. Van Dongen undoubtedly based his drawings on this edition. On this book: Ch. Snabilié, *Het Nieuws van den Dag*, 10 March 1904.

18.
Speenhoff 1939, pp. 334, 339.

19.
W.L. Brusse 1936.

20.
Gift of 11 September 1907 to the Archiv der Staatlichen Museen zu Berlin, Berlin, where registered as: 'Geschenkgeber ungenannt, Schätzwert: 75,- Mark' (Donor unknown, estimated value 75 DM). With thanks to Anita Beloubek-Hammer, Staatlichen Museen zu Berlin Preussischer Kulturbesitz, Berlin.

21.
Connaissance des Arts, no. 48 (extra number) p. 9; Brachlianoff 1989.

22.
Boijmans Van Beuningen Museum Annual Report, 1937, p. 7. In his letter to Hannema, dated 7 December 1936, Van Dongen mentions 45 drawings: Boijmans Van Beuningen Museum Archive, GA (Gemeentearchief – Municipal Archive) Rotterdam. The 1937 Annual Report and Hannema 1937, p. 10, mention 42 drawings. Purchase of the Charles Rappoport portrait mentioned in the 1937 Annual Report, p. 10. Hannema 1973, pp. 47-48, refers to the drawings being acquired from Van Dongen in Paris, together with the 'Rappoport', in 1936.

23.
Postcard from K. van Dongen to C. Scharten, 15 June 1905, mentions 4 paintings and 4 drawings being sent to Kunsthandel Buffa; NLMD, The Hague. Letter from K. van Dongen to S. Plate, Rotterdam Kunstkring, 6 April 1906, RKK Archive, GA Rotterdam. Another example is provided by the 'card' drawings which Van Dongen left for Octave Maus at Galerie Vollard, in connection with a possible exhibition at *La Libre Esthétique* in 1906 (which did not take place): letter from K. van Dongen to O. Maus, 22 January 1906, AHKB, Koninklijke Musea voor Schone Kunsten, Brussels, Inv. 15777; Ollinger-Zinque 1993, p. 139.

24.
Kyriazi 1971, p. 90. Works purchased 28 December 1906, including drawings such as *Les saltimbanques* (The acrobats) and *Le peuplier* (The poplar tree); Bernheim-Jeune Archives, Paris. The exhibition of drawings mentioned in a letter from K. van Dongen to Fénéon, auction at Sotheby's, London, *Impressionist and modern paintings*, 24 October 1984, no. 93.

25.
Quoted in Bazin 1933, p. 125, note 1. Subsequently cited in Chaumeil 1967, p. 12, with reference to Goujon, however without mentioning source. The quotation does not appear in Goujon's 1909 Salon Reviews: P. Goujon on Van Dongen in the *Gazette des Beaux-Arts*, 51 (1909), vol. 1, p. 397; vol. 2, p. 374. See also: Hoog 1971, p. 93, note 1; p. 97, note 12.

26.
Incorrect dating by Van Dongen: Chaumeil 1967, p. 170. For cut-up canvases see: Chaumeil 1967, p. 245. See: A. Chastel, 'Paris', *Art News*, 52 (1954), no. 9, p. 16, for reference to the cut-up canvas 'La belle Juana "dans ses dans lascives" au milieu des fauves' (The beautiful Juana 'dancing lasciviously' amidst the Fauvists), c. 1908 (Chaumeil 1967, fig. 1).

27.
Guth, 1949, p. 134.

28.
Letter from D. van Dongen to C. Lang, 15 July 1987, private collection: 'J'ai toujours entendu dire, non seulement par mes parents, mais aussi par mes grands-parents van Dongen et par le frère et les soeurs de mon père qu'il avait emporté à Paris tout ce qui l'intéressait [...] et qu'il avait détruit lui-même le reste à l'exception d'un carton contenant quelques documents de lui-même et de ses condisciples qu'il avait demandé à sa mère de brûler' (I have always heard, not only from my parents but also from my Van Dongen grandparents and my father's brother and sisters, that he took to Paris everything that interested him [...] and that he destroyed the rest himself, with the exception of a cardboard box containing several documents concerning himself and his fellow students, which he had asked his mother to burn).

29.
Perruchot 1958, p. 1. For Delfshaven see: Kleijn, 1873; Schilperoort 1909. Excavated circa 1400 by the city of Delft to create its own port on the Maas. Romer, 1979, p. 76: the area became independent in 1803 and gained municipal privileges in 1825; annexed by Rotterdam in 1886 owing to its poor economic situation. The buildings date principally from the 16th and 17th century. Johannes van Dongen (1838-1921) married Helena Francisca Geurts (1839-1917). Their children were Christina, born 27 October 1871; Kees, born 26 January 1877; Margaretha, born 5 November 1880; Jan, born 8 November 1883: directories and Rotterdam population register, GA Rotterdam.

30.
Guth 1949, p. 133; Perruchot 1958, p. 1 Application by J. van Dongen in 1877, maltster, population register, GA Rotterdam: anonymous, 'Gesprek met een cosmopoliet, Kees van Dongen, schilder en levensgenieter' (Conversation with a cosmopolitan, Kees Van Dongen, painter and epicurean), *Wereldkroniek*, 52 (1949) no. 27 (2 July); anonymous, 'Een "wilde" van tachtig jaar' (An eighty-year-old 'wild spirit' or Fauvist), *Haagse Post*, 2 February 1957. J. van Dongen's malting appeared in directories from 1888 onwards. For maltings and distilleries in Delfshaven see: Romer, 1979, pp. 79, 100; Kleijn 1873, pp. 385-409, 'Eene wandeling door Delfshaven in 1873' (A walk through Delfshaven in 1873).

31.
Guth 1949, p. 133; Perruchot 1958, p. 1: 'Le destin, pour moi, c'est le pays où je suis né. La couleur, la vie, la lumière!' (Destiny, for me, is the country where I was born. The colour, the life, the light!).

32.
Anonymous, 'Kees van Dongens eerste liefde' (Kees van Dongen's first love), *Week in beeld*, 2 July 1949; W.L. Brusse 1936, fol. 3.

33.
Schilperoort, 1909, p. 328. Tomas Anton Schilperoort (1882-1930), son of a Delfshaven chemist based at 49 Aelbrechtskolk; K. Komen, *Picasso in Holland. Parijs-Schoorldam 1905* (Picasso in Holland. Paris-Schoorldam 1905), Schoorl 1995, pp. 20, 41-50, 140-142; q.v. supplementary literature.

34.
Anonymous, 'Bij zijn zestigsten verjaardag' (On his sixtieth birthday), *Nieuwe Rotterdamsche Courant*, 26 January 1937. See also Guth, 1949, p. 133; Perruchot, 1958, p. 4.

35.
Letter to Fénéon, 1904, Inv. 860868, Getty Center, Santa Monica.

36.
Kleijn, 1873, p. 395.

37.
Guth 1949, p. 134; Chaumeil 1967, p. 38. The Academy's address was 92 Coolvest.

38.
The annual reports do not contain lists of all registered students, only end-of-year results of the successful students. For the Academy see: Academy 1914, Verheul 1926, Academy 1935, Maas 1951.

39.
J. Striening (1827-1903), writing on behalf of the Academy, to P. Haverkorn van Rijsewijk (president of the Rotterdam Kunstkring, January 1894-February 1897), letter of 18 September 1894; correspondence addressed to the board of the RKK, RKK Archives, GA Rotterdam.

40.
Exhib.cat., *Tentoonstelling van Levende Meesters* (Exhibition of Living Masters), Amsterdam (Stedelijk Museum), 14 September 1895: 'Schilderijen' (Paintings), no. 85, *Schip*; 'Teekeningen' (Drawings), no. 504, Sketch (watercolour).

41.
Johannes Leonardus Maria van Dongen (1883-1970) lived in Paris from 1904. Studied at the Academy during the academic years 1892/1893, 1893/1894. Student in 'Afdeeling B, Technische Wetenschappen' (Department B, Technical Sciences), in the 2nd and 3rd classes respectively.

42.
Striening taught at the Academy 1881-1903. F. Wouters et al., exhib.cat., *Jan Striening 1827-1903. Teekenmeester in Deventer en Rotterdam* (Jan Striening 1827-1903. Drawing master in Deventer and Rotterdam), Zwolle 1988, esp. pp. 34-48: H. Brouwer, P. Ratsma, 'Striening en de Rotterdamse Academie' (Striening and the Rotterdam Academy). Exhib.cat., *Rotterdam rond 1900. Tekeningen van J. Striening en zijn leerlingen* (Rotterdam around 1900. Drawings by J. Striening and his students), Rotterdam (Archiefwinkel), 1989. Verheul 1926, p. 20. The general director was G. Scholten, followed by A. Nolen from 1896.

43.
Anonymous, 'J. Striening', *Rotterdamsch Nieuwsblad*, 22 January 1897; Academy Annual Reports, 1882, p. 7, 1884, p. 13, 1885, pp. 12-13.

44.
Academy Annual Reports 1893, 1894: in 1892/1893 Van Dongen studied Freehand Drawing in the 4th class, and Industrial Art in the 1st class; in 1893/1894 he took Freehand Drawing in the 5th class and Industrial Art in the 2nd class. Complementary subjects in the Freehand Drawing department were Anatomical Drawing (taught by J.H.F.C. Nachtweh), Anatomy (taught by Dr. J.M. Dutilh), Perspective Drawing (D.G. Ezerman), History of the Visual Arts (Th. C. Simons).

45.
Letter to Fénéon, 1904, Inv. 860868, Getty Center, Santa Monica. See also: Niehaus 1942, p. 34.

46.
Academy Annual Report, 1888, p. 15. In 1896 A. Spoon was president of the Architecture and Industrial Art Division of the Rotterdam Kunstkring; Teychiné Stakenburg, 1985, p. 216.

47.
Academy Annual Report, 1914, pp. 32, 37.

48.
Koomen 1949, pp. 159-163: 'Twee vergeten schilders, A.H.R. van Maasdijk en Johannes Tavenraat' (Two forgotten painters, A.H.R. van Maasdijk and Johannes Tavenraat). Van Maasdijk (1856-1931) appointed in 1883, followed in G.H. Breitner's footsteps: Academy Annual Report, 1884, p. 10. J.G. Heijberg (1869-1952) was attached to the Academy as a drawing teacher from 1892: Annual Reports, 1892/93.

49.
Brusse 1927-I. H.P. Aletrino, 'Tentoonstelling in Boijmans over Kees van Dongen. Eerbetoon aan een grote zoon' (Kees van Dongen exhibition in Boijmans Van Beuningen Museum. Homage to a great son), *Algemeen Handelsblad*, 8 December 1967, quotes a former student Carl Eberle: 'Op zaterdagavond was er altijd modeltekenen op de Academie aan de Coolvest. Als ik me goed herinner was het Van Maasdijk die de naaktklasse onder zijn hoede had' (On Saturday evening there was always life drawing at the Academy on the Coolvest. If I remember correctly, it was Van Maasdikj who was in charge of the life class). Another former student of the Rotterdam Academy, the Haarlem painter H.F.Boot, told his student Kees Verwey, how highly Kees van Dongen was regarded at the Academy: oral information. A former resident of Rotterdam, Arie van Veen, in 'Rotterdamsche Kunstkring. Kees van Dongen', in the *Algemeen Handelsblad*, 13 June 1906: people looked up to Van Dongen – 'diè kon tekenen' (*he* could draw).

50.
Freehand Drawing department in 1892/1893: in class 2, H.J. Schotel (1874-1951); in class 3, J.H. Mastenbroek (1875-1945); in class 4, Van Dongen and Henri Bersenbrugge (1873-1959); in class 5, J. Linse jr. (1875-1930). Industrial Art department: in class 1, Van Dongen and J. P. Krulder (1878-1922); in class 2, J. Linse jr. For the 1893/1894 academic year, Freehand Drawing department: in class 4, Mastenbroek and Schotel; in class 5, Van Dongen and Krulder. Industrial Art department for 1893/1894: in class 2, Van Dongen en Krulder. Other artists at the Academy included P.C. de Moor (1866-1953) in 1883/1884: see Knoester 1988, p. 5; C.J. Addicks (1871-1962) in 1884-1888; M. Schildt (1867-1921) in 1880-1885. Successes and subsidies: Addicks, 1893/1894, won the silver medal for Freehand Drawing 1893/1894, and received a royal subsidy 1896/1899; J. Linse jr received the silver medal for Freehand Drawing 1894/1895; J.H. Mastenbroek won the 1897/1898 competition for Painting; M. Schildt received the 1891/1892 silver medal for Modelling, won the 1894/1895 Competition for Painting and received a royal subsidy 1893/97. For this information see: Academy Annual Reports; Scheen, 1969.

51.
Letter from the son of the first owner to the directors of Boijmans Van Beuningen Museum, 6 October 1967; exhibition archives of Boijmans Van Beuningen Museum, Rotterdam. To the left of the watercolour the De Ridder engineering works where Van Dongen's benefactor worked as an engineer; he rented a room from Kees' parents. Present location unknown. Compare exhib.cat. 1990 Paris, p. 82, *Delfshaven*, circa 1892.

52.
Letter from J. Striening on behalf of the Academy to P. Haverkorn van Rijsewijk, president of the RKK, 18 September 1894; RKK Archives, GA Rotterdam. Exhib.cat., *Israels-Tentoonstelling*, Rotterdam (Rotterdamsche Kunstkring; Pro Patria), 2-22 September 1894.

53.
Chaumeil 1967, fig. 4, a portrait of his father. See: the apostles and evangelists painted by Rembrandt after 1660, illus. in C. Brown et al., exhib.cat., *Rembrandt: De meester & zijn werkplaats* (Rembrandt: the master and his workshop), Amsterdam (Rijksmuseum) 1991, pp. 275-276. Chaumeil 1967, fig. 5, *Portret van een oude vrouw* (Portrait of an old woman), dated 1894 on back. Compare for both works exhib.cat. 1904 Paris (Vollard), no. 3, *Portrait de Jean van Dongen*, no. 5, *Vieille paysanne* (Old peasant woman); as 1894 in the Vollard catalogue.

54.
Perruchot 1958, p. 4; Chaumeil 1967, p. 39; S. (Charles Snabilié), 'Fransche Brieven' (Letters from France), in *Het Vaderland*, 3 December 1904: about Boijmans Museum.

55.
T. Schilperoort, 'Kees van Dongen', *De Telegraaf*, 21 November 1904, p. 2.

56.
De Voorhaven (Zondag) (The harbour on Sunday), oil on cardboard 33 x 25 cm: see exhib.cat. 1990 Paris, p. 83. This was no. 29 exhib.cat. 1904 Paris (Vollard) and no. 5, exhib.cat. 1908 Paris (Bernheim-Jeune). The other canvas at Vollard with this title *De Voorhaven*, no. 38, is probably Chaumeil 1967, fig. 3, and no. 5 in exhib.cat. 1908 Paris (Bernheim-Jeune). Described as 'een stemmingsvol wintergezicht' (a moody winter scene) in Cohen 1908. The *Landschap bij Delfshaven* (Landscape near Delfshaven), oil on cardboard, 25 x 32 cm, is no. 72 in exhib.cat. 1937 Amsterdam. Quotation T. Schilperoort, 'Kees van Dongen', *De Telegraaf*, 21 November 1904, p. 2.

57.
Anonymous (Johan de Meester), 'Kees van Dongen. II', *Nieuwe Rotterdamsche Courant*, 3 June 1906. Chaumeil 1967, p. 55, gives these sizes, with variations; format 3 en 4.

58.
Exhib.cat. 1904 Paris (Galerie Vollard), nos 9-11, 20-52; the second series entitled *La Hollande*, thereby indicating that these works were produced before 1897, and that Van Dongen painted little after this, until 1903. See also: exhib.cat. 1908 Paris (Bernheim-Jeune), nos 4-12 as 1895-1900. Chaumeil 1967, p. 55: Kahnweiler acquired various works here; 1907 or 1908 are more likely dates. See: Monod-Fontaine 1984, pp. 94-95; Kahnweiler 1982, pp. 48-49. Auction Paris, Drouot (J. Zapp), *Tableaux, aquarelles, gouaches & dessins ... composant la collection de la Galerie Kahnweiler* [sic] (Paintings, watercolours, gouaches & drawings ...comprising the collection of the Galerie Kahnweiler), 17-18 November 1921, nos 209-213; only general titles given such as 'Vue de Hollande' (Dutch view) See: exhib.cat. 1990 Paris, p. 83 for two Delfhavense scenes, provenance André Morin. After 1904 Paris (Vollard)

the early Delfhavense canvases were exhibited in 1908 Paris (Bernheim-Jeune), nos 4-12, and 1906 Rotterdam (Rotterdamsche Kunstkring), nos 4-8, 15.

59.
G.H. Breitner (1857-1923) worked at the Rotterdam Academy 1882-1883. Breitner in 1893-1897 represented in various exhibitions: Bergsma 1994, pp. 227-228. For Rotterdam add: *Tentoonstelling van schilderijen en andere kunstwerken* – De driejaarlijksche – (Exhibition of paintings and other works of art. The triennial), Rotterdam (Academie van Beeldende Kunsten en Technische Wetenschappen), May-June 1894, no. 59 *Plein bij avond* (Square in the evening), no. 60 *Op de heide* (On the heath); *Tentoonstelling van werken van leden van Arti et Amicitiae* (Exhibition of works by members of Arti et Amicitiae), Rotterdam (Rotterdam Kunstkring), April 1895, no. 6 *Artillerie* (Artillery), no. 7 *Heistellingen* (Building Site).

60.
Guth 1949, p. 134.

61.
Letter K. van Dongen to Fénéon, 1904; Inv. 860868, Getty Center, Santa Monica. Perruchot 1958, p. 1; Chaumeil 1967, p. 38. On Bolland see: W. Otterspeer, *Bolland. Een biografie*, Amsterdam 1995. On Bolland's attacks on the Catholic faith: pp. 147-152.

62.
Leaflet, January 1897, GA Rotterdam. J.P. Krulder left for Rome in November 1899; after 1900 he was in the Netherlands and Germany; in 1903 he was committed to an asylum. Koos Speenhoff: from 4 November 1898 his address in Rotterdam was Aert van Nesstraat 15; population register, GA Rotterdam; from 1898 his drawings appeared in *Woord en Beeld*. On his work in 1899 see: A.O., 'Speenhoff bij Oldenzeel te Rotterdam' (Speenhof at Oldenzeel in Rotterdam), *Elsevier's Geïllustreerd Maandschrift*, 23 (1913), vol. 45, pp. 279-280. A. de Haas, *Leven en levenskring van De heer J.H. Speenhoff, dichter-zanger (1869-1945). 't Was anders* (Life and circle of J.H. Speenhoff Esq., poet-singer (1869-1945). It was different), The Hague, 1971.

63.
Speenhoff 1939, p. 333. Anonymous, 'Vijf en twintig jaar dichter-zanger. Koos Speenhoff vertelt van zijn leven' (Twenty-five years a poet-singer. Koos Speenhoff recalls his life), an otherwise unspecified cutting [1928], GA Rotterdam: 'Ik kwam in aanraking met een Rotterdamsche vereeniging 'De Vrije Kunst'. Als amateur-schilder werd ik toegelaten en leerde Kees van Dongen kennen' (I came into contact with a Rotterdam association called 'Free Art'. I was admitted to the association as an amateur painter and met Kees van Dongen). Speenhoff 1939, p. 336: J. Linse jr. was also a member.

64.
Vrije Kunst 1897. F. Coenen jr., 'Litteratuur', *De Kroniek*, 3 (1897), p. 403; anonymous, 'Boekbeoordeling' (Book review), *Rotterdamsch Nieuwsblad*, 22 December 1897, 2nd part, p. 2; F.L. (F. Lapidoth), 'Nieuwe Boeken', *Elsevier's Geïllustreerd Maandschrift*, 13 (1903) vol. 25, p. 227-228.

65.
The names Siëbel, Joan ter Lecke, Conrad Verhaeren, G.M. v.d. M. are unknown, as are the musicians Jeanette Cijfer and Coenraad van Bos.

66.
J. Toorop, 'Over de Driejaarlijksche tentoonstellingen' (On the triennial exhibitions), *De Kroniek*, 16 February 1896; De Moor in *Kets*, 23 February 1896, no. 5, p. 40. Letter from J. Thorn Prikker to J. Borel, 6 December 1892, initial criticism of the Triennial; Joosten 1980, p. 87.

67.
On the Rotterdam Kunstkring see: Visser 1913, pp. 14-15; Teychiné Stakenburg 1985. On the Hague Kunstkring: T. van Kalmthout, 'De Haagsche Kunstkring 1891-1900', *De negentiende eeuw* 13 (1989), pp. 92, 94-95, 99; idem, 'Een gezellige en nuttige vereniging' (A convivial and useful association), pp. 21-39, in: E. Fernhout, H. Mühl, J. Verstegen (eds), *De Haagsche bohème op zoek naar Europa. Honderd jaar Haagsche Kunstkring* (The Hague bohemians in search of Europe. One hundred years of the Hague Kunstkring), Zutphen 1992; De Leeuw 1977.

68.
T. van Kalmthout, 'De ziekelijkheden van dit treurig eindje eeuw. De doorbraak van de kunst van het Fin-de-Siècle in de Haagsche Kunstkring' (The morbidity of this gloomy end of century. The breakthrough of Fin-de-Siècle art in the Hague Kunstkring), *Jaarboek Die Haghe*, 1989, pp. 131-145; on *Les XX* and *L'Association pour l'art*, pp. 133-134 (15 July-18 August). Redon, p. 141 (30 May-1 July 1894), p. 142. Exhib.cat. *Jan Toorop*, The Hague (Hague Kunstkring), 15 April-20 May 1894. Lecture delivered by E. Verhaeren on 19 April 1894. P. Verlaine: J.F. Heijbroek, A.A.M. Vis, *Verlaine in Nederland*, Amsterdam 1985, pp. 119-127. For Sar Joséphin Péladan see: lecture 12 November 1892 at Hague Kunstkring; Piet de Moor on this: A. Brunt, 'P. Cornelis de Moor', *Eigen Haard*, 36 (1910), no. 7, p. 125; Thorn Prikker on this: Joosten 1980, pp. 74-79 (letter 4, 27 November 1892). On Sar Péladan see: G. Imanse, J. Steen, pp. 26-28, in Blotkamp 1978. Also Ewers-Schultz 1996, pp. 21-29.

69.
Schilderijen-tentoonstelling (Exhibition of paintings by members of the Rotterdam Kunstkring), catalogue with a foreword about Symbolism by R. Stellwagen, Rotterdam (Rotterdam Kunstkring) 19 March-10 April 1893. On Stellwagen see: Joosten 1980, pp. 14-15.

70.
Knoester 1988, p. 15; Teychiné Stakenburg 1985, p. 216.

71.
Werken van de gebroeders Maris (Works by the Maris brothers), Rotterdam (Rotterdam Kunstkring), September 1893; *Israels-tentoonstelling* (Israels exhibition), Rotterdam (Rotterdam Kunstkring; Pro Patria); *Mauve-tentoonstelling* (Mauve exhibition), Rotterdam (Rotterdam Kunstkring), September 1895; *Werken van G.H. Breitner en Ed. Karsen* (Works by G.H Breitner and Ed. Karsen), Rotterdam (Rotterdam Kunstkring), 7 February-3 March 1897. For the same exhibitions in the Haagsche Kunstkring see: Bionda 1981, p. 59.

72.
Exhibitions: *Exposition d'estampes japonaises et d'objets d'art* (Exhibition of Japanese prints and objets d'art), Rotterdam (Rotterdam Kunstkring), December 1893; *Hedendaagsche toegepaste kunst uit binnen- en buitenland* (Contemporary industrial art from home and abroad), 9-24 November 1895; *Teekeningen, lithographieën en houtsneden door C. H. Shannon, C. S. Ricketts en W. Rothenstein* (Drawings, lithographs and woodcuts by C.H Shannon, C.S Ricketts and W. Rothenstein), April 1895; *Affiches* (Posters), January 1896; *Buitenlandse meesters van toegepaste kunst* (Foreign masters of industrial art), 11 October 1896; *Tentoonstelling van toegepaste kunst* (Exhibition of industrial art), 26 November-27 December 1896. Lecture delivered by August Vermeylen, 9 April 1894, reported in: 'Memorie betreffende de activiteiten van de Rotterdamsche Kunstkring in de periode maart 1893-juli 1913 (Recollections about the activities of the Rotterdam Kunstkring in the period March 1893-July 1913), manuscript 1913, RKK Archives, GA Rotterdam. Van de Kerckhove 1993, p. 38: Vermeylen was artistic director of this magazine. J. Venstermans, *August Vermeylen*, Brugge 1965, pp. 10-11.

73.
P. Koomen, 'P. Cornelis de Moor', *Nieuwe Rotterdamsche Courant*, 27 May 1936; quoted in Knoester 1988, p. 20, note 13.

74.
Knoester 1988, pp. 14-16; A. van Veen, 'P. Cornelis de Moor. Een beschouwing' (P. Cornelis de Moor. A consideration), *Elsevier's Geïllustreerd Maandschrift*, 10 (1900), vol. 20, pp. 97-116; A. Brunt, 'P. Cornelis de Moor', *Eigen Haard*, 12 February 1910, pp. 122-125. On Thorn Prikker: *Kets* no. 8, 15 March 1896, p. 58.

75.
A. de Kempenaar, *Vermomde Nederlandsche en Vlaamsche schrijvers* (Dutch and Flemish writers in disguise), Leiden 1928: 'prospectator' used as another pseudononym voor De Moor; see also Knoester 1988, p. 15 and note 13. Koomen 1936: also 'scrutator', and for De Moor on dance and drama.

76.
See *Kets*, 1896, no. 8 (15 March), p. 58; no. 2 (2 February), p. 16; no. 7 (8 March), p. 54. In 1897 De Moor himself exhibited at *La Libre Esthétique*. For this association: Ollinger-Zinque 1993, pp. 69-74. The first number of *Kets* appeared in February 1896, and was intended to temporarily replace another publication, *Abraham Prikkie*, which was not published from number 52, 19 January 1896 to 20 June 1896. In *Abraham Prikkie*, no. 51 (12 January) 1896, a drawing by De Moor; in the following number an announcement of his involvement with the publication.

77.
De Vlaamse School (The Flemish School), 10 (1897), p. 96; *Kets*, no. 7 (8 March), p. 54.

78.
M.T. Maugis, 'Portrait d'un artiste' (Portrait of an artist), unspecified newspaper cutting: 'J'avais déjà fait quelques petites explorations en Belgique' (I've already been exploring a little in Belgium); Kees van Dongen documentation, Musée National d'Art Moderne, Paris. J. Linse jr. lived in Brussels 30 May 1895-13 February 1897: population register, GA Rotterdam.

79.
Exhib.cat., *Werkende Leden* (Working members), 29 March-19 April 1896, nos 26-37.

80.
In May 1896 the first major strike occurred in Rotterdam, the dockers' strike. See *Morgenrood*, 4 (1896) no. 21, pp. 164-165; H. Romer 1981, fig. p. 94; R. Deinum, *'Verenigd door Vaart'. Gids van de bronnen betreffende het watertransport en havenbedrijven in het IISG en NEHA* ('United by Navigational Trade'. Guide to the sources relating to water transport and port companies in the ISSG and NEHA), IISG research papers 1994, p. 129.

81.
Exhib.cat., *Eerste keuze-tentoonstelling van Hollandsche aquarellen* (First selection exhibition of Dutch watercolours), Rotterdam (Rotterdam Kunstkring), September; J. Thorn Prikker, no. 47, *Fin d'une ère. Et la conscience de leur force donnera au peuple une élan vitale* (End of an era. And the awareness of their strength gave the people a vital momentum); J. Toorop, no. 48 *De zaaier* (The sower), no. 49 *Portret van den Heer Dr. Dorenbos* (Portrait of Dr Dorenbos Esquire), no. 50 *De zangen dezer tijden* (Today's songs). On *De zaaier*: A. Aurier, 1890, quoted in I. Gerards, E. van Uitert, 'Jan Toorop. Een 'fabuleuze bevattelijkheid' (Jan Toorop. A 'fabulous intelligence'); Symbolist creation: *Jong Holland*, 5 (1989), no. 1, p. 12 (with illus.). *De zangen dezer tijden*, black and coloured chalk, pencil, 320 x 585 mm, Otterlo Collection, Kröller-Müller Museum, inv. 803-19; Oxenaar 1968, p. 302; Blotkamp 1978, no. 159, p. 1772; Gerards 1994, p. 47, 40-50. *Fin d'une ère*, pencil, ink and watercolour, 720 x 1230 mm, Haags Gemeentemuseum Collection, The Hague, inv. T45-28. Previously exhibited in Brussels (Musée Moderne), *La troisième exposition annuelle de La Libre Esthétique* (The third annual exhibition of La Libre Esthétique), 22 February-10 March 1896. Joosten 1980, pp. 249-250, 302-303.

82.
Joosten 1980, p. 235 (letter 43, 30 November 1895).

83.
Ph. Mertens, 'De brieven van Jan Toorop aan Octave Maus' (The letters of Jan Toorop to Octave Maus), *Bulletin Musées Royaux des Beaux-Arts de Belgique*, 18 (1969), nos 3-4, pp. 192-193. Quoted in Gerards 1994. Blotkamp 1978, p. 172, for account of Toorop at *Tentoonstelling van werken van Toorop* (Exhibition of works by Toorop), Groningen (Museum van Oudheden) 1896.

84.
Anonymous (Johan de Meester), 'Aquarellen, Kunstkring. II.' (Watercolours, Kunstkring II) and 'Aquarellen, Kunstkring III.' (Watercolours, Kunstkring III), *Nieuwe Rotterdamsche Courant*, 20 and 29 September 1896.

85.
Tweemaandelijksch Tijdschrift, 2 (1895-1896), no. 2, p. 298 (letter 27 November 1892); Joosten 1980, p. 78, the song on p. 282, note 5.

86.
Tweemaandelijksch Tijdschrift, 2 (1895-1896) no. 4 (March), pp. 112-113; in Joosten 1980, p. 218, letter 35 (1 May 1895). See also E. van Uitert, 'Een kortstondige kentering. Beeldende kunst tijdens de eeuwwende' (A brief turning-point. Visual art during the Fin-de-siècle), pp. 185-211 in: A. Klukhuhn (ed.), *Eeuwwende 1900*, vol. I, Utrecht (Bureau Studium Generale) 1993.

87.
Van nu en straks (Today and Tomorrow), new series, 1 (1896), F. Domela Nieuwenhuis, 'Een omkeer in de zedelijke begrippen' (A revolution in moral concepts), pp. 100-122; idem. 'Het internationaal congres te Londen in 1896' (The London International Congress in 1896), pp. 310-340; idem. (The International Congress in 1896), *Van nu en straks*, new series 2 (1897) pp. 17-48. Vignettes of Toorop and Thorn Prikker in *Van nu en straks*, 1893-1894, no. 3. On this publication: Van der Kerckhove 1993 pp. 37-39.

88.
Van de Kerckhove 1993, pp. 62-63, fig. 39, H. van de Velde.

89.
De Vrankrijker 1972, pp. 68-69.

90.
F. Coenen jr., 'Litteratuur' (Literature), *De Kroniek*, 3 (1897), p. 403.

91.
Kropotkin 1987. The edition does not appear in studies on anarchism. The few copies publicly owned in the Netherlands appear to differ in details (additions to the cover, price, announcement of other titles on the back). Clearly, various editions were published.

92.
Thorn Prikker would only become familiar with the books published by Kropotkin in 1897; Joosten 1980, p. 256, letter 58 (spring 1897). On anarchism and Kropotkin: Joosten 1980, p. 231, letter 39 (25 October 1895); p. 247, letter 49 (28 April 1896).

93.
Van der Meulen 1901, p. 399. P. Kropotkin, *De anarchie. Philosophie en ideaal* (Anarchy. Philosphy and Ideal), Amsterdam (publisher 'Publicitas'), 1896.

94.
For the translations by F. Domela: Meyers 1993, p. 282: *Een woord aan de jongelieden (met levensschets)* (A word to youth – with life sketch), The Hague, 1885, Amsterdam 1893 (2nd edition; *De verovering van het brood* (The conquest of bread), Nijmegen 1894/Amsterdam 1895. Van der Voo translated Kropotkin's *De staat en zijn rol in de geschiedenis. Voordracht welke plaats had moeten hebben te Parijs op 7 maart 1896* (The state and its role in history. Discourse which should have been delivered in Paris on 7 March 1896), Amsterdam 1897, and *De onvermijdelijke anarchie* (The inevitable anarchy), Amsterdam 1899. The Brinkman catalogue lists a third translator, H.J. v. S; Van der Meulen 1901, p. 399. In 1904 I.I. Samson, publisher of *De Anarchie*, published Domela's, *De moderne wetenschap en het anarchisme* (Modern science and anarchy); Samson also published the anarchist paper *De Zweep* (1901-1903). On Domela's development: Meyers 1993; De Vrankrijker 1972, pp. 25-29, 67-77; leadership of Social Democratic Bond: De Vos 1967, pp. 78-81.

95.
Over B.P. van der Voo, De Vrankrijker 1972, pp. 59, 81-82. *De An-archie*, 1896-1898, no. 1 appeared on 14 March 1896. Editorial address: J. Sterringa, 9 Spaarndammerplein, Amsterdam. Number for 9 January 1897 gives Van Der Voo's address as: 2 Hugo de Grootstraat, Rotterdam; before this, Brussels.

96.
Jean Grave, *De stervende maatschappij en de anarchie* (The dying society and anarchy), Rotterdam 1896, with a foreword by F. Domela Nieuwenhuis.

97.
De An-archie, 2 (1897), no. 58 (17 April), p. 8. According to the advertisement, part of the translation appeared earlier in *De Anarchist*, a magazine published by J. Methöfer. This was a later publication by Samson. On *De Anarchist*: De Vrankrijker 1950, p. 78.

98.
Names mentioned in *De An-archie*: J.J. van Driel and Jac van Spanje.

99.
Letters Addicks, 23 January 1900: 'Die Heyenbrock schijnt wel een aardige vent te wezen' (That Heyenbrock seems to be a nice fellow). B.P. van der Voo, *In het polderland. Schetsen van het landschap en den plantengroei in de omstreken van Rotterdam* (In the polder land. Sketches of the landscape and plants growing in the environs of Rotterdam), with a foreword by Dr T.C. Winkler, illustrations by H. Heijenbrock, Amsterdam, 1898. See also: H. Heijenbrock, *Onze samenleving in woord en beeld* (Our society in words and pictures), with drawings after Steinlen, Gibson, Vaarzon Morel, Jan de Waardt, Amsterdam n.d. [1899]. This is the text of a social lecture which Heijenbrock gave in 1899-1900; announcements in *De Vrije Socialist*.

100.
Domela Nieuwenhuis 1910, p. 442; Meyers 1993, p. 284. Cohen on this in Cohen 1967, pp. 160-161: he names both Kropotkin and E. Réclus as influences on Domela. Alexander Cohen accompanied Domela Nieuwenhuis as an interpreter to the International Socialist Congress in London in 1896: Cohen 1961, pp. 79-80, where they met Kropotkin again. Letter from Cohen to Kaya Batut, July 1896; Cohen 1996; Meyers 1993, pp. 285-286.

101.
Meyers 1993, pp. 284-298: in December 1897 Domela left the Socialist Bond (before 1894 called the Social Democratic Bond). The first number of *De Vrije Socialist* appeared in 1898.

102.
See an illustration by Van Dongen in *De Vrije Socialist*, no. 26, 2 April 1904; a drawing by Van Dongen in the *Gedenkboek opgedragen aan F. Domela Nieuwenhuis* (Commemorative book dedicated to F. Domela Nieuwenhuis), Amsterdam 1904, p. 22; on this Domela Nieuwenhuis 1910, pp. 534-535. Toorop and Thorn Prikker also contributed. Domela regularly stayed in Paris: Wiessing 1960, pp. 198-199; Cohen, 1961, p. 202.

103.
Alexander Cohen (1864-1961) worked for *Recht voor Allen* from August 1887 through March 1888; Cohen 1967, pp. 127-129, 138-139. For the Social Democratic Bond see: De Vos 1967, p. 77. On the contact between Cohen and Domela: Cohen 1961, pp. 202-205 (in Paris); Cohen 1968, pp. 128-129 (in The Hague); R. Spoor, 'De burger en de bohémien. Alexander Cohen en Ferdinand Domela Nieuwenhuis (1887-1919)' (The burgher and the bohemian. Alexander Cohen and Ferdinand Domela Nieuwenhuis), *De As*, no. 89, January-March 1990. On Cohen in general: R. Spoor, 'Jozef Alexander Cohen', pp. 104-106, in J. Charité (ed.), *Biografisch woordenboek van Nederland* (Dutch Biographical Dictionary), vol. 3, The Hague, 1989; idem, 'Jozef Alexander Cohen', pp. 29-33, in M. Campfens et al. (ed.), *Biografisch woordenboek van het socialisme en de arbeidersbeweging in Nederland*, (Biographical Dictionary of Socialism and the Workers' Movement in the Netherlands) vol. 4, Amsterdam, 1990.

104.
The prison sentence, 6 months, for lese-majesty: Cohen 1967, pp. 141; in Paris on 12 May 1888: pp. 142-232; on Fénéon: pp. 187-188. Cohen knew Jean Grave and Elisée Réclus. He worked in Paris for *Recht voor Allen*, *Le Figaro*, the *Mercure de France*, various French anarchist publications such as *L'Endehors*, *Père Peinard*, *La Révolte*, *Revue Anarchiste*. Halperin 1988, pp. 262-263, pp. 271-271: on the contact between Fénéon and Cohen; pp. 302, 310: Van Dongen and Fénéon. Van Dongen on Fénéon: Perruchot 1958, p. 4.

105.
In Cohen's letters and memoirs there is no mention of Van Dongen before 1900; confirmed by R. Spoor. On Cohen's exile on 24 December 1893: Cohen 1967, pp. 218-232. On his stay in England, December 1893-May 1896: Cohen 1961, pp. 11-74; pp. 31-33 on Kropotkin; pp. 77-127 on return to the Netherlands, May 1896, his imprisonment, August 1896-7 February 1897, and subsequent stay in The Hague. In *De Anarchie* 1 (1896), no. 25 (29 August); no. 48 (6 February), p. 3, on Cohen in the Netherlands. Cohen returned to Paris on 14 July 1899: Cohen 1961, p. 127. Letter from Dolly van Dongen to E. Hild, 13 June 1985, fol. 2: it was probably Cohen who helped Guus Preitinger and K. van Dongen in 1899 to find housing; elsewhere she mentions S.J. ten Cate in this connection.

106.
P. Signac: Cachin 1971, p.83. M. Luce: Chaumeil 1967, pp. 66-69, 77. *Les Temps Nouveaux*: J. Grave, *Le mouvement libertaire sous la 3e république d'un révolté*, Paris 1930, p. 219; Dardel 1987, pp. 25, 45; Leighton 1990, p.615, 618; Oppler 1976, p. 189. For Picasso: Leighton 1989, p. 72. Shapiro 1976, pp. 51-52; Olivier 1933, p. 87: la 'bande Picasso'. Criticism of Leighton's view of Picasso's anarchism: Richardson 1991, pp. 237, 540 note 1; on the influence of Kropotkin, Nietzsche and others in Barcelona: pp. 129-130. Chaumeil 1967, p. 77: for Luce en Signac.

107.
Dardel 1987, p. 25; Giry 1981, pp. 13-14. Chaumeil 1967 mentions Van Dongen's interest in anarchy around 1900 in connection with *L'Assiette au Beurre*, p. 66; see also Shapiro 1976, pp. 30-31.

108.
Wiessing 1960, p. 192.

109.
De Vrankrijker 1972, pp. 81-82; p. 94 ff.; Herbert 1961, passim.

110.
Herbert 1960, pp. 479-482: on the autonomy of art in combination with a left-wing position; Herbert 1961, pp. 180-192; Leighton 1989. General: J. Maitron, *Histoire du mouvement anarchiste en France 1880-1914*, Paris 1951; A. Springer, 'Terrorism and anarchy: late 19th century images of a political phenomenon in France', *Art Journal*, summer 1979, pp. 261-266.

111.
Kropotkin 1897, p. 13: importance of free development; p. 14: the personal will is 'the most powerful factor' in the ideal society, which is based both politically and morally on the necessity of communism'. Compare: Domela Nieuwenhuis 1910, p. 450, on the importance of powerful and heroic personalities; p. 364, for his admiration for Kropotkin.

112.
Letter from K. van Dongen to Addicks, sent from Paris, September 1901, Fondation Custodia Paris.

113.
B. Ciquel, 'Van Dongen retrouve son passé' (Van Dongen recalls his past), *Paris Match*, 10 October 1959, no. 548, p. 77: 'Picasso n'a pas été convaincu. Il se souvient toujours de "Kees" le Kropotkine inspiré du Bateau-Lavoir' (Picasso has not been convinced. He still remembers the inspired 'Kees Kropotkin' of the Bateau Lavoir).

114.
Apollinaire 1960, p. 67, in 'Le Salon des Indépendants', *La Revue des Lettres et des Arts*, 1 May 1908: 'M. Van Dongen nous transporte chez des géants qui résolvent la question sociale par l'impudeur. Il nous laisse toujours sous une impression pénible. Il prostitue ses plus nobles et ses plus belles couleurs à des hontes citadines qu'il remarque en étranger' (M. van Dongen transports us to a circle of giants who resolve the social question through immodesty.
He always leaves us with a painful impression. He prostitutes his noblest and loveliest colours to urban forms of shame which he observes abroad). Van Dongen's canvases at the 1908 Salon included 2 still lifes, 2 landscapes, 1 painting of a ship, and also the *Lutteuses*, female wrestlers in the Bal Tabarin: Chaumeil 1967, black-and-white fig. no. 64.
The monumental canvas, *La fleur rouge* (The red flower), may also have been added. See also: Apollinaire 1960, p. 154: 'M. Van Dongen fait des progrès dans la banalité, mais ses dons de peintre sont évidents' (M. Van Dongen is making progress in the field of banality, but his painterly gifts are evident), Salon d'Automne, 1910.

115.
Warnod 1947, p. 101: Van Dongen whistled anarchist tunes in the Bateau-Lavoir for his infant daughter in her crib; Dolly van Dongen enjoyed a free upbringing. See also: Salmon 1945, p. 39: 'Il lui est toujours resté quelque chose de cette température proudhonienne ou kropotkinienne, esprit "conquête du pain"' (He has always retained something of that Proudhon or Kropotkin temperament, that "bread-conquering" spirit'). Dorgelès 1963, p. 15: on Van Dongen who removed the milk from Montmartre doorsteps in the morning. Van Dongen 1960, p. 46: 'we were all anarchists without throwing bombs'.

116.
Guth 1949, p. 134. Loosjes-Terpstra 1987, p. 233, note 1.

117.
Kunstzaal Oldenzeel, exhibitions included Van Gogh (1892 en 1896), H. Heijenbrock (1897), Haagsche School artists (1897), Toorop (1898 and 1899). For a Van Wisselingh exhibition in the Maas Hotel, *Rotterdamsch Nieuwsblad*, 25 June 1897. Works of art were also occasionally exhibited in the Tijdingzaal of the *Rotterdamsch Nieuwsblad*; reported in newspapers; artists such as Isaac and Jozef Israels, J.H. Mesdag, the Maris brothers, Toorop and De Moor. Also exhibitions at the Kunstclub, 16 Geldersche kade (quayside).

118.
J. Verheul, *Het aesthetisch genootschap te Rotterdam. Een herinnering aan den werkkring van het genootschap gedurende de 25 jaren van zijn bestaan, 1877-1903* (The aesthetic society of Rotterdam. A memoir of the society's working environment during the 25 years of its existence, 1877-1903), Rotterdam 1934, and *Jaarverslagen* (Annual Reports).

119.
Exhib.cat., *Affiches* (Posters), January 1896; exhib.cat., *Tentoonstelling van buitenlandsche meesters* (Exhibition of foreign masters), October 1896; lecture by H.G. Ibels, 26 November 1896, on which correspondence with Snabilié committee minutes, 17 September 1896; RKK Archives, GA Rotterdam.

120.
Jan C. de Vos and Willem van Korlaar. The company performed a programme inspired by the naturalism of André Antoine's *Théâtre Libre*; I thank Henk Gras, who works as a researcher in the field of Rotterdam theatre. M.G. Kemperink, *Nederlands toneel in het Fin-de-siècle 1890-1900* (Dutch theatre during the Fin-de-siècle 1890-1900), Amsterdam 1995. On cultural life in Rotterdam: articles in, E.O.H.M. Ruempol (ed.), *Gedenkboek Rotterdam 1328-1928 uitgegeven ter gelegenheid van het 600-jarig bestaan van de stad Rotterdam* (Commemorative volume, published to mark the 600th anniversary of Rotterdam), Rotterdam 1928; about the theatre, P. Koomen, 'Konstrycke Verpoosingh', pp. 479-509. See also: Ch. Cocheret 1955.

121.
A. Stuyvesant, 'On Rotterdam', *Woord en Beeld*, 1 (1896), pp. 59-65, quoted on p. 62. Also, L.H.J. Angenot, *De toekomstige loop der bevolking in Nederland en in het havengebied van Rotterdam* (The future course of the population in the Netherlands and in the port district of Rotterdam), Rotterdam, 1934. P. van Laar, 'Bouwers in de "natte" 1850-1990. Geschiedenis van een Rotterdamse haveninfrastructuur' (Builders in the 'wet' 1850-1990. History of a Rotterdam port infrastructure) in *Op de groei gemaakt. 'Geriefelijkheden voor een wel-ingerichte stad'. Anderhalve eeuw gemeentewerken Rotterdam* (Allowing for growth. 'Facilities for a well-organized city.' 150 years of Rotterdam public works), Rotterdam, 1996, at press. The port works were constructed from 1880 by the city of Rotterdam (later the Gemeentelijk Havenbedrijf – the City Port Authority).

122.
P. Haverkorn van Rijsewijk, introduction in exhib.cat., *Israelstentoonstelling*, Rotterdam (Rotterdamsche Kunstkring/Pro Patria), September 1894: 'En dan nog dit. Rotterdam moge naar 't zielentaal de tweede stad van Nederland zijn, ten aanzien der schilderkunst is zij zelfs niet de derde of vierde. Nooit heeft die kunst er gebloeid' (And now this. Rotterdam may be the second city in the Netherlands, in terms of inhabitants, but as far as painting is concerned it's not even the third or the fourth. Art has never flourished there); J. de Vries et al., *Pieter Haverkorn van Rijsewijk*, Amsterdam 1996; see also: M.J. Brusse, *Rotterdamsche zedeprenten*, Rotterdam 1921.

123.
Letter to Fénéon 1904, Inv. 860868, Getty Center, Santa Monica. C. Snabilié, 'Brieven uit Parijs' (Letters from Paris), *Nieuws van den Dag*, 4 March 1898: on these travel offers.

124.
Perruchot 1958, p. 4.

125.
Perruchot 1958, p. 4.

126.
Le Peuple (Brussels), 9 June 1931.

127.
L'Image 1 (1897), no. 11 (October), pp. 341-343. The illustrations are followed by a list of contents; the page numbering is incorrect. The illustrations remain unknown.

128.
Georges de Feure (1868-1943), an artist's name used by Georges Joseph van Sluijters, who was involved in the magazine from the very beginning: *L'Image*, no. 1 (December), also no. 3 (February), no. 6 (May), no. 8 (July).

129.
Millman 1993, p. 6.

130.
Undated cutting from the Dutch paper *Nieuws van den Dag*, May 1899, press documentation, RKD, The Hague.
F. Melchers (Paris), 'Over C.[P.] Cornelis de Moor' (On C.[P.] Cornelis de Moor), *Vlaamse School*, 1899, pp. 185-187. De Moor left for Paris on 18 February 1898: population register, GA Rotterdam; he returned temporarily to Rotterdam in August 1898 to draw the Coronation celebrations: *Rotterdamsch Nieuwsblad*, 18 August 1898; remained in Paris until sometime in 1900: Knoester 1988, p. 20. Other introductions possibly made via Franz Melchers, a friend of De Moor, who was also in Paris, or Charles Snabilié.
See: Bulée (Ch. Snabilié), 'Nederlandsche artisten te Parijs, Georges de Feure' (Dutch artists in Paris, Georges de Feure), *De Amsterdammer*, no. 1085, 10 April 1898, pp. 2-3; idem, 'Georges de Feure (Van Sluyters), *Elsevier's Geïllustreerd Maandschrift*, 10 (1900) vol. 19, pp. 481-495.

131.
Millman 1993, pp. 9-15, p. 72; examples of book decoration: p. 80 (no. 81), p. 89 (no. 104). In 1897 publication of a volume with 10 lithographs and cover by De Feure: X. Privas, *Chimères et grimaces* (Chimeras and grimaces), 1897; a series of 10 lithographs *Femmes damnées* (Damned women) after Baudelaire was under preparation. See: *L'Estampe et l'Affiche* (The print and the poster), 1 (1897), p. 130 and 2 (1898), p. 10; Millman 1993, p. 7, for illustrations in magazines; also contributions in *Le Figaro illustré, Les Maîtres d'Affiche.*

132.
Bulée (Ch. Snabilié), 'Nederlandsche artisten te Parijs, Georges de Feure', *De Amsterdammer*, no. 1085, 10 April 1898, pp. 2.

133.
Founded by André Marty, publisher of *L'Estampe originale*, c. 1894. Millman 1993, p. 16, p. 75 (no. 74), p. 83 (no. 87). Van Dongen mentioned in an article, 'Memories of Van Dongen', c. 1950, otherwise unspecified, p. 78, furniture drawings for *Galerie de l'Art Moderne*, in the rue Royale under supervision of Jansen: press documentation, RKD The Hague. This gallery not listed in Paris directories. Possibly the reference to *L'Artisan Moderne* is oblique. Weisberg 1986, p. 145, for the start of Galerie Bing; pp. 56-57, for J. Meier-Graefe's *La maison moderne.*

134.
Le Sourire, 4 (1902), no. 121, 15 February, p. 4. O. Gerdeil, 'Un atelier d'artiste' (An artist's studio), in *L'Art Décoratif*, no. 40, pp. 144-148. Milmann 1993, p. 24, a photograph of De Feure and his associates in 1901. In 1901 De Feure received the Legion of Honour, reported in the Dutch paper *Nieuws van den Dag*, 9 December 1901. This homage may have directly provoked Van Dongen's criticism of him (see the small line right on De Feure's suit).

135.
Examples of 1902 reviews: Millman 1993, p. 28; Weisberg 1986, p.256. Previously, in 1900, *La Critique* refers to first reviews: no. 136, 20 October 1900, p. 160.

136.
Brusse 1927-II. The home address of Siebe Johannes Ten Cate (1858-1908) was 4 Faubourg du Temple, his studio address 65 rue de Malte.

137.
Ten Cate attended the Drawing Academy in The Hague, and the Rijksacademie in Amsterdam. Taught by Anton Mauve, friends with Van Gogh and Anton van Rappard.
Ch. Snabilié, 'Siebe ten Cate', *De Amsterdammer*, no. 1509, 27 May 1906; idem, *Het Vaderland*, 22 March 1901, in response to an exhibition at Bernheim-Jeune; idem, 'Siebe ten Cate', *Elsevier's Geïllustreerd Maandschrift*, 8 (1898), vol. 16, pp. 481-493; C.L. ten Cate, *Genealogie van de Friese takken der van oorsprong Doopsgezinde familie ten C(K)ate uit Borne* (Genealogy of the Frisian branches of the originally Mennonite family ten C(K)ate from Borne), Utrecht 1985, p. 395. April-May 1892 exhibited in Rotterdam, Kunstclub Geldersche Kade; July 1897 at Van Wisselingh in Rotterdam, *Rotterdamsch Nieuwsblad*, 25 June 1897. Pastels by Ten Cate in, 'Pastels du Musée Carnavalet', *Bulletin du Musée Carnavalet*, 35 (1982), nos 1-2, pp. 16-23.

138.
Carel Jan Willem Snabilié (1856-1927), lived in Paris, in Montmartre, since May 1895. Address in 1896, 3 rue d'Orchamps; in 1898, 10 rue Lamarck.

139.
Bulée (Ch. Snabilié), 'Uit Parijs' (From Paris), *De Amsterdammer*, 27 March 1898; S. (Ch. Snabilié), 'Fransche brieven' (Letters from France), *Het Vaderland*, 18 February 1905; idem, 'Fransche brieven', *Het Vaderland*, 19 December 1908.

140.
Snabilié wrote for *De Amsterdammer*, *Elsevier's Geïllustreerd Maandschrift*, *Nederland* and French publications *Mercure de France*, *Le Figaro illustré*, *Art et Décoration*. He employed the pseudonyms, Bulée (from his mother's maiden name Bulaeus), Lutetius and Lutetiana, from the Latin name for Paris. In the Dutch daily *Nieuws van den Dag*, 'Brieven uit Parijs' (Letters from Paris); in *Het Vaderland*, 'Fransche brieven', signed S'.

141.
The Dutch-French Society (Nederlands-Fransche Vereniging) founded in June 1903; Snabilié was a committee member and librarian. In 1904 secretary of the subdivision Art and Science; in February 1905 transformed into the Dutch Society (Nedelandsche Vereniging). The aim was to foster Dutch cultural life in Paris. For invitation of the French press to the Vollard exhibition of Kees van Dongen 1904, see: Snabilié, 'Fransche brieven', *Het Vaderland*, 29 October 1904; 3 December 1904. On the Society see: *Neerlandia*, 1904, no. 12, p. 169; *Nieuws van den Dag*, 13 February 1905; *De Telegraaf*, 24 October 1905. Banquets held for such figures as Philippe Zilcken on 3 May 1901 and Georges de Feure on 9 December 1901: *Algemeen Handelsblad*, 6 May 1901; *Nieuws van den Dag*, 9 December 1901. Snabilié presented on his seventieth birthday with an album of drawings by such artists as Jan Toorop, H.G. Ibels and Isaac Israels.

142.
On Le Barc de Boutteville: G. Geffroy, 'Un marchand', *Le Journal*, 22 October 1897, pp. 1-2, quoted in Chaumeil 1967, p. 47; *Le Temps*, 14 October 1897, p. 3; C. Guy, 'Le Barc de Boutteville', *L'Oeil*, no. 124, April 1965.

143.
Ch. Snabilié, 'Uit Parijs', *De Amsterdammer*, 27 March 1898, p. 4.

144.
See also: *Nieuwe Rotterdamsche Courant*, 4 January 1894: 'De heer S. ten Cate geeft [...] impressies, waaronder twee nocturnes op de boulevards met paars-blauw en rood verlichte kiosken' (S. ten Cate Esq. produces [...] impressions, which include two nocturnes on the boulevards with purple-blue and red-lit kiosks). See for the silhouette as *tache* (blot): Van Gogh, G.H. Breitner, G. de Nittis, later Albert Marquet, etc.; on this: E. van Uitert, De Bodt 1995, p. 148.

145.
Exhib.cat. 1897 Paris, 'Cornelis van Dongen, no. 22. Aquarelle'; Vollard Archives, Vollard address book begins from the firm's inception, ms 1421 (4, 11). Under C: 'Cornelis T.M. van Dongen, 65 rue de Malte'; under T: 'Ten Cate, 65 rue de Malte'; the sales ledgers show that Vollard handled various works by Ten Cate; Bibliothèque Musée du Louvre, Paris.

146.
Anatole France, foreword to exhib.cat. *Exposition d'ouvrages peints, dessinés ou gravés par Th.-A. Steinlen* (Exhibition of paintings, drawings and engravings by Th.-A. Steinlen), Paris (Place Saint Georges 32), November-December 1903. France's designation was quoted in several reviews and acquired a life of its own.

147.
Brusse 1927-1. Also C. Scharten, 'Kees van Dongen', *De Amsterdammer*, no. 1461, 25 June 1905.

148.
Guth 1949, p. 134

149.
F. Lapidoth, *Fransche teekenaars* (French draughtsmen), The Hague, n.d. [1894]; previously appeared as articles in *De Nederlandsche Spectator*. An anthology with commentary in *De Amsterdammer*, anonymous (Ch. Snabilié?), 'Fransche teekenaars', I and II, no. 978, 22 March 1896, p. 6; no. 979, 29 March 1896, pp. 6-7.

150.
Th. Molkenboer, 'Aanplakbiljetten' (Posters), *De Amsterdammer*, no. 1033, 11 April 1897, p. 7, for four poster exhibitions in Amsterdam; see note 119.

151.
See also: Brusse 1904, pp. 496-497. Only a few people were early collectors of Steinlen's illustrations; see, J. Veth, 'Opstandigheid in prenten' (Rebellion in prints), in *Tweemaandelijksch tijdschrift*, 1894-1895, vol. I, pp. 142-145; N.H. Wolf, 'Th.A. Steinlen. Tentoonstelling Frans Buffa & Zonen Amsterdam', (Th.A. Steinlen. Exhibition at Frans Buffa & Zonen Amsterdam), *De Kunst*, 6 (1913), no. 299, pp. 33-40.

152.
Joosten 1980, p. 247, letter 94, 28 April 1896; in 1895 the *Chambard* was praised in *De Kroniek* as extremely unusual, Henkels 1993, p. 170. Joosten 1980, p. 132, letter 14, 1 July 1893; Thorn Prikker also mentions in this letter that he often inquired in vain for this type of publication at Jozef Blok's bookshop in The Hague.

153.
Brusse 1904, pp. 490-491. exhib.cat. *Tentoonstelling van Fransche, Duitsche en Engelsche journalistieke prentkunst waaronder 70 oorspronkelijke teekeningen van Steinlen georganiseerd door de vereniging 'Kunst aan het Volk'* (Exhibition of French, German and English journalistic illustrations, including 70 original drawings by Steinlen, organised by the association 'Art to the People'), Amsterdam (Stedelijk Museum), November 1904. For this exhibition see: Henkels 1993, pp. 172-180.

154.
G. (G.H. Marius), 'Haagsche Kunstkring', *Het Vaderland*, 16 February 1899; Henkels 1993; esp. pp. 164, 170, 274, note 23.

155.
Brusse 1904, p. 494-495. Jean-Louis Forain, asked about his exhibition, replied 'in the kiosk': Cate 1988, p. 115.

156.
Lethève 1961, pp. 241-254, 'Journaux Parisiens ayant publié des caricatures sous la troisième république (1870-1940)' (Parisian newspapers which published caricatures during the Third Republic). For circulation figures for the daily press: Bellanger 1972, pp. 7-31; Hiekisch-Picard 1986, p. 18. P. Melot, 'Les journaux d'humour' (The humorous papers), *Le Vieux Papier*, no. 173, p. 188: new papers produced in response to the 1900 World Fair.

157.
Illustrated press in general: Hiekisch-Picard 1986; Lethève 1961. For importance of illustrations: esp. pp. 46, 65, 241-254. Eardel 1987 for *Les Temps Nouveaux*. For portfolios of prints and special print editions: Boyer 1988, pp. 115-169; esp. p. 126 for *La Plume*; pp. 115, 161 for *Le Chambard Socialiste* and *La Feuille*. For circulation figures see: De Crauzat 1913, nos 117-159, 200-213. The lithographs were published by E. Kleinmann, Paris. For *La Plume*, see: Van Deputte 1994, with references; for *La Revue Blanche*, Jackson 1960.

158.
Cate 1982, pp. 109-130; Cate 1988, pp. 36-39. Caillaud 1985, pp. 206-208 for the advertising kiosks (*kiosques à affiches*).

159.
Halpérin 1988, p. 261. Quotation from F. Fénéon, 'Chez les barbouilleurs. Les affiches en couleurs' (Among the daubers. Colour posters), *Le Père Peinard*, 30 April 1893. Halpérin 1988, p. 33, for Fénéon's interest in 'the street'.

160.
Cohen 1967, pp. 198-200, Cohen 1961, p. 79; Snabilié 1900, pp. 165, 169-170. W.A. Paap, *Vincent Haman*, Amsterdam 1936 (1898), p. 117, for an interior with posters by French draughtsmen. For this rage see: anonymous (C. Snabilié?), 'Aanplakbiljetten en verzamelaars' (Posters and collectors), in *De Amsterdammer*, no. 1026, 21 February 1897, p. 4. In 1897 posters in Paris were stamped with a text warning against theft or private sale.

161.
Th.A Steinlen, *La rue. Affiches Charles Verneau* (The street. Charles Verneau posters), 1896, colour litho, 238 x 304 cm, illus. in Schultze 1994, p. 387; Cate 1982, 118-120; Le Men 1993, p. 77. The street as part of the artist's life: Cate 1988, pp. 18-27.

162.
Le Men 1993, esp. pp. 4-46; with references to the iconography of various 'types'.

163.
Fields 1984. R. de Leeuw, 'Jean-François Raffaëlli', *Van Gogh Bulletin*, 1994, no. 1, pp. 10-13. For distribution: Joris Karl Huysmans, *Croquis Parisiens* (Parisian sketches), Paris 1880; and Fields 1984, pp. 70, 296-302. J.F. Raffaëlli, *Les types de Paris* (Parisian types), Paris 1889, a publication for which Raffaëlli requested the collaboration of a large number of naturalistic writers, and produced 179 drawings of his own. Fields 1984, pp. 286, 290-291, for Vincent van Gogh, letters in June and July 1885. For the term 'caracterisme' see: J.F. Raffaëlli in, 'Etude des mouvements de l'art moderne et du beau caractériste' (Study of the movements of modern art and of the fine character artist), exhib.cat., *Catalogue illustré des oeuvres de Jean-François Raffaëlli*, Paris (28 bis avenue de l'Opera) 1884. For Ten Cate, G.H. Marius in 1908: undated cutting: press documentation, RKD, The Hague.

164.
Van Gogh and *The Graphic*: R. Pickvance, exhib.cat., *English influences on Vincent van Gogh*, London (The Arts Council) 1974; Van Heugten 1996, pp. 176-178. Raffaëlli and *The Graphic*, Fields 1984, p. 175. Herbert 1961, p. 181, on Raffaëlli, who was not the 'peintre de banlieue' (painter of the suburbs), he was taken for. Fields 1984, pp. 100-115, 281, esp. p. 117, on the 'déclassé' (person of reduced social status).

165.
Caillaud 1985. Rearick 1985, pp.174-176, for the emergence of illustrations and street plans to present the city.

166.
T.J. Clark, *The painting of modern life. Paris in the art of Manet and his followers*, London 1985; Herbert 1988, pp. 14-32, and 33-38 for the 'Flâneur'; esp. also p. 24 for Joris-Karel Huysmans' review, 'L'exposition des Indépendants en 1880', which advocates 'la vie moderne' (modern life) as subject. Ch. Baudelaire, 'Le peintre de la vie moderne', *Le Figaro*, 26 November, 29 November, 3 December 1863; included in idem, *Curiosités esthétiques. L'Art romantique*, Paris 1986,

pp. 453-502. E. and J. de Goncourt esp., *Manette Salomon*, Paris 1867. See also E. Duranty, *La nouvelle peinture: à propos du groupe d'artistes qui expose dans les Galeries Durand-Ruel* (The new painting: in connection with the group of artists exhibiting in the Galeries Durand-Ruel), Paris n.d. [1876]. For Breitner see: Hefting 1970, pp. 38-40, 59-65, 90. For I. Israels: Wagner 1985, pp. 22-23, 48.

167.
M.J. Brusse, 'Onder de menschen. Isaac Israels. II' (Among the people. Isaac Israels. II), *Nieuwe Rotterdamsche Courant*, 17 October 1934, in which Israels admires a drawing by Van Dongen: 'een knip in de Scharensteeg' (a glance into the Scharensteeg alley). I. Israels with Van Dongen in Paris around 1903-1904: Wagner 1985, pp. 65-88, p. 52 for the portrait of Van Dongen by I. Israels; Chaumeil 1967, p. 23, fig. 7. Van Dongen on the meeting: anonymous, 'Bij Kees van Dongen, de man die weg wou en dat van anderen niet begrijpt' (The world of Kees van Dongen, the man who wanted out...), *Nieuwe Haagsche Courant*, 11 June 1949.

168.
Anatole France, foreword exhib.cat. *Exposition d'ouvrages peints, dessinés ou gravés par Th.-A. Steinlen* (Exhibition of paintings, drawings and engravings by Th.A. Steinlen), Paris (Place Saint Georges 32) November-December 1903, p. 10. For the Montmartre artists: Cate 1988, pp. 8-20; Herbert 1961, pp. 192-195.

169.
Th.-A. Steinlen (1859-1923), Gill 1982; Cate 1982, esp. pp. 38, 45 for *Le Mirliton*. A. Bruant, *Dans la rue. Chansons et monologues*, Paris, n.d. [1888] and idem *Dans la rue. chansons et monologues*, vol. 2, Paris 1895. See Gill 1982, p. 15.

170.
Le Chambard Socialiste, Gill 1982, pp. 106 ff.; Cate 1982, p. 89; Steinlen drawings, under the pseudonym 'Petit Pierre', in December 1893-July 1894. Publication (*Chambard* is argot for upheaval and revolution) followed A. Vaillant's bomb attack on the Chambre des Députés, 9 December 1893. For J. Grave: Dardel 1987, p. 45.

171.
Gill 1982, pp. 140-156; in total 25 numbers; 17 drawings by Steinlen, 6 devoted to the Dreyfus Affair; Cate 1982, pp. 96-107. Appeared as a supplement with the daily newspaper *L'Aurore*, which also printed 'J'accuse' (I accuse) by E. Zola.

172.
De Crauzat 1913, no. 660, pp. 182-195; Gill 1982, pp. 68-71; Cate 1982, pp. 38-41; Hiekisch-Picard 1986, pp. 27-29. J. Pennell, *Modern Illustration*, London 1895, p. 54: 'It is especially in "Gil Blas" that the best French work is now to be found', quoted in, Gill 1982, pp. 22, 35, note 37. See also: F.L. Emanuel, *The illustrators of Montmartre*, London 1904, p. 3 and pp. 8-9, for Steinlen and *Gil Blas*.

173.
Dardel 1987, pp. 14-15 for subscriptions to left-wing papers. Bellanger 1972, pp. 381-382, for circulation figures.

174.
Gill 1982, pp. 16-17, 71, 76.

175.
Anatole France, foreword exhib.cat. *Exposition d'ouvrages peints, dessinés ou gravés par Th.-A. Steinlen*, Paris (Place Saint Georges 32) November-December 1903, p. 10. Also in Cate 1982, p. 23.

176.
J. Reibrach, 'Les trottins', *Gil Blas Illustré*, 8 (1898), no. 13, 1 April, p. 2. Steinlen and naturalist literature, Gill 1982, pp. 71-72.

177.
M.J. Brusse, 'Th. Steinlen en zijn prentkunst' (Th. Steinlen and his engravings), *Nieuwe Rotterdamsche Courant*, 18 December 1923. Also M.J. Brusse (introduction), *Liedjes van Alex de Haas*, Rotterdam [after 1941], p. 5 on his collection: lithograph by Toulouse-Lautrec, portrait of Aristide Bruant; collections of stories by Bruant. For a description of streets by Brusse see: Brusse 1901, p. 69. Example of Snabilié's work in: Bulée, 'Lutetiana', *Nederland*, 50 (1898), vol. 3, pp. 459-472.

178.
M.J. Brusse, 'Onder de menschen. Th. Steinlen en zijn prentkunst', *Nieuwe Rotterdamsche Courant*, 18 December 1923; the poster advertised *Le Coupable* by F. Coppée. R. Bargiel, C. Zagrodzki, *Steinlen affichiste: catalogue raisonné* (Steinlen the poster artist: catalogue raisonné), Lausanne 1986, no. 26. M.J. Brusse (patron for children's society 'Pro Juventute'), *Nieuwe Rotterdamsche Courant*, December 1901-July 1902; see J. Charité (ed.), 'Marie-Joseph Brusse', *Biografisch woordenboek van Nederland*, Amsterdam 1985, p. 81. Published in 1903 as a book with cover drawings by Steinlen; M.J. Brusse, *Boefje. Naar het leven verteld* (Boefje. A true-life story), Rotterdam 1903; see Van Faassen 1993, p. 104, no. 2; led to contact between Brusse en Steinlen.

179.
Brusse 1904, p. 508.

180.
Philippe 1908, p. 731. See Philippe 1901; Freeman 1990, p. 64, for a letter from Marquet to Henri Manguin, about the refusal of the drawings and his work on these in the summer of 1904.

181.
Bulée (Ch. Snabilié), *Jean Lefort. Een greep uit het Parijsche leven* (Jean Lefort. A random selection of Parisian life), with a foreword by Mr H. Louis Israëls, Amsterdam (E.L.E. van Dantzig) 1900. Two volumes in one cover, 448 pp.; one edition sewn, the other in de luxe binding with a parchment spine. Reviews: anonymous (F. Lapidoth), 'Jean Lefort, door Bulée' (Jean Lefort, by Bulée), *Elsevier's Geïllustreerd Maandschrift*, 11 (1901), vol. 21, p. 152; Th.P., 'Jean Lefort, door Bulée', *De Amsterdammer*, 1901, no. 1235 (24 February), pp. 4-5; Wolfgang, 'Jean Lefort', *De Nederlandsche Spectator*, 9 March 1901, pp. 79-80. I thank A. Putman for this information.

182.
Foreword H. Louis Israëls (a journalist colleague, Paris correspondent for *Het Handelsblad*) in Bulée 1900. The model was possibly: W.G.C. Byvanck, *Parijs 1891. Notities*, Leiden 1892. F. Xau (1852-1899), director of *Le Journal* was possibly the model for part of Jean Lefort's life.

183.
Bulée 1900, I, pp. 33, André Ibels; I, p. 169 H.G. Ibels.

184.
J. Hanssen O'Toole, 'Henri-Gabriel Ibels: Nabi journaliste', *Gazette des Beaux-Arts*, 124 (1982) vol. 99, pp. 31-38; Boyer 1988, pp. 144-158. For Ibels' programme for the *Théâtre Libre*, see: G. Aitken, exhib.cat. *Artistes et théâtres d'avant-garde. Programmes de théâtre illustrés. Paris 1890-1900* (Avant-garde artists and theatres. Illustrated theatre programmes. Paris 1890-1900), Pully (Musée de Pully) etc., 1991, pp. 24-29. H.G. Ibels et al., *Les demi-cabots. Dessins de H.-G. Ibels. Le café-concert, le cirque-les forains* (The provincial actors. Drawings by H.G. Ibels. The café concert, the circus, fairs), with texts by G. d'Esparbes, A. Ibels, M. Lefèvre, G. Montorgueil, Paris 1896. For André Ibels the covers of *Les chansons colorés*, Paris 1894, and *Les cités futures*, Paris 1895.

185.
H. Ryner, *André Ibels (Esquisse d'un 'Endehors' à l'aube du XXe siècle)* (André Ibels – Sketch of an 'Outsider' at the dawn of the twentieth century), Conflans-Honorine 1927, p. 9. For Vlaminck see: Herbert, James D. 1992, p. 218; in particular on anarchism see: *Le Libertaire*, no. 73, 13-20 July 1901, pp. 2-3. In *La Critique* A. Ibels' *Critiques sentimentales. James Vibert, sculpteur*, 1898; *Talentiers, ballades libres*, 1899. On publications by Ibels: Bulée 1900, I, pp. 71-73, 126. For A. Ibels in *La Critique*, see appendices in the years 1898 (nos 69, 73, 77, 87-89), 1899 (nos 95-99, 105, 115), 1899 (no. 117). In 1899, nos 95-99, his study of Judas ('Judas de Kayroth') was published; in Bulée 1900, I, p. 126 designated as 'Judas le Sauveur' (Judas the Saviour).

186.
The *Mercure de France* mentioned in Snabilié, *Les Archives de la Jeunesse Gauloise*. See Bulée 1900, I, pp. 126-127, 134-142. The editorial offices of the *Mercure de France* were in the rue de l'Echaudé, which corresponds with the route description in Bulée 1900, pp. 133-134. On Snabilié's article on Montmartre, Bulée 1900, II, p. 114 (not traced). For his collaboration with A. van Bever, editorial secretary of the *Mercure de France*; H.G.M. Prick, *De briefwisseling tussen Lodewijk van Deyssel en Albert Verwey*, vol. III, The Hague 1986, p.70. Ibels would publish little in the *Mercure* (Bulée 1900, I, p. 141). See *Tables* on the magazine 1890-1896, 1897-1904; a single contribution by Ibels in 1897, vol. 25, p. 97. It is also possible that Snabilié combined information about the *Mercure de France* and *La Critique*. Herbert 1961, p. 100, on the left-wing slant of the *Mercure de France* and *La Plume*.

187.
Première exposition de l'oeuvre dessinée et peinte de T.A. Steinlen (First exhibition of drawings and paintings by T.A. Steinlen), Paris (La Bodinière) 10 April-15 May 1894. *Exposition H.G. Ibels*, Paris (La Bodinière) 6 November-15 December 1894. For *La Bodinière*, the exhibition hall of the *Théâtre de l'Application*, see; Cate 1988, p. 38. For Snabilié's visits to this and *Le Salon des Cent* (*La Plume*) see: Bulée 1900, respectively I, 204-205; I, pp. 132-133; II, 46-47. See also: Lapidoth 1894, pp. 99-106 on Ibels; p. 106, as anarchist draughtsman. In *La Plume* by André Ibels, *Les chansons colorées, poésies*, Paris (Bibliothèque de 'La Plume') 1894.

188.
Bulée (C. Snabilié), 'Parijsche silhouetten. H.G. Ibels' (Parisian silhouettes. H.G. Ibels), *De Amsterdammer*, no. 995 (19 July) 1896, pp. 3-4; Ibels' exhibition at the Hague Kunstkring, January 1895. In a letter from the Kunstkring to Snabilié, 13 October 1896, mention of a possible follow-up lecture by Ibels for the Kunstkring; see, copy books, Hague Kunstkring Archive, GA The Hague. The lecture held in Rotterdam, 26 November 1896.

189.
H.G. Ibels in *L'Assiette au Beurre* from 1901; Dixmier 1974, pp. 351-357. Chaumeil 1967, p. 72.

190.
Mendès mentioned in: anonymous (F. Lapidoth), 'Jean Lefort, door Bulée', *Elsevier's Geïllustreerd Maandschrift*, 11 (1901), vol. 21, p. 152. See Bulée 1900, as 'Droze', I, pp. 34-35, 118-119. For *Le Figaro Illustré* and Valadon ('Cavard' in the book), Bulée 1900, I, pp. 36, 44-51; II, pp. 54-62, 115. In 1898 Snabilié wrote in *Le Figaro Illustré* under the pseudonym 'Lutétius' and was correspondent for this magazine at the Coronation celebrations in Amsterdam (1898); GA Amsterdam, Hartkamp Collection. For Deschamps see: Van Deputte 1994; also for F. Rops (1833-1898) and Deschamps and (1863-1899) Ibels at *La Plume*; see pp. 16, 54-57. Snabilié in Bulée 1900, on F. Rops (als Bernard van der Stap), I, pp. 37, 169-170, 200; on Deschamps, I, pp. 132-133, 200-209; II, pp. 45-47.

191.
Bulée 1900, I. pp. 136-139. As novel figure also mentioned in anonymous (F. Lapidoth), 'Jean Lefort, door Bulée', *Elsevier's Geïllustreerd Maandschrift*, 11 (1901), vol. 21, p. 152.

192.
Saint-Georges de Bouhélier (1876-1947) 1946, esp. pp. 262-308; idem, *Les Eléments d'une Renaissance Française*, Paris 1899 (assembling a collection); a novel which illustrates its ideas, idem, *Histoire de Lucie*, Paris 1902. For naturalism see: Maurice Le Blond, 'Saint-Georges de Bouhélier', *Les Hommes d'Aujourd'hui*, 1899, no. 439, pp. 1-4; F.C.Jr. (Frans Coenen), 'Littérature. Revue Naturiste; Essai sur le Naturisme; Documents sur le Naturisme' (Literature. Naturalist review; essay on naturalism; documents on naturalism), and idem, 'Littérature. Le Naturisme, l'art sacré et réel' (Literature. Naturalism, sacred and realistic art),

De Kroniek, 1897, in respectively April, pp. 132-133, May, pp. 140-141. Also T.B. (Jan ten Brink), 'Uit de studeercel' (From the study cell), *Elsevier's Geïllustreerd Maandschrift*, 7 (1897) vol. 13, p. 19-20. Oppler 1976, pp. 198-199. Survey in: M. Décaudin, *La crise des valeurs symbolistes* (The crisis of symbolist values), Toulouse 1960.

193.
Exhib.cat., Paris 1990, p. 126; Saint-Georges de Bouhélier, *Choix des poésies*, Paris 1933, frontispiece. In the Archives & Musée de la Littérature, Koninklijke Bibliotheek Albert I, Brussels, a letter from G. Kahn to E. Verhaeren, 25 November 1910, on a banquet for De Bouhélier. Van Dongen was also a member of the organizing committee. I thank Fabrice van de Kerckhove for this information.

194.
G.H. Marius, *De Hollandsche schilderkunst in de negentiende eeuw*, The Hague, 1903, p. 518

195.
Chapsal 1963, p. 45. See also: Salmon 1945, p.39

196.
J.H. Mastenbroek, *Vertelt zijn herinneringen ter gelegenheid van zijn zeventigsten verjaardag* (Reminisces on the occasion of his seventieth birthday), Rotterdam, Antwerp 1946, pp. 24-25, 32. Mastenbroek was in England in 1895-1896; in 1898 he had a studio at Oudedijk 203 (1), together with J. Linse jr. and Jan Weiland. For Chris Addicks, who took over Van Dongen's studio on the Groenendaal: letters to Addicks, Fondation Custodia, Paris. See the portrait of Addicks by Van Dongen, annotated 'September 1898'; Inv. KvD 26, Boijmans Van Beuningen Museum, Rotterdam.

197.
Speenhoff 1939, pp. 334-335. Tobacco factory belonging to Louis Dobbelman.

198.
Speenhoff 1939, pp. 333, 335.

199.
Scheffer 1981, pp. 260-261. From 1890 illustrations in the newspaper, which from 1894 were topical and commented on news reports. On printing processes: J. de Zoete, *Zomaar een plaatje? De introductie van nieuwe illustratietechnieken in Nederland in de negentiende eeuw* (Just a picture? The introduction of new illustration techniques in the Netherlands in the nineteenth century), n.p. 1991. Chaumeil 1967, p. 48. Letter from K. van Dongen to Fénéon, Inv. 860868, Getty Center, Santa Monica.

200.
Rotterdams Nieuwsblad Collection, Rotterdam: seven drawings of virtually the same format, 322 x 245 mm.; two of these appeared in the *Rotterdamsch Nieuwsblad: Avenue Concordia*, 8 June 1899; *'t Boymanshuis*, 15 May 1899. Originally owned by a porter who worked for Van Dongen's father, acquired in 1942; letter 28 January 1957, Rotterdams Nieuwsblad Archive. The old archive was destroyed in the May 1940 bombing of Rotterdam. Scheffer 1981, p. 261: artists possibly W.H. van der Nat and S.C. Tinbergen.

201.
Inauguration of the monarch, 31 August 1898. Drawings in *Rotterdamsch Nieuwsblad*, 15 August-13 September 1898. Van Dongen wrote on this anonymously, in 'Kees van Dongen weet nog alles van vroeger' (K.v.D. knows all about what went on before), *Rotterdamsch Nieuwsblad*, 28 May 1949. In the letter to Fénéon (1904) Van Dongen says that he made drawings for the paper, before 1897; these have not been found in the paper. The queen visited the city on 9 June and 26 September 1899.

202.
Studies of his art academy, 17 May 1899. Van Dongen referred to the series as *Langs de Schie/De spoorbrug van de Ceintuurbaan/no 5; Langs de Schie/no 3/Een bloemkwekerij; Kijkjes op de bloemenmarkt no 1; Pinksterbloemmarkt/Kijkjes op de bloemenmarkt/no 2* (Views along the river Schie, of a plant nursery, at the flower market, etc.). The drawing titled *De vaandeldrager van de eerewacht* (The flag-bearer of the guard of honour) is also numbered, as *no. 28*; fig. in Van Adrichem 1989, p. 14. The drawing dates from 1899.

203.
Anonymous, 'Bij Kees v. Dongen, de man die weg wou en dat van anderen niet begrijpt' (The man who wanted out...) *Nieuwe Haagsche Courant* (newspaper), 1 June 1949.

204.
Brusse 1927-I.

205.
A.J.Z., 'An interview with Kees van Dongen', *Eindhovens Dagblad* (local daily paper), 28 May 1949.

206.
Juliana Augusta Johanna Preitinger (1878-1946). Student at the Academy, Department of Freehand Drawing, the academic years 1896/1897 and 1897/1898, *Jaarverslagen* (Annual Reports). In a filmed interview with Martin van Dalen, summer 1987, Dolly van Dongen stated that her mother had lessons at the Academy for 5 years; she referred to a letter from the director A. Nolen, dated September 1899, confirming this.

207.
Exhib.cat. 1904 Paris (Vollard), no. 15; cp. exhib.cat. 1906 Rotterdam, no. 41: *Naakt* (Nude), 1898. The *Portrait d'une Zélandaise* (Portrait of a girl from Zeeland), exhib.cat. 1990 Paris, p. 82 (as 1898), by Vollard, no. 14, as 1896, which corresponds with the Symbolist influences on Van Dongen at that time.

208.
See on Addicks the following: K. Hazelzet, 'Schilderijen in Rotterdam, C.J. Addicks' (Paintings in Rotterdam...), *De Tijd*, 3 June 1942; P. Koomen, 'C.J. Addicks in de kunst. Van Zanten', *Algemeen Handelsblad* (daily paper), 27 May 1942. On Schildt see: N.H. Wolf, 'Martinus Schildt', *Elsevier's Geïllustreerd Maandschrift* (illustrated monthly), 11 (1901), vol. 21, pp. 155-164. In 1900 Schildt won the silver medal at the World Exhibition in Paris for a painting showing washerwomen, titled *Les lessiveuses*; in 1901 this won a gold medal in Munich and was then acquired for the Neue Pinakothek in Munich, Inv. 8187, p. 252 in G. Hopp et al., *Impressionisten, Postimpressionisten und Symbolisten. Volständige Katalog*, Munich (Neue Pinakothek) 1990. Both artists regularly showed their work at the Exhibitions of Living Masters.

209.
W.L. Brusse 1936.

210.
Brusse 1927-I,II,III. On M.J. Brusse (1873-1941) see the anonymous article 'Van De Koo tot Brusse. 25 jaren Onder de Menschen', *Haagsche Post*, 3 April 1923, p. 532. H. Wanting, 'M.J. Brusse, 1873-1941', in Ch. A. Cocheret, W.F. Lichtenauer, *Bekende Rotterdammers door hun stadgenoten beschreven* (Famous Rotterdammers described by their fellow citizens), Rotterdam 1951, pp. 105-124. J. Charité (ed.), 'Marie-Joseph Brusse', *Biografisch woordenboek van Nederland* (Biographical Dictionary of the Netherlands), Amsterdam 1985, pp. 81-83. Scherphuis 1991, p. 44; he began his career as a journalist in Amsterdam working for the dailies *De Amsterdammer* and *De Telegraaf*.

211.
On Willy Brusse (1879-1937) see: S. Hubregtse, 'De gebroeders Brusse, hun fonds en de context', pp. 7-16 in Van Faassen 1993. The Brusse family, 70 Diergaardesingel.

212.
Brusse 1927-I; W.L. Brusse 1936-37.

213.
First serials published in 1899 (later ones titled 'Onder de Menschen' (Among the people)). First important reportage in 1893, describing a conflict in Rotterdam harbour, see: Scherphuis 1991, p. 44. Literary publications in P.H. Muller, D. Kramer, 'Bibliographie XVIII. M.J. Brusse', *Opwaartsche Wegen*, 7 (1929-1930), pp. 379-384; in addition, M.J. Brusse, ''n Sterfgeval' (A Death), *Elsevier's Geïllustreerd Maandschrift* (monthly magazine), 8 (1898), vol. 15, pp. 23-38; idem, 'Dirk Haspels vertelt van zijn leven', *Woord en Beeld* 5 (1900), pp. 219-238. J. Charité (ed.), 'Marie-Joseph Brusse', *Biografisch woordenboek van Nederland* (Biographical Dictionary of the Netherlands), Amsterdam 1985, p. 81. Influence of Zola, M.J. de Meester, 'Letterkundige Kroniek. Vijf-en twintig jaar Onder de Menschen' (Literary Chronicle. Twenty-five Years in the World), *Nieuwe Rotterdamsche Courant* (Rotterdam daily), 31 August 1919. Herman Heijermans the Dutch writer was also an example in the national daily *De Telegraaf*; see the anonymous article, 'De "Onder de Menschen"-maker van de N.R.Crt.', *Het Leven*, 14 (1919), no. 39, p. 1262.

214.
Brusse 1927-I.

215.
For details and photographs see: A.T., 'Een buurt, die gaat verdwijnen' (Death of a neighbourhood), *Wereldkroniek*, 15 (1909), pp. 229-233. M.J. Brusse, 'Polder-herinneringen van een oud- van politiepostcommandant in de Zandstraatbuurt' (Memories of an ex-policeman in the Zandstraat district), *Nieuwe Rotterdamsche Courant*, esp. 15 and 18 March 1933.

216.
Van Vree 1991, with literature references.

217.
Brusse 1912; second enlarged edition Brusse 1917. The articles 'In den polder' (In polderland) were published as a result of a decision by the city council, published in the daily *Nieuwe Rotterdamsche Courant*, in November-December 1910, and on 2 January 1912. Five drawings by K. van Dongen were published in Brusse 1917; see in this connection Brusse 1927-I 'waarvan er nòg verscheiden mijn werkkamer sieren' (...my workroom which is adorned with several [pictures].' Four drawings by Van Dongen that were in Brusse's possession in 1935 at the art dealer's Kunsthandel Buffa, exhib.cat. 'Amsterdam geëxposeerd', 1935 Amsterdam. In connection with this exhibition see the correspondence in RKK Archive, Inv. 328d, GA Rotterdam. See also: J. Brusse, 'Als zoontje van M.J. Brusse' (As the son of M.J. Brusse) in the local weekly *De Groene Amsterdammer*, 22 December 1956, p. 12.

218.
Brusse 1901, p. 69.

219.
Letter to Fénéon 1904, Inv. 860868, Getty Center, Santa Monica: a brothel on the Red Sand (Zandstraat). See also the anonymous article, 'Een wilde van tachtig jaar' (A Fauvist at the age of Eighty), *Haagse Post*, 2 February 1957; Chaumeil 1967, p. 41; F.X.M.S., 'Kees van Dongen in Amsterdam', *Het Leven* (Life), 16 April 1927, p. 495, Van Dongen reported in Amsterdam about the Zandstraat: 'hoe mooi het toen daar ook was' (it was so attractive there at that time).

220.
Perruchot 1958, p. 4.

221.
W.L. Brusse 1936, fol. 1; W.L. Brusse 1936-1937, fol. 1.

222.
First article in the paper *Nieuwe Rotterdamsche Courant*, Sunday 4 June 1899, second sheet, p. 1; last one, ibid., 3 August 1899. Shortly thereafter the series appeared as a book – according to the foreword at the request of many readers, see Brusse 1899. Mentioned as the first 'book series' in N.H. Wolf, 'M.J. Brusse "Onder de menschen" te water en te land', *Wereldkroniek*, 10 (1904), no. 46, pp. 721-722.

223.
Scherphuis 1991, p. 46, as a result of the series the official job recruitment centres were set up and the homes for sailors were improved. See Brusse 1911, in the introduction to the 7th impression of *Van af- tot aanmonsteren*, Brusse 1899. Brusse was not a member of a political party; his brother Willy was active in the SDAP, forerunner of the Dutch Labour party; see S. Hubregtse, 'De gebroeders Brusse, hun fonds en de context', p. 7 in Van Faassen 1993.

224.
Brusse 1899, pp. 80-96 on the Zandstraat in Rotterdam. Drawing printed in Brusse 1917 (not in Brusse 1912), no. 5, signed and dated lower right: *VDongen./99*. See Brusse 1899, pp. 74-75 for Toon and Bakker; p. 7, the *veelkleurige sjaal*, (many-coloured scarf) that Brusse also acquired.

225.
Brusse 1901, p. 73 as 'Catrientje' (Katy), in Brusse 1907, pp. 14-15.

226.
Brusse 1899, pp. 80-81.

227.
Brusse 1901, pp. 72-73.

228.
The help given by the organizations 'Jeruël' and 'Mordechaï' is described. For the centre see: the foreword in Brusse 1901. Brusse's mother was on the committee of an organization to help women, the *Onderlinge Vrouwenbescherming*; Scherphuis 1991, p. 46; see also a letter from K. van Dongen to Herman Schotel (1874-1951), n.d. [1903]; private collection, on Brusse's mother: 'zoo lief [...] dat ze gevallen meisjes helpt' (such a kind and loving person ... that she helps fallen women).

229.
Brusse 1907, pp. 135-148, quotation p. 137. This section is added, together with 'Zangeresjes' (Singers) pp. 33-45, to the accounts of welfare work in this neighbourhood, earlier published by Brusse in 1901. The story may have been written in connection with Van Dongen's visit to Rotterdam in 1907. See a description of Van Dongen in Brusse 1927-I, which helps identify the painter here as Kees van Dongen.

230.
M.J. Brusse, 'Onder de menschen. Isaac Israels. II', in the paper *Nieuwe Rotterdamsche Courant*, 17 October 1934.

231.
For Zandstraat see: Brusse 1917, pp. 5-9, p. 34: not until later did he come to realise the criminal side of this district; idem, 'M.J. Brusse interviewt M.J. Brusse' (Brusse interviews Brusse) (1929), in a catalogue from the publishers W.L. & J. Brusse.

232.
M.J. Brusse, 'Onder de Menschen. Isaac Israels', article in the paper *Nieuwe Rotterdamsche Courant*, 13 and 17 October 1934; idem, 'Polder-herinneringen van een oud- van politiepostcommandant in de Zandstraatbuurt' (Memories of an ex-policeman from the Zandstraat area) in the paper *Nieuwe Rotterdamsche Courant*, 15 March 1933, here mentioned: Kees van Dongen, Isaac Israels and Paul Signac.

233.
M.J. Brusse 1917, pp. 6-7 and pp. 77, 79. The dance hall owned by Chr. Nielsen was at 15 Zandstraat, according to the 1899 directory. The reference in Brusse 1935 about this visit says that the owner was called Posthuma.

234.
The packet of letters, including drawings, was destroyed when the city of Nijmegen was bombed in September 1944.

235.
Letter from Brusse to Jacobus Funke, director of the daily paper *Het Nieuws van den Dag*, 19 December 1899; M.J. Brusse Archive, NLMD The Hague.

236.
Brusse 1927-I.

237. H.J. Scheffer, *Willem Smalt, kruidig chroniqueur* (Willem Smalt, a spicy narrator), Rotterdam 1963, pp. 37-55; Scheffer 1987, pp. 235-236; Van Faassen 1993, 53-62 with reference to illustrated book publications; Veth 1905, 1921, 1941; J. Veth 1905, pp. 232-237; De Vrankrijker 1950. Rotterdam papers and magazines such as *Abraham Prikkie* (1891-1896) and *De Ware Jacob* (1901-1916) were published either earlier or later.

238.
A selection of illustrated Dutch magazines appears in G.W. Ovink, *Het aanzien van een eeuw. De periode 1856-1956 weerspiegeld in 950 illustraties uit de voornaamste Nederlandse familiebladen* (The period 1856-1956 reflected in 950 illustrations from the leading magazines), Haarlem n.d., pp. 323-325. Art magazines are not included in J. Hemels, R. Vegt, *Het geïllustreerde tijdschrift in Nederland. Bron van kennis en vermaak, lust voor het oog. Bibliografie deel I: 1840-1945* (The Illustrated Magazine in Holland ... 1840-1945), Amsterdam 1993. See *Woord en Beeld* (Word and Image), for J. de Meester, G. van Hulzen, M.J. Brusse; illustrations by K. Speenhoff, Piet de Moor and the Steinlen disciple Louis Raemaekers. For Louis Raemaekers, see A. de Ranitz, *Met pen en potlood als wapen* (Armed with pen and pencil), thesis Amsterdam 1989.

239.
J. Sillevis et al., exhib.cat., Rodin, The Hague (Museum Het Paleis), Laren (Singer Museum) 1995, pp. 79-90, for the Rodin exhibition in the Rotterdam Kunstkring, 29 June-30 July 1899. G. (G.H. Marius), 'Haagsche Kunstkring', *Het Vaderland*, 16 February 1899, including Th.A. Steinlen, Adolphe Willette, Odilon Redon, Henri de Groux, Félicien Rops. Letter from K. van Dongen to Addicks, 24 January 1900, Fondation Custodia, Paris, in which Van Dongen mentions his hope of finding work for this. See the guide to the exhibition, Israëls 1900. In 1899 Guus Preitinger had completed her studies.

240.
Van Dongen on 4 October 1899 'officially' (note made by an official, not reported by Van Dongen himself) signed out of the population register as having departed for Paris; population register, GA Rotterdam.

241.
Brusse 1927-II; postcard from Kees van Dongen to G. Preitinger, dated 25 September 1899; private collection.

242.
Letter to Addicks, December 1899, Fondation Custodia, Paris.

243.
Letter to Addicks, September 1901, Fondation Custodia, Paris.

244.
See for a summary the anonymous article, 'Bij Kees v. Dongen, de man die weg wou en dat van anderen niet begrijpt' (Talking to Kees van Dongen, the man who wanted out...) in the paper *Nieuwe Haagsche Courant*, 1 June 1949. Letters Addicks, December 1899; 24 January 1900; September 1901; Fondation Custodia, Paris.

245.
Brusse 1927-II.

246.
For C. Pissarro (1830-1903) see Chr. Lloyd (ed.), *Studies on Camille Pissarro*, London & New York 1986. For Pissarro's published drawings see: Dardel 1987, pp. 15-16; for example p. 21, *La charrue*, a lithograph from 1901, showing a farmer ploughing, reminiscent of Millet. On Van Gogh and Millet see L. van Tilborgh, S. van Heugten, Ph. Conisbee, exhib.cat., *Van Gogh & Millet*, Amsterdam (Rijksmuseum Vincent van Gogh) 1988.

247.
Van Heugten 1996, p. 252. *Tentoonstellingen van teekeningen van Vincent van Gogh* (Exhibitions of Vincent van Gogh's Drawings), Rotterdam (Rotterdamsche Kunstkring) 23 December 1900-10 February 1901.

248.
Postcard from K. van Dongen to G. Preitinger in Paris, sent from the Dutch seaside resort of Scheveningen, 15 February 1901; private collection. 'Je brief heb ik ontvangen maar waarom stuur je ze naar Rotterdam ik ben steeds in Scheveningen' (I received you letter but why do you write to me in Rotterdam – I'm still in Scheveningen).

249.
Postcards from K. van Dongen to Guus Preitinger, stamped respectively 3 and 6 March 1901, sent from Amsterdam, private collection. In Amsterdam at the house of Christina Kuenen, a friend of Sanne Bruinier; 46 Van Baerlestraat. In the postcard dated 6 March, M.J. Brusse is mentioned. The celebrations lasted from 5 until 9 March 1901; Hartkamp Collection, GA Amsterdam. On 7 February 1901 Queen Wilhelmina and Prince Hendrik, Duke of Mecklenburg-Schwerin were married. The illustrations were not published; *Nieuws van den Dag*, 25 January 1902; undated newspaper cutting, January 1902, 'Illustrator tegen uitgever' (Illustrator versus publisher), RKD The Hague. Van Dongen's lawyer, P. Drooglever Fortuyn, was the husband of Hélène Bruinier, the sister of Sanne Bruinier.

250.
Postcards to G. Preitinger sent from the Dutch seaside resort of Scheveningen, 15 February, 15 and 16 March 1901, private collection. Address of Sanne Bruinier (1875-1951): 6 Haringstraat, Scheveningen, see: Bruinier 1993, p. 127. For Van Dongen and Bruinier in Paris, June 1900, October 1901: Bruinier 1993, pp. 107, 157. Bruinier 1993, pp. 150, 157, 179, September 1901 Kees and Guus in Scheveningen; p. 179, no contact between Van Dongen and Thorn Prikker. On Bruinier and Thorn Prikker (1899-1902) see: Bruinier 1993, pp. 18-21 and passim.

251.
Postcard to G. Preitinger in Paris, from the Dutch seaside resort of Scheveningen, postmark 16 March 1901, private collection: 'Morgenochtend ga ik naar Mesdag' (Tomorrow morning I'll go and see Mesdag). J.H. Kraan, 'De particuliere kunstverzameling van H.W. Mesdag' (The private art collection of H.W. Mesdag), *Oud Holland*, 104 (1990), nos 3-4, pp. 305-327. See also: Thorn Prikker's appreciation of Millet in Joosten 1980, letter 27 November 1892, no. 4, pp. 81-82.

252.
Postcard to G. Preitinger in Paris, from the Dutch seaside resort of Scheveningen, dated 15 March 1901, private collection: 'Ik ben Looyen zijn moeder aan 't schilderen maar 't goeie mensch poseert nog minder goed dan jij' (I'm painting a portrait of Looyen's mother but the dear woman is even worse at posing than you are). The architect J.D. Looyen (1876-1944) was in Paris in 1900-1901; see Bruinier 1993, pp. 43, 56-57, 94-96, 106-107, 120, 123, 150, 165, 167; p. 56: Looyen gave Guus Preitinger (drawing?) lessons; he was a friend of Georges de Feure and Charles Snabilié. See Israëls 1900, drawings for maps and plans, done by J.D. Looyen.

253.
Postcard to G. Preitinger, from Rotterdam, postmark 2 March 1901, private collection: 'Je suis en train de peindre le portrait de mon père. Ça marche bien' (I'm busy painting a portrait of my father – it's going well).

254.
Postcard from K. van Dongen to G. Preitinger from the Dutch seaside resort of Scheveningen, postmarked 16 March 1901, private collection.

255.
Anonymous (Snabilié), 'Brieven uit Parijs, 24 april 1901' (Letters from Paris, 24 April 1901) in the Dutch paper *Het Nieuws van den dag*, 29 April 1901. Exhib. 1901 Paris, no. 1407 *Femme assise* (Seated woman).

256.
Anonymous, 'Een Hollandsch talent' (A Dutch talent) in the local paper *De Zutphense Courant*, no. 153, 1 July 1901. Article partially copied by the paper *Nieuwe Rotterdamsche Courant*, 2 July 1901.

257.
See N.H. Wolf, 'Th.A. Steinlen. Tentoonstelling Frans Buffa & Zonen Amsterdam' (Exhibition of Steinlen at Buffa's), *De Kunst*, 6 (1913), no. 299, p. 40, about a portrait of K. van Dongen painted by Th.A. Steinlen; no illustration, present location unknown.

258.
Pieter Dupont (1870-1911); Ch. Snabilié, 'P. Dupont', *Elsevier's Geïllustreerd Maandschrift*, 11 (1901), vol. 21, pp. 371-382, esp. p. 376 about their meeting. Dupont 1947, was in Paris 1896-December 1897, autumn 1898-1901; in 1902 in Auvers-sur-Oise, afterwards in Amsterdam. Bruinier 1993, pp. 85, 97-98, visit to Dupont in May 1900.

259.
Brusse 1904, pp. 504-505. Dupont 1947, no. 84, *Portret Th.-A. Steinlen*, 1900-1901, copper engraving, 305 x 245 mm.

260.
Cohen 1961, p. 127, (return from exile) pp. 131-241, period in Paris, period as correspondent for the Dutch daily *De Telegraaf* (September 1906-September 1917), see Nord 1981, p. 17. Also wrote for the French papers *Le Figaro, Mercure de France, Le Temps.*

261.
Halperin 1988, p. 302. Portrait drawing of Cohen by Van Dongen, fig. in A. Cohen, *Uitingen van een reactionnair (1896-1926)* (Exclamations of a reactionary), Baarn 1929, frontispiece, c. 1901. There was a portrait of Fénéon by Van Dongen drawn c. 1904, fig. in J. Paulhan, *Félix Fénéon ou le critique* (F. Fénéon or the critic), Paris 1945, p. 61 (whereabouts unknown). Cohen in *La Revue Blanche*, 11 (1900), vol. 22 (May-August); 23 (September-December); 12 (1901), vol. 26 (September-December). In 1896 Cohen published translations of the Dutch writer Multatuli in *La Revue Blanche*; I thank R. Spoor for this information.

262.
J. Roullet, 'Petitjean', *La Revue Libre*, 1901/1902, pp. 157-162; Dorgelès 1947, pp. 130-131; Georges-Michel 1954, p. 73. J. Adhémar, 'Les journaux amusants et les premiers peintres cubistes' (Humorous papers and the first cubist painters) in *L'Oeil*, 1955, no. 4, pp. 40-43. R. Bachollet, 'Juan Gris', pp. 15-26, in exhib.cat., *Juan Gris et les dimanches de Boulogne*, Boulogne-Billancourt (Musée Municipal) 1987. M. Melot, 'Le modèle impossible. Ou comment le jeune Pablo Ruiz abolit la caricature' (The impossible model, or, how the young Pablo Ruiz abolished caricature), pp. 68-87, esp. p. 82, in Léal 1991.

263.
Jackson 1960, pp. 18-21, and pp. 23, 112 on anarchism; p. 27: the Natansons were owners from 1891, Alexandre Natanson was director; Thadée and Louis-Alfred Natanson were on the board of editors. For *La Revue Blanche* see: G. Beruier, *La Revue Blanche, ses amis, ses artistes* (The *Revue Blanche*, its friends, its artists), Paris 1991; B. Waller, G. Seiberling, exhib.cat., *Artists of the Revue Blanche*, Rochester (Memorial Art Gallery) 1984. *La Revue Blanche*, 12 (1901) vol. 24: vignettes of Pierre Bonnard, Paul Ranson, Félix Vallotton; in vol. 25 of Pierre Bonnard, Paul Signac and K.X. Roussel; a full sheet drawing of Rippl-Ronaï; in vol. 26 vignettes of Albert Marquet, Paul Signac, K.X. Roussel, Félix Vallotton.

264.
On the (political) leanings of the *Revue Blanche* see: Jackson 1960, pp. 14-16, 21-27, 33-38, 109-112; on Léon Blum see: esp. pp. 27, 81-83; for the *Nabis*, Jackson 1960, pp. 38, 63-72; Halperin 1988, p. 300; Oppler 1976, pp. 199-200, naturalism as a reaction to Symbolism; see also pp. 91-92 (drawing style of Derain, Marquet, Matisse, Van Dongen related to Bonnard's later sketches in ink). For Marius-Ary Leblond in *La Revue Blanche*, 12 (1901), vol. 25, and 14 (1903), vol. 30.

265.
Halperin 1988, pp. 42, 140, 190-193, 300. Jackson 1960, p. 25 for (political) leanings of the *Revue Blanche*; esp. Fénéon, pp. 95-99; Romain Coolus, pp. 119-120; Charles-Louis Philippe, pp. 126-128; Léon Blum, p. 120.

266.
Auction Paris, Drouot (F. Lair Dubreuil), *Tableaux modernes, aquarelles, pastels...collection Alexandre Natanson*, 16 May 1929, nos 64-68; no. 68, *Au bal de l'Opéra*, not published. The drawings in *La Revue Blanche*, 12 (1901), vol. 25, respectively in nos 15 July 1901, p. 465 (*L'escalier de l'Opéra*), 15 August 1901, p. 615 (*Femme vue de dos*), p. 625 (*Le fiacre*), p. 643 (*Le musicien*). Titles taken from those at the auction of Natanson, 1929. *L'escalier de l'Opéra*, again in vol. 26, 15 September 1901, p. 144; *Femme vue de dos*, in vol. 30, January 1903, p. 90; *Le fiacre*, in vol. 30, January 1903, p. 134. *Femme vue de dos*, in 1901 as vignette under J. Madeline, 'Dans les regards' ('From the glances' – about a woman who imagines herself to be a courtesan because of the looks she receives). Again in 1903 as a vignette under Félix Le Dantec, 'La virulence du sexe' (The virulence of sex), pp. 81-90.

267.
See also Carco 1921, p. 43.

268.
Dixmier 1974, pp. 15-25 on Schwarz; p. 22 for citation of André Salmon; pp. 335-336 a comparable remark from the draughtsman Paul Jove. Beside the special number Van Dongen made 8 drawings for the paper. His last contribution was *Le Maroc* in no. 140, 5 December 1903, p. 2347.

269.
On printing processes in general see: Dixmier 1974, pp. 39-42; Gill 1982, pp. 22-28; Cate 1982, pp. 77-81. M.J. Brusse, 'Onder de Menschen. Albert Hahn II' (Among the People...) in the Dutch daily *Nieuwe Rotterdamsche Courant*, 14 September 1911. Brusse 1904, p. 507 with reference to Steinlen.

270.
Richardson 1991, pp. 193-202, Vollard exhibition, contributions to *Frou-Frou;* Gordon 1974, p. 36: 64 paintings, 65 drawings. On Picasso's illustrations see: P. Daix, 'Quand Picasso dessinait pour la presse parisienne' (When Picasso made drawings for the Parisian press), *Les Lettres Françaises*, 3 March 1971, pp. 24-45; M. Melot, 'Le modèle impossible' (The impossible model) in Léal 1991, pp. 82-83: *Frou-Frou*, nos 44, 46 and 48 (15 and 31 August, 14 September) 1901.

271.
Dixmier 1974, p. 278: the price for one number varied from 700 to 1000 francs; Chaumeil 1967, p. 72: Van Dongen received the fee of 800 francs.

272.
Chaumeil 1967, pp. 70-72. No illustrations by Van Dongen in *Frou-Frou*. Chaumeil, p. 71, references to *Le Rab'lais* are incorrect; the cover drawing in Chaumeil (fig. 31) is not by Van Dongen, nor are the illustrations in no. 48 (13 January 1903); probably by A. Méria. For *Gil Blas* see: Georges-Michel 1967; this contains six drawings by Van Dongen. For Van Dongen commenting on making illustrations for papers, see: Guth 1949, p. 135; Perruchot 1958, p. 4.

273.
Van Dongen made drawings for these papers in 1902-1904; in 1905 for *L'Indiscret, Les Temps Nouveaux, La vie pour rire* (drawings previously published in *La Caricature*). He also made incidental illustrations for *Le Rire, Sans-Gêne* and *L'Oeil*. Lethève 1961, pp. 241-250, general list of magazines. See also P. Melot, 'Les journaux d'humour et la presse galante à la Belle Epoque' (Humorous papers and gossip columns in the belle epoque), *Le vieux papier*, no. 173, October 1955, pp. 185-195; Hiekisch-Picard 1986, pp. 235-237 bibliography.

274.
M. Melot, p. 83 in Léal 1991, on *Le Journal pour Tous*; Richardson, Steinlen and Picasso, p. 173; P. Dittmar, 'Steinlen et le jeune Picasso' (Steinlen and the young Picasso), *Revue de l'Art* 1985, no. 68, pp. 85-91. Cate 1982, p. 83. A. Blunt, Ph. Pool, *Picasso. The formative years. A study of his sources*, London, New York 1962.

275.
Dardel 1987, 45; Leighton 1990, p. 618. The metro drawings in *L'Assiette au Beurre*, no. 125, 22 August 1903. For general themes see: Dixmier 1974; Hiekisch-Picard 1986.

276.
Winkel 1986: no index for the drawn contributions. Scheffer 1987, pp. 233-239. Illustrations by Van Dongen in nos 11, p. 60 and 20, p. 109 (colour), and as cover for nos 33, 35, 38, 40, 43. The drawing in Winkel 1986, p. 32 is not by Van Dongen. Winkel, pp. 136-137, list of special numbers; the number by Van Dongen is missing. For an illustration by Van Dongen in the Dutch paper *Het Volk*, 17 August 1902, see Henkels 1975, p. 24; Van Adrichem 1989, p. 15.

277.
Winkel 1986, p. 27, note 8 and p. 145, note 66 about the meeting. On Henri Dekking (1871-1939) see: Scheffer 1981, pp. 252-255, p. 279; his period working for the Dutch daily *Rotterdamsch Nieuwsblad* from December 1892, from 1900 as art critic, see: in memoriam articles in the Dutch dailies *Nieuwe Rotterdamsche Courant* and *Rotterdamsch Nieuwsblad*, 9 October 1939. Scheffer 1987, p. 234: Dekking seen as the link between those involved with the publication *De Ware Jacob*. Winkel 1986, passim, for Schotel and Speenhoff. Joop Siedenburg (1875-1961), who is frequently mentioned, started working for the paper in 1903 and became editor in chief in October 1903: Winkel 1986, pp. 22-23; Heyting 1994, pp. 110-113.

278.
E. Delacroix, *Les massacres de Scio*, 1824, Paris, Musée du Louvre. P. Hecht, 'Sara Lichtenstein, Delacroix and Raphael', *Simiolus*, 11 (1980), nos. 3-4, pp. 186-195.

279.
J. Véber, 'Les camps de reconcentration au Transvaal' (The concentration camps in Transvaal), *L'Assiette au Beurre*, 1 (1901), no. 26, 28 September. Dixmier 1974, pp. 44, 187-188, 220-221. The Dutch edition (which did not include the page 'Albion') is mentioned in Van der Meulen 1912; this and Van der Meulen 1901 list other Dutch publications dealing with the Boer War. See also R.C. van Caenegem et al. (ed.), *Grote Winkler Prins encyclopedie*, vol. 4, Amsterdam, Brussels, 1979, pp. 460-461.

280.
Announced as a special number *De Ware Jacob*, 1 (1901/1902), no. 38, 21 June, p. 205; a drawing from the series, titled *De kleine vreugd en het groote leed* (Small joy, huge grief) was published on the cover of *De Ware Jacob*, 1 (1901/1902) no. 40, 5 July, p. 216. The number was published in Rotterdam, printed by Helios, a firm specialising in photo-zincography and autotype, at 113 Binnenrotte.

281.
Edward VII succeeded his mother Queen Victoria on her death on 22 January 1901; the coronation was on 9 August 1902. See also the announcement in *De Ware Jacob*, 1 (1902), no. 38, 21 June, p. 205: 'In de loop dezer maand verschijnt "De Vrede" extra-nummer van De Ware Jacob, ontworpen en geteekend door Kees van Dongen, ter gelegenheid van den "vrede", en ook met het oog op de kroningsfeesten in Engeland' (An extra number of *De Ware Jacob* will be published this month, designed and illustrated by Kees van Dongen, to mark the "Peace" and also in connection with the coronation in England).

282.
Brusse 1927-III: Van Dongen as illustrator at an evening party in The Hague, at Jonkheer Joan Roëll's. Brusse described the illustration drawn as a result of this party, which appeared in *Le Canard Sauvage*, 1 (1903), no. 2,

28 March 1903. The sketch that accompanies the text, made during the evening party, is drawn on letter paper from the Haagsche Journalistenvereeniging, the Hague Society of Journalists. See for another drawing of the same event the auction, London Sotheby's, *Impressionist and modern drawings and watercolours*, 5 December 1979, no. 230.

283.
Letter to Herman Schotel (1874-1951), ex-pupil of the Rotterdam Academy, n.d. [1903], private collection. Schotel drew in a similar style to Van Dongen's, and also for *De notekraker*, *De Ware Jacob*, and *De Wereldkroniek*. The illustration was in *Gil Blas Illustré* on 3 July 1903, p. 8.

284.
L. Schotting, H. Spiekman, *Arm Rotterdam. Hoe het woont!, hoe het leeft!* (Poor Rotterdam! What a place to live in!) (with illustrations by H. Schotel), Rotterdam 1903; see Van Faassen 1993, no. 14, p. 107. For H. Spiekman (1874-1917) see: Chr.A. de Ruyter-de Zeeuw, *Hendrik Spiekman. De grondvester van de Rotterdamse Sociaal-Democratie* (Founder of the Rotterdam Social Democrats) The Hague 1971.

285.
D.J.A. Westerhuis, *Prisma Latijns citatenboek* (Prisma Book of Latin Quotations), Utrecht/Antwerp 1957, p. 54, no. 506. The motto was well-known and was often used in a metaphorical sense, Snabilié 1900, p. VII.

286.
Schilperoort 1905, p. 736. September 1903 to Amsterdam, in 1904 to Paris; not certain which month he arrived; certainly there in October. Worked for the Dutch papers *De Telegraaf*, *Op de Hoogte*, *Nieuwe Rotterdamsche Courant*. See Komen 1995, pp. 19, 49-53; on p. 41 the author suggests Schilperoort's first journalistic work in Paris was in March 1904, but no confirmation of this. Richardson 1991, pp. 376-382.

287.
Guth 1949, p. 135; Van Dongen 1960, p. 45; Chaumeil 1967, p. 91. Anonymous 'Kees van Dongen' s first love,' *Week in Beeld*, 2 July 1949, p. 14: 'Ik werd de vertrouweling van het circuspubliek en kreeg zo de gelegenheid de exotische circusfiguren uit te schilderen' (I became a trusted figure among the circus public and so I was able to paint the exotic circus folk), S. (Ch. Snabilié), 'Fransche brieven' (Letters from France), *Het Vaderland*, 3 December 1904. For Picasso see: M. Richet, 'Bateleurs et cirque dans l'oeuvre dessiné de l'époque rose' (Acrobats and circus in the drawings of the rose period), pp. 108-125, in Léal 1991. Richardson 1991, pp. 381-387.

288.
Halpérin 1988, p. 358, Fénéon was appointed in about November 1906. The sale was on 28 December 1906; Bernheim-Jeune Archives, Paris. Kyriazi 1971, p. 90 mentions 14 watercolours, among which the series depicting clowns.

289.
Guth 1949, pp. 135-136; Perruchot 1958, p. 4; Van Dongen 1960, p. 46. Letter Fénéon 1904, Inv. 860868, Getty Center, Santa Monica.

290.
Ch. Saunier, *Revue Universelle*, 15 April 1904: 'Coin singulier de Rotterdam dont Van Dongen exprime le caractère avec force' (An unusual corner of Rotterdam which Van Dongen reveals with strength and power). Ciolkowski, 'Les Indépendants', *La Revue Libre*, 15 April 1904, p. 175; cited in Chaumeil 1967, p. 78.

291.
See *Au bal musette*, auction London, Christie's, *Impressionist and modern watercolours and drawings*, 6 December 1983, no. 178. For *Coin de bal masqué*, no. 2285 at the Salon, see Ch. Morice, 'le XXe Salon des Indépendants', *Mercure de France*, 1904, p. 417.

292.
T. Schilperoort, 'Kees van Dongen', *De Telegraaf* (Dutch daily), 21 November 1904. On the Vollard exhibition see: letter from K. van Dongen to C. Scharten, 21 November 1904: (and now I have my "horses" from the exhibition) 'Verder heb ik er nu mijn "paarden" van de Salon d'Automne'; NLMD, The Hague.

293.
Besson 1967. Also Chaumeil 1967, pp. 77-78.

294.
F. Fénéon, 'Van Dongen', exhib. cat. 1904 Paris (Vollard); cited in Halperin 1970, pp. 243-244.

295.
For Matisse as a Primitivist and Fauvism in general, see: Flam 1984, pp. 211-239; references to other literature. The seminal publication on the subject by R. Goldwater, *Primitivism in modern art* (1938) provided a sense of coherence for what was initially a largely formal analysis of this influence, cp. Rubin 1984. For the importance of the individual expressive style see: Shiff 1984, pp. 162-174.

296.
L. Vauxcelles, 'Le vernissage des Indépendants' (The opening of the Salon des Indépendants), *Gil Blas*, 21 February 1904, p. 1: 'Beaucoup de bonnes choses, mais rien de très neuf. [...] le néo-impressionisme piétine' (Plenty of good, interesting pieces, but nothing really new ... a kind of stagnant neo-Impressionism). M. Fouquier, 'Les petits salons. Les Indépendants', *Le Journal*, 21 February 1904, p. 5: refers to 'un chaos pictural', the Salon had little of interest to show and Pointillism and Impressionism were on their last legs. Ch. Morice, 'le XXe Salon des Indépendants', *Mercure de France*, 1904, pp. 409-110: 'Mais ce qui, longuement germé, s'épanouit enfin et s'impose à l'évidence, c'est la lassitude d'une formule accomplie et épuisée, c'est le besoin du nouveau' (...what has germinated for a long time and finally opened to reveal itself, is the lassitude of a formula that has been perfected and exhausted: it is the need for something new). See also: anonymous (Marius-Ary Leblond), 'Société des Artistes Indépendants', *Les Arts de la Vie*, 1 (1904), no. 3, pp. 192-193: 'Indépendants! en quoi le sont-ils? la plupart imitent quelqu'un' (Independent? In what way? Most of them are imitating someone else).

297.
See also Thiébault-Sisson, 'Le Salon des Indépendants', *Le Temps*, 23 February 1904, p. 2: 'Il leur est impossible, avec une technique aussi tyrannique, de se varier' (it is impossible for them, because they have a technique that is so strict and tyrannical, to introduce variations) with reference to the work of Van Rysselberghe, Luce, Cross, and Signac; also, Ciolkowski, 'Les Indépendants', *La Revue Libre*, 15 April 1904, p. 176: 'peinture qui semble toujours en peine de démonstration, et d'où l'émotion est si complètement bannie' (painting that always appears to be at pains to demonstrate something, and which has completely banished all feeling).

298.
Camoin after the death of G. Moreau in this studio; Gassier 1983, p. 12. For the prizes won by this group see Pip, 'Carnets de Paris. Le Salon des Indépendants', *La Nouvelle Revue*, vol. 27, 1 March 1904, no. 106, p. 132; R. Marx, 'Le Salon des Artistes Indépendants', *La Chronique des Arts et de la Curiosité*, no. 9, 27 February 1904, p. 71; L. Vauxcelles, 'Le vernissage des Indépendants', *Gil Blas*, 21 February 1904, p. 1.

299.
Ch. Morice, 'Le XXIe Salon des Indépendants', *Mercure de France*, (1905), vol. 54, p. 550.

300.
See Dagen 1986, p. 55 for Van Dongen. *Mercure de France*, 1905, vol. 56, 1 August, pp. 346-359. The questionnaire confirmed the 'anarchism' and 'disorder' that had already been observed in art, and a widespread preference for Cézanne.

301.
Denis 1912, 'De la gaucherie des primitifs', pp. 167-173, previously in *Les Arts de la Vie*, July 1904; 'L'influence de Paul Gauguin', *L'Occident*, October 1903, pp. 161-166; 'De Gauguin, de Whistler et de l'excès des théories', *L'Ermitage*, 15 November 1905, pp. 192-202, esp. pp. 192-193 on Gauguin, p. 197 on Cézanne.

302.
Marius-Ary Leblond, 'L'art sauvage', *Les Arts de la Vie*, 1 (1904) vol. 2, pp. 83-90; Dagen 1986, pp. 36-37.

303.
L. Vauxcelles, 'Le Salon des Indépendants', *Gil Blas*, 23 March 1905: after visiting 'Serre A', Vauxcelles and some literary friends – Marius-Ary Leblond, F. Fénéon, Thédore Duret and the artist Henri Matisse walked slowly along the river Seine. On Leblond and the *Revue Blanche* see *La Revue Blanche*. Chaumeil 1967, p. 219: Van Dongen was a subscriber to 'Argus'; p. 117, he saved the press cuttings in *cahiers*; Chaumeil was able to examine these exercise books (the earliest press cuttings that Chaumeil refers to dated from 1898).

304.
Marius-Ary Leblond, *Peintres de races*, Brussels 1909, Vincent van Gogh, pp. 1-23; in 1905 De Bouhélier visited the Van Gogh exhibition in Amsterdam; Saint-Georges de Bouhélier 1946, p. 266. On Van Gogh and 'gaucherie' see: M. Rummens, 'Van Goghs expressieve onhandigheid' (Van Gogh's expressive awkwardness), *Jong Holland*, 10 (1994), no. 4, pp. 27-39. On Van Dongen and Van Gogh see: Ch. Saunier, 'Le Salon des Indépendants', *La Plume*, April 1905, p. 333; Ch. Morice, 'Art Moderne', *Mercure de France*, 1905, vol. 58, p. 451.

305.
Séries de vues de la Tamise à Londres (1900 à 1904) (Views of the river Thames at London), Paris (Galeries Durand-Ruel), 9 May-4 June 1904. The series was completed in France, Callen 1973, pp. 33-38; see also under P. Signac.

306.
Anonymous (Marius-Ary Leblond), 'Exposition Claude Monet', *Les Arts de la Vie*, 1 (1904), vol. 1, pp. 390-391. On the importance of Impressionism in the early years of Fauvism see: Oppler 1976, pp. 39-82. Monet exhibition in 1904 and its importance, so far not mentioned. For general importance of Impressionism see also: the replies to Morice's questionnaire, Dagen 1986, pp. 57-58 (Ch. Camoin), 73-74 (P. Sérusier).

307.
C. Scharten (1878-1950), 'Kees van Dongen' in Dutch daily *Algemeen Handelsblad*, 29 November 1904. On Scharten as correspondent in Paris, see Wiessing 1960, pp. 172, 190.

308.
C. Scharten, 'Van Dongen', *Algemeen Handelsblad*, 20 October 1904; on the interior see: Scharten in the Dutch weekly *De Amsterdammer*, no. 1461, 25 June 1905, p. 7.

309.
C. Scharten, 'Kees van Dongen', *De Amsterdammer*, no. 1461, 25 June 1905, p. 7. Idem, 'Herinneringen uit ons leven en aan enkele groote figuren die wij in Holland en daarbuiten hebben gekend' (Reminiscences about our life and some of the famous people we have known both in Holland and abroad), manuscript lecture, n.d.; I thank Lien Heyting for this information. Lecture and letters to Scharten, NLMD, The Hague. The lecture was delivered to the Rotterdamsche Kunstkring, Rotterdam on 3 June 1927; minutes recorded, RKK Archive, GA Rotterdam.

310.
Letter from K. van Dongen to C. Scharten, sent from Fleury-en-Bière, June 1905 (after 25 June); further, a letter from Van Dongen to Scharten, 8 December 1904: 'Heel veel dank voor uw zeer sympathiek artikel' (Thank you very much for your most friendly article); letters in NLMD, The Hague.

311.
Scharten in *De Amsterdammer*, 25 June 1905; see both articles for the other citations.

312.
'Le masque rouge' (Tabaran?), *L'Action*, 27 March 1905, p. 1.

313.
Ch. Morice, 'Le XXIe Salon des Indépendants', *Mercure de France*, (1905), vol. 54, pp. 547-548.

314.
The new merry-go-rounds, G. Geffroy, 'Le plaisir d'été', *Revue Illustré*, 1906, vol. 2; Ch. Snabilié, 'Brieven uit Paris' (Letters from Paris), *Het Nieuws van den Dag*, 30 November 1908. On the circuses, idem, 'Brieven uit Parijs', *Nieuws van den Dag*, 4 July 1898. Illustrations in *Le Journal amusant*, 10 August 1901, no. 111, p. 2; *Le monde illustré*, 47 (1903), vol. 2, cover no. 2414, 4 July 1903 (fig.); 48 (1904), vol. 1, p. 495. In general see: Z. Gourarier, *Manèges d'autrefois*, Paris 1991; C. Py, C. Ferenczi, *La fête foraine d'autrefois, les années 1900*, Paris 1987. Rearick 1985, p. 172.

315.
Schilperoort 1905, p. 738. Another positive (anonymous) voice (H. Wiessing): 'De Salon des Indépendants (Van Gogh)', *Algemeen Handelsblad*, 13 April 1905; L. Vauxcelles, 'Le Salon des Indépendants', *Gil Blas*, 23 March 1905.

316.
Postcard to Scharten, sent from Fleury-en-Bière, 15 June 1905 (postmarked), NLMD, The Hague.

317.
Postcards sent from Paris, postmarked 25 June 1905 and 27 August 1905; private collection.

318.
Henkels 1975. Postcard from O. van Rees to P. Picasso in Paris, 25 July 1905 (postmarked), sent from Fleury-en-Bière; Musée Picasso, Paris.

319.
H. Wiessing, 'Tentoonstelling Kees van Dongen', article in the Dutch paper *Algemeen Handelsblad*, 31 October 1905. Chaumeil 1967, p. 132.

320.
Chaumeil 1967, p. 132: the canvas was bought in 1905 by Georges Viau.

321.
A. Alexandre, 'La vie artistique. Les petites expositions', *Le Figaro*, 3 November 1905. Ch. Morice, 'Art Moderne', *Mercure de France*, 1905, vol. 58, p. 451. L. Vauxcelles, 'Exposition Kees van Dongen', *Gil Blas*, 26 October 1905.

322.
Wiessing 1960, p. 190: took over from Scharten as from 1 January 1905.

323.
Letter from Kaya Batut (1871-1959) to A. Cohen, no. 180 in, 'Alexander Cohen. Brieven en documenten 1888-1961' (letters and documents) collected by R. Spoor, typescript IISG Amsterdam. Kaya Batut returned in January 1905. In 1904 Cohen was asked by the French government to carry out comparative research studies of the educational and health systems in French Indo-China and the Dutch East Indies. Cohen and Kaya Batut had been living together since August 1893 and were married on 23 March 1918. See R. Spoor, 'Jozef Alexander Cohen', pp. 29-33, in M. Campfens et al. (ed.), *Biografisch woordenboek van het socialisme en de arbeidersbeweging in Nederland* (Biographical Dictionary of Socialism and the Workers' Movement in the Netherlands), vol. 4, Amsterdam 1990.

324.
La Revue Blanche, 1 and 15 May 1898; 1 July 1898. Published in book form by the magazine in 1899; Oppler 1976, p. 84.

325.
Exposition Paul Signac Venise Hollande Paris Provence, Paris (Galerie Druet) 13-31 December 1904. See also *Exposition Luce*, Paris (Galerie Druet) 12-26 March.

326.
Koomen 1949, pp. 72-73, offprint 'Tentoonstellingen. Kees van Dongen.' *Weekblad van Rotterdam* (1927). In connection with a visit to the Vollard exhibition in 1904, Koomen reported: 'he [Van Dongen] lived on a cul-de-sac in Montmartre – where incidentally I once encountered Matisse at his studio. The latter – already an artist of considerable reputation – nevertheless came to take a look at the work of the Dutchman.' They met in 1904 or 1905. In the autumn of 1905 Koomen was again in Paris, p. 74. Van Dongen on Matisse as his most important artistic contact, Chapsal 1963, p. 45.

327.
On Matisse and neo-Impressionism: Bock 1981; Monod-Fontaine 1993, pp. 63-67. See also Y.-A. Bois, 'On Matisse: The blinding', *October*, 68 (spring 1994), pp. 61-121. Van Dongen: L. Vauxcelles, 'La vie artistique', *Gil Blas*, 28 September 1905: 'Van Dongen, néo-impressioniste hollandais.'

328.
Félix d'Anner, 'Le Salon des Indépendants', *L'Intransigeant*, 28 March 1905, p. 3; Chaumeil 1967, pp. 83-84. R. Lestrange, 'Exposition aux artistes indépendants', *Le Tintamarre*, 22 April 1905, pp. 1-2. Ch. Saunier, 'Le Salon des Indépendants', *La Plume*, 15 April 1905, p. 333.

329.
Chaumeil 1967, p. 98.

330.
H. Wiessing, 'Tentoonstelling Kees van Dongen' in the Dutch paper *Algemeen Handelsblad*, 31 October 1905. On Van Gogh and Fauvists (not Van Dongen) see: O'Laoghaire 1992.

331.
See note 321 for Alexandre and Vauxcelles.

332.
L. Vauxcelles, 'Salon d'Automne', *Gil Blas*, 17 October 1905; included in Dagen 1994-II, pp. 28-30.

333.
Anonymous (Ch. Snabilié), 'Brieven uit Parijs' (Letters from Paris) in the Dutch paper *Het Nieuws van den Dag*, 6 November 1905; idem, 'Fransche brieven', *Het Vaderland*, 4 November 1905. 'Masque Rouge' (Tabaran?) sought in vain (!), see 'Notes d'art. Le Salon d'Automne', *L'Action*, 18 October; 18 November 1905.

334.
A. Lantoine, 'Le Salon d'Automne. Deuxième article', *La Fédération Artistique*, 32 (1905), no. 4, 29 October, p.28.

335.
So formulated recently in Freeman 1990, p. 13, and in Freeman 1995, p. 12; in a summary on pp. 23-24 Van Dongen's name is missing. See Chaumeil 1967 for opinions about Van Dongen and Fauvisme, pp. 87-90. The position defended in Chaumeil 1952, and 1961. The conclusions drawn are repeatedly based on inaccurate dating and identifications. The first general publications on Fauvism, Puy 1907 does not mention Van Dongen, Salmon 1912 does mention him; in Salmon p. 14: Marquet as a marginal figure.

336.
Exposition, Paris (A. Prath & P. Maynier), 1-31 December 1905, included among other works by Van Dongen 'Un Carrousel', no. 29. L. Rosenthal, *Chronique des Arts*, no. 38, 9 December 1905, p. 318.

337.
Chaumeil 1967, p. 93: late 1905 as the date of moving house, no source. First document with the new address, a letter from K. van Dongen to O. Maus, 1906 [early January]: 'Si je ne suis pas à l'Impasse Girardon je suis à mon atelier 13 Rue Ravignan' (If I'm not at Impasse Girardon then I'll be at my studio on rue Ravignan); AHKB Archive, Koninklijke Musea voor Schone Kunsten Brussels, Inv. 15776; Ollinger-Zinque 1993, p. 139. Letter from K. van Dongen to Mej. Plate, committee member of RKK, 14 May 1906: 'Wilt u ook zoo goed zijn verdere correspondentie aan mijn atelier 13 rue Ravignan, Paris XVIII te adresseeren daar de post daar meer geregeld komt dan in de Impasse' (Would you kindly forward my post to rue Ravignan rather than the Impasse...); RKK Archive, Rotterdam.

338.
On Picasso-Van Dongen, Chaumeil 1967, p. 93-96; Olivier 1933, p. 87; Richardson 1991, p. 376, basing what he wrote on Chaumeil and Olivier. On the contacts in the Bateau-Lavoir: Salmon 1912, p. 12; Salmon 1945, p. 24: saw Matisse there; Salmon 1961, p.192. Olivier 1933, p. 87-88: Vlaminck visited Van Dongen there. See Vlaminck 1943, p. 264: he met Van Dongen for the first time in the Bateau-Lavoir. Chaumeil 1967, p. 96: Van Dongen did not sympathise with G. Apollinaire and M. Jacob; became friends with Salmon (also living there), Dorgelès, and Mac Orlan. Derain hardly ever saw Van Dongen: see letter from A. Derain to H. Matisse, dated 1 January 1907, Kellermann 1992, p. LI.

339.
Van Dongen's reticence, Warnod 1947, pp. 155-157; Salmon 1961, p. 196. On the *Lapin Agile*, Carco 1927, pp. 53-54; Carco 1953, pp. 22-23. The artist did not often frequent the restaurant opposite the Bateau Lavoir, the Azon, see Salmon 1961, p. 193. Van Dongen does refer to gatherings with 'Père Frédé (Frédéric Gérard) in *Le Lapin Agile*, rue des Saules; anonymous article 'Memories of Van Dongen', p. 78, Press Documentation RKD The Hague; anonymous, 'Bij Kees v. Dongen, de man die weg wou en dat van anderen niet begrijpt' (The man who wanted out...) *Nieuwe Haagsche Courant*, 1 June 1949. For *Le Lapin Agile* see Richardson 1991, pp. 371-373; Seigel 1986, pp. 339-340.

340.
Chaumeil 1967, pp. 76-102. Giry 1981, pp. 83-87, 132-134, 174-180.

341.
L. Vauxcelles, 'Le Salon d'Automne' (Salle III), *Gil Blas*, 5 October 1906; E. Charles, 'Le Salon d'Automne', *La Liberté*, 5 October 1906 (according to him 'Salle IV': 'C'est ici le lieu de réunion, le "Salon carré" des novateurs les plus audacieux [...] Raoul Dufy, Othon Friesz, Derain, Henri Matisse, de Vlaminck et Kees van Dongen, occupent tout un côté de la salle.' (Here in the Salon Carré are the most audacious and revolutionary painters ... and Kees van Dongen ...).

342.
E. Charles, 'Le Salon des Indépendants II', *La Liberté*, 23 March 1906. See also 'Masque Rouge' (Tabarant?), 'Le Salon des Indépendants', *L'Action*, 21 March 1906.

343.
L. Vauxcelles, 'Le Salon des Indépendants', *Gil Blas*, 20 March 1906, on Room 6. For Vlaminck beside Van Dongen see: A. Antoine, 'L'Art à Paris. 22e Exposition des Artistes Indépendants', *La Fédération Artistique*, 33 (1906) no. 25, 25 March 1906.

344.
Anonymous (H. Wiessing), 'Salon des Artistes Indépendants' in the Dutch paper *Algemeen Handelsblad*, 10 April 1906. H. Pellier, 'Le Salon des Indépendants', *La Petite République*, 20 March 1906 ('les notes parfois violentes'). E. Charles, 'Le Salon des Indépendants II', *La Liberté*, 23 March 1906: 'des prodigieuses et énigmatiques débauches de couleur' (excessive and enigmatic splurges of colour).

345.
Salon des Indépendants 1906, no. 4984, *Aux Folies-Bergères*. Exhib. cat., *Centenaire de Verhaeren*, Brussels (Bibliothèque Royale de Belgique) 1955, p. 83, Inv. CAB.V.12. Description

in, anonymous (Ch. Snabilié), 'Brieven uit Parijs' (Letters from Paris) in the Dutch paper *Het Nieuws van den Dag*, 26 March 1906. Marthe Verhaeren in a manuscript which has a sketch of the painting, acquired by Verhaeren around 1907; possible dating therefore 1906; Archives and Musée de la Littérature, Koninklijke Bibliotheek, Brussels. Several documents in this collection which confirm the contact between Van Dongen and Verhaeren (after 1917). Paul Aron, who dealt with a publication of the reviews by Verhaeren, has so far found no references to Van Dongen. On Verhaeren see: J. Marx, 'Pour une biographie critique d'Emile Verhaeren', in R. Trousson, L. Somville, *Lettres de Belgique. En hommage à Robert Frickx*, 1992, pp. 145-157; I thank Fabrice van de Kerckhove for this information.

346.
Kuku, Salon des Indépendants 1906, no. 4985. Anonymous (H. Wiessing), 'Salon des Artistes Indépendants' article in the Dutch paper *Algemeen Handelsblad*, 10 April 1906. For the use of Kuku as a pet name for Dolly van Dongen see: a postcard from Alexander Cohen to Guusje (Dolly) van Dongen, 21 January 1906, sent from Elspeet, to the holiday address of M.J. Brusse: 'Dag kleine Kuku, groetjes van Henkje Brusse...' (Hallo, little Kuku, best wishes from Henkje Brusse) (oldest son of M.J. Brusse). See A. Cohen, *Brieven 1888-1961, bezorgd door Ronald Spoor* (Letters ...), Amsterdam 1996. Cohen was witness in April at the registration of the birth of Augusta (Dolly) van Dongen (18 April 1905-4 September 1987), Cohen 1961, p. 199.

347.
The number 51 written in blue chalk on the central slat of the stretcher refers to the Van Dongen exhibition in the Rotterdamsche Kunstkring in 1906; letter from K. van Dongen to S. Plate, 14 May 1906; RKK Archive, GA Rotterdam. A detailed description in F. L. (Frits Lapidoth), 'De vierjaarlijksche te Rotterdam. Kees van Dongen. W. de Zwart', *Nieuwe Courant*, 2 June 1906. Mus.cat., *Musée d'Art Moderne Troyes. Donation Pierre et Denise Lévy. Peintures*, Troyes 1988, no. 327, Inv. MNPL 327, as *Le Moulin de la Galette*. In exhib. cat. 1967 Paris, no. 11, as *La Matchiche*; correct spelling is *La Mattchiche*, no. 4988, Salon des Indépendants 1906. On the 'Maxixe': Willy, 'Danses', *Revue Illustrée*, 21 (1906), vol. 1, in *La Lanterne magique*, no page numbers. Anonymous, 'Parijs, dat danst' (Paris is dancing) in the Dutch paper *De Telegraaf*, 6 November 1906: 'De Maxixe is hier de dans à la mode geworden' (The Maxixe dance is all the fashion here).

348.
L. Vauxcelles, 'Le Salon des Indépendants', *Gil Blas*, 20 March 1906 ; C. Le Senne, 'Le théâtre au Salon des Indépendants', *Revue Théâtrale*, 5 (1906), no. 55 (April), p. 1422.

349.
A. Cohen brought photographs with him from his trip to Java, showing Indonesian dancing, see: 'Danses et musiques de l'Archipel Malais', *L'Illustration*, 127 (1906), no. 3292, 31 March, pp. 194-195.

350.
Rearick 1985, pp. 91, 183. S. (Ch. Snabilié), 'Fransche brieven' in the Dutch paper *Het Vaderland*, 22 February 1904. A.M., 'Frankrijk' (France) in the Dutch paper *De Telegraaf*, 20 February 1904.

351.
Letter from K. van Dongen to Mej. Plate, committee member for the Rotterdam Kunstkring, 6 April 1906; Rotterdam Kunstkring Archives, GA Rotterdam.

352.
Ch. Morice, 'Le XXIIe Salon des Indépendants', *Mercure de France*, vol. 60, pp. 535-537. Cited in Flam 1993, p. 233.

353.
Flam 1993, pp. 233-234.

354.
Letter from K. van Dongen to H. Matisse, 17 September 1906; Matisse Archives, Paris.

355.
Fourcade 1993, no. 35.

356.
Fig. *La ballerina borgne*, in exhib.cat. 1990 Paris, p. 112. Exhib.cat. 1959 Nice, no. 9, on verso of the stretcher originally: 'Salon de 1906'. L. Vauxcelles, 'Le Salon d'Automne', *Gil Blas*, 5 October 1906: 'des clownesses chlorotiques en maillot chair' (anaemic female clowns in flesh-coloured leotards). Anonymous (H. Wiessing), 'De Salon d'Automne', *Het Handelsblad*, 29 October 1906: 'een "mademoiselle Léda", fideel en guitig' (a 'mademoiselle Léda', merry and mischievous). H. Eon refers to the influence of Matisse's *Le bonheur de vivre*, in which 'each woman's body is enveloped with a halo' on other artists showing work at the Salon. He doubtless included Van Dongen here; H. Eon, 'Le Salon d'Automne', *Le Siècle*, 5 October 1906.

357.
Matisse, Perry 1993, pp. 58-59, as the expression of Primitivism and Naturalism, and the influence of a novel by André Gide on *Nu bleu. Souvenir de Biskra* (1907). See *Les demoiselles d'Avignon* (1907), Leighton 1990, for Primitivism, African art and anarchism. On Derain and a pure representation of nature see: Andral 1994, p. 72; Freeman 1990, pp. 40-41, 92 (summer 1906), 97 (November-December 1906).

358.
Kyriazi 1971, p. 92, letter from K. van Dongen to F. Fénéon, early February 1908.

359.
Daniel Henry [Kahnweiler], 'Kees van Dongen', pp. 12-14, in exhib.cat. 1919 Düsseldorf: 'Ich ging zu ihm. Im Atelier eines Freundes hatte er seine Bilder untergebracht: Impasse Girardon. Dort entrollte er mir auf dem Fußboden riesige Leinwände, lief mit nackten Füßen darüber hin' (I went to visit him. He had installed his paintings in a friend's studio ... there he unrolled in front of me across the floor huge canvases and he walked over them with bare feet).
Not in Kahnweiler 1982.

360.
Exhib.cat. Paris 1990, p. 86. Van Dongen in this painting, Guth 1949, p. 133. Chaumeil 1967, p. 54.

361.
Saint-Georges de Bouhélier, foreword, exhib.cat. 1908 Paris (Kahnweiler), 2-28 March pp. 2-3.

362.
Visit to the circus *Cirque Médrano* with Picasso, Guth 1949, p. 135. Frequented by Van Dongen in 1908, Niehaus 1942, p. 34. Colour illustration of *L'Ecuyère*, M. Jover, 'Van Dongen le dernier des Fauves', p. 17 in, *Van Dongen, Beaux-Arts, hors série*, 1990. *L'Ecuyère* was exhibited in December 1908 at Bernheim-Jeune's, as 1908, no. 60; described by Cohen 1908: 'een teer circus-rijdstertje in roze-tricot en gazen fladder-rokje, een been over het àndere gekruist, peinzend, dofzwart van ongezadeld paard, fel-inbijtend op wit van achtergrond' (a fragile girl on a horse, wearing pink tights and a gauze tutu, one leg crossed over the other, thoughtful, the unsaddled horse a dull black contrasting sharply with the white background).

363.
Perry 1993, esp. pp. 46-54, 62-81: for influences of naturalism on Matisse and Nietzsche on Derain, Vlaminck and Die Brücke; see Oppler 1976, pp. 195-204 (A. Gide; naturalisme, Nietzsche); Giry 1981, pp. 14-16. These ideas were important for Van Dongen's development from about 1906 when his communication with Matisse and Vlaminck was more intense and when he also came into contact with *Die Brücke* artists (1908). Max Pechstein in Paris in 1908: Moeller 1990, p. 318, in Dorn 1990; Chaumeil 1967, p. 116-117; Freeman 1990, p. 106.

Catalogue

1. *Zelfportret* (Self-portrait), 1895
Oil on canvas
92 x 60 cm
Signed and dated lower right: *Kees van Dongen. 95*
In brush with black gouache on reverse of canvas before lining (pre 1976): *Kees van Dongen/Delfshaven/januarie 1895*; the same in other handwriting on the new canvas
PROVENANCE:
Augusta (Dolly) van Dongen (1905-1987), Paris; Musée National d'Art Moderne, Centre Georges Pompidou, Paris, 1976 (gift of Dolly van Dongen)
EXHIBITIONS:
1967 Paris, no. 1 (fig.); 1969 Marseilles, no. 2 (fig.); 1971 Tucson, no. 36 (fig.); 1972 Paris, no. 2; 1981 Utrecht, no. 59 (fig.); 1990 Paris, p. 87 (fig.)
LITERATURE:
Kyriazi 1971, fig. 1; Sutton 1971, p. 38, fig. 4; Hulton 1977, p. 134
COLLECTION:
Musée National d'Art Moderne, Centre Georges Pompidou, Paris, Inv. AM 1976-1056

2. *Zelfportret* (Self-portrait), c. 1905
Brush with black ink, watercolour, white gouache
837 x 610 mm
COLLECTION:
Private collection

3. *Retour des champs* (Return from the fields), c. 1896
Watercolour over pencil sketch, black chalk, white gouache
226 x 300 mm
Signed lower right in black chalk: *v Dongen.*; white gouache over signature: C. *v Dongen*; centre right in pencil: *water.*
Label on reverse of cardboard to which drawing is attached: *Galerie Kahnweiler, 28 rue Vignon, 28/no 811* (?); in boxed letters: *11355* (Inv. Ville de Paris, Beaux-Arts)
Special features: also known as *Boeufs* (Oxen)
PROVENANCE:
Daniel-Henry Kahnweiler (1884-1979), Paris; auction Paris, Drouot (J. Zapp), *Tableaux, aquarelles...composant la collection de la Galerie Kahnweiller* [sic], 4 July 1922, no. 37 (?); Mathilde Amos (1881-1967), Paris; Musée d'Art Moderne de la Ville de Paris, Paris, 1955 (gift of Mathilde Amos)
EXHIBITIONS:
1976 Montrouge, no. 46
COLLECTION:
Musée d'Art Moderne de la Ville de Paris, Paris, Inv. AMD 682

In this youthful self-portrait, Van Dongen painted himself standing at the window of his studio in his parental home. Ships' masts can be seen in the background. The expressive style of his painting has always caused surprise. A photo of the painting, taken around 1950, shows clearly that Van Dongen painted various parts of it at a later date. (fig. p. 16) Some parts, in particular the face, he accentuated by using strong brushstrokes, which gave it more expression. In both states it is an interesting canvas.

The defiant pose of the painter, then 18 years of age, is imposing. Van Dongen has the same stance in a photo of his class at the academy, which was probably taken at his graduation in 1895. (fig.) The self-portrait which was painted around this time is a self-assured debut. The painting has this sort of self-confident feel about it, created partly by the head being held up high and the upright, defiant pose. It reminds the onlooker of other artists' portraits, his fellow countryman G.H. Breitner springs most readily to mind, a portrait almost certainly influenced by photography. The most typical feature of Van Dongen's rendition, the flat, deep-blue silhouette form of the figure and the pronounced light-dark contrast, should however be attributed to the artist himself. Paying particular attention to the effect of the light, he painted the contour and the translucent material of the suit, in a shade of light blue. More traditional in terms of lighting and unmistakably due to his experiments with technique inspired by Rembrandt are his *Portrait of Emma Hanken* and *Nu au fauteuil*. Emma Hanken was a fellow student at the Rotterdam Academy at the time, a class below Van Dongen. She was portrayed by him in classical costume. The painting was on show at the exhibition mounted in honour of the fiftieth anniversary of the Academy in 1901. The Dutch-toned nude, portrayed in a seated position, was painted by Van Dongen in 1896; a drawing showing the same model has been conserved too. (fig.) That year a drawing prize was awarded for this subject at the Academy, won by his friend Chris Addicks. It may be the competition referred to by Van Dongen in his letter to Fénéon in 1904, when he claimed that his drawing, which had a hole in it, was disqualified on the grounds of poor presentation. Other reasons for its being disregarded were Van Dongen's unflattering view of the nude, as can be seen in the painting and the preliminary sketch, and the strong linear style of drawing which estranged Van Dongen from the academic ideal.

On the back of the original passe-partout accompanying this watercolour – on which a farmer returning home on horseback is portrayed – there was a Kahnweiler Gallery label. It was most probably the watercolour *Retour des champs* which changed hands at one of the auctions of the Kahnweiler Collection in 1922. The dating, c. 1895-1896 is partly due to the stylistic similarities between this canvas and a portrait of a girl from Zeeland which Van Dongen painted in 1896.[1] The vague silhouette forms and these subjects are in some ways Symbolist in style. This forms the beginning of a following stage in Van Dongen's development in which he ceased to paint.

1. Exhib.cat. 1990 Paris, p. 82

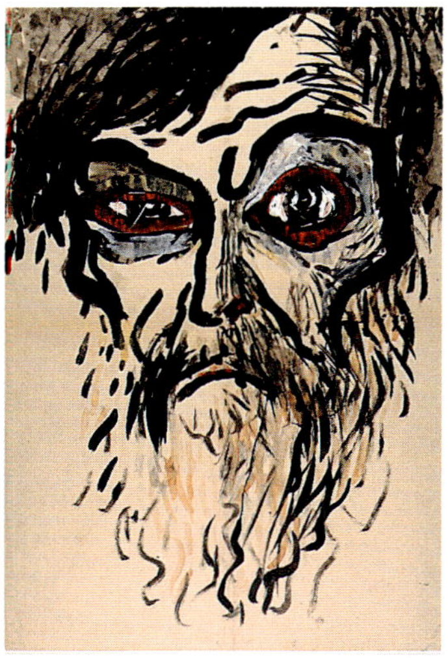

2. *Self-portrait*, c. 1905

4. *Portret Emma Hanken* (Portrait of Emma Hanken) (1874-1911), c. 1895
Oil on canvas
94 x 46 cm
Signed twice upper left: *van Dongen*
On stretcher a black-printed label: *Academie van Beeldende Kunsten en Technische Wetenschappen./1851-1901.*, marked in pen with brown ink: *Kees van Dongen Paris/Emma Hanken Oppert 98/Rotterdam./*[idem]*/Geschilderd portret.*; a black-printed label numbered: *71*

EXHIBITIONS:
1901 Rotterdam (ex. catalogue)

COLLECTION:
Private collection

5. *Nu au fauteuil* (Nude in an armchair), 1896
Oil on canvas
35 x 35 cm
Signed lower right: *van Dongen*
Signed on reverse of canvas in brush with ink: *Kees van Dongen*; dated on stretcher in brush with ink: *1896*; label on reverse of canvas with annotation in black chalk: *mort aux vaches/Van Dongen*; on stretcher a black-printed label: *BERNHEIM JEUNE & CIE/Experts près de la Cour d'Appel/25, Boulevard de la Madeleine/36, Avenue de l'Opéra et 15, Rue Richepanse/NO*; marked in pen with brown ink: *99 du catalogue/Kees van Dongen/"Nu au fauteuil"*; label with blue chalk: *716*

PROVENANCE:
Auction Paris, Palais Galliera (E. Ader), *Tableaux modernes, aquarelles...*, 12 June 1964, no. 60 (fig.); auction Paris, Drouot (C. Delorme), *Estampes, aquarelles, dessins...*, 7 March 1973, no. 19 (fig.); auction London, Sotheby's, *Impressionist and modern art...*, 13 October 1993, no. 44 (fig.); private collection

EXHIBITIONS:
1904 Paris, Galerie Vollard, no. 12 (*Femme nue*); 1973 Brussels, (fig.)

LITERATURE:
Chaumeil 1967, fig. 12, p. 316

COLLECTION:
Private collection

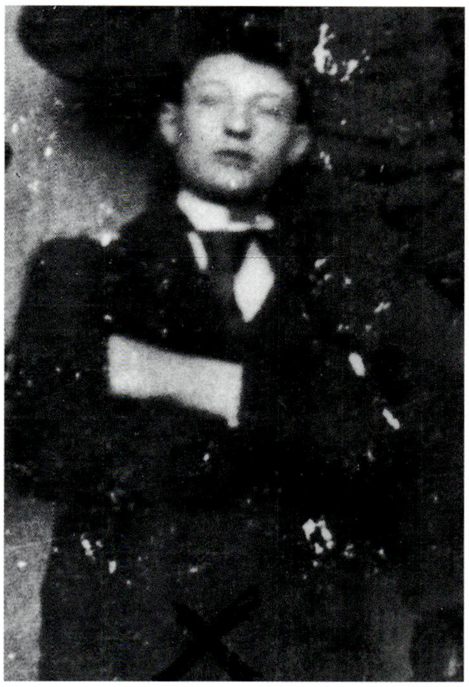

Photo portrait, c. 1895
Detail from a group photo, Academie van Kunsten en Technische Wetenschappen, Rotterdam

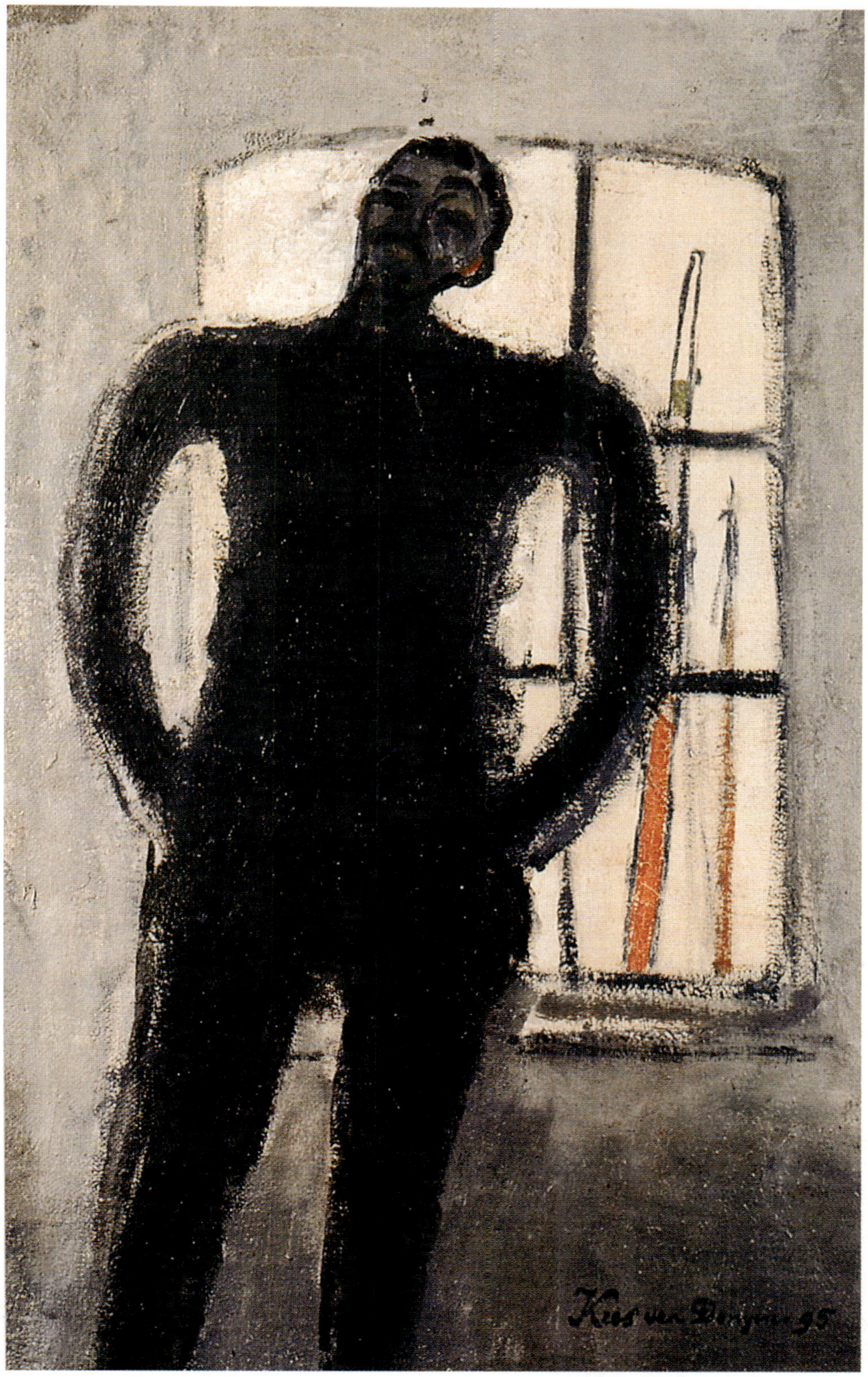

1. *Self-portrait*, 1895

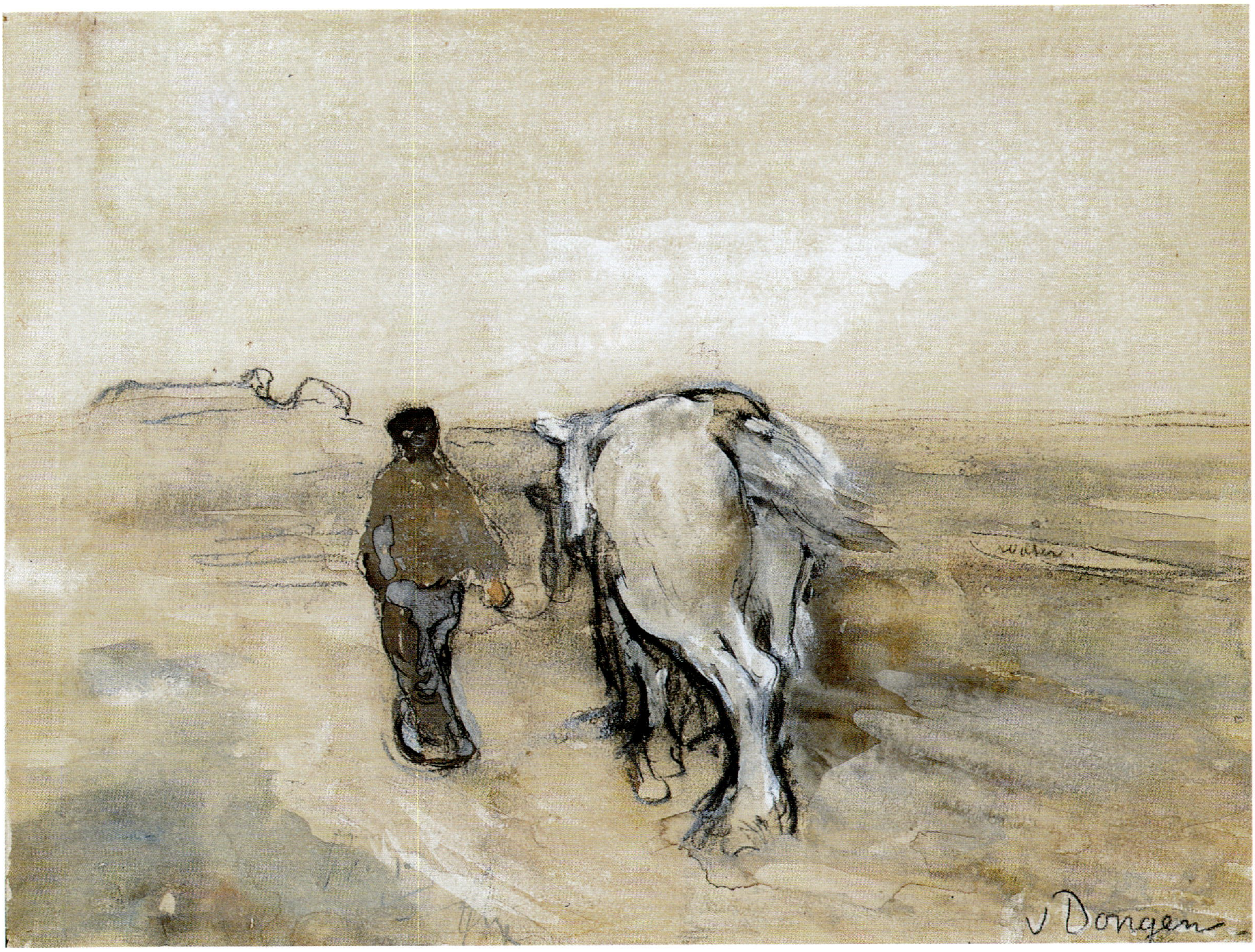

3. *Retour des champs*, c. 1896

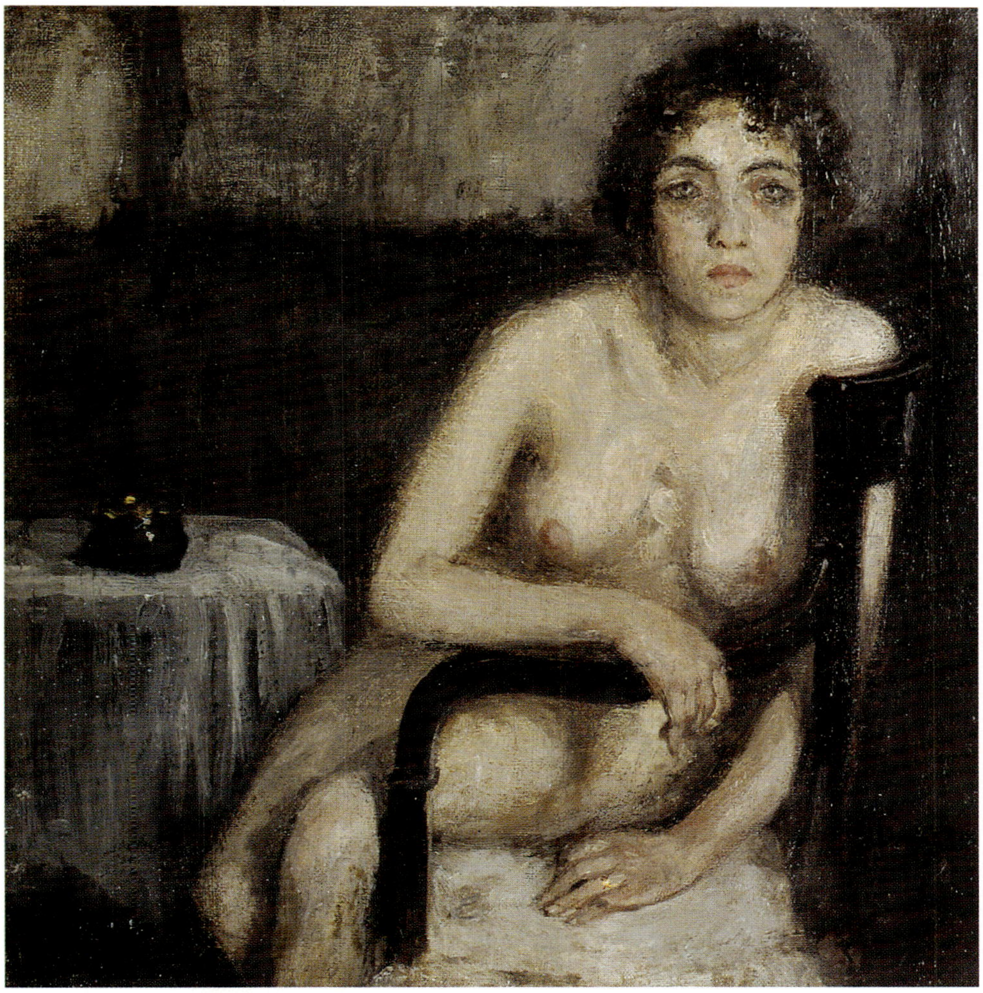

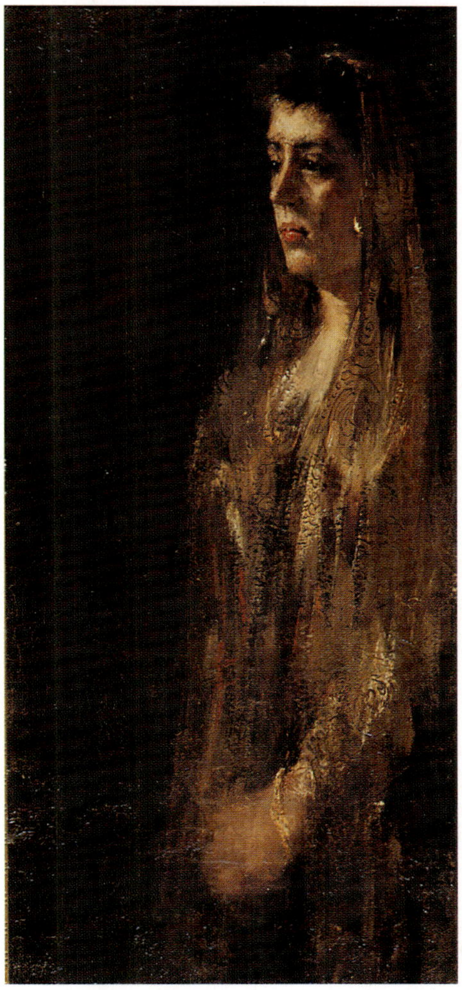

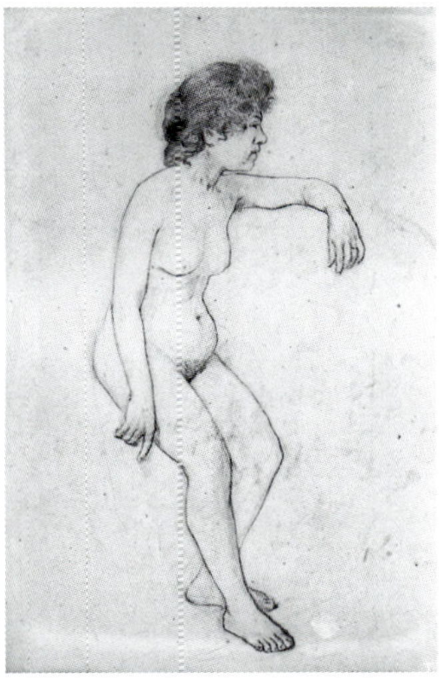

Nude study, c. 1895
Black chalk, 350 x 230 mm

5. *Nu au fauteuil*, 1896

4. *Portrait of Emma Hanken* (1874-1911), c. 1895

6. *Jonker-Frans* (Baron Frans), 1897
Illustration in the magazine:
Vrije Kunst. Tijdschrift voor poëzie, proza, beeldende kunst, muziek, kritiek, filosofie (eerste deel)
Published by the Leden der Vereeniging 'Vrije Kunst' (members of the 'Free Art' Association) Rotterdam (Rotterdamsche Uitgevers-maatschappij), 1897. Text by H. Bosch de Lateren (Pieter Cornelis de Moor), 'Jonker Frans', pp. 17-82
COLLECTION:
Amsterdam, University Library, Inv. Y 3358

The society called *Vrije Kunst* (Free Art) was founded in January 1897, its premises were to be found at 68 Wijnstraat in Rotterdam. The members included various Rotterdam artists, writers, poets, musicians, an architect and an actor. The idea behind the founding of the society was no doubt to promote mutual cooperation and rapprochement between the different art forms. This supported the symbolist idea that, along these lines, a spiritually more elevated form of art could be achieved. The founders also seemed to have been keen on the ideal of community art. In the brochure presenting the society, they stated their aim of anchoring art in the life of the community. Not a great deal ever came of this. The only tangible evidence of this ideal the society left behind is to be found in a book *Vrije Kunst I* (Free Art I). In this edition, which appeared around December 1897 and was projected as being the first of a series, can be found poetry, prose, a play, illustrations and an occasional piece of music. Two contributions, those made by Piet de Moor and Koos Speenhoff, are remarkable for their revolutionary zeal. These are the texts which were illustrated by Kees van Dongen. In the play by Piet de Moor 'Jonker Frans' (Baron Frans), the death of the nobleman (his own choosing), after leading a debauched life, is used to represent the decline of the old class structure. In the illustration for this piece, Van Dongen, inspired by the art of Jan Toorop, gave a symbolist representation of the essence of the plot: to the left the baron, next to him a woman who, by means of the snakes, represents Evil, and underneath this, indicating ruin, is a skull. The other two symbolist drawings by Van Dongen illustrate Speenhoff's trilogy, 'Visioen' (Vision), 'Der generatie einde, een profetie' (The end of a generation, a prophecy) and 'Geluk' (Luck). (fig.) The first one does not represent a Roman Bacchanal – even though this may be the first association which springs to mind – but according to the text represents tradespeople, 'four men with wild, filthy, curly hair ranting and raving', who are killing the three women, personifications of Religion, Chastity and Wisdom. Death is also awaiting the men, who represent society motivated by profit; only after death can pure happiness, and a simple life in harmony with nature commence. (fig.)

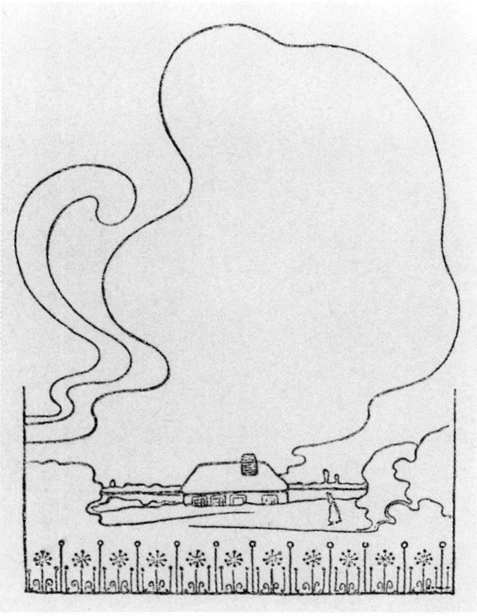

Vignette accompanying J.H. Speenhoff, 'Geluk', *De Vrije Kunst*, Rotterdam 1897, p. 238

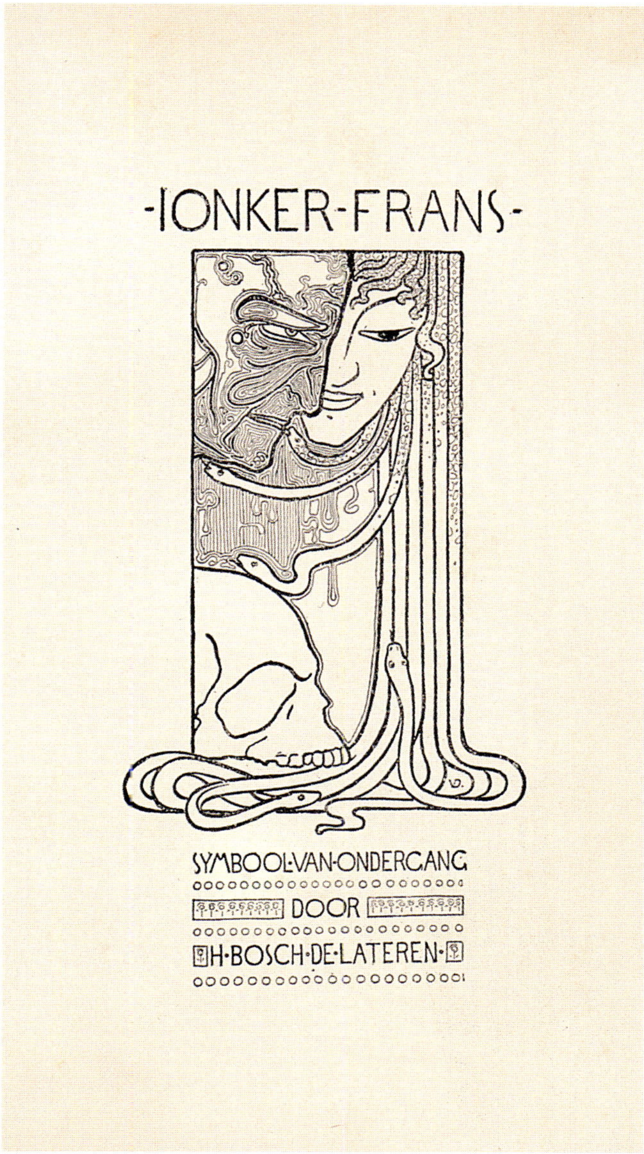

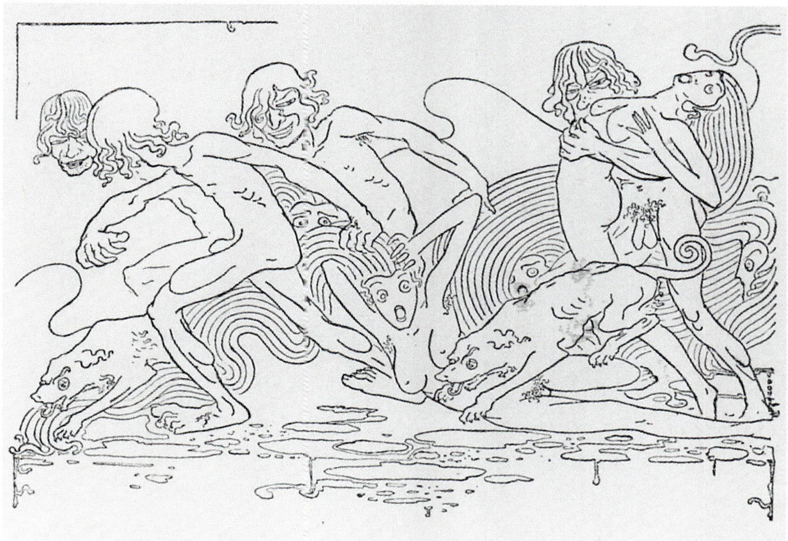

6. *Jonker Frans*, 1897

Illustration accompanying J.H. Speenhoff, 'Visioen', *De Vrije Kunst*, Rotterdam 1897, p. 227

7. *Intérieur pauvre* (Impoverished interior), 1898
Pen and brush with black ink, grey wash, watercolour, white gouache
376 x 259 mm
Signed and dated lower right with pen in black ink: *van Dongen/98 -*; in blue chalk lower right on the cardboard to which the drawing is attached: 2.
Reverse of cardboard annotated in red chalk: *Intérieur pauvre/30/*
PROVENANCE:
Boymans Museum, Rotterdam, 1936 (gift of the artist; letter from Kees van Dongen to D. Hannema, 7 December 1936, GA (Gemeentearchief – Municipal Archive) Rotterdam
EXHIBITIONS:
1962 Breda, no. 42
LITERATURE:
Hannema 1937, p. 10; Hannema 1973, p. 48; Boymans Museum Annual Report 1937, p. 7; Cocheret 1948, p. 5
COLLECTION:
Boijmans van Beuningen Museum, Rotterdam, Inv. KVD 2

8. *Souvenir Groenendaal* (Remembrance of Groenendaal)
Jour de pluie, visites à mon atelier
(Rainy day, visitors at my studio), 1898
Pen and brush with black ink, grey wash
392 x 279 mm
Unsigned; lower right annotation in blue chalk: *Souvenir-Groenendaal-*; lower right annotation in pen with black ink: *JOUR DE PLUIE/VISITES A./MON ATELIER*; under the figures in pen with black ink: *SCHILTD./SPEENHOF/KRULLERT.*
Special features: paper cut off at three corners
PROVENANCE:
Gift of the artist to the publisher Ad Donker (1908-1986), Rotterdam, c. 1949; private collection
LITERATURE:
1951 Cocheret (fig.); 1949 Engers, p. 4 (fig.)
COLLECTION:
Private collection

No photographs of Van Dongen's Rotterdam studios have been preserved. The drawing *intérieur pauvre* which probably depicts one of his earlier studios also reminds us that we should not expect too much of the decor. In his recollections of the artist, W.L. Brusse noted that the Delfshaven studio – situated in the malting belonging to Van Dongen's father – contained little more than 'a table and a rickety stool.'[1] Perhaps this is the studio depicted in the drawing. However, the studio in Groenendaal and the following one in Batavierenstraat were extremely spartan too according to those who witnessed them at the time. The only signs of luxury which are mentioned are a brass chandelier and candelabra which were bought by the artist Johan Mastenbroek when Van Dongen left for Paris. The atmosphere he created owed a lot to his reduced means but as M.J. Brusse wrote, Van Dongen was attracted by 'the lived-in feeling, the dilapidated structure, the weather-beaten tonality of a ramshackle facade, although there would still be a row of plants blooming in the windowsill in cleanly scrubbed red pots.'[2] This sombre ambience is to be found in the watercolour drawings. The second interior clearly shows the studio at 25 Groenendaal as the title *Souvenir Groenendaal* would suggest. Van Dongen worked there from May 1898 to April 1899, after which he moved to Batavierenstraat. In the foreground can be seen – smartly dressed in a suit – the older, already successful painter Martinus Schildt, who rented a studio above Van Dongen. Behind him is the poet-singer Koos Speenhoff, artistically attired in a wide-brimmed hat and a long cape. In front of the black wall Van Dongen had painted himself (thus allowing his models to be seen at their best) the shabby figure of Johan Krulder has been placed, Van Dongen's classmate at the Academy, of whom nothing is known apart from a few book decorations he made. In the small pot on the table there is a variety of drawing pens, at the time Van Dongen's daily work-material.

1.
W.L. Brusse 1936
2.
Brusse 1927-1

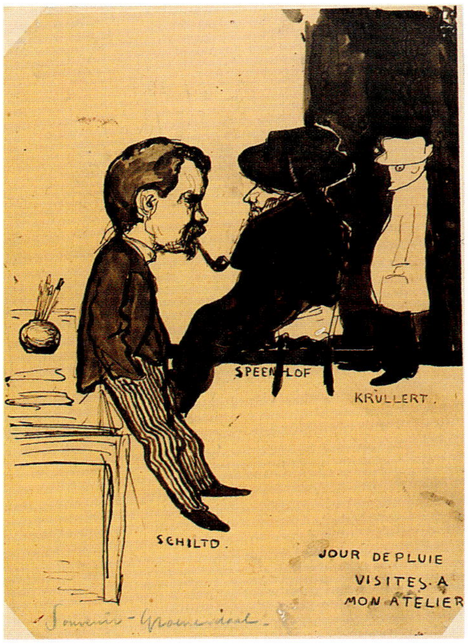

8. *Souvenir Groenendaal*, 1898

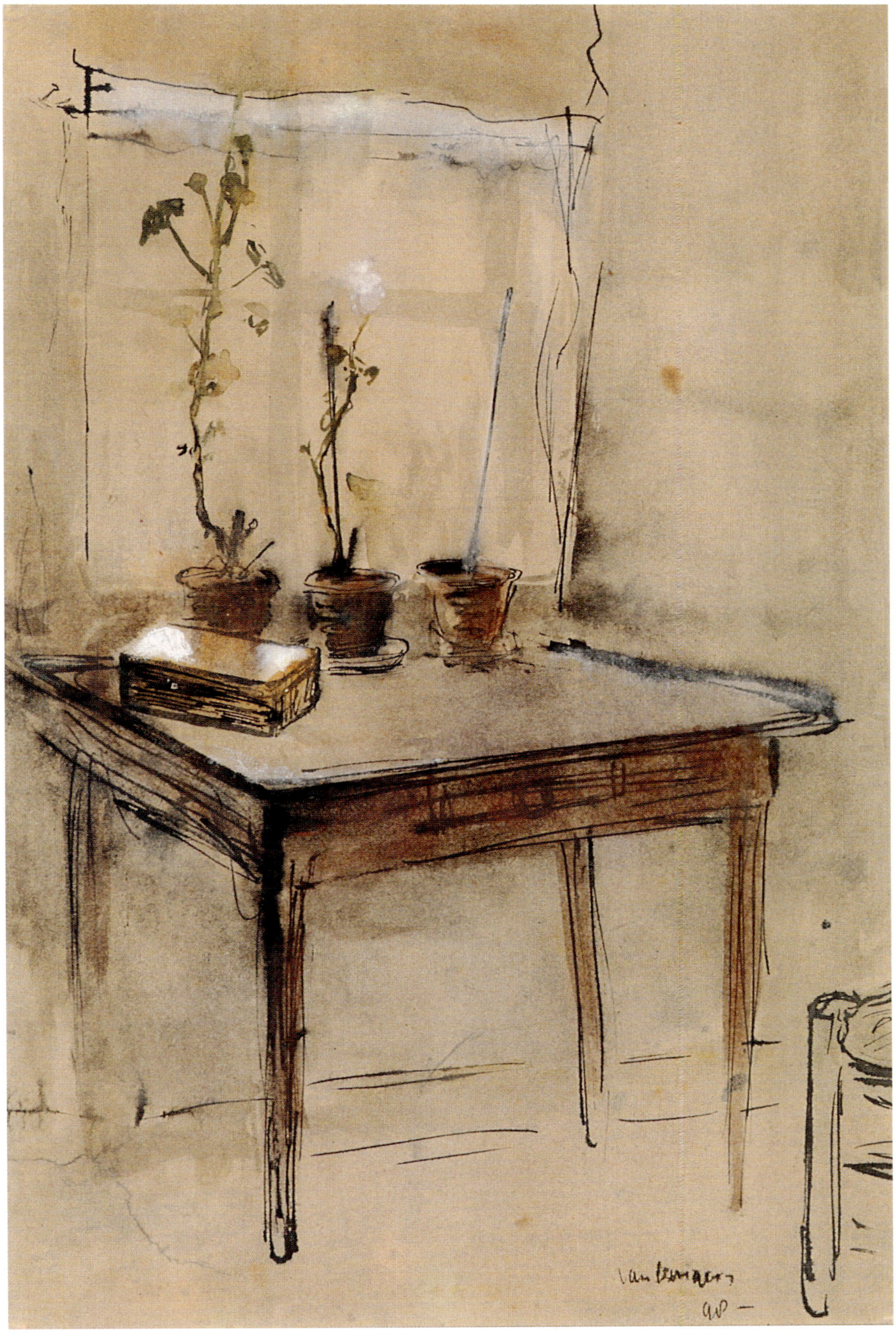

7. Intérieur pauvre, 1898

9. *Au music-hall* (At the music hall), 1898; 1905
Watercolour and gouache over initial design in brush and black ink
650 x 540 mm
Signed lower centre in brush with blue gouache: *V.D.*;
at top in brush with black ink: *WILHELMINA PORT*
On reverse of original frame a black-printed label:
GALERIE CHARPENTIER/76 FAUBOURG SAINT-HONORE-PARIS/EXPOSITION/VAN DONGEN/CINQUANTE ANS DE PEINTURE/-MCMXLII-; another black-printed label: *GALERIE CHARPENTIER/76 FAUBOURG SAINT-HONORE/PARIS*;
marked in pen with black ink: *VAN DONGEN/n°206-Au Music-Hall (1894)*

PROVENANCE:
Galerie Charpentier, Paris, 1942; auction Paris, Drouot (J. Hoebanx, E. Couturier), *Cent soixante-dix oeuvres modernes*, 9 December 1992 (fig.).

EXHIBITIONS:
1942 Paris, no. 206

COLLECTION:
Private collection

This colourful rendition of a hall filled with spectators was exhibited by Van Dongen at the Gallery Charpentier in 1942 under the title *Au music-hall.* It is a title which raises questions. The title at the top left-hand corner, *WILHELMINA PORT*, belies the idea that this portrays a theatre audience. The designation would seem to point to some sort of activity related to a harbour which then raises the questions of which one and the nature of the occasion for which the drawing was made. The city of Rotterdam houses only a Wilhelminakade, not a Wilhelminaport. However, two nearby towns, Vlaardingen and Schiedam, do have ports of this name which started their activities in 1895 and 1916 respectively. The Koningin Wilhelminahaven in Vlaardingen was given its name on the occasion of the inauguration of Queen Wilhelmina on 31 August 1898 and it is probable that the drawing depicts a festive gathering in honour of the naming of this port.[1] The first composition on paper, done in pencil and black ink, dates it to this time. Stylistically, this sketch in ink is closely linked to the drawings Van Dongen made in 1898-1899 for the *Rotterdamsch Nieuwsblad* and the piece may have been produced as part of his work for this newspaper. The type of hat the lady in the centre is wearing, with feathers and a flower, suggests it should be dated to this period.[2] In all likelihood, Van Dongen filled the drawing in with gouache and watercolour to make it more attractive, around 1905. This type of expressive use of colour can also be seen in circus drawings like *La parade foraine*, which was signed in almost exactly the same way with a monogram in cobalt blue. (cat. 100) In view of the open space left in the bottom right-hand corner of the drawing Van Dongen may have been considering giving it a second function as a poster announcing a theatre production or something similar. This may be what the later title refers to.

1.
M. A. Struijs, *Het gevolg van een kloek besluit. Het ontstaan van de Koningin wilhelminahaven te Vlaardingen*, Vlaardingen 1995.

2.
P. de Cantelaus, 'Douze ans de chapeaux forcés', *Le monde illustré*, no. 2557, 31 March 1906, pp. 206-207.

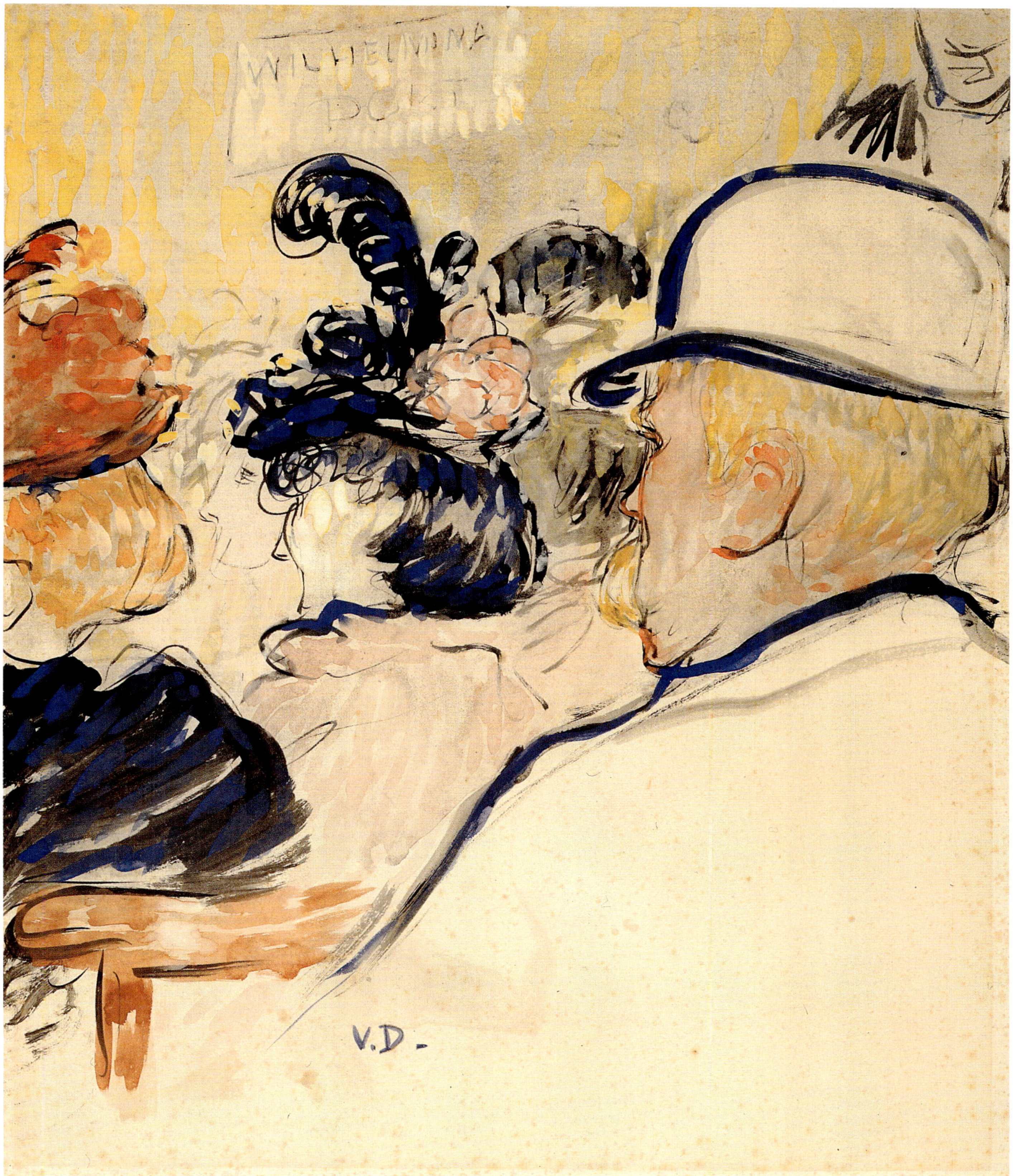

9. *Au music-hall*, 1898; 1905

10. *Binnenrotte, Rotterdam*, 1899
Black chalk, watercolour
291 x 463 mm
Annotated and signed upper left in black chalk: *Binnerotte-/vDongen*
Signed in blue chalk on the reverse of the cardboard to which the drawing is attached: *Van Dongen 1*
PROVENANCE:
Boymans Museum, Rotterdam, 1936 (gift of the artist; letter from Kees van Dongen to D. Hannema, 7 December 1936, GA Rotterdam)
LITERATURE:
Hannema 1937, p. 10; Hannema 1973, p. 48; Boymans Museum Annual Report 1937, p. 7
COLLECTION:
Boijmans Van Beuningen Museum, Rotterdam, Inv. KVD 5

11. *Lijnbaanstraat, Rotterdam*, 1899
Black chalk, watercolour accents
290 x 463 mm
Signed and annotated lower right in black chalk: *VD 99./Lynbaanstraat.*
Special features: the drawing is attached to cardboard
PROVENANCE:
Boymans Museum, 1936 (gift of the artist; letter from K. van Dongen to D. Hannema, 7 December 1936, GA Rotterdam)
LITERATURE:
Hannema 1937, p. 10; Hannema 1973, p. 48; Boymans Museum Annual Report 1937, p. 7
COLLECTION:
Boijmans Van Beuningen Museum, Rotterdam, Inv. KVD 6

12. *Rotterdamsche vrouwen* (Rotterdam women), 1899
Black chalk, watercolour
462 x 290
Signed lower right in black chalk: *VDongen.*
Special features: the drawing is attached to cardboard
PROVENANCE:
Boijmans Van Beuningen Museum, Rotterdam, 1936 (gift of the the artist; letter from Kees van Dongen to D. Hannema, 7 December 1936, GA Rotterdam)
LITERATURE:
Hannema 1937, p. 10; Hannema 1973, p. 48; Boymans Museum Annual Report 1937, p. 7
COLLECTION:
Boijmans Van Beuningen Museum, Rotterdam, Inv. KVD 12

13. *Lijnbaanstraat, Rotterdam*, 1899
Black chalk, watercolour accents
305 x 475 mm
Signed and annotated lower right in black chalk: *VD/Lynbaanstraat.*
PROVENANCE:
Auction Geneva, Galerie Motte, *Vente aux enchères publiques*, 8-9 November 1969, no. 399; Milan, Finarte, *Arte moderna e contemporanea*, 28 March 1992, no. 79; private collection, 1992
COLLECTION:
Private collection

The first drawings made by Kees van Dongen of prostitutes in Zandstraat, the Rotterdam red-light area, or of Lijnbaanstraat and the Binnenrotte nearby, were made in 1899. They are straightforward drawings with little embellishment. The shabby look of the streets and the women haggling outside, or half concealed in a doorway or window, waiting for their clients, were sketched by Van Dongen in a few rough continuous lines in black chalk on coarse paper. Colour has only been added here and there using watercolour. In a similar way, from 1899 onwards the writer and journalist M.J. Brusse wrote newspaper articles about the diversions of the Zandstraat area. This was also the year he made friends with Van Dongen and the two of them were impressed by the artistry of Steinlen. Brusse typified the women in his newspaper articles as 'squinting behind the transparent curtain' next to the lamplight of a 'round white gaslight lamps' and the 'brightly coloured light of oil lamps, in long festoons, surprisingly reflected in the muddy cobblestones'. The painter and the writer must have roamed around this entertainment area on numerous occasions, an area most frequented by passing seamen, and would no doubt have inspired one another's work. Brusse claims that Van Dongen made hundreds of sketches there. Apart from in 1899, Van Dongen also captured the area on paper in later visits. A pre-dating of a drawing is occasionally provided by an illustration in a French magazine for which an earlier Zandstraat study had been used as a departure point. (fig.) Also in Brusse's book about the Zandstraat district, published in 1912 in response to the municipal council's decision to demolish the area, a couple of drawings by Van Dongen were included. (fig.) These proved to be from Brusse's own collection and can be dated to different years. The lithograph portrait that Van Dongen made of the writer Brusse whilst the latter was staying with him in Paris also bears witness to their friendship. Only a few prints are known to have been made of this lithograph. One example in the collection of the Haags Gemeentemuseum has the number 10 in the margin and is probably the last print in the series.

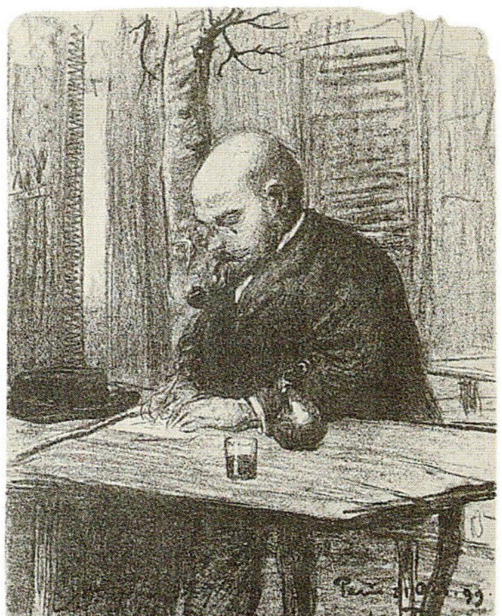

16. *Portrait of the writer-journalist Marie Joseph Brusse*, 1899

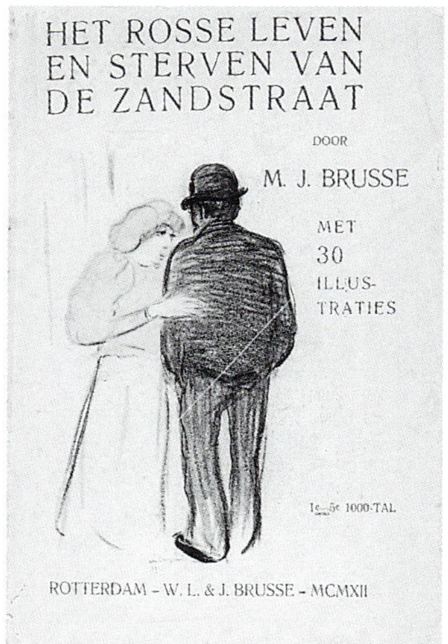

Illustration on cover, 1899
M.J. Brusse, *Het rosse leven en sterven van de Zandstraat*, Rotterdam (W.L. & J. Brusse) 1912

14. *Le bout de la route* (The end of the road), 1899
Black chalk, watercolour
443 x 270 mm (present size)
Initialled in black chalk lower right: *V.D.*; centre in yellow-ochre watercolour: *CAFÉ/SPORT*

PROVENANCE:
Galerie de Berri, Paris, 1955; auction Paris, Drouot (M. Boscher), *Tableaux Modernes*, 4 December 1957, no. 43 (John van der Klip collection, Galerie de Berri, Paris); private collection 1957

LITERATURE:
Loosjes-Terpstra 1987, p. 24, p. 233 note 2

COLLECTION:
Private collection, Paris

15. *Rotterdam, de Zandstraat* (Zandstraat in Rotterdam), 1899
Black chalk, brown wash, watercolour and white gouache accents
442 x 283 mm
Signed and annotated lower left in blue chalk: *vDongen-/Rotterdam. De Zandstraat.*
Signed on verso in pen and ink: *Kees van Dongen./10. Impasse Gi[rardon]/(M*

PROVENANCE:
Boymans Museum, Rotterdam, 1936 (gift of the artist; letter from Kees van Dongen to D. Hannema, 7 December 1936, GA Rotterdam)

EXHIBITIONS:
1901 Rotterdam, no. 25 (as *Rotterdam*)

LITERATURE:
Hannema 1937, p. 10; Hannema 1973, p. 48; Boymans Museum Annual Report 1937, p. 7

COLLECTION:
Boijmans Van Beuningen Museum, Rotterdam, Inv. KVD 4

16. *Portret van de schrijver-journalist Marie Joseph Brusse* (Portrait of the writer-journalist Marie Joseph Brusse; 1873-1941), 1899
Lithograph on light-grey paper
495 x 359 mm
Signed and dated lower right: *Paris 21 Oct. 99./van Dongen*; pencil annotation in the margin lower right: *no IX*

PROVENANCE:
J.H.J. Mellaart, The Hague; Rijksprentenkabinet, Rijksmuseum, Amsterdam, 1940 (gift of J.H.J. Mellaart)

COLLECTION:
Rijksprentenkabinet, Rijksmuseum, Amsterdam, Inv. P 40: 1857

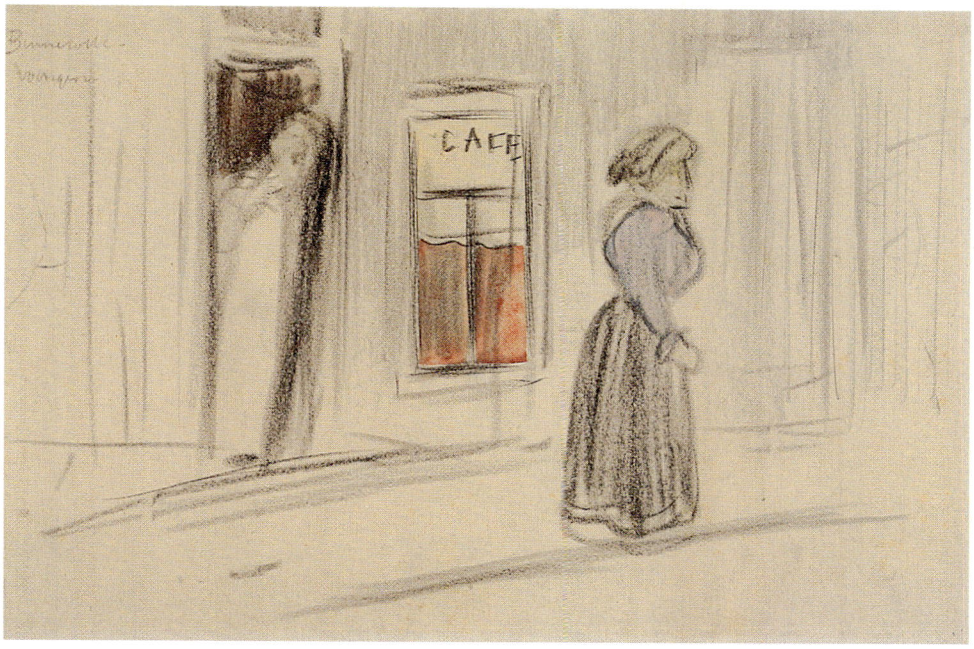

10. *Binnenrotte, Rotterdam, 1899*

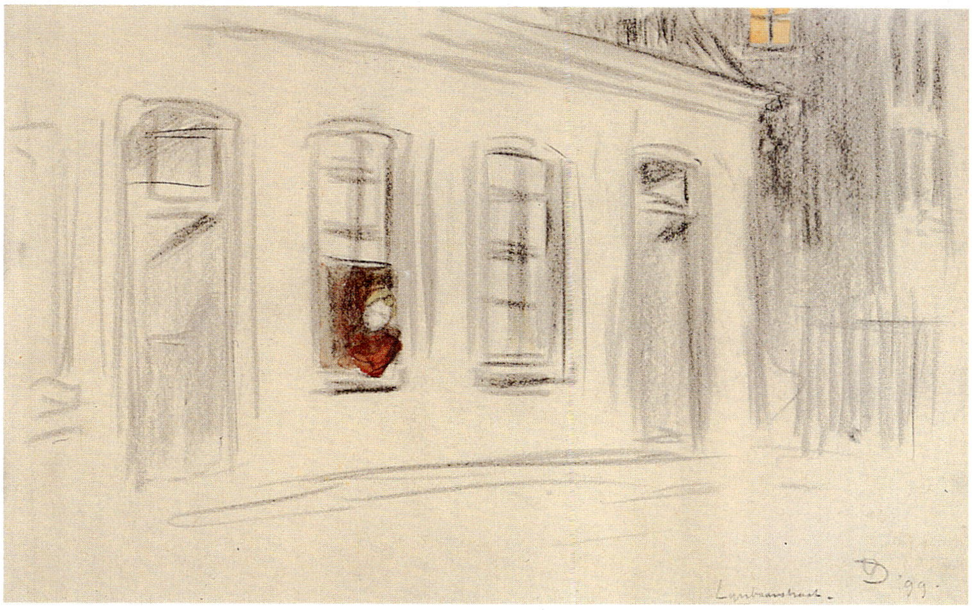

11. *Lijnbaansstraat, Rotterdam, 1899*

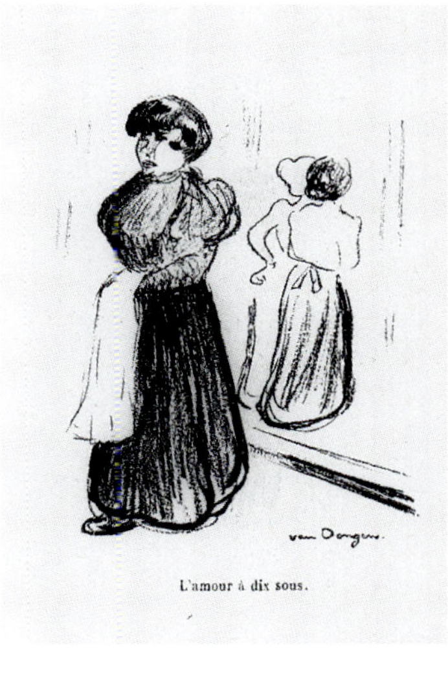

L'amour à dix sous, 1903
Illustration in *La Vie en Rose*, no. 104, 10 October 1903, p. 5

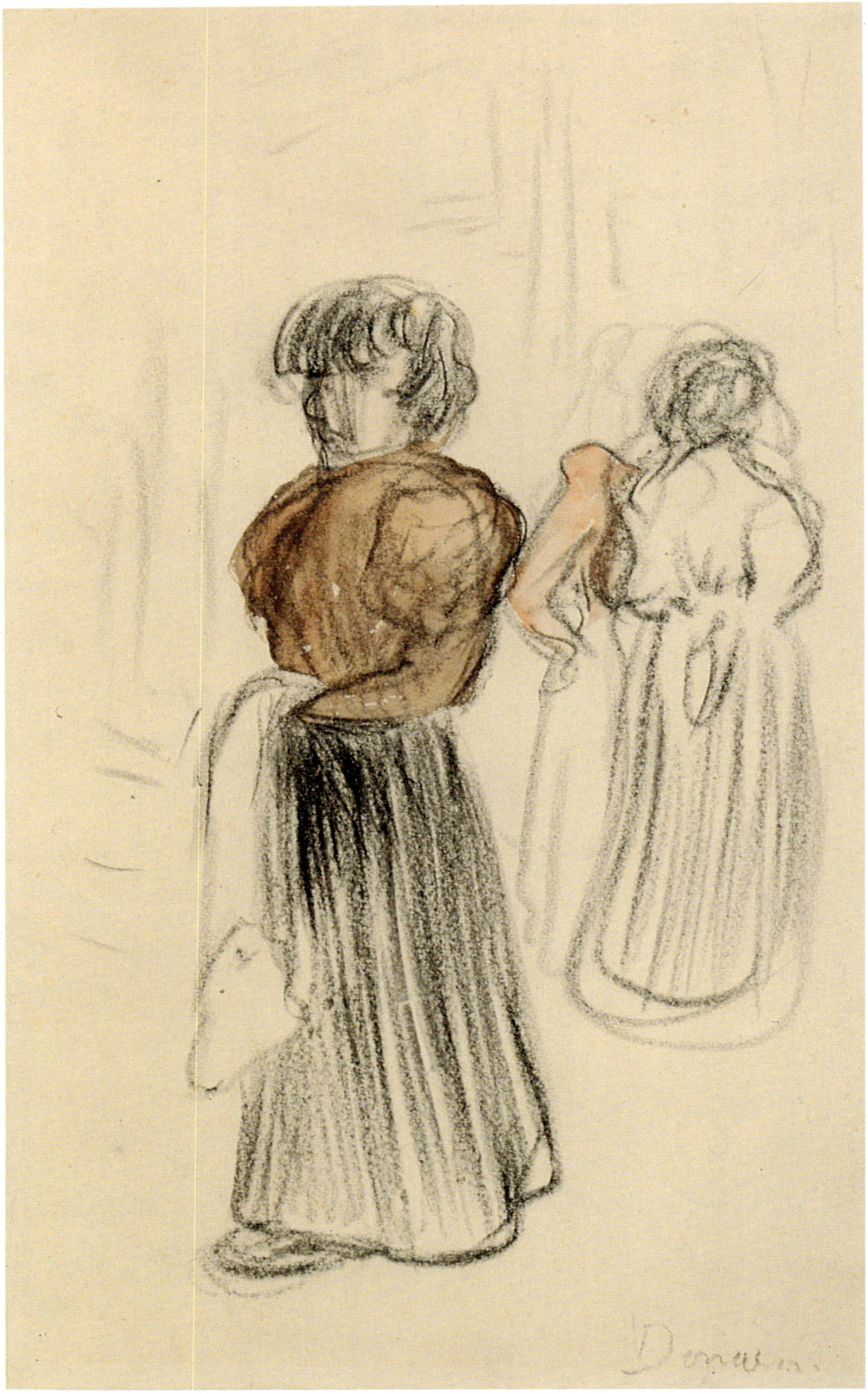

12. *Rotterdam women*, 1899

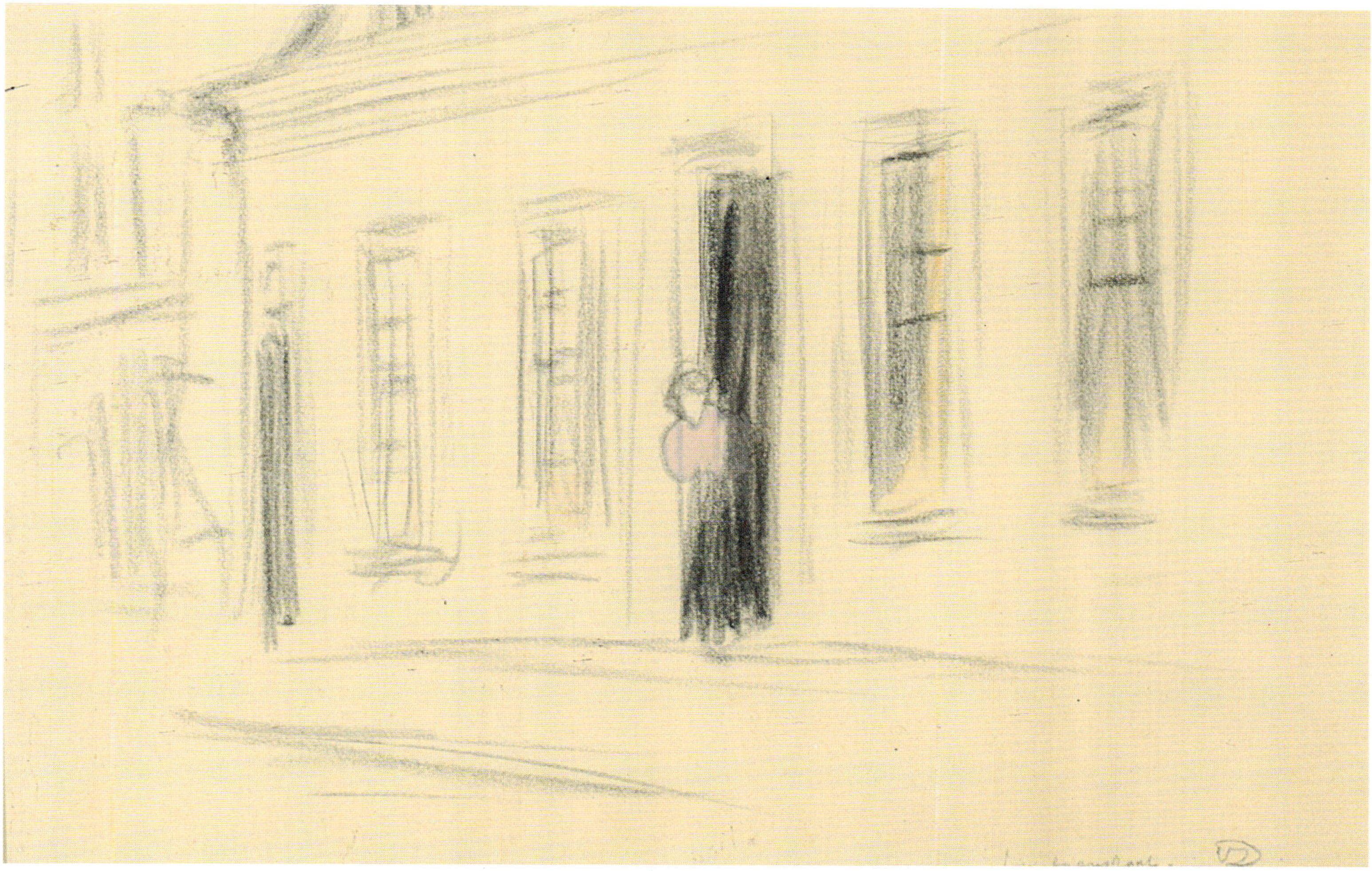

13. *Lijnbaanstraat, Rotterdam*, 1899

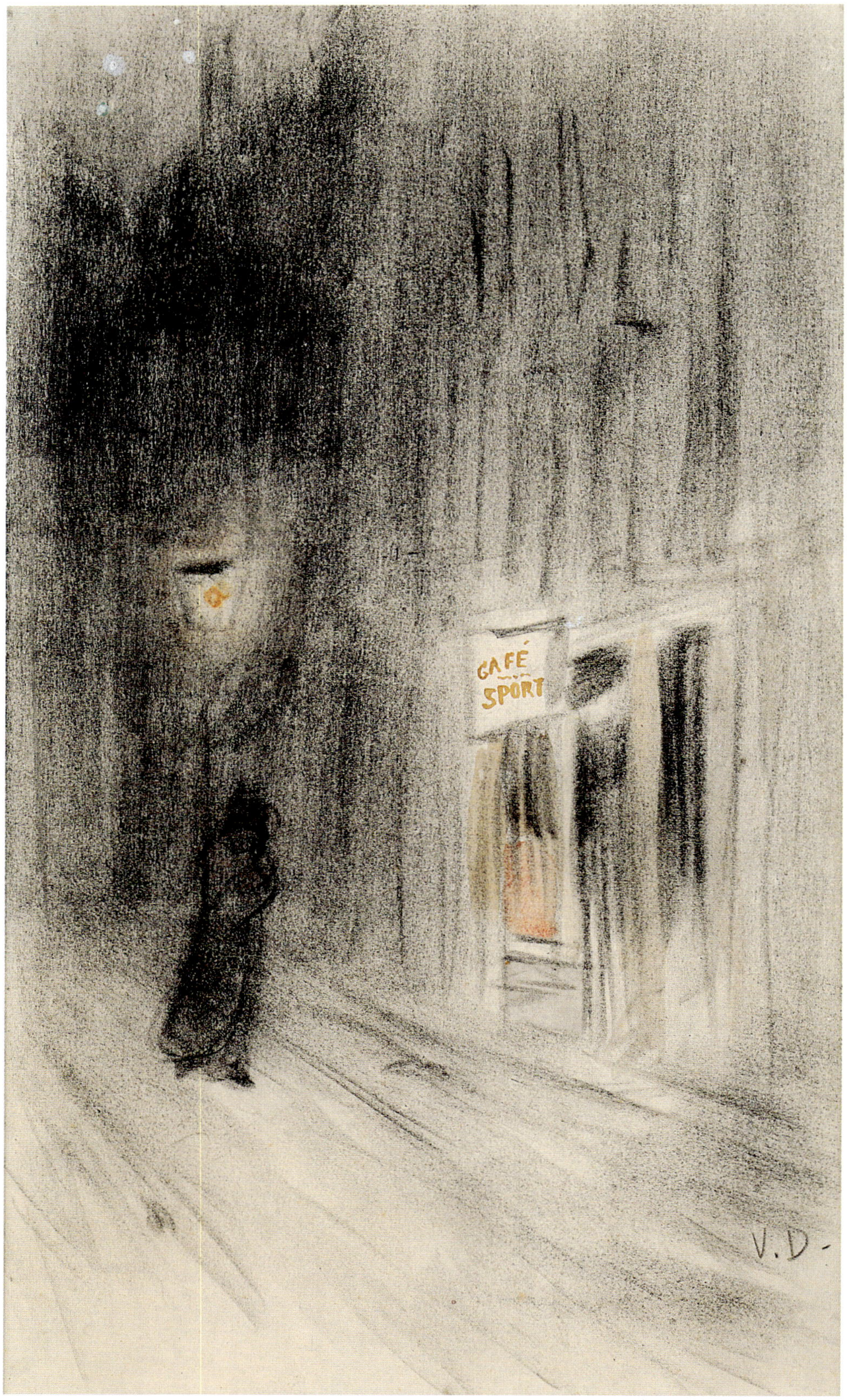

14. *Le bout de la route*, 1899

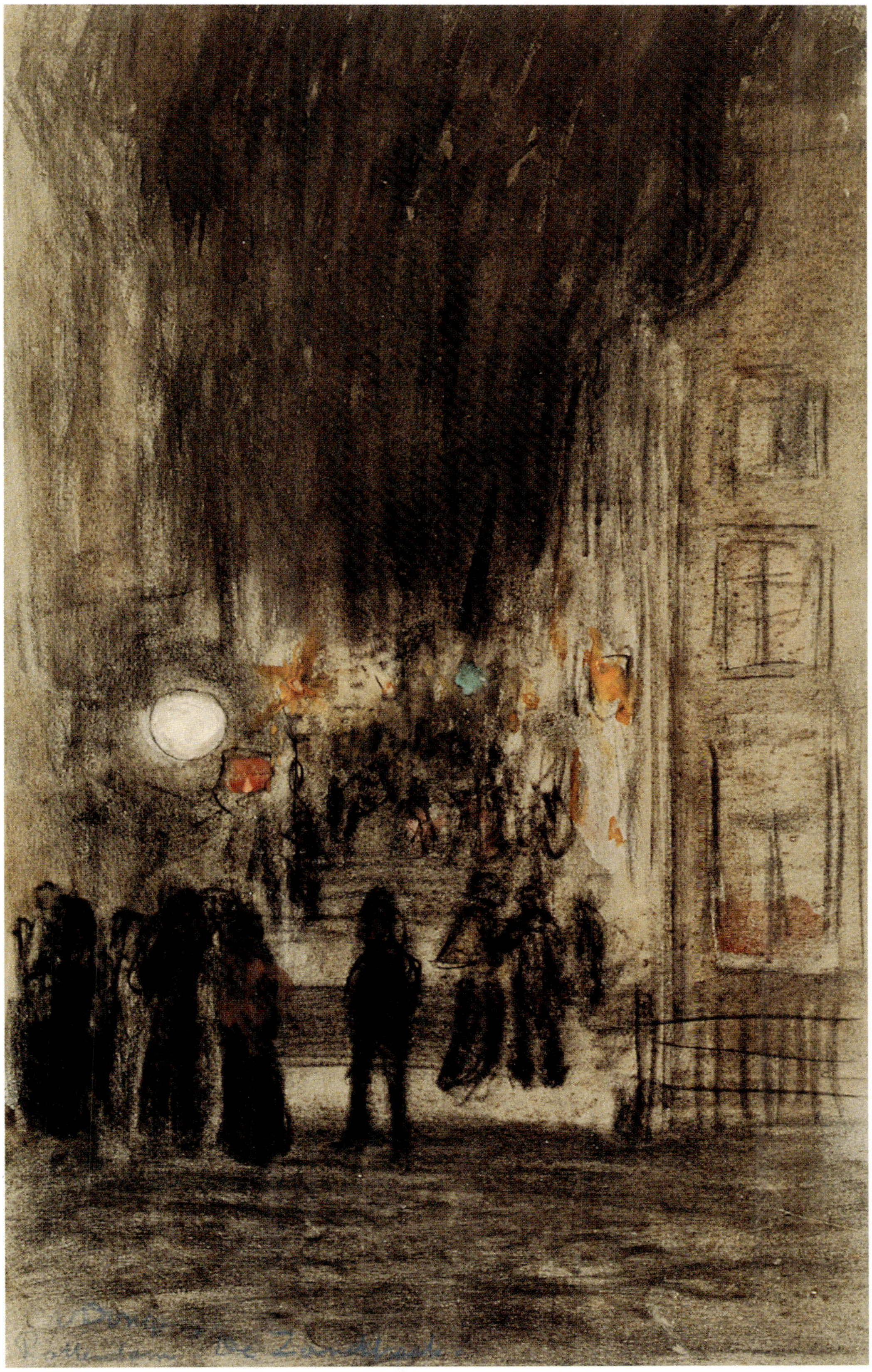

15. *Rotterdam, de Zandstraat*, 1899

17. *Brief van Kees van Dongen aan de kunstenaar Chris Addicks* (Letter from Kees van Dongen to the artist Chris Addicks)
6 December 1900
Handwritten letter, pen in brown ink, 1 sheet folded double, 4 pages of writing, 1 illustrated
207 x 265 mm
On page 1 place and date: *Montmartre 6 December 00.*; addressed to: *Vieux*; followed by other handwriting: *(C.J. Addicks)*; signed on p. 3: *Kees van Dongen.*; address on page 4: *10. Impasse Girardon/Montmartre.-Paris.*
At bottom of page 4 in pen and brown ink: *Schets van het atelier van Kees van Dongen in Montmartre* (Sketch of Van Dongen's studio in Montmartre)
PROVENANCE:
Joop Siedenburg (1875-1961), Amsterdam, after 1949 (gift of Chris Addicks); Henk Siedenburg (1908-1990), Amsterdam, 1961 (bequest J. Siedenburg; see letter from H. Siedenburg to C. van Hasselt, 25 January 1977, Fondation Custodia, Paris); Fondation Custodia, Paris, 1977
LITERATURE:
Heybroek 1987, p. 333, note 6; Van Berge-Gerbaud 1994, no. 85 (fig.)
COLLECTION:
Collection Frits Lugt, Institut Néerlandais, Paris, Inv. 1977-A 696

18. *Parijsch stadsgezicht* (Parisian cityscape), 1900
Black and red chalk, watercolour, white gouache
454 x 287 mm
Signed lower right in black chalk: *van Dongen-*; annotation lower right in blue chalk: *Paris*; on the omnibus in black chalk: *Mt JAQUE MONTMARTRE*
PROVENANCE:
Auction Amsterdam, De Zon (L. Gijselman & zoon), *Inboedels uit verschillende nalatenschappen*, 20 April 1943, no. 3891; Rijksprentenkabinet, Rijksmuseum, Amsterdam, 1943
Rijksprentenkabinet, Rijksmuseum, Amsterdam, Inv. 1943 A 2

19. *Boulevard extérieur*
c. 1900
Black chalk, brown-grey wash, watercolour, white gouache
350 x 298 mm
Signed lower right in black chalk: *van Dongen.*; annotated lower right in blue chalk: *Boulevard Extérieur.*
PROVENANCE:
Auction Amsterdam, Mak van Waay, *Oude en moderne schilderijen...uit verschillend nederlandsch bezit*, 21-24 December 1943, no. 473; Rijksprentenkabinet, Rijksmuseum, Amsterdam, 1943
COLLECTION:
Rijksprentenkabinet, Rijksmuseum, Amsterdam, Inv. 1943 A 68

20. *Le Chiffonier* (The rag-and-bone man), c. 1900
Black chalk, watercolour accents
190 x 295 mm (present size)
Signed lower right in watercolour: *van Dongen*; lower left in black chalk: *V.D.*
On reverse of frame in blue: *Van Dongen/"Le Chiffonnier"/n° 313* (Inv. Dolly van Dongen)
PROVENANCE:
Dolly van Dongen (1905-1989), Paris; private collection, Le Havre, 1989
EXHIBITIONS:
1982 Saint-Antoine; 1983 Paris, no. 26
COLLECTION:
Private collection, Le Havre

21. *Au marché* (At the market), c. 1900
Black chalk
125 x 195 mm (present size)
Signed lower left in pencil: *van Dongen.*
PROVENANCE:
Auction New York, Parke-Bernet, *Modern paintings, drawings, watercolors*, 7 March 1968, no. 24; private collection
COLLECTION:
Private collection

When Van Dongen writes the here depicted letter to the Dutch painter Chris Addicks in December 1900, he has already been in Paris for more than a year. (fig.) He probably arrived there for the second time at the end of September 1899. (fig.) The letter illustrates that Van Dongen was still interested in news about his Rotterdam friends: the artist asks about Addick's latest work and wants to know how Krulder, Speenhoff and Schildt are getting on. It is one of the few letters in which Van Dongen informs them about his own activities in Paris. It becomes clear that although he portrays himself in a sketch at the end of the account as being engaged in painting, at that time he devoted himself more to drawing: 'I have made quite a few sketches in the streets, those sort of instantaneous works, a chalk or ink thumbnail sketch, apply a bit of colour to it, and there it is – ready in a jiffy.' Brusse too described how when Van Dongen was in Paris he went out almost every day with his sketch book to capture life on the streets. The types he encounters are tramps, lonely drudges, and women of the streets, seen here on a bench on an almost deserted boulevard in the suburbs. The traffic at a road junction in the city is drawn in a lively way. Almost the same composition, somewhat larger and furnished with a few more figures, was used by Van Dongen for the cover of the book which he recommended in his letter, *Jean Lefort. Een greep uit het Parijsche leven* (fig.): 'a book recently appeared in Holland with a title print of mine on it...the book itself is quite nice particularly for people who are interested in Paris...it is what you would call an 'experienced' little book, the writer has had all the experiences and is himself the hero of the book.' Van Dongen's cover illustration, a sketch of the busy boulevard traffic is an image of the city which regularly recurs in the book by the author, Charles Snabilié, Dutch correspondent in Paris. It is a snatch from busy Paris life which at the same time is a metaphor for the daily rhythm of the large city, 'doing business, making a profit, the struggle for life.'[1] The city must also have been experienced this way by Van Dongen. His first success in material terms was a long way off at that moment. The attic which Van Dongen had furnished as his studio on Impasse Girardon, which it would appear from the sketch looked out onto the Sacré-Coeur and the Moulin de la Galette, was 'nice enough', but the space was limited: you can 'only stand up straight on one side.'

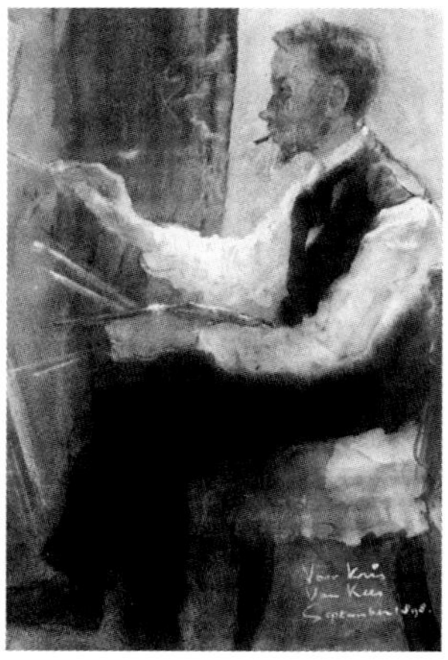

The painter C.J. Addicks in his studio, 1898
Watercolour, black chalk, body colour, 332 x 331 mm
Boijmans Van Beuningen Museum, Rotterdam

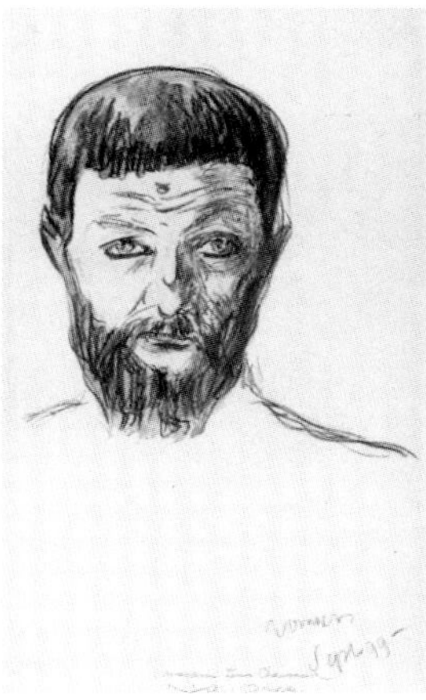

Self-portrait, 1899
Black chalk, watercolour, 450 x 230 mm
Private collection

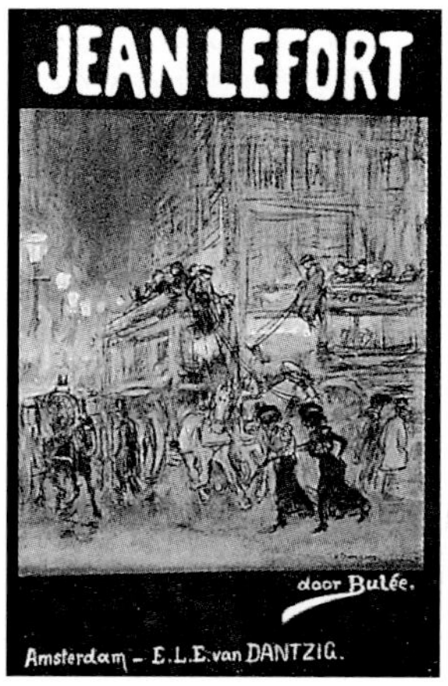

Illustration on cover, 1900
Bulée (Charles Snabilié), *Jean Lefort, Een greep uit het Parijsche leven*, E.L.E. van Dantzig, Amsterdam n.d. (1900)

1. Bulée 1900, I, pp. 70-71. See also on *Jean Lefort*, cat. pp. 36-7

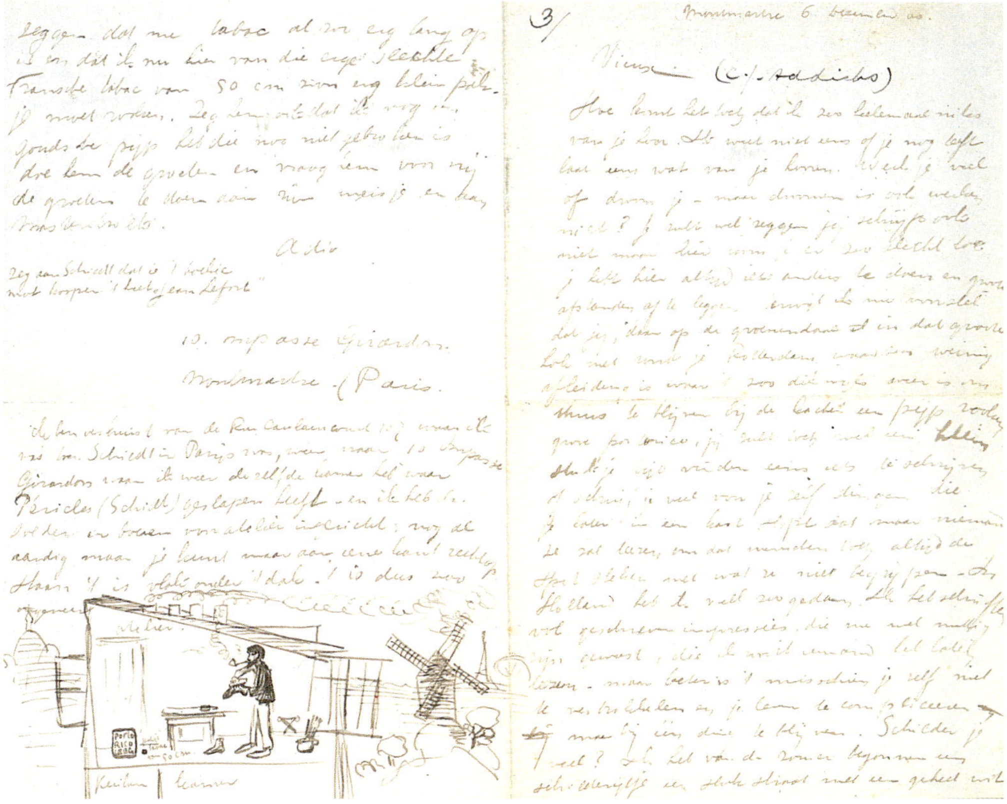

Montmartre 6 December 00.

10. impasse Girardon.
Montmartre / Paris.

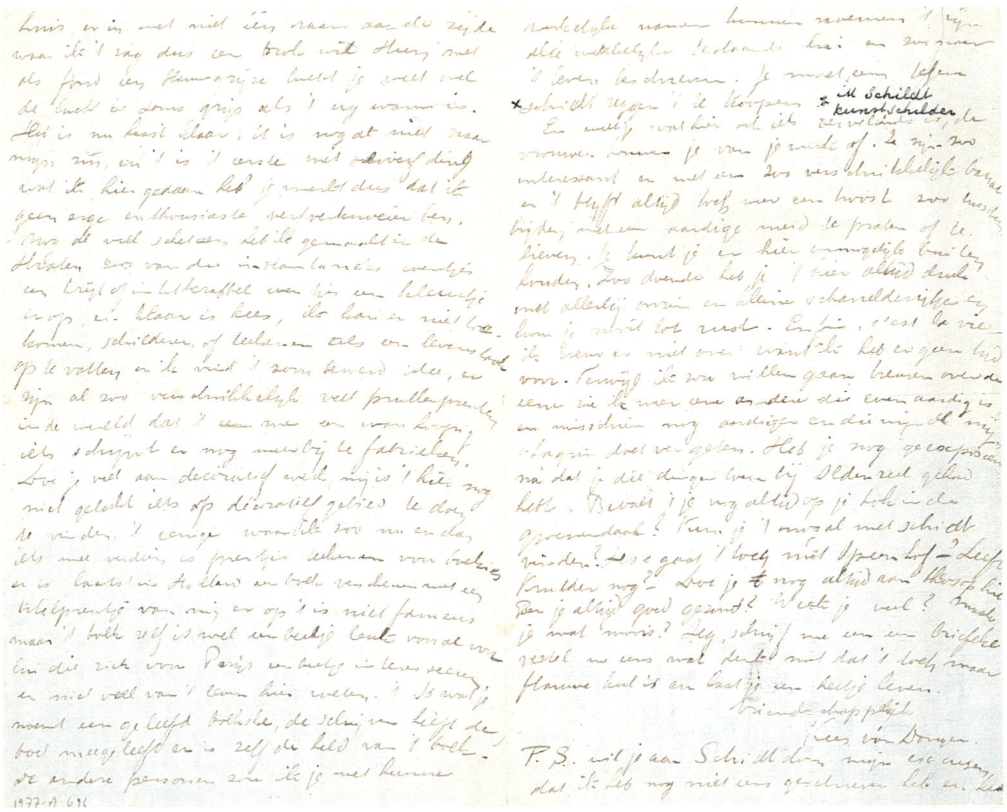

Kees van Dongen.

17. *Letter from Kees van Dongen to the artist Chris Addicks, 6 December 1900*

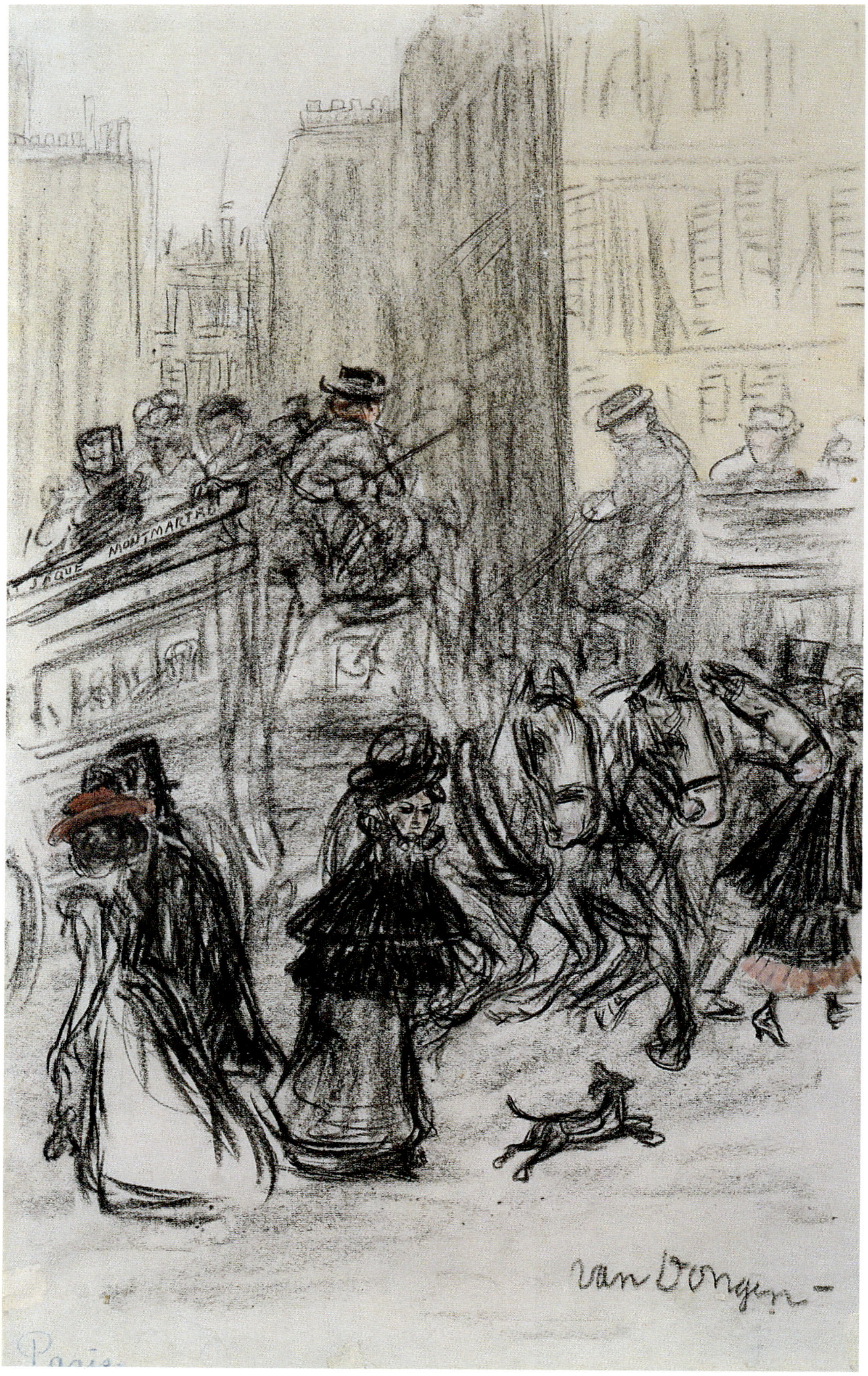

18. *Parisian cityscape*, 1900

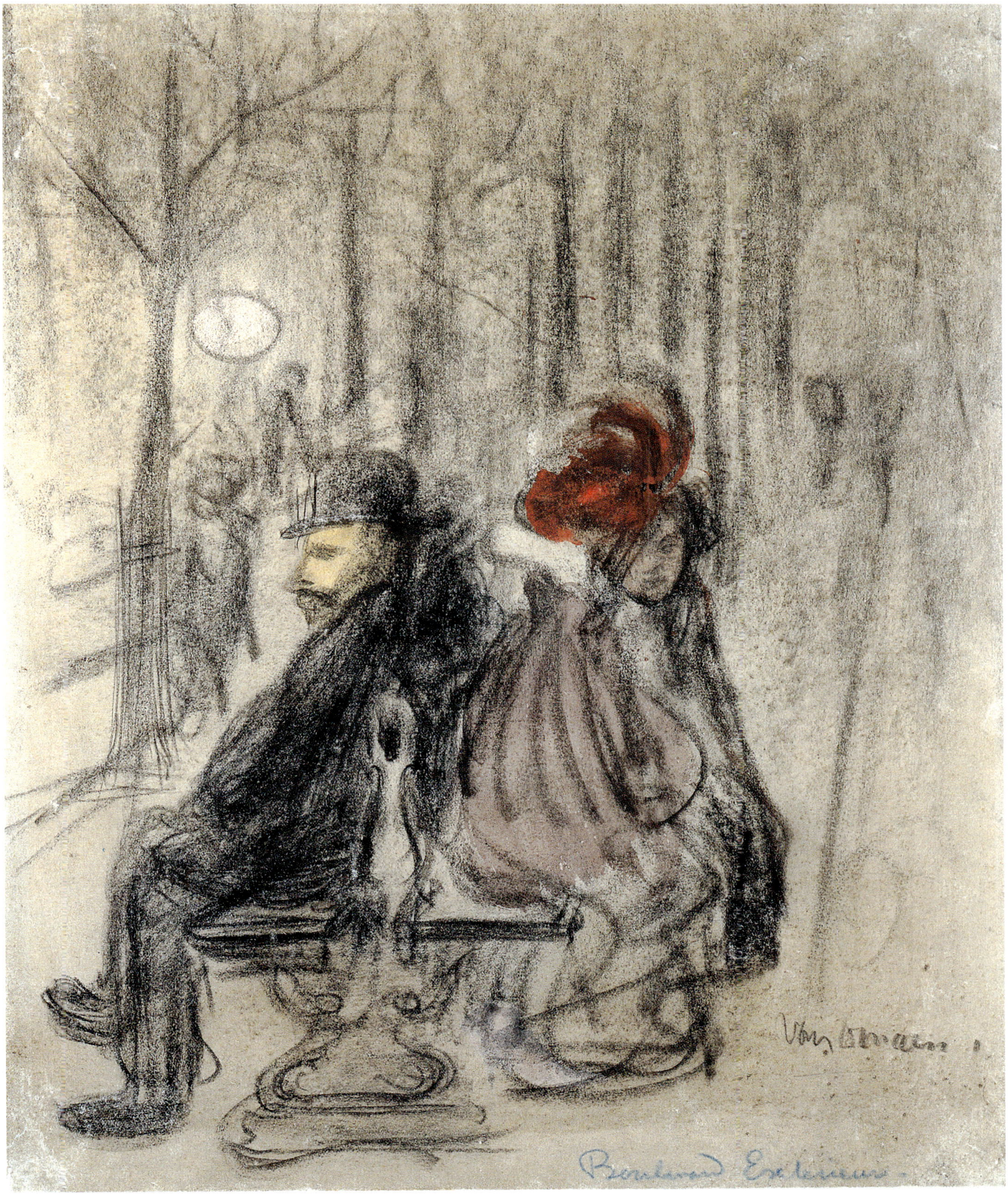

19. *Boulevard extérieur*, c. 1900

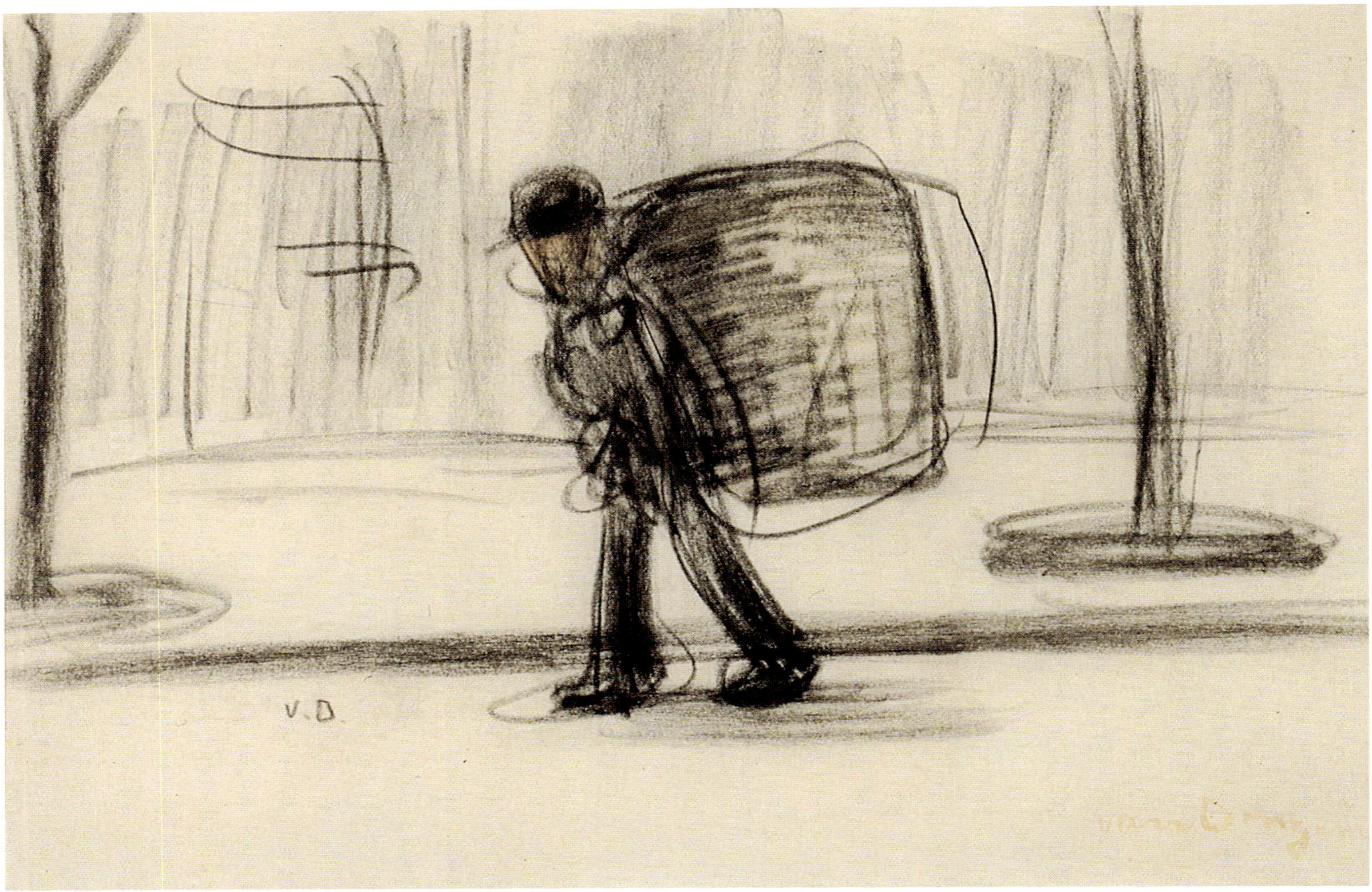

20. *Le chiffonnier*, c. 1900

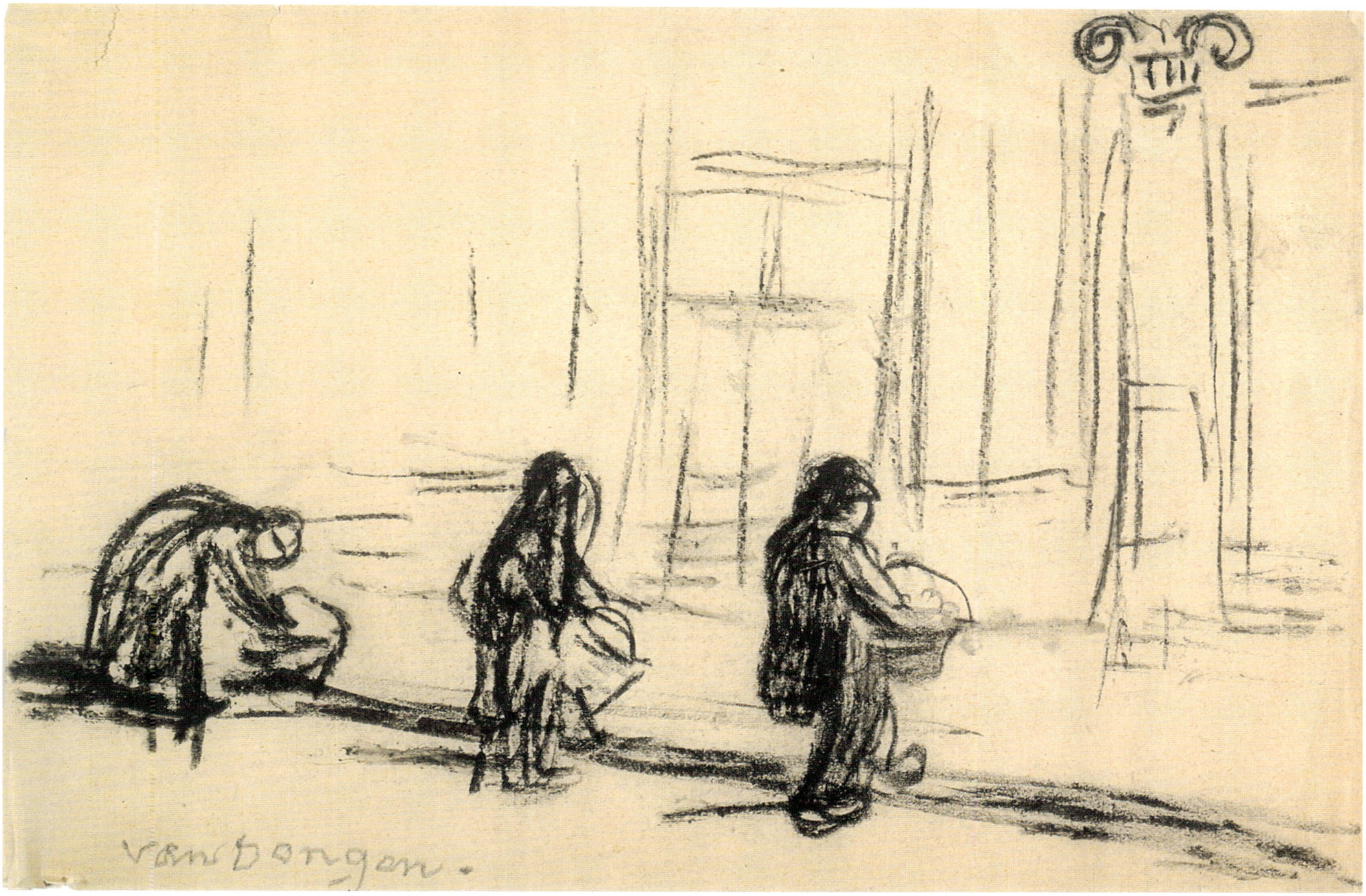

21. *Au marché*, c. 1900

22. *Les chevaux de Paris* (The Horses of Paris), 1900
Black chalk, watercolour, white gouache
292 x 462 mm
Signed and dated lower right in watercolour: *VDongen/1900*; annotated lower right in blue chalk: *Les chevaux de Paris*.
Handwriting on reverse of original frame: *Van Dongen/villa Said 29/Paris XVI* (note made by Rijksbureau voor Kunsthistorische Documentatie – RKD, The Hague)
provenance
J.C.W. Cossaar (1874-1966), The Hague; his daughter J.J. Cossaar, The Hague, 1966; private collection, 1969
LITERATURE:
Hopmans 1992, p. 43, fig. 11
COLLECTION:
Private collection

23. *Deux chevaux attelés* (Two harnessed horses), c. 1900
Black chalk, watercolour, white gouache
123 x 195 mm
Signed and dated lower right in watercolour: *van Dongen/1900*
PROVENANCE:
Félix Fénéon (1861-1944), Paris; Musée Léon Dierx, Saint-Denis, 1911-1912 (gift of Félix Fénéon on the founding of the Musée d'Art et d'Histoire/Musée Léon Dierx, Saint-Denis, at the request of Marius-Ary Leblond)
COLLECTION:
Musée Léon Dierx, Saint-Denis, La Réunion, Inv. 450/73

24. *Straatscène met kar en paard*
(Street scene with horse and cart), 1900
Black chalk, watercolour, white gouache
275 x 370 mm
Signed lower right in black chalk: *Van Dongen.*; in black chalk upper right: *VINS LIQUERS*
PROVENANCE:
Boymans Museum, Rotterdam, 1936 (gift of the artist; letter from Kees van Dongen to D. Hannema, 7 December 1936, GA Rotterdam)
EXHIBITIONS:
1947 Eindhoven, no. 130
LITERATURE:
Doelman 1947 (fig.); Hannema 1937, p. 10; Hannema 1973, p. 48
Boymans Museum Annual Report 1937, p. 7
COLLECTION:
Boijmans Van Beuningen Museum, Rotterdam, Inv. KVD 15

25. *Chemin de halage* (Tow-path), c. 1901
Brush in black ink over pencil sketch
150 x 350 mm
Signed lower right in blue chalk: *VD* (in ligature)
PROVENANCE:
Auction Amsterdam, Sotheby's, *Modern and contemporary art*, 27 May 1993, no. 267 (fig.); auction London, Sotheby's, *Impressionist, modern and contemporary art...*, 23 March 1994, no. 16 (fig.)
COLLECTION:
Private collection

Around 1900 Van Dongen made some more drawings in black chalk and ink of horses pulling carts and other vehicles. One of these drawings, dated 1900, was given the title *Les chevaux de Paris* and shows that several of these horse drawings were probably designed to be part of a series. (fig.) In these sheets it is clear that Van Dongen wanted to accentuate above all else the effort the animals had to put into pulling the heavily laden vehicles, usually coal wagons, although he also gave a glimpse of the surroundings too. Undoubtedly, he also represented the daily toil of the Parisian labourers and ordinary people. This is unmistakeably the aim of a drawing which Van Dongen donated to F. Domela Nieuwenhuis in 1904 for inclusion in the commemorative book celebrating 25 years of his work for the socialist periodical *Recht voor Allen* (Justice for All): in it can be seen that the life of a woman with two children is similar to that of the visibly exhausted workhorse. (fig.) In a similar way, the Dutch graphic artist Pieter Dupont, also working in Paris at that time, portrayed the workhorse in several drawings and engravings. In a number of letters he makes critical comparisons between the way the animals and the labourers were worked to death during their long exhausting day: 'just reflect for a moment...how much luxury can be squandered due to savings brought about by floggings.'[1] His pastel *L'attelage*, which has captured a calmer moment, was acquired by Boymans Museum in 1898.[2] (fig.)

1.
W.F. Dupont, *Pieter Dupont, Een Nederlandsch graveur. Zijn leven en werken*, Oisterwijk 1947, p. 43.
2.
Tentoonstelling van schilderijen en andere kunstwerken (The exhibition of works of art of Living Masters held every four years), Rotterdam (Academie van Beeldende Kunsten en Technische Wetenschappen) 1898, no. 87.

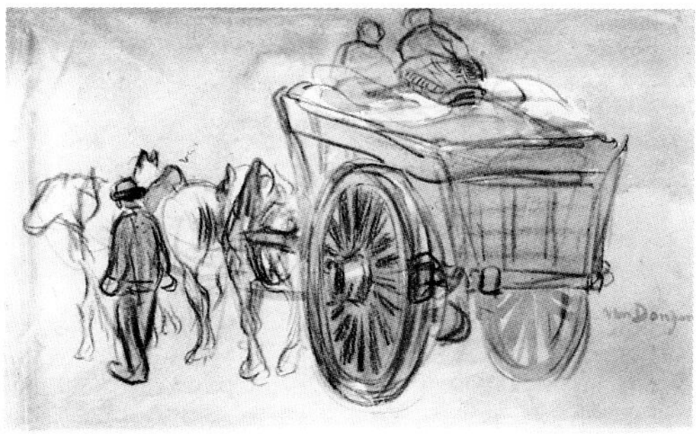

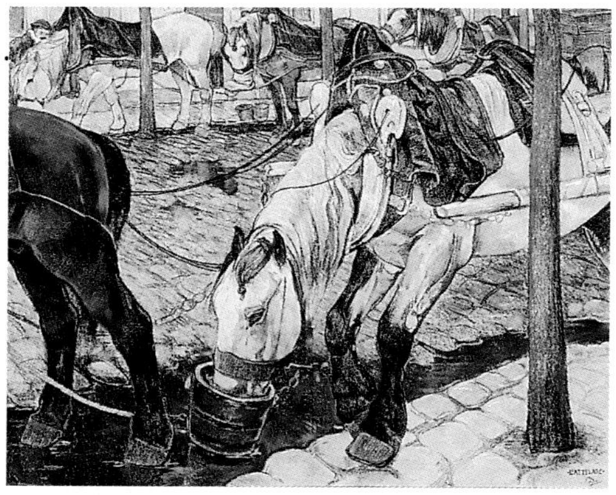

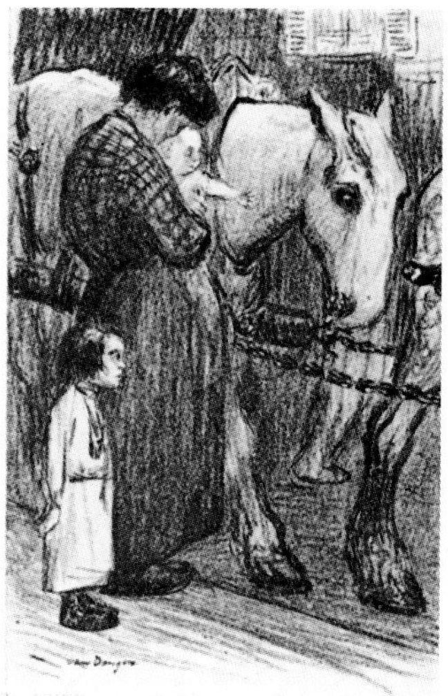

Cart with horses, 1900
Black chalk, water colour, 260 x 420 mm,
Boijmans van Beuningen Museum, Rotterdam

P. Dupont, *L'Attelage*, 1898
Pastel on light brown paper, 610 x 775 mm,
Boijmans Van Beuningen Museum, Rotterdam

Woman with children in front of harnessed horses, c. 1902
Illustration in *Gedenkboek opgedragen aan F. Domela Nieuwenhuis*, Amsterdam 1904, p. 22

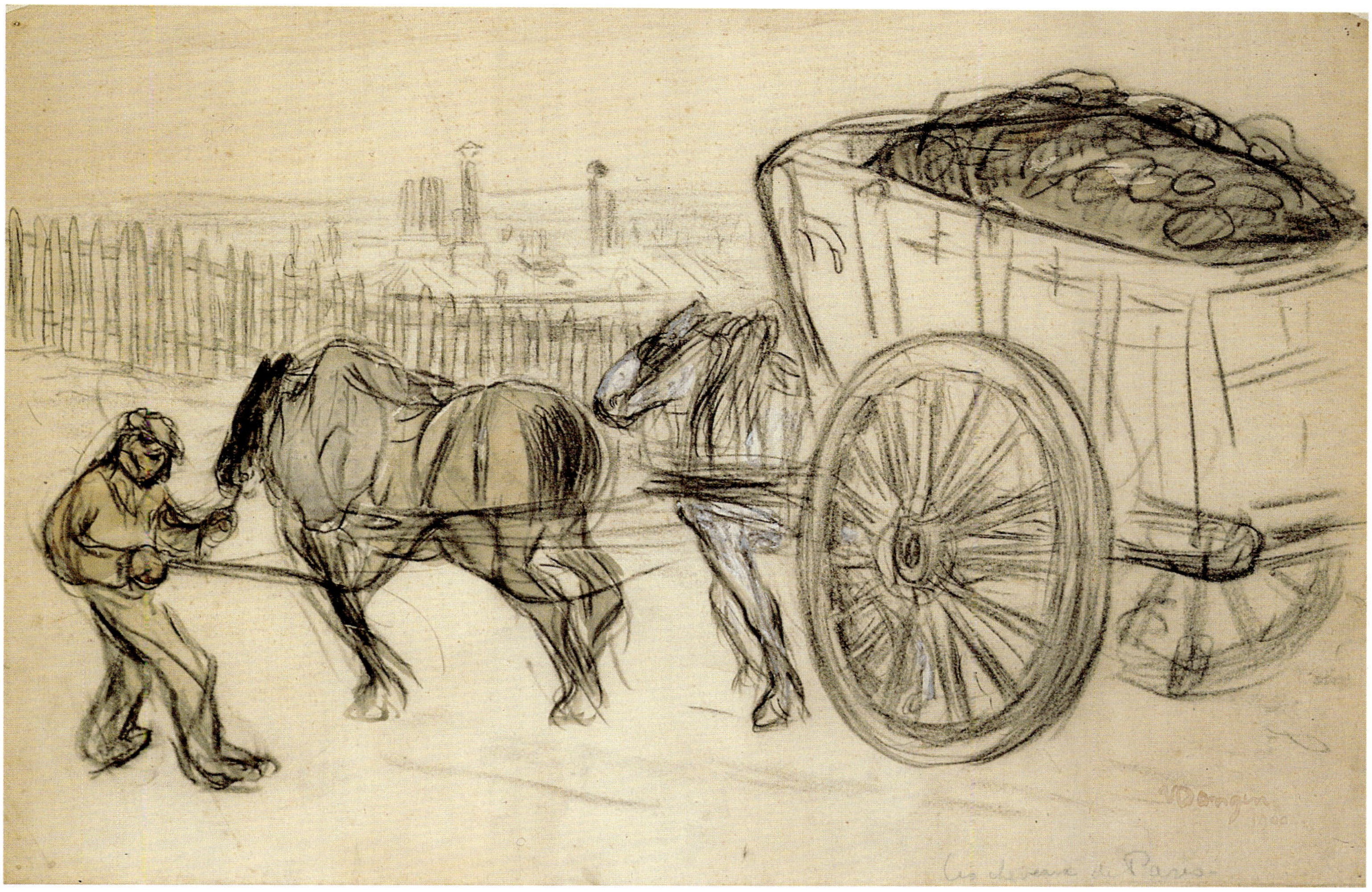

22. *Les chevaux de Paris*, 1900

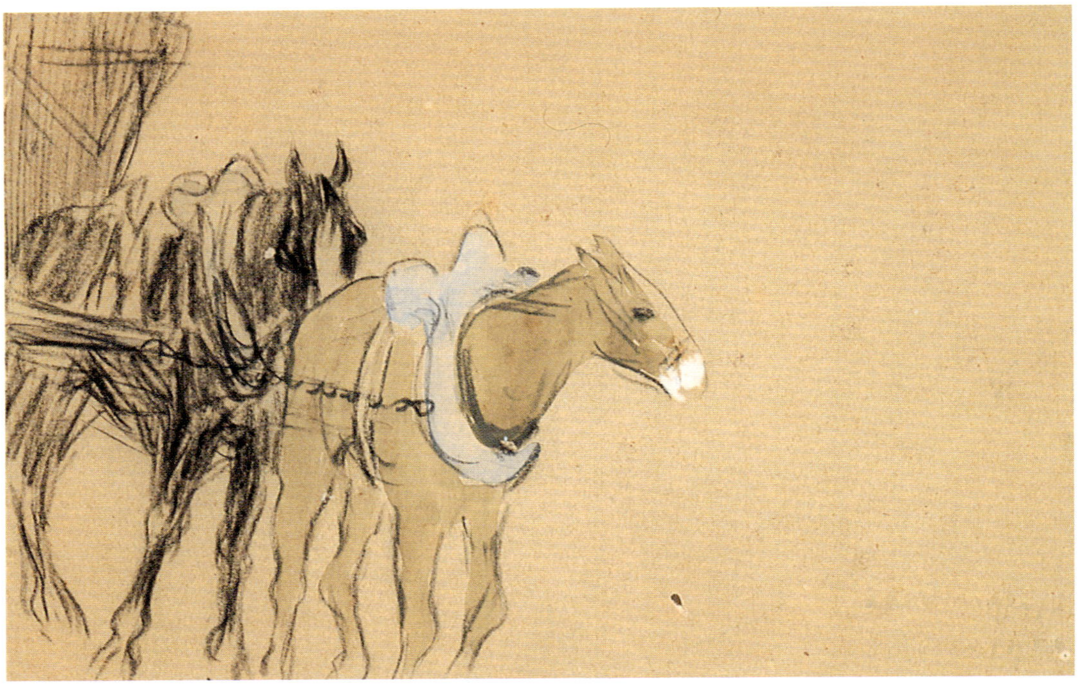

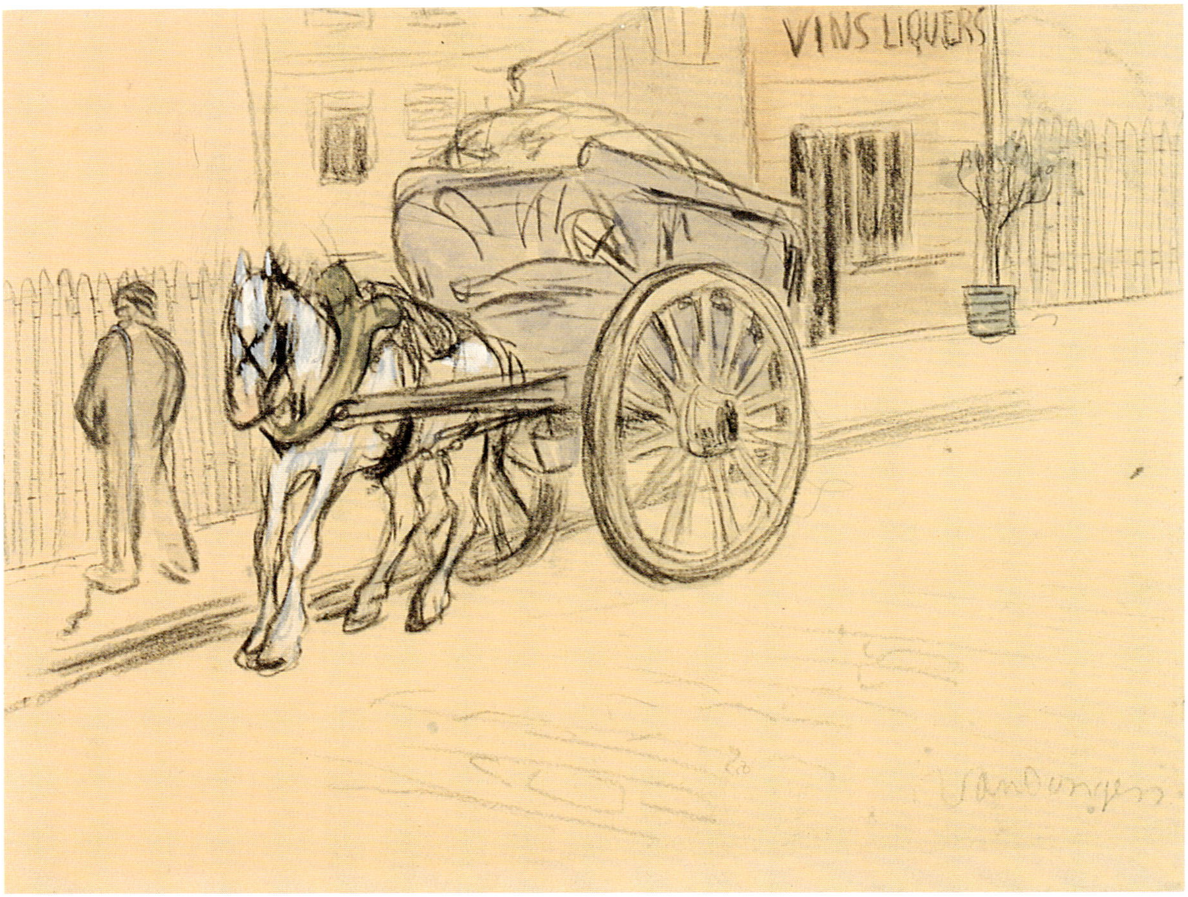

23. *Deux chevaux attelés*, c. 1900

24. *Street scene with horse and cart*, 1900

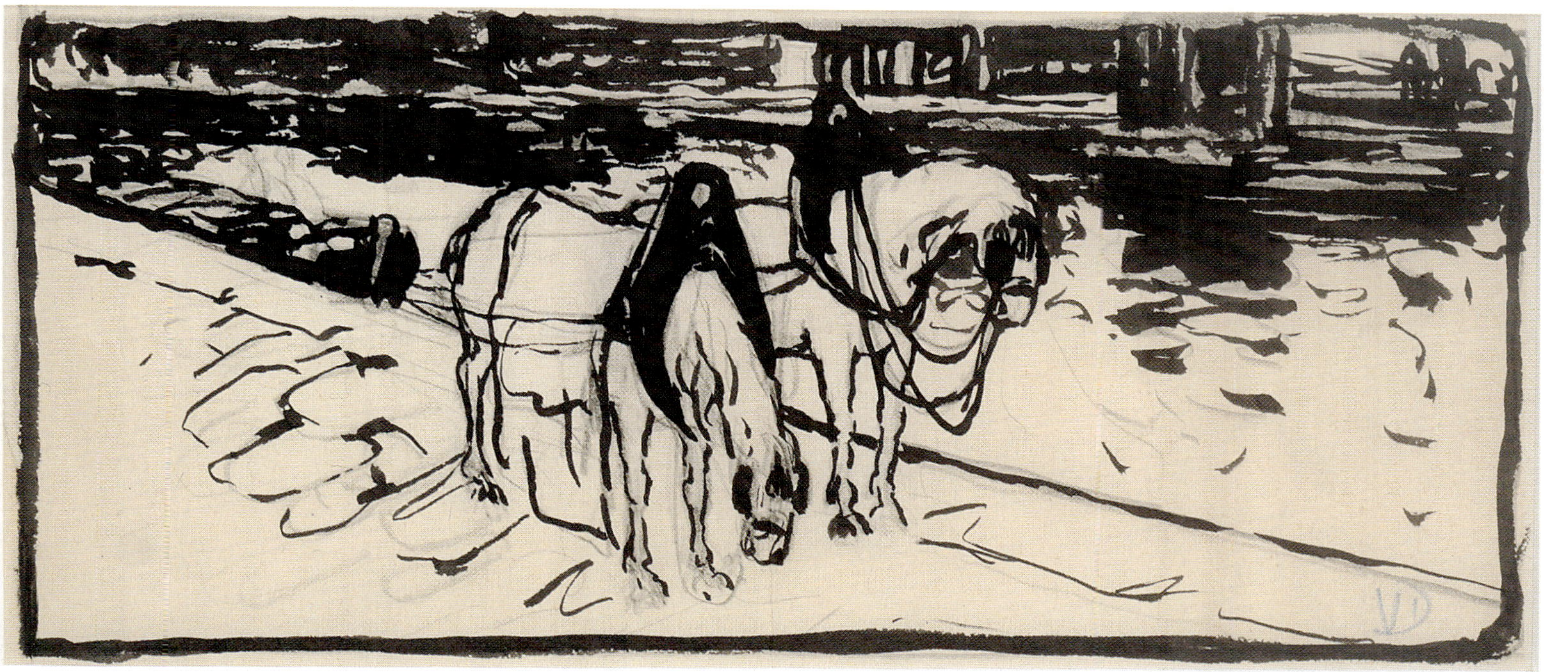

25. *Chemin de halage*, c. 1901

26. *Zelfportret* (Self-portrait), 1900
Brush in black ink, grey wash, watercolour
270 x 470 mm
Signed and dated in brush with grey: *vanDongen/1900.*

PROVENANCE:
Auction London, Sotheby's, *Impressionist and modern drawings...*, 11 December 1969, no. 208 (fig.); art dealers' Roland, Browse & Delbanco, London, 1969; Jonathan Leaver, UK, 1972; art dealers' Roland, Browse & Delbanco, London, 1973; Constance B. and Carroll L. Cartwright, 1974

EXHIBITIONS:
1070 London, no. 27 (fig.); 1971 Tucson, no. 40 (fig.)
1990 Paris, p. 21 (fig.)

LITERATURE:
Sutton 1971, p. 38, fig. 5; Thorson 1979, vol. I, fig. 5

COLLECTION:
Constance B. and Carroll L. Cartwright

This superb self-portrait turned up at an auction in London in 1969 and was acquired by Roland, Browse & Delbanco. One of the partners at this art gallery, Lillian Browse, thinks she can remember that there was a companion piece depicting Van Dongen's wife Guus Preitinger. Not a single trace has been found of this work. In the self-portrait, the 23-year old artist gave himself a searching gaze, thereby achieving a somewhat reserved look. The way the artist has selected to frame the composition places all the emphasis on the eye. The composition seems to have been chosen in this way from the outset: the watercolour and ink on the picture runs over the edges of the sheet and was therefore not cut out later. The artist has also given the entire work a finishing frame, also in watercolour (concealed by the passe-partout). The portrait could have been made for a special occasion, like the World Exhibition in Paris of 1900, but nothing is known to corroborate this. References to the self-portrait have not been found in letters or other documents. The fairly fluent brush technique used, with watered-down ink and watercolour, was increasingly taking the place of chalk drawing around that time. It is a more expressive technique which was easy to reproduce, and perhaps Van Dongen was influenced in his choice by the ink drawings of artists like Pierre Bonnard or Félix Vallotton which he would have seen in the illustrated periodicals of the time. The drawings which Van Dongen subsequently produced in 1901 for *La Revue Blanche* and *L'Assiette au Beurre* are also mainly designed in ink, filled in with watercolour and chalk.

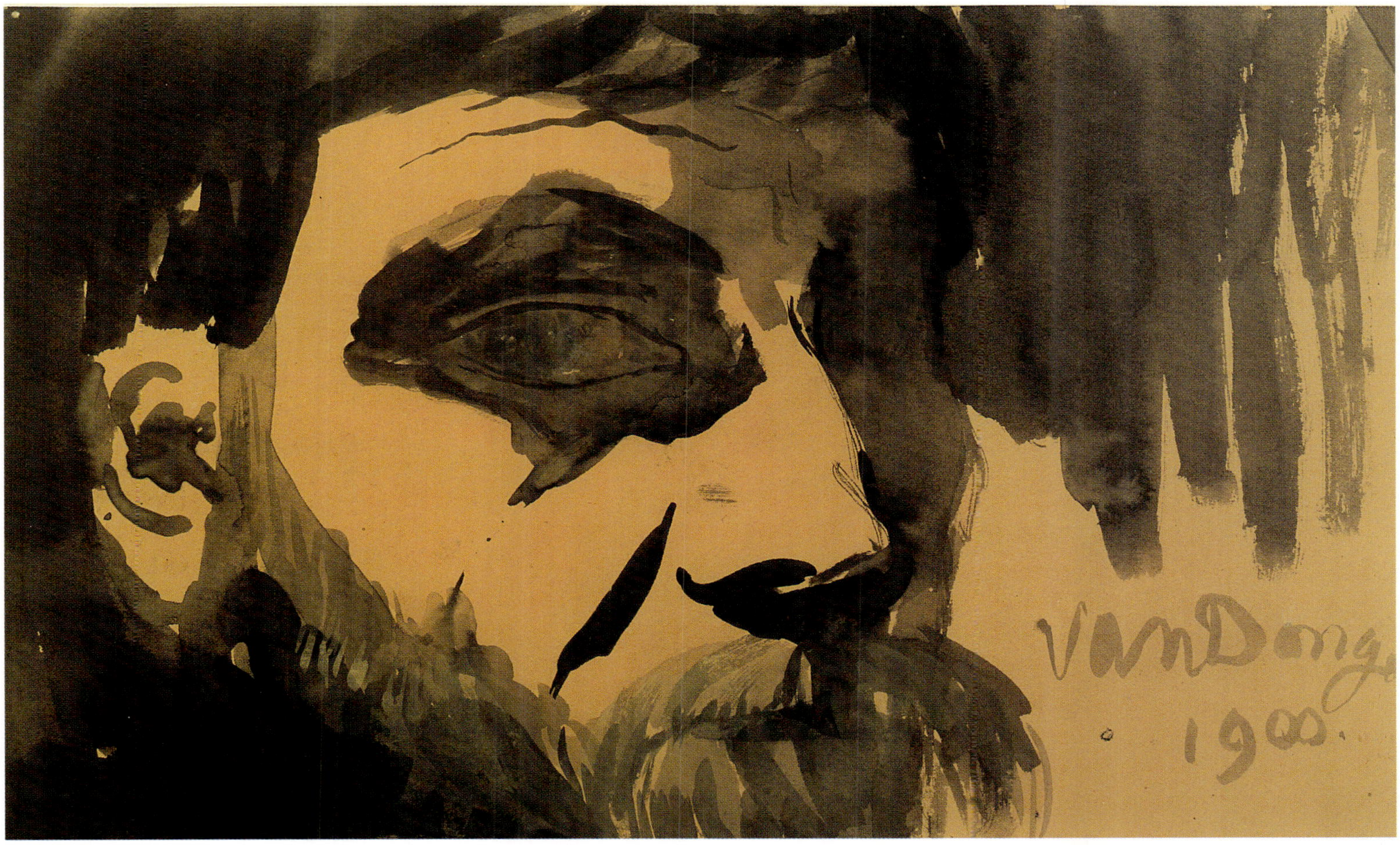

26. *Self-portrait*, 1900

27. *La nuit, Paris* (Night, Paris), c. 1900-1901
Black chalk, brush in black ink, grey wash, watercolour, gouache accents
267 x 450 mm (present size)
Signed lower left in brush with white gouache: *van Dongen.*
On reverse of frame in pen: *Maxwell Galleries*

PROVENANCE:
Maxwell Galleries, San Francisco; Donald D. and Sybil Harrington, Phoenix; Phoenix Art Museum, Phoenix 1964 (gift of D. and S. Harrington)

LITERATURE:
Harithas 1965, pp. 39-40 (fig.)

COLLECTION:
Phoenix Art Museum, Phoenix, Inv. 64.222

1. De Bodt 1995, p. 148.
2. Rearick 1985, passim, esp. pp. 164-166; Ives 1989, pp. 130-134.

In *La nuit, Paris* passers-by can be seen late at night on a dimly-lit square or a city park with only a few bare trees and a kiosk for adornment. The figures are like silhouettes on a wash background, placed on the paper over a cursory contour line in black chalk like stains, *taches*. Then one part is given more detail using an occasional dab of colour and a brushstroke.[1] The fact that some areas have not been filled in any further strengthens the effect of movement which is also suggested by Van Dongen's use of a few well-chosen strokes of chalk. At the time this was a tried and tested stylistic device. This sort of street scene with lamplight emanating dimly into the night is a direct reminder of depictions by artists like Steinlen and Siebe ten Cate, whose drawings Van Dongen knew well. This type of scene has associations with a whole group of works which have the city and its population as their theme. It is a genre which enjoyed increasing popularity at the end of the nineteenth century, greatly influenced by the increase in the number of foreign visitors drawn to Paris by the World Exhibition and the entertainment in Montmartre.[2] Van Dongen, however, did not portray the joyous side of modern city life, he was more attracted by the low life; some of the passers-by out late are prostitutes; those putting up the festive lights are malnourished labourers; the *forains*, circus folk, are pallid lonely figures illuminated only by the pale evening light. This type of drawing showing Van Dongen's interest in the emission of a limited source of light was also produced in Rotterdam during his following visit to the Netherlands. (fig.)
The sheet, *La nuit, Paris* is part of a generous donation made by Mr and Mrs Donald D. Harrington to the Phoenix Museum of Art which also includes works by Monet, Degas, Camille Pissarro, Redon, Bonnard, Marquet, Dufy and Derain.

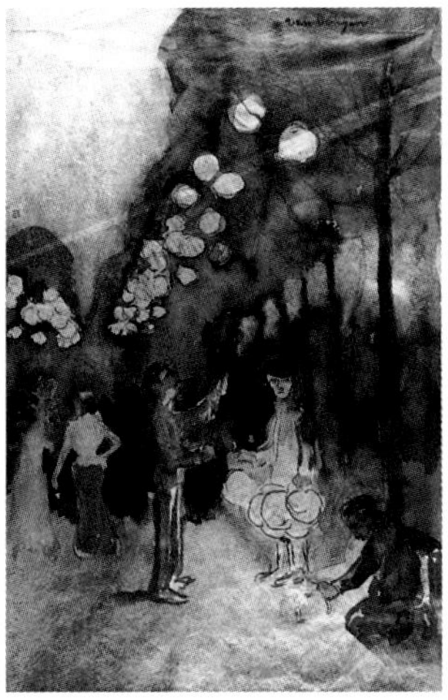

La fête à Montmartre, c. 1901
Watercolour, 450 x 275 mm

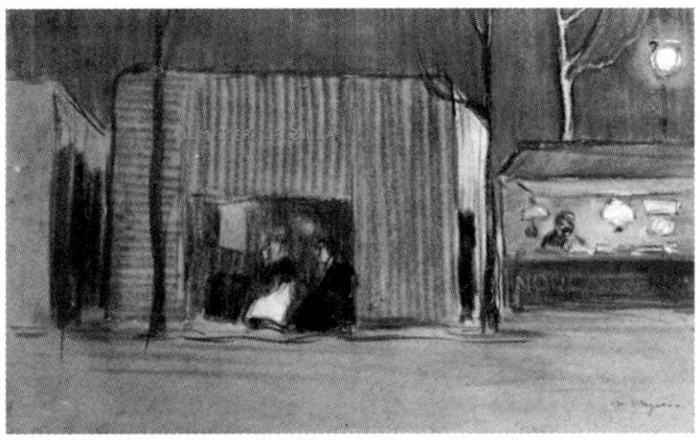

Baraque foraine, c. 1901
Black and coloured chalk, 265 x 450 mm

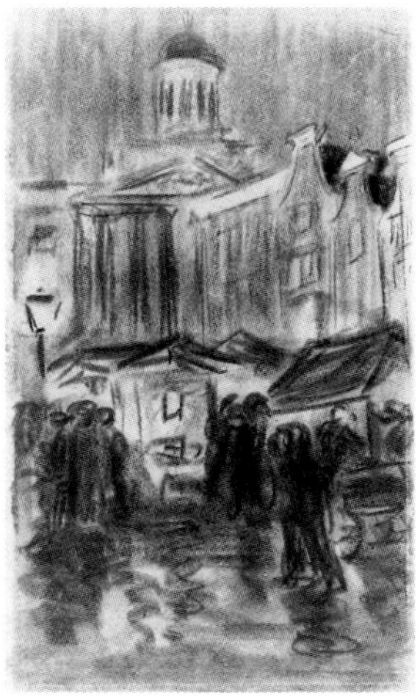

View of the Botersloot and the town hall, 1901
Black and coloured chalk, watercolour, 450 x 274 mm
GA Rotterdam, Rotterdam

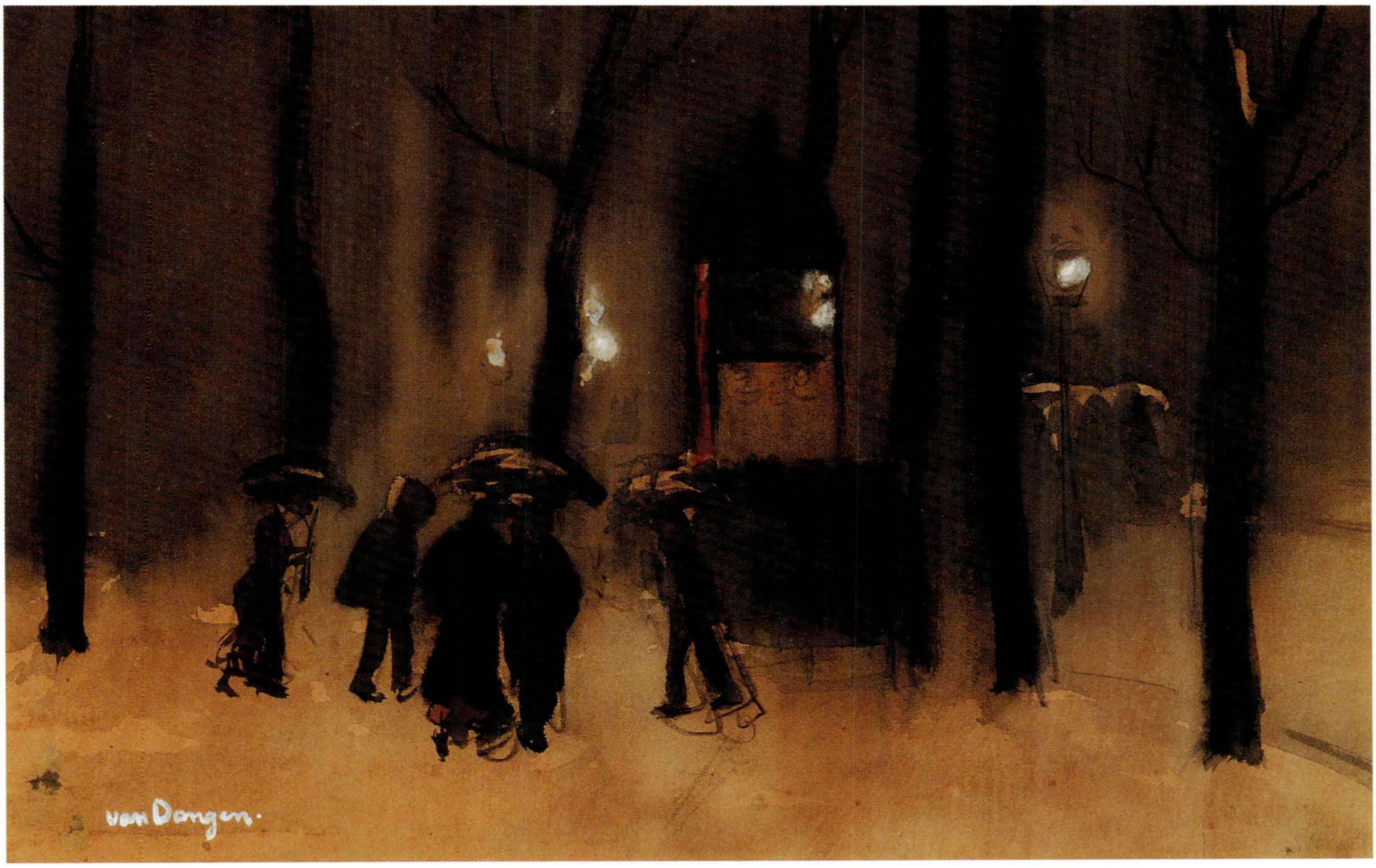

27. *La nuit, Paris*, c. 1900-1901

28. *Feesten-Amsterdam. Het Singel*
(Festive Amsterdam. The Singel), 1901
Pen and brush with black ink over pencil sketch, corrections in white gouache
203 x 128 mm
Signed lower right in pen with black ink: *v.Dong*; annotated lower left in grey ink: *Amsterdam/5 maart 1901/Singel.*
Annotated on reverse in pen with black ink: *Amsterdam (fêtes)/5 mars 01.*
Special features: 2 small cards have been preserved with the 8 drawings on this subject, bearing the annotation in blue chalk: *Elseviers Maandschrift feesten-Amsterdam n° 1.*; and: *Elseviers Maandschrift feesten-Amsterdam n° 2*
PROVENANCE:
Jean François van Royen (1878-1942), The Hague; private collection
COLLECTION:
Private collection

29. *Feesten-Amsterdam. De koets*
(Festive Amsterdam. The coach), 1901
Pen and brush with black ink over sketch in blue chalk
128 x 203 mm
Signed lower right in brush with black ink: *v.Dongen.*
PROVENANCE:
Jean François van Royen (1878-1942), The Hague; private collection
COLLECTION:
Private collection

30. *Feesten-Amsterdam. Wij fiere feest*
(Festive Amsterdam. We make merry), 1901
Pen and brush with black ink over pencil sketch, white gouache
223 x 128 mm
Signed lower right in brush with black ink: *vDongen.*; annotated below in pen with black ink: *Wij fiere feest zoo as 't nog nooit in Holland is gewees.*; in pencil on the window: *FIJNE VLEESWAREN*; at the top in pencil: *Wij fiere feest zoo as 't nog nooit in Holland is gewees.*
PROVENANCE:
Jean François van Royen (1878-1942), The Hague; private collection
COLLECTION:
Private collection

The young Queen Wilhelmina became officially engaged on the 16 October 1900 to Duke Hendrik van Mecklenburg, whom she married on 7 February 1901 in the Hague. The celebrations paying tribute to the royal couple took place in Amsterdam from 5 to 9 March 1901 and commenced with a festive entry into an illuminated city. According to a newspaper report, Van Dongen was commissioned at the beginning of 1901 by *Elsevier's Geïllustreerd Maandschrift* to make 12 to 15 drawings of the festivities for the newspaper at a fee of eighty guilders. For this purpose Van Dongen stayed in Amsterdam for about a week, after which he returned to his address in Scheveningen to complete the drawings. This is confirmed in a postcard dated 15 March: 'Before the 18th the Elsevier drawings must be ready. I am therefore extremely busy at the moment.'[1] The illustration-drawings were handed in on time, but it would appear from a report about the legal action which followed (as a result of non-payment) that the editor, the artist Philippe Zilcken, had rejected the drawings and that they were therefore not placed.[2] Fortunately eight of them have been preserved. (fig.) The subjects they represent, which primarily concern the entry parade and the illuminations, suggest they are the first of the series. The drawings are all made with pen and brush in black ink over a cursory design in pencil or blue chalk on light beige paper. The sketches of the women are charming, sheltering under their umbrellas, showing a characteristic gesture of the hand as they try to prevent their skirts getting wet; the groups of musicians and singers on the streets have the same appeal. The smooth scrawls show with what dexterity Van Dongen could already put together scenes like *De gouden koets* (The golden coach) and with what ease he typified the merrymakers. He introduced variations to his ink technique as the dry rubbing on the skirts shows.

1.
Postcard to G. Preitinger, postmarked 16 March 1901, private collection.
2.
Het Nieuws van den Dag, c. 10 and 25 January 1902.

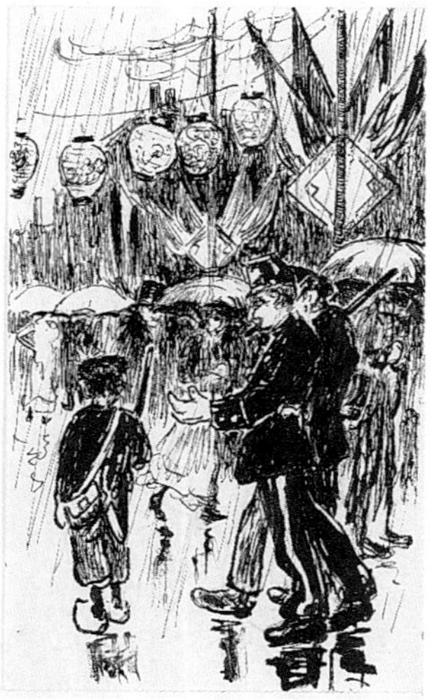

Police and crowds, 1901
Pen and brush in black ink, blue chalk,
203 x 127 mm

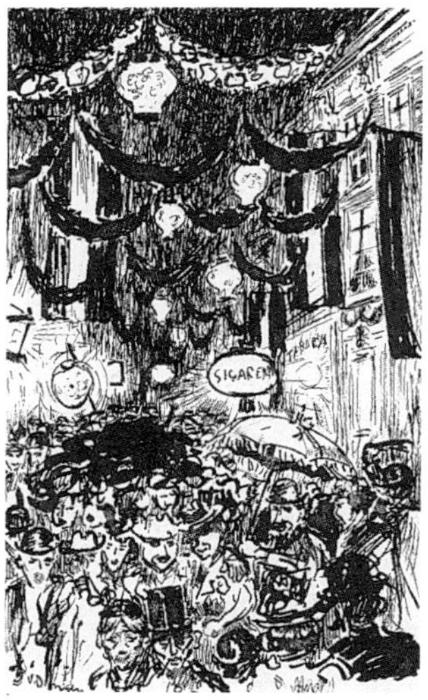

Kalverstraat decorated, 1901
Pen and brush in black ink, blue chalk,
203 x 127 mm

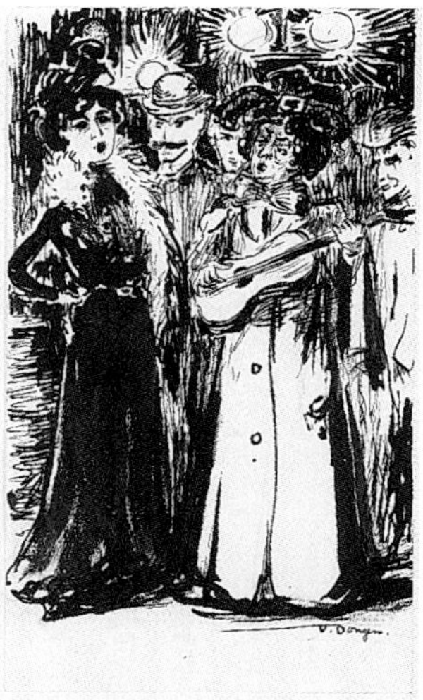

Groups of musicians, 1901
Pen and brush in black ink,
204 x 127 mm

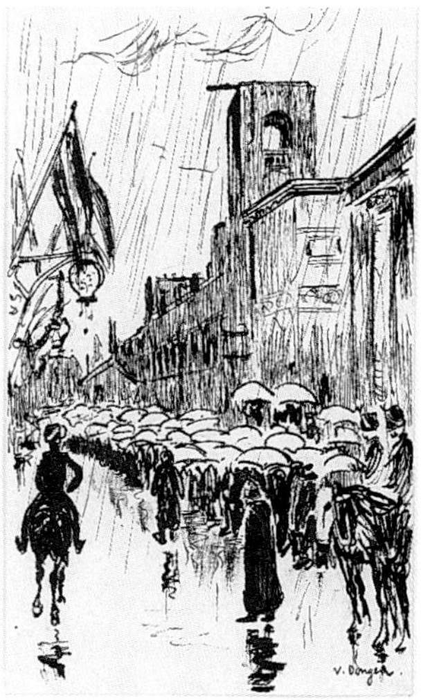

Crowds near the exchange, 1901
Pen and brush in black ink, blue chalk,
203 x 127 mm

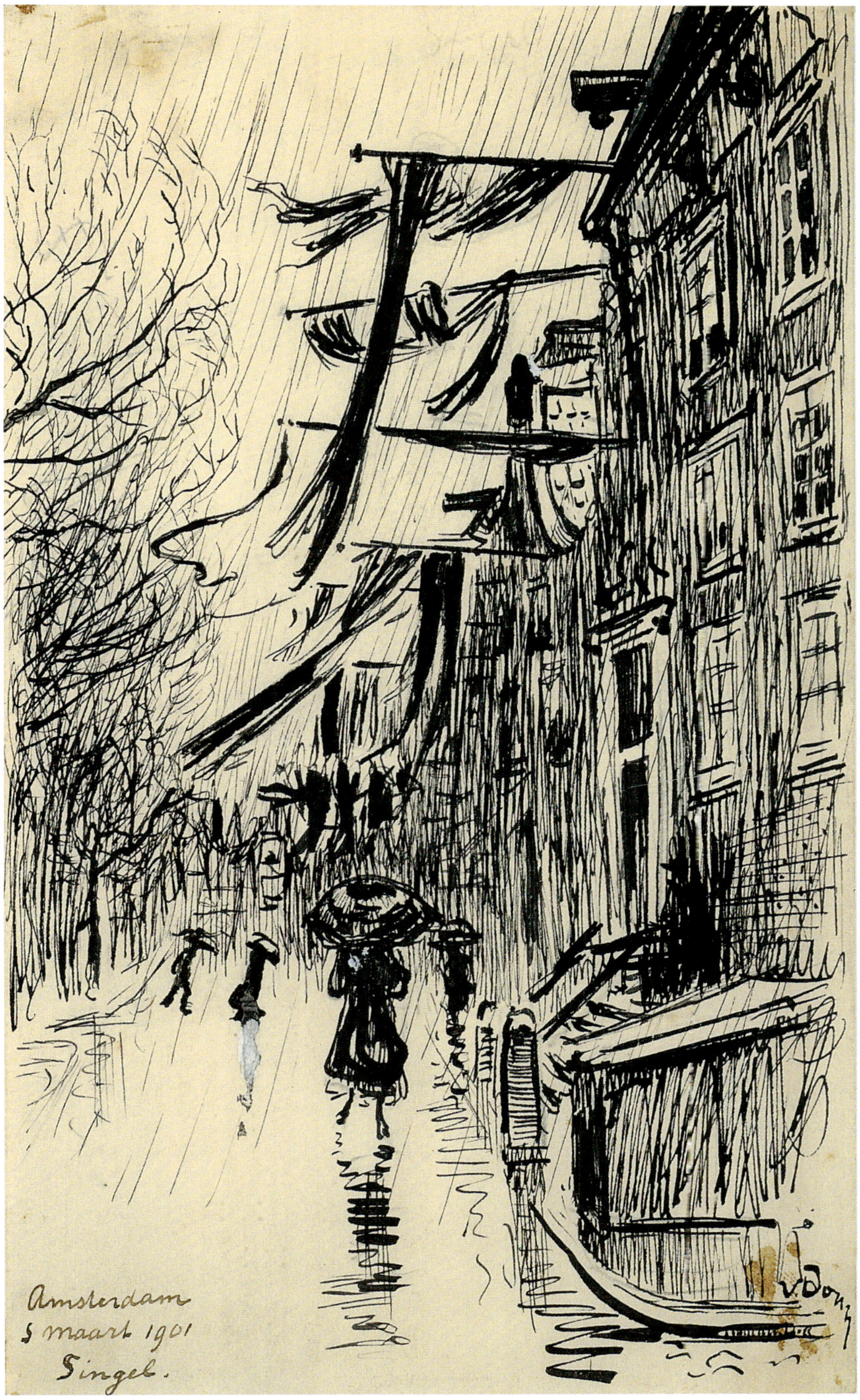

28. *Festive-Amsterdam. Het Singel*, 1901

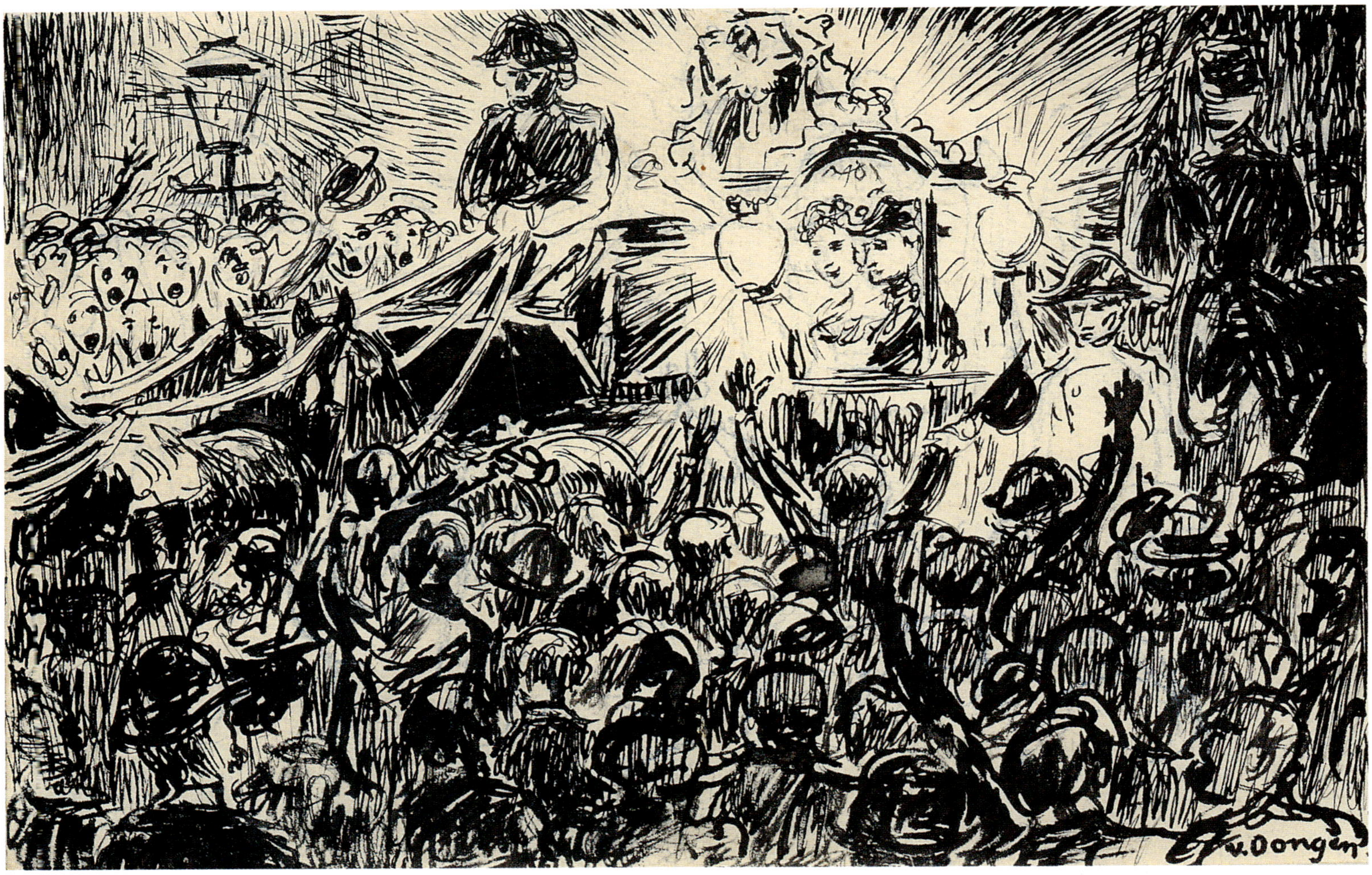

29. *Festive-Amsterdam. The coach*, 1900

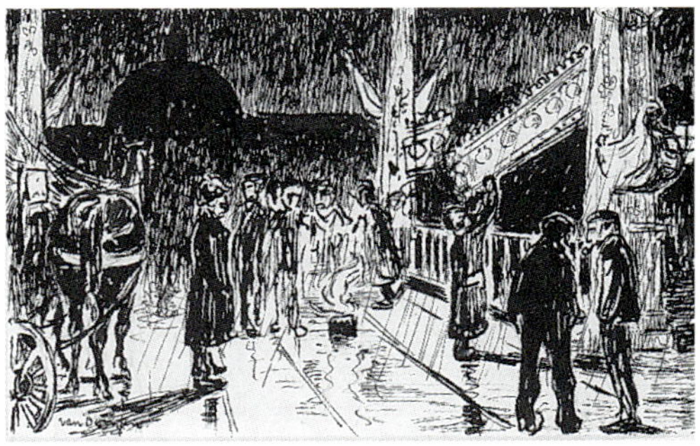

Decorations, 1901
Pen and brush in black ink, pencil, 128 x 203 mm

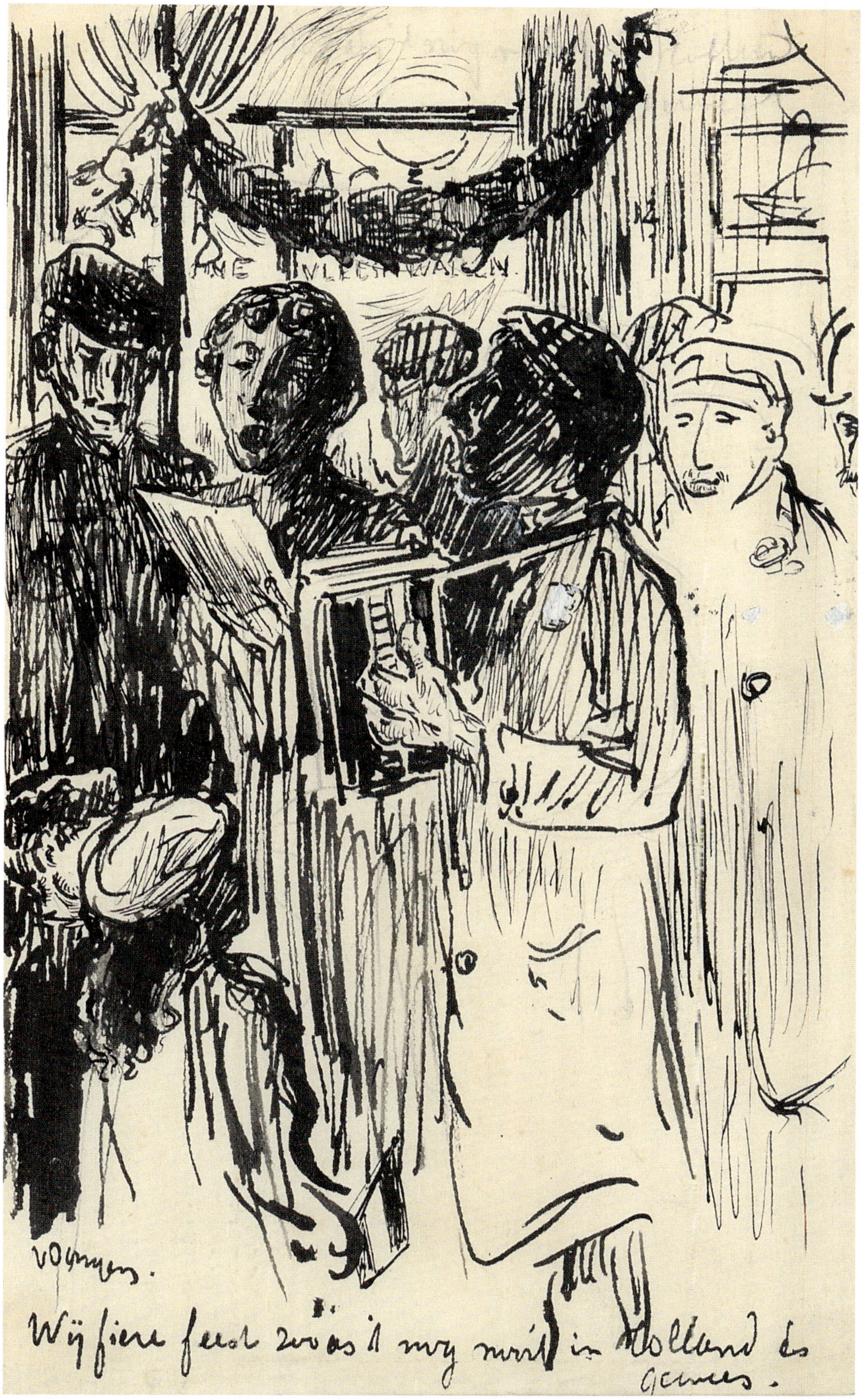

30. *Festive-Amsterdam. We make merry*, 1901

31. *Portret van de vader van de kunstenaar*
(Portrait of the artist's father), Jan van Dongen (1838-1921)
1901
Black chalk, grey wash, watercolour
446 x 265 mm
Signed lower right in black chalk: *v Dongen*; blue chalk on reverse of cardboard to which the drawing is attached: *35*

PROVENANCE:
Boymans Museum, Rotterdam, 1936 (gift of the artist; letter from Kees van Dongen to D. Hannema, 7 December 1936, GA Rotterdam)

EXHIBITIONS:
1907 Amsterdam, C.M. van Gogh, no. 42; 1940 Rotterdam, no. 65

LITERATURE:
Hannema 1937, p. 10; Hannema 1973, p. 48; Boymans Museum Annual Report 1937, p. 7

COLLECTION:
Boijmans Van Beuningen Museum, Rotterdam, Inv. KVD 1

32. *Portret van zijn vader* (Portrait of his father)
Jan van Dongen (1838-1921)
1901
Oil on canvas
65.5 x 80 cm
Signed lower left: *van Dongen.*
On reverse of lining canvas attached in 1995, annotation in grey oil: *Portrait de/Jan van Dongen*; blue chalk upper left: *56.* Signed and numbered on the stretcher in grey: *Kees van Dongen/n°2*; a black-printed label: *BERNHEIM JEUNE & CIE/Experts près de la Cour d'Appel/25, Boulevard de la Madeleine/36, Avenue de l'Opéra et 15, Rue Richepanse/N°*; marked in pen with brown ink: *13 du catalogue/Kees Van Dongen/"Portrait"*; later handwriting in pencil: *1902*; a black-printed label: *GALERIE CHARPENTIER/76 FAUBOURG SAINT-HONORE-PARIS/EXPOSITION/VAN DONGEN/CINQUANTE ANS DE PEINTURE/-MCMXLII-*; remains of label marked with ballpoint pen: *Anc. Coll. Romain Coolus*

PROVENANCE:
Romain Coolus (1868-1952), Paris; Pierre Monart, c. 1960; Auction, Enghien-les-Bains (Champin, Lombrail), 23 June 1985, no. 266; private collection

EXHIBITIONS:
1904 Paris, Vollard, no. 17; 1906 Rotterdam, RKK, no. 55; 1908 Paris, Bernheim-Jeune, no. 13; 1942 Paris, Charpentier, no. 1

COLLECTION:
Private collection

In the Boijmans Van Beuningen Museum Collection is to be found a finely drawn portrait of the artist's father, Johannes van Dongen, depicted with a full beard and a pipe in his mouth. It appears to be a preliminary study for a painted version which was created in February-March 1901. This becomes clear from a postcard Van Dongen sent to Guus Preitinger from Rotterdam on the 2nd March 1901: 'je suis en train de peindre le portrait de mon père. Ça marche bien!'[1] The painting was then first exhibited in 1904 at Galerie Vollard and is dated to 1901 in the accompanying catalogue. At the following solo exhibition of Van Dongen's in 1906 at the Rotterdam Kunstkring in Rotterdam, the portrait was shown once again. The number 56 which has been put on the back of the canvas in blue chalk would appear to refer to this exhibition. This comes to light from a letter Van Dongen sent to a member of the Board of the Kunstkring for this event on 14 May 1906 in which he had enclosed a numbered hand-written list of the exhibits: 'the numbers [on the list] are in blue chalk on the back of the things [the paintings].'[2]

It was not the first, and by no means the last, portrait that Van Dongen painted of his father. An early likeness, with a Rembrandtesque fall of light, was created around 1894. In 1907 and 1909 two more portraits followed: the first, the father in a striped shirt, is painted somewhat in the manner of Van Gogh; the second is a more monumental portrait in a splendid cobalt-blue and light grey colour scheme. In all these depictions made after 1900 the coarse hands of the maltster and the long full beard are a dominant element in the composition. The portraits are evidence of the respect Van Dongen felt for his father and the bond that existed between them. This emerges from several other sources too. In a conversation about an exhibition in 1949, Van Dongen asserted that he took after his father most of all, whom he furthermore called revolutionary, but 'not quite enough to follow his own insights.'[3] The master explained to Paul Guth: 'Everything I know, I know because of my father.'[4] Jan van Dongen is said to have been an amateur draughtsman himself.[5]

1.
Postcard to G. Preitinger, postmarked 2 March 1901, private collection.

2.
Letter to Mej. S. Plate, 14 May 1906, RKK Archives, Rotterdam.

3.
Wereldkroniek, 2 July 1949.

4.
Guth 1949, p. 134. 'Tout ce que je sais, je le sais par mon père'

5.
H.P. Aletrino, 'Exhibition in Boymans on Kees van Dongen. Homage to a great son'. *Algemeen Handelsblad*, 8 December 1967.

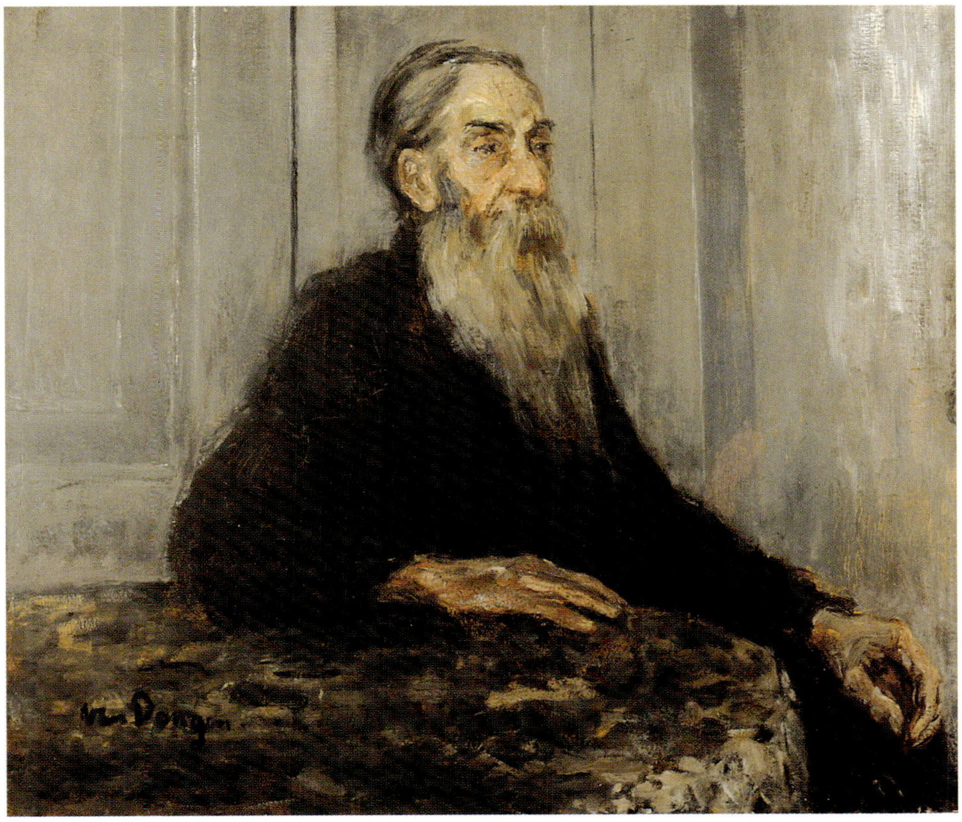

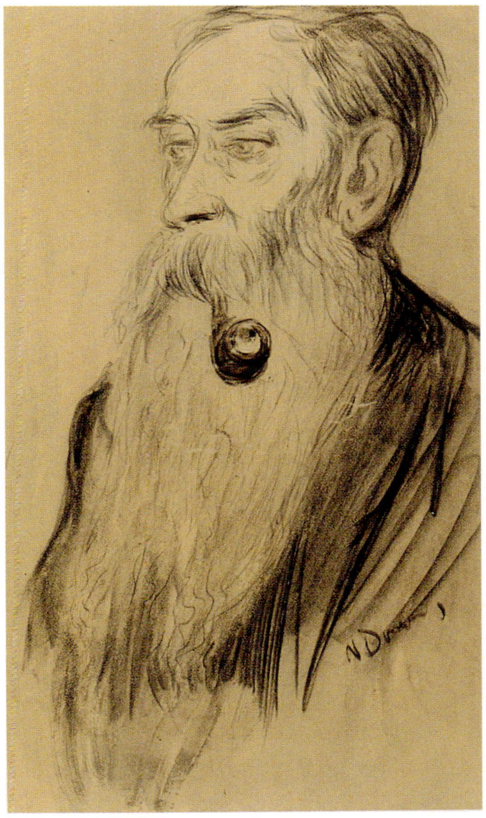

32. *Portrait of his father Jan van Dongen (1838-1921)*, 1901

31. *Portrait of the artist's father*
Jan van Dongen (1838-1921), 1901

33. *Femme vue de dos* (Woman viewed from back), 1901
Brush in black ink, black chalk
284 x 183 mm (present size)
Signed lower right with brush in black ink over signature in black chalk: *van Dongen.*
Special features: also known as *Elégante de dos* (Elegant woman from the back)
Drawing for vignette published in *La Revue Blanche*, vol. 25 (May-August) 1901, p. 615; reprinted in 1903, vol. 30 (January-April), p. 90
PROVENANCE:
Alexandre Natanson (1876-1936) Paris, 1901; auction Paris, Drouot (F. Lair Dubreuil), *Tableaux modernes, aquarelles, pastels...composant la collection Alexandre Natanson*, 16 May 1929, no. 65 (awarded to M. Marbeau); auction Paris, Drouot (Guy Loudmer), *Importants tableaux modernes*, 20 November 1988, no. 103 (fig.); private collection, Paris
COLLECTION:
Private collection, Paris

34. *L'escalier de l'Opéra* (Staircase at the Opera House), 1901
Black chalk, brush in black ink
312 x 272 mm
Signed lower right in black chalk and brush in black ink: *van Dongen.*
Special features: also known as *L'entrée du café concert* (Entrance to the café-concert) and *Soirée à l'Opéra* (Evening at the Opera)
Illustration for *La Revue Blanche*, 1901, vol. 25 (15 July), p. 465; reprinted in 1901, vol. 26 (15 September), p. 144
PROVENANCE:
Alexandre Natanson (1876-1936) Paris, 1901; auction Paris, Drouot (F. Lair Dubreuil), *Tableaux modernes, aquarelles, pastels...composant la collection Alexandre Natanson*, 16 May 1929, no. 64 (awarded to M. Manuel); auction Paris, Drouot (H. Baudoin), *Livres modernes et anciens, tableaux anciens...provenant des collections de Messieurs M..F...*, 25 April 1931, no. 88; auction Paris, Drouot (Arcole), *Dessins, tableaux modernes, sculptures*, 11-12 April 1989, no. 64 (fig.); Kunsthandel Ivo Bouwman BV, The Hague; Stoppenbach & Delestre, London, 1989
EXHIBITIONS:
1989 London, Stoppenbach & Delestre, no. 26 (fig.); 1995 New York, no. 35
COLLECTION:
Private collection

35. *Au bal de l'Opéra* (At the opera ball), 1901
Black chalk, pen and brush in black ink
322 x 245 mm
Signed lower left with brush in black ink: *van Dongen.*
Special features: blind-stamped watermark below: *VIDALON FILS*; also known as *La soirée* (The soiree)
PROVENANCE:
Alexandre Natanson (1876-1936) Paris, 1901; auction Paris, Drouot (F. Lair Dubreuil), *Tableaux modernes, aquarelles, pastels...collection Alexandre Natanson*, 16 May 1929, no. 68; auction Paris, Drouot (H. Baudoin), *Livres modernes et anciens, tableaux anciens...collections de Messieurs M..F...*, 25 April 1931, no. 91; P. Boisson, Chartres; auction Paris, Drouot (O. Rieunier, I. Bailly-Pommery), *Dessins et tableaux anciens, dessins et tableaux modernes...*, 23 March 1993, no. 27 (fig.); auction London, Sotheby's, *Impressionist and modern art...*, 13 October 1993, no. 38 (fig.); private collection
COLLECTION:
Private collection

Van Dongen made a total of five illustrations for the periodical *La Revue Blanche*. Four of them were spread over a number of issues. (fig.) The first of the series, *L'Escalier de l'Opéra* appeared in the 15 July 1901 issue. The drawing which was not published, *Au bal de l'Opéra*, was specified as belonging to the group when the collection of Alexandre Natanson was auctioned in 1929. The representations are drawn with pen and brush in black ink on smooth white paper and were reduced to a third of their original size using a zincographic procedure before being printed in the newspaper.

Three of the sheets have the traditional *Bals de l'Opéra* as their theme. These carnival balls would seem to have been held at court from the beginning of the fourteenth century, and after a few interruptions, including the period of the French revolution, were reintroduced in the nineteenth century and became known as *Bals de l'Opéra*.[1] In the final quarter of that century the festivities took place in the new Opéra building by Charles Garnier. This included four evenings of festivities in total: two as a prelude to the official long period of fasting in Lent, a third during the Carnival days, and the last during the semi-fasting period (*mi-carême*).[2] The fancy-dress balls were famous for the temporary liaisons formed between high-class gentlemen and women of easy virtue. For the latter, the *domino*, a long coat was advisable (to conceal identity), as was wearing a mask or a so-called *loup*, a lace veil to hide the face. It was customary for many of the rendezvous to take place on the steps of the Opéra building. This moment of encounter is rendered by Van Dongen in the *Revue Blanche* illustration. Subsequently Van Dongen devoted several independent drawings to this subject. (fig.) The only work not to show a ball is *L'avant-scene* which shows the Opéra instead. The drawing can be dated to 1902 on the basis of the style and signature.

1.
F. Duquesnel, 'Ressuscitons les Bals de l'Opéra', *Le Journal*, 4 April 1914; J. Landre, 'Les Bals de l'Opéra', *Touche à tout*, February 1914; Bulée 1900, II, pp. 181-182. See also Herbert 1988, pp. 130-132; Frèches 1991, pp. 206-07.
2.
S. (Snabilié), 'Letters from France', *Het Vaderland*, 11 March 1905.

36. *Devant l'Opéra* (In front of the Opera House), c. 1901
Black chalk, grey wash over entire sheet, watercolour, white gouache accents
277 x 450 mm
Signed lower right in brush with black ink over signature in blue chalk: *van Dongen*; annotated in blue chalk on reverse: *devant l'Opéra*
PROVENANCE:
Emma Hanken (1874-1911), c. 1901 (gift of the artist); private collection
EXHIBITIONS:
1949 Amsterdam, no. 13; 1967 Paris (Rotterdam, ex. catalogue)
COLLECTION:
Private collection

37. *Le domino* (The domino cloak), 1901
Black chalk, watercolour, brush with black ink, grey wash, white gouache
443 x 274 mm
Signed lower right in brush with black ink: *van Dongen.*; numbered on reverse of frame: 34
Special features: also known as *Personnages* (Characters) and *A l'Opéra* (At the Opera)
PROVENANCE:
Germaine Henry (1904-), Paris, before 1967; Musée d'Art Moderne de la Ville de Paris, Paris, June 1976 (gift of Germaine Henry, Robert Thomas)
EXHIBITIONS:
1908 Paris, Bernheim-Jeune, no. 72; 1912 Brussels, Giroux, 1952 Rennes, no. 46; 1967 Paris, no. 7 (fig.); 1976 Paris, no. 122 (fig.); 1981 Nice, no. 32
LITERATURE:
Diehl 1968, p. 23 (fig.)
COLLECTION:
Musée d'Art Moderne de la Ville de Paris, Paris, Inv. AMD 682

38. *Sortie de l'Opéra* (Leaving the Opera), 1901
Black chalk, watercolour, white gouache
459 x 270 mm
Signed lower centre with black chalk: *V.D-*; pencil: *564*.
Special features: the drawing is lined
PROVENANCE:
Galerie Deva Mbez, Paris; auction London, Sotheby's, *Impressionist and modern paintings...*, 22 February 1989, no. 44; art dealers' Frost & Reed, London, 1989 (Inv. D 166275); private collection, USA, 1992
EXHIBITIONS:
1989 London, Frost & Reed
COLLECTION:
Private collection, USA

39. *L'Avant-scène* (The Front Line), c. 1902
Brush with black ink, watercolour
450 x 280 mm
Signed lower centre in brush with black ink: *Kées*
Black-printed label on reverse of frame: *GALERIE RAPAIRE/ Le Continental, Place des Moulins MONTE-CARLO*; marked in typing: *Kees VAN DONGEN/"L'avant-scène"/Encre de Chine et gouache,/vers 1900/45 cm x 28 cm.*; label with typing: *V.D. 13* (Inv. Galerie Rapaire)
PROVENANCE:
Georges Rapaire, Monte-Carlo, 1962 (acquired from the artist); Galerie René Rapaire, Monte-Carlo, 1967; auction Paris, Palais Galliéra (G. Loudmer et al.), *Importants tableaux modernes*, 28 November 1971, no. 68 (fig.); auction London, Sotheby's, *Impressionist and modern drawings...*, 26 June 1985, no. 323 (fig.); auction Lokeren, Galerie De Vuyst, 19 October 1985, *Oude en moderne kunst*, 19 October 1985, no. 390 (fig.); auction Lokere, Galerie De Vuyst, *Oude en moderne kunst*, 18 October 1986, no. 421 (fig.); auction Lokeren, Galerie De Vuyst, *Oude en moderne kunst, dl 2*, 7 October 1989, no. 417 (fig.); auction Lokeren, Galerie De Vuyst, *Oude en moderne kunst, dl 2*, 16 March 1991, no. 426 (fig.)
COLLECTION:
Private collection

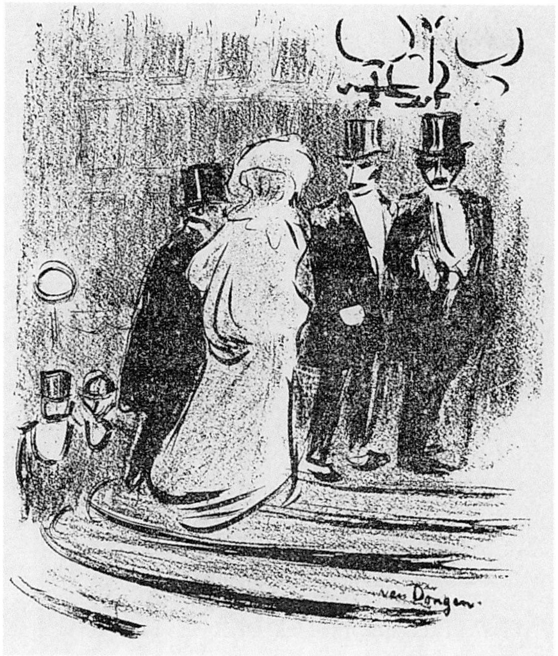

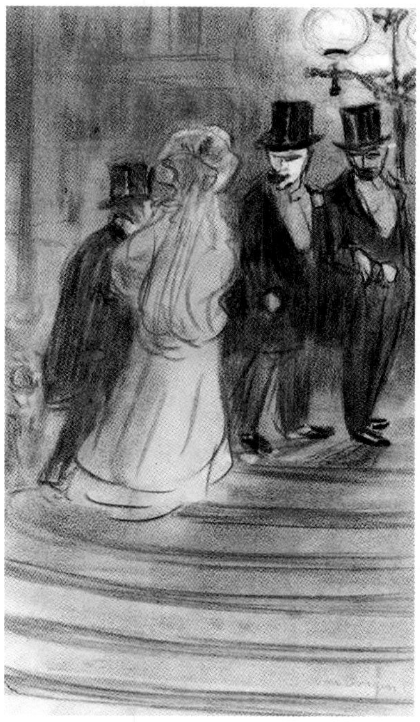

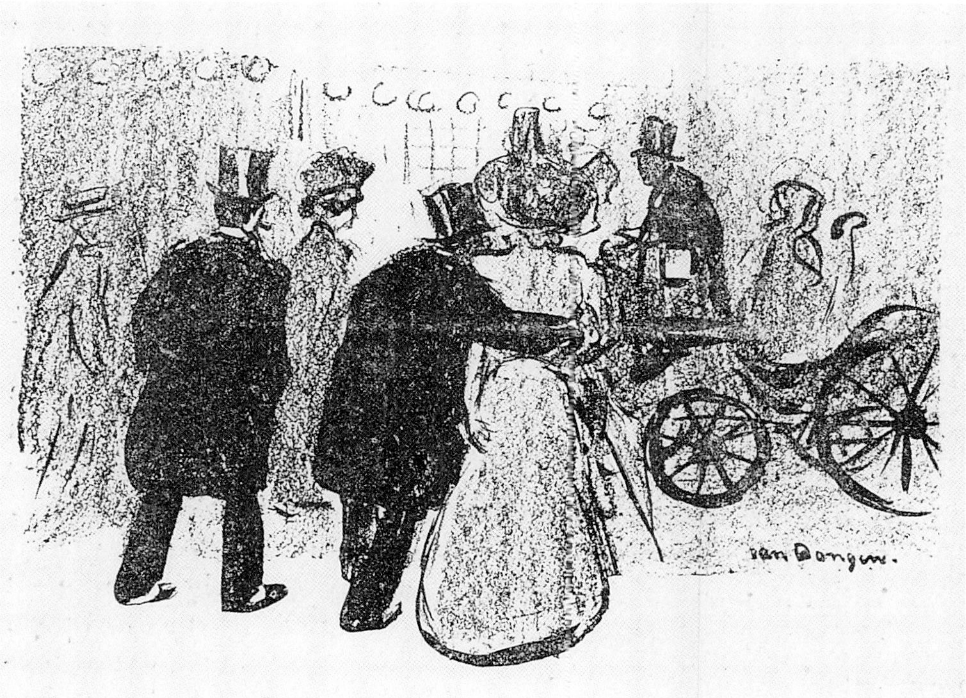

L'escalier de l'Opéra, 1901
Illustration in *La Revue Blanche*, 1901, vol. 25 (15 July), p. 465

Grand soirée à l'Opéra, 1901
Black chalk, watercolour, body colour, 425 x 245 mm

Le fiacre, 1901
Illustration in *La Revue Blanche*, 1901, vol. 25 (15 August), p. 625

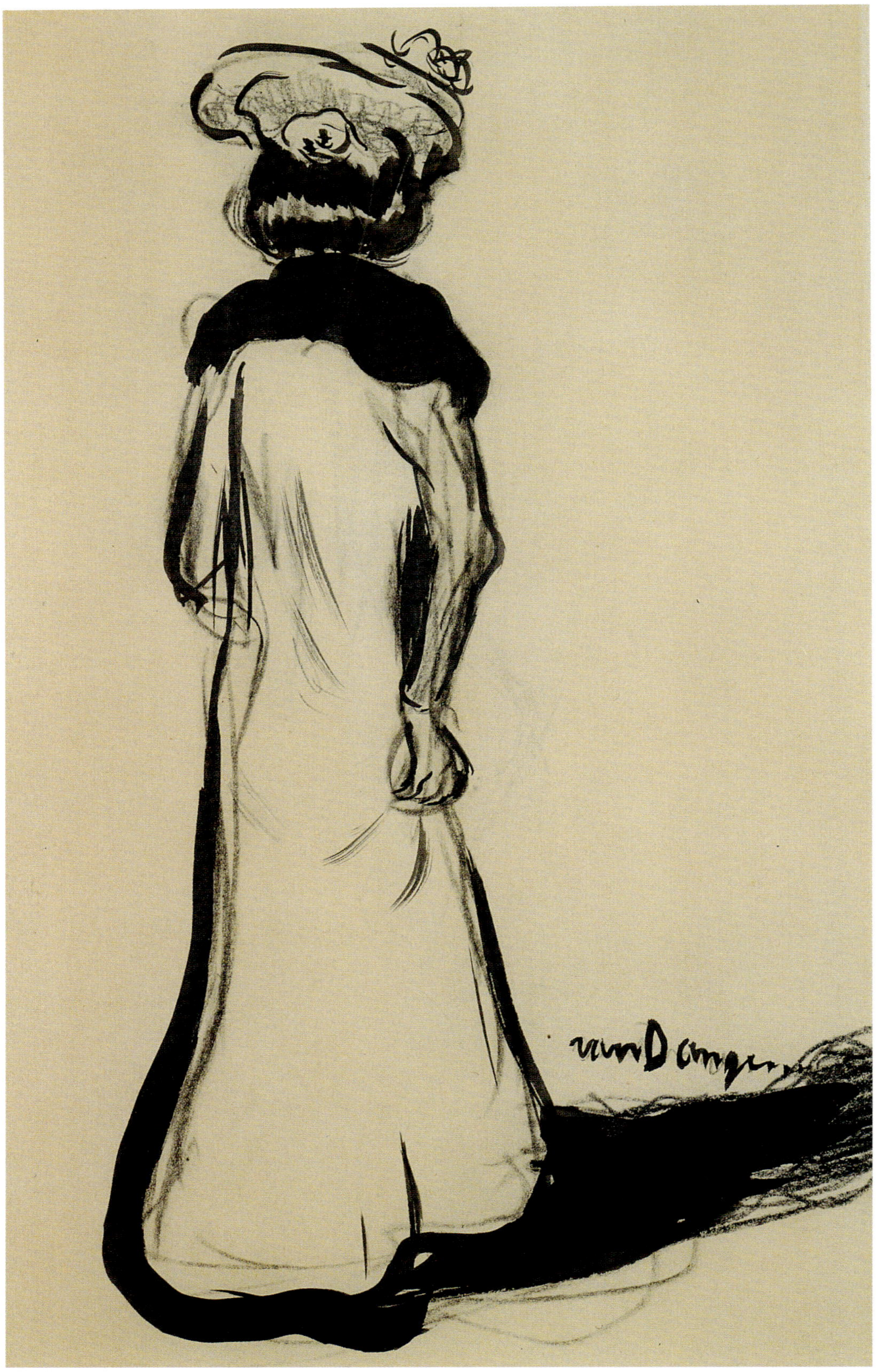

33. *Femme vue de dos*, 1901

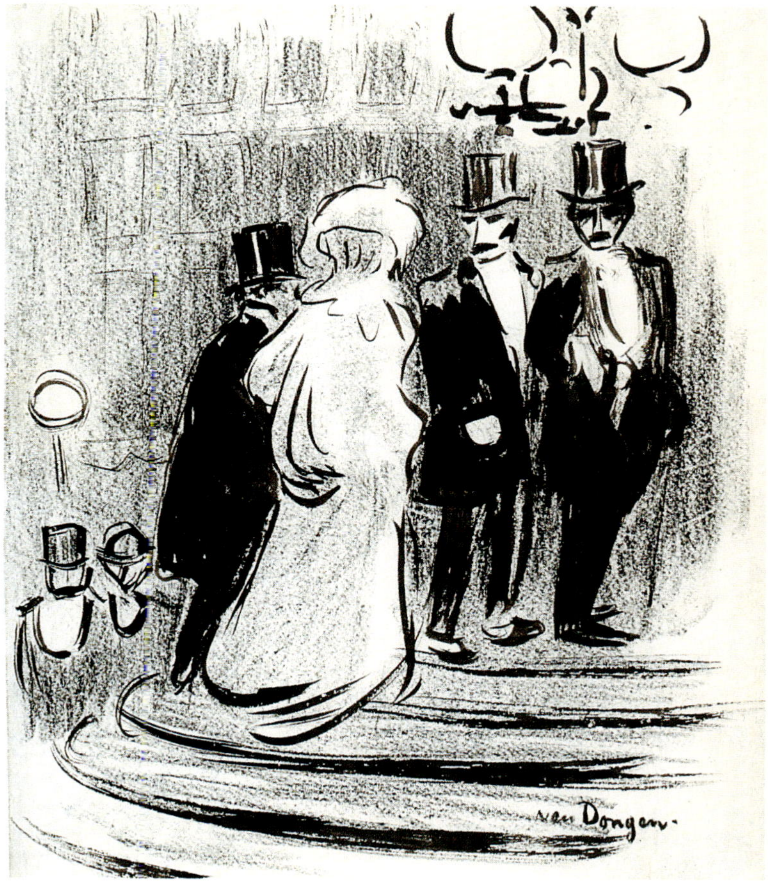

34. *L'escalier de l'Opéra*, 1901

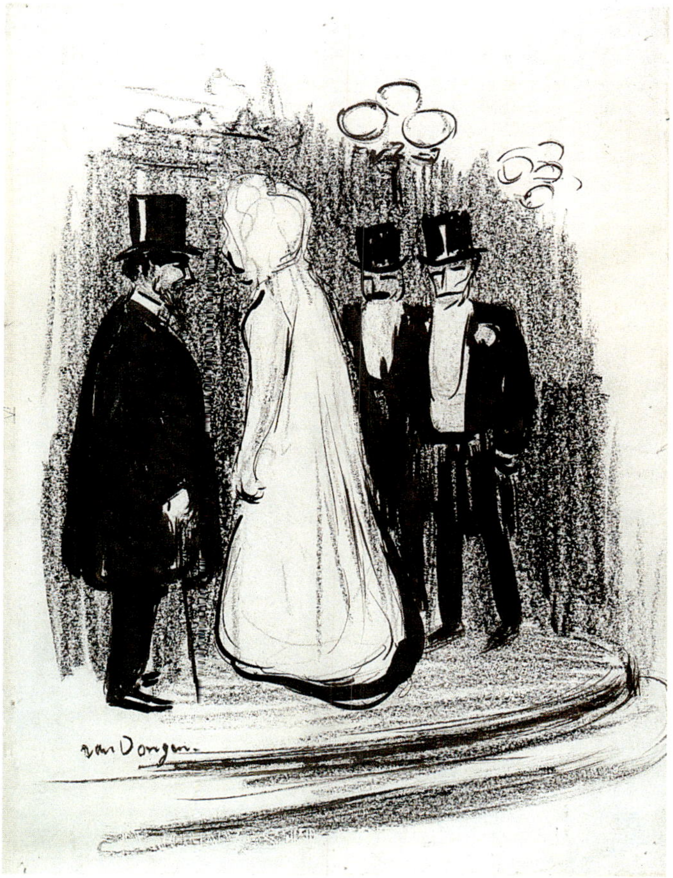

35. *Au bal de l'Opéra*, 1901

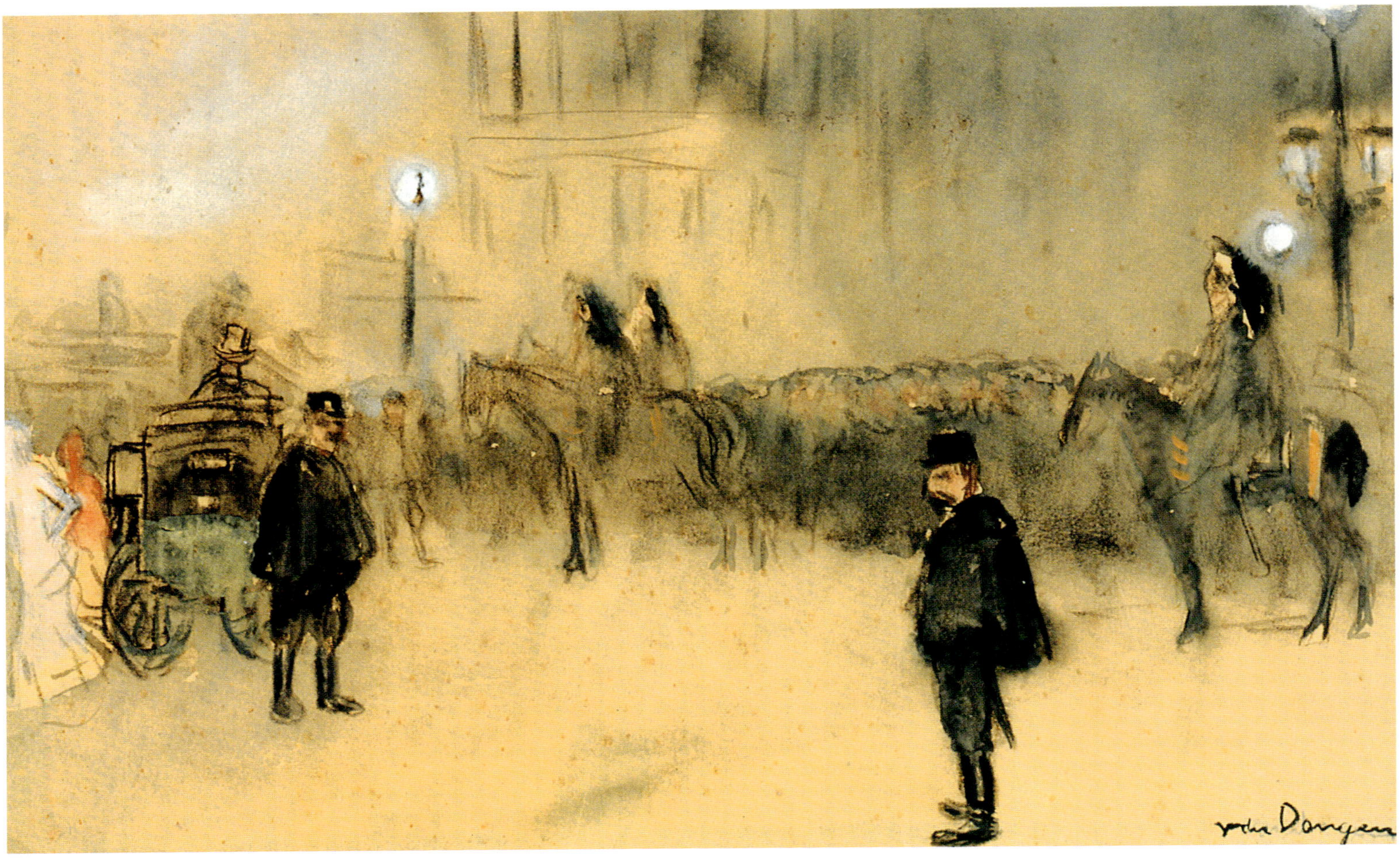

36. *Devant l'Opéra*, c. 1901

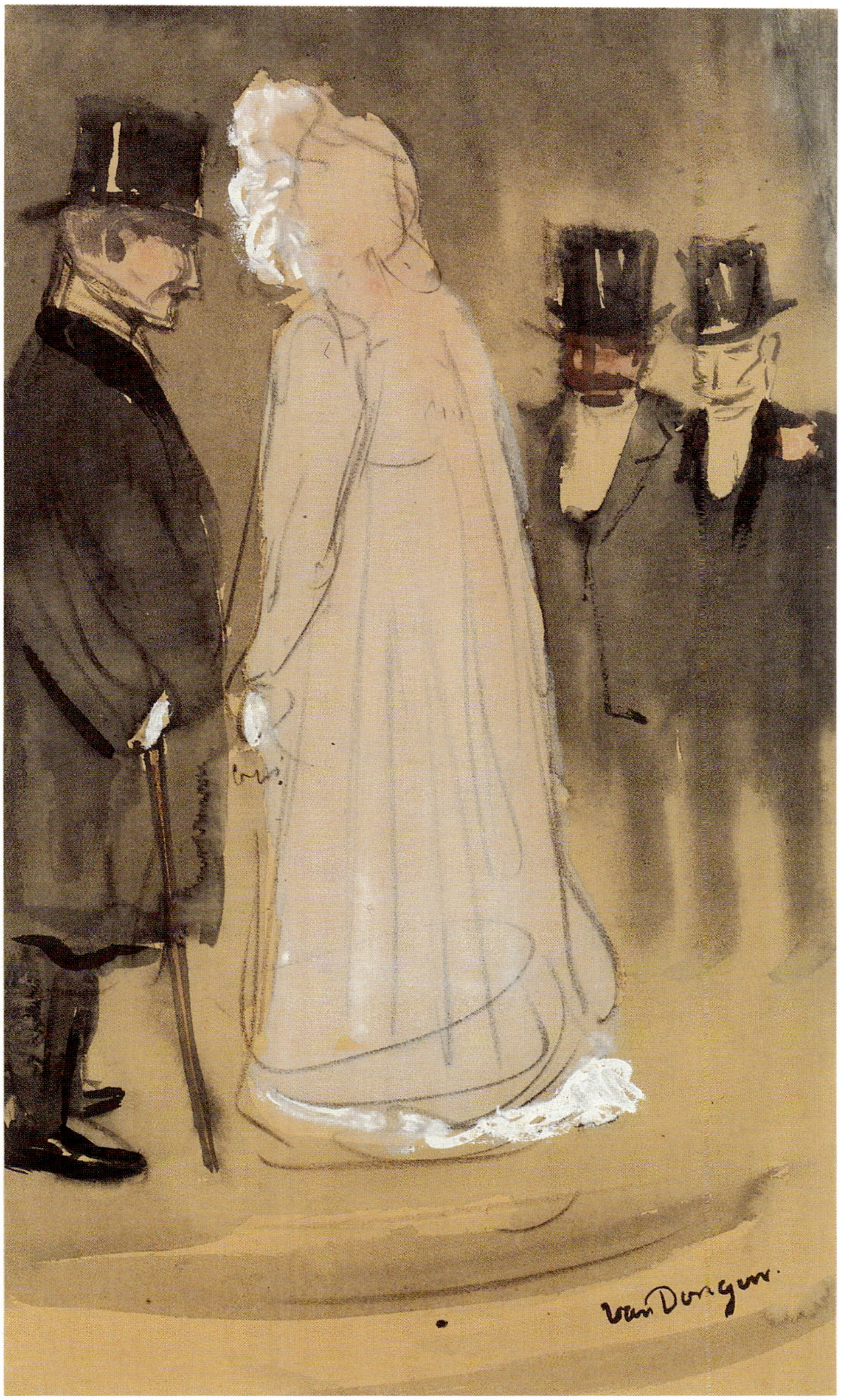

37. *Le domino*, 1901

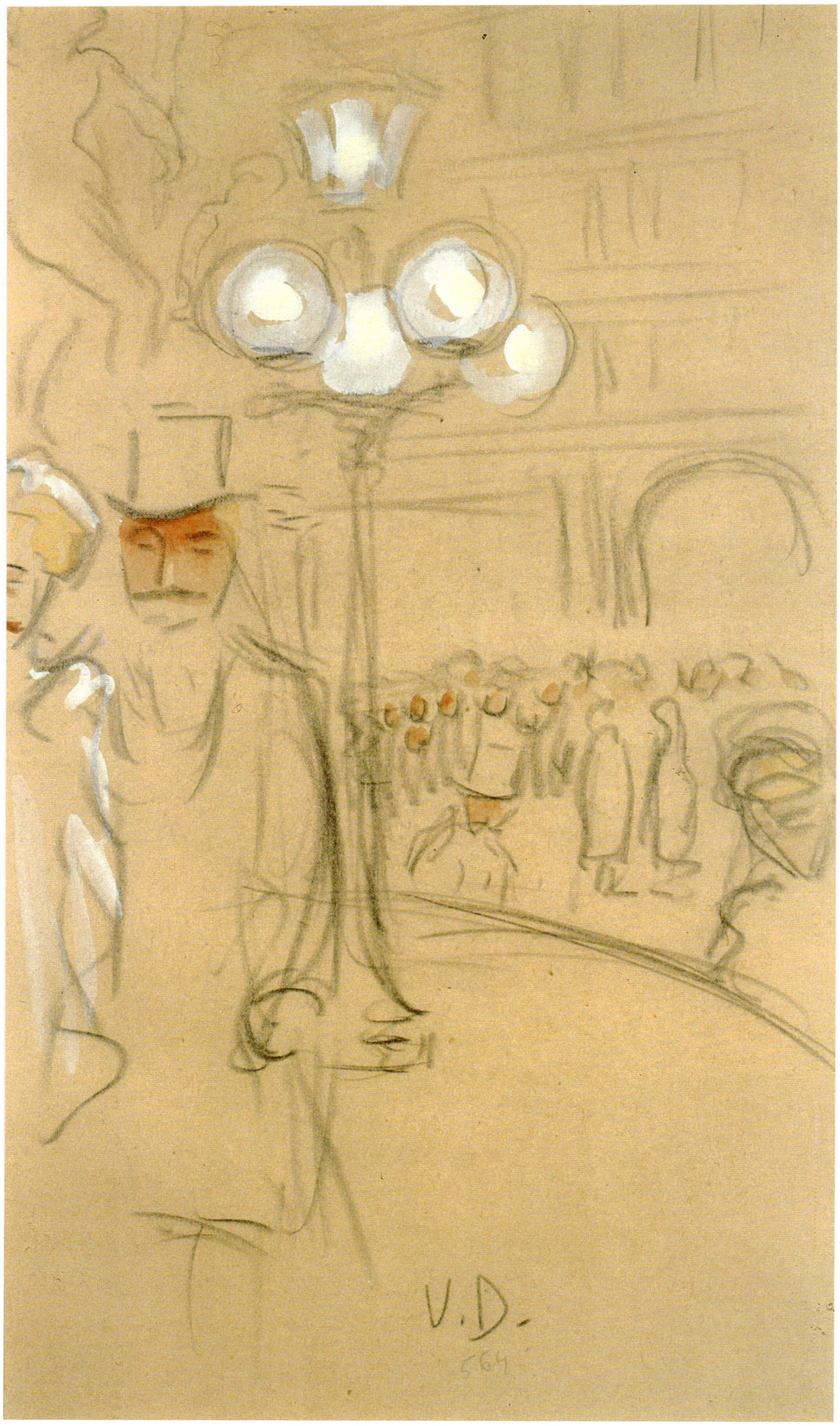

38. *Sortie de l'Opéra*, 1901

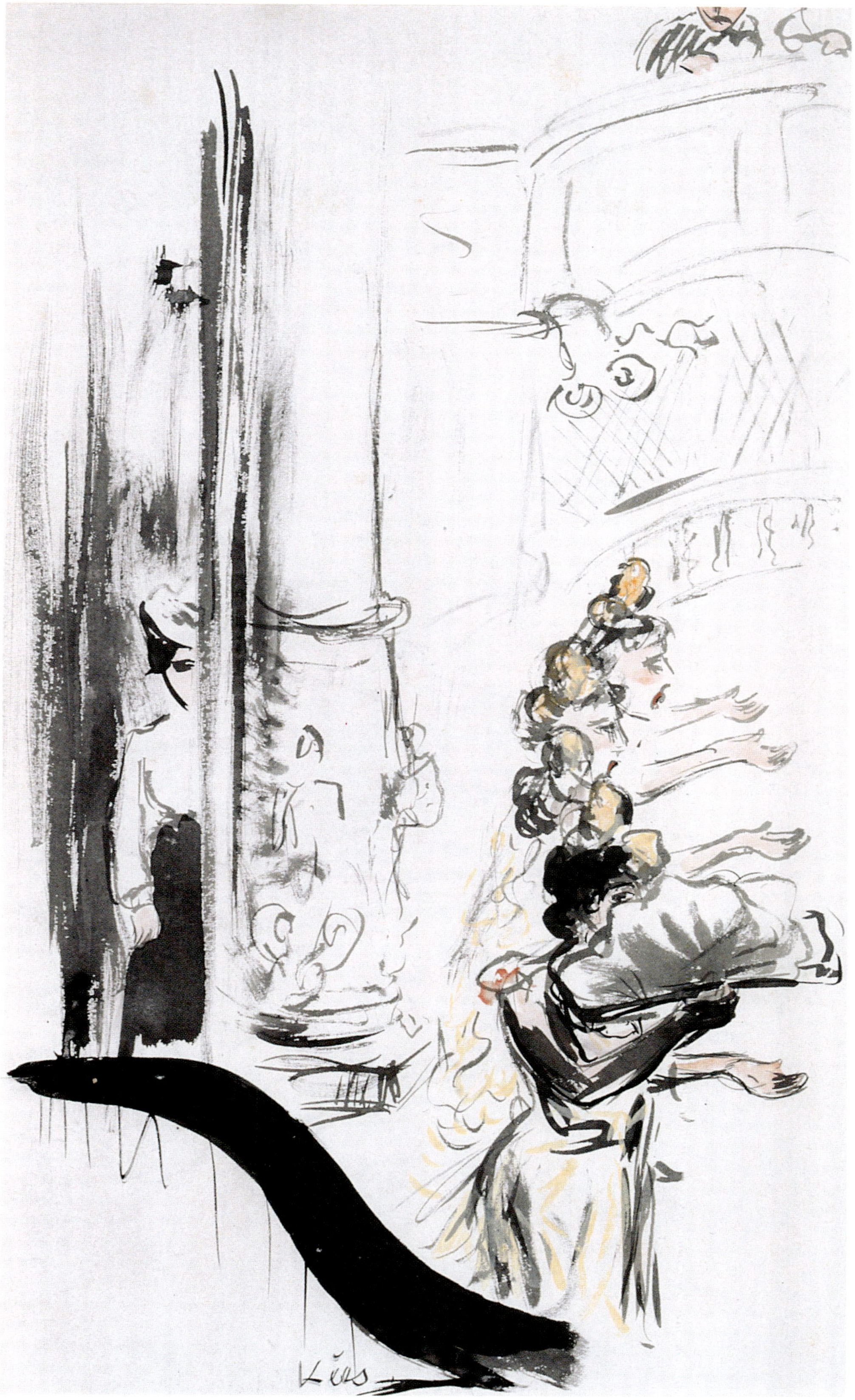

39. *L'Avant-scène*, c. 1902

40. *Le mépris* (Contempt), 1901
Blue chalk, brush with black ink, grey wash, watercolour, on grey-green paper
584 x 460 mm (present size)
Signed lower right in brush with black ink: *VD.* (in ligature); annotated lower left in brush with black ink over black chalk: *l'amant l'a vite laché/'y restait la fille/avec son enfant.*, lower right brush with black ink: *Ier fantôme./(Le mépris)*; at right border in blue chalk
Preliminary study for *Premier fantôme (Le mépris). L'amant part. La fille reste...avec son enfant!* (First spectre – Contempt. The lover leaves. The girl is left...with his child!) in *Petite histoire pour petits et grands nenfants, L'Assiette au Beurre*, no. 30, 26 October 1901, p. 461a
PROVENANCE:
Auction Versailles, Hôtel Rameau (G. Blache), *Tableaux modernes*, 6 December 1970, no. 53; Galerie Paul Vallotton, Lausanne, 1971; private collection
EXHIBITIONS:
1971 Lausanne, no. 24; 1990 Paris, p. 234 (fig.)
LITERATURE:
Kyriazi 1971, illus. 16
COLLECTION:
Private collection

41. *La pauvreté* (Poverty), 1901
Blue chalk, watercolour, brush with black ink, grey wash, on grey-green paper
460 x 580 mm (present size)
Signed lower right in brush with black ink: *VD.* (in ligature); annotated lower left in brush with black ink over blue chalk: *l'enfant avait soif-et sa mère avait faim-/y avait pas d'argent.*; upper right brush with black ink: *2eme fantôme (la pauvreté)*; upper centre in blue chalk: *l'assiette au Beurre.*; upper left in blue chalk: *4-* (crossed out with black chalk); followed by black chalk: *3-*; border in brush with black ink over blue chalk
Special features: the sheet comprises 2 pieces of paper
Preliminary study for *Deuxième fantôme (La Pauvreté). L'enfant a soif. La mère a faim. Le lait est tari. L'argent s'est enfui!* (Second spectre – Poverty. The child is thirsty. The mother is hungry. Her milk has dried up. Her money is gone!) in *Petite histoire pour petits et grands nenfants, L'Assiette au Beurre*, no. 30, 26 October 1901, p. 462
PROVENANCE:
Auction Versailles, Hotel Rameau (G. Blache), *Tableaux modernes*, 14 March 1971, no. 55; Galerie Paul Vallotton, Lausanne, 1971; private collection
EXHIBITIONS:
1971 Lausanne, no. 26; 1990 Paris, p. 213 (fig.)
LITERATURE:
Kyriazi 1971, fig. 18
COLLECTION:
Private collection

42. *L'abandon* (Desertion), 1901
Blue and red chalk, watercolour, brush with black ink, grey wash, on grey-green paper
578 x 490 mm (present size)
Unsigned; annotated lower right in brush with black ink: *elle allait chercher/son ancien amant/il l'a donné cent sous/et dit, va t'en.*; in black chalk upper right: *4* (crossed out with blue chalk); in black chalk below: *11*
Preliminary study for *Le père, relancé, donne cent sous à condition qu'on ne vienne plus l'embêter* (The father of the child, pestered by the girl, gives her a hundred sous on condition that she never bothers him again) in *Petite histoire pour petits et grands nenfants, L'Assiette au Beurre*, no. 30, 26 October 1901, p. 462a
PROVENANCE:
Auction Versailles, Hôtel Rameau (G. Blache), *Tableaux modernes*, 6 December 1970, no. 51 (fig.); Galerie Paul Vallotton, Lausanne, 1971; private collection
EXHIBITIONS:
1971 Lausanne 1971, no. 18; 1990 Paris, p. 234 (fig.)
LITERATURE:
Kyriazi 1971, fig. 17
COLLECTION:
Private collection

43 *Péripatéticiennes au café* (Streetwalkers in a café), 1901
Blue and black chalk, pen and brush with black ink, grey wash, watercolour
628 x 484 mm (present size)
Signed lower centre in brush with black ink: *van Dongen*; annotated lower left in blue chalk: *il faut vivre pourtant.*; black chalk lower left: *6.*; blue chalk: *21x29*
Special features: blind-stamped watermark below: *B CRAYON-ANCNE MANUFRE CANSON & MONTGOLFIER-VIDALON-FILS-ANNONAY*
Drawing for *Il faut bien vivre pourtant!* (Well, you've got to make a living!) in *Petite histoire pour petits et grands nenfants, L'Assiette au Beurre*, no. 30, 26 October 1901, p. 463bis
PROVENANCE:
Auction Versailles, Hôtel Rameau (G. Blache), 6 December 1970, *Tableaux modernes*, 5 December 1970, no. 48 (fig.); Galerie Paul Vallotton, Lausanne, 1971; private collection
EXHIBITIONS:
1971 Lausanne, no. 20; 1990 Paris, p. 213 (fig.)
LITERATURE:
Hoog 1971, p. 93; Kyriazi 1971, fig. 13
COLLECTION:
Private collection

44. *Péripatéticiennnes* (Streetwalkers), 1901
Black chalk, watercolour and gouache accents
265 x 5 mm (present size)
Signed lower right in black chalk: *Kées van Dongen*
On reverse of original frame a black-printed label: *GALERIE CHARPENTIER/76, RUE DU FG SAINT-HONORÉ-PARIS/Anjou 57-61 – 34-82/VAN DONGEN/1949*; numbered twice, in black and red chalk: *627*; red chalk: *6476*
PROVENANCE:
Galerie Charpentier, Paris, 1949; auction Paris, Drouot (Ader, Picard, Tajan), *Dessins, aquarelles, pastels, gouaches...*, 4 July 1990, no. 17 (fig.); 'La Galerie' Paris, 1990
EXHIBITIONS:
1943 Bordeaux, no. 133; 1949 Paris, no. 2
COLLECTION:
'La Galerie', Paris

45. *La réussite* (Success), 1901
Blue and black chalk, brush in black ink, grey wash, watercolour
634 x 485 mm (present size)
Signed lower right with brush in black ink: *van Dongen*; upper right brush with black ink: *PRINTEMPS*; on the packages in the carriage: *BON MAR/CHE/PRINTEMPS*; in black chalk lower centre: *7-*; in blue chalk: *21 x 25*
Drawing for *Elle finit par gagner des vingt francs ... qu'elle dépense* (She ends up making some twenty francs...which she spends) in *Petite histoire pour petits et grands nenfants, L'Assiette au Beurre*, no. 30, 26 October 1901, p. 464
PROVENANCE:
Auction Versailles, Hôtel Rameau (G. Blache), *Tableaux modernes*, 6 December 1970, no. 47 (fig.); Galerie Paul Vallotton, Lausanne, 1971; private collection
EXHIBITIONS:
1971 Lausanne, no. 21; 1990 Paris, p. 234 (fig.)
LITERATURE:
Kyriazi 1971, fig. 15
COLLECTION:
Private collection

46. *La maladie* (Illness), 1901
Blue chalk, brush in black ink, grey wash, watercolour on grey-green paper
570 x 455 mm (present size)
Signed lower right in brush with black ink: *VDongen.* (in ligature); annotated upper right in brush with black ink: *3eme fantôme./(la maladie)*; lower centre in brush with black ink: *ohé.*; right border in blue chalk
Preliminary study for *Troisième spectre (La Malade) Ohé!* (Third spectre – The sick woman – Hello there!) in: *Petite histoire pour petits et grands nenfants, L'Assiette au Beurre*, no. 30, 26 October 1901, p. 464bis
PROVENANCE:
Auction Versailles, Hôtel Rameau (G. Blache), *Tableaux modernes*, 6 December 1970, no. 52; Galerie Paul Vallotton, Lausanne, 1971; private collection
EXHIBITIONS:
1971 Lausanne, no. 22; 1990 Paris, p. 234 (fig.)
LITERATURE:
Hoog 1971, p. 94, fig. 3; Kyriazi 1971, fig. 21
COLLECTION:
Private collection

47. *La mort* (Death), 1901
Black, blue and red chalk, pen and brush with black ink, grey wash, watercolour
622 x 485 mm (present size)
Signed centre right in brush with black ink: *vanDongen*; upper right in brush with black ink: *COURONNES.*; lower right in black chalk: *9.*; in blue chalk below: *un grain sur tout le dessin, excepté le parapluie [tekening] et le banc [tekening]*
Special features: at top blind-stamped watermark: *B CRAYON-ANCNE MANUFRE CANSON & MONTGOLFIER-VIDALON-FILS-ANNONAY*
Drawing for *Quatrième spectre – La Mort. Elle s'en est allée un jour à Saint-Ouen* (Fourth spectre (Death). One day she departs for Saint-Ouen) in *Petite histoire pour petits et grands nenfants, L'Assiette au Beurre*, no. 30, 26 October 1901, p. 465
PROVENANCE:
Auction Versailles, Hôtel Rameau (G. Blache), *Tableaux modernes*, 6 December 1970, no. 55; Galerie Paul Vallotton, Lausanne, 1971; private collection
EXHIBITIONS:
1971 Lausanne, no. 17; 1990 Paris, p. 235 (fig.)
LITERATURE:
Kyriazi 1971, fig. 22
COLLECTION:
Private collection

48. *La destinée* (Fate), 1901
Blue chalk, brush with black ink, grey wash, watercolour, on grey-green paper
585 x 446 mm (present size)
Signed lower right in brush with black ink: *VD.* (in ligature); annotated lower left in brush with black ink: *faut bien que j'fasse,/c'est dit l'enfant,/comme a fait maman.*; right borderline in blue chalk
Preliminary study for *Il faut bien que j'fasse, s'est dit l'enfant, comme a fait maman!* (I had to do it, the child told herself, just like mummy did!) in *Petite histoire pour petits et grands nenfants, L'Assiette au Beurre*, no. 30, 26 October 1901, p. 465bis
PROVENANCE:
Auction Versailles, Hôtel Rameau (G. Blache), *Tableaux modernes*, 6 December 1970, no. 50 (fig.); Galerie Paul Vallotton, Lausanne, 1971; private collection
EXHIBITIONS:
1971 Lausanne, no. 19; 1990 Paris, p. 235 (fig.)
LITERATURE:
Kyriazi 1971, fig. 14
COLLECTION:
Private collection

49. *Et elle a eu aussi des amants!* (And she had lovers too!)
1901
Black and coloured chalk, brush with black ink
635 x 490 mm
Signed lower right in brush with black ink: *Kées van Dongen.*
Special features: also known as *Couple arrivant au café* (Couple arriving at the café)
Drawing for *Et elle a eu aussi des amants!*, in *Petite histoire pour petits et grands nenfants*, *L'Assiette au Beurre*, no. 30, 26 October 1901, p. 466

PROVENANCE:
Auction New York, Sotheby's, *Impressionist and modern paintings, drawings...(part II)*, 9 November 1994, no. 150 (fig.); private collection

COLLECTION:
Private collection

50. *Au café* (At the café), c. 1901
Brush with black ink, grey wash, watercolour
217 x 210 mm
Signed lower left in brush with black ink: *V Dongen.*; over brush with grey: *VD*

PROVENANCE:
Musée des Beaux-Arts de Lyon, 1917 (acquired from the artist with the assistance of the Chazière Foundation)
Musée des Beaux-Arts de Lyon, Lyons, Inv. B 1176-4

51. *L'automne* (Autumn), 1901
Black chalk, brush with black ink, grey wash, watercolour, corrections in white gouache
630 x 485 mm (present size)
Signed lower left in brush with black ink: *van Dongen.*; annotated lower left in black chalk: *même pas/les ouvriers*; in black chalk lower right: *14*
Annotated on verso in pen and black ink: *mais quand son feu était brulé/son automne est venu/on ne l'a plus voulu.*
Special features: at top blind-stamped watermark: *B CRAYON-ANC^{NE} MANUF^{RE} CANSON & MONTGOLFIER-VIDALON-FILS-ANNONAY*
Drawing for *Le feu consumé, vint l'automne... On n'en voulait plus* (When the fire had burned out, autumn came...There was no more passion) in *Petite histoire pour petits et grands nenfants*, *L'Assiette au Beurre*, no. 30, 26 October 1901, p. 467bis

PROVENANCE:
Auction Versailles, Hôtel Rameau (G. Blache), *Tableaux modernes*, 14 March 1971, no. 54 (fig.); Galerie Paul Vallotton, Lausanne, 1971; private collection

EXHIBITIONS:
1971 Lausanne, no. 25; 1990 Paris, p. 235 (fig.)

LITERATURE:
Kyriazi 1971, fig. 19

COLLECTION:
Private collection

52. *Cocotte* (Prostitute), 1901
Blue and black chalk, pen and brush with black ink, grey wash, watercolour
620 x 495 mm (present size)
Signed and dated lower right in brush with black ink: *van Dongen/1901.*; annotated lower left in blue chalk: *la voie des parents-/regarde pas ça c'est qu'une cocotte.* (rest of text under the frame)
Drawing for *Cocotte*, in *Petite histoire pour petits et grands nenfants*, *L'Assiette au Beurre*, no. 30, 26 October 1901, p. 468bis

PROVENANCE:
Auction Versailles, Hôtel Rameau (G. Blache), *Tableaux Modernes*, 14 March 1971, no. 52 (fig.); Galerie Paul Vallotton, Lausanne, 1971; private collection

EXHIBITIONS:
1971 Lausanne, no. 23; 1990 Paris, p. 235 (fig.)

LITERATURE:
Kyriazi 1971, fig. 20

COLLECTION:
Private collection

Van Dongen's name as an artist was established through one commission, the request from the publisher-director S. Schwarz for him to illustrate an entire issue of the periodical *L'Assiette au Beurre*. This number entitled *Petite histoire pour petits et grands nenfants* came out on 26 October 1901. It was the thirtieth edition of the paper which first appeared in 1901. As was usual for this periodical, sixteen pages including the front cover were illustrated by Van Dongen; printed to fill the entire page. (fig.) They portray the life history of a mother and daughter forced by their reduced circumstances into a life of prostitution. Their sad destiny is represented by Van Dongen by so-called 'phantoms' (fantômes) like 'rejection', 'poverty', 'illness' and 'death' which add emphasis to the theme. What is unique is that both the independent drawings used for the prints as well as a great number of studies which preceded them have been saved. They allow us a glimpse of the way Van Dongen worked and the printing method he used. Contrary to what is often assumed, Van Dongen prepared his work for the issue very carefully. The sketches show that he studied different poses beforehand and for some parts drew upon earlier scenes like *Au café*. The studies on light green paper like *Le mépris*, or *La pauvreté* were probably used by Van Dongen in his presentation of the project. On a few of these drawings text corrections have been added in different handwriting, possibly by Schwarz himself or by one of the authors involved with the paper like Anatole France or Jehan Rictus. Despite the editorial remarks at the end of the periodical that drawings once used would not be returned, it would seem that they made an exception for Van Dongen. The original drawings would appear to have been altered by the artist after publication, having been filled in with watercolour just like the prints. It is very likely that Van Dongen subsequently sold the drawings; together with various preliminary studies they were auctioned in batches at Blache's in Versailles.

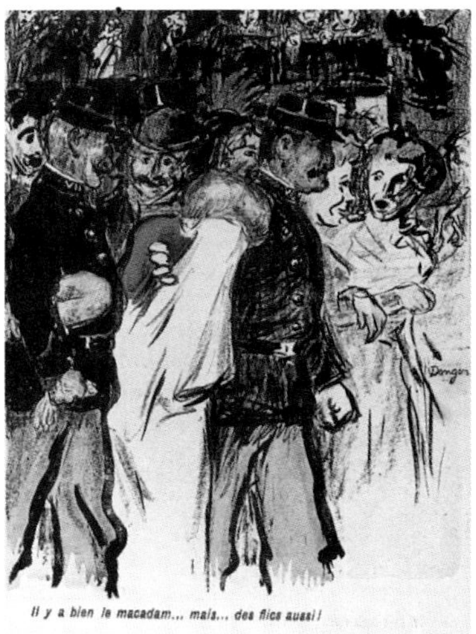

Il y a bien le macadam
L'Asiette au Beurre, no. 30, 26 October 1901, p. 463 bis

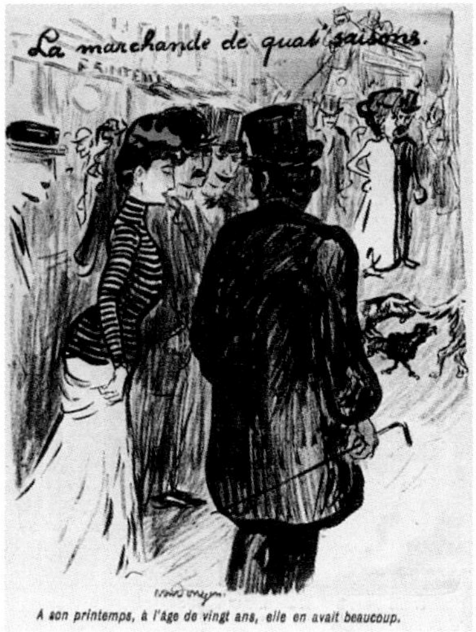

La marchande de quat' saisons
L'Asiette au Beurre, no. 30, 26 October 1901, p.466bis

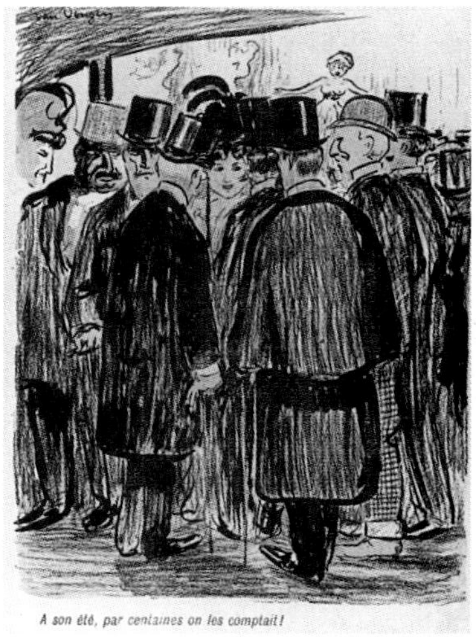

A son été
L'Asiette au Beurre, no. 30, 26 October 1901, p.467

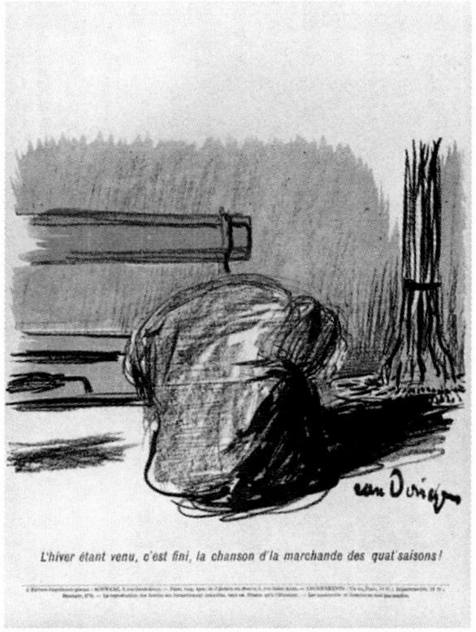

L'hiver
L'Assiette au Beurre, no. 30, 26 October 1901, p.468

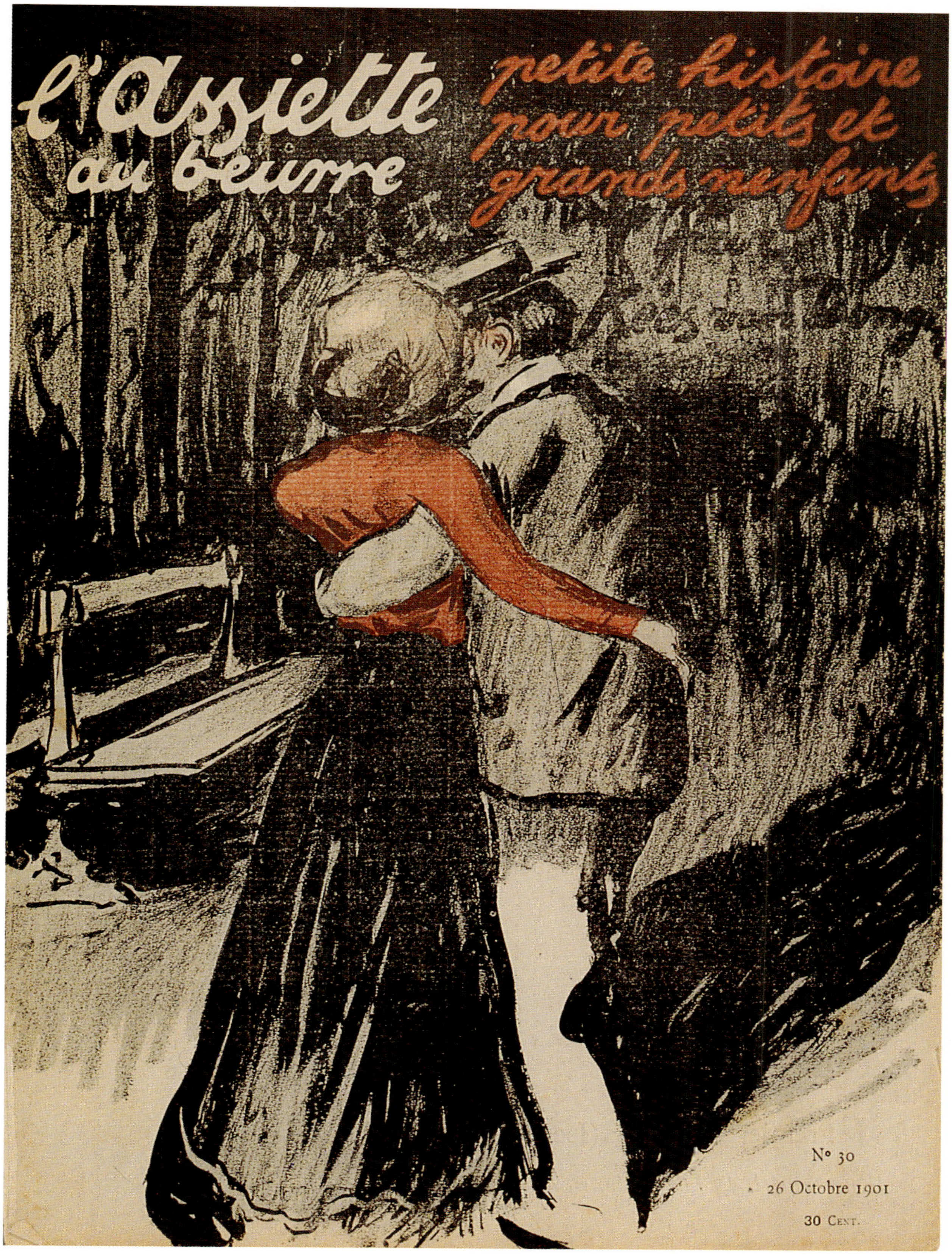

Cover *L'Assiette au Beurre*, no. 30

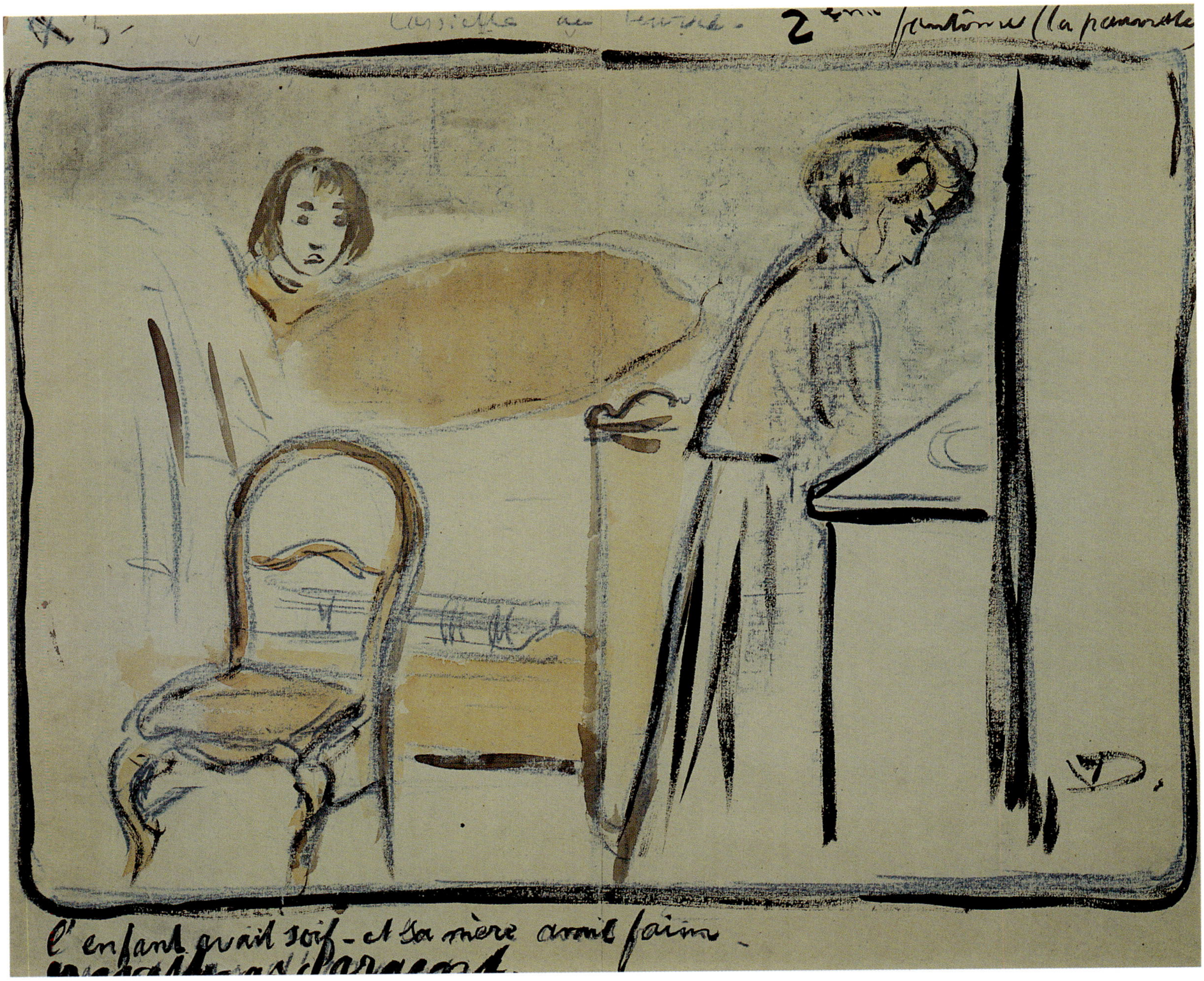

41. *La pauvreté*, 1901

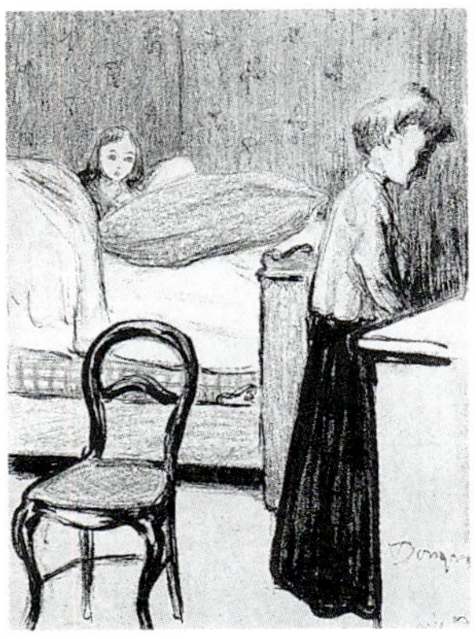

La pauvreté, *L'Assiette au Beurre*, no. 30, 26 October 1901, p.462

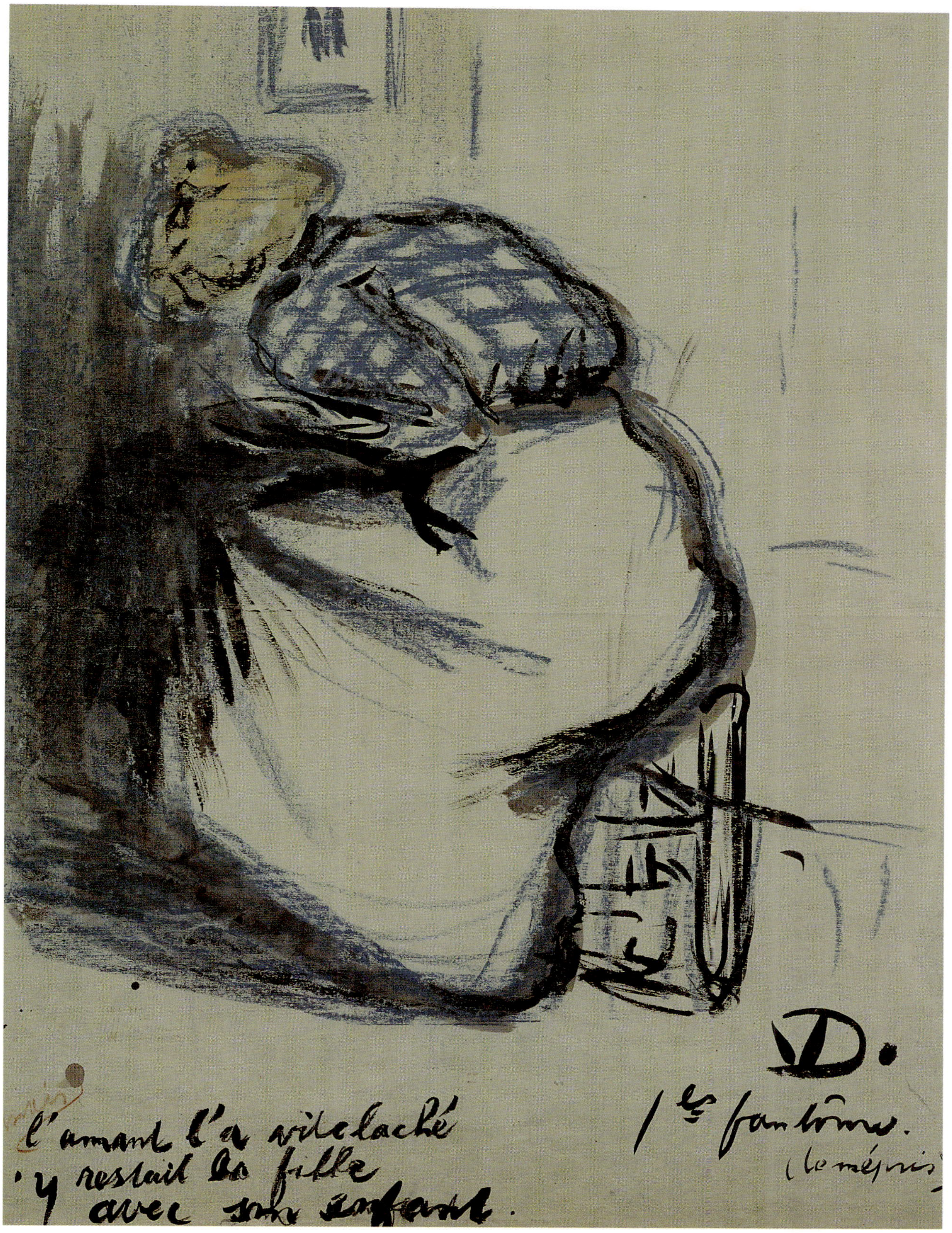

40. *Le mépris*, 1901

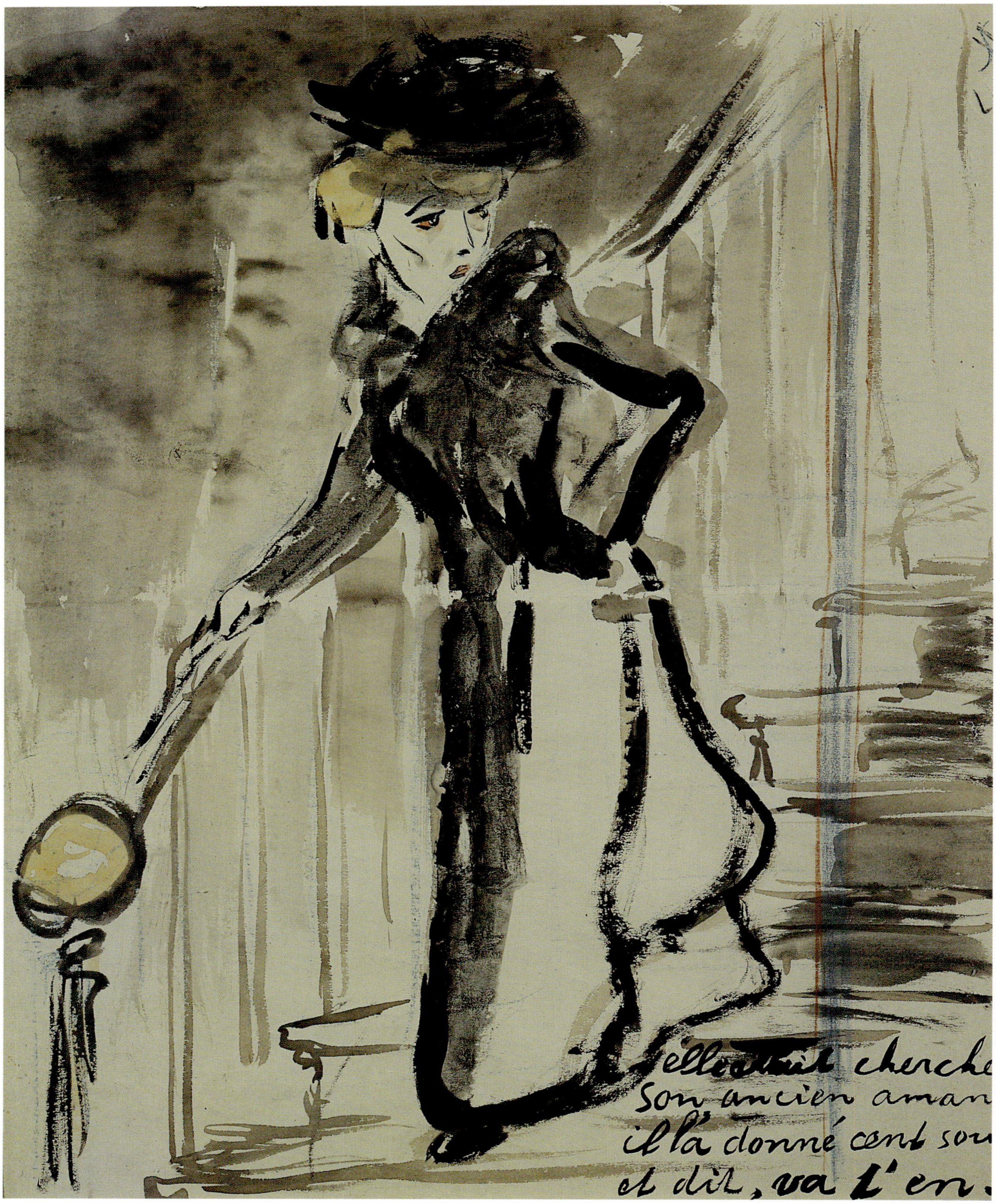

42. *L'abandon*, 1901

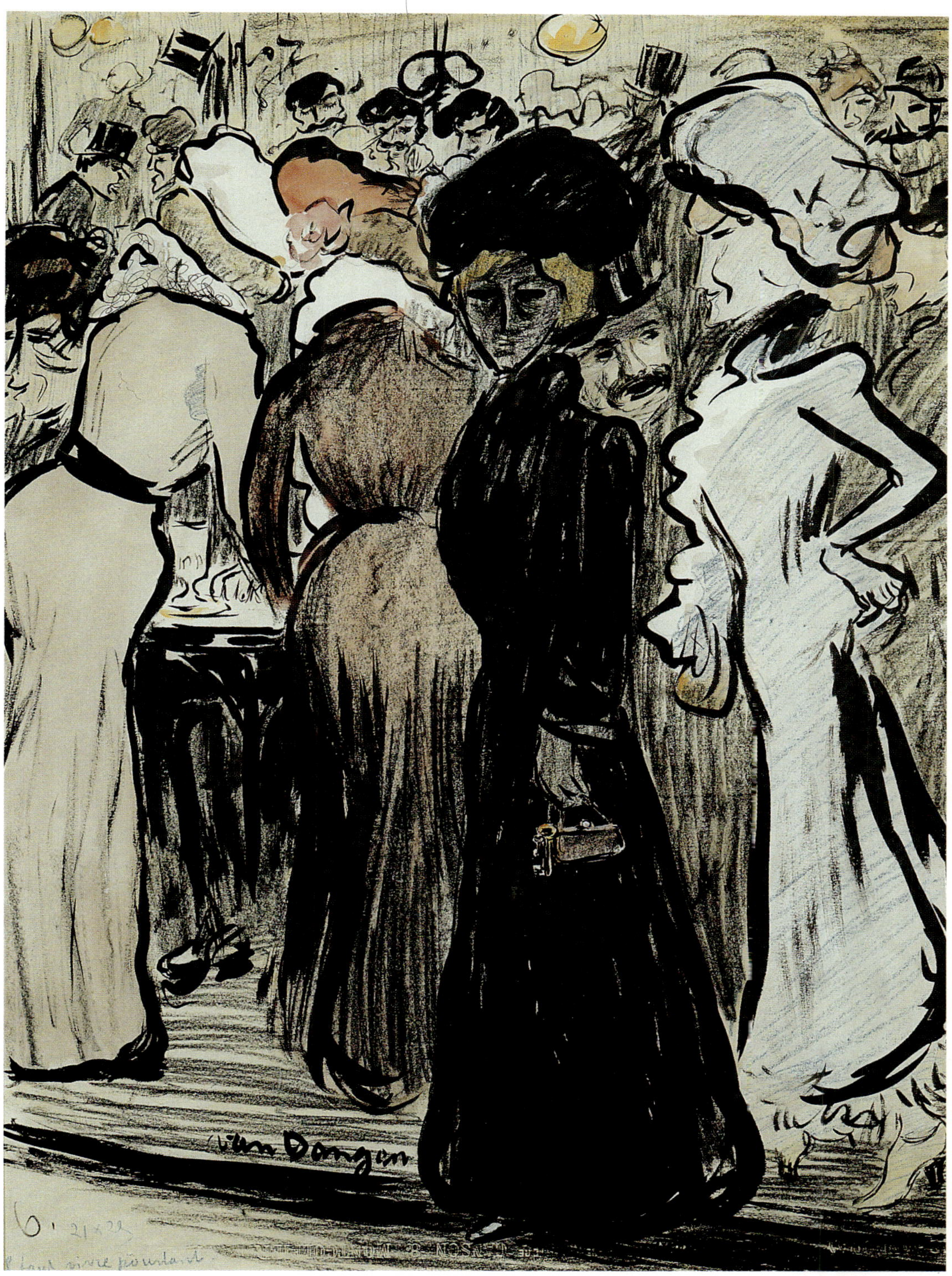

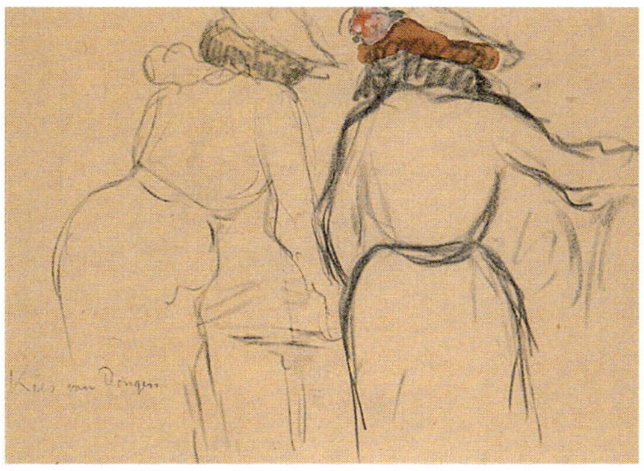

44. *Péripatéticiennes*, 1901

43. *Péripatéticiennes au café*, 1901

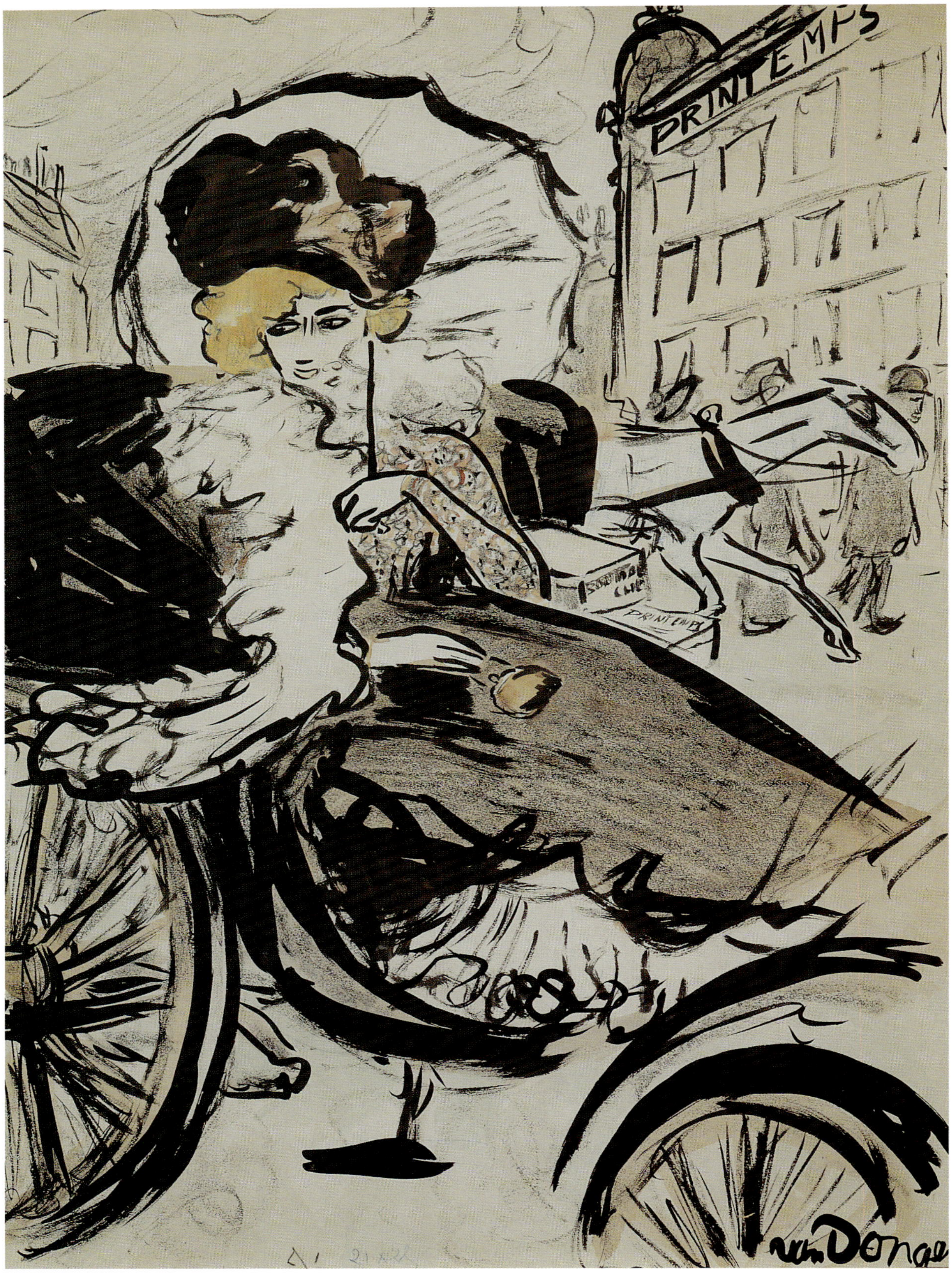

45. *La réussite*, 1901

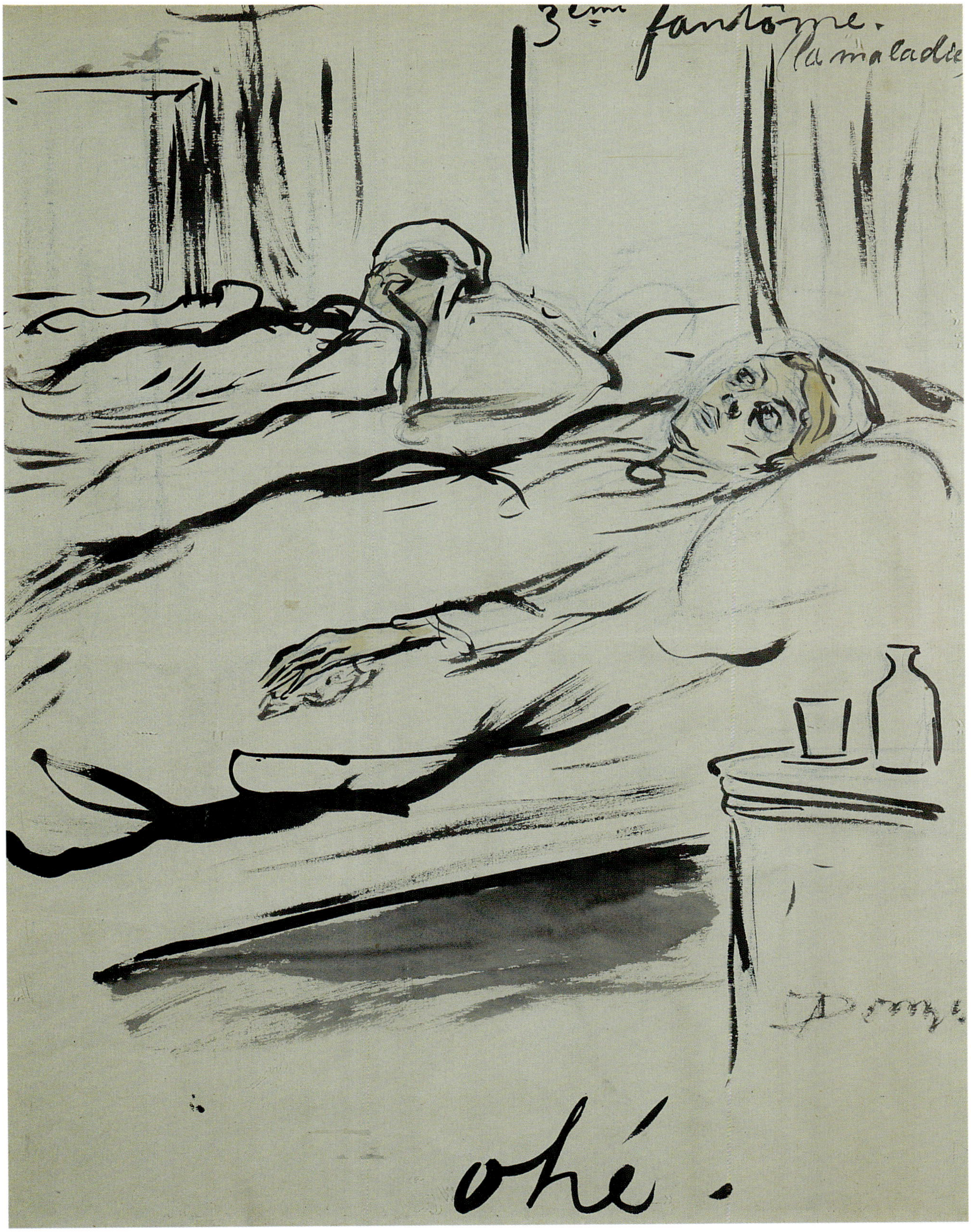

46. La maladie, 1901

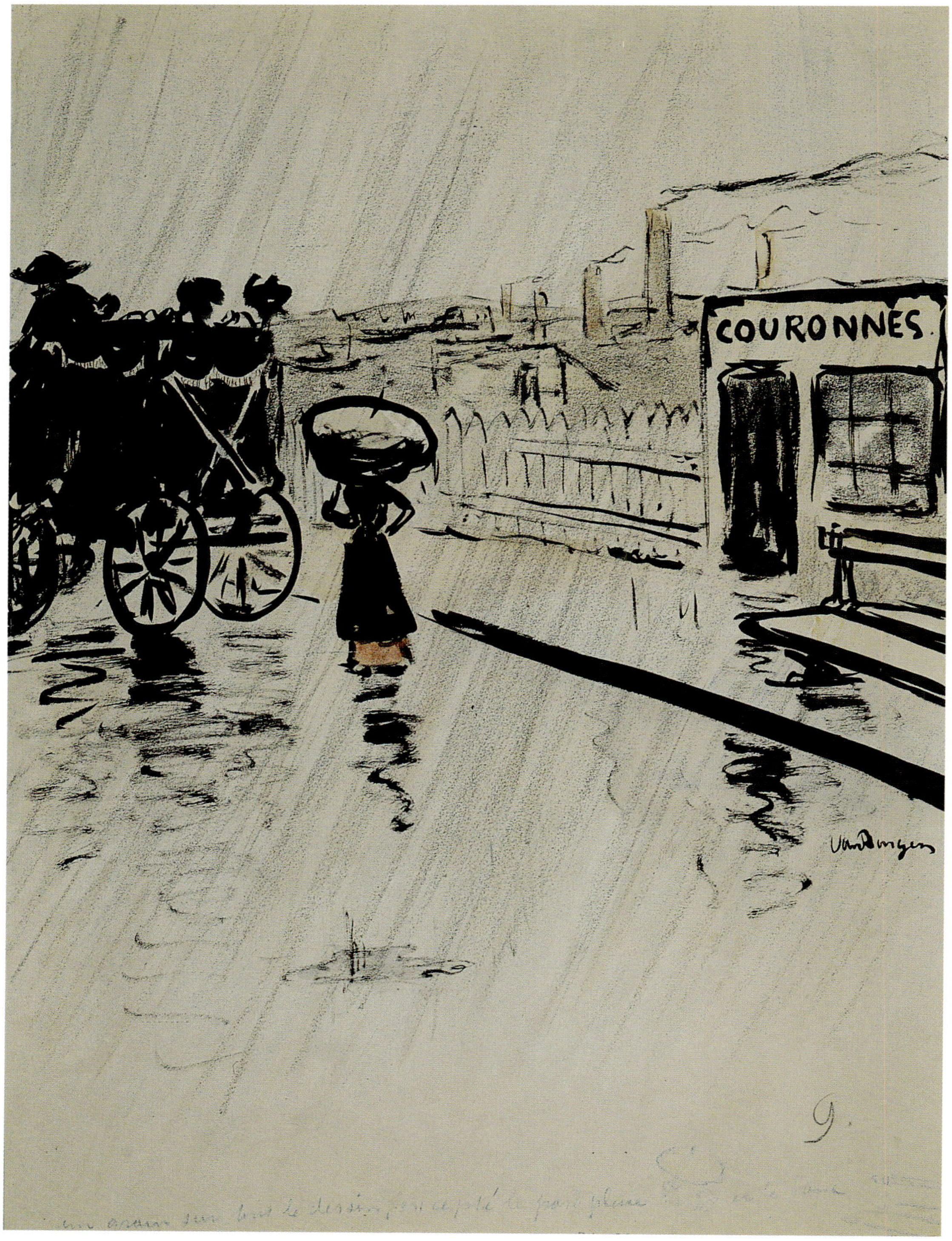

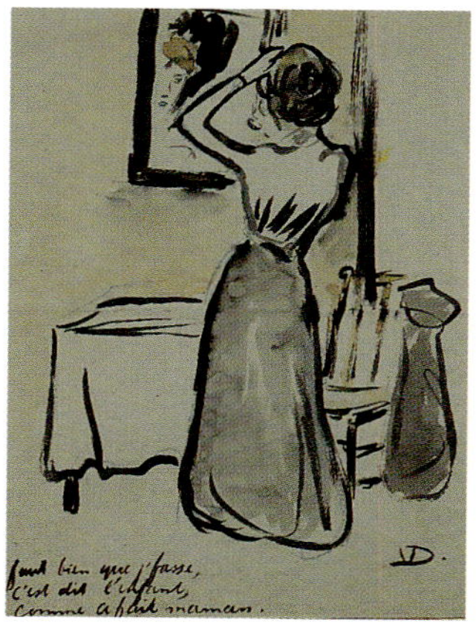

47. *La mort*, 1901

48. *La destinée*, 1901

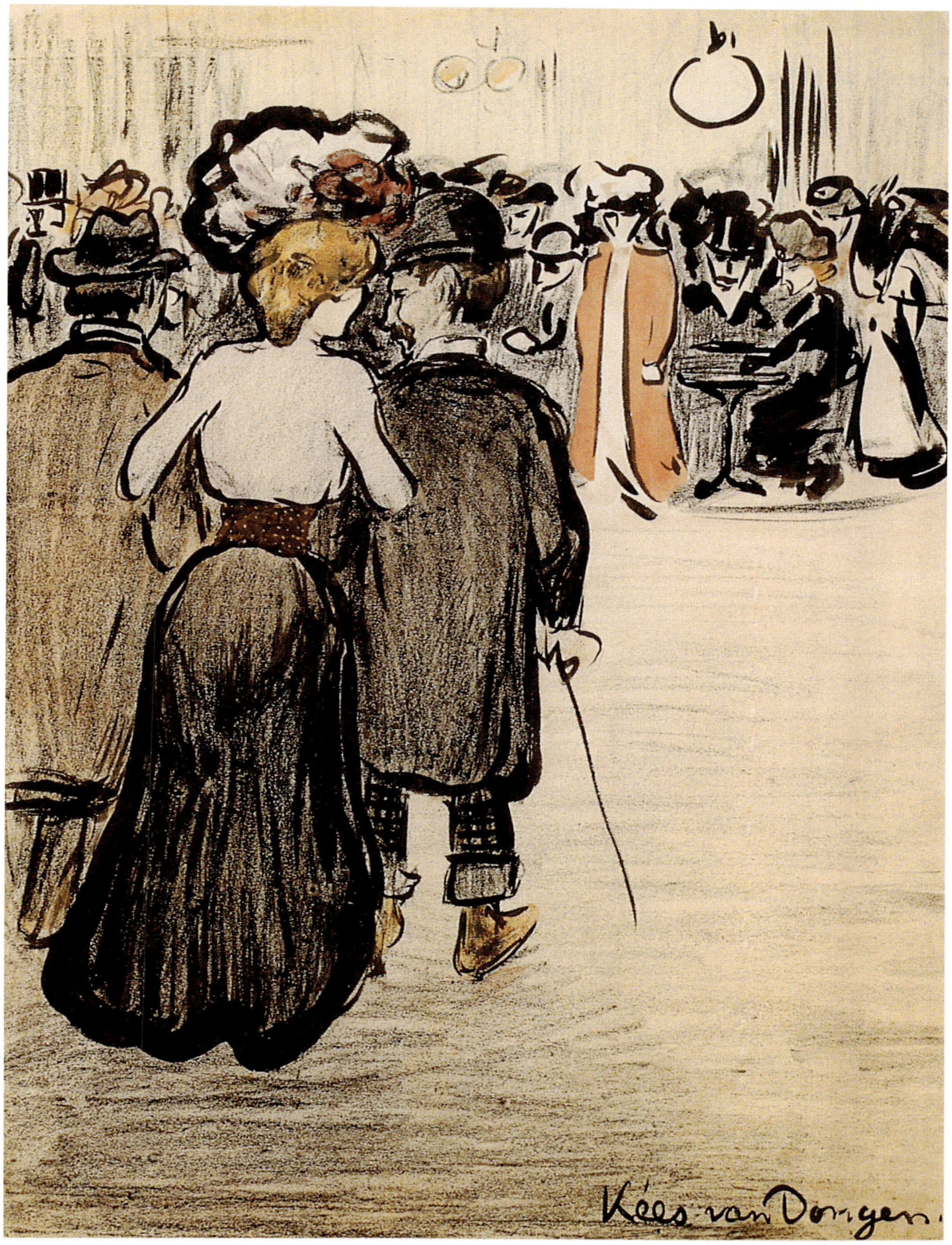

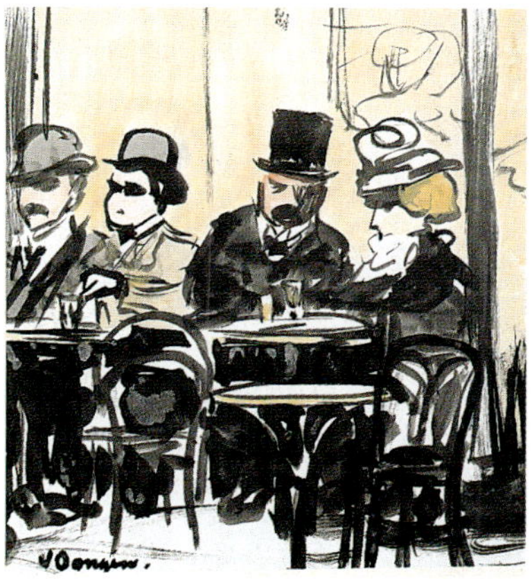

50. *Au café*, c. 1901

49. *Et elle a eu aussi des amants!*, 1901

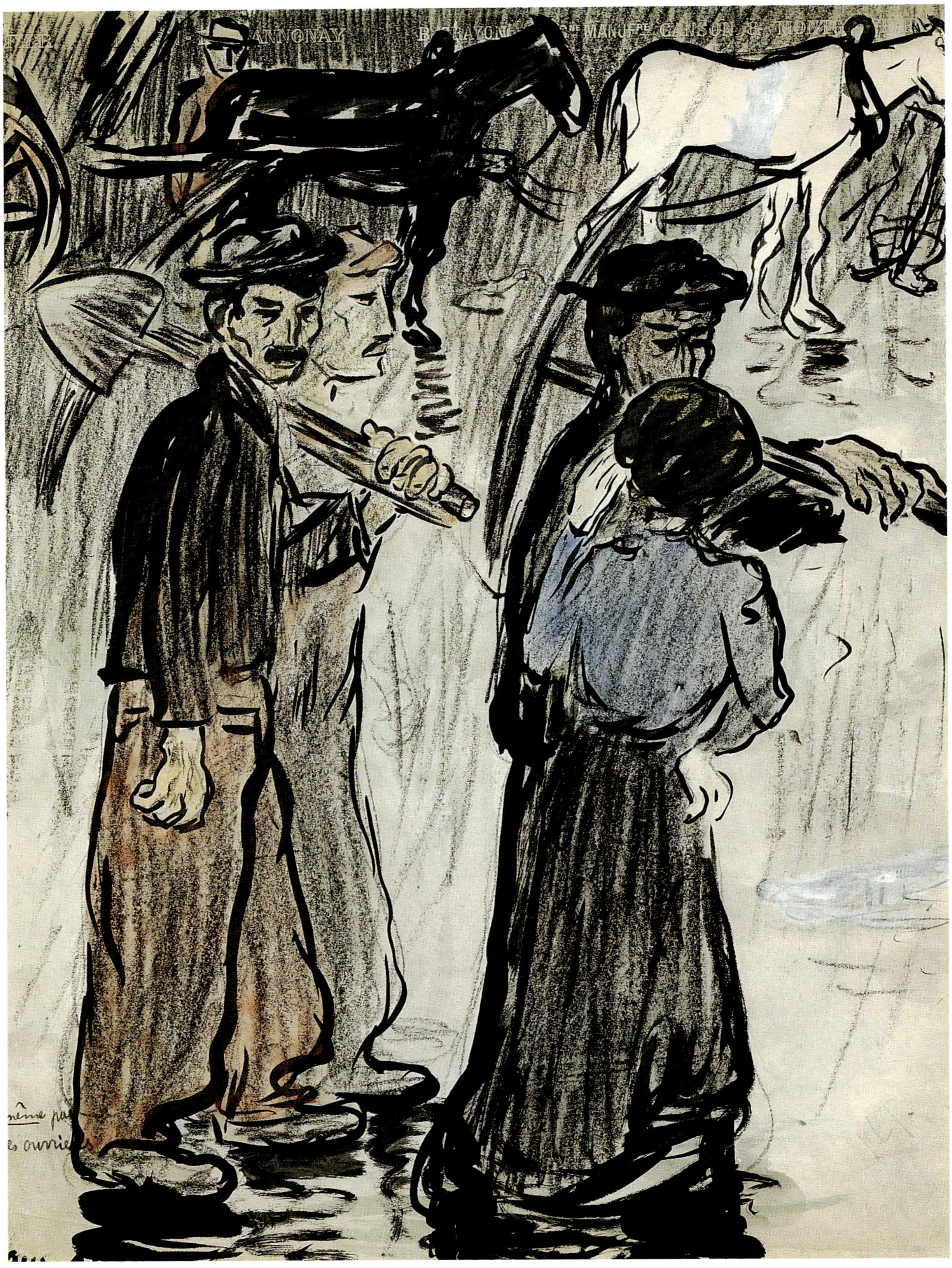

51. *L'automne*, 1901

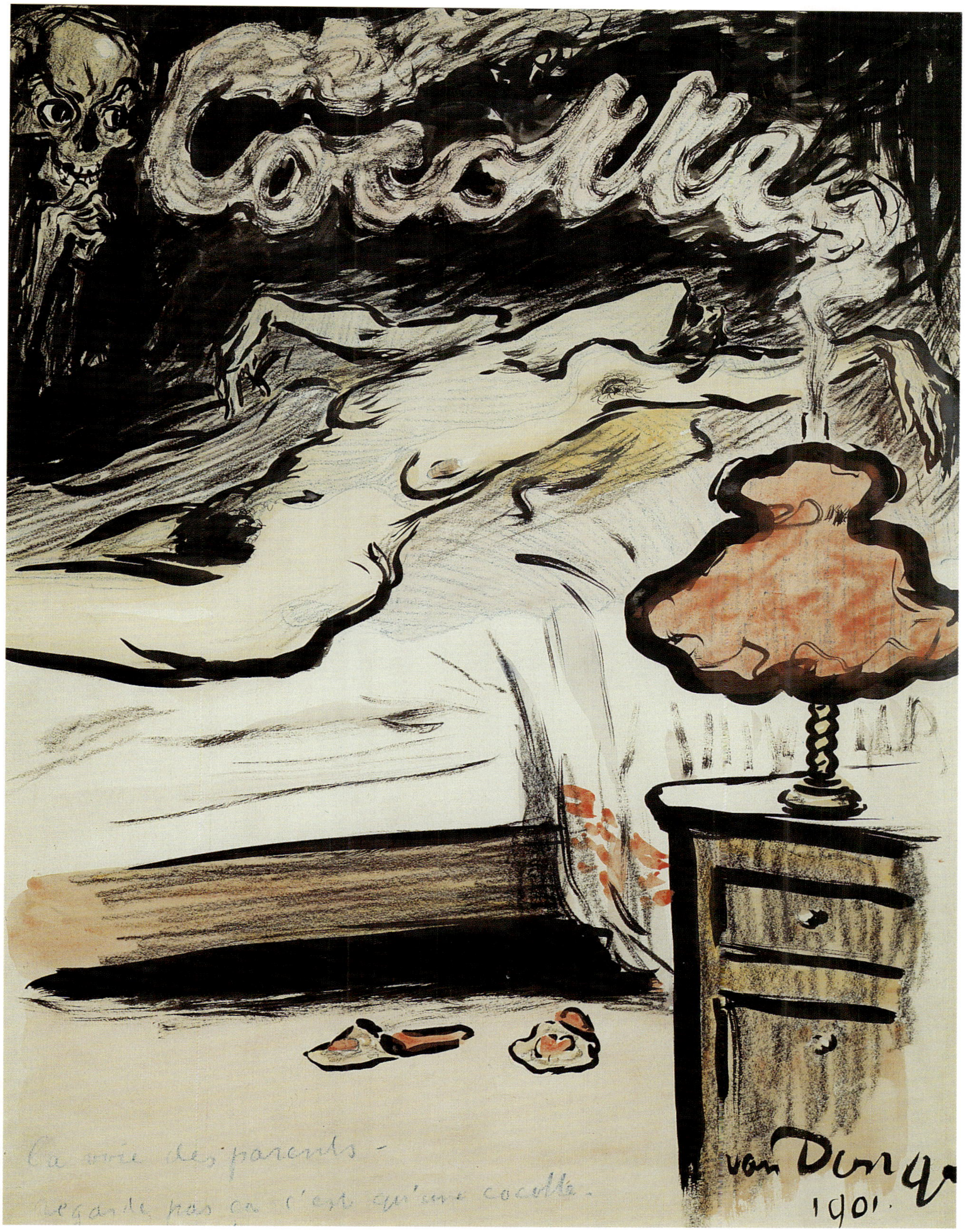

52. *Cocotte*, 1901

53. *Sieste* (Siesta), c. 1902
Black chalk
280 x 449 mm (present size)
Signed lower right in black chalk: *van Dongen.*;
annotated lower left in blue chalk: *Sieste-*
PROVENANCE:
Auction Paris, Drouot (M. Rheims), *Estampes, dessins anciens...*, 23 November 1953, no. 125; Galerie Fricker, Paris; J. Reiss, London; auction London, Sotheby's, *Impressionist and modern paintings, drawings...*, 19 July 1963, no. 98 (fig.); Mr and Mrs Sidney E. Cohn, New York; auction New York, Sotheby's, *19th & 20th Century drawings & watercolors*, 17 December 1969, no. 56 (fig.); Mr. and Mrs. Irving Moskovitz
COLLECTION:
Mr and Mrs Irving Moskovitz

54. *Vrouw in bed* (Woman in bed), c. 1902
Black chalk, watercolour
264 x 445 mm
Signed lower right in black chalk: *v Dongen.*
PROVENANCE:
Anonymous gift to the Nationalgalerie, Staatliche Museen zu Berlin, Berlin
EXHIBITIONS:
1958 Berlin, no. 24
COLLECTION:
Kupferstichkabinett, Staatliche Museen zu Berlin, Berlin, Inv. SdZ no. 1

The woman abandoned by her lover, left without any support from family and friends, reduced to street prostitution out of sheer desperation, appears to be a subject that was portrayed by Van Dongen more than once around 1901-1902. The beautiful, 'classical' drawing in black chalk of a woman reclining entitled *Sieste*, would seem to link up thematically with this sort of image. Another related drawing of a woman on a bed, which has been part of the collection of the National Gallery of Berlin since 1907, is also an indication of this as the scene was developed by Van Dongen for the periodical *L'Indiscret* and in it was given the title *L'abandonnée*. (fig.) The drawing *Femme à l'éventail*, of which there is a preliminary study in the Musée de Beaux-Arts in Lyons, offers the next example of Van Dongen's affiliation with the destiny of the fallen woman. (fig.) Compared to the *L'Assiette au Beurre* drawings, these can be called modest. The outlines of the figures are careful but at the same time flowing, with a lively use of line, drawn in black crayon; the surfaces are austere and filled in quite uniformly with watercolour. The drawings demonstrate how Van Dongen had become more proficient in the art of drawing. It is likely that he had already familiarized himself with the art of Degas or Toulouse-Lautrec.

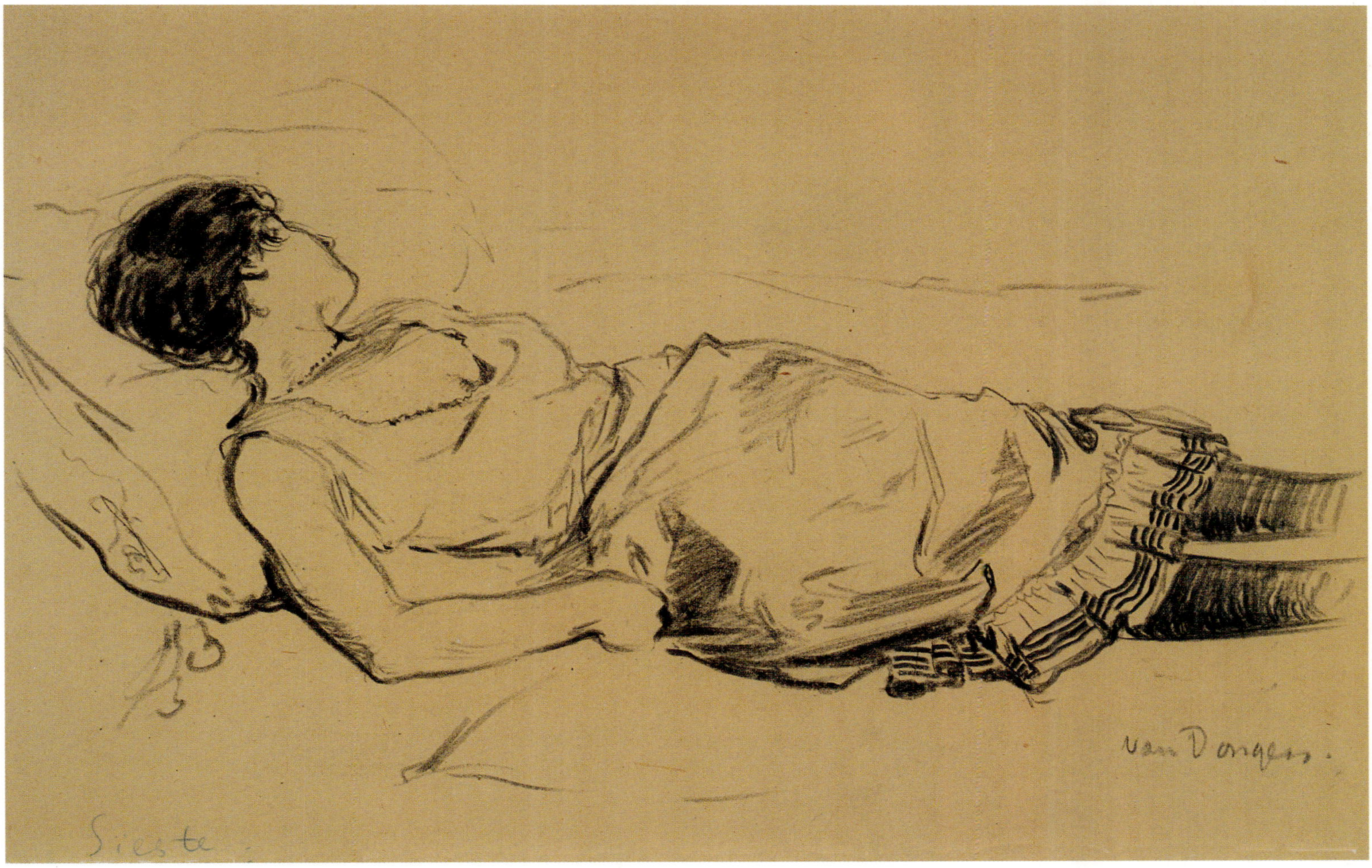

53. *Sieste*, c. 1902

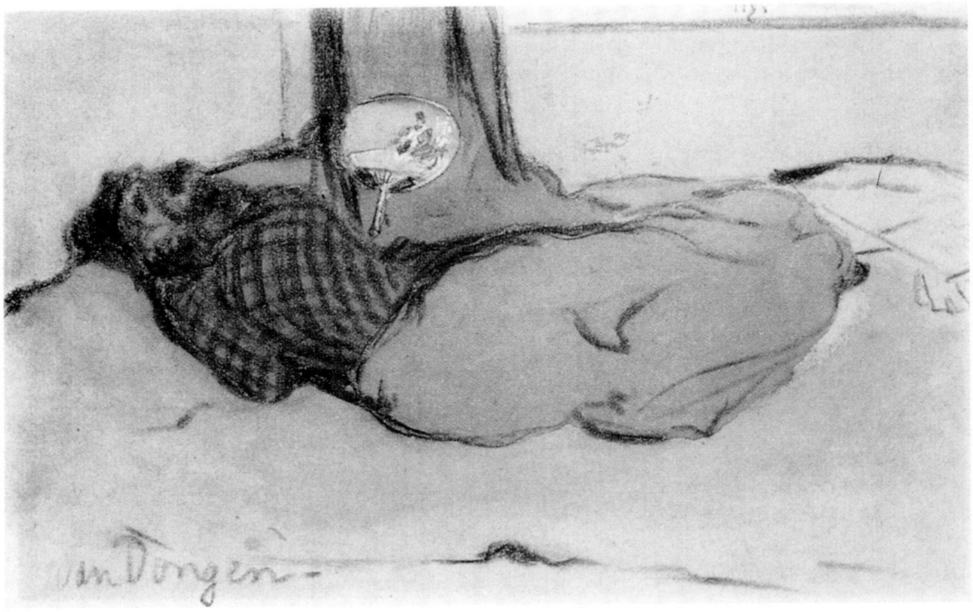

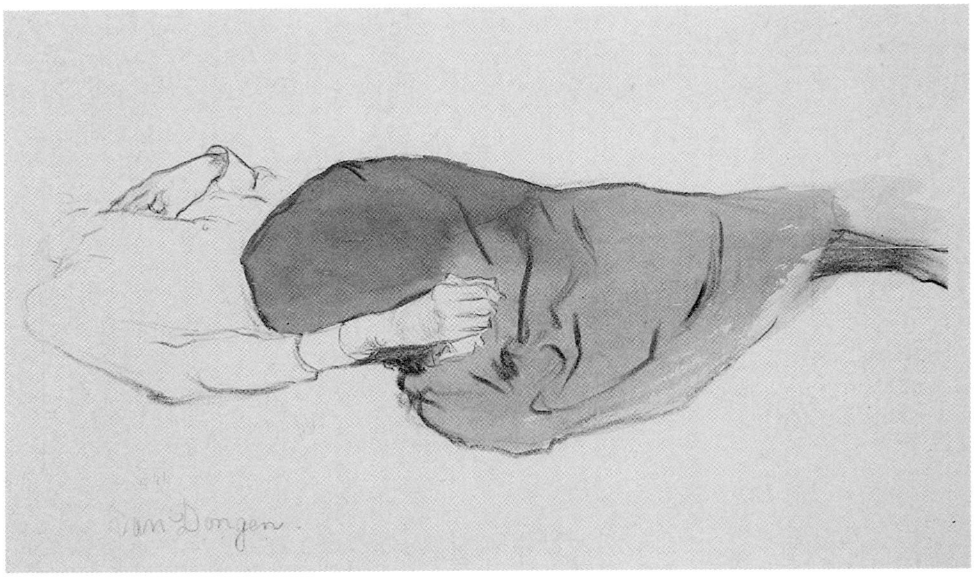

Femme à l'éventail, c. 1902
Black chalk, watercolour, body colour, coloured chalk, 275 x 445 mm

Femme allongée, c. 1902
Black chalk, watercolour, body colour, coloured chalk, 263 x 448 mm
Musée des Beaux-Arts de Lyon, Lyons

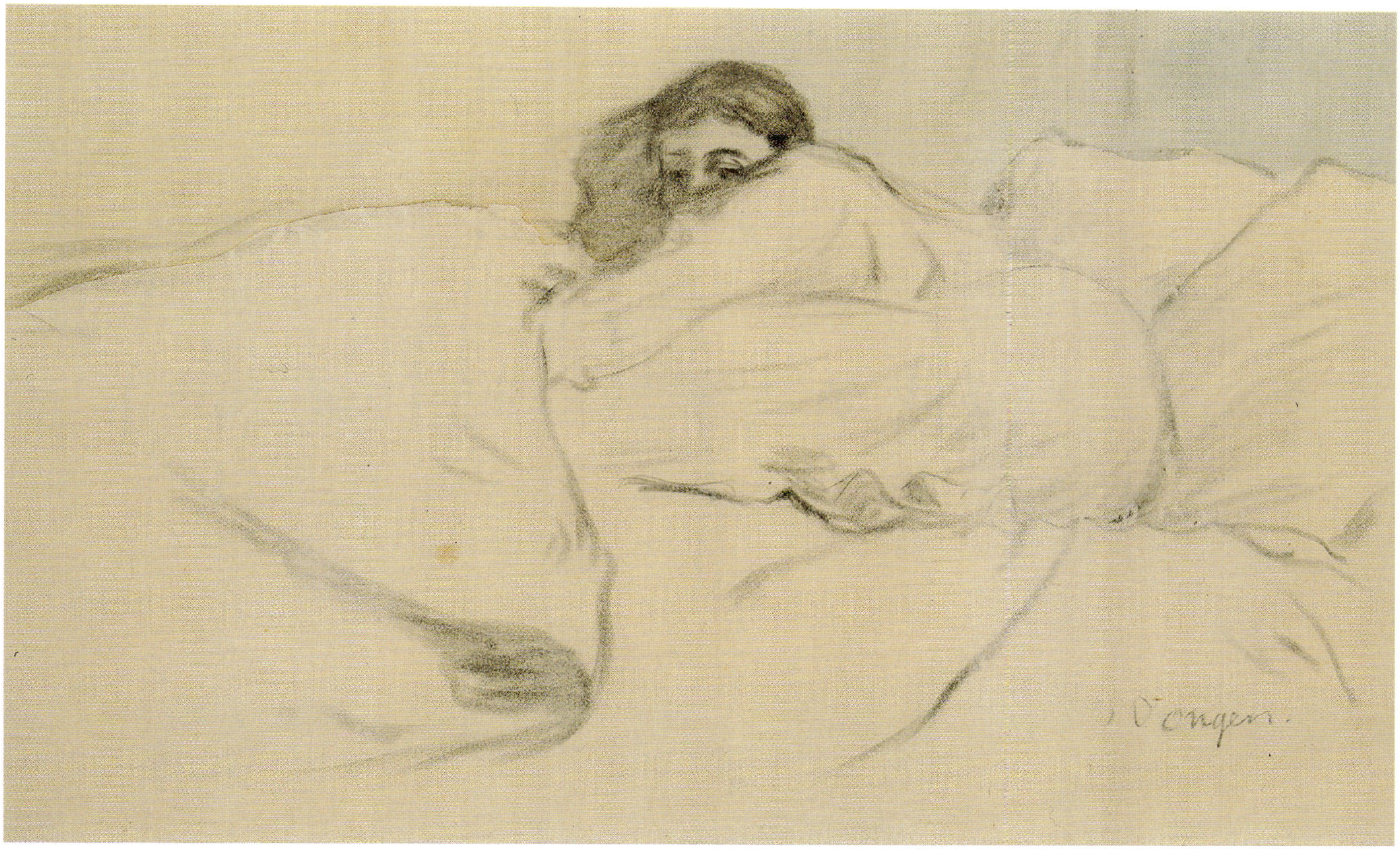

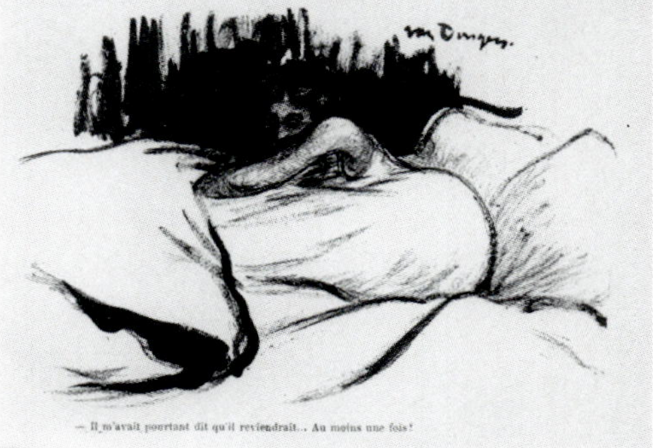

L'abandonnée, 1902
Illustration in *L'Indiscret*, no. 5,
19 February 1902, p. 21

54. *Woman in bed*, c. 1902

55. *L'entrée de l'église* (In front of the church), c. 1902
Black chalk, grey wash, watercolour, white gouache
227 x 305 mm
Signed lower left in orange and dark-red chalk: *VDongen*; annotated on back in black chalk: *Entree de l'Eglise*; numbered in black chalk: *276-*
Special features: also known as *Scène de rue* (Street scene)
PROVENANCE:
Galerie Charpentier, Paris, 1942; auction Versailles, Hôtel Rameau (G. Blache), *Tableaux modernes*, 14 December 1961, no. 12b (ex. catalogue, auction ledger for 14 December 1961); private collection
EXHIBITIONS:
1942 Paris, no. 154
COLLECTION:
Private collection

56. *Place de l'Opéra*, c. 1902-1903
Black chalk
103 x 133 mm
Signed lower right in black chalk: *V.D.*; dated lower left in black chalk over pencil: *1903*; annotated below in black chalk: *Chanteurs ambulants/place de l'opéra.*
PROVENANCE:
Auction, France; Connaught Brown, London, c. 1988; Jane B. and Leonard S. Meranus, Cincinnati, 1995
EXHIBITIONS:
1942 Paris, no. 170 (?); 1943 Bordeaux, no. 138 (?)
COLLECTION:
Jane B. and Leonard S. Meranus, Cincinnati, Ohio, USA

57. *Straatscène* (Street scene), c. 1902
Black chalk on squared paper
127 x 164 mm
Signed lower right in black chalk: *VAN Dongen-*
On reverse: *Drie paarden voor een rijtuig gespannen*, impression from a sketch in black chalk: lower right in ballpoint pen: *PJ*
Special features: torn right edge and squared paper suggest this is probably a page from a notepad. The letters 'PJ' indicate that the drawing appears to have been sent as a *pièce jointe* (enclosure) with a letter.
PROVENANCE:
Private collection, Los Angeles; auction London, Sotheby's, *Impressionist, modern and contemporary paintings...*, 23 October 1985, no. 18 (unsold); Teresa Longyear and David Bull, Washington, 1982
COLLECTION:
Teresa Longyear and David Bull

The drawing *L'entrée de l'église* – which at first sight is merely a fluent street sketch – possesses a social element just like the drawings described earlier. It depicts street-singers hoping to be given a reward for their performance. The lady shrouded in light blue in the foreground belongs, quite unmistakably, to a different social class and contrasts with the darker group of singers on the right in more than just a formal sense. The scene is smoothly sketched and appears to have been built up from chalk scratches and ink stains. The mixture of watercolour and body colour in the woman's robe, creating a sort of open-and-closed veiled effect, is a technique which Van Dongen regularly applied at the time. The *Streetscene*, a notepad sketch of a woman in front of a group of harnessed horses, has, on the reverse side, a light print of a study with horses in front of a carriage. This sketch appears to have served as the model for the drawing *Pigalle-Halle aux Vins*, a title which indicates the dual termini of the omnibus portrayed. (fig.)
The drawings show how Van Dongen went to work: the scribblings done on the street outside on squared paper, called *Place de l'Opéra* and the *Streetscene*, were afterwards developed into independent, more stage-managed drawings and filled in with watercolour, while maintaining their sketchy appearance.

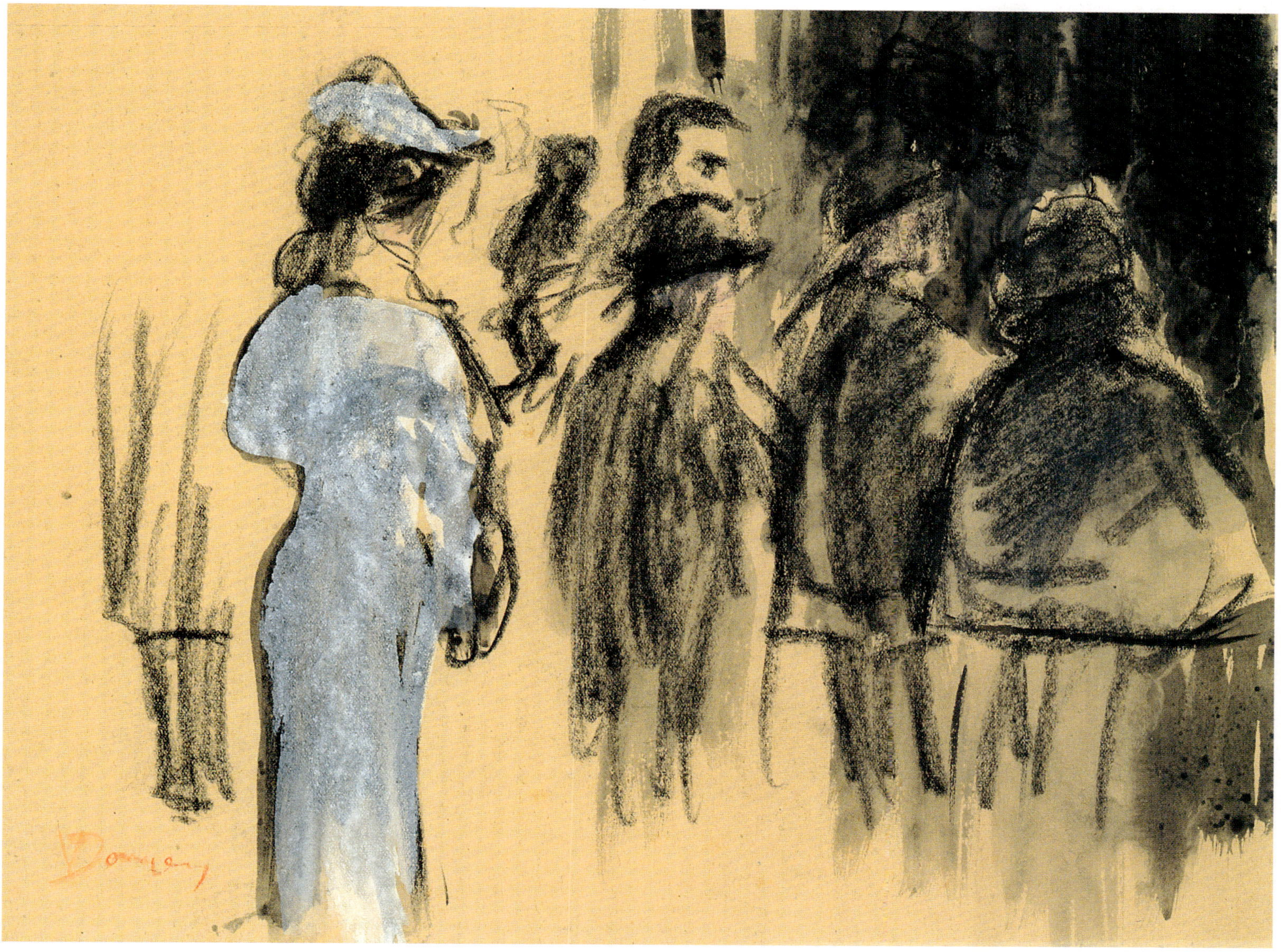

55. *L'entrée de l'église*, c. 1902

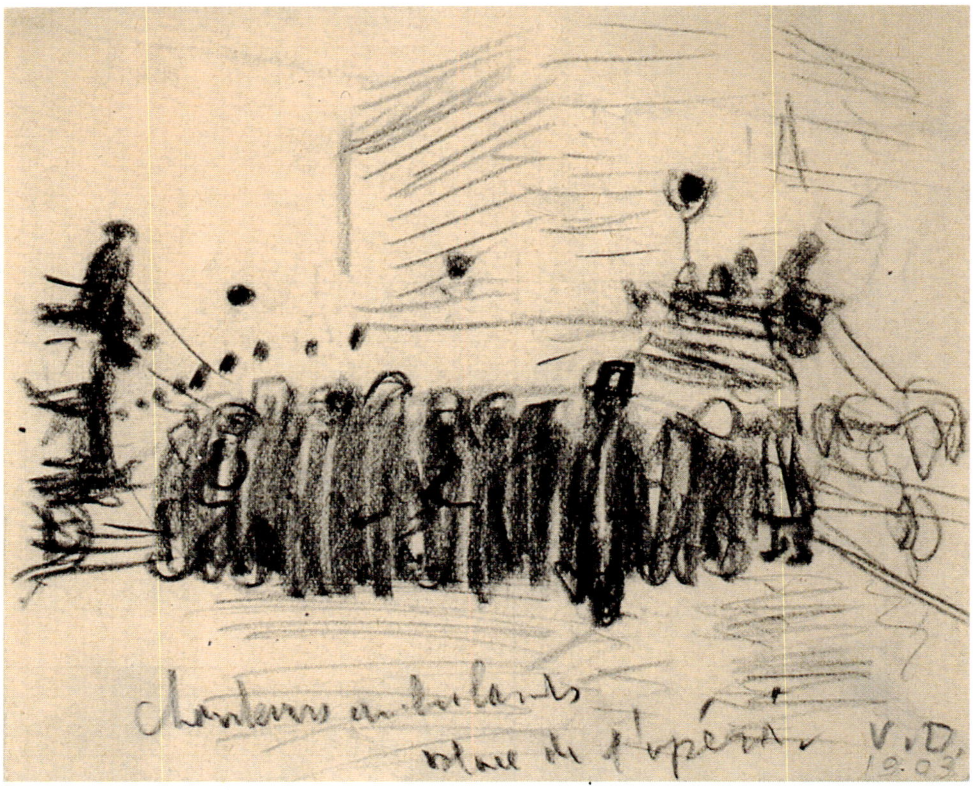

56. *Place de l'Opéra*, c. 1902-1903

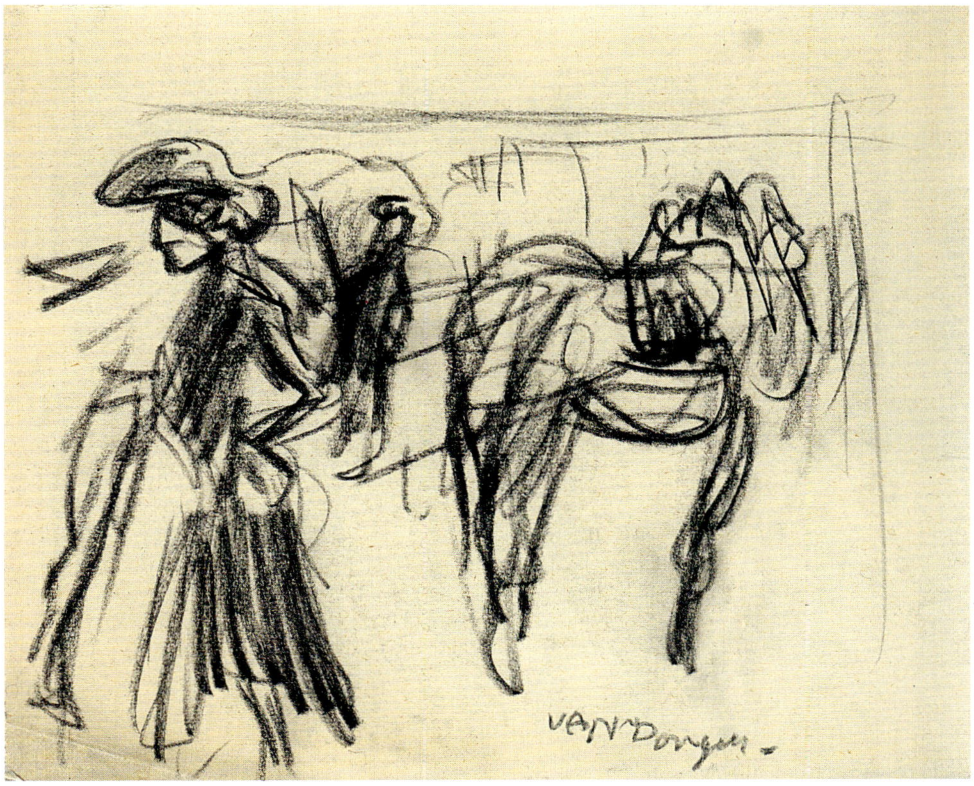

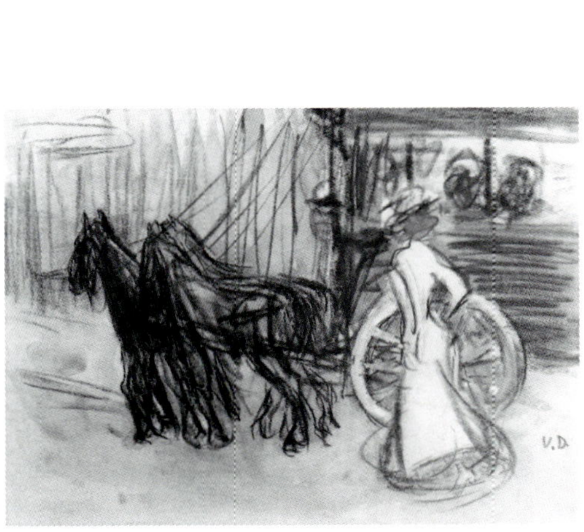

Pigalle-Halle aux Vins, 1902
Black chalk, watercolour, coloured chalk, 240 x 340 mm

57. *Streetscene*, c. 1902

At the end of December 1901 and beginning of 1902 Kees van Dongen once again spent some time in Rotterdam. His stay may have been related to his artistic contribution to the newly founded periodical *De Ware Jacob*. It is equally likely that the miscarriage suffered by his wife Guus Preitinger in December 1901 was the direct reason for his trip. The drawings of a milkmaid and the smooth cameo of snow-movers and farmers seen from the back in which the outlines have been drawn with a few continuous strokes – their feet in a sort of loop – show what by then had become the typical Van Dongen style. The drawings after the milkmaids possess a supreme charisma. (fig.) This subject later came in very handy for Van Dongen when he was in Paris – although it might have been quite coincidental. At the beginning of January 1902 the Parisian daily newspaper *Le Matin* launched into the scandal of milk dilution with great fervour, an affair which was subsequently handled by the entire Parisian press.[1] The Dutch journalist Snabilié also covered it in his 'Brieven uit Parijs' (Letters from Paris).[2] The case involved the milk-workers, the *garçons-laitiers*, who were accused of creaming off and watering down the milk with water from city fountains or other impure sources during its nightly transportation from the city reservoirs to the sales points. The high level of mortality among Parisian children was said to be a direct consequence of this practice. In February the periodical *L'Assiette au Beurre* devoted a whole number to the affair, with contributions from almost all its regular staff. Van Dongen drew a witty retort for *La Vie pour Rire*, for which his Rotterdam milkmaid came in very handy. (fig.) For *Le Matin* the milk question brought more than publicity alone. The money deposited in a fund set up by the paper for a *Ligue pour la Défense de la Vie Humaine*, is alleged to have ended up in the coffers of the newspaper.

58. *Melkmeid* (Milkmaid), c. 1902
Watercolour
456 x 271 mm
Signed lower right in grey: *van Dongen.*
Special features: the drawing is mounted on cardboard; also known as *Werkvrouw met blauw emmer* (Charwoman with blue bucket)
PROVENANCE:
Boymans Museum, Rotterdam, 1936 (gift of the artist; letter from Kees van Dongen to D. Hannema, 7 December 1936, GA Rotterdam)
EXHIBITIONS:
1940 Rotterdam, no. 67; 1947 Eindhoven, no. 131
LITERATURE:
Doelman, p. 7 (fig.); Hannema 1937, p. 10, fig. 9; Hannema 1973, p. 48; Boymans Museum Annual Report 1937, p. 7; Loosjes-Terpstra, 1987, p. 26
COLLECTION:
Boijmans Van Beuningen Museum, Rotterdam, Inv. KvD 10

59. *Sneeuwscheppen* (Shovelling snow), c. 1902
Black chalk, grey wash, watercolour
264 x 450 mm
Signed lower right in black chalk: *van Dongen*
In blue chalk on reverse of cardboard on which drawing is mounted: *41-*
PROVENANCE:
Boymans Museum, Rotterdam, 1936 (gift of the artist; letter from Kees van Dongen to D. Hannema, 7 December 1936, GA Rotterdam)
EXHIBITIONS:
1907 Amsterdam, C.M. van Gogh, no. 47; 1947 Eindhoven, no. 129
LITERATURE:
Hannema 1937, p. 10; Hannema 1973, p. 48; Boymans Museum Annual Report, 1937, p. 7; Schilperoort 1905, p. 7 (fig.)
COLLECTION:
Boijmans Van Beuningen Museum, Rotterdam, Inv. KVD 11

60. *Les deux Hollandais* (The two Dutchmen), c. 1902
Black chalk, watercolour
411 x 270 mm
Signed lower right in orange gouache: *v Dongen.*
Special features: the drawing is mounted on cardboard
PROVENANCE:
Auction Paris, Drouot (C. Robert), *Tableaux modernes. Lithographies, dessins...*, 2 October 1970, no. 36; P. Monart, 1970
COLLECTION:
P. Monart

1. Dixmier 1974, pp. 250-251; *L'Eclair*, 24 January 1902; *Le Figaro*, 6 February 1902.
2. Ch. Snabilié, 'Brieven uit Parijs', *Het Nieuws van den Dag*, 20 January 1902.

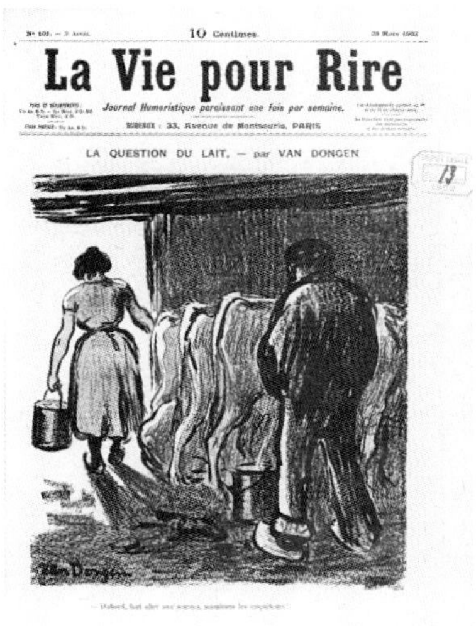

La question du lait (The milk question), 1902
Illustration in *La Vie pour Rire*, no. 101,
29 March 1902

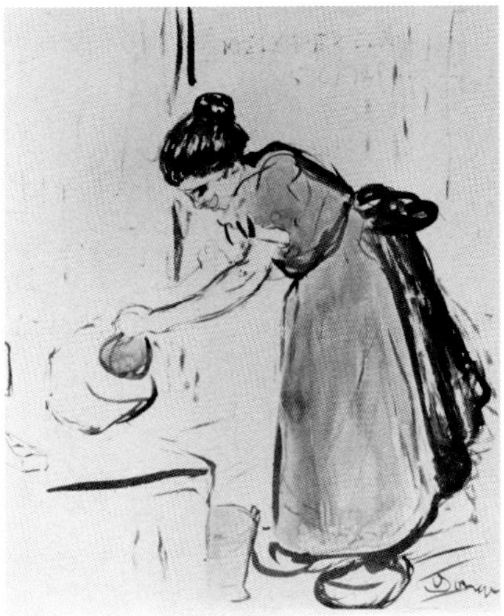

La laitière Hollandaise, c. 1902
Brush in black ink, watercolour, 670 x 545 mm

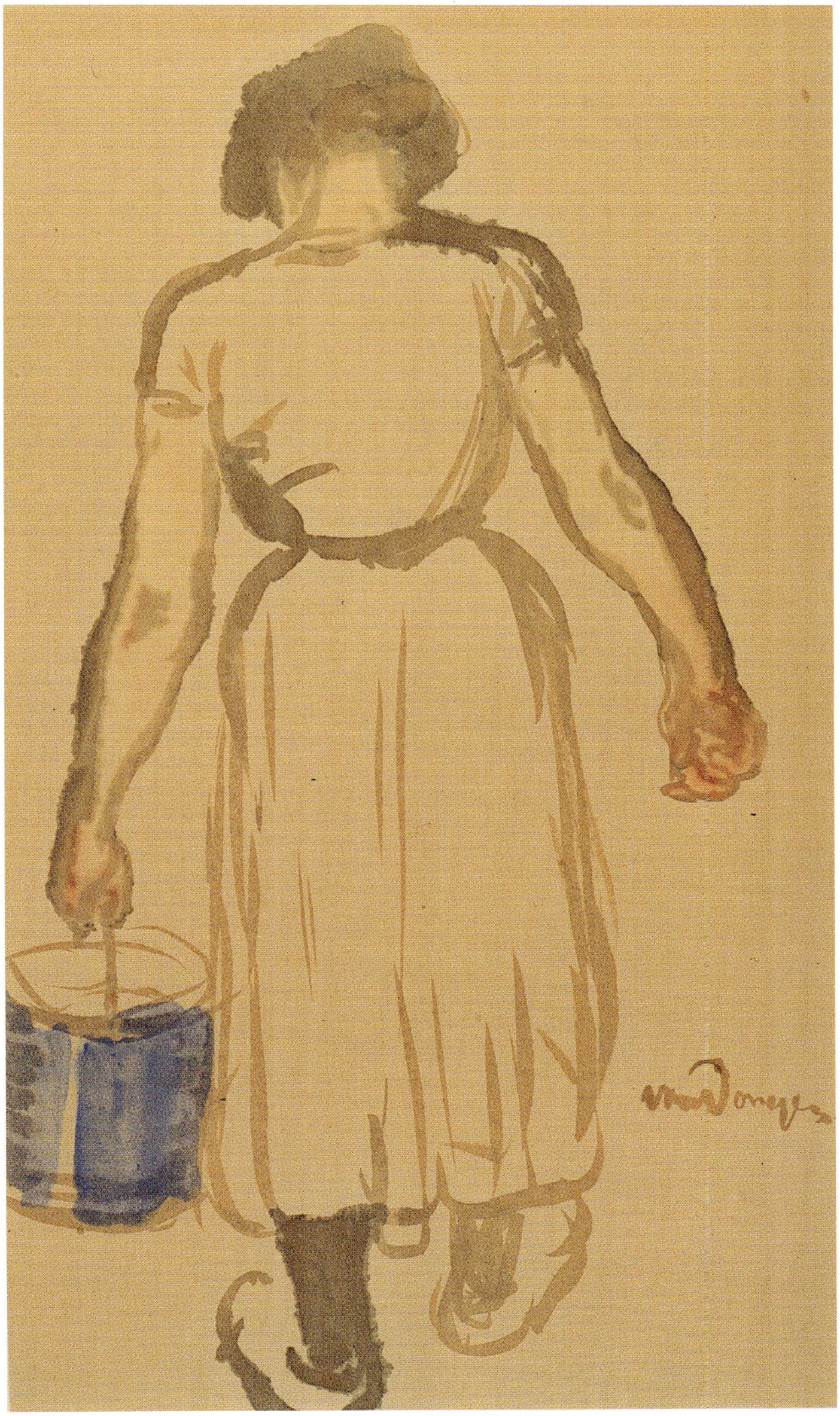

58. *Milkmaid*, 1902

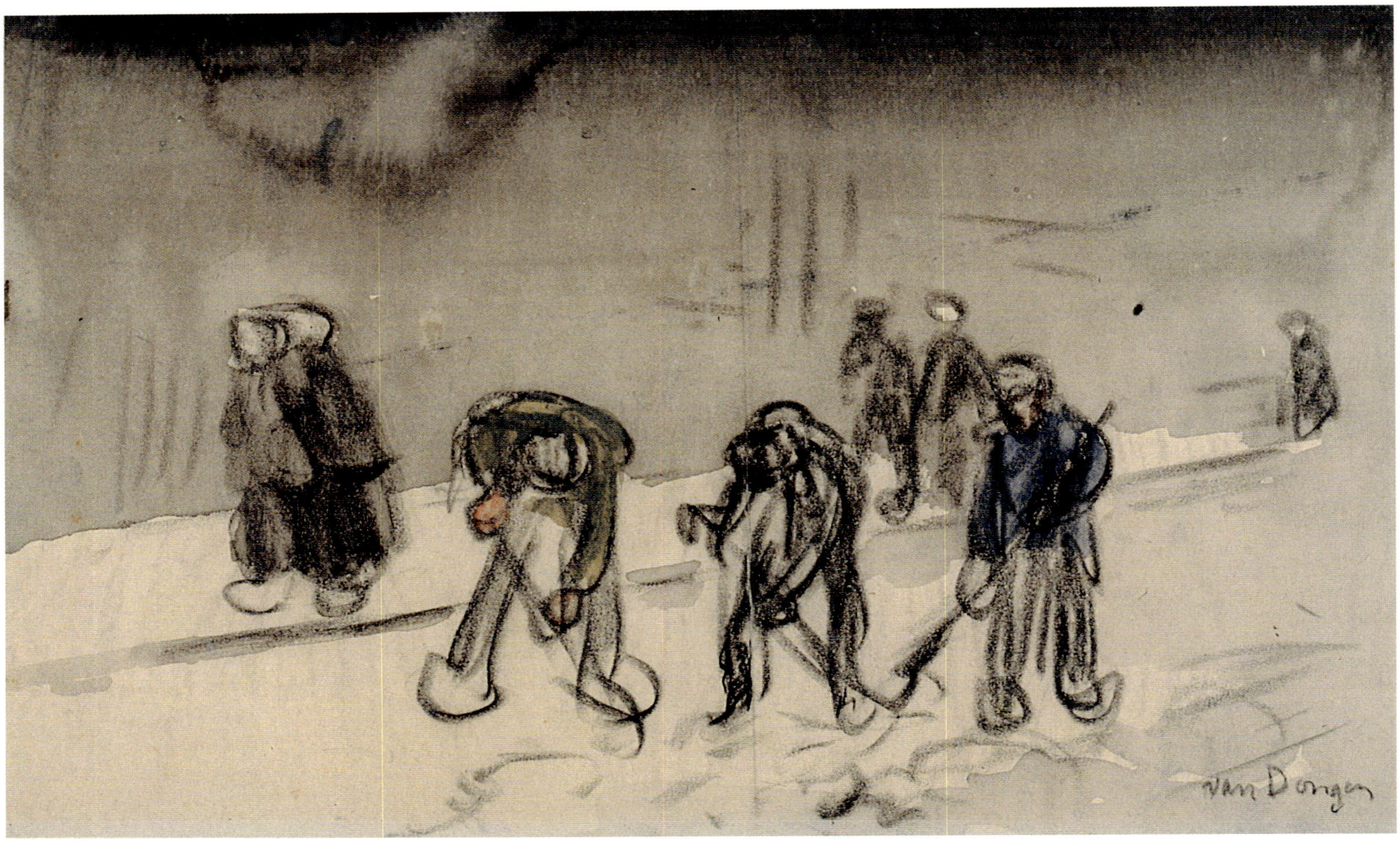

59. *Shovelling snow*, c. 1902

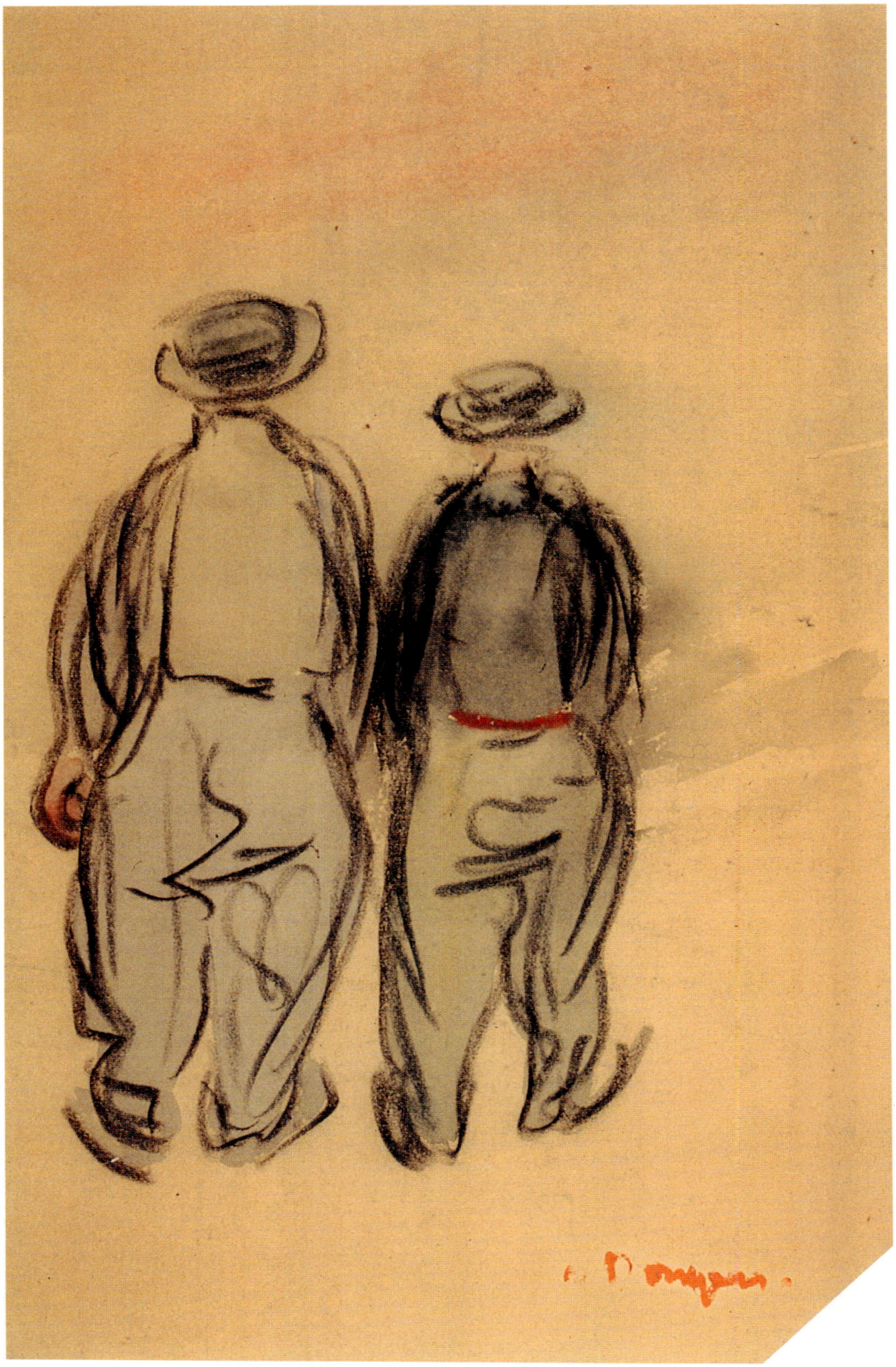

60. *Les deux Hollandais*, c. 1902

61. *Moeder en zus van de kunstenaar*
(The artist's mother and sister), c. 1902
Blue and black chalk over pencil sketch, pen and brush with black ink, white gouache
460 x 310 mm
Signed lower right in brush with black ink: *van Dongen.*
On reverse of frame annotated in ballpoint pen: *Ce dessin réprésente le portrait/de ma mère et de ma soeur/Christine-dessiné en 1896/van Dongen*; in black chalk: *Kees van Dongen/ 10 Impasse Girardon/Montmartre*; a red-printed label: *GALERIE MOOS/GENEVE*, with number in black: *5211*
Special features: lower right a watermark with caduceus and 'C F' in shield

PROVENANCE:
Galerie Max Moos, Geneva; Kunsthandel E.J. van Wisselingh, Amsterdam, 1979 (Inv. T 9359); private collection, 1979
Private collection

62. *Guus en profil* (Guus in profile)
Portrait of Guus Preitinger (1878-1946), c. 1902
Black chalk, pencil
354 x 245 mm
Signed lower right in black chalk: *Kées.*

PROVENANCE:
Dolly van Dongen (1905-1989), Paris (Inv.no. 970); private collection

LITERATURE:
Kyriazi 1971, p. 17 (fig.)
R. Benaïm

The drawing of his mother and his younger sister Christine (born in 1871) in a Dutch snowy landscape, must have been very precious to Van Dongen. The work of art hung, in the rich frame now surrounding the drawing, amidst top paintings in Van Dongen's house in Monaco and afterwards ended up in private hands through Max Moos' gallery. On the back of the frame Van Dongen identified the subject and recorded the date 1896 as the year of its creation. A more plausible date would be around 1901-1902. The drawing was presented by Van Dongen as an illustration for the literary supplement *Le Journal pour Tous*, which appeared on 6 February 1902 with a caption that has nothing to do with the subject of the drawing. (fig.) The artist had given instructions to the printer to roughen up the blue chalk surfaces. These surfaces can be seen in the illustration as grey. It was also printed in a more centred version so that Van Dongen's signature had to be placed at an angle.

The fluent, sketched portrait of Guus Preitinger built up of a few black chalk lines, shows the woman Van Dongen was to marry on 11 July 1901, and must have been created around that time. It may have been a souvenir portrait that Van Dongen had drawn as a reminder of a trip he and Guus made to the Netherlands in 1902. Among the Erich Heckel collection in the Brücke Museum in Berlin, a lithograph portrait of a woman by Van Dongen dated 'Paris 1902' is to be found that shows stylistic similarities. (fig.) The dating of the portrait of Guus is suggested by the signature 'Kées', which appears in exactly the same way on an illustration-drawing Van Dongen made in 1902 for *De Ware Jacob*.

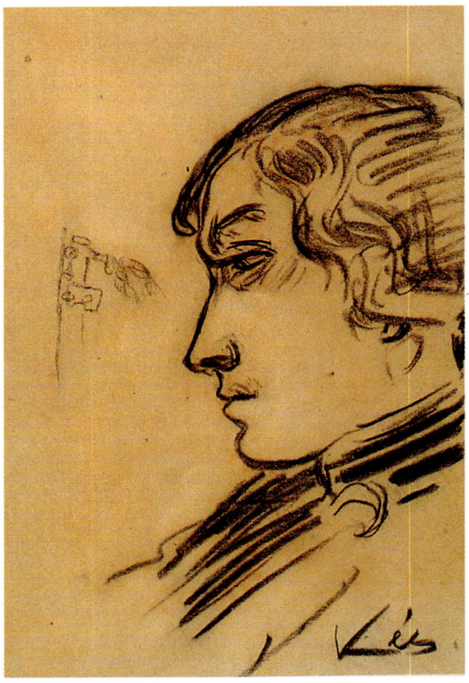

62. *Guus en profil*
Portrait of Guus Preitinger (1878-1946), c. 1902

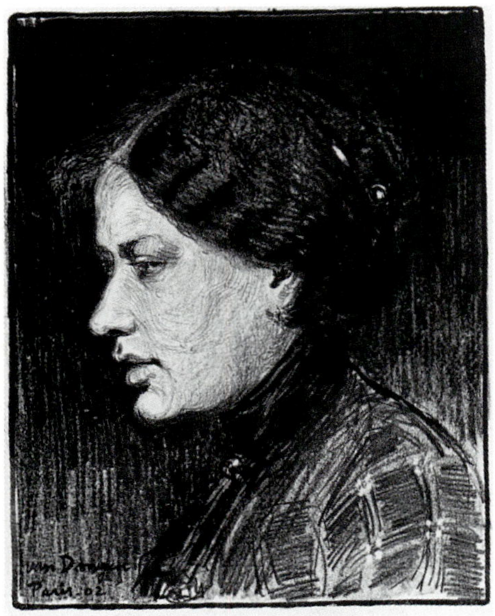

Profile of an unknown woman, 1902
Lithograph, 30 x 24 cm, Brücke Museum, Berlin

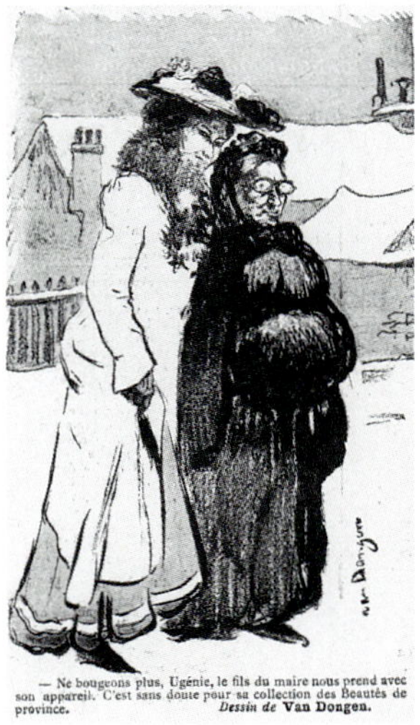

Ne bougeons plus, Ugénie..., 1902
Illustration in *Le Journal pour Tous* no. 6, 6 February 1902, p. 4

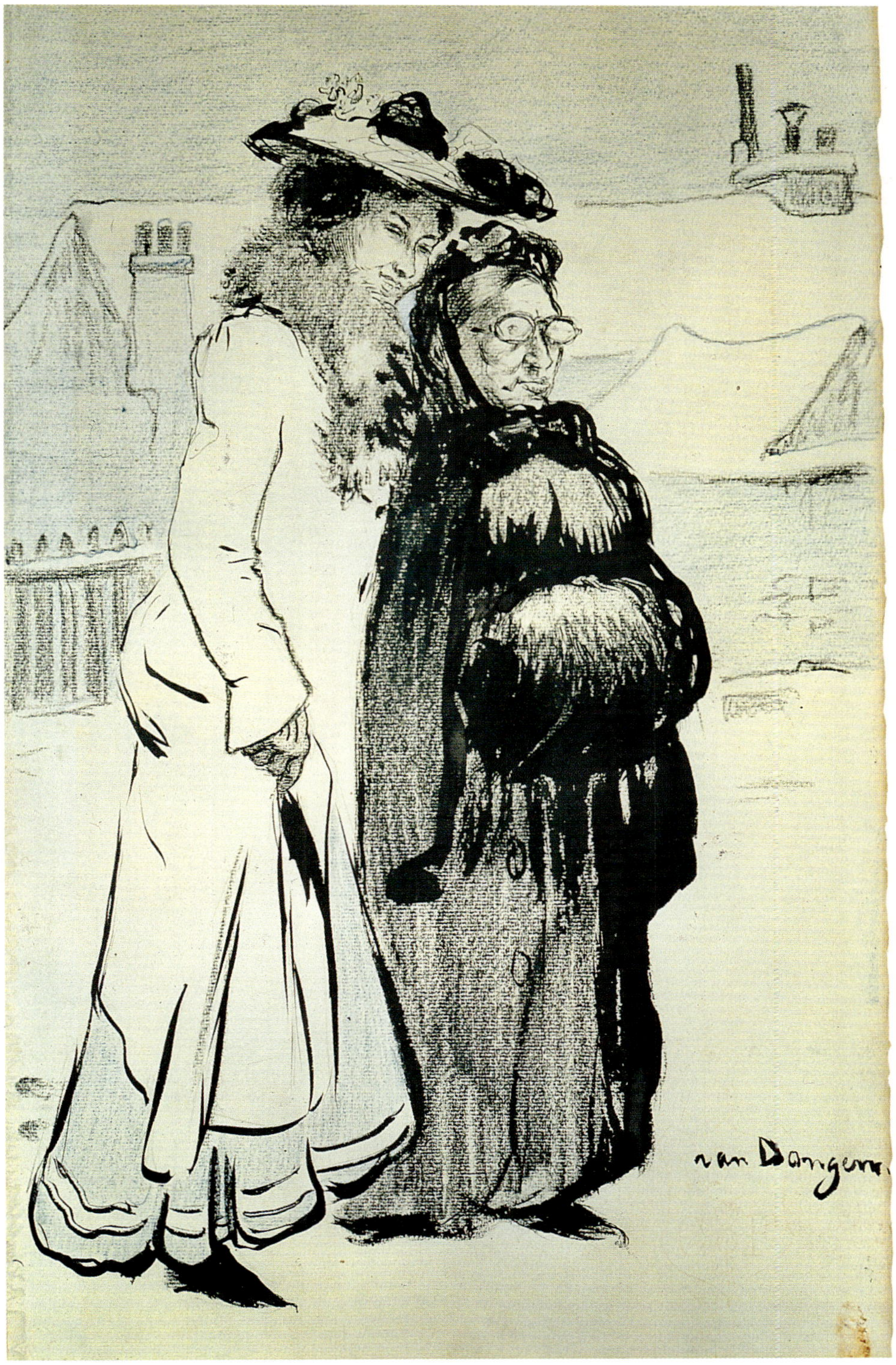

61. *The artist's mother and sister*, c. 1902

63. *Rue chaude à Rotterdam* (Red-light street in Rotterdam), c. 1902
Black chalk, watercolour
284 x 442 mm
Signed upper right in black chalk: *van Dongen.*; in black chalk lower centre: *V.D.*; in black chalk, colour notes in French spread over the sheet: *rouge/rouge/vert*; and number: *41*
Signed and dated in blue chalk on reverse of cardboard on which drawing is mounted: *van Dongen/-Rue chaude à Rotterdam*; in red chalk: *Hollande)*; in blue chalk: 38-
Special features: also known as *Zandstraat Rotterdam*
PROVENANCE:
Boymans Museum, Rotterdam, 1936 (gift of the artist; letter from Kees van Dongen to D. Hannema, 7 December 1936, GA Rotterdam)
EXHIBITIONS:
1940 Rotterdam, no. 66
LITERATURE:
Van Gelder 1958, p. 81, fig. 215
Hannema 1937, p. 10
Boymans Museum Annual Report 1937, p. 7
Loosjes-Terpstra 1987, p. 23, fig. 17
COLLECTION:
Boijmans Van Beuningen Museum, Rotterdam, Inv. KVD 7

64. *In de nes* (In the Nes), c. 1902
Black chalk, pen with black ink, grey wash, watercolour, white gouache
450 x 275 mm
Signed and dated lower right in black chalk: *van Dongen./1898.*; in grey over signature: *Kées*; black chalk upper left: *[C]AFE*
Note in ballpoint pen lower right on cardboard on which drawing is mounted: *In de Nes*; on the reverse customs stamp (?) in purple ink: *Paris* (partially illegible)
PROVENANCE:
W.J.R. Dreesmann (1885-1954), Amsterdam, c. 1949-1951; Historisch-topografische Atlas, GA Amsterdam, 1960 (?)
LITERATURE:
Dreesmann 1951, p. 798
COLLECTION:
Historisch-topografische Atlas, GA Amsterdam, Inv. Dreesmann Collection XXXIV-1006C

65. *De Zandstraat, Rotterdam* (Zandstraat in Rotterdam), c. 1902
Black chalk
430 x 260 mm
Signed lower right in black chalk: *van Dongen -*; over note in blue chalk: *voor Herman/Schotel/vriendschap/ Kées*; in black chalk upper left: *H.OLSEN*
PROVENANCE:
Dolly van Dongen (1905-1989), Paris; private collection; auction Paris, Drouot (Loudmer), *Tableaux modernes et sculptures*, 7 June 1993, no. 105 (fig.); auction London, Sotheby's, *Impressionist and modern art...*, 13 October 1993, no. 40 (fig.)
EXHIBITIONS:
1971 Tucson, no. 37 (fig.)
LITERATURE:
Kyriazi 1971, p. 13 (fig.); Sutton 1971, p.38, fig. 3; Diehl 1971, p. 88
COLLECTION:
R. Benaïm

These drawings which once again have the Zandstraat neighbourhood as their subject, must have been created in around 1901-02. The figures portrayed are different from the earlier drawings in that they are situated more in the neighbourhood and are somewhat caricatural. The artist also seems to have had more of an eye for the entertainment in the neighbourhood. In a drawing like *Rue chaude* the prostitutes and pimps are standing around in groups on the street waiting good-naturedly for customers, the scene of *Le bal* portrays enjoyment at a dance-hall. In *Rue chaude* Van Dongen used bright colours and noted the specifications for them in French, which also indicates the date at which they were made, which must have been after 1900. He used a few of the figures sketched in this drawing for an illustration-drawing which in March 1902 appeared on the cover of the French satirical journal *La Caricature*. (fig.) The title, *Les élections approchent*, refers to the imminent elections for the French parliament. 'Enfin, pendant quelques mois, nous allons être tranquilles... Waldeck a besoin d'nous pour les élections' the caption reads (We'll have things quiet for a few months...Waldeck needs our cooperation). The remark may be a reference to the so-called 'rafles', police raids to pick up unregistered prostitutes, which may have been temporarily halted to win votes. A few of the places can be identified. The drawing dedicated to Herman Schotel, *De Zandstraat*, portrays the 'Bierhuis' (literally Beer house) run by H. Olsen at number 75. The pub 'de Nightlamp' was on the corner of Zandstraat and Peperstraat. It was a celebrated nightclub where the riff-raff gathered after other establishments had closed and where, according to the chief of police, 'artists' hung around as a integral part of their studies.[1] The man sitting on the chair in front of the window was apparently an infamous character, nicknamed 'the horse thief'. The ladies in front of the pub in the drawing *In de Nes*, one of the streets in Amsterdam known for its nightlife, were despite Van Dongen's (later designated) title more likely to be found in the Rotterdam red-light area.

1.
M.J. Brusse, 'Polder-herinneringen van een oud-politiecommandant in de Zandstraatbuurt' (Recollections of a policeman in the Zandstraat area), I, VIII, *Nieuwe Rotterdamsche Courant*, 15 March, 8 April 1933.

66. *Le bal* (The ball), c. 1902
Brush in black ink, grey wash, over sketch in black chalk
424 x 285 mm
Signed lower right in black chalk: *van Dongen.*
PROVENANCE:
Auction Versailles, Hôtel Rameau (G. Blache), *Tableaux modernes*, 19 June 1985, no. 35; auction Auch-en-Gascogne, Hôtel des Ventes, (A. Briscadieu), *Nombreux et importants dessins...*, 29 June 1988, no. 75 (fig.); auction London, Christie's, *Impressionist and modern watercolours...*, 29 November 1988, no. 333 (fig.); Christoph Czwiklitzer (1914-1992), 1988; private collection
COLLECTION:
Private collection

67. *Café de Nightlamp* (The Nightlamp Café), c. 1902
Black chalk, watercolour, brush in black ink
460 x 285 mm (present size)
Lower left remains of signature in black chalk in artist's handwriting: *D...en.*; completed and dated in pencil in other handwriting: *van Dong/1895.*; in black chalk upper centre: *CAFE/DE/NICHTLAMP/LOGEMENT*; in blue chalk upper right: *n°1.* (crossed out in black chalk)
On reverse of frame in red chalk: *no.3/M.J. Brusse Hillergersberg/Zandstraat/Rotterdam*
PROVENANCE:
M.J. Brusse (1873-1941), Rotterdam; private collection
EXHIBITIONS:
1935 Amsterdam (ex. catalogue)
LITERATURE:
Brusse 1912, p. 8; Brusse 1917, fig. 3
COLLECTION:
Private collection

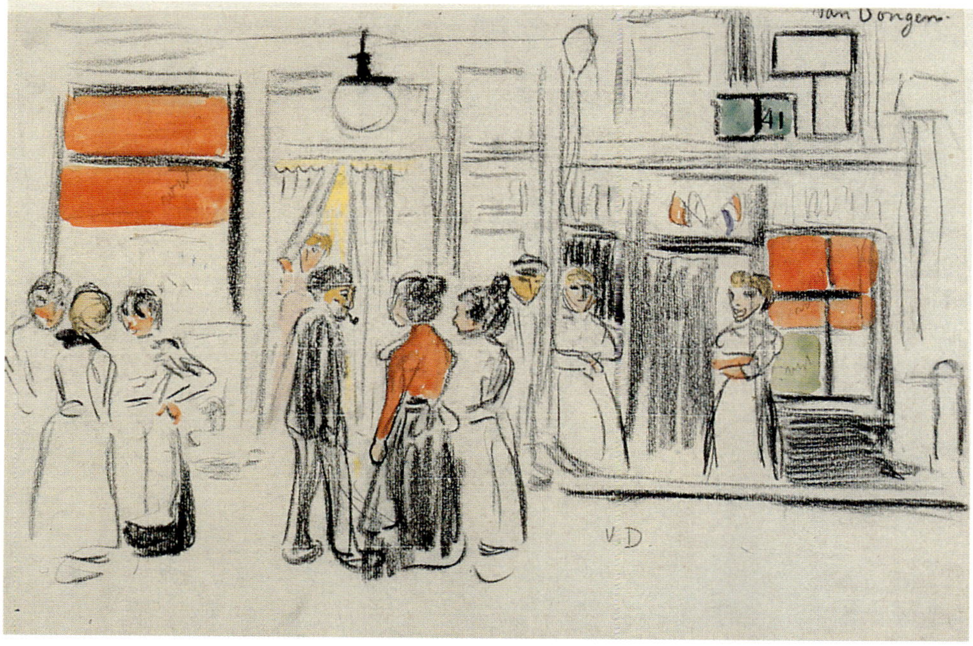

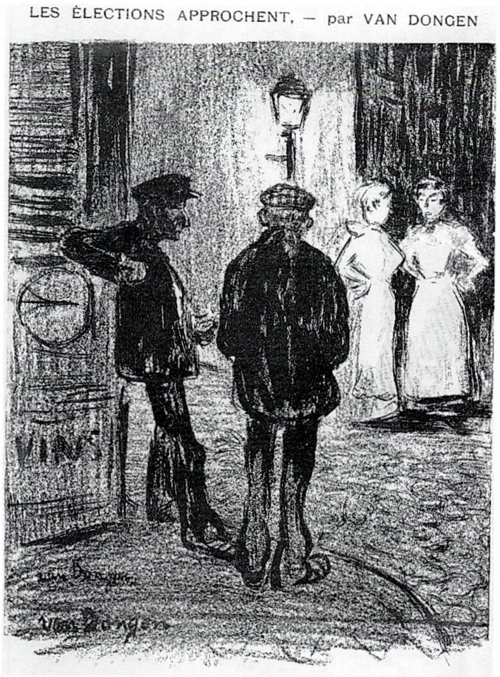

Les élections approchent, 1902
Cover *La Caricature*, no. 1157, 1 March 1902

63. *Rue chaude à Rotterdam*, c. 1902

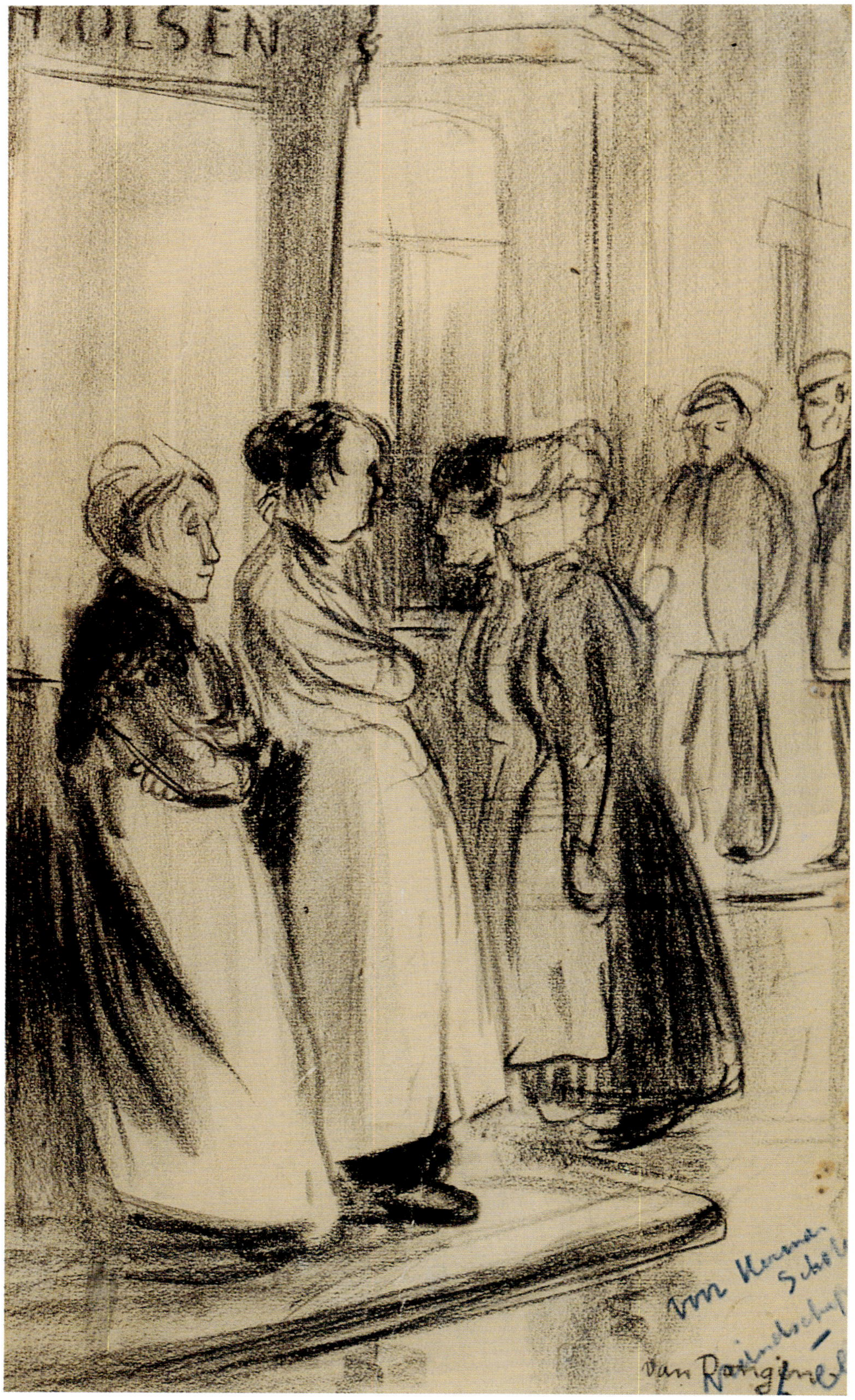

65. *De Zandstraat, Rotterdam*, c. 1902

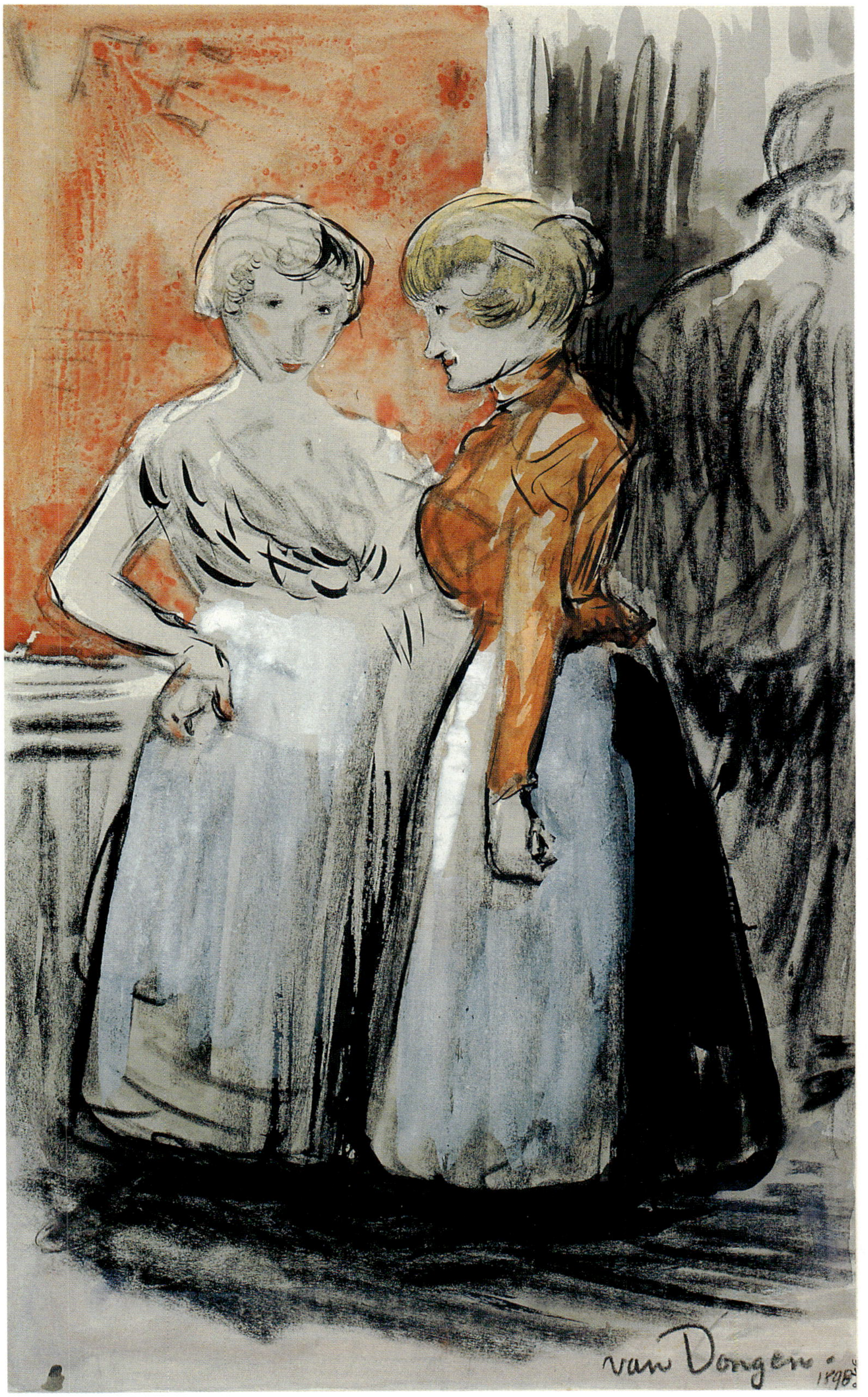

64. *In de nes*, c. 1902

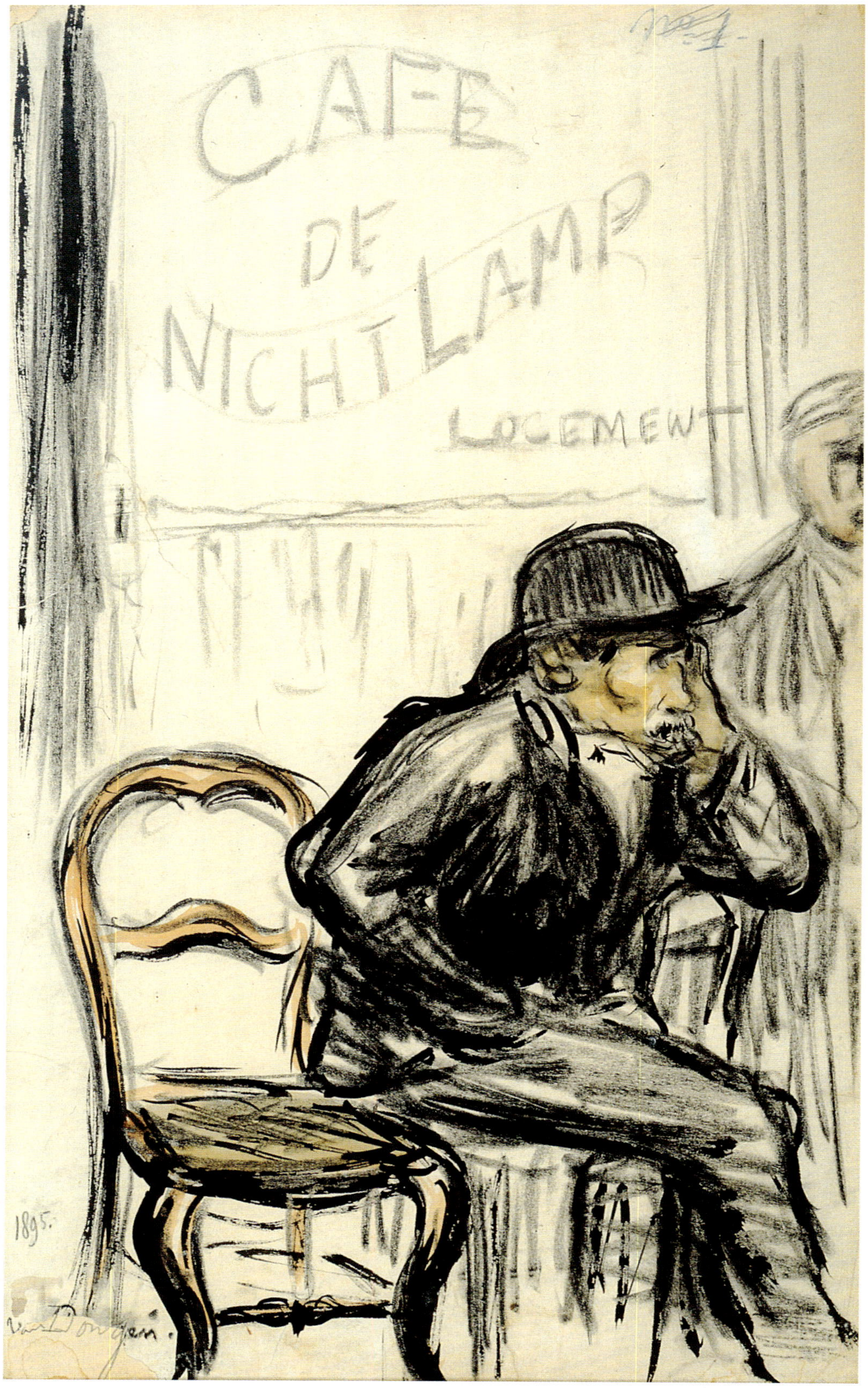

67. *Café de Nightlamp*, c. 1902

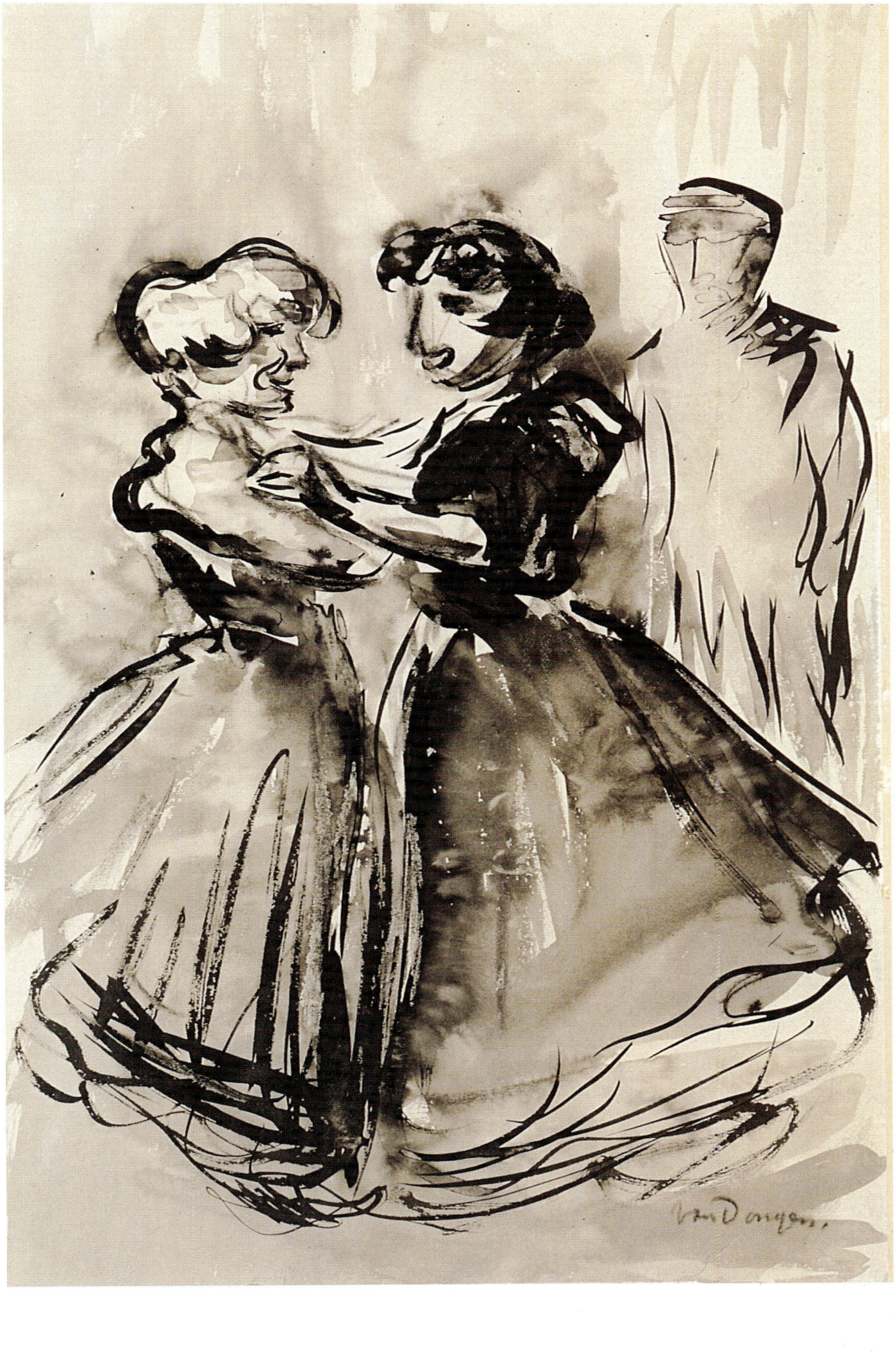

66. *Le bal*, c. 1902

68. *Vrede* (Peace)
Extra editon of *De Ware Jacob*
June 1902
16 drawings including cover. Published by the Nederlandsche Kiosken-Maatschappij, Rotterdam. Printed by Cliché Hélios, Rotterdam
PROVENANCE:
Antiquarian bookshop Niek Waterbolk, Utrecht
COLLECTION:
Boijmans Van Beuningen Museum, Rotterdam

On 21 June 1902, what was then the most important Dutch satirical periodical *De Ware Jacob* announced the publication of a special number illustrated throughout by Kees van Dongen. This extra number, entitled *Vrede* (Peace), was published in addition to the regular weekly edition and could be bought separately. The publication has not been heard of up to now because it was not included in the compiled editions of the periodical which are to be found in the Dutch public collections. This Peace number and the prostitution number brought out by *L'Assiette au Beurre* in 1901 are the only two periodicals illustrated entirely by Van Dongen. Undeniably, they are a testimony to Van Dongen's level of social engagement. The *Ware Jacob* number in particular bears witness to his anarchic disposition. In the publication Van Dongen gave a critical commentary of the Boer War, the conflict between the South African republic Transvaal and the Orange Free State and Britain, which began in October 1899 and officially ended on 31 May 1902. The title *Vrede* is meant to be ironic: peace between the states was forced at the cost of great human sacrifice. The sad result is the subject of the first print. Cecil Rhodes, former leader of the British South Africa Company who had colonized various areas in South Africa and brought them under British rule – and who was partly responsible for the Boer War – is represented here as a skeleton (Rhodes died in March 1902) and surrounded by countless numbers of coffins. Parodying Hamlet's soliloquy 'To be or not to be' he asks Queen Victoria's skull (the queen had died in January 1901), what will it be: 'War or peace?' The scene expresses the futility of the conflict. Another explicitly critical rendering is the representation 'Zoo was 't. Zoo zal 't zijn' (That's how it was. That's how it will be) in which a black man is portrayed on the left, representative of the indigenous population, treated by a Boer as a slave, and on the right can be seen how the black slave and the Boer are both equally subjugated by an English armed soldier. This representation runs contrary to the general consensus which was that the heroic Boers were seen as victims of the imperialistic and all powerful British. On the two following pages Van Dongen depicts the soldiers on both sides in an almost identical way and ironically portrays them as heroes. The following images of the mutilated soldiers, remains of those who had been killed, and the widow with her child, speak for themselves. Together they form a general indictment against war. The only conflict which Van Dongen would support, going by one of the main illustrations in the number *De Kroning* (The Coronation) would be that of the people against the British ruler, King Edward VII. In this drawing Van Dongen appears to be inciting an anarchic uprising against the king, successor to Queen Victoria: the crown which would have been presented to the king at the coronation ceremony in August 1902 is thrown into the air by the personification of anarchy. One wonders whether the pro-Boer Dutch public would have shown much appreciation for Van Dongen's vision as portrayed in *Vrede*.

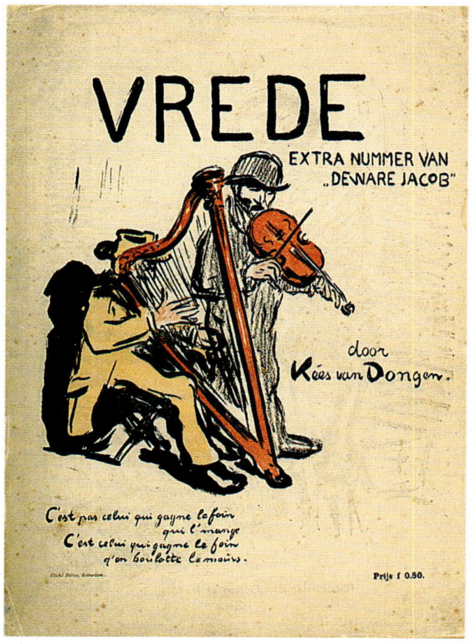

Cover *Vrede* extra edition of *De Ware Jacob*

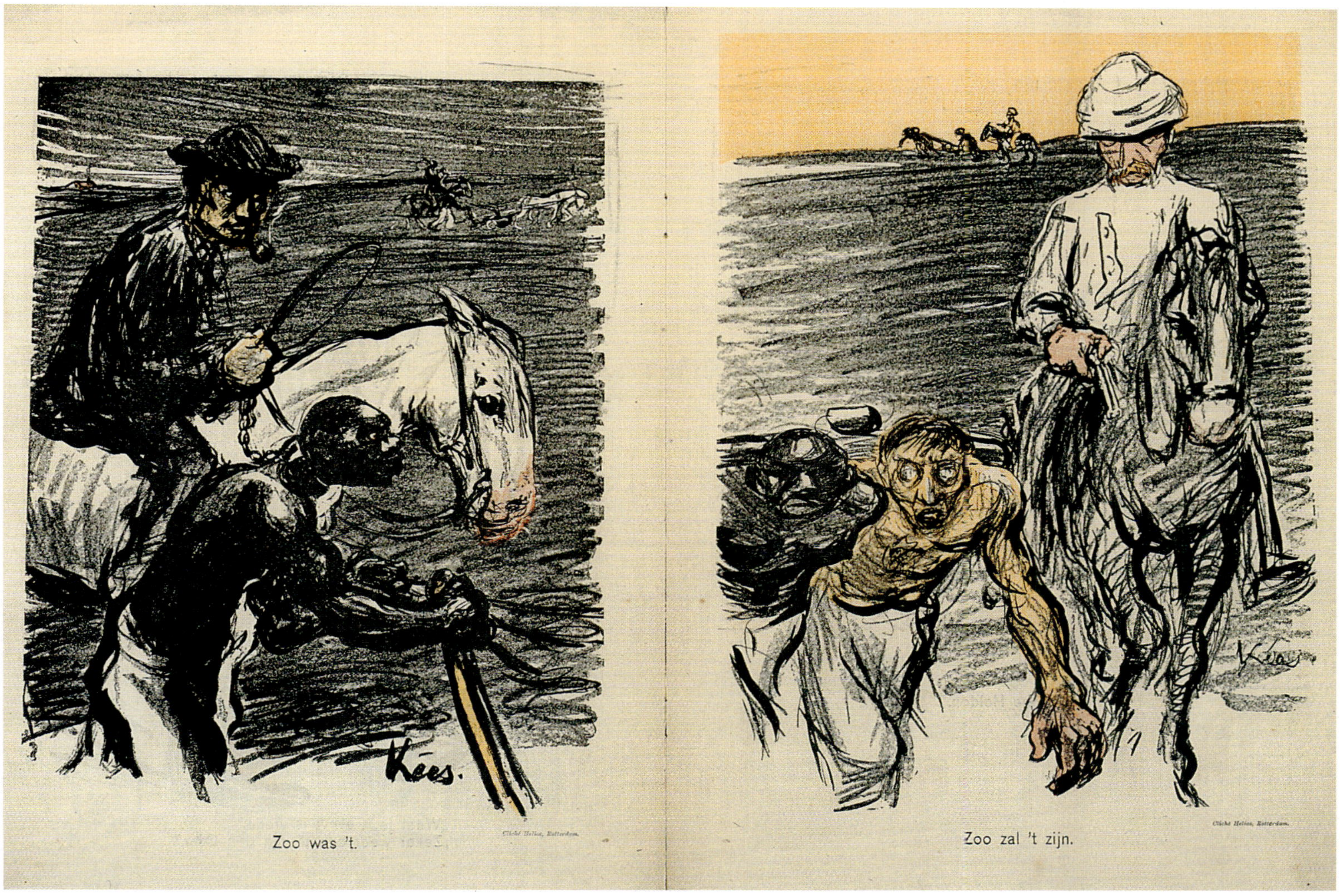

68. *That's how it was. That's how it will be*, June 1902, illustration in *Vrede*, Extra number *De Ware Jacob*

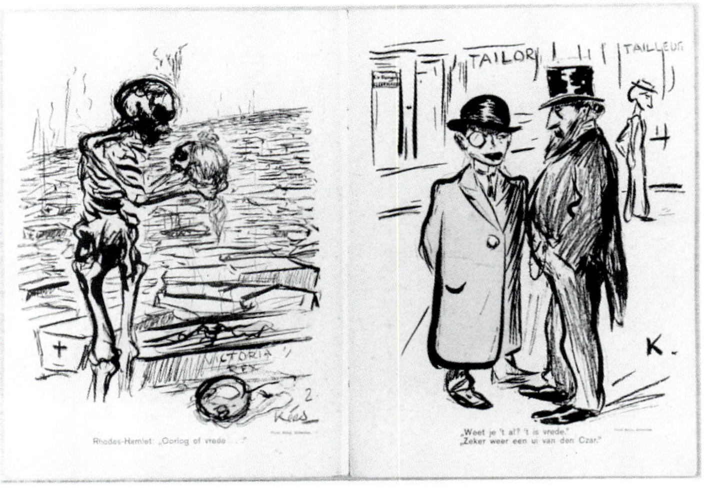

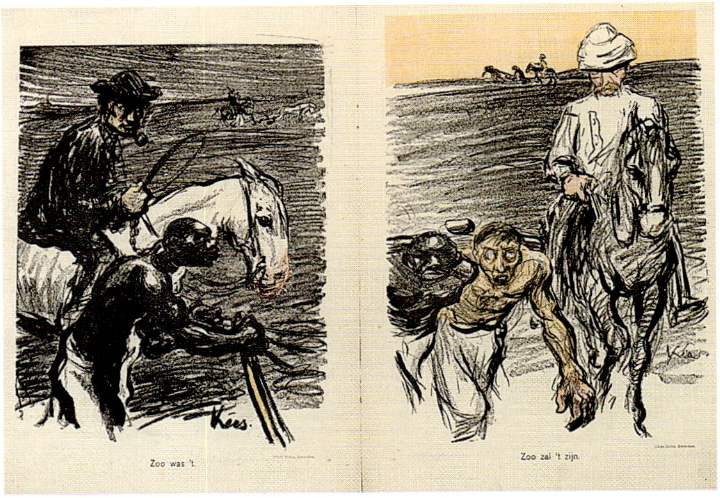

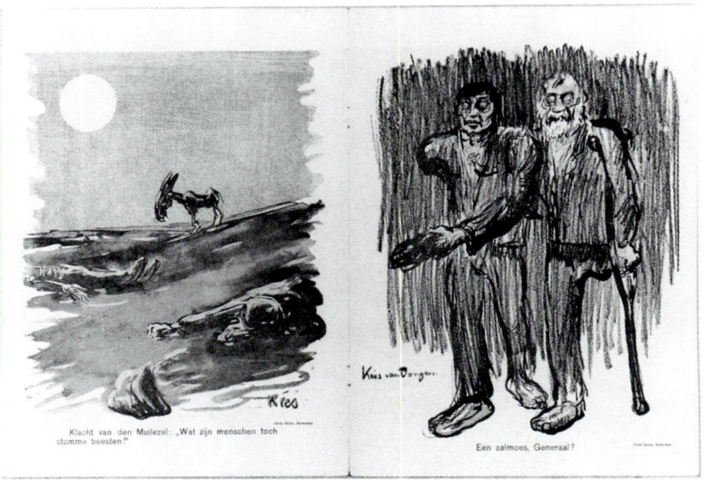

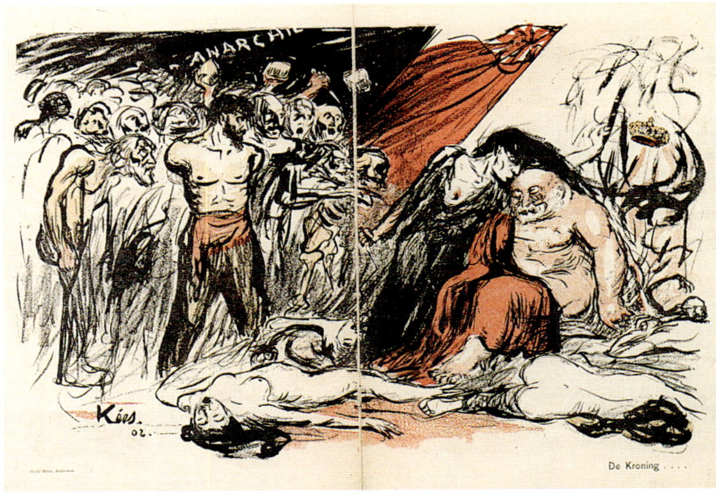

Rhodes-Hamlet: 'War or Peace...'
'Have you heard? there is peace. Must be one of the Tsar's jokes.'

The mule's complaint! 'Aren't people stupid animals!'
Charity, General?

That's how it was. That's how it will be

The Coronation...

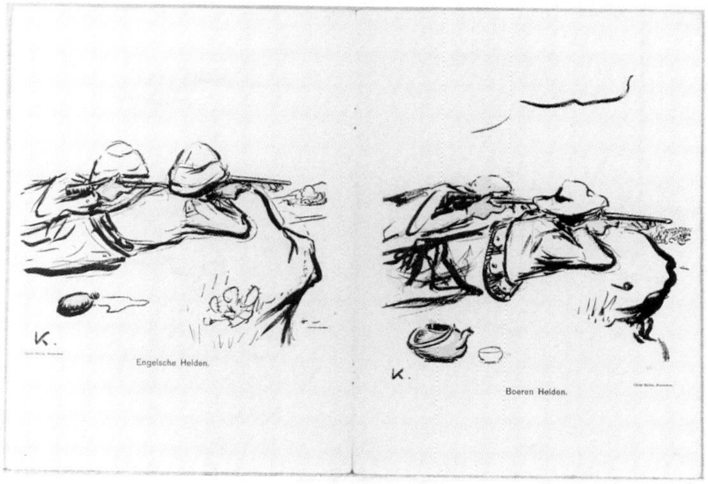

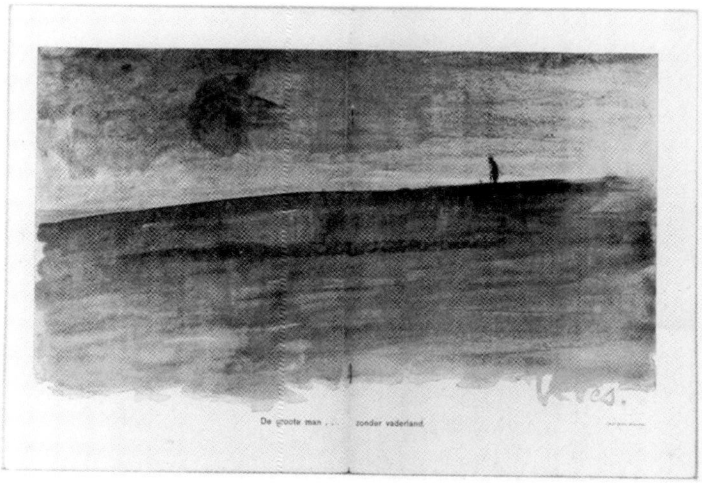

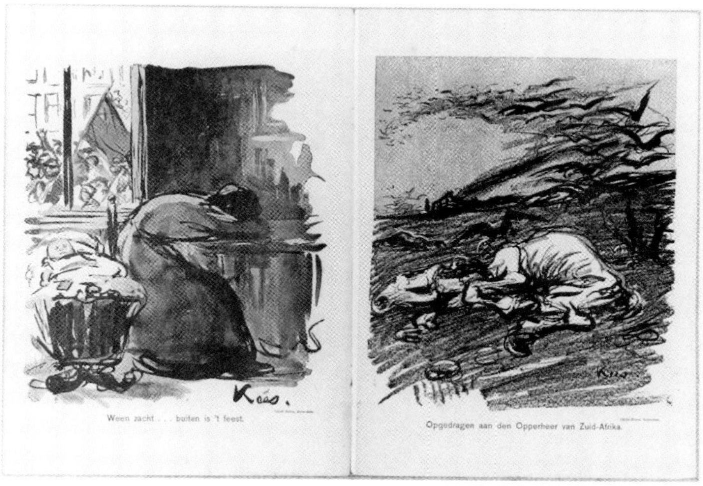

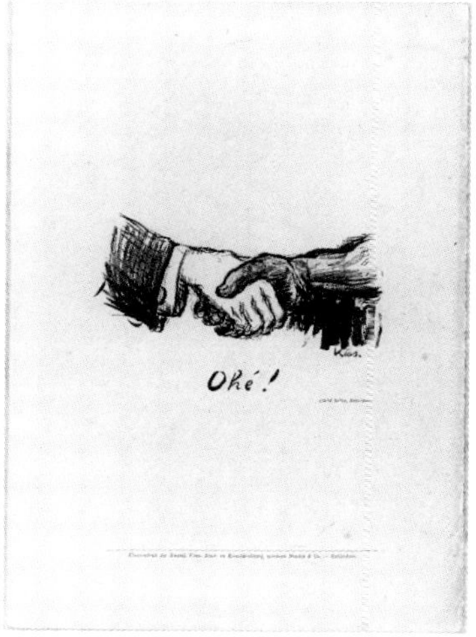

English Heroes. Boer Heroes

The great man... with no homeland

Be quiet... outside it's a party
Dedicated to the ruler of South Africa.

Ohé!

69. *Buveuse d'absinthe* (Woman drinking absinthe), c. 1902
Brush with black ink, grey wash, over sketch in black chalk, watercolour, gouache
410 x 605 mm (present size)
Signed lower left with brush in grey: *Van Dongen*
On reverse of frame a label with printed, blue ornamented border; marked with pen in brown ink: *N°68/Van Dongen./ Buveuse d'Absinthe*; a label with printed blue edges; marked in pen with brown ink: *n°11./Kees van Dongen/buveuse d'absinth*; note in pencil: *Dr Cerf/...* [illegible]
PROVENANCE:
Dr Jean Cerf, Brussels; Mevrouw Jean L'Hoest-Cerf, Brussels; auction Antwerp, Guillaume Campo, *Moderne schilderijen*, 6-9 April 1976, no. 637; private collection
COLLECTION:
Private collection (with assistance of BVBA Stefan Campo, Antwerp)

70. *Les vieux et la mort* (The old folks and death), c. 1902
Brush with black ink, grey wash, over sketch in blue chalk, white gouache, on brown discoloured paper
580 x 720 mm (present size)
Signed lower left in brush with brown: *Kées*; annotated lower centre in brush with brown: *Les vieux et la mort*
On reverse of frame a black-printed label: *GALERIE CHARPENTIER/76 FAUBOURG SAINT-HONORE-PARIS/EXPOSITION VAN DONGEN/CINQUANTE ANS DE PEINTURE/-MCMXLII-*; blank label with red chalk: *B/8*
PROVENANCE:
Gift of Kees and Marie-Claire van Dongen to the Musée Toulouse-Lautrec, Albi, June 1961
EXHIBITIONS:
1941 Paris, Galerie Charpentier, no. 207; 1943 Bordeaux, no. 92; 1959 Geneva, no. 12; 1960 Albi, no. 61; 1981 Nice, no. 35; 1991 Toulouse, no. 120 (fig.)
Musée Toulouse-Lautrec, Albi, Inv. 425

71. *Zittende man* (Seated man), c. 1903
Pen and brush with black ink, white gouache over sketch of figure wearing hat
410 x 278 mm
Signed lower right in brush with black ink: *van Dongen.*; over signature in blue chalk
PROVENANCE:
Erich Heckel (1883-1970), Hemmenhofen; Brücke-Museum, Berlin, 1966-1969 (gift of Erich Heckel)
LITERATURE:
Brücke Archives 1970, p. 49
COLLECTION:
Brücke-Museum, Berlin, Inv. 753/66

72. *Femme à la voilette* (Woman with a veil), 1903
Black chalk, brush with black ink, watercolour
298 x 233 mm
Signed lower right in black chalk: *van Dongen.*; lower right pen in black ink: *Inv. 579.* (Inv. Jacques Doucet); lower right stamp in grey ink: *M.N.* (Musées Nationaux)
PROVENANCE:
Jacques Doucet (1853-1929), Paris; his sale, Hôtel Drouot (A. Desvouges), Paris, *Aquarelles, pastels & dessins modernes*, 28-29 December 1917, no. 333; Gaston Migeon, Paris, 1917; his sale, Drouot (H. Baudoin), Paris, *Tableaux modernes, aquarelles, pastels...*, 18-21 March 1931, no. 101; Carle Dreyfus (1875-1952), Paris 1931; Musée National d'Art Moderne, Centre Georges Pompidou, Paris, 1953 (bequest C. Dreyfus)
EXHIBITIONS:
1953 Paris, no. 303; 1954 Paris, no. 220; 1957 Pau, no. 68; 1958 Luxembourg, no. 78; 1959 Villeneuve sur Lot, etc., no. 60; 1962 Mexico, no. 138; 1963 Stockholm, no. 134; 1974 Paris, no. 183 (fig.); 1981 Nice, no. 33
COLLECTION:
Musée National d'Art Moderne, Centre Georges Pompidou, Paris, Inv. AM 1872 D

The drunken woman, *The absinthe drinker*, who has collapsed spread-eagled on the ground, appears to be challenging death: she is offering the skull a glove with a welcoming gesture. It is not a happy sight, nor is Van Dongen's rendering of it. Little colour has been applied to this predominantly ink-drawn, monumental drawing; the deep red must have been used to underline the dramatic content of the scene. The consumption of spirits in France, particularly absinthe, rose enormously in the last quarter of the nineteenth century. This increase was the result of commercial enterprise, low prices, but more significantly of social change. Frequenting pubs and cabaret establishments became a regular way of life for a broad cross-section of society during the *belle époque*, a trend which became increasingly common among women too.[1] The popularity of the pale-green coloured absinthe became the butt of criticism in left-wing circles. The rage for it was profitable for those dealing in it as it was a product which could easily be tampered with ending in disastrous consequences for the users. 'The green fairy' was only banned by law relatively late in France, in 1915. The drawing of a woman walking along the street in high spirits is related to *The absinthe drinker* in both representation and technique and demonstrates that Van Dongen explored the subject as a theme. (fig.)

Death also appears in a drawing with two figures sitting at the table; the candle of life is blown out by the woman on the left. The depiction is not very clear, but that their demise is the result of a poverty-stricken existence seems more than likely. The drawing of the sinister-looking man and the woman in the veiled hat can be traced to 1903; the dating of the last drawing relies upon an illustration drawing. (fig.)

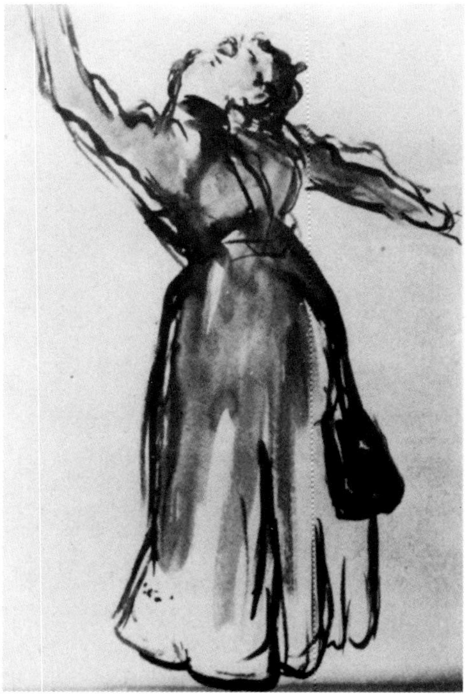

Femme, c. 1902
Ink, watercolour, 550 x 365 mm

1. Herbert 1988, pp. 72-74; M.R. Marrus, 'Social drinking in the *belle époque*', *Journal of Social History*, 7 (winter 1974) no. 2, pp. 115-141.

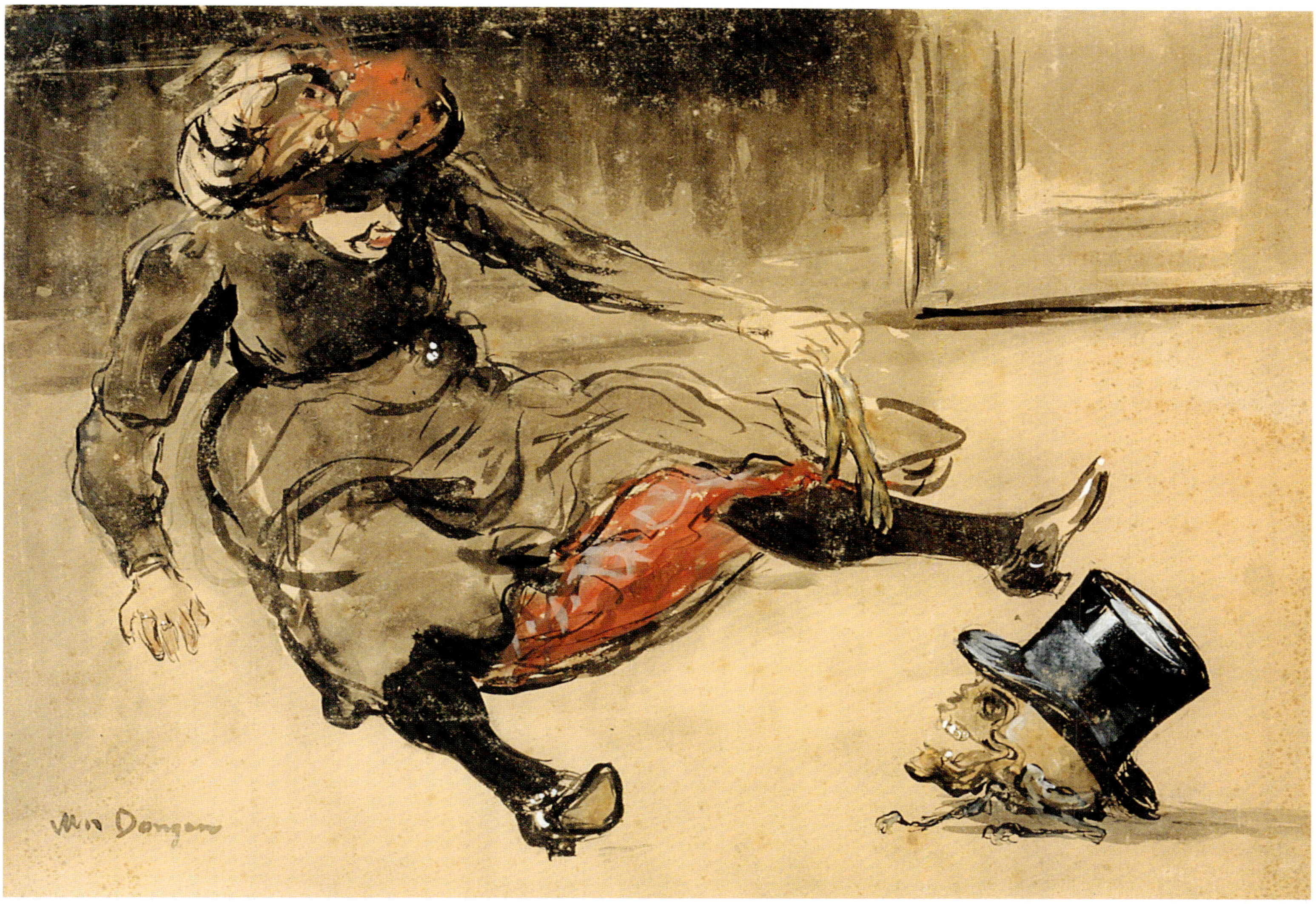

69. *Buveuse d'absinthe*, c. 1902

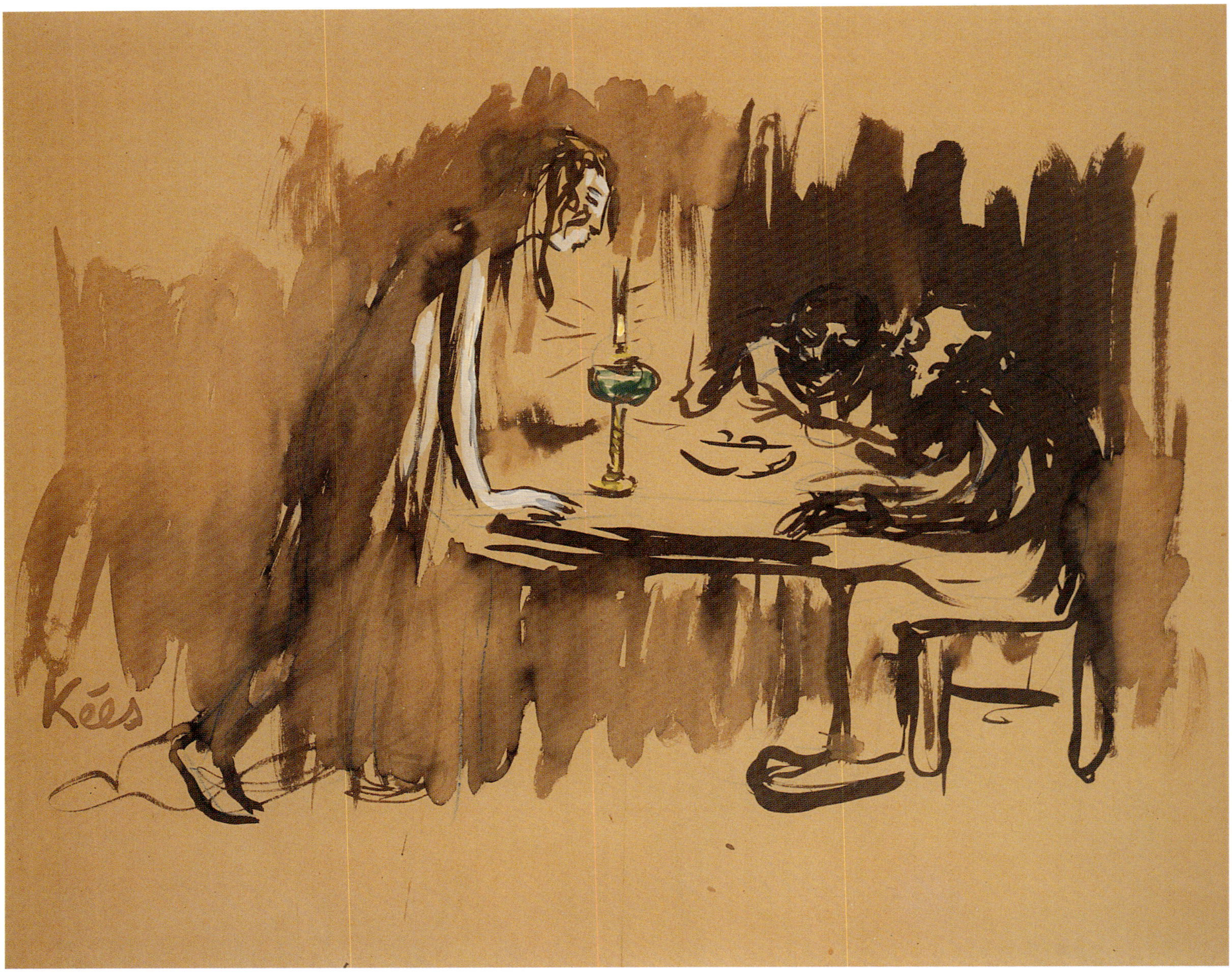

70. Les vieux et la mort, c. 1902

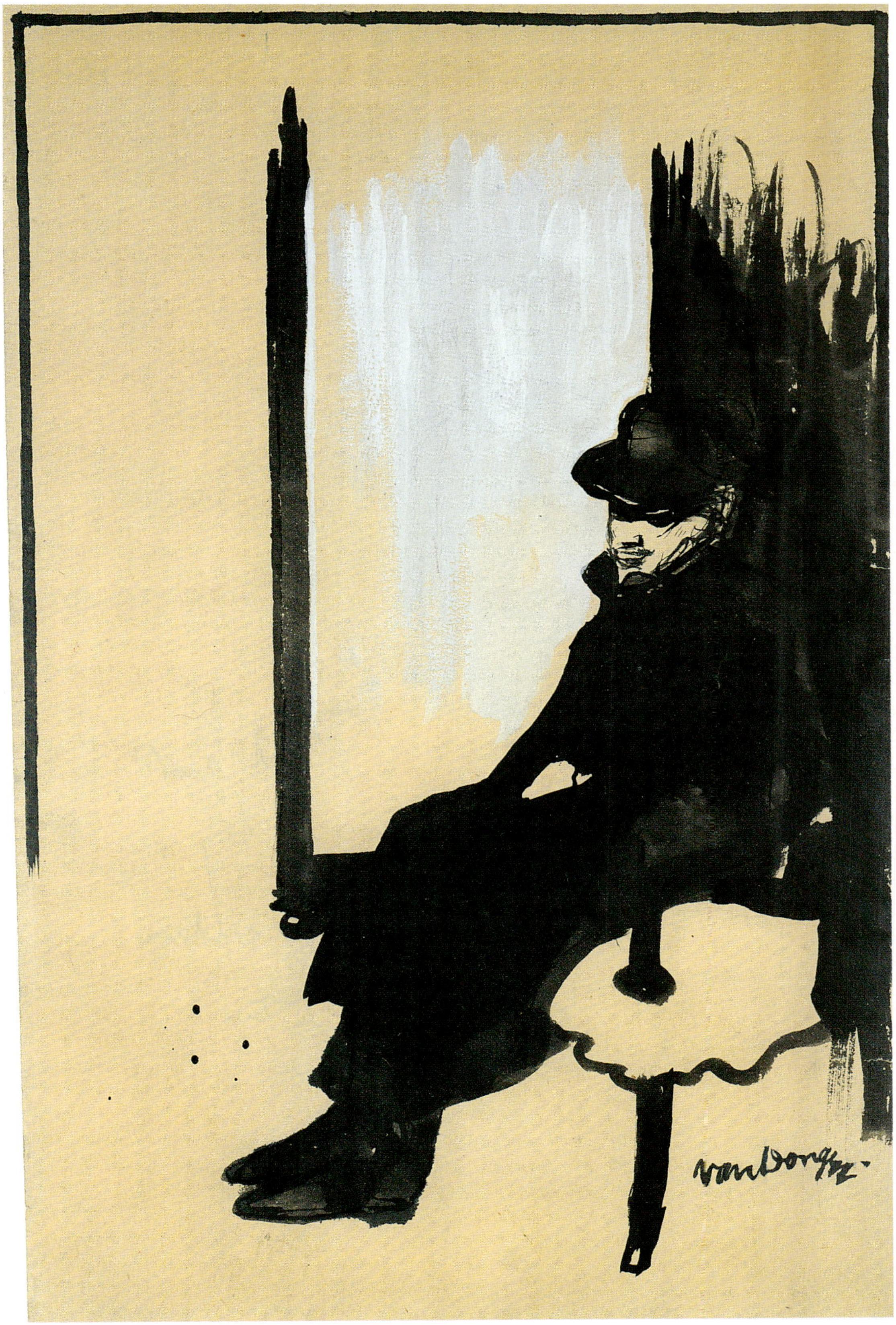

71. Seated man, c. 1903

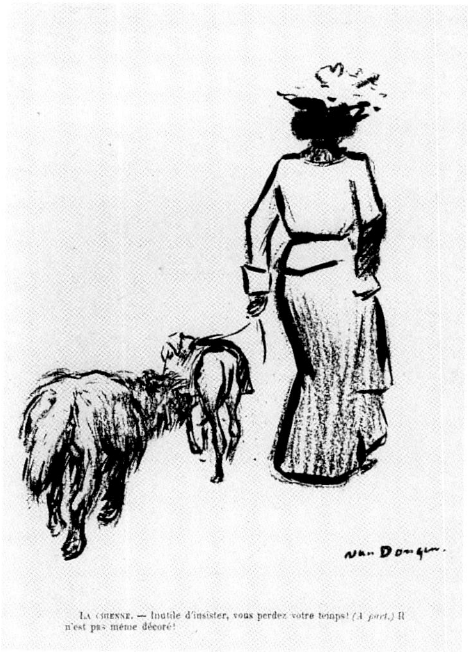

La chienne, illustration in *L'Indiscret*, no. 89, 30 September 1903, p.32

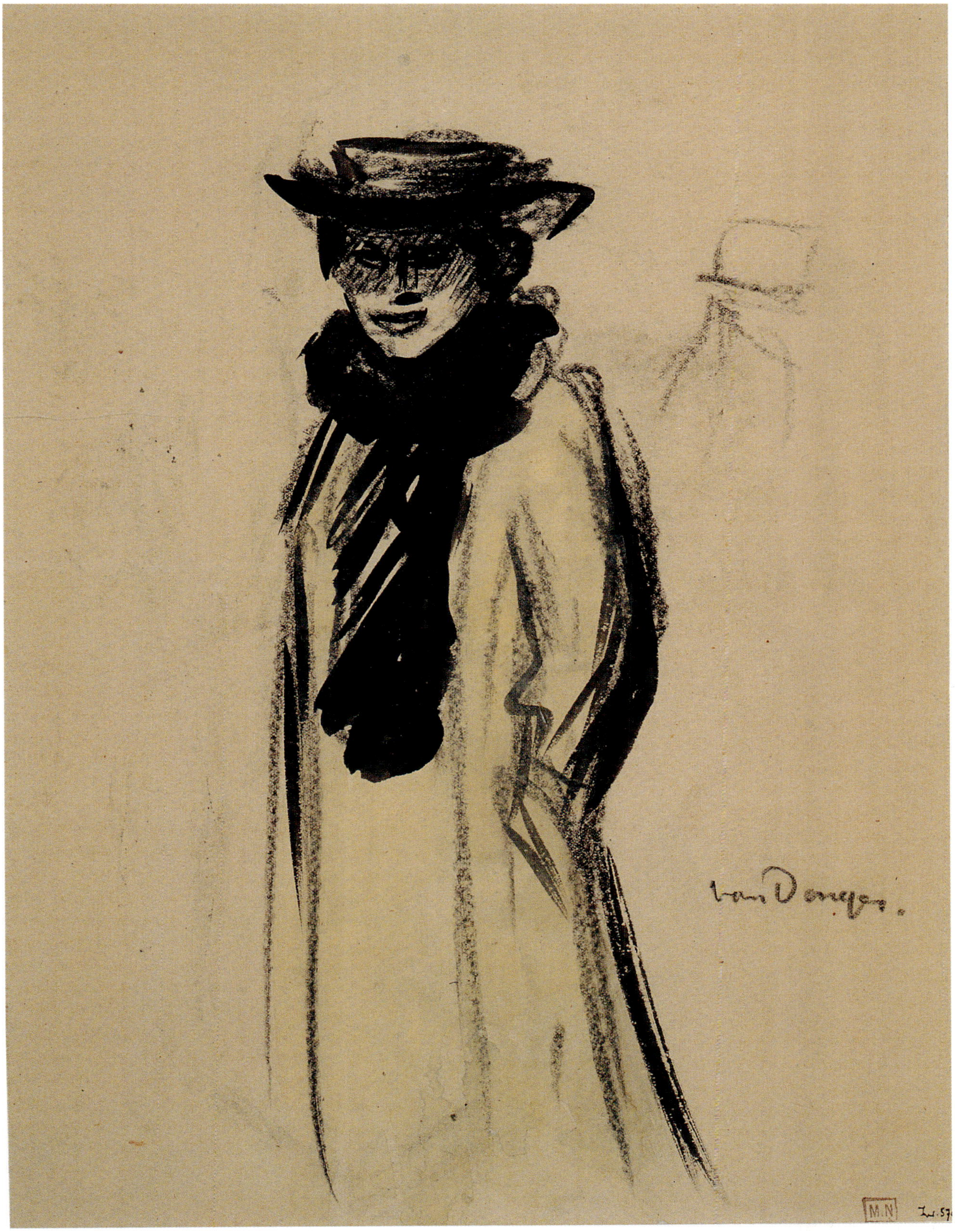

72. *Femme à la voilette*, 1903

73. *Le vagabond* (The vagabond), 1903
Black chalk
318 x 240 mm
Signed lower left in red chalk: *vanDongen*
Annotated on reverse in pencil: *le Vagabond*
Blue chalk on reverse of frame: *Le Vagabond*; a blue-printed label: *GALERIE/"COULEUR DU TEMPS"/9, Rue Arsène-Houssaye, PARIS-VIIIe*; marked with pen in black ink: *Van Dongen/Le vagabond-dessin-*; a label with typed letters (text from earlier original label): *GALERIE CHARPENTIER/76, Faubourg Saint-Honoré-Paris/EXPOSITION/VAN DONGEN/Cinquante ans de peinture/-MCMXLII-*; in pencil: *n°213*.
Special features: also known as *Zelfportret met cape* (Self-portrait with cape)
PROVENANCE:
Galerie Charpentier, Paris, 1942; Galerie Couleur du temps, Paris, c. 1950; P. Monart, c. 1970
EXHIBITIONS:
1942 Paris, no. 213
COLLECTION:
P. Monart

74. *Marins et filles* (Sailors and girls), 1903
Brush with black ink, grey wash, watercolour
437 x 274 mm (present size)
Signed lower right in brush with black ink: *van Dongen* (ink has run)
Special features: upper left and lower left corners cut off
PROVENANCE:
Auction Pau (L.F. Ducousso, J.P. Gestas), *Dessins, aquarelles, pastels, tableaux anciens...*, 6 December 1987; Kunsthandel Ivo Bouwman, The Hague; Stoppenbach & Delestre, London, 1987; private collection, 1988
EXHIBITIONS:
1988 London, no. 11 (fig.)
COLLECTION:
Private collection

75. *Les filles de Zandstraat* (The Zandstraat girls), 1903
Brush with black ink, grey wash, watercolour, gouache
565 x 493 mm
Signed lower right in black chalk: *V.D.*
PROVENANCE:
Dumac Collection, Roermond, 1957; Fotouhi & Schenkein, New York; Kunsthandel Ivo Bouwman, The Hague, 1986; auction New York, Sotheby's, *Impressionist and modern drawings...*, 12 May 1987, no. 117 (fig.); auction Paris, Drouot (Loudmer), *Importants tableaux modernes*, 23 November 1987, no. 47 (fig.); auction Versailles, Galerie des Chevau-Légers (P. and O. Perrin, et al.), *Tableaux et sculptures modernes et contemporains*, 13 March 1988, no. 63 (fig.); auction London, Christie's, *Impressionist and modern paintings...(part II)*, 30 June 1992, no. 112 (fig.); auction London, Sotheby's, *Impressionist and modern art...*, 26 October 1994, no. 2 (fig.); auction Paris, Drouot Montaigne (P. Cornette de Saint-Cyr), *Importants tableaux modernes et contemporains*, 14 December 1995-March 1996, no. 14 (fig.)
EXHIBITIONS:
1957 Roermond, no. 55 (fig.); 1986 The Hague (no catalogue)
COLLECTION:
Private collection

In one of his articles on Kees van Dongen, Brusse mentioned how, to his great surprise, after not having heard from the artist for a long time, he suddenly spotted him in the Hague at a distinguished soirée, a formal evening reception held at Jonkheer Joan Roëll's house, former minister of Foreign Affairs.[1] Neither the date of this visit nor that of the party are further specified. A drawing which resulted from this evening in which, according to Brusse, 'two drowsy, rotund, mutton-chop whiskered footmen with tasselled- shouldered livery' appear, is in its representation related to the illustration which Van Dongen published in March 1903 in the left-wing periodical *Le Canard Sauvage*: *Les défenseurs de la reine de Hollande*. (fig.) Apart from this sketch, two other drawings and an illustration must be mentioned which would seem to be linked to one of the two occasions when Van Dongen stayed in the Netherlands in 1903.[2] At the above-mentioned party, Van Dongen was introduced as an illustrator and was described as concealed in 'a wide rumpled woollen cape' which hung 'right down to his muddy shoes'. In this apparel, looking like 'a highwayman, an alarming anarchist and activist, with a long beard and long hair' Van Dongen was said to have wanted to show his 'unconventional independence and anti-socialness.' This description fits in neatly with the drawing the artist made of himself in the cape which Brusse referred to as the *dalles-dekker* (literally, mess-concealer). It was this stay in the Netherlands which sparked off the extremely fine, lively sketches in ink and watercolour of entertainment in the Zandstraat district. (fig.) These drawings can quite rightly be characterized as a series. Life on the streets glimpsed at different times is represented in the drawings, as if the artist had made them on the spot while walking through the neighbourhood. The spontaneous hand also seems to point to this method. Nothing could be further from the truth. Studies in black chalk were made beforehand and the large drawings were probably developed in Paris on the basis of these sketches. It is interesting that several of Van Dongen's characterizations of the girls can be found in Brusse's Zandstraat stories: the girls with flowing hairdos waiting aimlessly for customers or flaunting themselves in their Sunday best, with an air of self-satisfaction in 'patent leather shoes with pink or sky-blue lacy stockings.' These colours show up on Van Dongen's drawings as beautifully matte next to the parts where the black ink has been applied in its undiluted form. It is a colour effect that Van Dongen obtained by adding a little body colour to the watercolour paint.

1.
Brusse 1927, I and II.
2.
See pp. 53.

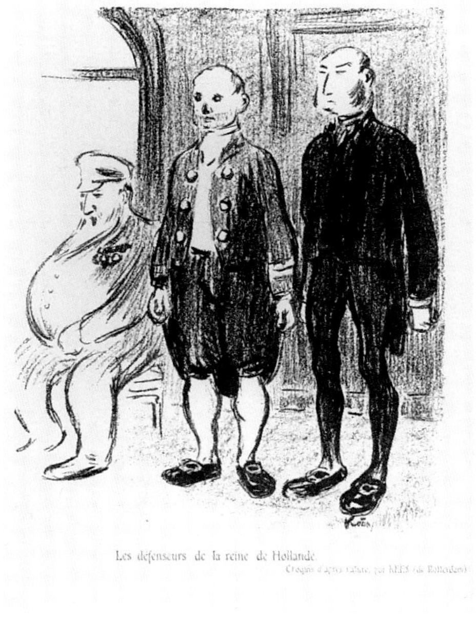

Les défenseurs de la reine de Hollande, 1903
Illustration in *Le Canard Sauvage*, no. 2 (28 March 1903), p. 12

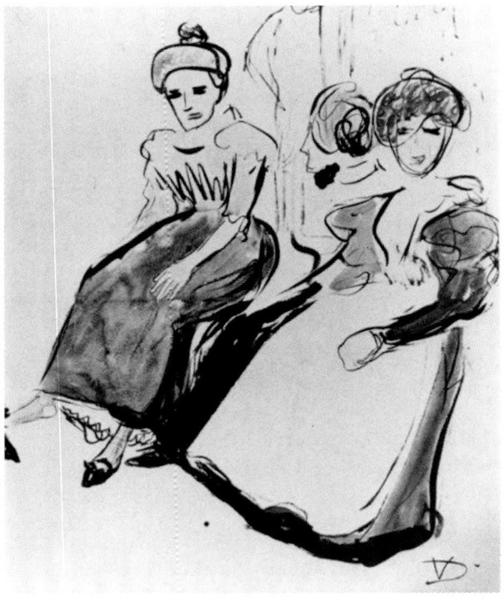

Les trois filles, 1903
Ink, watercolour, 650 x 560 mm

76. *Fille de Zandstraat* (Girl from Zandstraat), 1903
Brush in black ink, watercolour
535 x 230 mm
Initialled lower right in black chalk: *V.D-*; annotated in pencil lower right on the paper on which the drawing is mounted: *Zandstraat Rdam*
PROVENANCE:
Kees van Dongen, Monaco, 1962 (artist's certificate); auction Saint-Etienne (Imbert & Carlier), 26 March 1994, no. 11; auction New York, Sotheby's, *Impressionist and modern paintings...*, 28 September 1994, no. 39; auction Saint-Dié (M. Guérin), 5 February 1995, no. 114; auction Paris, Drouot (F. Briest), *Tableaux modernes,...*, 21 March 1995, no. 205; private collection, France
COLLECTION:
Private collection, France

77. *La mère* (The mother), c. 1903
Watercolour, brush with black ink, grey wash
680 x 560 mm (present size)
Signed lower right in black chalk: *van Dongen.*
Annotated on reverse of frame in blue chalk: *Lou* [?] *mère*; in black chalk: *Rotterdam 1895*; a printed label: *GALERIE CHARPENTIER/76 FAUBOURG SAINT-HONORÉ-PARIS/EXPOSITION VAN DONGEN/CINQUANTE ANS DE PEINTURE/-MCMXLII-*; blank label with red chalk: *B/10*
Special features: also known as *Les deux femmes* (The two women)
PROVENANCE:
Presented by Kees and Marie-Claire van Dongen to the Musée Toulouse-Lautrec, Albi, June 1961
EXHIBITIONS:
1942 Paris, no. 202; 1943 Bordeaux, no. 94; 1960 Albi, no. 60; 1981 Nice, no. 34; 1991 Toulouse, no. 119 (fig.)
COLLECTION:
Musée Toulouse-Lautrec, Albi, Inv. 424

78. *La jupe verte* (The green skirt), 1903
Brush in black ink, grey wash, watercolour, gouache
652 x 525 mm
Signed lower right in black chalk: *V.D.*
Special features: also known as *La fille verte* (The girl in green)
PROVENANCE:
Auction Paris, Galerie Charpentier (M. Rheims), *Tableaux modernes, dessins... Collection Pierre Bonnard*, 23 February 1954, part II, (*Divers amateurs*), no. 51bis; Galerie de l'Elysée, Paris, 1954; The Mayor Gallery, London, 1954; Sir Robert Adeane (1905-1979), London, 1954; his wife Jane Adeane (1932-1992), 1979; Tate in East Anglia Foundation (Lady Adeane Bequest), Castle Museum, Norwich, 1993
EXHIBITIONS:
1942 Paris, no. 200; 1943 Bordeaux, no. 100; 1962 Manchester, no. 36; 1994 Norwich, no. 2 (fig.)
COLLECTION:
Tate in East Anglia Foundation, Castle Museum, Norwich, Inv. 3.L1993.3

79. *Dans la rue* (In the street), 1903
Brush in black ink, grey wash, watercolour
671 x 565 mm
Signed lower left in pen with black ink: *V.D.*
PROVENANCE:
Auction Paris, Galerie Charpentier (M. Rheims), *Tableaux modernes, dessins... Collection Pierre Bonnard*, 23 February 1954, part II (*Divers amateurs*), no. 51 (fig.); Galerie de l'Elysée, Parijs, 1954; The Mayor Gallery, London, 1954; Sir Robert Adeane (1905-1979), London, 1954; his wife, Jane Adeane (1932-1992), 1979; Tate in East Anglia Foundation (Lady Adeane Bequest), Castle Museum, Norwich, 1993
EXHIBITIONS:
1942 Paris, Charpentier, no. 204; 1962 Manchester, no. 37; 1994 Norwich, no. 1 (fig.)
LITERATURE:
Adeane 1962, p. 722 (fig.)
COLLECTION:
Tate in East Anglia Foundation, Castle Museum, Norwich, Inv. 2.L1993.3

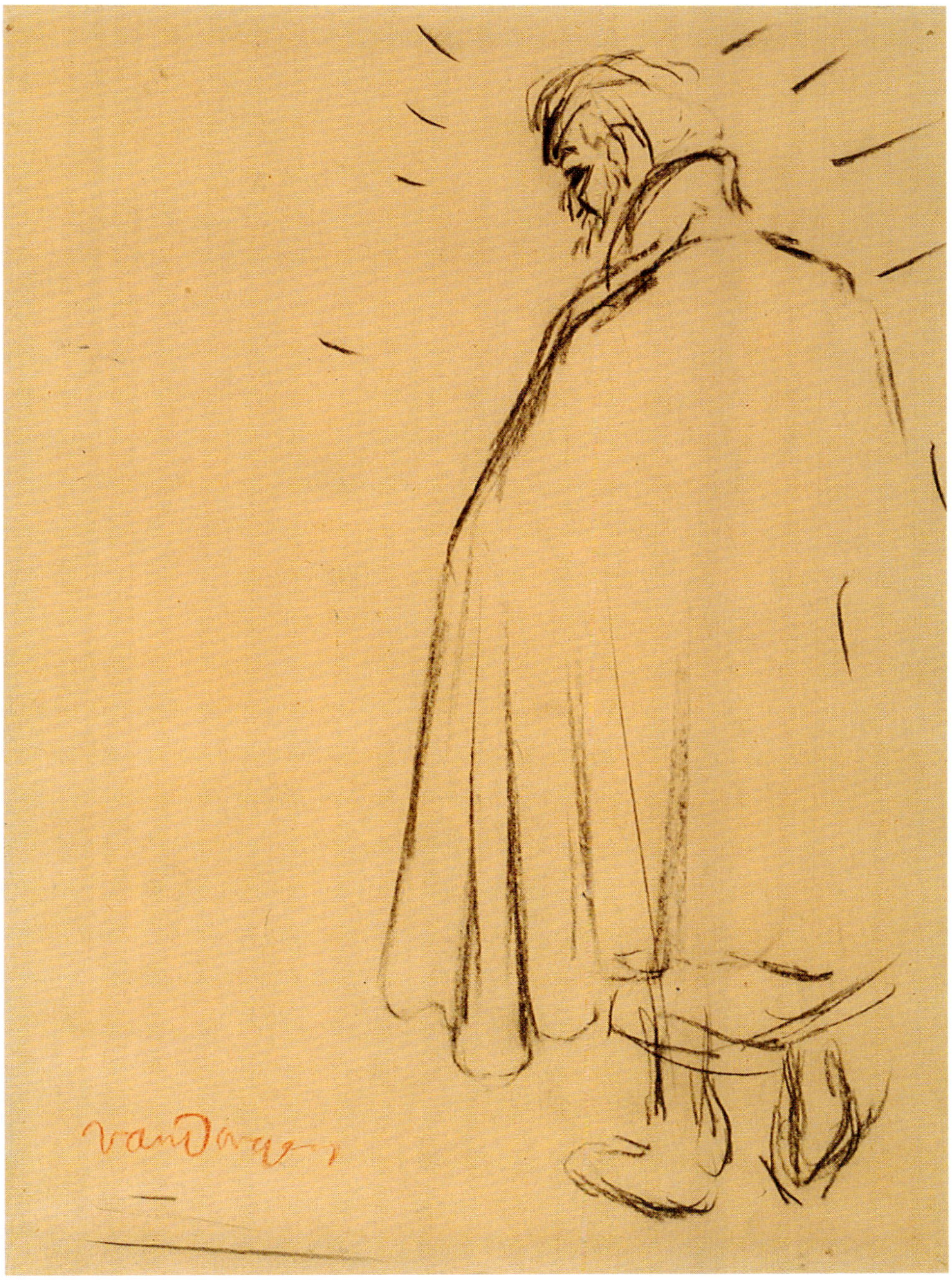

73. *Le vagabond*, 1903

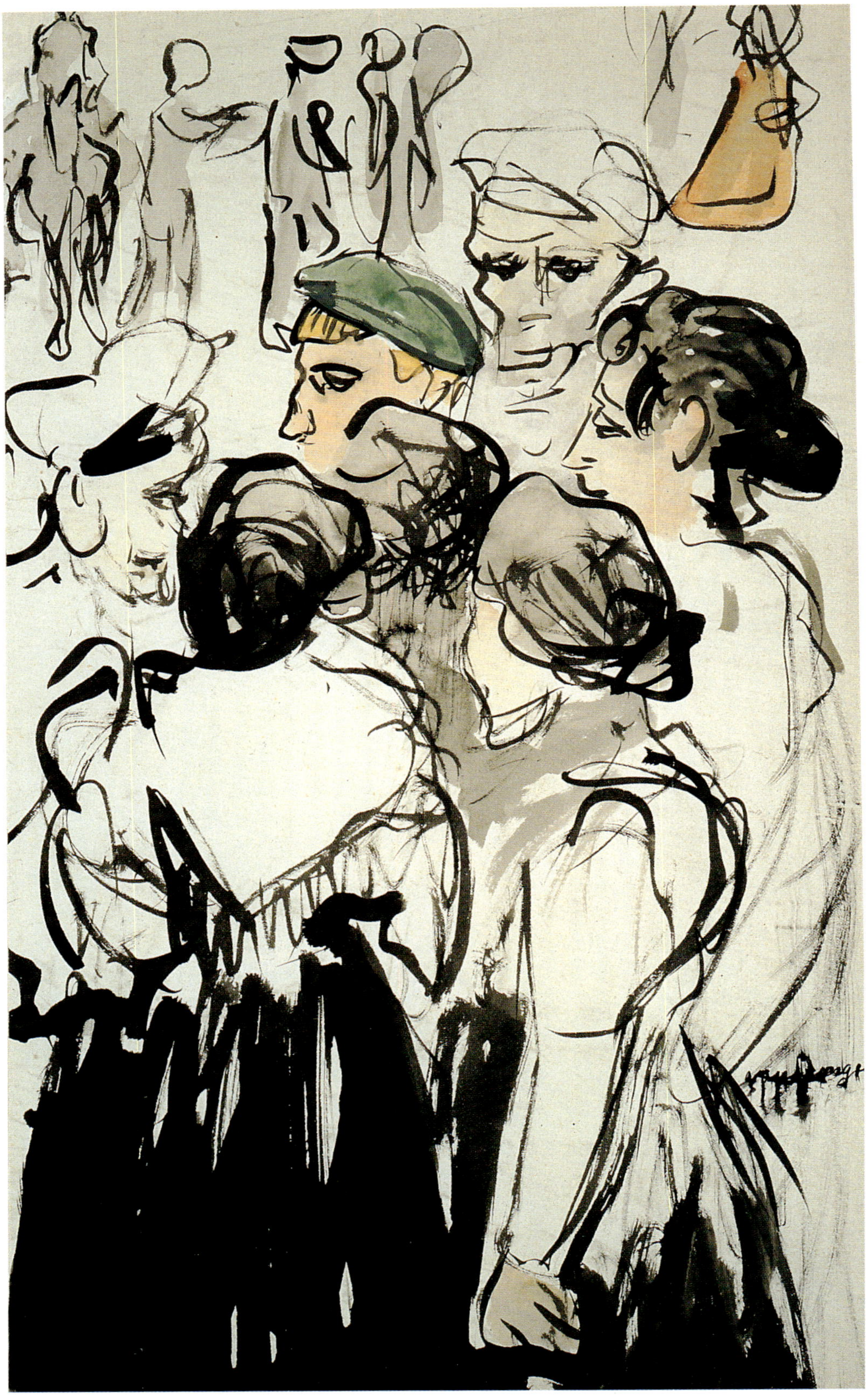

74. Marins et filles, 1903

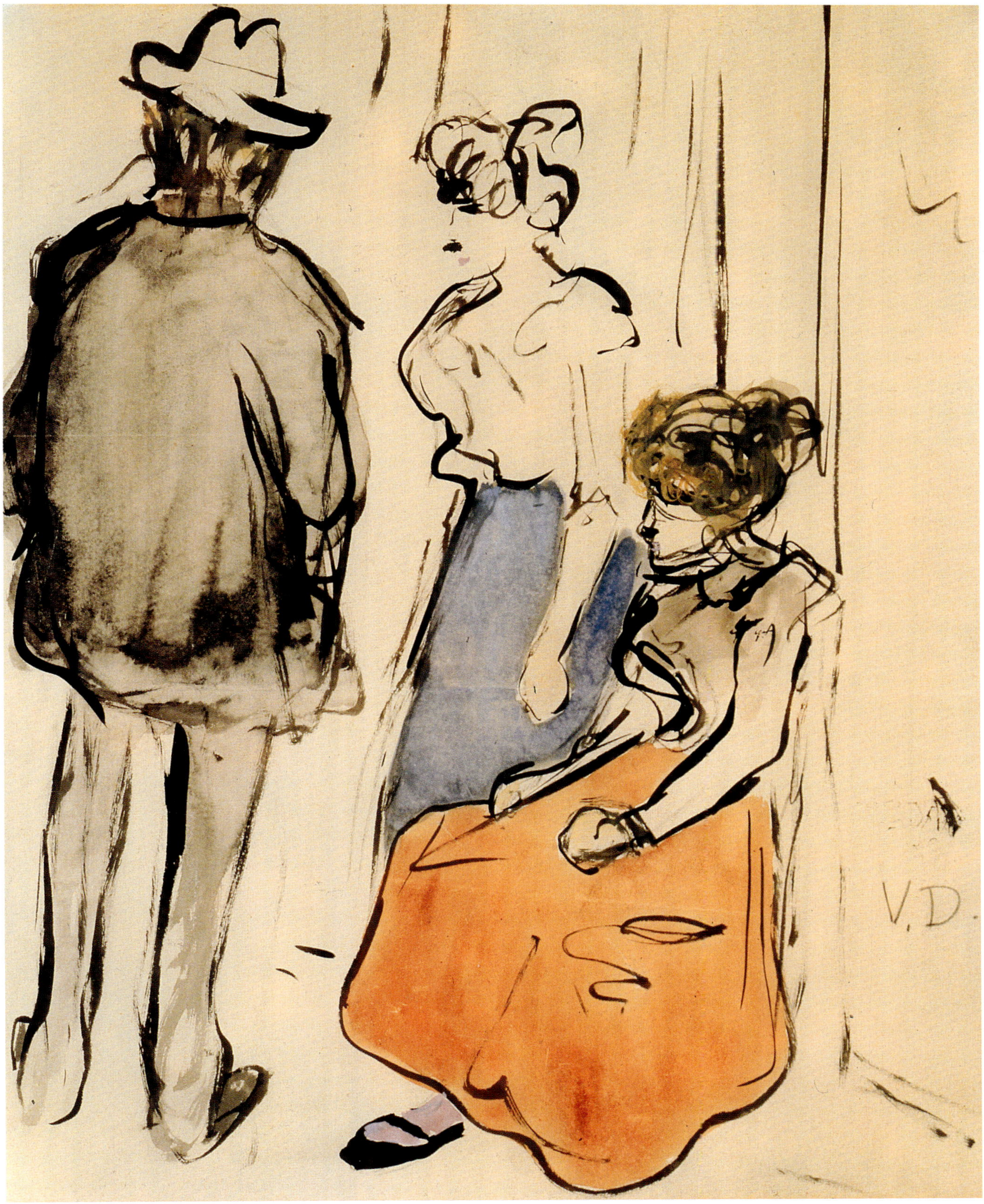

75. *Les filles de Zandstraat*, 1903

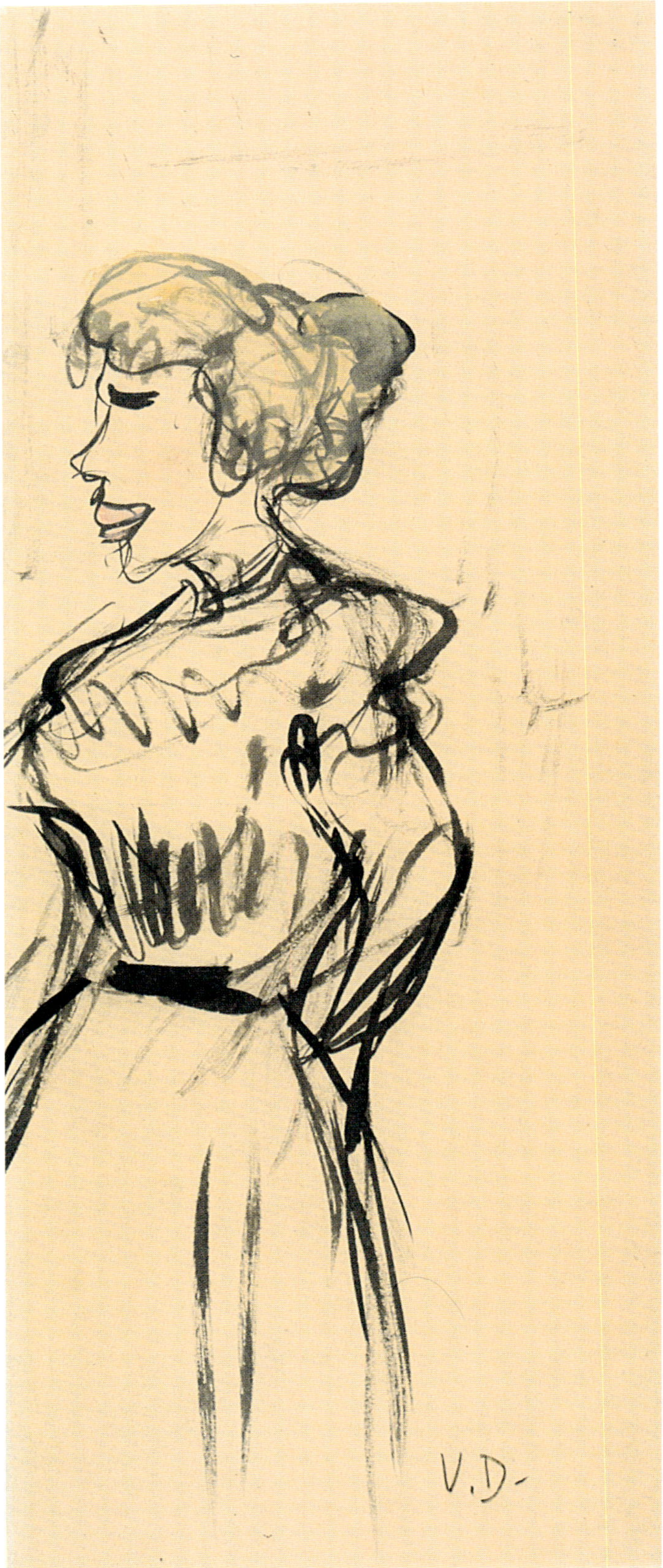

76. *Fille de Zandstraat*, 1903

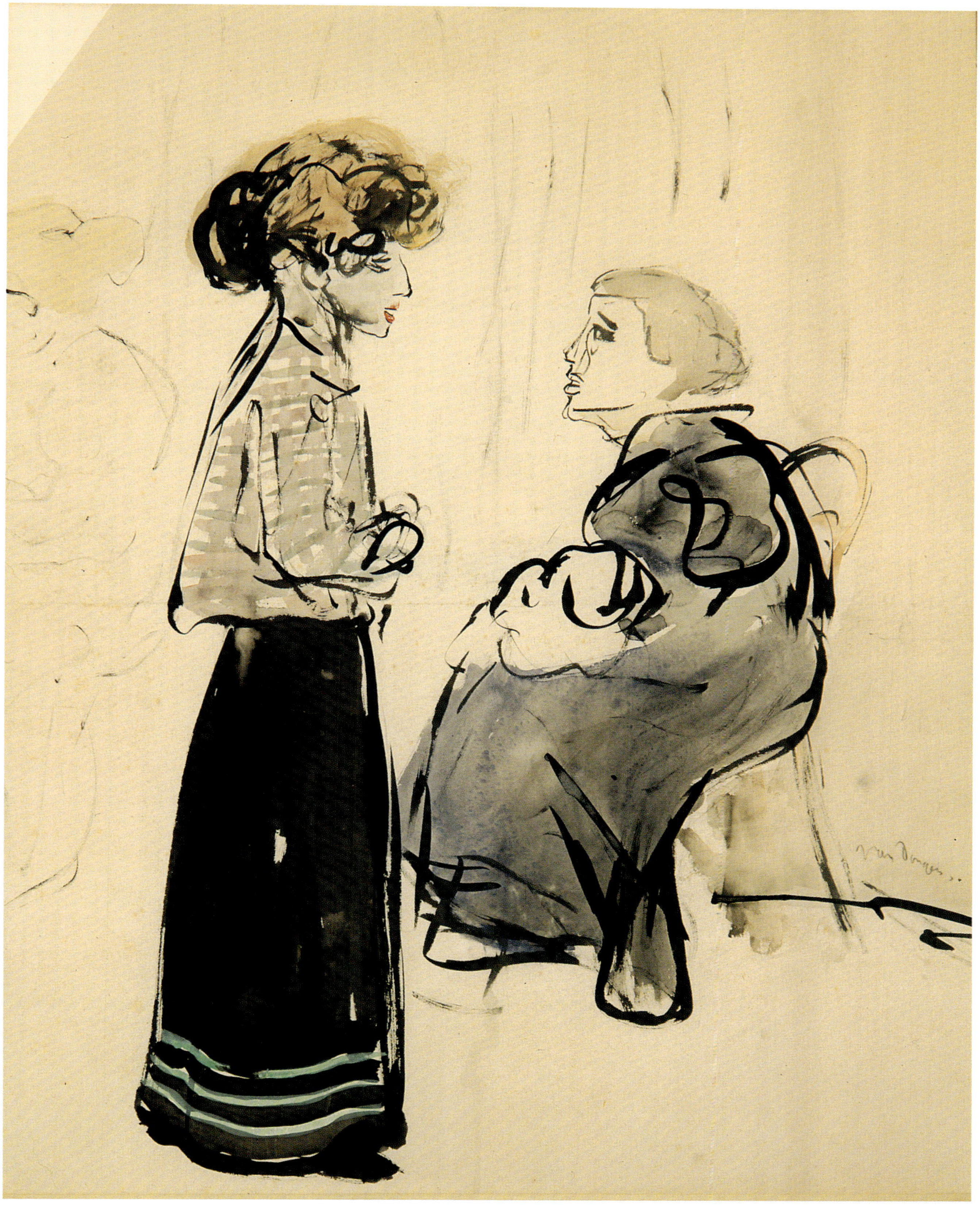

77. *La mère.* c. 1903

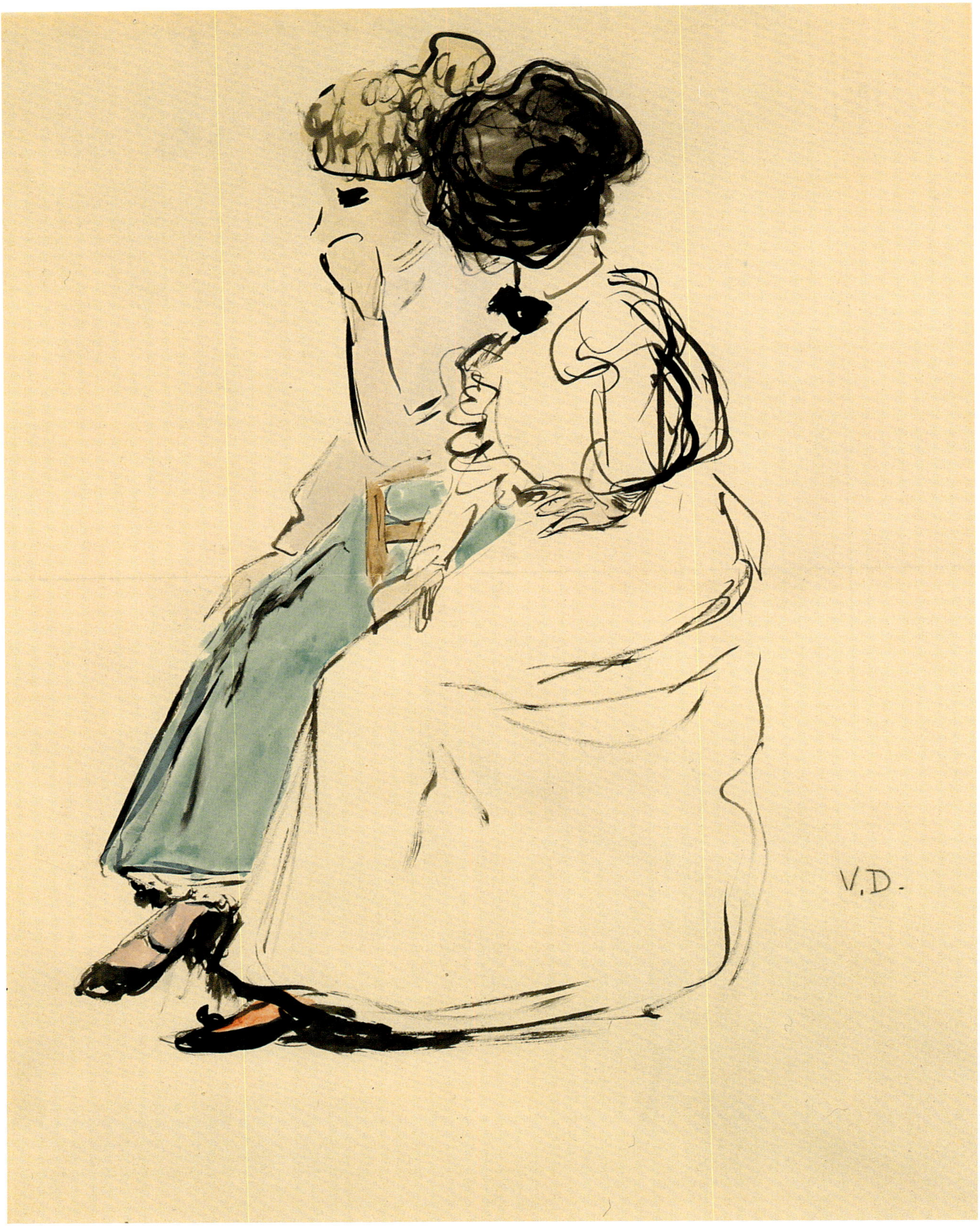

78. La jupe verte, 1903

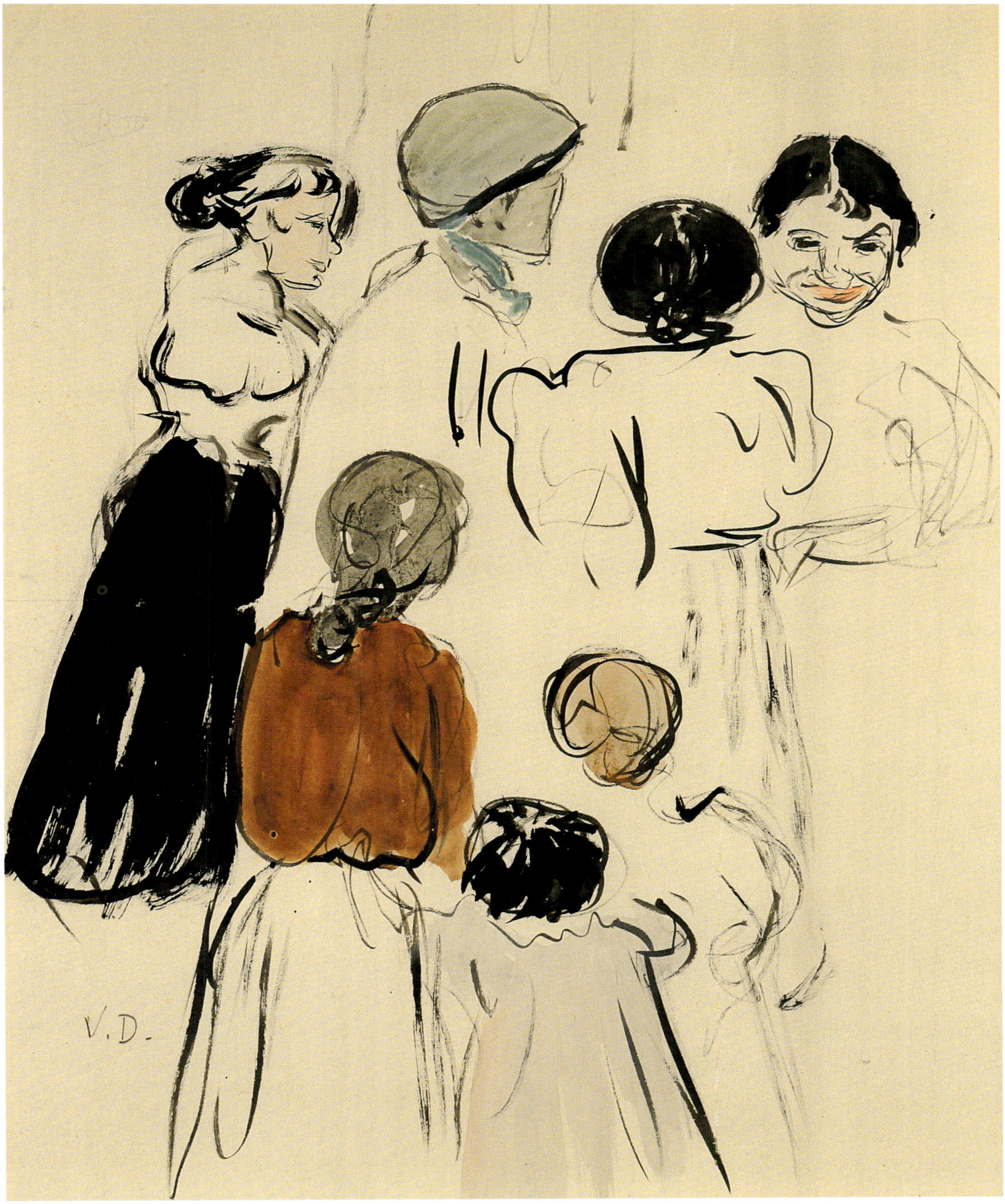

79. Dans la rue, 1903

80. *Femme se chaussant* (Woman putting on a shoe), c. 1903
Brush in black ink, grey wash, over sketch in blue chalk, watercolour, on light-brown discoloured papier
288 x 478 mm
Signed lower right in brush with black ink: *van Dongen*
PROVENANCE:
Emanuele Sarmiento (?-1936), Grenoble-Paris; Petit Palais, Paris, 1936, (gift of Count Emanuele Sarmiento); Musée d'Art Moderne de la Ville de Paris, Paris
EXHIBITIONS:
1936 Paris, no. 60; 1976 Montrouge, no. 50; 1990 Paris, p. 90 (fig.)
LITERATURE:
Escholier 1936, pp. 60-61
COLLECTION:
Musée d'Art Moderne de la Ville de Paris, Paris, Inv. AMD 209

81. *Staand naakt, kniestuk* (Standing nude, three-quarter length), c. 1903
Brush with black ink, grey wash, watercolour
413 x 259 mm
Signed lower right in brush with grey: *VD.* (in ligature)
Special features: corners cut off at an angle; drawing is mounted on cardboard
PROVENANCE:
Anonymous gift, 11 September 1907, to the Nationalgalerie, Staatliche Museen zu Berlin, Berlin
COLLECTION:
Kupferstichkabinett, Staatliche Museen zu Berlin, Berlin, Inv. SdZ nr 3

82. *Gehurkte vrouw* (Crouching woman), c. 1903
Pen and brush with black ink, grey wash, watercolour, white gouache
426 x 254 mm
Signed in black chalk: *van Dongen.*
Special features: the drawing is mounted on cardboard
PROVENANCE:
Anonymous gift, 11 September 1907, to the Nationalgalerie, Staatliche Museen zu Berlin, Berlin
EXHIBITIONS:
1958 Berlin, no. 25
COLLECTION:
Kupferstichkabinett, Staatliche Museen zu Berlin, Berlin, Inv. SdZ no. 2

83. *Le sommeil* (Sleep), c. 1903
Watercolour
440 x 540 mm
Signed lower right in light-brown watercolour: *van Dongen.*
PROVENANCE:
Auction London, Christie's, *Impressionist and modern water-colours and drawings*, 29 June 1982, no. 143 (Marie-Claire van Dongen Collection) (fig.); auction London, Christie's, *Impressionist and modern watercolours...*, 22 March 1982, no. 132 (fig.); auction London, Christie's, *Impressionist and modern watercolours and drawings*, 4 December 1984, no. 155 (fig.); private collection
EXHIBITIONS:
1978 Tokyo, no. 53 (fig.); 1981 Nice, no. 17 (fig.)
COLLECTION:
Private collection

84. *Femme allongée* (Reclining woman), c. 1903
Black chalk, watercolour, white gouache
282 x 456 mm
Signed lower left in grey watercolour: *van Dongen*
PROVENANCE:
Musée des Beaux-Arts de Lyon, 1917 (acquired from the artist with the assistance of the Chazière Foundation)
EXHIBITIONS:
1989 Lyons, no. 131 (fig.)
COLLECTION:
Musée des Beaux-Arts de Lyon, Lyons, Inv. B 1176-a

85. *Femme devant une cheminée* (Woman in front of a fireplace), c. 1903
Blue chalk, brush with black ink, grey wash, watercolour, white gouache
442 x 283 mm
Signed lower right in black chalk: *V.D.*
PROVENANCE:
Musée des Beaux-Arts de Lyon, 1917 (acquired from the artist with the assistance of the Chazière Foundation)
EXHIBITIONS:
1949 Arles, no. 117
COLLECTION:
Musée des Beaux-Arts de Lyon, Lyons, Inv. B 1176-b

86. *Zittende vrouw* (Seated woman), c. 1903
Pen and brush in black ink, grey wash over pencil sketch, watercolour
451 x 283 mm
Signed upper right in black chalk: *van Dongen.*
PROVENANCE:
Galerie Pétridès, Paris; art dealer Tjerk Wiegersma, Paris, March 1974; private collection
EXHIBITIONS:
1988 Deurne, no. 32 (fig.)
COLLECTION:
Private collection

87. *Femme nue se coiffant* (Nude woman doing her hair), c. 1903
Brush with black ink, grey wash, watercolour, white gouache
452 x 273 mm (present size)
Signed lower right in pen with black ink: *vanDongen.*
PROVENANCE:
Auction London, Christie's, *Impressionist and modern water colours and drawings*, 1 December 1981, no. 326 (fig.); auction London, Christie's, *Impressionist and modern watercolours and drawings*, 27 March 1984, no. 129 (fig.); private collection
COLLECTION:
Private collection, London

88. *Staand naakt* (Standing nude), c. 1903
Brush with black ink, grey wash, watercolour
451 x 284 mm
Signed lower right in yellow watercolour: *vanDongen*
Special features: the drawing is mounted on cardboard
PROVENANCE:
Galerie Huguette Berès, Paris, 1965; art dealer Roland, Browse & Delbanco, London, 1967; Oscar Kimmelman, New York, 1968; Galerie Jean Tiroche, New York (?); auction New York, Christie's, *Impressionist and modern paintings, drawings and sculpture*, 16 February 1989, no. 19 (fig.); Margo and Irwin Winkler, 1989
EXHIBITIONS:
1967 London, no. 5 (fig.)
COLLECTION:
Margo and Irwin Winkler

89. *Femme au lit* (Woman lying on bed), c. 1903
Pen and brush with black ink, grey wash, watercolour
370 x 517 mm (present size)
Signed lower centre in brush with black ink: *van Dongen*; remains of annotation lower centre: *L.. F..*
COLLECTION:
Galerie Lesieutre, Paris

90. *Torse* (Torso), c. 1903
Brush with black ink, watercolour
680 x 420 mm
Signed lower right in black chalk: *V.D.*
Special features: upper corners cut off
PROVENANCE:
Auction Geneva (Galerie Motte), *Trois ventes aux enchères publiques*, 27-29 June 1969, no. 338 (fig.); private collection
EXHIBITIONS:
1959 Geneva, no. 14 (fig.); 1960 Albi, no. 67 (fig.); 1976 Genève, no. 39; 1976 Montrouge, no. 49; 1978 Tokyo, no. 62 (fig.); 1979 Cannes; 1990 Osaka, no. 45 (fig.)
COLLECTION:
Private collection

91. *Couple*, Zelfportret met vrouw (Self portrait with wife), c. 1903
Watercolour, brush with black ink
580 x 676 mm
Signed lower right in brush with grey: *Kées-*; later signed again in brush with black ink: *van Dongen.*; lower right in pencil: *409*
On reverse of cardboard on which drawing is mounted, in brown chalk: *5*
EXHIBITIONS:
1959 Geneva, no. 107; 1960 Albi, no. 89 (fig.); 1976 Montrouge, no. 56
LITERATURE:
Schilperoort 1905, p. 738 (fig.)
COLLECTION:
Private collection

The drawings of women, naked or clothed, making their toilet or absorbed in their daily work, take you by surprise. A few reproductions are known from earlier exhibitions, but most of these drawings have never been exhibited before. Two drawings came through a donation to the Nationalgalerie in Berlin as early as 1907 and after the Second World War they ended up in the East Berlin section of the museum which meant that they did not become well known. Most of the other drawings turned up in several private collections through auctions; a few pieces were acquired by the Musée des Beaux-Arts in Lyons by means of a special fund as early as 1917. Félix Fénéon praised the series in the introduction for the Van Dongen-Vollard exhibition in 1904 as being extremely expressive, and described how beautifully the artist had secured on paper the movements of the bodies through an open and agile use of lines. A second appreciative description of the series came from the hand of Van Dongen's old fellow-townsman, Tom Schilperoort: 'seldom have I seen drawings that have released such emotions.' In this article, published in 1905, he praised the style of drawing applied by Van Dongen, the way he sketched the figures using just a few lines and surfaces after which 'a few colours were used to emphasize one or two things'. After this no further attention was paid to the works in other publications, undoubtedly because they were never exhibited as a series. Around 1904, the artist did seem to be planning to do just this, as is indicated by a poster-design with a nude featuring prominently in the foreground. (fig.) The drawings can be dated around 1903 based on descriptions by contemporaries. This date can be corroborated by illustrations which were included in the periodical *La Vie en Rose* in 1903, although the captions are meaningless and were probably added by the editor. (fig.) The drawing *Femme se chaussant* appears to be a later version of a more detailed, illustration-drawing, which was placed in a periodical in 1902. (fig.)

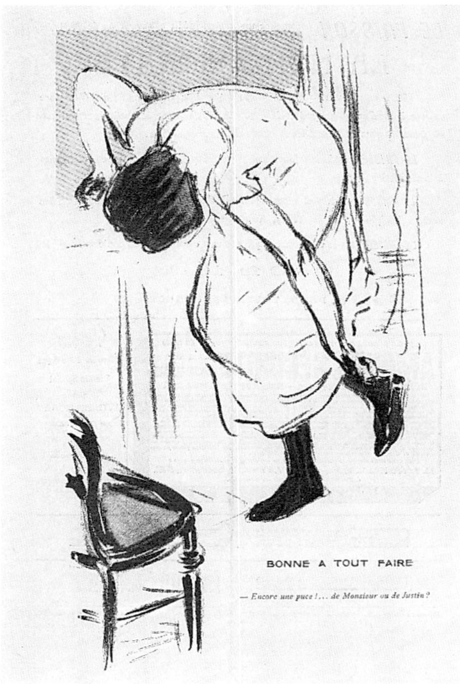

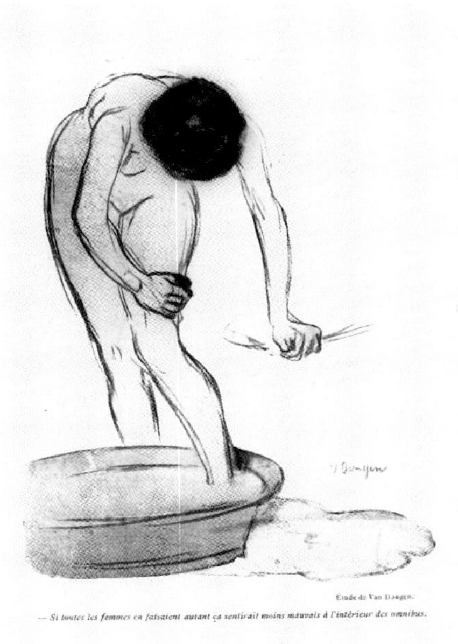

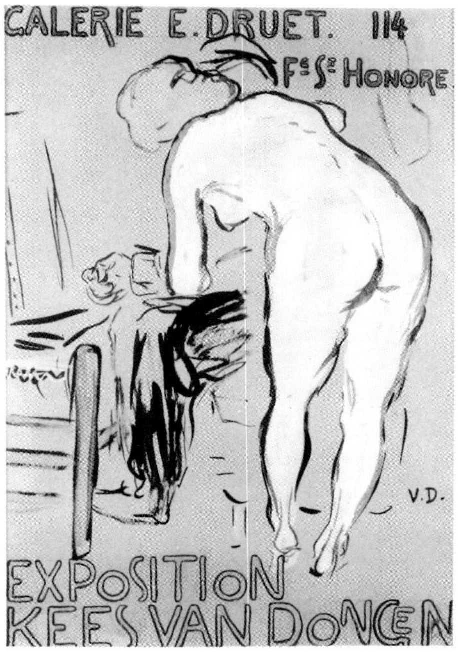

Si tous les femmes..., illustration in *La Vie en Rose*,
no. 94, 1 August 1903, p.14

Bonne à tout faire, illustration in *La Vie en Rose*,
no. 87, 13 July 1903

Design of poster, *Exposition Kees van Dongen*, c. 1904
Black chalk, ink, gouache, 830 x 605 mm

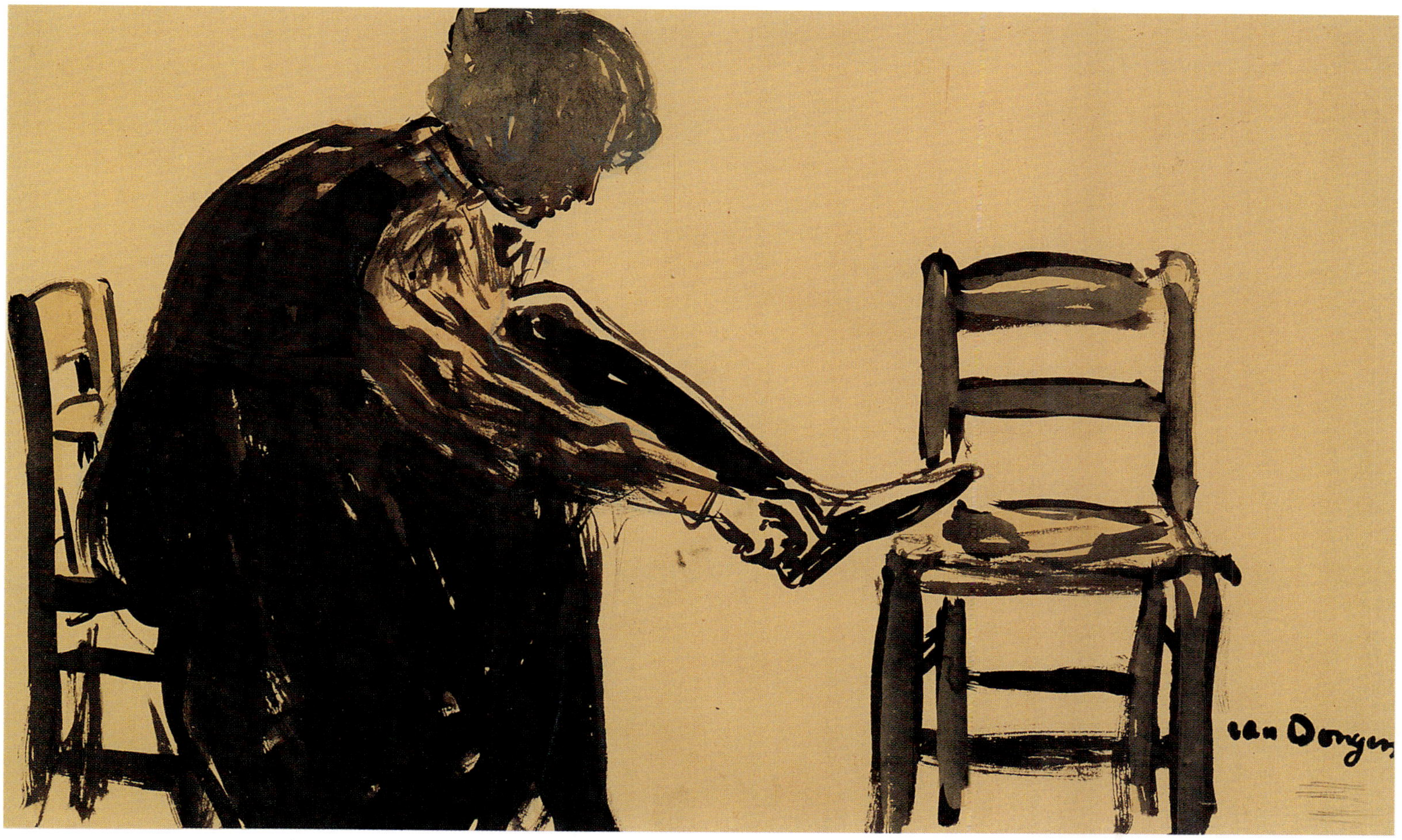

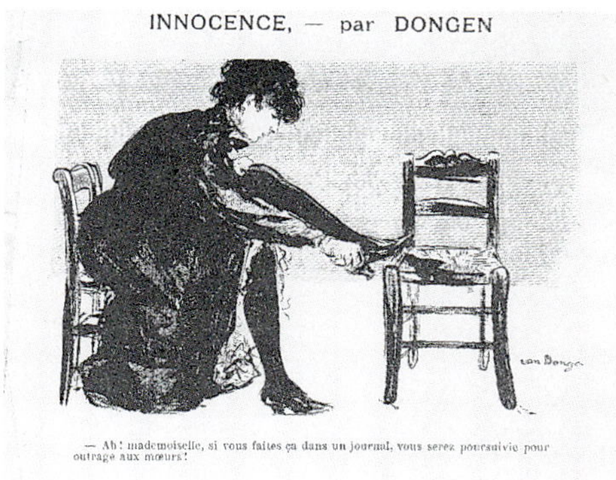

Innocence, illustration in *La Caricature*, no. 1154,
8 February 1902, p. 42

80. *Femme se chaussant*, c. 1903

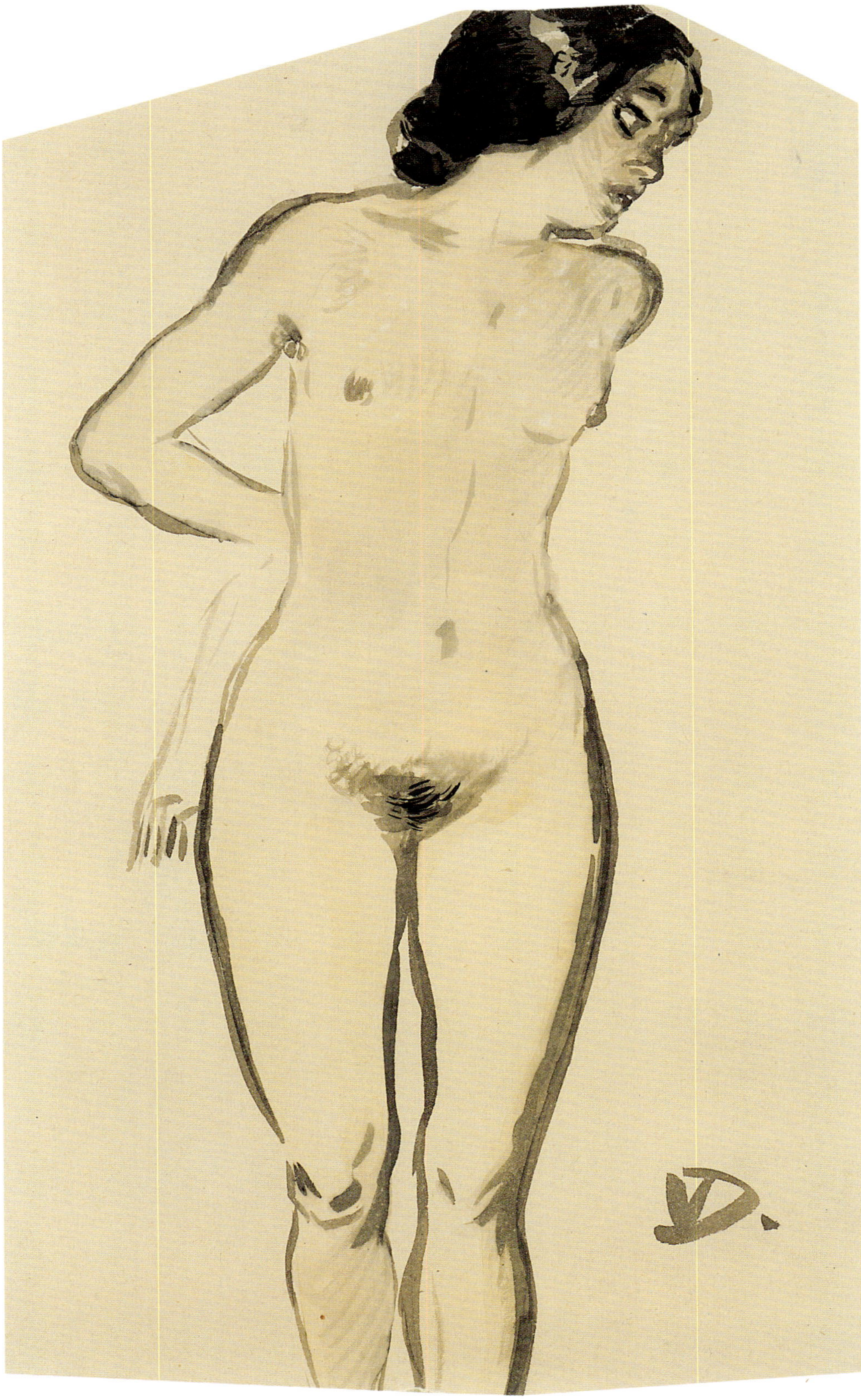

81. *Standing nude, three-quarter length*, c. 1903

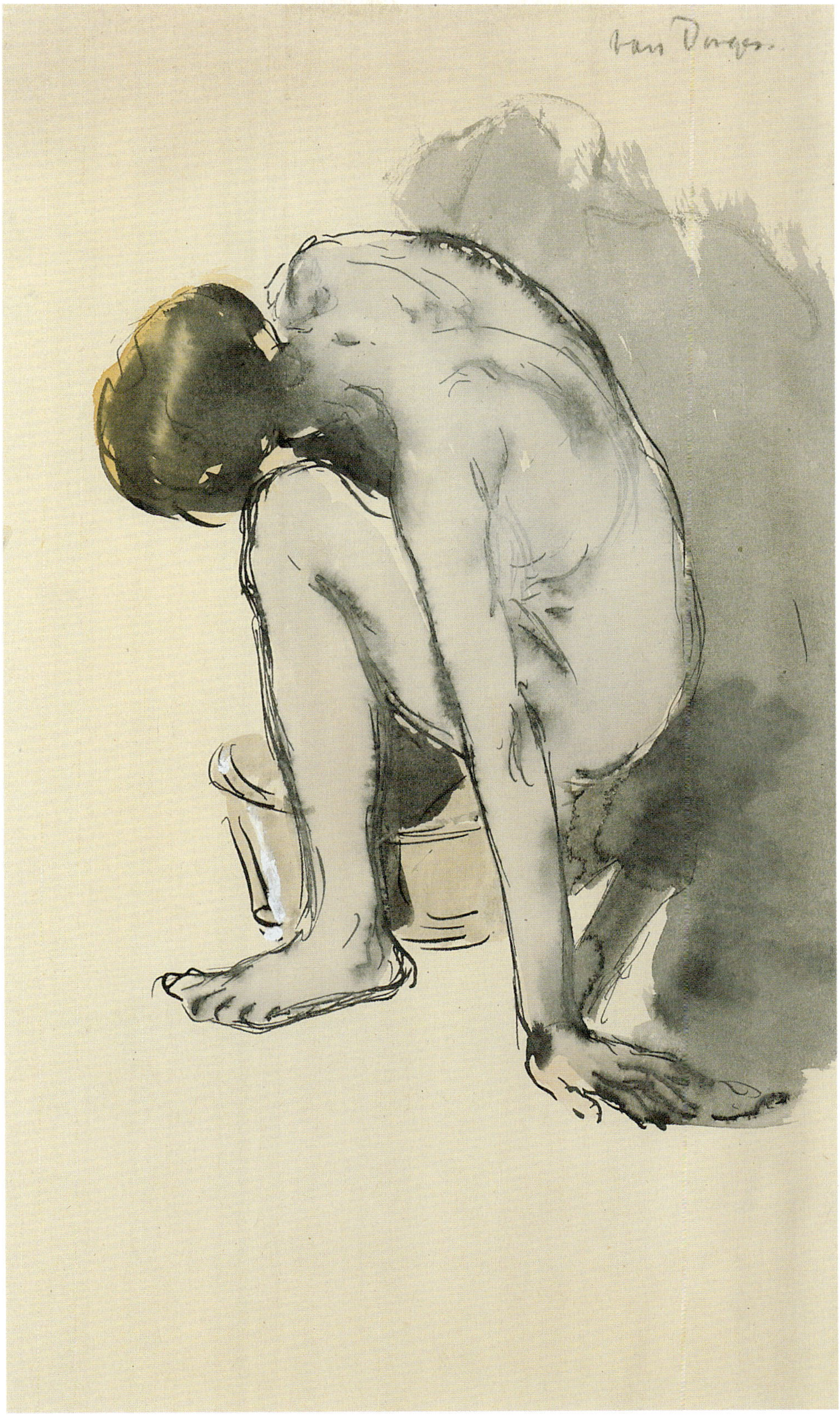

82. *Crouching woman*, c. 1903

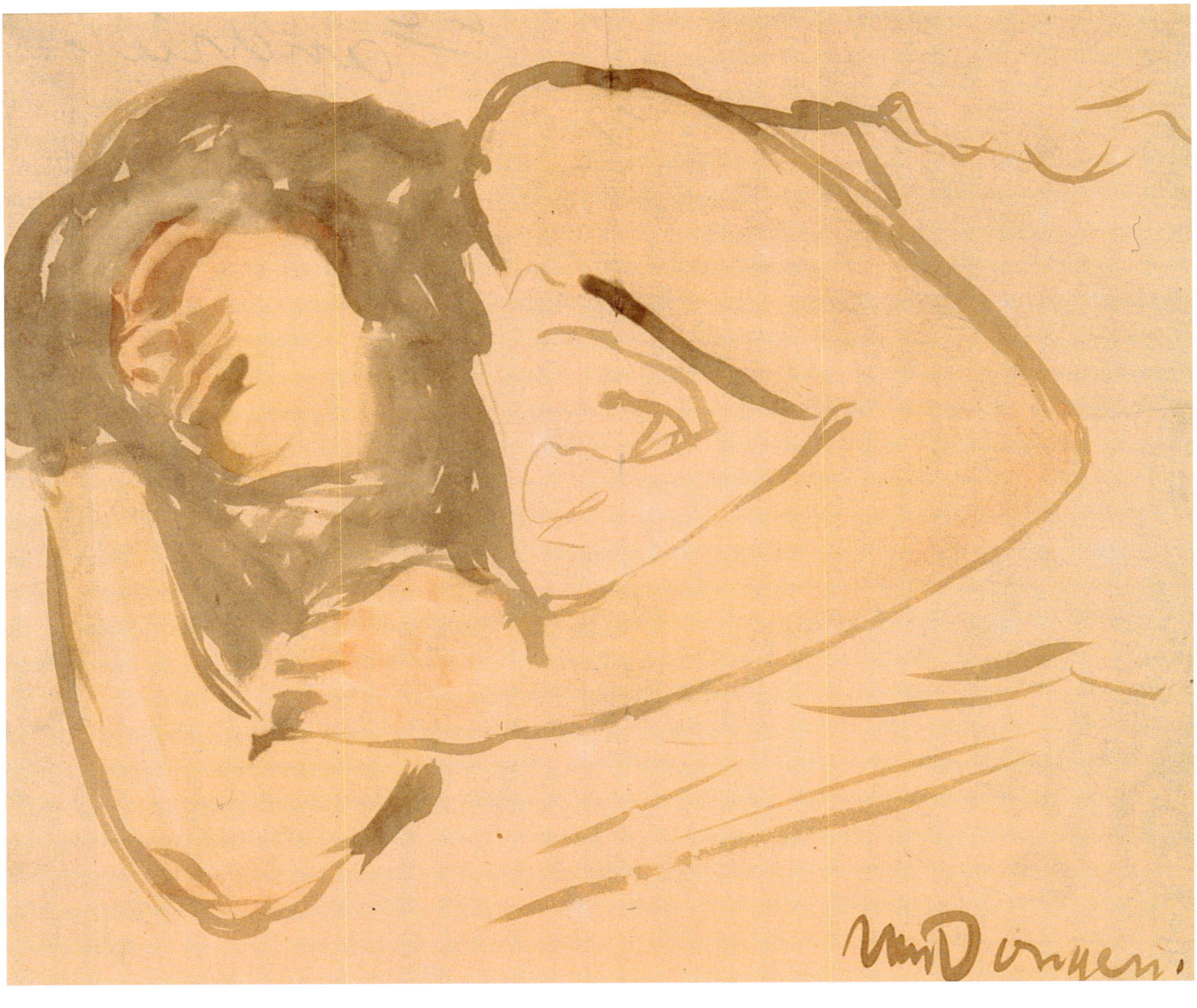

83. *Le sommeil*, c. 1903

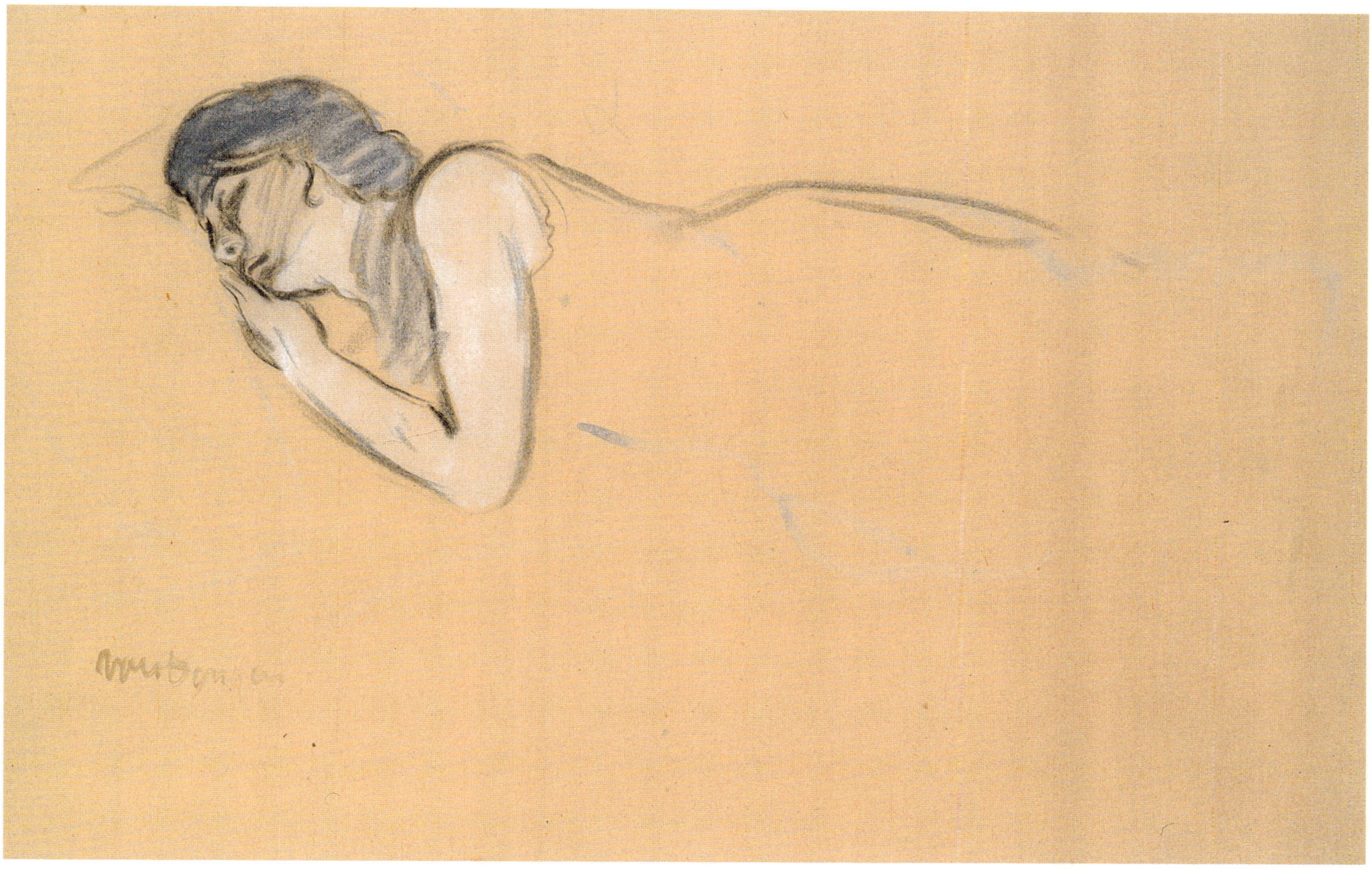

84. *Femme allongée*, c. 1903

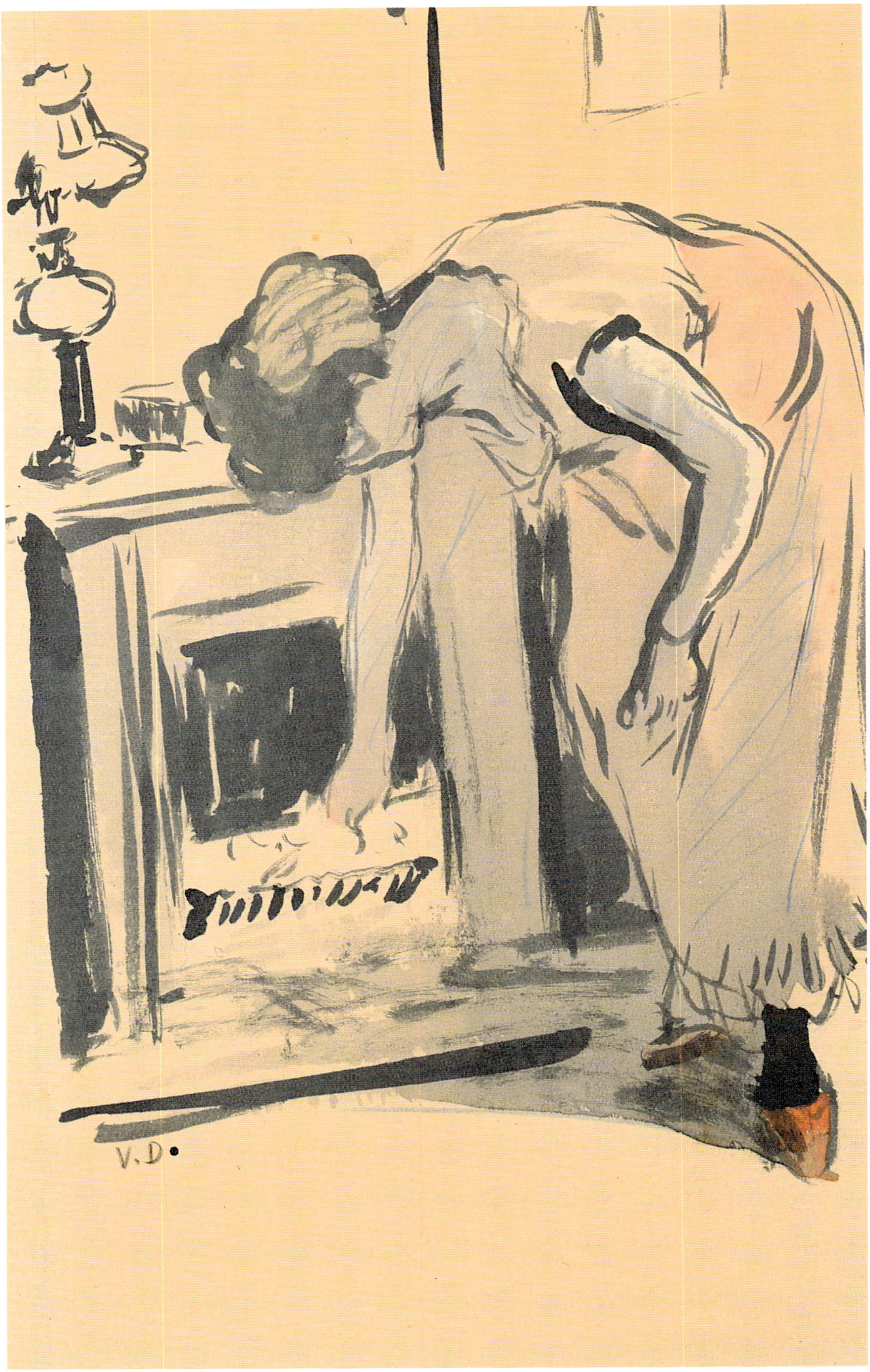

85. *Femme devant une cheminée*, c. 1903

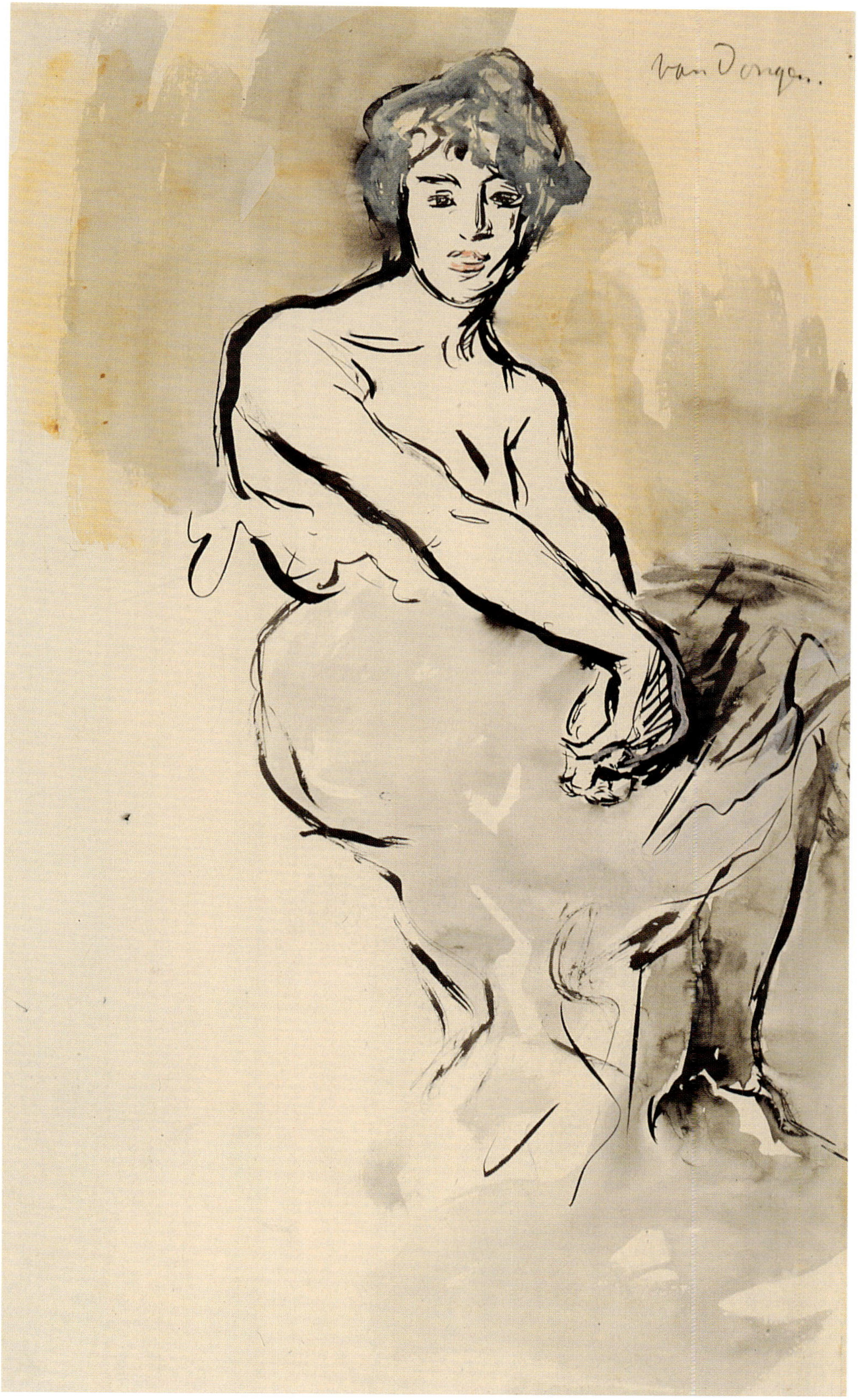

86. *Seated woman*, c. 1903

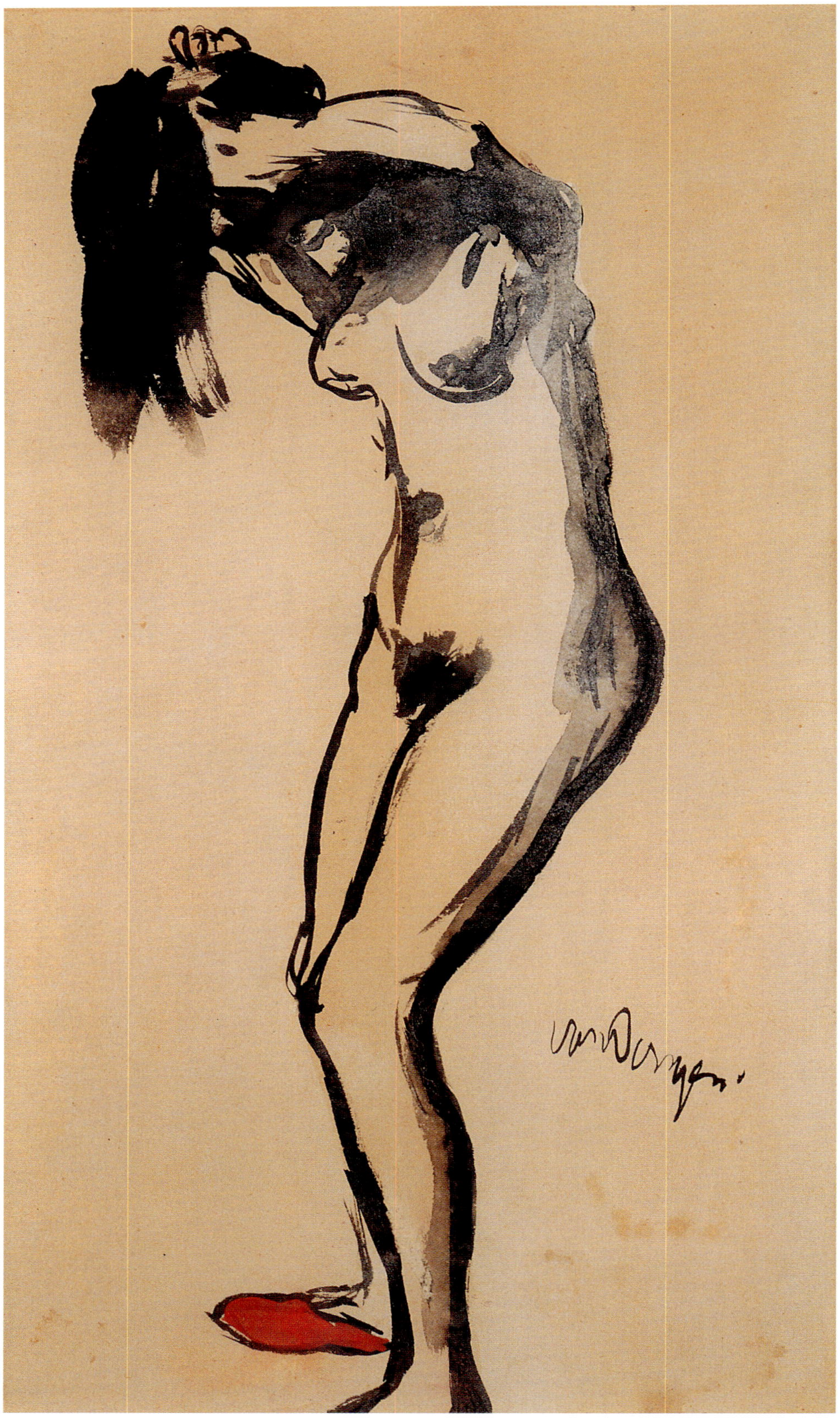

87. *Femme nue se coiffant*, c. 1903

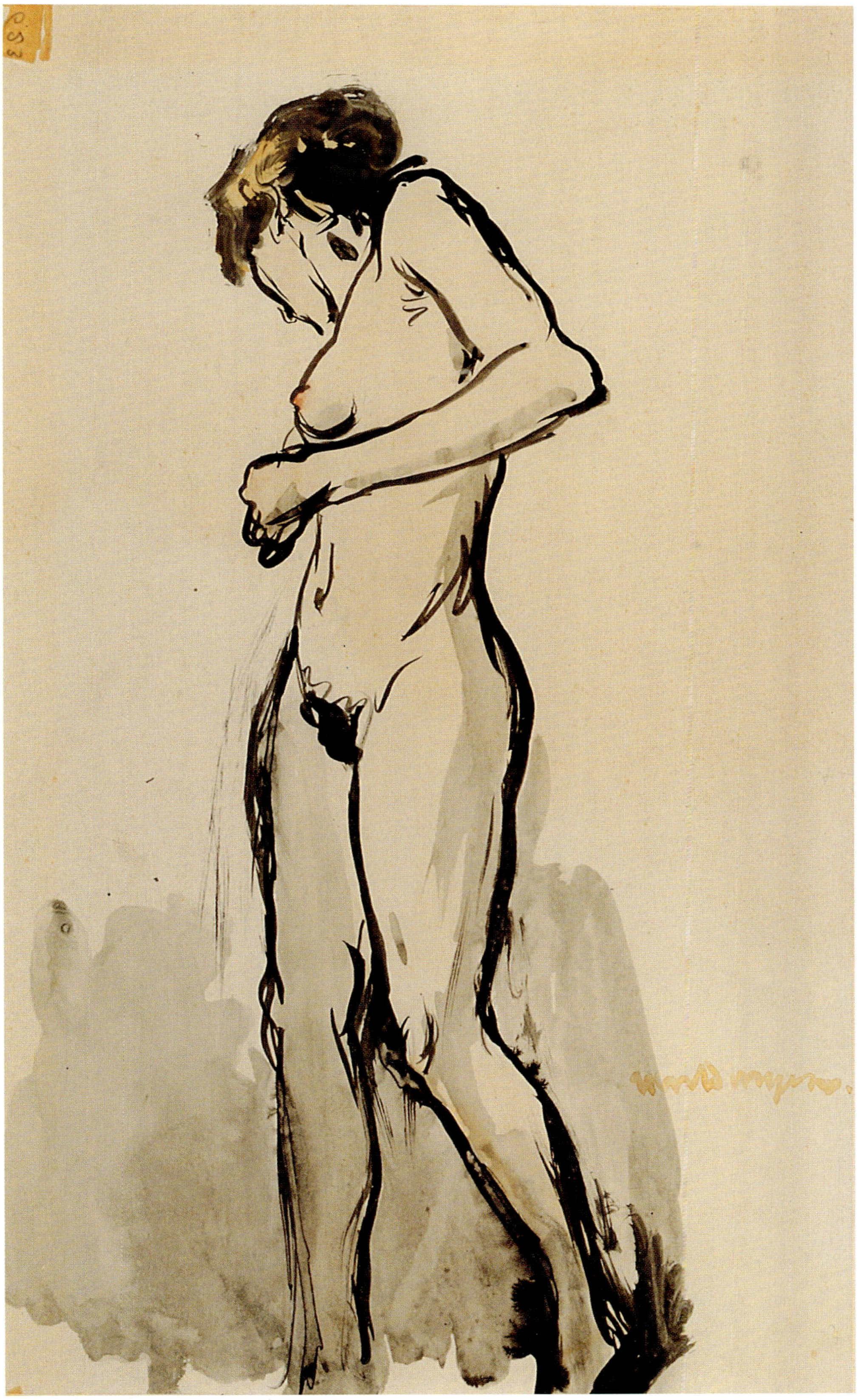

88. *Standing nude*, c. 1903

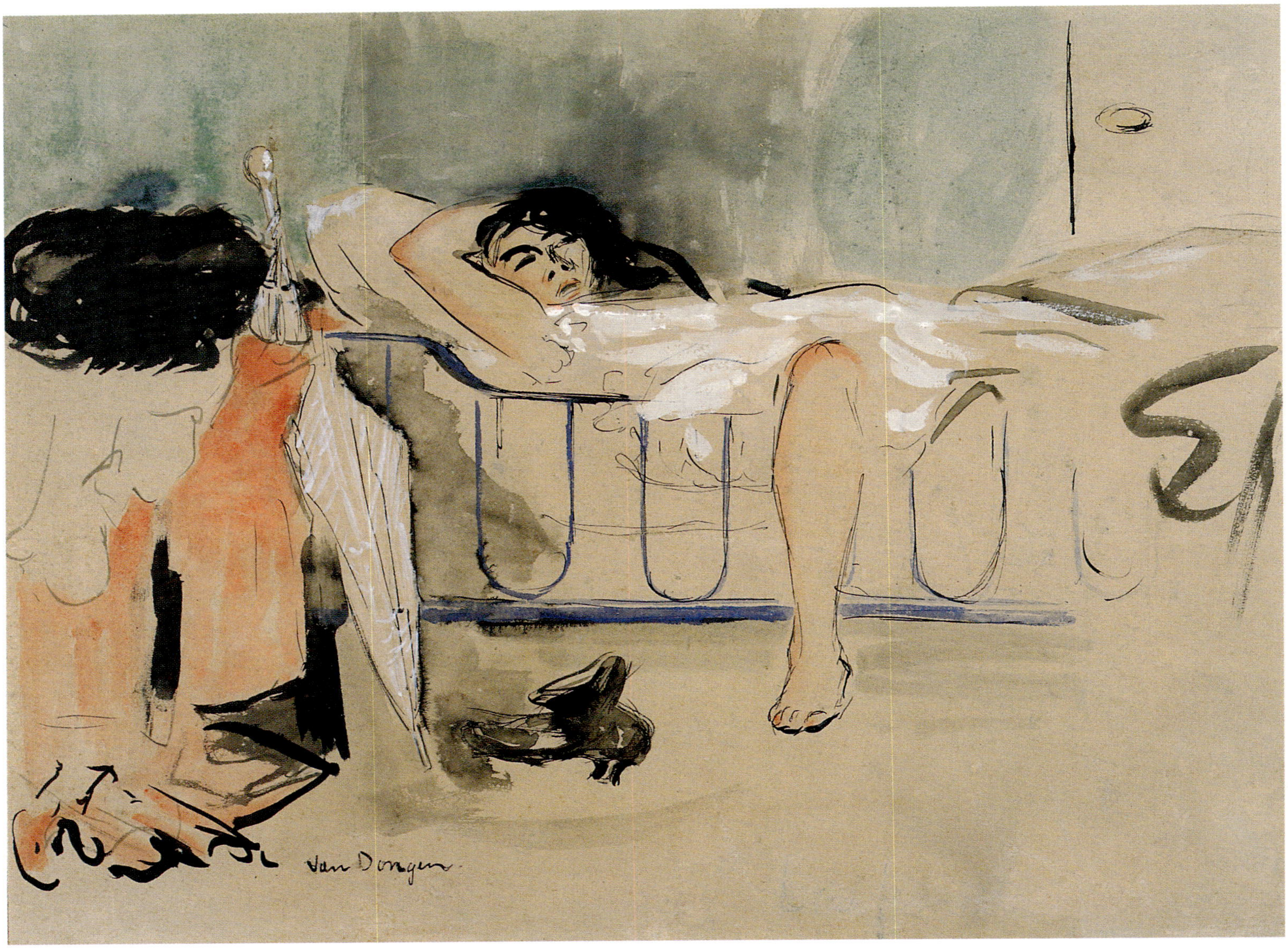

89. *Femme au lit*, c. 1903

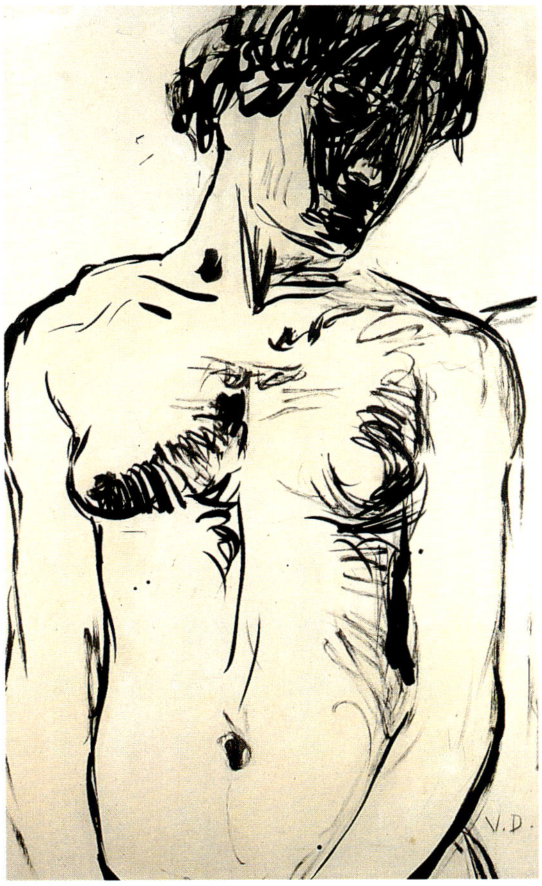

90. *Torse*, c. 1903

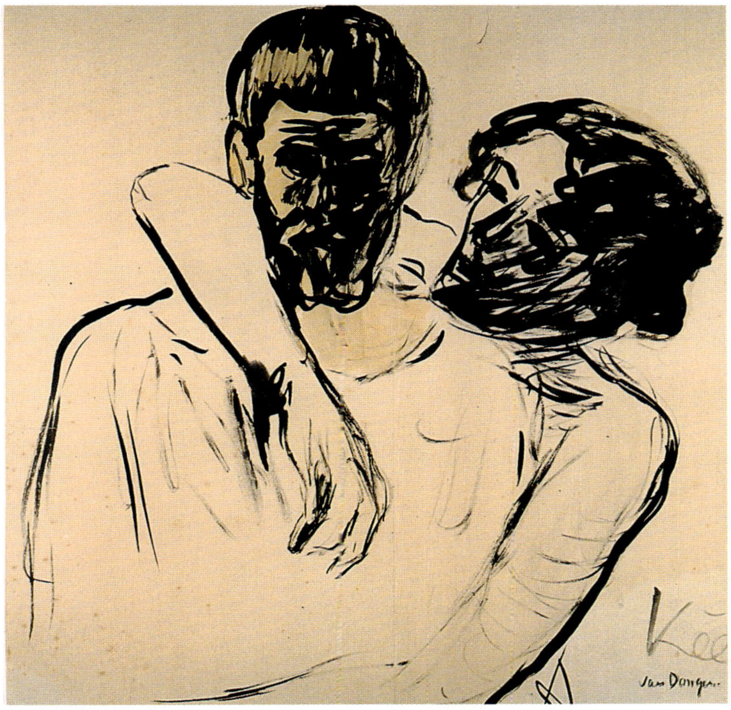

91. *Couple*
Self-portrait with wife, c. 1903

92. *Maison à Montmartre* (House in Montmartre), c. 1903-1904
Oil on canvas
65 x 46 cm
Signed lower right: *V.D.*
Special features: the canvas is lined
PROVENANCE:
Henriette Reuchlin-Lucardie (1877-1970), 8 June 1906 (via the Rotterdam Kunstkring, GA Rotterdam); Boymans Museum, Rotterdam, 1936 (gift of H. Reuchlin-Lucardie, on loan to Boijmans Van Beuningen Museum since 1930)
EXHIBITIONS:
1904 Paris, Vollard, no. 61; 1906 Rotterdam, RKK, no. 43; 1967 Paris (Rotterdam, ex. catalogue); 1969 Charleroi, no. 109 (fig.); 1971 Tucson, no. 50 (fig); 1979 Amsterdam, no. 98
1989 Rotterdam, p. 17 (fig.); 1992 Rotterdam, no. 42 (fig.); 1995 Tokyo, no. 48 (fig.)
LITERATURE:
Loosjes-Terpstra 1987, p. 25; Ebbinge Wubben 1963, pp. 40-41; Ebbinge Wubben 1972, p. 210, fig. 3; Van Veen 1906, p. 6
COLLECTION:
Boijmans Van Beuningen Museum, Rotterdam, Inv. 1171

93. *Le Sacré Coeur*, 1904
Oil on canvas
46 x 55 cm
Signed lower left: *van Dongen-*
Signed on reverse of stretcher in oils: *van Dongen-*; annotated in brush with grey ink: *Le "Sacré Coeur-"*; on reverse of canvas upper left in blue chalk 27; over this in red chalk: 72; rectangular stamp in purple (illegible)
Special features: also known as *Vue de Montmartre* (View of Montmartre) and *Vue de Paris* (View of Paris)
PROVENANCE:
Kunsthandel M.L. de Boer, Amsterdam, September 1955 (Inv. 3275; label on reverse); Paul Citroen, Wassenaar, c. 1960; private collection, France; private collection
EXHIBITIONS:
1904 Paris, Vollard, no. 82; 1906 Rotterdam, RKK, no. 26; 1908 Paris, Bernheim-Jeune, no. 21; 1957 Amsterdam, no. 39; 1960 Amsterdam, no. 32
LITERATURE:
Chaumeil 1967, p. 317, fig. 35; Loosjes-Terpstra 1987, p. 25, fig. 20; Scharten 1905, p. 1461 (fig.); Van Veen 1906, p. 6
COLLECTION:
Private collection

In the years between about 1896 and 1903 Van Dongen only produced a few paintings. At that time, both for both artistic and ideological reasons, he preferred to make drawings. Part of the explanation for Van Dongen's preference can be found in a couple of letters he wrote from Paris to his friend in Rotterdam, Chris Addicks, in 1900. In the letter of December 1900 he remarked that he was 'not a very enthusiastic dabbler with paint' and did most of his drawing outside on the streets. (cat. 17) In September 1901 he indicated that this choice was prompted by ideal motives: 'Anyway what is churning out paintings all about, it's serving luxury and that at a time when poverty surrounds you wherever you care to look. You make yourself and the world even poorer for the benefit of a few money-grubbers who have the resources to enjoy paintings.... I have always worked on the supposition that it is better to work as much as possible for the general good, for the community as a whole, and not for just a few calculating, or non-calculating, bandits. This is why I draw for papers and have abandoned painting although, on occasions, I still do a little for myself.' This viewpoint imbued with a great amount of social conscience was not abandoned by Van Dongen in 1903, but he did seem to separate artistic and ideological questions more rigorously to smooth the path for his interest in painting, which had in fact never completely disappeared. Van Dongen must have realized that if he was to play a role of any importance in the history of avant-garde art he would have to show his talents as a painter. It is difficult to determine when exactly Van Dongen started painting again. On the basis of his first exhibition entries in 1904 and his stylistic development, the time can be probably set at spring-summer 1903. The canvas *Maison à Montmartre*, that without doubt represents a building on the cul-de-sac Impasse Girardon – perhaps the house in which the artist himself was lodging – must have been created in the early summer of 1903 – if the fresh greenery and the bright light are anything to go by. This painting together with the two following paintings, *Le Sacré-Coeur* and *Trouville. La Mer*, were some of the exhibits in Van Dongen's first solo exhibition which took place at Galerie Vollard in 1904; in the catalogue the paintings were recorded as being made in the period '1902-1903-1904'. The canvases of the Sacré-Coeur and the sea can be dated more precisely. In his foreword in the catalogue Félix Fénéon indicated that Van Dongen had worked on two series in oils that year, one with the sights of Paris, seen from the hills of Montmartre, and another of the sea off Normandy: 'la mer sans l'anecdote d'une falaise ou d'une barque, la mer qui suffit à elle-même.' In these town and sea impressions Van Dongen has painted the roofs and the waves as a composition of coloured surfaces. Occasionally he embarked upon a more narrative element, like the ship in *Trouville. La Mer*. This ship also appears in a black chalk drawing of a mussel gatherer on the beach, a drawing which also belongs to a series and was exhibited under the title 'Moulières' at Vollard's. (fig.) On two other drawings from the series Van Dongen specified the place he had worked as: 'Le Pratier, en face Villerville.' The painting entitled *Femme cousant* is stylistically related to the canvases in the above-mentioned series. It might very well be that it portrays a woman reading; a painting with a similar title, dated 1904, was exhibited by Van Dongen in 1908 at Berheim-Jeune's.

94. *Trouville. La mer* (Trouville. The sea), 1904
Oil on canvas
28.5 x 35 cm
Signed lower right: *VD.* (in ligature)
Signed on reverse of canvas in brush with blue: *van Dongen*; numbered in blue chalk: *21*; customs stamp in black: *5*; annotated on stretcher in brush with black ink: *Trouville (La Mer).*; on reverse of frame white label marked in ballpoint pen: *hr Eilers*; black-printed label: *E.J. VAN WISSELINGH & Co./ROKIN 78 & 80 AMSTERDAM TELEFOON 32757/TABLEAUX MODERNES, AQUARELLES, ET EAUX-FORTES ORIGINALES*; marked in typed letters: *1146X/Kees van Dongen/Trouville la Mer*; and note in pen with blue ink: *ZIE AB Loosjes-Terpstra afb 21*; on reverse of frame in blue chalk: *UTRILLO*

PROVENANCE:
Mevrouw M.Th. van Berckel, Hulshorst 1957; Kunsthandel E.J. van Wisselingh, Amsterdam, 1957 (Inv. S 7839); private collection

EXHIBITIONS:
1904 Paris, Vollard, no. 97 or no. 98; 1906 Rotterdam, RKK, no. 21

COLLECTION:
Private collection

95. *Femme cousant* (Woman sewing), c. 1904
Oil on cardboard
33 x 27 cm
Signed lower right: *van Dongen*
Signed on stretcher in brush with black: *van Dongen*; in blue chalk on reverse of canvas: *18*; in red chalk: *35/Honfleur*
Special features: also known as *Femme assise* (Seated woman)

PROVENANCE:
Daniel-Henry Kahnweiler (1884-1979), Paris: auction Paris, Drouot (J. Zapp), *Tableaux, gouaches & dessins...composant la collection de la Galerie Kahnweiller* [sic], 13-14 June 1921, no. 97 (awarded to Grassat representing the Kahnweiler syndicate); Daniel-Henry Kahnweiler, Paris, 1921 (Inv. 25565); Musée National d'Art Moderne, Centre Georges Pompidou, Paris, 1984 (gift of Louise and Michel Leiris)

EXHIBITIONS:
1984 Paris, no. 203 (fig.); 1985 Saint-Tropez, no. 10 (fig.); 1989 Saitama, p. 63 (fig.); 1994 Düsseldorf, p. 275 (fig.)

LITERATURE:
Chaumeil 1967, p. 55; Monod-Fontaine 1984, p. 131; Peters 1994, pp. 15, 26, 204

COLLECTION:
Musée National d'Art Moderne, Centre Georges Pompidou, Paris, Inv. AM 1984-679

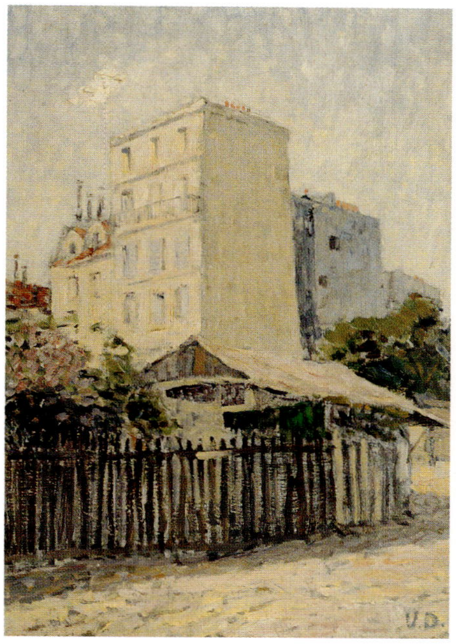

92. *Maison à Montmartre*, c. 1903-1904

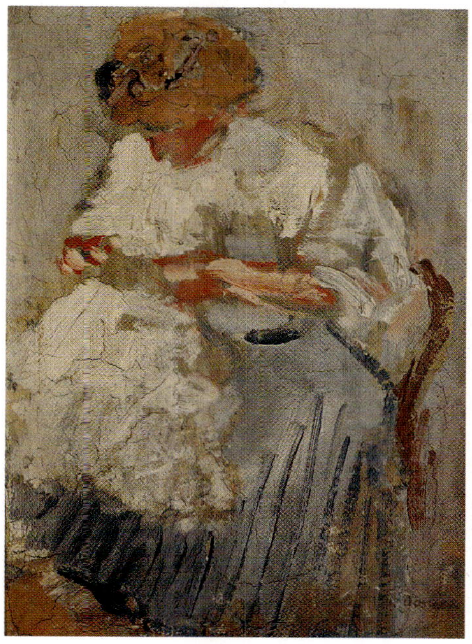

95. *Femme cousant*, c. 1904

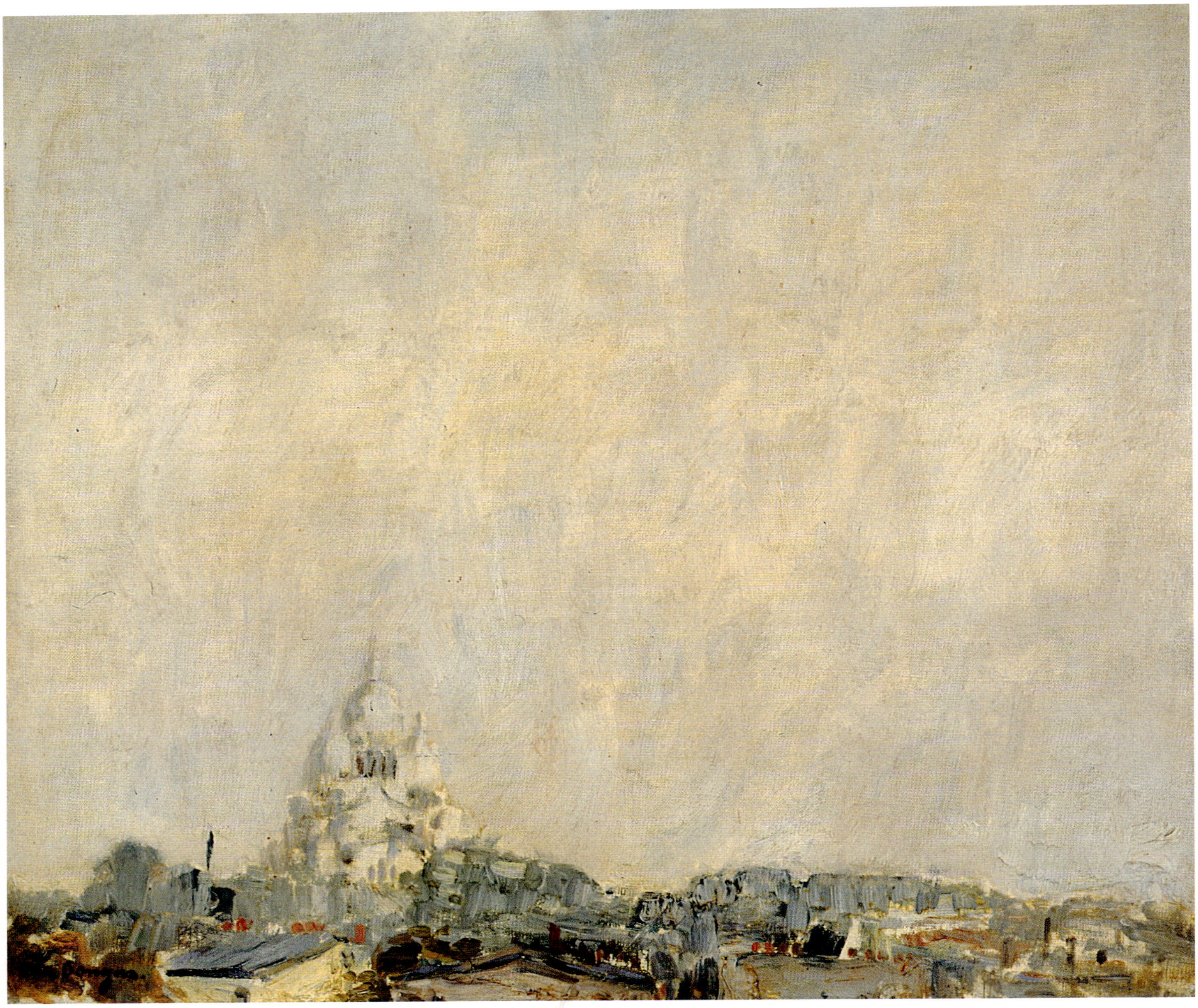

93. *Le Sacré Coeur*, 1904

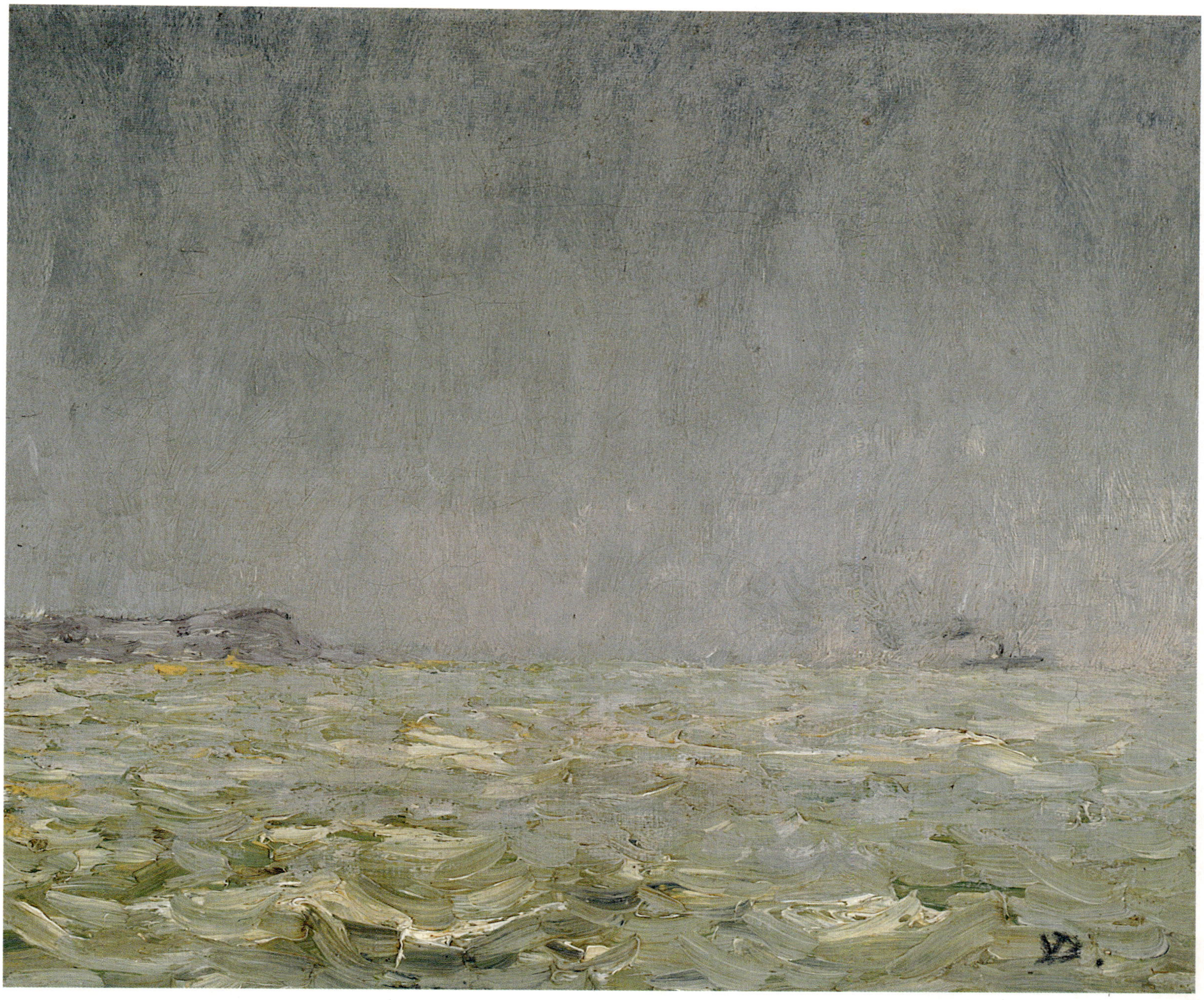

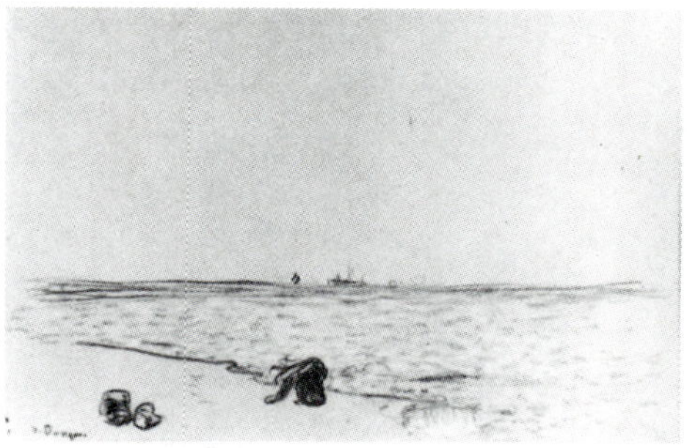

Ramassage de coquillages sur la plage, 1904
Pastel, black chalk, 280 x 450 mm

94. *Trouville. La mer*, 1904

96. *Saucisse et Pépino* (The clowns Sausage and Gamp), 1904
Brush with black ink, watercolour, white gouache
605 x 382 mm
Signed upper left in green watercolour: *van Dongen.*
Special features: also known as *Les bouffons* (The buffoons)
PROVENANCE:
Galerie Bernheim-Jeune, Paris, 28 December 1906 (Inv. 15334, Bernheim-Jeune Archives); Galerie Vildrac, Paris; William Preston Harrison (1869-1940), Los Angeles, 1926; Hood Museum of Art, Dartmouth College, Hanover, May 1938 (gift of William and Ada Preston Harrison)
EXHIBITIONS:
1904 Paris, Vollard, no. 18; 1908 Paris, Bernheim-Jeune, no. 69; 1912 Brussels, Giroux; 1971 Tucson, no. 6 (fig.); 1975 Dartmouth, no. 26
COLLECTION:
Hood Museum of Art, Dartmouth College, Hanover, USA, Inv. W.940.43

97. *Staande clown* (Standing clown), c. 1904
Brush with black ink, white and coloured chalk
413 x 286 mm
Signed centre right in blue chalk: *V.D*
PROVENANCE:
Boymans Van Beuningen Museum, Rotterdam, 1936 (gift of the artist; letter from Kees van Dongen to D. Hannema, 7 December 1936, GA Rotterdam)
LITERATURE:
Hannema 1937, p. 10; Hannema 1973, p. 48; Boymans Museum Annual Report 1937, p. 7
COLLECTION:
Boijmans Van Beuningen Museum, Rotterdam, Inv. KvD 25

98. *Une gymnaste* (A gymnast)
1904
Black chalk, watercolour, white gouache
155 x 105 mm
Signed upper right in red watercolour: *VD.* (in ligature)
PROVENANCE:
Félix Fénéon (1861-1944), Paris; Musée Léon Dierx, Saint-Denis, La Réunion, 1911- 1912 (gift of Félix Fénéon on the founding of the Museum of Art and History, the Musée Léon Dierx, in Saint-Denis, at the request of Marius and Ary LeBlond)
COLLECTION:
Musée Léon Dierx, Saint-Denis, La Réunion, Inv. 450/73

99. *Le cirque* (The circus), 1905
Oil on paper over sketch in black chalk
320 x 496 mm
Signed lower right in oils: *V.D.*
PROVENANCE:
Esmérian Collection, Paris; Galerie Bernard Lorenceau, Paris, c. 1958; Galerie Félix Vercel, Paris; private collection, 1984
EXHIBITIONS:
1973 Paris, no. 8 (fig.)
COLLECTION:
Private collection

In 1904-1905 Van Dongen drew a series of works on paper with clowns and acrobats as its theme. It is in the period that he worked as a porter and stooge among the audience for the *forains* (circus) company Chez Marseille. His familiarity with this ambulant Parisian circus group allowed him to draw its members during their performances. Van Dongen also depicted the so-called parade, the moment before the performance when the artists presented their acts to attract an audience. (fig.) The drawings mainly in ink and watercolour, like *Saucisse et Pépino* and *Marie Cochon* can be dated to 1904. (fig.) That was the year that Van Dongen exhibited them at Galerie Vollard; these drawings along with a couple of works from the series made in 1906 were obtained by Félix Fénéon for Galerie Berheim Jeune. The colourful impressions and the acrobats on horseback – the ears and head of the animal are to be seen in the foreground of *Les écuyères du cirque Médrano* – were created in 1905-1906. (fig.) These funfair and circus scenes show, more than the Zandstraat figures or the nudes, a completely different Van Dongen; both palette and iconography have changed completely. The clowns and acrobats were chosen out of admiration for the power and litheness of their bodies. There is little to be found of the symbolism familiar to art history of the clown as a social outcast, as represented by Daumier or Rouault. Neither is there a relation with Picasso's subtly-drawn circus groups which portray life in a more general sense. Van Dongen's renditions are both explorations in colour, and exercises in complementary contrast and expression through colour (a couple of works are painted in oil on paper). Through these experiments in Neo-Impressionist technique, Van Dongen developed from 1905-1906 an expressive, Fauvist style of painting, as can be seen in the acrobats on horseback whom he studied in the then extremely popular Cirque Médrano.

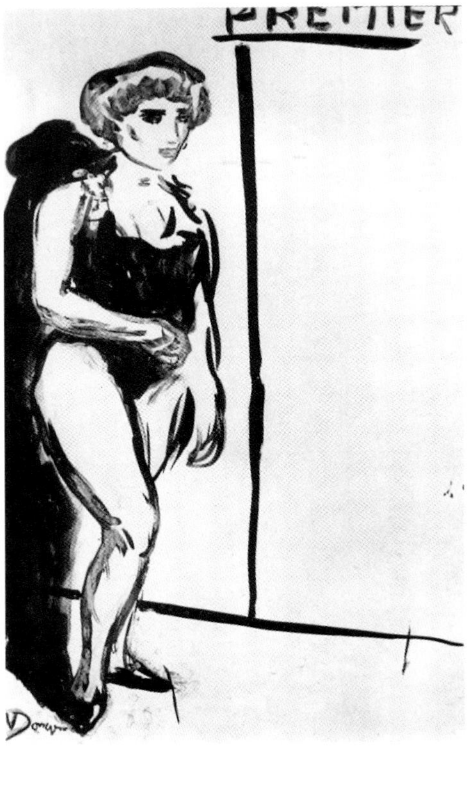

Marie Cochon, 1904
Ink, watercolour, 610 x 380 mm

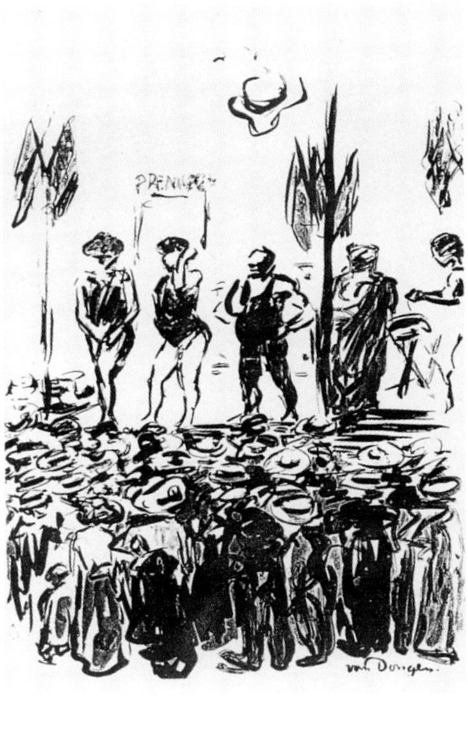

La parade, 1904
Ink, watercolour, 630 x 390 mm

100. *La parade foraine* (The fairground parade), 1905
Watercolour, gouache
485 x 630 mm
Signed centre left in blue: *V.D.*
Special features: also known as *Parade du cirque* (Circus parade)

PROVENANCE:

Daniel-Henry Kahnweiler (1884-1979), Paris (according to auction in Amsterdam, 1965); Kunsthandel d'Audretsch, The Hague, 1937; Kunsthandel E.J. van Wisselingh, Amsterdam, 1937 (Inv. A 5823); Kunsthandel d'Audretsch, The Hague, 1938; Van de Weg, the Netherlands; auction Amsterdam, S.J. Mak van Waay (H.S. Nienhuis), *Kunstveiling 165*, 16 December 1965, no. 27 (fig.); Kunsthandel M.L. de Boer, Amsterdam, 1965 (Inv. 6677); I. Hellenberg (Hall Establishments), Paris 1968; private collection, Neuilly-sur-Seine; private collection

EXHIBITIONS:

1937 Amiens, (according to auction in Amsterdam, 1965); 1938 Utrecht, no. 17

COLLECTION:

Private collection

101. *Les écuyères du cirque Médrano* (The Médrano Circus riders), c. 1905-1906
Oil on paper on cardboard
730 x 600 mm
Signed centre left: *van Dongen.*

PROVENANCE:

Auction Paris, Palais Galliera (R.-P. Oury), *Tableaux, aquarelles, pastels...*, 9 December 1960, no. 54 (fig.); auction London, Sotheby's, *Impressionist and modern paintings... (part II)*, 2 December 1987, no. 175 (fig.); private collection

EXHIBITIONS:

1972 Paris, no. 3; 1990 Paris, p. 95 (fig.)

LITERATURE:

Kyriazi 1971, fig. 24

COLLECTION:

Private collection

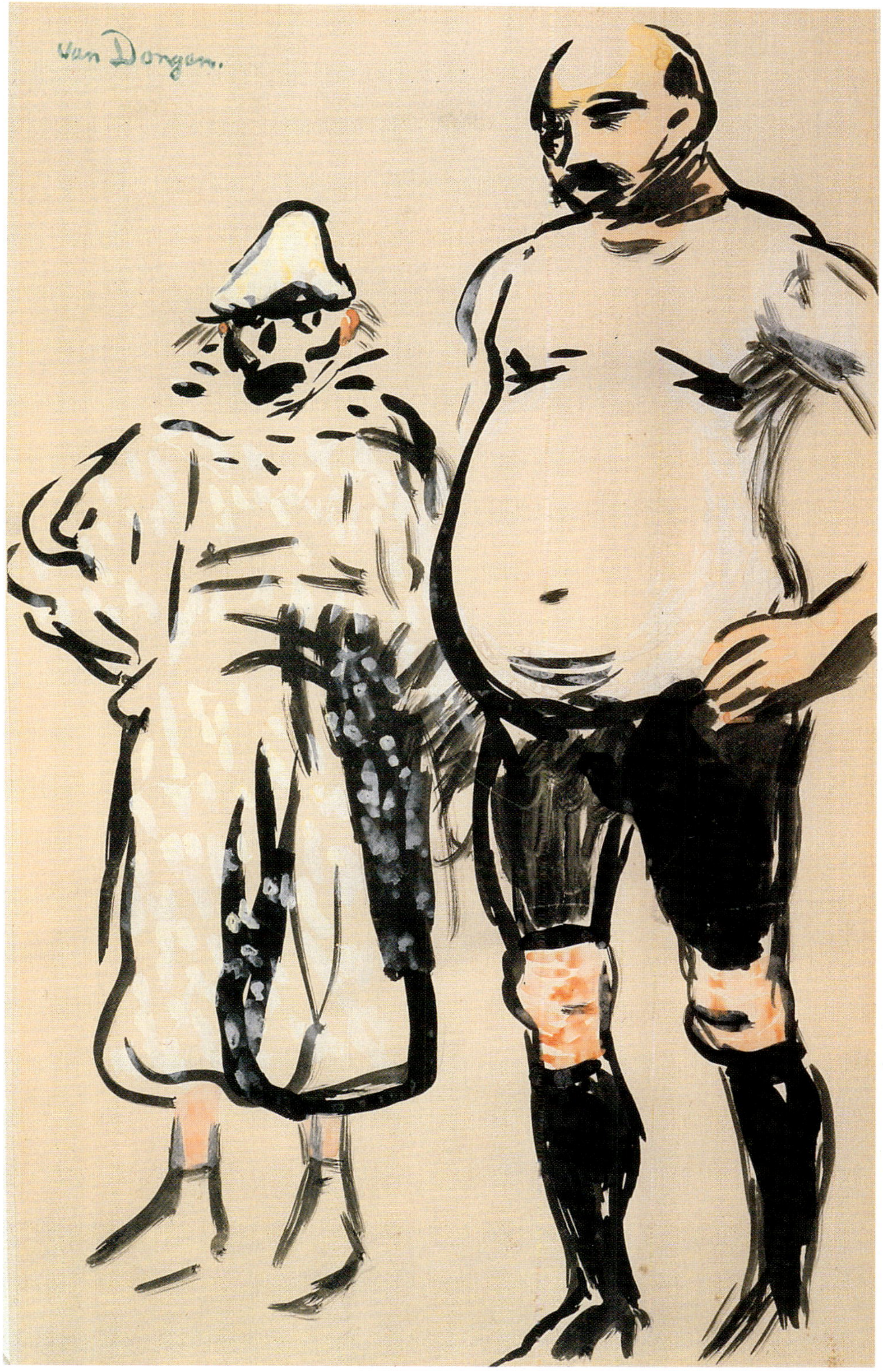

96. *Saucisse et Pépino*, 1904

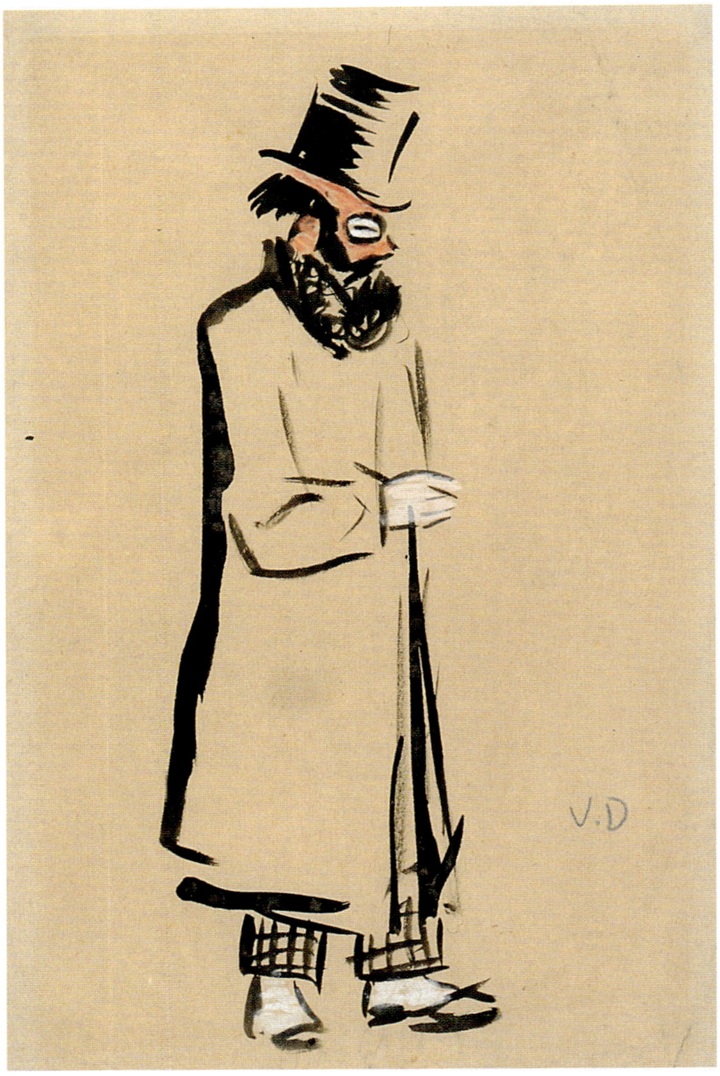

97. *Standing clown*, c. 1904

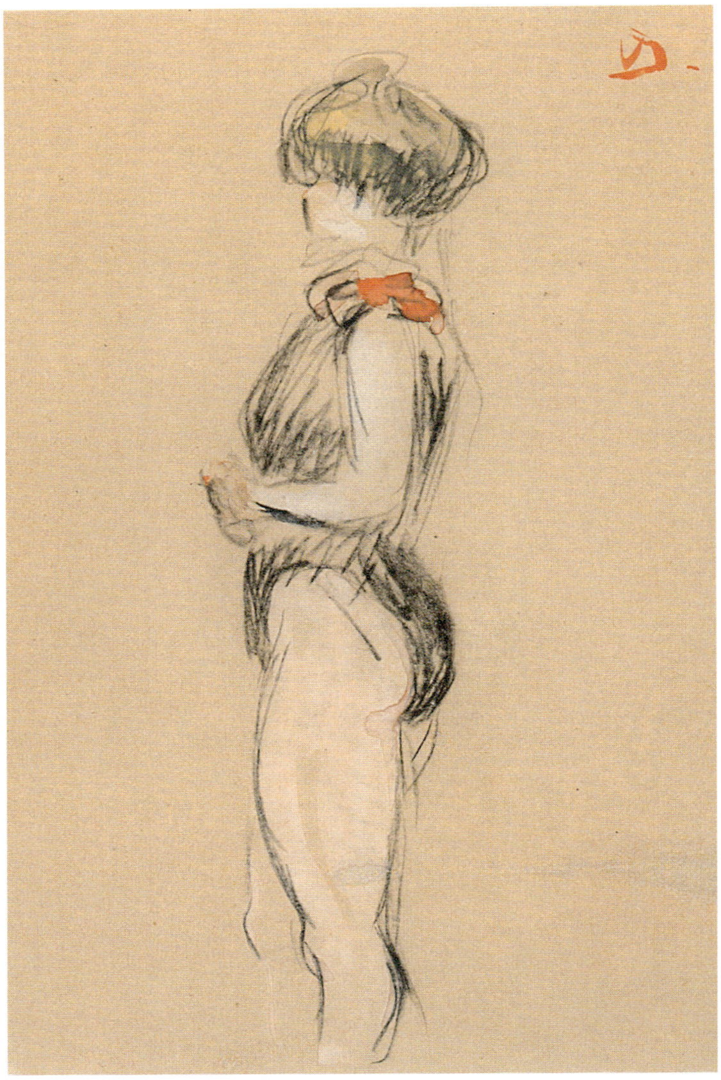

98. *Une gymnaste*, 1904

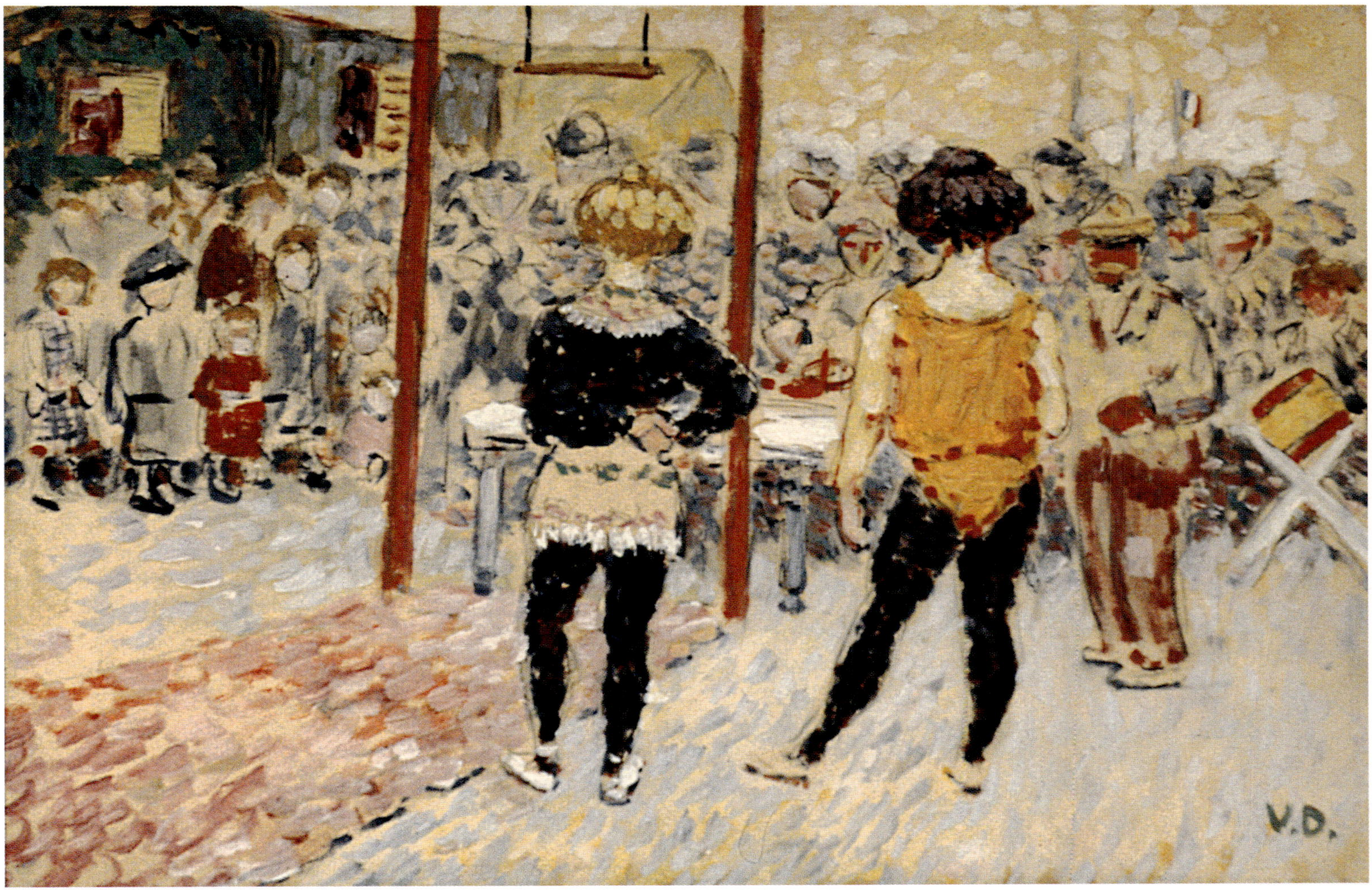

99. *Le cirque*, 1905

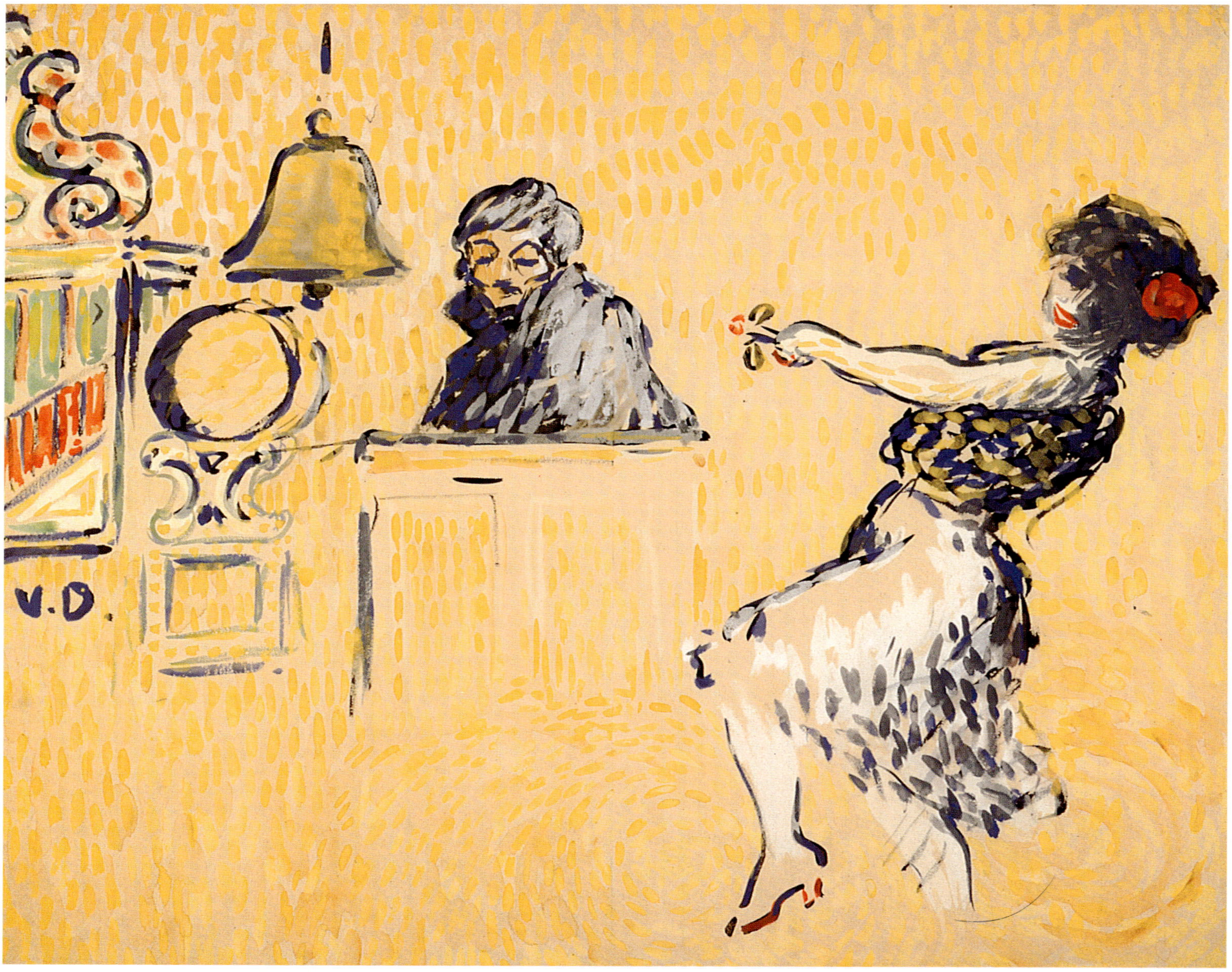

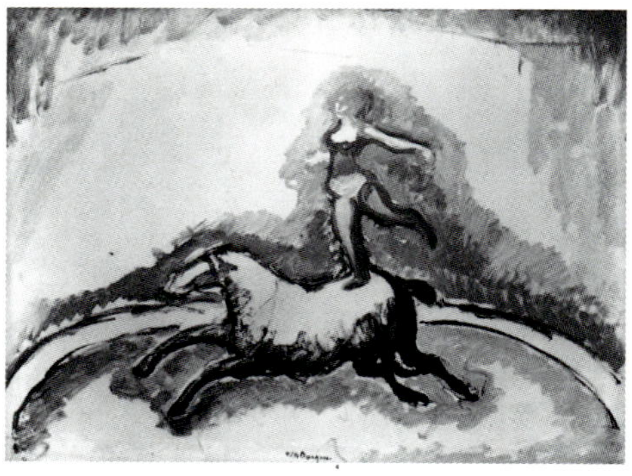

L'écuyère, c. 1905-1906
Oil on canvas, 73.7 x 100.4 cm

100. *La parade foraine*, 1905

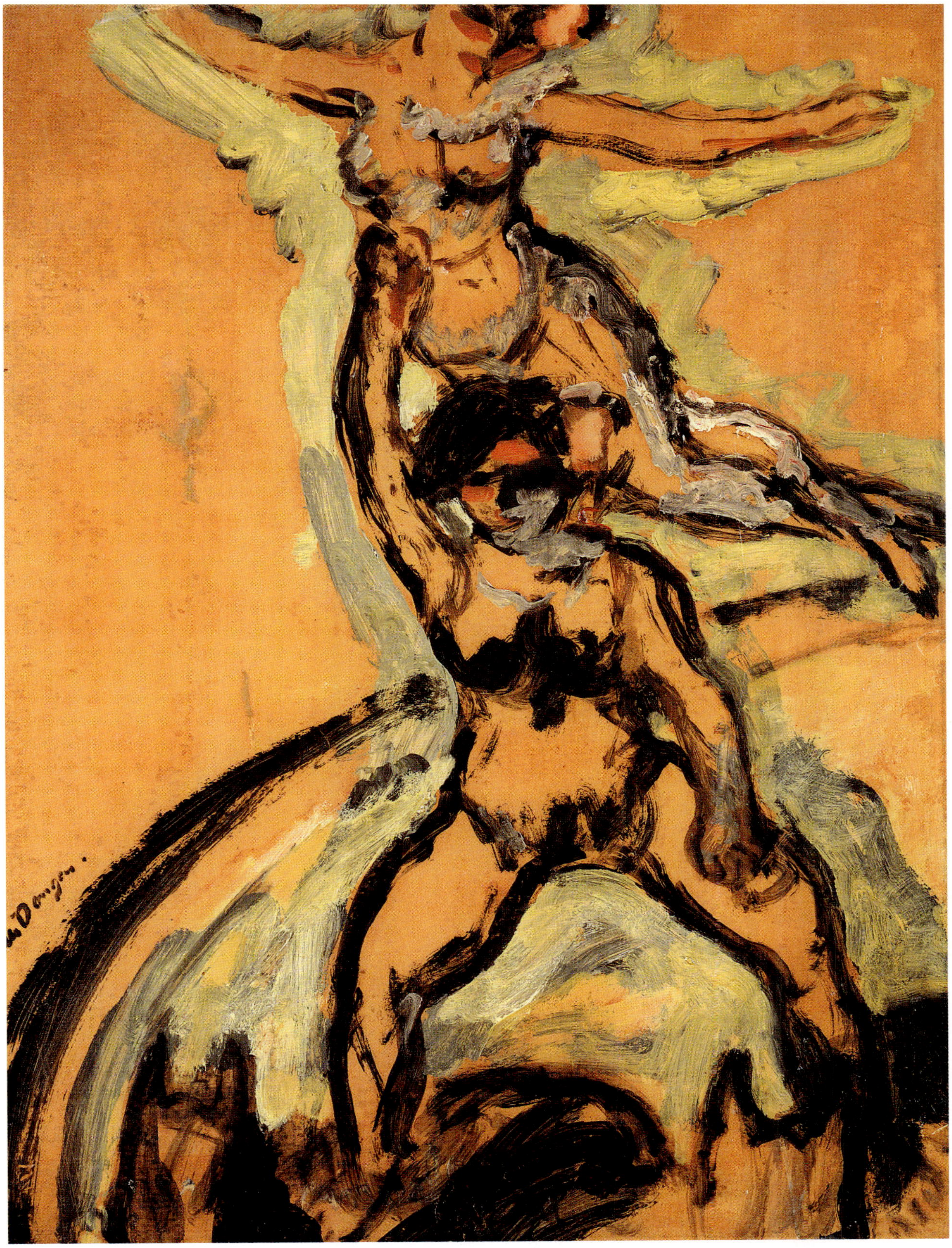

101. *Les écuyères du cirque Médrano*, 1905-1906

102. *Le peignoir rose* (The pink peignoir)
Portrait of Marie Kalff (1874-1959)
1904-1905
Oil on canvas
33 x 54,7 cm
Signed lower left: *VD.*
On stretcher a blue-printed label with purple stamp: *LA PEAU DE L'OURS*; marked in pen with black ink: *Van Dongen n° 34, 05/Femme au peignoir rose*; annotated on stretcher in brush with black ink: *Kees van Dongen/Le peignoir rose*

PROVENANCE:
'La Peau de l'Ours', Paris, 1905 (purchased for this association by André Level from Berthe Weill); auction Paris, Drouot (Henri Baudoin), *Collection de La Peau de l'Ours. Tableaux modernes*, 2 March 1914, no. 13 (acquired by Affoelter); auction Paris, Drouot (F. Lair Dubreuil), *Collection Jules Chavasse. Tableaux, aquarelles...*, 22 June 1922, no. 9 (fig.); Léon Clerc; his heirs, Santiago, Chile; Galerie Paul Vallotton, Lausanne, 1988 (Inv. 76792); private collection, Lausanne; auction London, Sotheby's, *Impressionist and modern paintings... (part II)*, 5 December 1990, no. 116 (fig.); auction London, Sotheby's, *Impressionist and modern drawings...(Part II)*, 1 July 1992, no. 121 (fig.); Kunsthandel Borzo, 's-Hertogenbosch, 1992; private collection, 1992

EXHIBITIONS:
1905 Paris, Berthe Weill, no. 53; 1988 Lausanne, no. 65 (fig.); 1980 Paris, p. 96 (fig.)

LITERATURE:
Level 1959, pp. 16, 20

COLLECTION:
Private collection

103. *Repos* (Rest)
1904-1905
Brush with black and brown watercolour, on brown discoloured paper
275 x 456 mm
Signed lower right in yellow-white watercolour: *V.D.*; pen with ink lower right: *Inv.n° 734* (Inv. Jacques Doucet); pencil on reverse: *VIII/100f*

PROVENANCE:
Jacques Doucet (1853-1929), Paris; his sale Paris, Drouot (A. Desvouges), *Aquarelles, pastels & dessins modernes*, 28-29 December 1919, no. 333 (acquired by Affoelter); Jules Chavasse (1858-1919; L.1430), Sète, 1917; auction Paris, Drouot, (A. Desvouges), *Estampes & dessins...composant la collection de M. J.-C. de C.* (Jules Chavasse), 6 June 1919, no. 258; private collection

COLLECTION:
Private collection

The painting titled *Le peignoir rose* was painted by Van Dongen in 1904-1905. In terms of style, particularly the way in which the dressing gown has been made with palette-knife strokes and swift dabs over the black background, the canvas is related to *Le boniment*, the entry with which Van Dongen focused attention on himself at the *Salons des Indépendants* of 1905. *Le peignoir rose* was exhibited by Van Dongen in January 1905 at Galerie Berthe Weill and afterwards acquired by André Level for the association *La peau de l'ours*. This group of investors, who had joined forces under the leadership of André Level in 1904, was founded to acquire Modern art and at the same time to support contemporary artists. The works they bought were to be auctioned ten years later. This auction took place in March 1914 and was a great success. After auction, Van Dongen's painting ended up in the collection of Jules Chavasse, who not long afterwards acquired one of the preliminary studies. The painting *Le peignoir rose* portrays the Dutch actress Marie Kalff. Reclining on a divan, the actress is studying her role; the manuscript she is reading from is bound in red whilst the pencil helps her to keep her eye on the right line in the passage. Marie Kalff had been in Paris since the summer of 1900 and was having acting lessons from Aurélien Lugné-Poe. Under his direction she played different roles at the Théâtre de l'Œuvre; in 1904 she was employed for a season by André Antoine, director of the Théâtre Libre. Afterwards she acted with success for various companies in plays by people like Georges de Bouhélier and Henri-René Lenormand. Van Dongen portrayed her at an earlier period. That canvas, whose present location is unknown, was sent in to the Salon d'Automne of 1904, but the press criticized it: 'Fortunately, Marie Kalff is hanging in a corner of the corridor...it is very ugly, it doesn't look like anything at all.'[1] The portrait of 1905 can be seen as a second attempt. The different preliminary studies make it clear that Van Dongen prepared the painting carefully. (fig.) The sketches show different poses and were probably, in view of the clothing the actress is wearing, drawn at the same posing session. The question arises as to whether Van Dongen was acquainted with the canvas *Woman reading* painted by his fellow countryman Isaac Israels, which in terms of composition and fluent hand reminds one of Van Dongen's *Peignoir rose*. (fig.) Isaac Israels settled in Paris in 1904 and lived in a studio on the edge of Monmartre, on the Boulevard Clichy. The artists were friends: Van Dongen's portrait was painted by Israels around 1904-1905; also a number of street sketches by the pair on the same subject have been preserved.[2] After 1904 Van Dongen's style of painting took another turn and the artist started to show an affiliation to the French avant-garde, whilst Israels remained true to his Dutch roots. An interesting detail worth mentioning is that Van Dongen's preliminary drawing *Repos*, together with the pen drawing *Robe japonaise* by Matisse (Salon d'Automne, 1905), originally belonged to Jacques Doucet and the drawings probably hung in the same room at the collector's house.

1.
Anonymous (C. Scharten), *Algemeen Handelsblad*, 16 October 1904.

2.
Wagner 1985, pp. 52, 65-67.

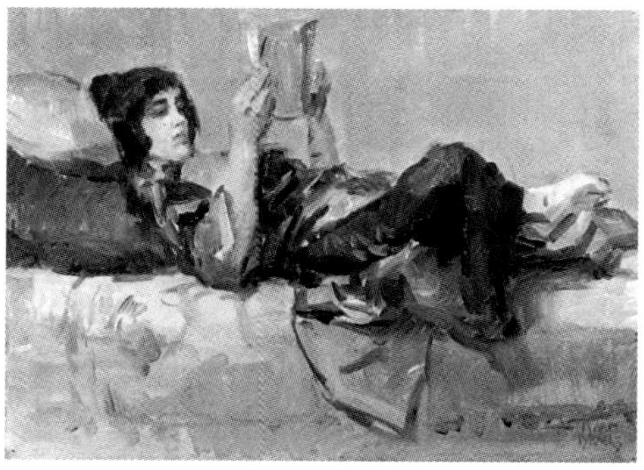

I. Israels, *Lezende vrouw*, c. 1904
Oil on canvas, 37.5 x 53 cm

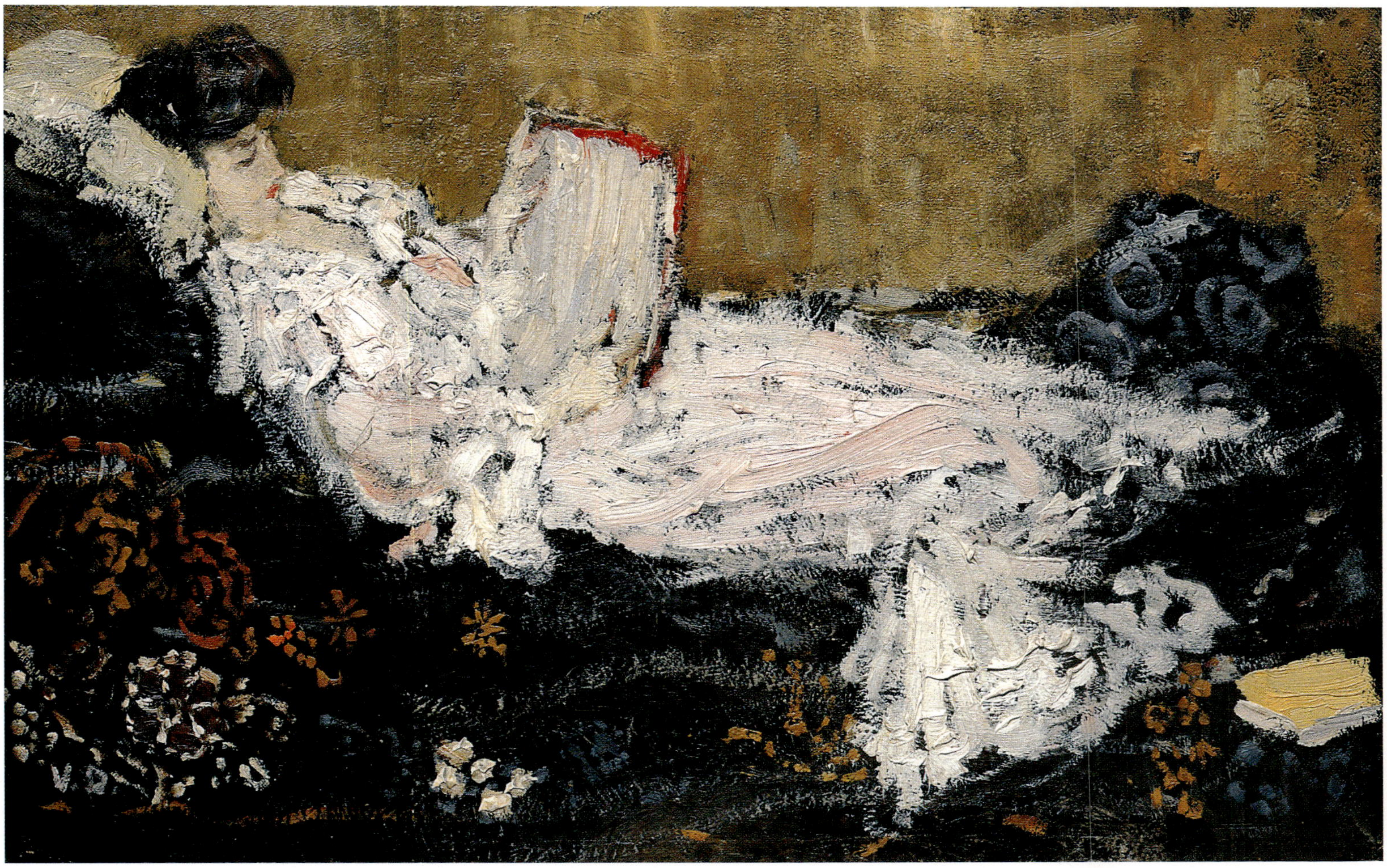

102. *Le peignoir rose*
Portrait of Marie Kalff (1874-1959), 1904-1905

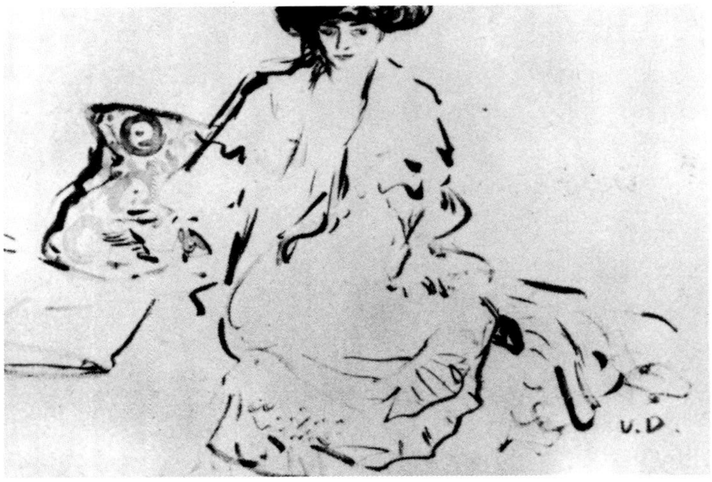

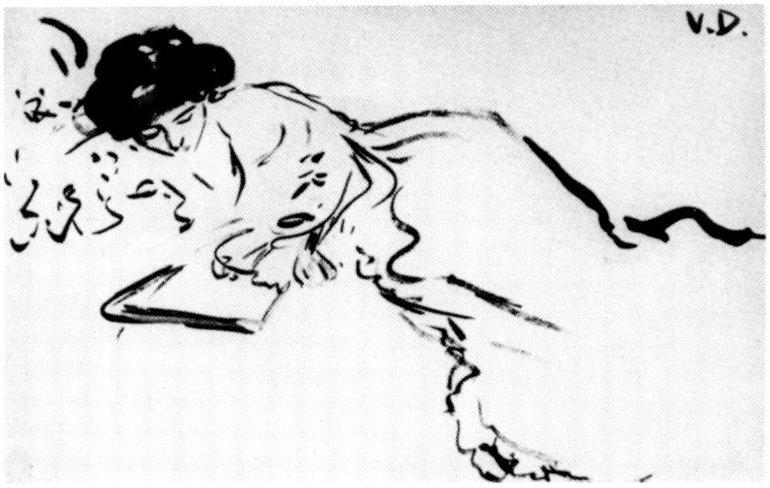

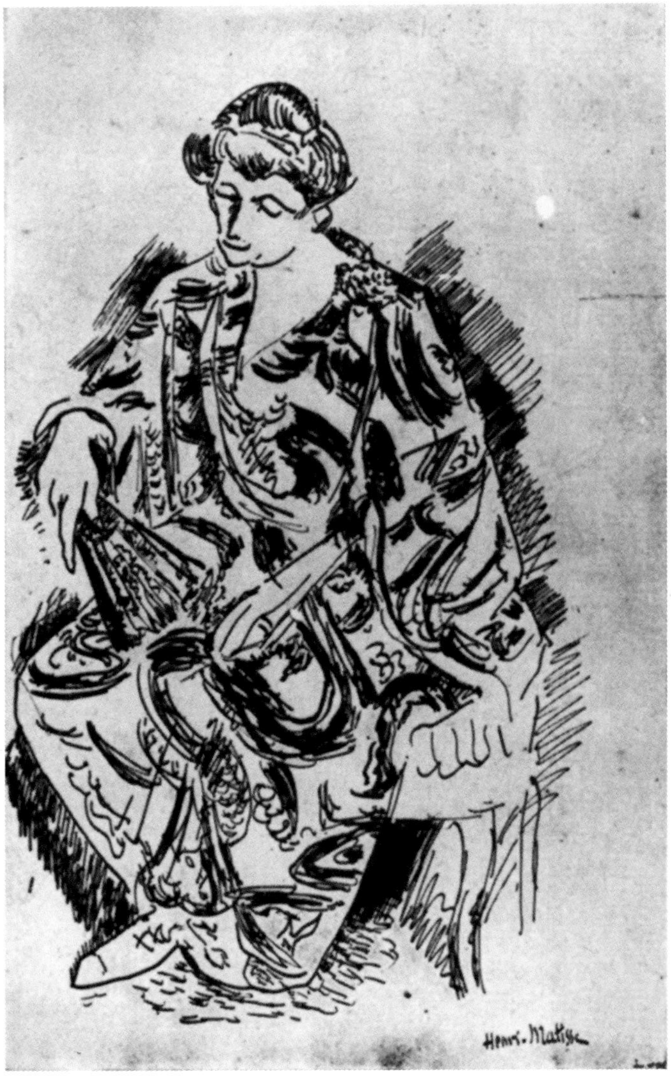

Femme assise au coussin bleu, 1904-1905
Watercolour, 290 x 440 mm

Elégante, 1904-1905
Ink, body-colour, 290 x 464 mm

Henri Matisse, *Madame Matisse en robe japonaise*, 1905
Pen and brush in ink, 492 x 310 mm

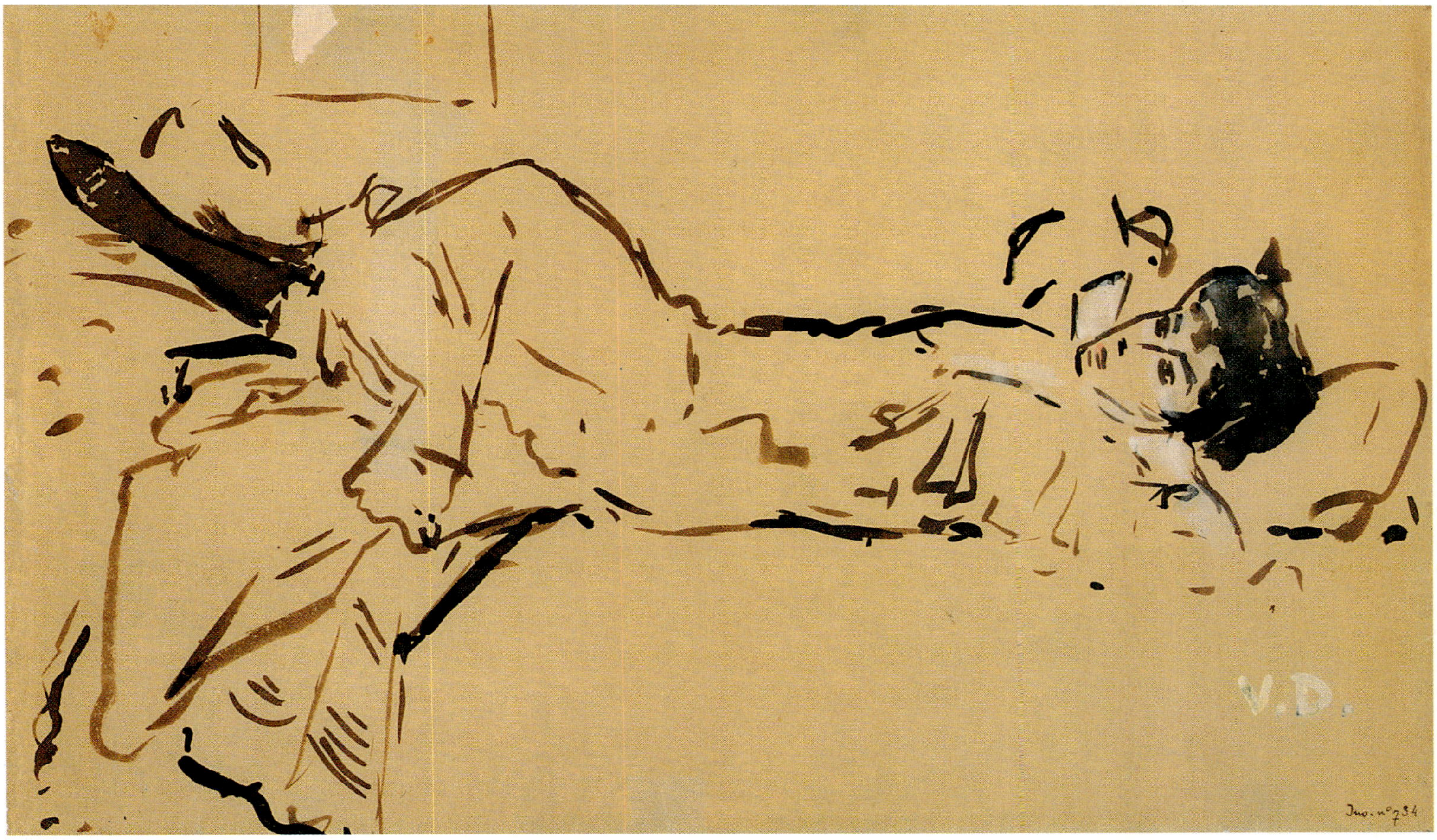

103. *Repos*, 1904-1905

104. *Un carrousel* (A merry-go-round), 1905
Oil on canvas
46 x 55 cm
Signed lower left: *van Dongen*
On stretcher a printed label with blue border: *KESTNER-GESELLSCHAFT/HANNOVER/Nr.*; marked with pen in black ink: 302

PROVENANCE:
Daniel-Henry Kahnweiler Collection (1884-1979), Paris (Inv. 600, Paul Cassirer-Archiv, Kahnweiler Archive); Kunsthandel d'Audretsch, The Hague, 1938 (according to exhib.cat. 1938 Utrecht); auction Paris, Galerie Charpentier (A. Bellier), *Tableaux modernes*, 3 June 1954, no. 79; Galerie Paul Pétridès, Paris, 1954 (label on reverse); auction London, Sotheby's, *Impressionist and modern paintings ...(part II)*, 2 December 1987, no. 174 (fig.); private collection

EXHIBITIONS:
1905 Paris, Indépendants, no. 4095 or no. 4096; 1919 Berlin, Cassirer, no. 3; 1919 Hamburg, Galerie Commeter; 1919 Düsseldorf, Flechtheim, no. 4; 1920 The Hague; 1922 Hannover, no. 36; 1938 Utrecht, no. 16; 1967 Paris, no. 14 (fig.); 1990 Paris, p. 92 (fig.); 1991 Boston, no. 26 (fig.)

LITERATURE:
Chaumeil 1967, fig. II; Kyriazi 1971, fig. 25

COLLECTION:
Private collection

105. *Carrousel des cochons* (Merry-go-round of pigs), 1905
Brush with black ink, watercolour, gouache
382 x 608 mm
Signed lower centre in brush with black ink: *van Dongen.*; pencil lower right: *13*
Special features: the drawing is mounted on cardboard

COLLECTION:
Private collection

'Everyone makes landscapes, but it takes guts and willpower to make something from twirling light emanating from those tremendous electric balls of white light...in daring to represent that Bacchanal of light and life, bold and violent as the whole thing is, the personality of the artist comes most powerfully to the foreground', was the view of the journalist Tom Schilperoort in his article on Van Dongen published in 1905.[1] Van Dongen's first exploration of this subject, the *manèges des cochons* – steam merry-go-rounds with wooden pigs illuminated by electric lights – were to be seen in November 1904 at the exhibition in Galerie Vollard. They are sketches in ink and watercolour like the drawings *Le manège* and *Manège des cochons* in which the spectacle of light and movement is depicted in a strikingly free manner – so aptly characterized by a critic as 'scribbled-down movements'. (fig.) Van Dongen did not concern himself with details but was determined to capture the revolving light and its effect. He indicated the crowd at the bottom of the drawing once again as a dark mass so that attention would be drawn mainly to these aspects. He is said to have made the works on the spot watching a street funfair, sheet for sheet, sitting somewhere in an upstairs room of a pub: tearing up the drawings which did not turn out quite right. After the Vollard exhibition, Van Dongen's showed two paintings on this subject, at the Salon des Indépendants of 1905, including *Un carrousel*. Through this entry he qualified as an up-and-coming young artist: *un maître nouveau*. The spontaneous direct hand, as if it were compelled by the movement, and presentation by means of the colour, were the modes of expression favoured by the avant-garde at that moment. It is remarkable that Van Dongen did not portray a merry-go-round with a more diverse menagerie – with ostriches, lions or elephants, as were popular at the annual, more chic funfair at Neuilly – but chose a carrousel with pigs instead. In making this choice he emphasized the common aspect, the exuberance and licentiousness of this frivolous amusement which was reflected in the pigs. His preference links up with the interest for primitive cultures and folk art that was then current. Van Dongen's interest in electric, modern white light was also in vogue. (fig.) This is 'the latest thing' the Dutch critic Wiessing thought, 'no one has approached the essence of our age more closely than he has.'[2] Prominent French critics like Arsène Alexandre and Louis Vauxcelles also labelled Van Dongen's representations as modern – 'une formule nouvelle'. Just how daring Van Dongen's approach was becomes clear by comparison with other representations of this subject. The Dutch painter Isaac Israels, for example, went in for a more staged scene in his funfair, more composed, and at the same time aimed at a more faithful representation of reality. (fig.) The compositions by Nicolas Tarkhoff, a Russian artist working in Paris, were strongly influenced by Impressionism in which light, movement and colour are the components which catch the eye, as in Van Dongen's pieces: however, the works do not achieve the same modern result. (fig.) By abandoning the representation of reality and by applying himself to the more formal aspects of art, Van Dongen was in fact able to forge links with the avant-garde.

1.
Schilperpoort 1905, p. 738.

2.
Anonymous (H. Wiessing), *Algemeen Handelsblad*, 31 October 1905.

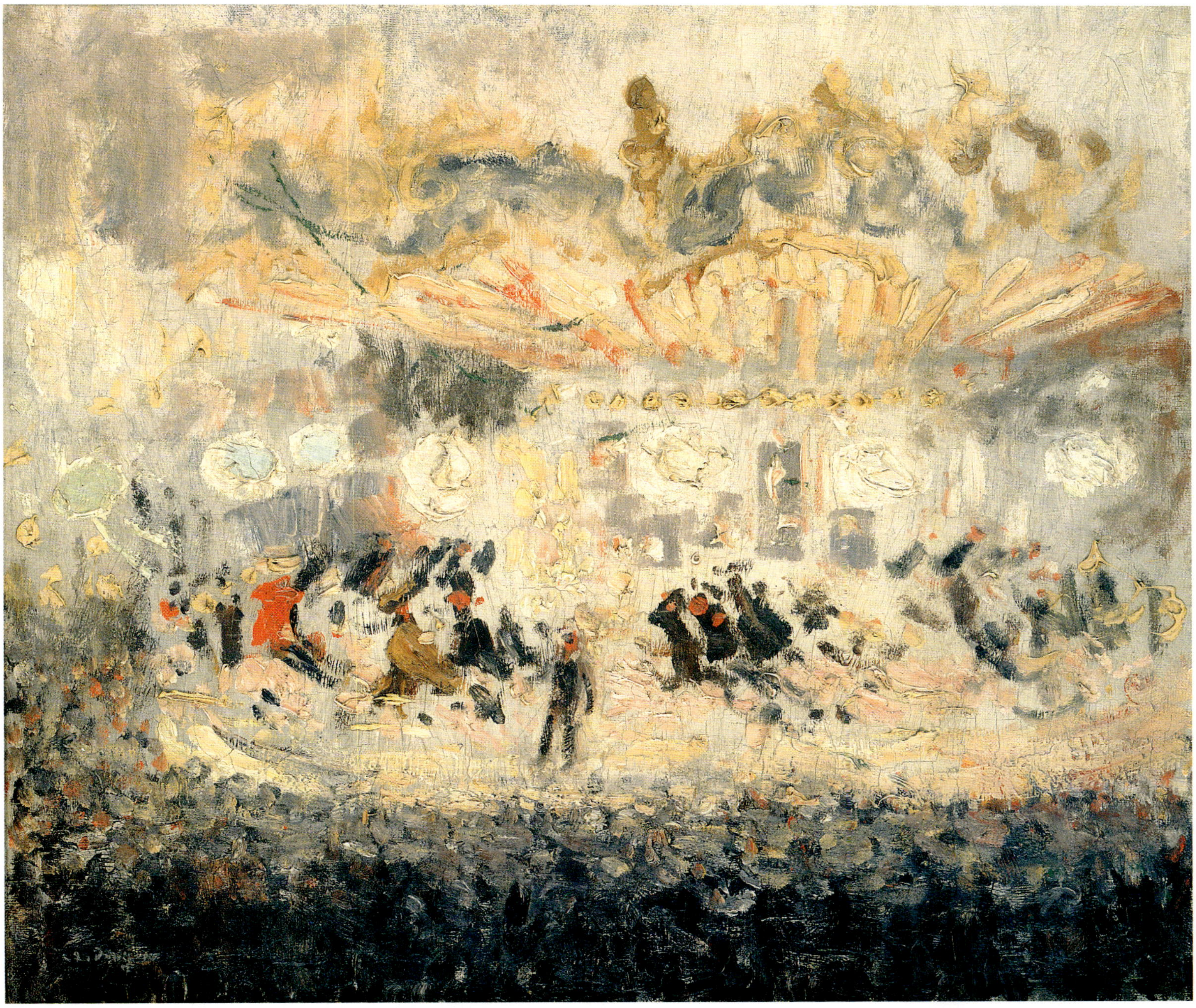

104. *Un carrousel*, 1905

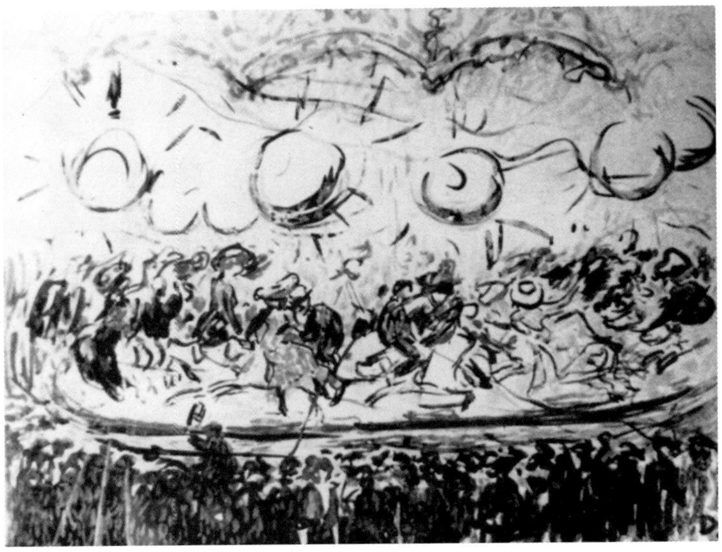

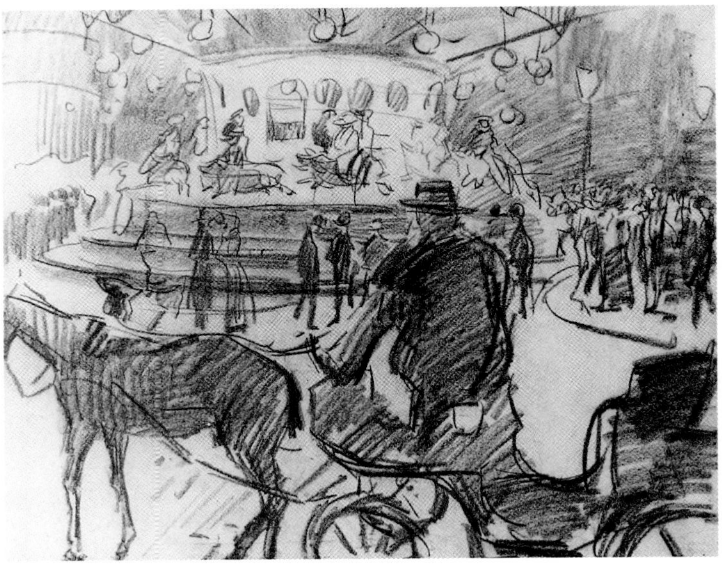

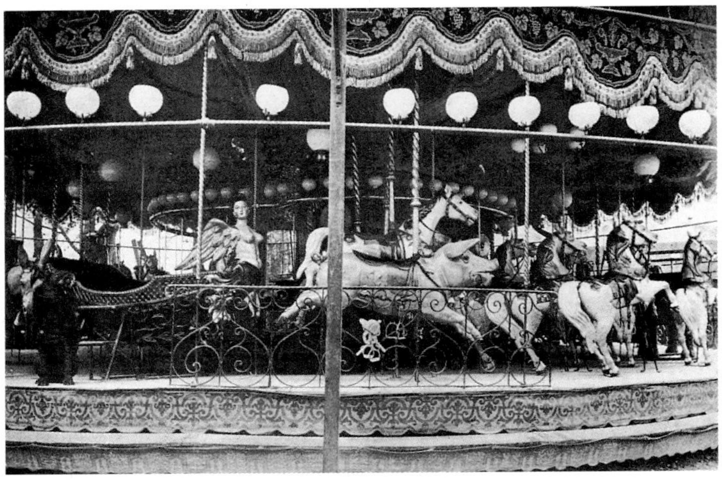

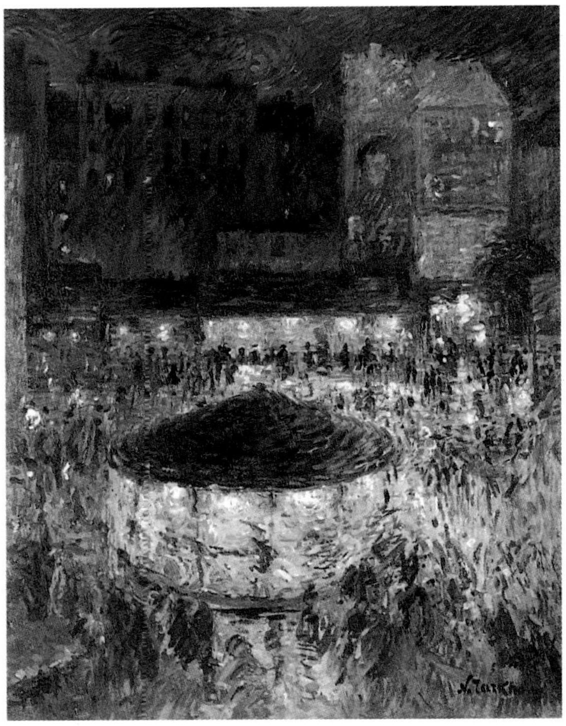

Le manège, 1905
Ink, watercolour, bocy colour, 482 x 610 mm

Le manège nouveau style, fig. in *La Revue Illustré*, part II, 1906

Isaac Israels, *Waiting coachman at the fair*, c. 1904-1905
Black chalk, 480 x 620 mm

N. Tarkhoff, *Fête fcraine*, 1905
Oil on canvas, 82 x 65 cm, Petit Palais, Musée d'Art Moderne, Genève

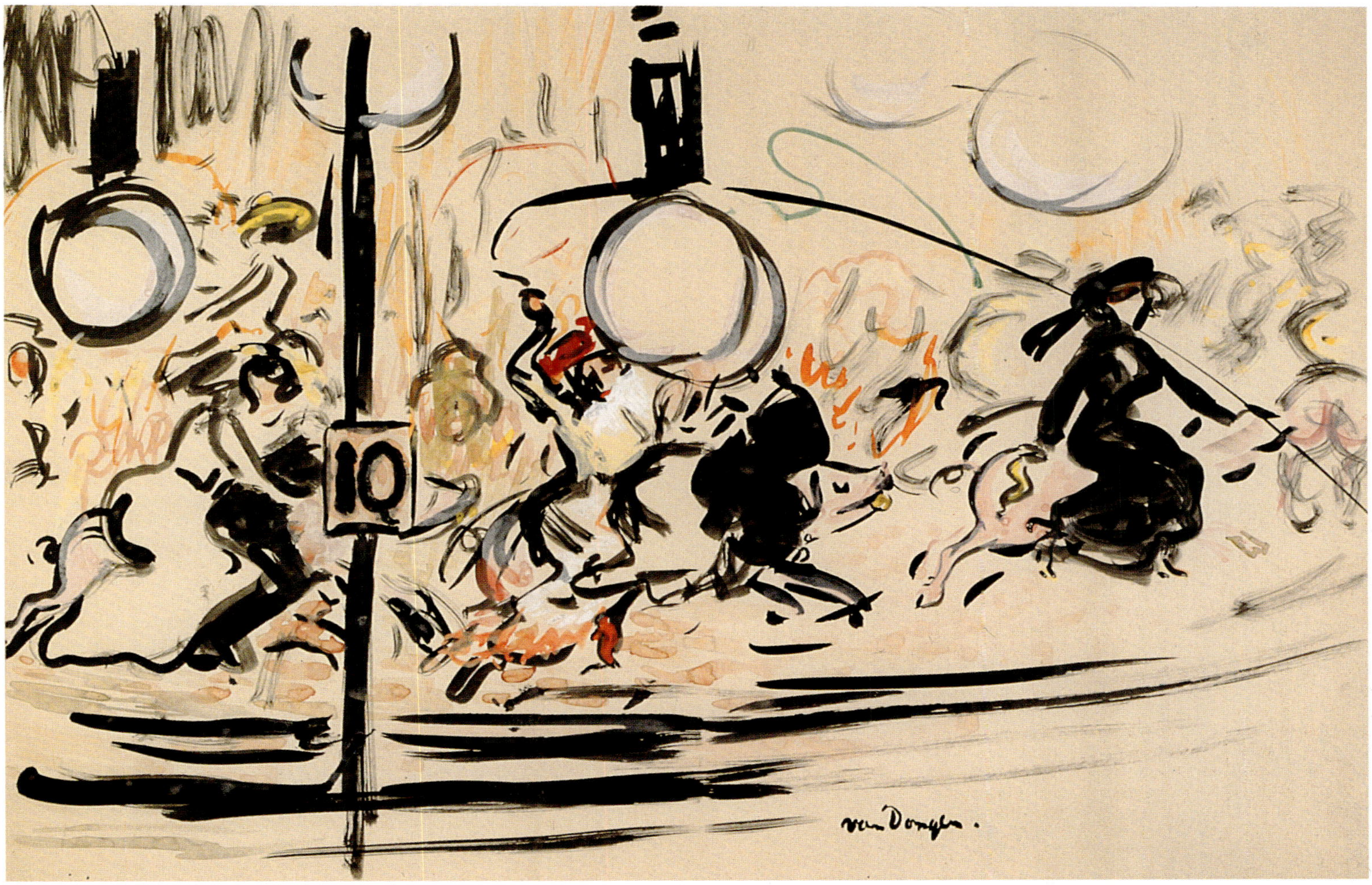

105. *Carrousel des cochons*, 1905

106. *L'épouvantail* (The scarecrow), 1905
Coloured chalk
310 x 464 mm
Signed lower right in blue chalk: *V. Dongen*
In blue chalk on reverse of cardboard on which the drawing is mounted: 29-
Special features: also known by its Dutch title *De vogelverschrikker*
PROVENANCE:
Boymans Museum, Rotterdam, 1936 (gift of the artist; letter from Kees van Dongen to D. Hannema, 7 December 19, GA Rotterdam)
EXHIBITIONS:
1907 Amsterdam, C.M. van Gogh, no. 38 (?); 1908 Toulouse, no. 23; 1989 Rotterdam, (ex. catalogue)
LITERATURE:
Hannema 1937, p. 10; Hannema 1973, p. 48; Boymans Museum Annual Report 1937, p. 7
COLLECTION:
Boijmans Van Beuningen Museum, Rotterdam, Inv. KvD 17

107. Le peuplier (The poplar tree), 1905
Pastel chalk
500 x 310 mm
Signed lower right in dark-blue chalk: *van Dongen.*; annotated in purple chalk lower left: *Cely-*
On reverse of frame a green-printed label on yellow paper: *EMIL RICHTER Dresden*; marked in pen with blue ink: *Van Dongen/peuplier/E 76*; a note in pen and ink: *N°15337/ Van Dongen/le Peuplier*; label from Albi exhibition, 1960, no. 68
PROVENANCE:
Galerie Bernheim-Jeune, Paris, 28 December 1906 (Inv. 15337); Maître Jean Sirgan, Toulouse, c. 1960; auction New York, Sotheby's, *Impressionist and modern paintings, drawings and sculpture*, 2 October 1991, no. 14 (fig.); private collection
EXHIBITIONS:
1908 Dresden, Emile Richter; 1908 Paris, Bernheim-Jeune, no. 76; 1912 Brussels, Galerie Giroux; 1960 Albi, no. 68
LITERATURE:
Kyriazi 1971, p. 90
COLLECTION:
Private collection

108. *Maaimachine met paarden in een korenveld* (Harvester and horses in a cornfield), 1905
Pastel chalk
286 x 340 mm
Signed lower right in pink chalk: *van Dongen*
Special features: the drawing is mounted on cardboard
PROVENANCE:
Boymans Museum, Rotterdam, 1936 (gift of the artist; letter from Kees van Dongen to D. Hannema, 7 December 1936, GA Rotterdam)
EXHIBITIONS:
1906 Rotterdam, RKK, no. 67 (*La Faucheuse* – The reaper) (?); 1989 Rotterdam, (ex. catalogue)
LITERATURE:
Hannema 1937, p. 10; Hannema 1973, p. 48; Boymans Museum Annual Report 1937, p. 7
COLLECTION:
Boijmans Van Beuningen Museum, Rotterdam, Inv. KvD 31

109. *Lieuses* (Women binding sheaves), 1905
Pastel chalk
305 x 464 mm
Signed lower right in pink chalk: *van Dongen*; annotated lower left in purple pastel: *Lieuses-*; in blue chalk on reverse of cardboard on which drawing is mounted: 28-
PROVENANCE:
Boymans Museum, Rotterdam, 1936 (gift of the artist; letter from Kees van Dongen to D. Hannema, 7 December 1936, GA Rotterdam)
EXHIBITIONS:
1907 Amsterdam, C.M. van Gogh, no. 37; 1908 Toulouse, Télégramme, no. 22; 1989 Rotterdam, (ex. catalogue)
LITERATURE:
Hannema 1937, p. 10; Hannema 1973, p. 48; Boymans Museum Annual Report, 1937, p. 7
COLLECTION:
Boijmans Van Beuningen Museum, Rotterdam, Inv. KvD 32

In the summer months of 1905, Van Dongen, his wife Guus and their daughter Guusje (Dolly), who was born in May that year, stayed with an artist couple Otto van Rees and Adya Dulith in Fleury-en-Bière. Fleury was in the middle of the countryside, 'close to Barbizon but fortunately there aren't any painters living there', Van Dongen informed the writer Carel Scharten in the middle of June. The stay in the country was undoubtedly for the benefit of the two Guuses; the artist himself 'thought it was alright, but not wonderful.' This remark can be read in a following letter to Scharten, also in the collection of the Nederlands Letterkundig Museum in The Hague, which was embellished by Van Dongen with the picture of an old woman under a sketched roof of a house. Gradually his interest in the outdoor life expanded and he made a whole series of drawings and paintings in the area directly surrounding the village. A part of this series is devoted exclusively to the harvest, showing scenes like reaping, binding up the corn in sheaves, and, after these had been stacked, the threshing. (fig.) At that time in Fleury this was carried out by a steam thresher as is shown in the sketch with brush and black ink *Harvesting near Fleury-en-Bière*. (fig.) A new feature is Van Dongen's use of pastel chalk; the first drawings using this technique were made in Fleury. This method of work may have been suggested to him by Otto van Rees. Before leaving for Paris in the autumn of 1904, this artist worked for a few months with Jan Toorop in Domburg and, on his suggestion, had practised a method of drawing inspired by Neo-Impressionism. Van Rees drew several sheets himself in Fleury in the 'dot and line technique'. The retrospective of Van Gogh's work also proved to be important for the two artists; it was held in the spring of 1905 at the Indépendants. The paintings which Van Dongen exhibited in October-November 1905 entitled 'Une saison' at Galerie Druet, including *La vigne*, show the influence of his famous Dutch predecessor. The stooping figure painted between the vines is characteristic of Van Dongen, and can be compared to the type of figure he sketched on the letter to Scharten.

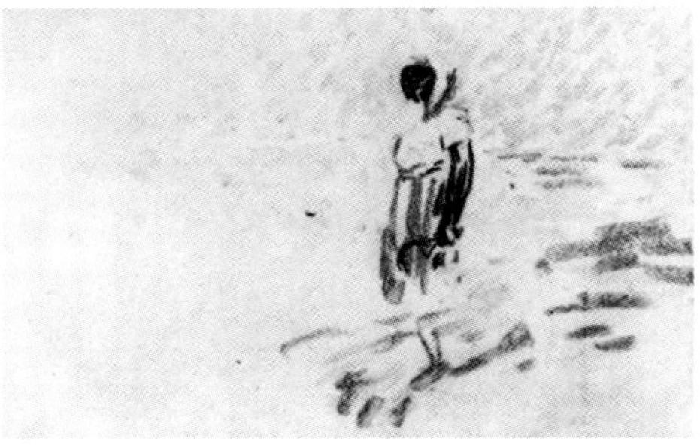

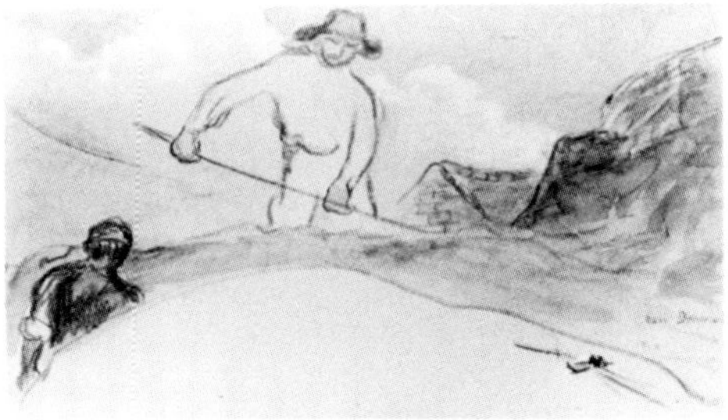

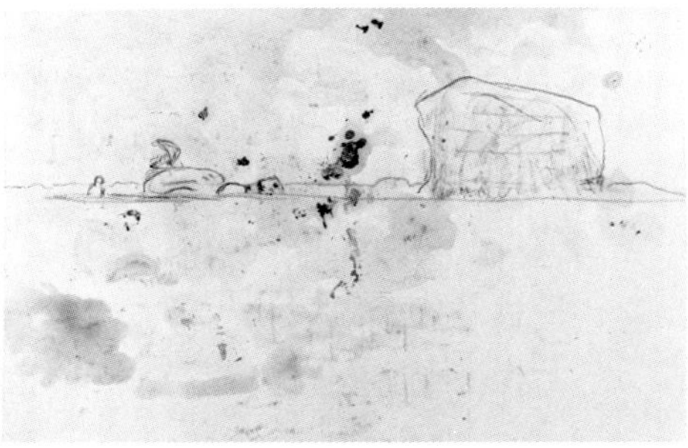

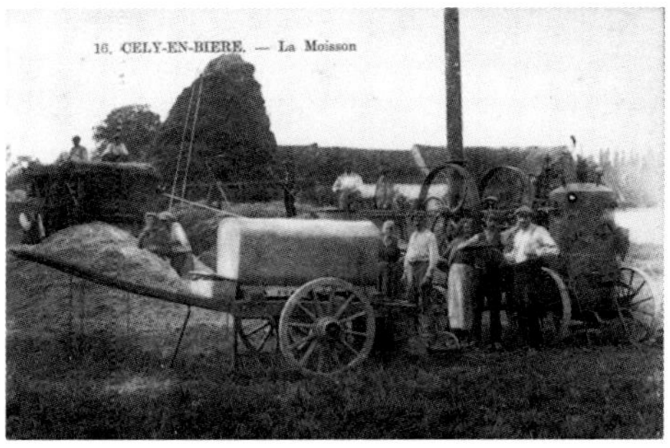

La moissonneuse, 1905
Pastel, 290 x 445 mm

La meule, 1905
Black chalk, watercolour, 270 x 450 mm

Harvesting farmers, 1905, verso *Farm at Fleury*
Black chalk, 326 x 500 mm, verso *Huizen onder een bewolkte lucht*, Boijmans Van Beuningen Museum, Rotterdam

Postcard *Cély-en-Bière*, (near Fleury), c. 1905
Otto van Rees estate

110. *Letter from Kees van Dongen to Carel Scharten*
June 1905
Handwritten letter, pen with black ink, 1 sheet, drawing in purple chalk on the left
400 x 312 mm
Upper right place and date: *Fleury...Juni/05*; signed below: *Kees-*, with annotation of place: *à Fleury en Bière. (Par Perthes)/Seine de Marne-*
PROVENANCE:
Gift of the heirs of Carel Scharten to the NLMD, The Hague
COLLECTION:
Nederlands Letterkundig Museum en Documentatiecentrum, The Hague, Inv. S 00255 B2

111. *La vigne* (The vine), 1905
Oil on canvas
46 x 55 cm
Signed upper right: *V.D.*
Signed on stretcher in yellow paint: *05. Kees van Dongen.*; annotated in green paint on reverse of canvas: *La Vigne*; numbered in blue chalk: 39; upper centre of stretcher remains of a label from Galerie Druet, Paris (1905 exhibition)
PROVENANCE:
Pablo Picasso (1881-1973), Paris, c. 1906; gift of Picasso's heirs to the French State, 1973; Museum Picasso, Paris, 1985
EXHIBITIONS:
1905 Paris, Druet, no. 4; 1906 Rotterdam, RKK, no. 38; 1978 Paris, no. 37 (fig.); 1990 Paris, p. 99 (fig.)
LITERATURE:
Besnard-Bernadac 1985, p. 250 (fig.)
COLLECTION:
Musée Picasso, Paris, Inv. RF. 1973-92

112. *Akker in de omgeving van Fleury-en-Bière*
(Field in the neighbourhood of Fleury-en-Bière), 1905
Pastel chalk
465 x 305 mm
Signed lower left in red chalk: *van Dongen*
PROVENANCE:
Marie-Claire van Dongen, Monaco; private collection, Paris
EXHIBITIONS:
1906 Rotterdam, RKK, no. 65 (*Paysage Fleury* – Fleury Landscape) (?); 1908 Toulouse, Télégramme, no. 20 (*Champ à Fleury* – Field at Fleury) (?)
COLLECTION:
Private collection, Paris

113. *Oogst nabij Fleury-en-Bière* (Harvesting near Fleury-en-Bière), 1905
Blue chalk, brush with black ink
335 x 555 mm
Signed lower right in pink chalk: *van Dongen*
PROVENANCE:
Marie-Claire van Dongen, Monaco; Françoise Marquet, 1990
Françoise Marquet Collection

114. *Hooischelf met boeren* (Haystack with farm labourers), 1905
Black chalk
399 x 305 mm
Signed lower left in blue chalk: *V.D*
Special features: the drawing is attached to cardboard
PROVENANCE:
Boymans Museum, Rotterdam, 1936 (gift of the artist; letter from Kees van Dongen to D. Hannema, 7 December 1936, GA Rotterdam)
LITERATURE:
Hannema 1937, p. 10; Hannema 1973, p. 48; Boymans Museum Annual Report 1937, p. 7
COLLECTION:
Boijmans Van Beuningen Museum, Rotterdam, Inv. KvD 34

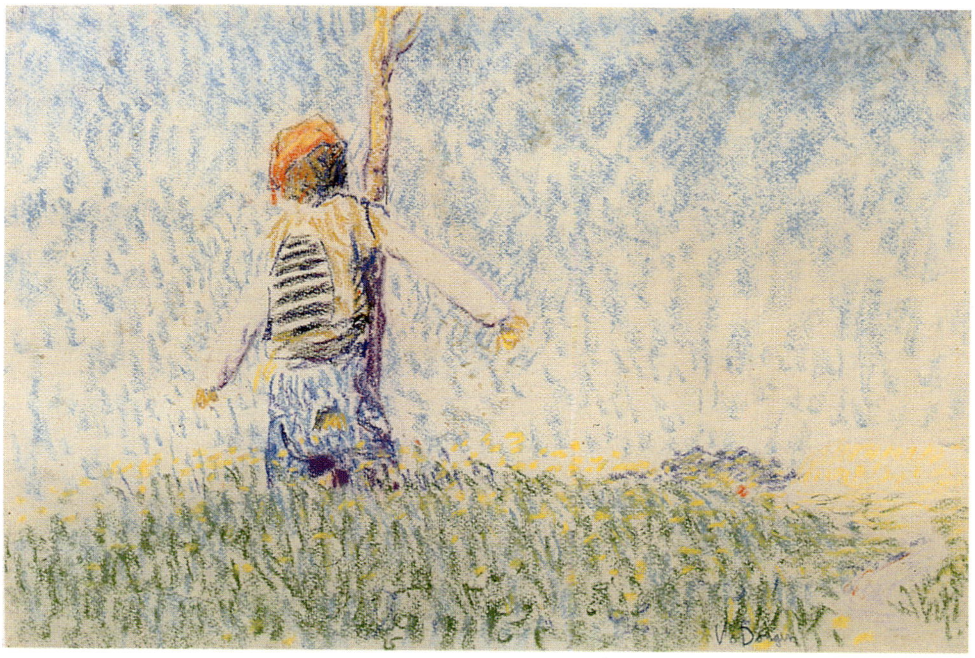

106. *L'épouvantail*, 1905

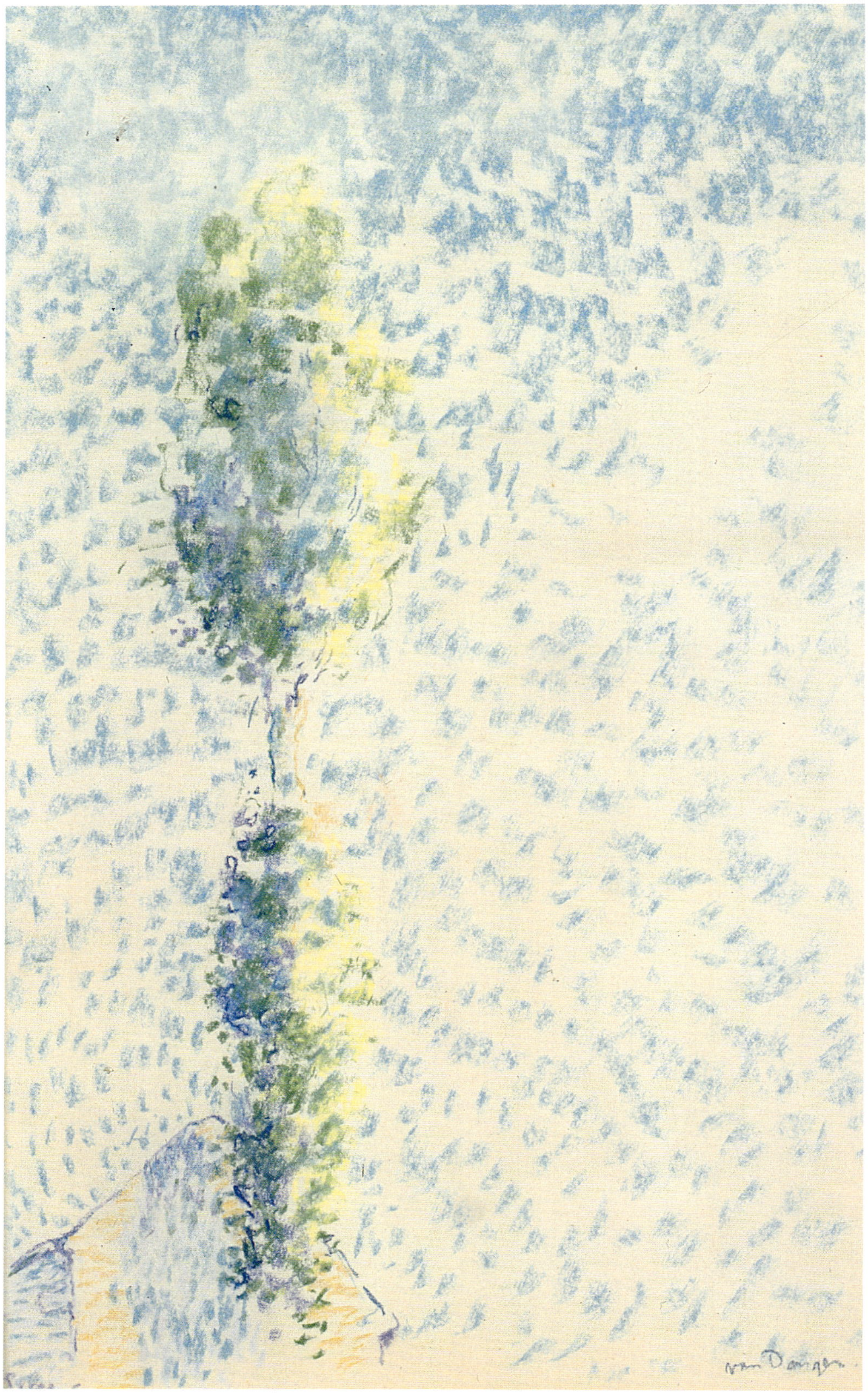

107. *Le peuplier*, 1905

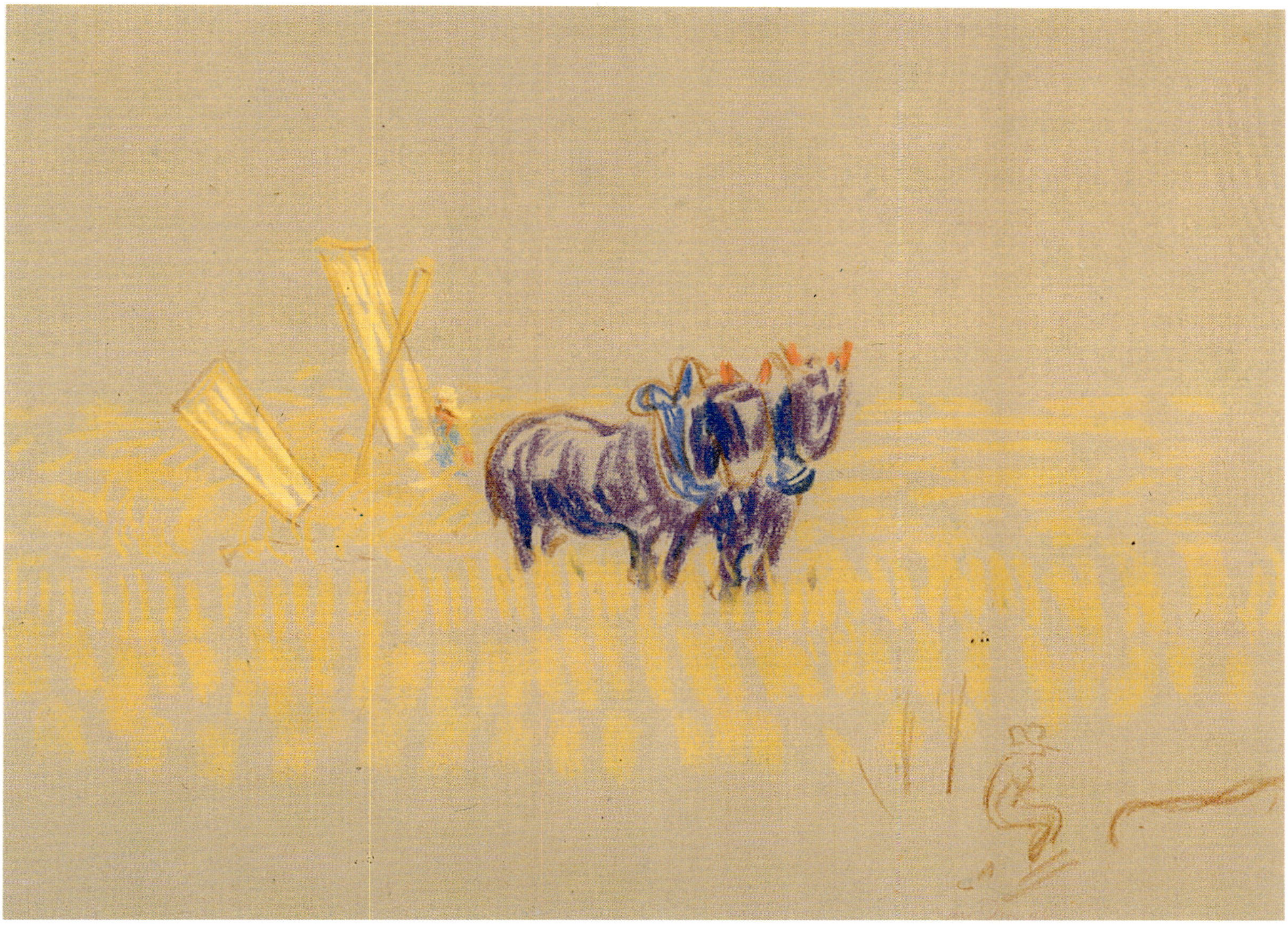

108. *Harvester and horses in a cornfield*, 1905

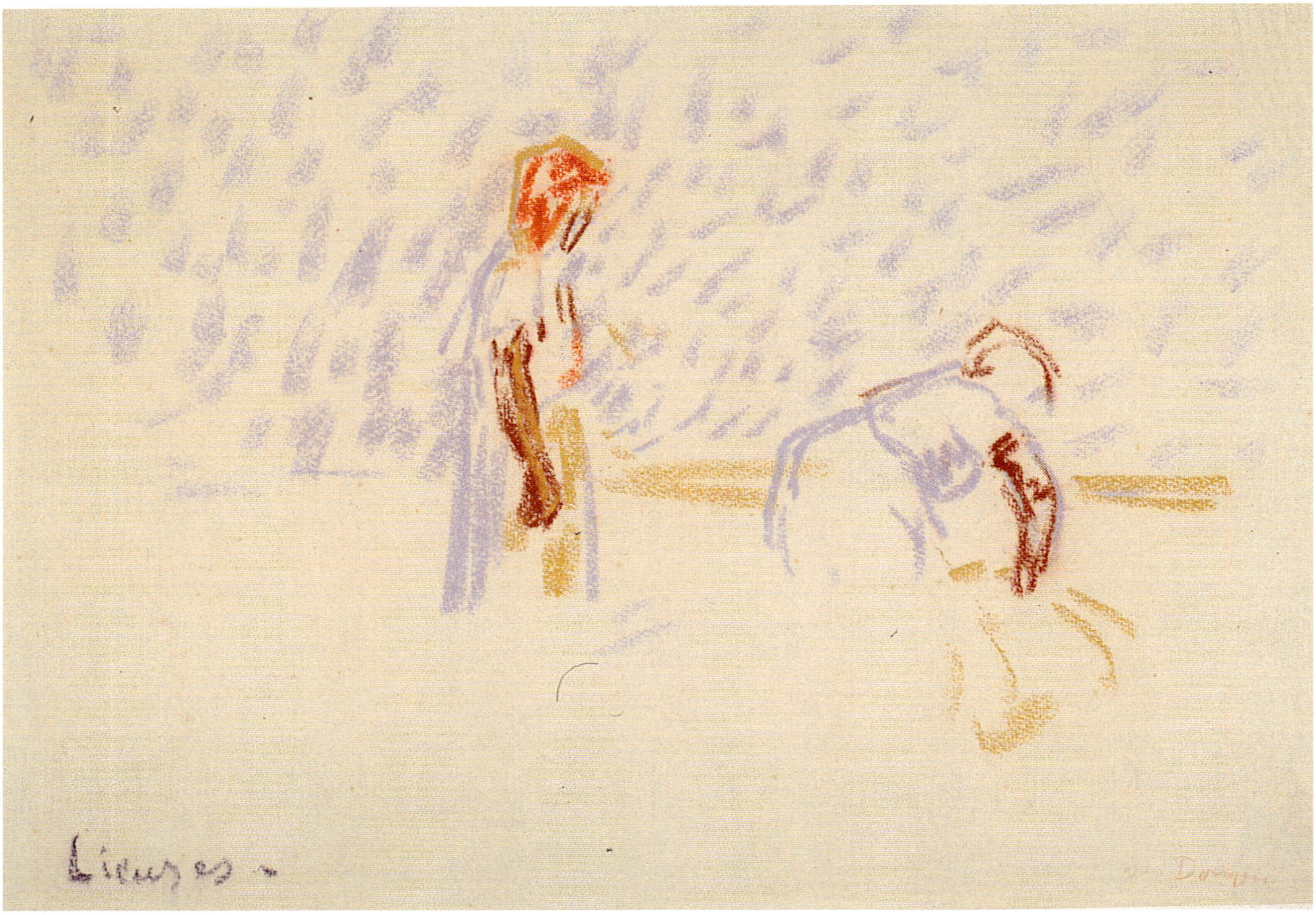

109. *Lieuses*, 1905

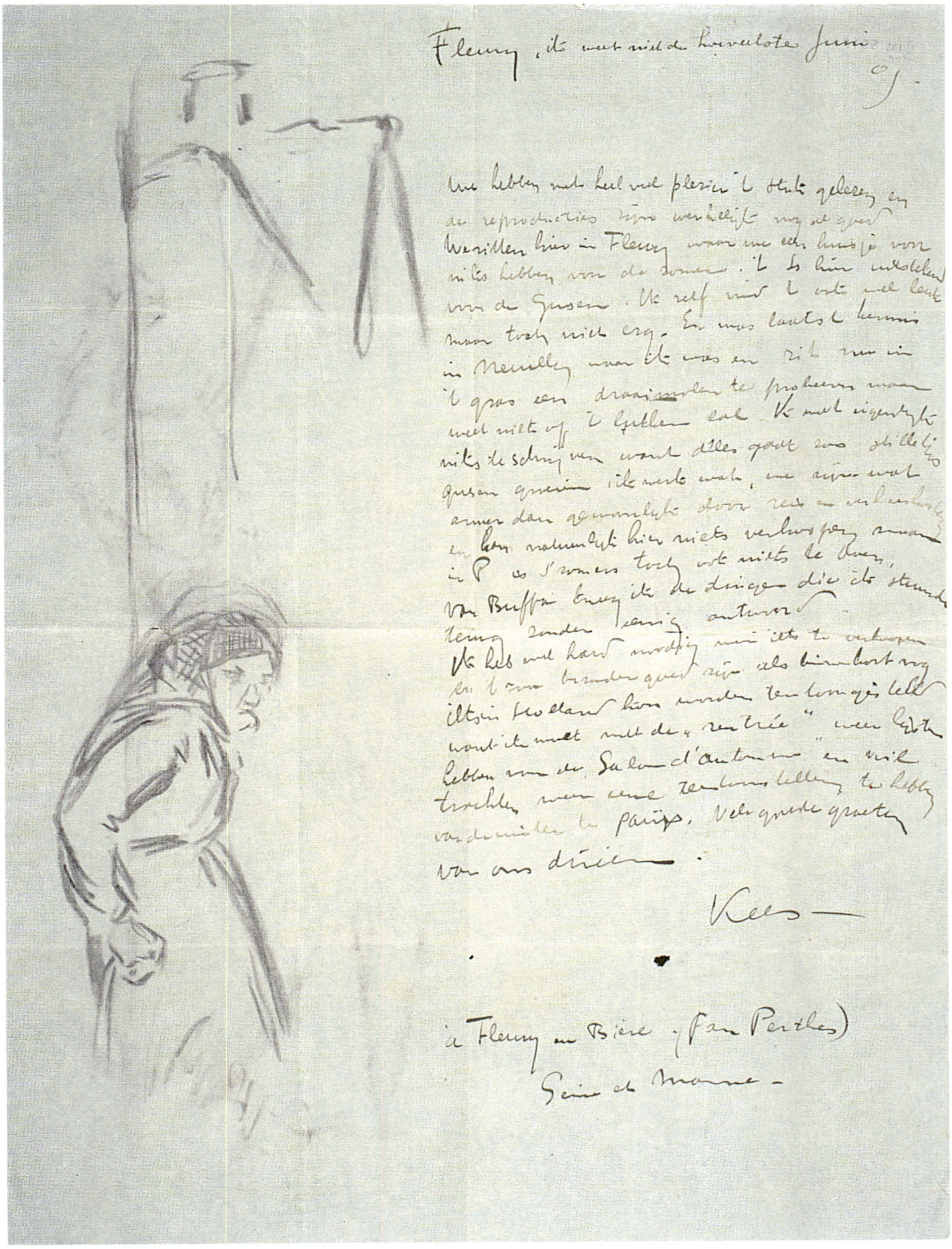
Fleury, ik weet niet de hoeveelste Juni 05.

We hebben met heel veel plezier 't stuk gelezen en
de reproducties zijn werkelijk nog al goed
We zitten hier in Fleury waar we een huisje voor
niets hebben voor de zomer. 't Is hier uitstekend
voor de Guusen. Ik zelf vind 't ook wel leuk
maar toch niet erg. Er was laatst kermis
in Neuilly waar ik was en zit nu in
't gras een draaimolen te probeeren maar
weet niet of 't lukken zal. Ik weet eigenlijk
niets te schrijven want alles gaat zoo stilletjes
Guus en Guusje ik werk wat, we zijn wat
armer dan gewoonlijk door reis en verhuizing
en kan natuurlijk hier niets verkoopen maar
in P. is 's zomers toch ook niets te doen.
Van Buffa kreeg ik de dingen die ik stuurde
terug zonder eenig antwoord
Ik heb wel hard noodig om iets te verkoopen
en 't zou bijzonder goed zijn als binnenkort nog
iets in Holland kon worden tentoongesteld
want ik weet niet de „rentrée" weer gezien te
hebben van de Salon d'Automne en zal
trachten weer eene tentoonstelling te hebben
van de middag te Parijs. Veel goede groeten
van ons drieën.

Kees —

à Fleury en Bière (par Perthes)
Seine et Marne —

110. *Letter from Kees van Dongen to Carel Scharten, June 1905*

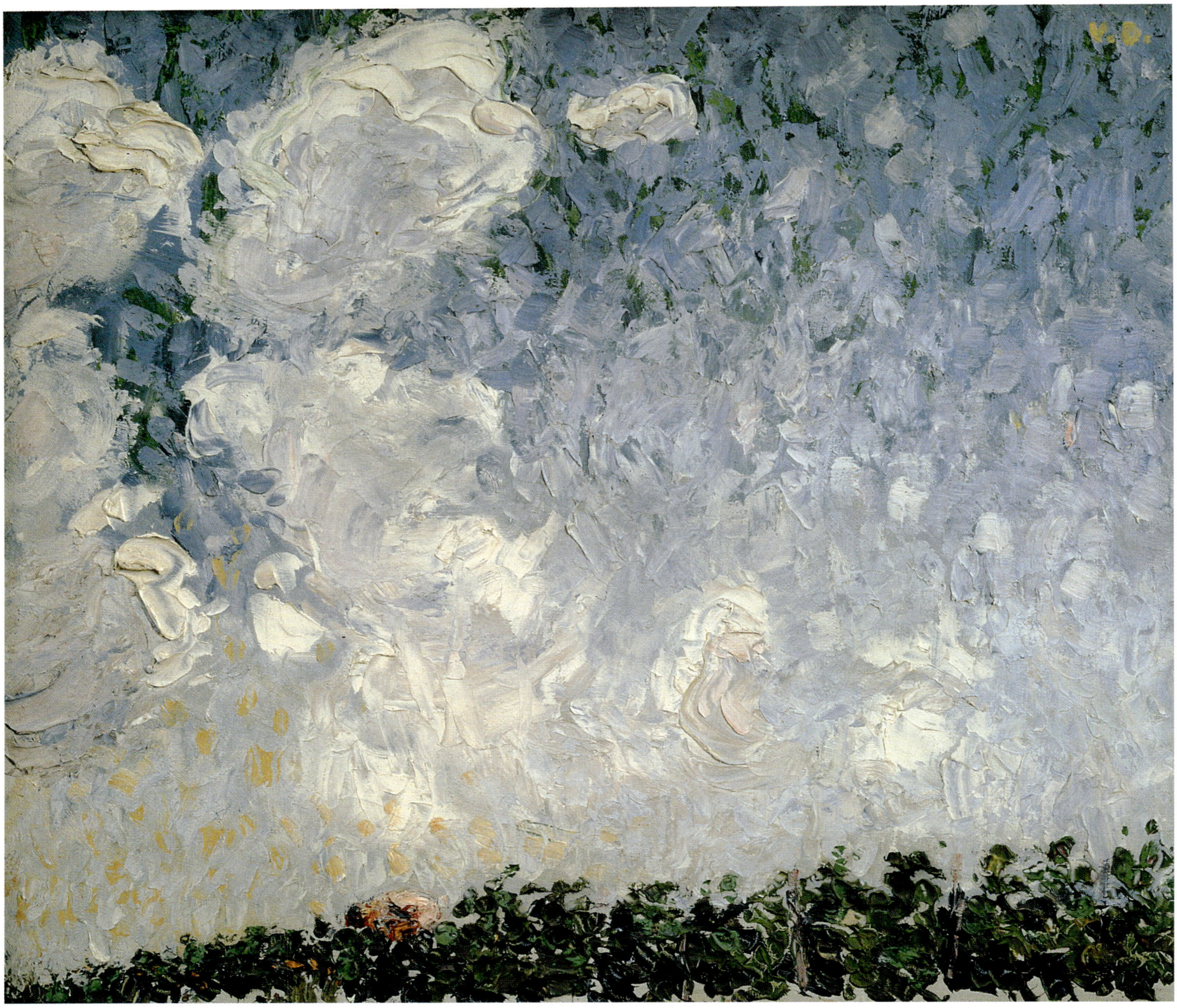

111. *La Vigne*, 1905

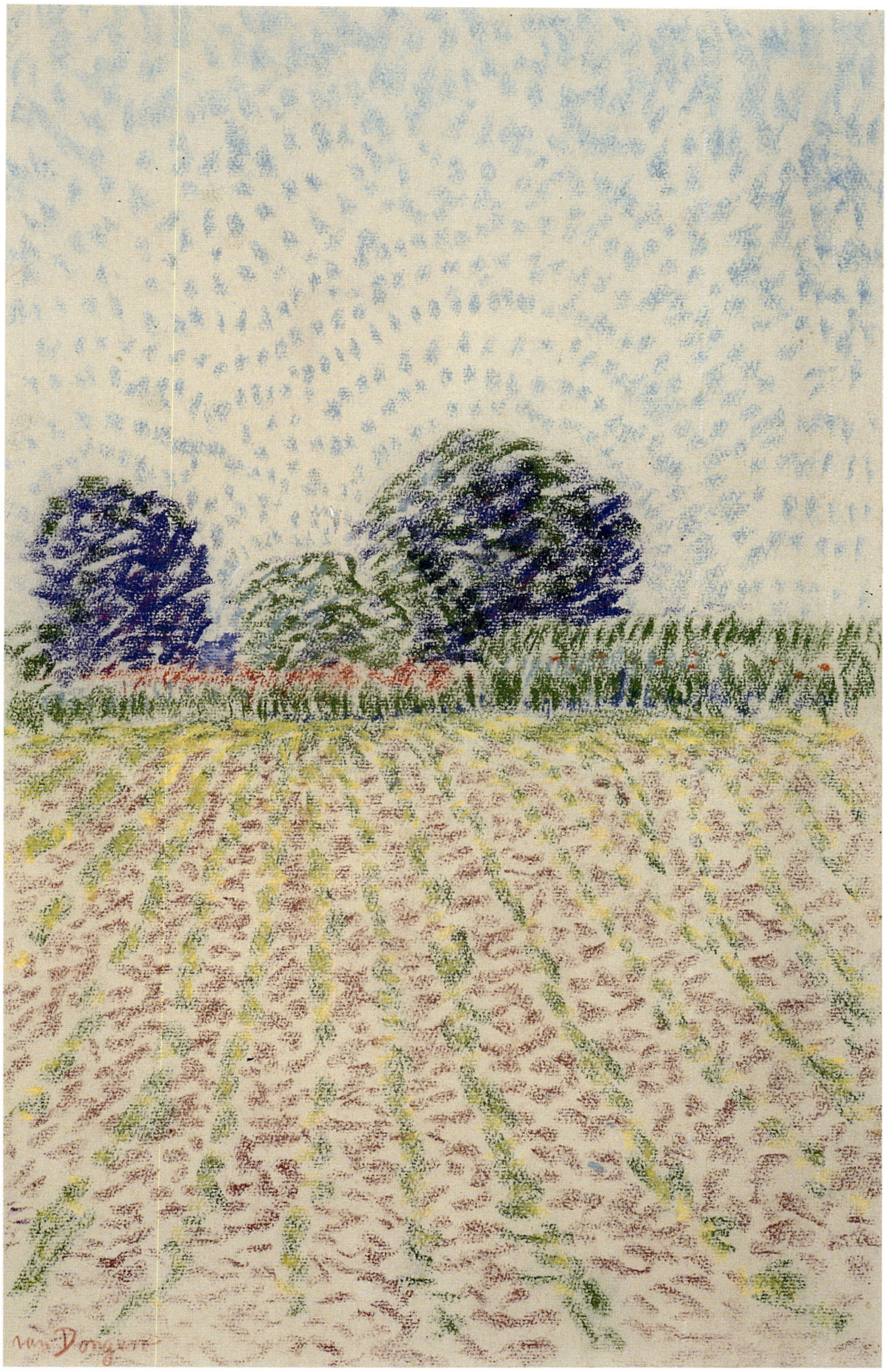

112. *Field in the neighbourhood of Fleury-en-Bière*, 1905

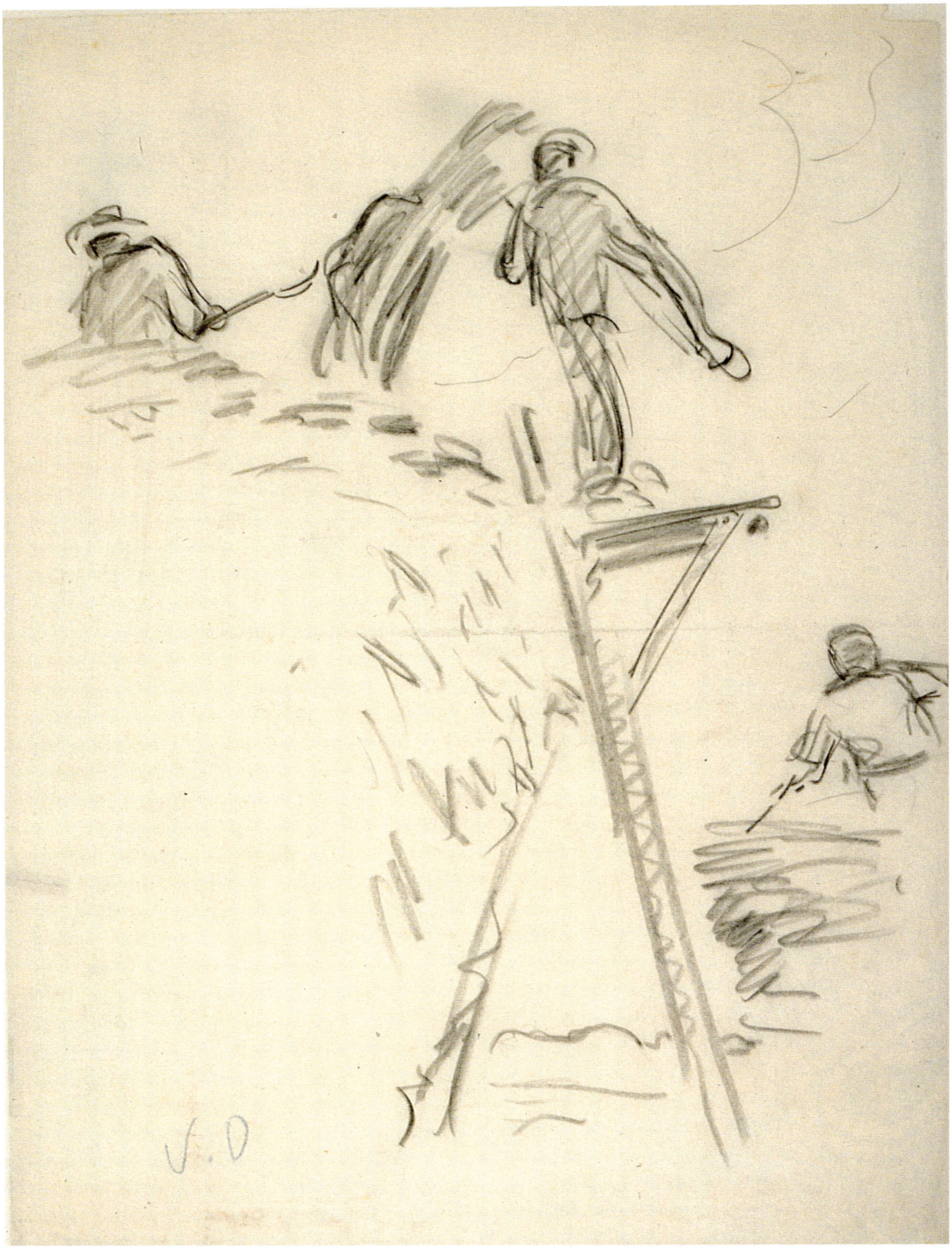

114. *Haystack with farm labourers*, 1905

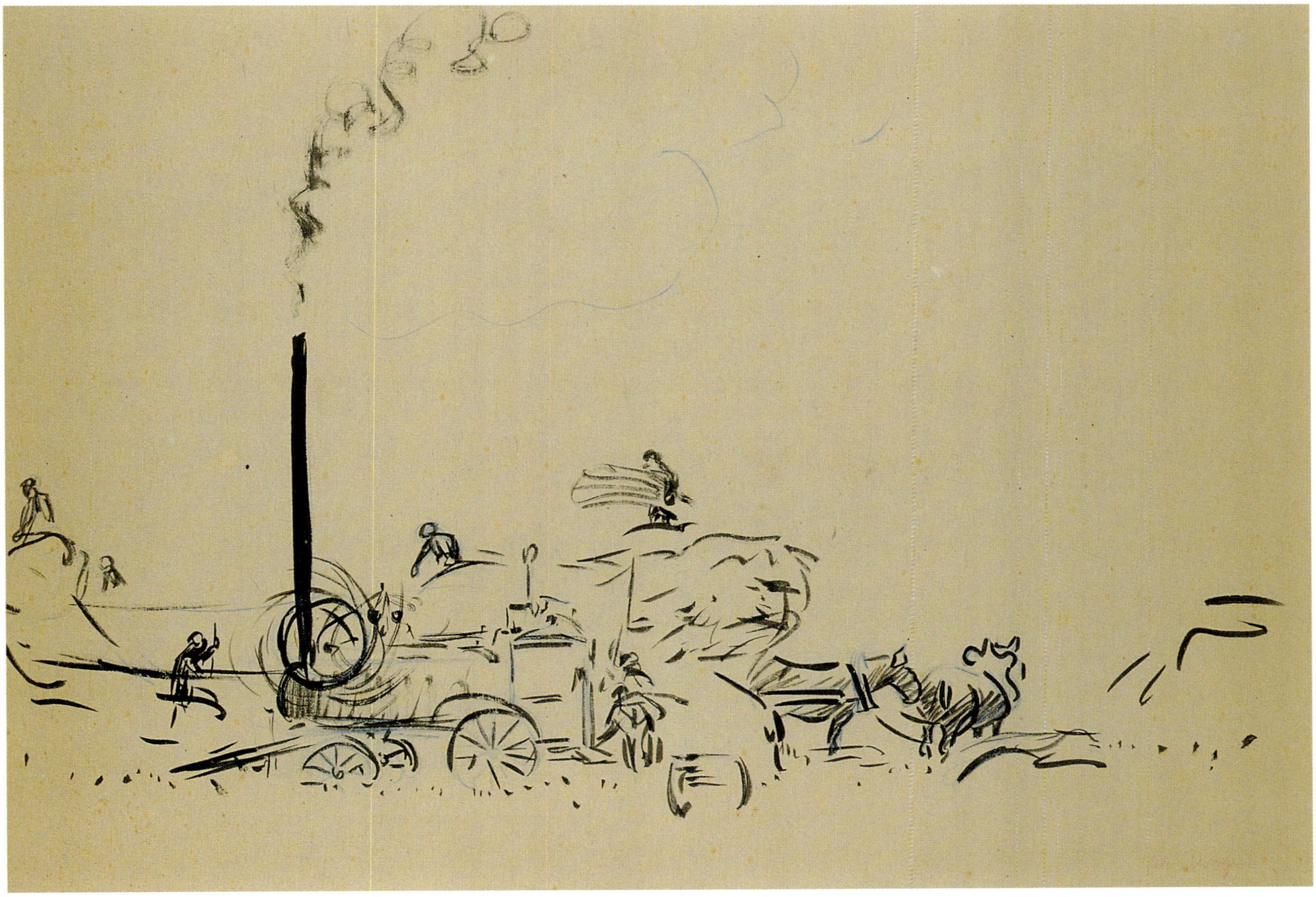

113. *Harvesting near Fleury-en-Bière*, 1905

115. *A la Galette* (At the Moulin de la Galette), 1906
Chalk pastel
481 x 632 mm
Signed lower right in blue chalk: *van Dongen*
Special features: has lining
EXHIBITIONS:
1906 Paris, Indépendants, no. 4987; 1959 Geneva, no. 118; 1967 Paris, no. 15
COLLECTION:
Private collection, Monaco

1.
A.M., 'Mardi-gras', *De Telegraaf*, 20 February 1904.
2.
C. Le Senne, 'Le théâtre au Salon des Indépendants', *Revue Théâtrale*, no. 55 (April) 1906, p. 1422.
3.
Letter K. van Dongen to Mej. S. Plate, 30 March 1906, GA Rotterdam

The pastel *A la Galette* depicts the interior of the famous place of entertainment, the Moulin de la Galette in Montmartre. (fig.) Van Dongen exhibited the drawing together with a painting on the same subject entitled, *A la Galette*, a canvas of monumental proportions, at the Salons des Indépendants of 1906. The works are the results of a great number of studies which he made in that dance-hall at the time. The owner, Auguste Debray, allowed the artists to enter free of charge: the drawings and paintings that were created as a result of their visit only served to increase the fame of the Moulin de la Galette. Van Dongen's interest for this subject is confirmed by a few postcards from him to Guus in the summer months of 1905 (in private ownership), as well as the memories of Fernande Olivier, with whom the artist became acquainted in 1906, the year that he moved into a studio in the Bateau-Lavoir. Van Dongen has placed the dance-hall public in the foreground on both the drawing and painting – for the painting a slightly higher vantage point has been chosen – on the right a part of the orchestra balcony can be seen. In a Salon review the women waiting around angling for a partner were characterized as 'prostitutes with their apache friends' – the scum of the night. The dance-hall however was also frequented by 'labourers, minor civil servants, women shop assistants and working women' and this too would have been represented by Van Dongen.[1] His renditions differ a great deal from those of the more famous paintings which Renoir, Toulouse-Lautrec and Picasso made of the terrace and the interior of the Moulin de la Galette. In the painting *A la Galette* Van Dongen depicted the sultry atmosphere of the hall through a crisscross of heads and flirting expressions and painted the scene in a Neo-Impressionist derived brushstroke and palette. But what is most striking is the energy he put into the representation of light: the electric chandeliers, 'glowing coloured suns', take up more than half of the canvas. The bright white glow of what at that time was a new form of lighting is represented by Van Dongen as a shower of loose, mainly blue and yellow strokes, that swathed the hall in blue light, making the faces pale and the make-up pronounced. Van Dongen's depictions were only known up to the present from descriptions: the pastel drawings are in private ownership and have only been exhibited a few times; Van Dongen cut the painting into pieces in the fifties and sold the parts as independent works. When the pieces of the painting – with the aid of a photograph which appeared in the *Revue Théâtrale* in 1906 – are reconstructed to form a whole, the canvas appears originally to have measured 130 x 200 cm.[2] (fig.) It was clearly meant to be a 'Salon piece', painted to attract attention. In a letter addressed to the Rotterdam Kunstkring Van Dongen wrote about the canvas: 'the most typical are the larger [pieces] including a painting of the Moulin de la Galette – at the present moment being shown at the Société des Artistes Indépendants and which I would very much like to show in Holland.'[3] The painting *A la Galette* was indeed exhibited in May-June 1906 in Rotterdam – it figures as number 62 in the catalogue – and has either through this showing or through his presence at the Salon des Indépendants inspired Dutch artists like Jan Sluijters and Leo Gestel to make comparable pictures.

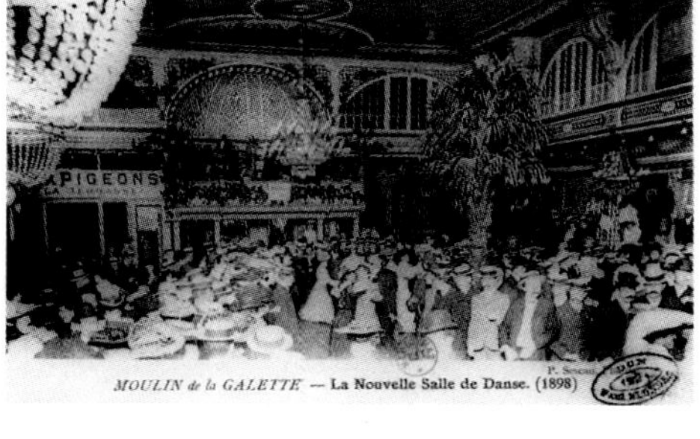

Interior Moulin de la Galette, c. 1898
Photo Bibliothèque Nationale, Paris

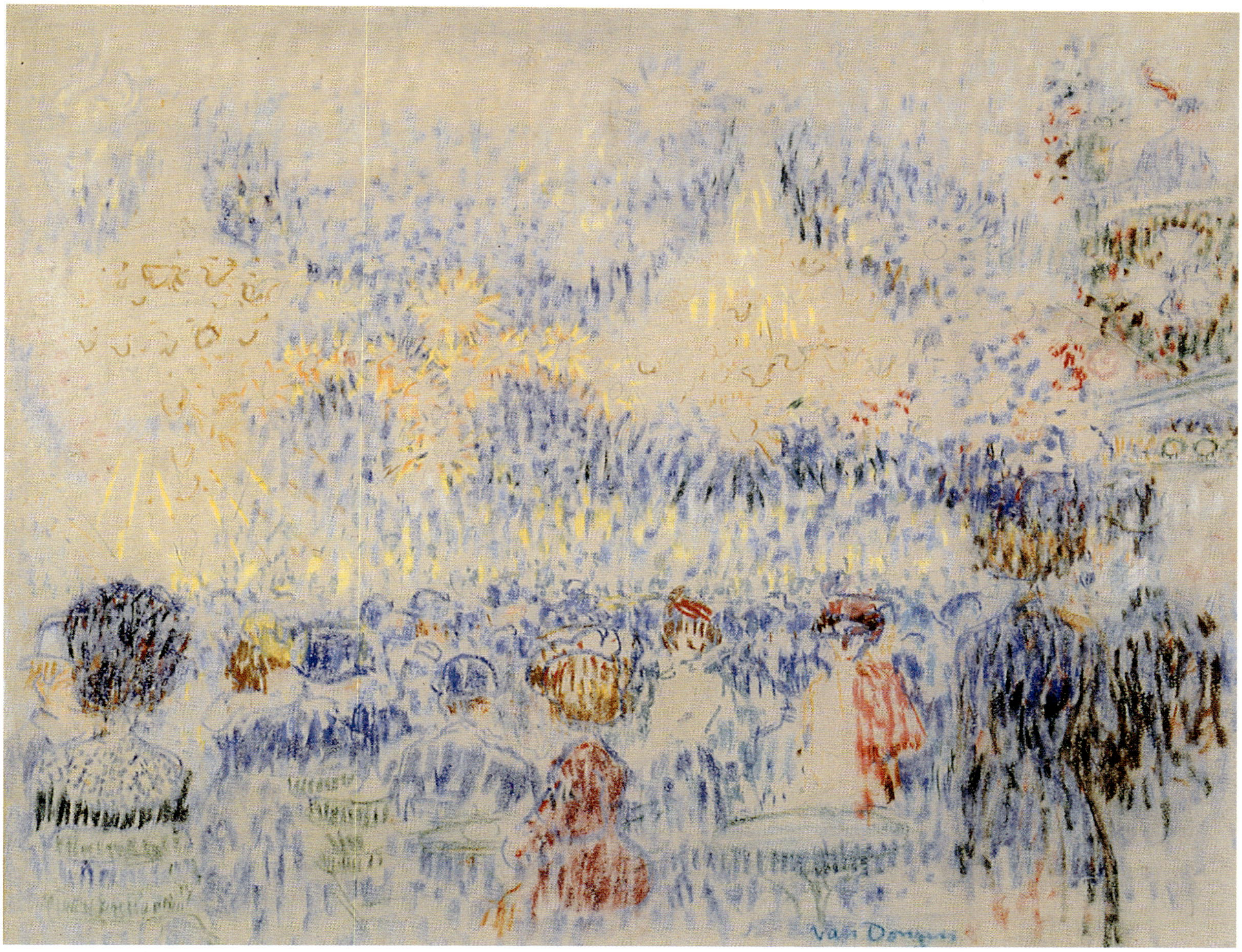

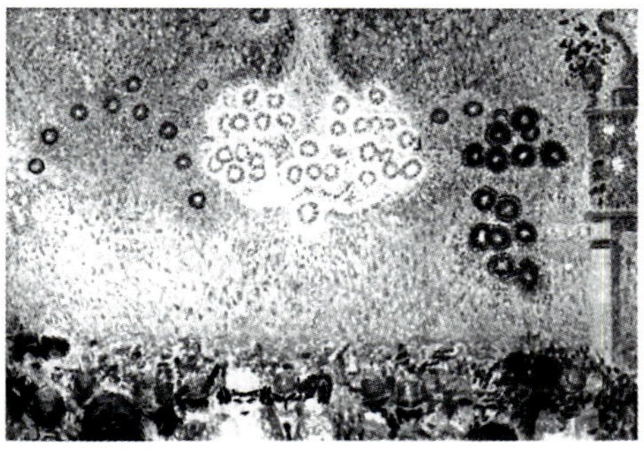

A la Galette, 1906
Oil on Canvas, c. 130 x 200 cm

115. *A la Galette*, 1906

116. *La jarretière* (The garter), 1906
Oil on canvas
73 x 92 cm
Signed lower left: *van Dongen*
Signed on reverse of stretcher in pink watercolour: *Kees van Dongen*; annotated in blue chalk: *La Jarretière*; in blue chalk: *8191*; notes in light-brown watercolour (crossed out): *N° 6*; in blue chalk: *3776*; in pink watercolour (painted over in white) *Une femme en gris*

PROVENANCE:
Galerie Bernheim-Jeune, Paris, 28 December 1906, bought from the artist (Inv. 15318; Bernheim-Jeune Archives); Paul Signac (1863-1965), Paris, 27 February 1907 (through Bernheim-Jeune); private collection

EXHIBITIONS:
1985 Saint-Tropez, no. 14 (fig.); 1989 Rotterdam, no. 8 (fig.); 1990 Paris, p. 74 (fig.)

LITERATURE:
Cachin 1971, p. 86, fig. 77. Kyriazi 1971, p. 90

COLLECTION:
Private collection

After Van Dongen's scenes of popular amusement at funfairs and dance-halls painted in a neo-impressionist style, *La jarretière* comes as a surprise as it is an entirely different canvas. It has not been drawn with short brushstrokes, but with large areas of colour, and the nude figure is encircled by a broad blue contour line. The background is designed in one tone. An indication of a sofa or platform on which the woman has perched herself is missing, giving the impression that the cushion on the left is floating in mid-air. The mysteriousness of the canvas is strengthened by the strange shortening of the right arm, and by the absence of a great deal of the model's face, concealed by a wide-brimmed hat. The nude must have been painted fairly shortly after the Salon des Indépendants of 1906; a closer inspection under the last layer of paint reveals an earlier version in swift brushstrokes: the method of work which Van Dongen still employed at the beginning of 1906. Furthermore, the canvas, according to a specification by the artist on the reverse side, had been stretched over the old stretcher of the painting *Une femme gris*. Van Dongen sent a picture with this title to the Salon des Indépendants of 1906. Finally, the wide blue outline indicates that it was made after the Spring Salon. The model for this new approach of Van Dongen's was the monumental painting *Le bonheur de vivre* exhibited by Henri Matisse at the same Salon de Indépendants. (fig.) Seeking a form of expression in which there would also be room for 'the line', a composition element which had been subordinate in the Neo-Impressionism of Signac, Matisse decided to change his technique in the winter of 1905-1906. Around *Le bonheur de vivre*, set in an arcadian landscape, he drew figures with wide coloured contours, resembling areas of shadow or auras. It was an experiment on the part of Matisse, and one he was criticized for.[1] He never used this method again with the same stylistic incoherence. It inspired Van Dongen, who greatly admired Matisse's impressive canvas, to embark upon his own application of the coloured contour, which he sometimes broadened to a sort of halo, and more than Matisse, used it as an expressive element in his compositions.

The painting *La jarretière* was acquired in 1907 by Paul Signac through the Bernheim-Jeune gallery. This fact, as well as the painting itself, evokes a great number of questions: not long before in a letter to Charles Angrand dated 14 January 1906, Signac had condemned the use of 'thumb-thick' lines by Matisse in *Le bonheur de vivre*, speaking of it with repugnance as being like the 'worst Ranson' (a Nabis artist).[2]

1.
Flam 1993, pp. 226-235.
2.
Bock 1981, p.124, note 64; Flam 1993, pp. 234-235.

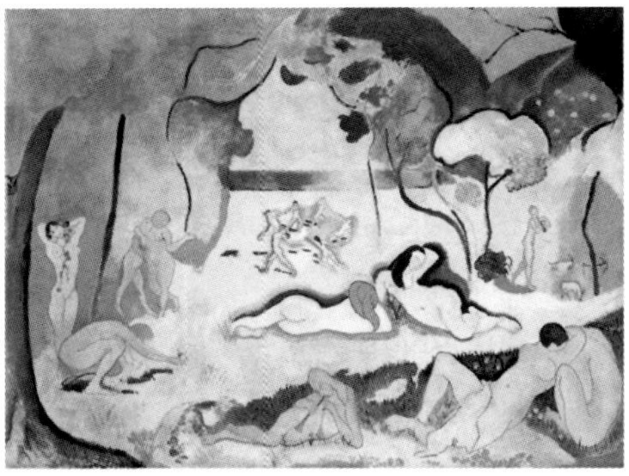

H. Matisse, *Le bonheur de vivre*, 1906
Oil on canvas, 175 x 241 cm
The Barnes Foundation, Merion

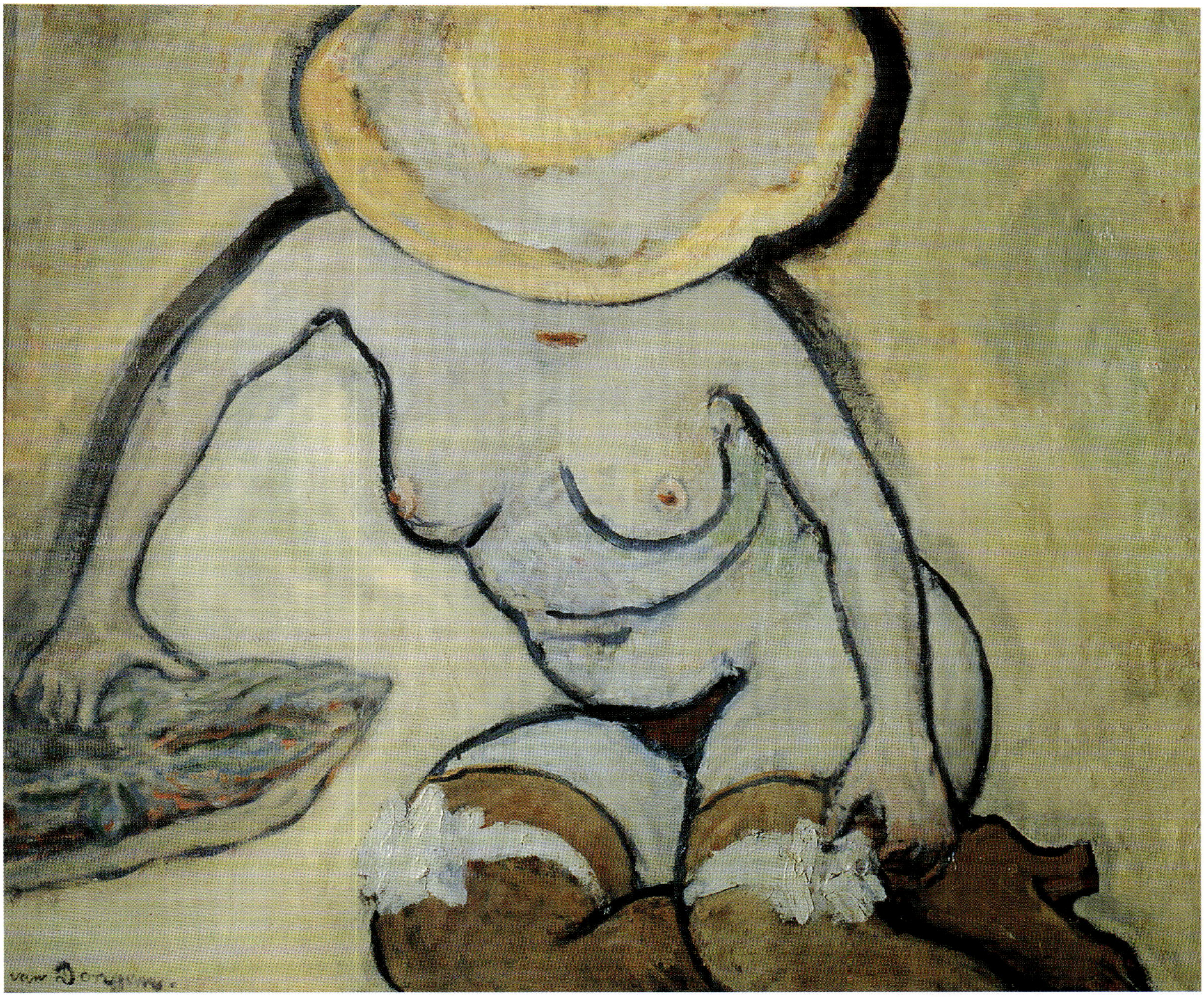

116. *La jarretière*, 1906

117. *Brief van Kees van Dongen aan Félix Fénéon*
(Letter from Kees van Dongen to Félix Fénéon), 1907
Handwritten letter, pen with black ink, 2 sheets, folded double, written and illustrated on 2 sides,
260 x 210 mm
At top of page 1 place of sender: *Rotterdam*; addressed to: *Mes chers amis.* (Félix and Fanny Fénéon); upper left in Félix Fénéon's handwriting: *[Kees/van/Dongen]*; annotated centre right on verso of p. 1: *Kees (le chauffeur)*, signed on verso of p. 2: *Kees*
Illustrations in pen and ink, p. 1: *De kunstenaar werkend aan een besneeuwd doek* (The artist working on a snowy canvas); p. 1 verso: *Van Dongen kolen op het vuur van een kachel gooiend* (Van Dongen throwing coals on the fire in a stove); p. 2: *Van Dongen en zijn vader zich warmend voor een kachel* (Van Dongen and his father warming themselves in front of a stove); p. 2 verso: *Van Dongen en zijn vader kolen scheppend* (Van Dongen and his father shovelling coal)
PROVENANCE:
Félix Fénéon (1861-1944), Paris; Jean Paulhan (1884-1968), Paris, c. 1945-1947; heirs of Jean Paulhan, 1968 (kept in the Jean Paulhan/IMEC Archives, Paris)
LITERATURE:
Halperin 1988, pp. 339-340 (fig.)
COLLECTION:
Jean Paulhan/IMEC Archives, Paris

118. *Op de boot* (On the boat), 1907
Black, blue and red chalk
539 x 338 mm
Signed lower right in blue chalk: *V.D.*
Special features: the sheet has been folded double; when unfolded it measures 539 x 680 mm
Drawing on the inside of the sheet: *Zeilboot met molen op de achtergrond* (Sailboat with windmill in the background), coloured chalk; signed lower right in blue chalk: *V.D.*
PROVENANCE:
Boymans Museum, Rotterdam, 1936 (gift of the artist; letter from Kees van Dongen to D. Hannema, 7 December 1936, GA Rotterdam)
EXHIBITIONS:
1947 Eindhoven, no. 132; 1957 Rotterdam
LITERATURE:
Hannema 1937, p. 10; Hannema 1973, p. 48; Boymans Museum Annual Report 1937, p. 7
COLLECTION:
Boijmans Van Beuningen Museum, Rotterdam, Inv. KvD 8

119. *De Maas à Schiedam* (The river Maas at Schiedam), 1907
Blue, black and red chalk, with scratching
340 x 538 mm
Signed lower right in blue chalk: *V.D.*; annotated upper left in red chalk: *Schiedam.* Annotated on reverse in black chalk: *Rotterdam/De Maas a Schiedam*
PROVENANCE:
Boymans Museum, Rotterdam, 1936 (gift of the artist; letter from Kees van Dongen to D. Hannema, 7 December 1936, GA Rotterdam)
EXHIBITIONS:
1989 Rotterdam, (ex. catalogue)
LITERATURE:
Van Gelder 1958, p. 81, fig. 216; Hannema 1937, p. 10; Hannema 1973, p. 48; Boymans Museum Annual Report 1937, p. 7
COLLECTION:
Boijmans Van Beuningen Museum, Rotterdam, Inv. KvD 29

120. *Achtersteven van een aak* (Stern of a barge), 1907
Oil on cardboard
598 x 726 mm
Signed lower right in oil *van Dongen.*; lower right in blue chalk: 40
Special features: 3 nail holes in upper and lower edge
PROVENANCE:
Boymans Museum, Rotterdam, 1936 (gift of the artist; letter from Kees van Dongen to D. Hannema, 7 December 1936, GA Rotterdam)
EXHIBITIONS:
1989 Rotterdam, (ex. catalogue)
LITERATURE:
Hannema 1937, p. 10; Hannema 1973, p. 48; Boymans Museum Annual Report 1937, p. 7
COLLECTION:
Boijmans Van Beuningen Museum, Rotterdam, Inv. KvD 41

On 19 January 1907 Kees van Dongen sent a postcard to Félix Fénéon from Delfshaven with nothing but an exclamation mark and his address on it.[1] Apparently, he wanted Fénéon to send him a message from Paris. The postcard is interesting because of the date: from this it becomes clear that Van Dongen was in the Netherlands from the middle of January 1907. He was to stay until the middle of August. His sojourn in his home country lasted altogether more than six months. In between, in the month of June, Van Dongen paid a visit to England – possibly because of an exhibition.[2] One of the reasons for his stay in the Netherlands concerned tracking down work by Vincent van Gogh for a future exhibition at the Bernheim-Jeune gallery; this was the topic of the correspondence between Van Dongen and Fénéon who had worked for this art gallery since the end of 1906.[3] The direct reason for his journey may have been Guus' poor health. However, in view of the preparations made before Van Dongen left (in the correspondence between Ludovic-Rodo and his brother Lucien Pissarro, his forthcoming journey to England is mentioned as early as January 1907), and another message from Van Dongen in Rotterdam to Fénéon, in which he writes that he has not achieved a great deal (*je n'ai pas encore travaillé beaucoup*), it must be concluded that Van Dongen's journey was motivated by artistic considerations. It may have been that prior to his departure there had already been talk about a possible exhibition at Bernheim-Jeune's, partly as a report of his stay in Holland. This did not take place until December 1908, but it is referred to in the correspondence from August 1907.[4] The drawings which Van Dongen made during his stay in the Netherlands reveal a sketchy, summarizing style of drawing. The sketches are clearly aiming at the effect of line, a specific form of shading or colour. With a few penstrokes Van Dongen denotes the decoration on a hat or the shape of a mouth. (fig.) The studies in oils on paper depicting a three-master and a barge demonstrate how Van Dongen's manner of painting developed further in the Netherlands: he continued to imitate reality but to interpret it more freely using a colourful palette. (fig.) During the months of May and June Van Dongen was accompanied by the painters Maximilien Luce and Ludovic-Rodo Pissarro. Luce drew a series of harbour views in Rotterdam; Ludovic-Rodo the portrait of the singer Modiesko, among others. A few postcards confirm that the painters worked in Dordrecht and Amsterdam, from where Van Dongen probably made the drawing *Une fête en Hollande*. It was Van Dongen's last extended sojourn in the Netherlands. The landscapes drawn here were successful, but the pictures with figures in them are more fascinating. In the period after 1907, Van Dongen's paintings were less inspired by nature. He may already have shared the opinion of his French friends. Luce felt that you could not work well in the Netherlands due to the rain and hard wind. The Dutch countryside did have its own unique character, but was monotonous: 'it's so flat! fields, canals, windmills, no trees. You know, if there aren't any fine skies to look at, then there's hardly anything left at all!'[5]

121. *Une fête en Hollande* (A celebration in Holland), 1907
Black and dark-blue chalk, watercolour
456 x 320 mm
Signed lower right in purple watercolour: *van Dongen.*
Signed and annotated on reverse in blue chalk: *van Dongen/Une fête en Hollande-*; upper left in red chalk: *23*
PROVENANCE:
Boijmans Van Beuningen Museum, Rotterdam, 1936 (gift of the artist; letter from Kees van Dongen to D. Hannema, 7 December 1936, GA Rotterdam)
EXHIBITIONS:
1957 Rotterdam, (no catalogue); 1962 Breda, no. 43;
LITERATURE:
Hannema 1937, p. 10; Hannema 1973, p. 48; Boymans Museum Annual Report 1937, p. 7
COLLECTION:
Boijmans Van Beuningen Museum, Rotterdam, Inv. KvD 3

122. *Koningin Wilhelmina en Prins consort* (Queen Wilhelmina and the Prince Consort), 1907
Brush with brown ink, watercolour, gouache, white gouache
449 x 412 mm
Signed lower right in black chalk: *V.D.*; lower centre in brush with black ink: *HET VOLK*
On reverse of cardboard on which drawing is mounted a torn white label marked in pencil: *[...]lmina en Prins consort*
EXHIBITIONS:
1964 Lyons, no. 72 (fig.)
COLLECTION:
Private collection

1. Postcard to F. Fénéon, postmarked 19 January 1907, Inv. 860868, Getty Center, Santa Monica.
2. Letter from L.R. Pissarro to L. Pissarro, 1 July 1907, Ashmolean Museum, Oxford.
3. Kyriazi 1971, p. 92.
4. Postcard from K. van Dongen to Guus, postmarked 31 August 1907, private collection; Kyriazi 1971, pp. 92, 102.
5. J. Bouin-Luce, D. Bazetoux, *M. Luce. Cat. raisonné*, Paris 1986, p. 122.

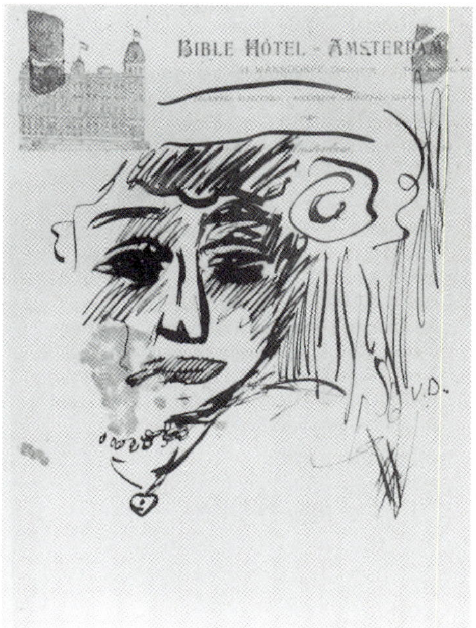

Etude pour tête de femme, 1907
Pen and ink, 285 x 215 mm

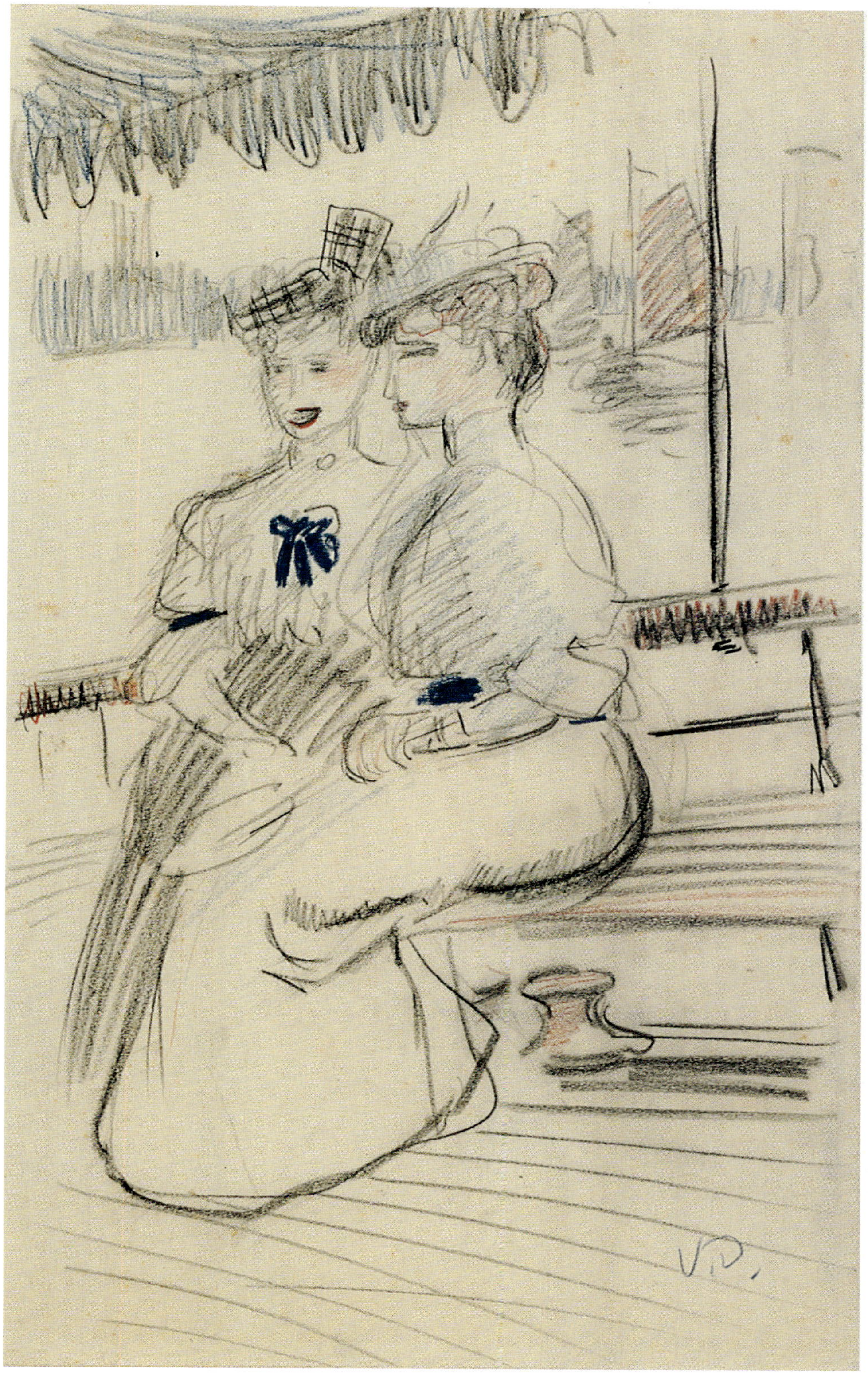

118. *On the boat*, 1907

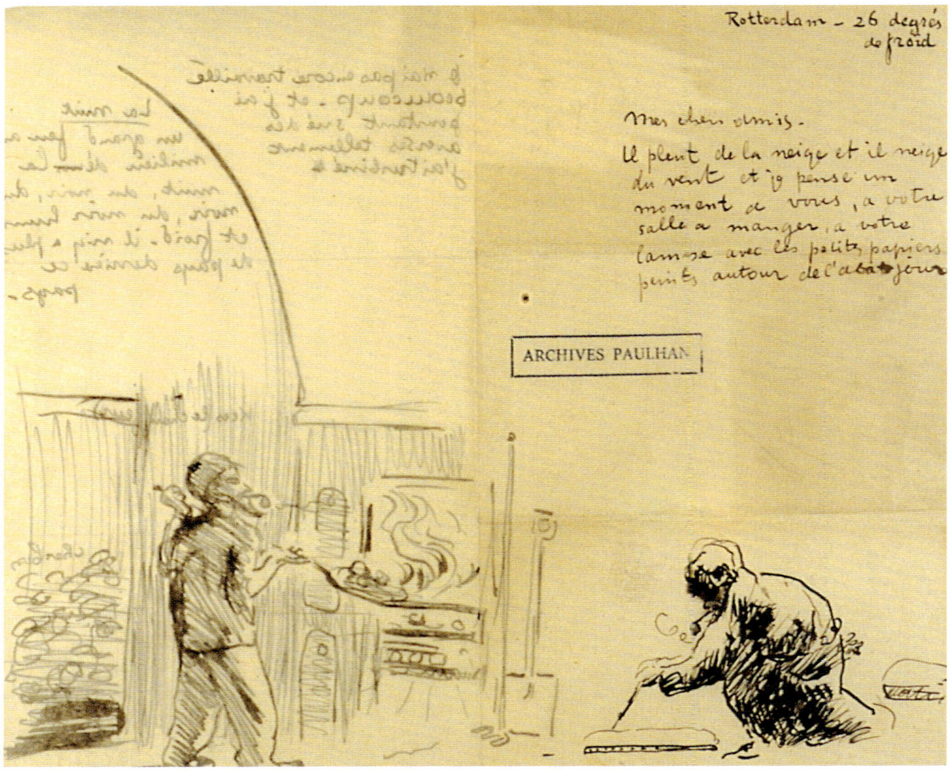

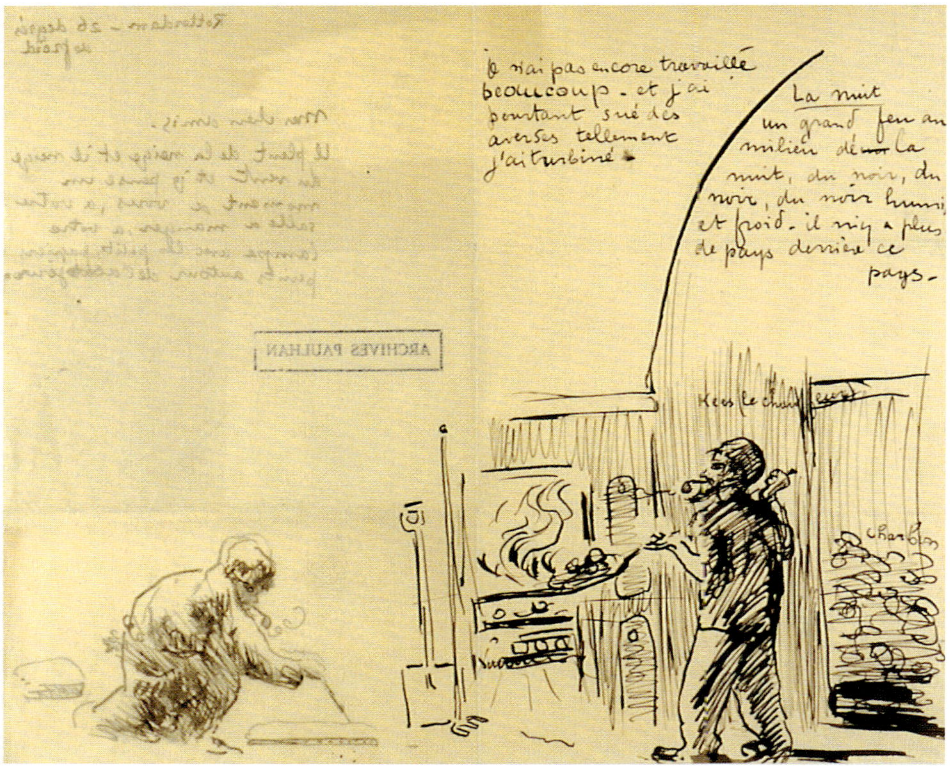

117. *Letter from Kees van Dongen to Félix Fénéon, 1907*

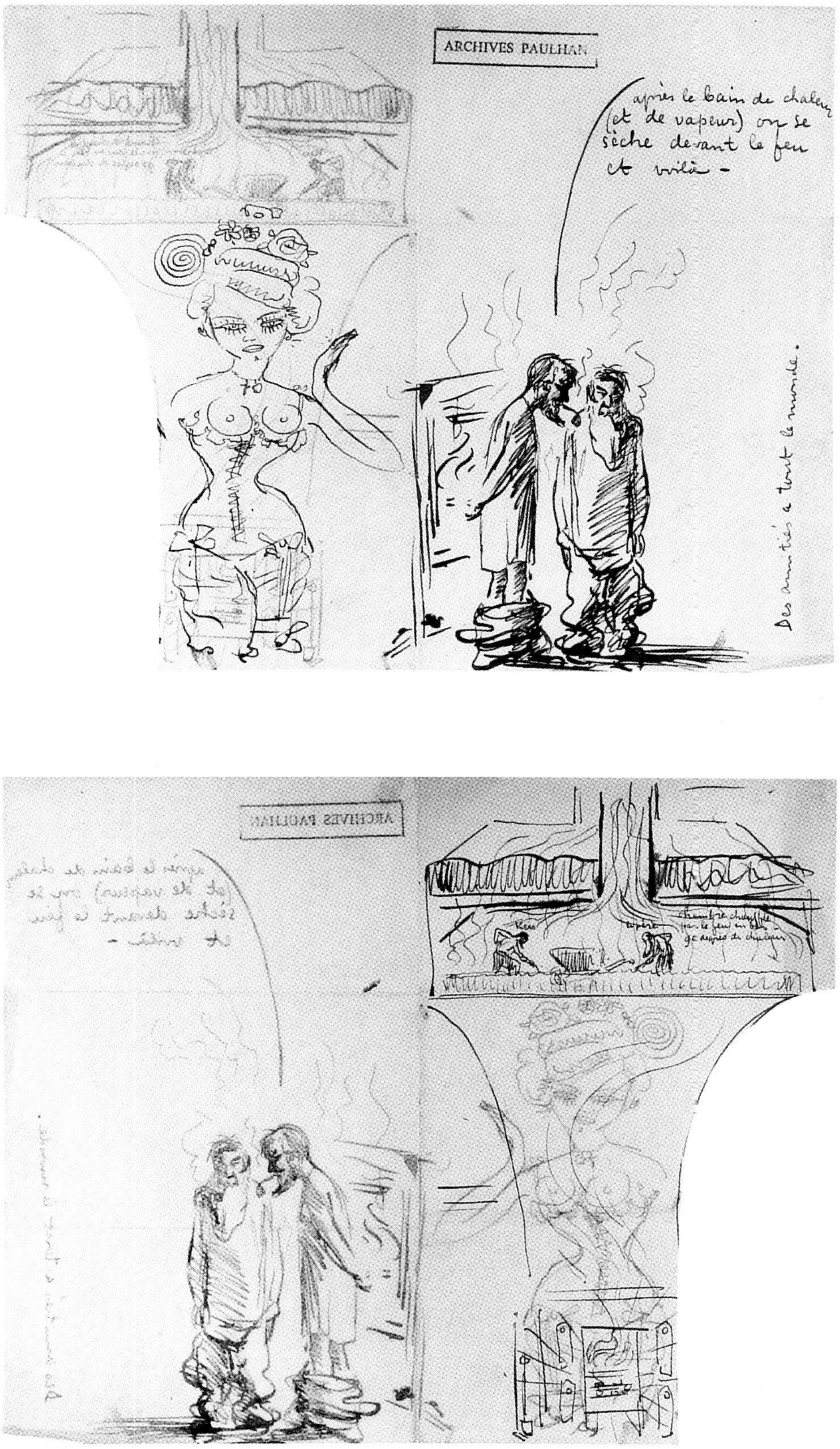

117. *Letter from Kees van Dongen to Félix Fénéon*, 1907

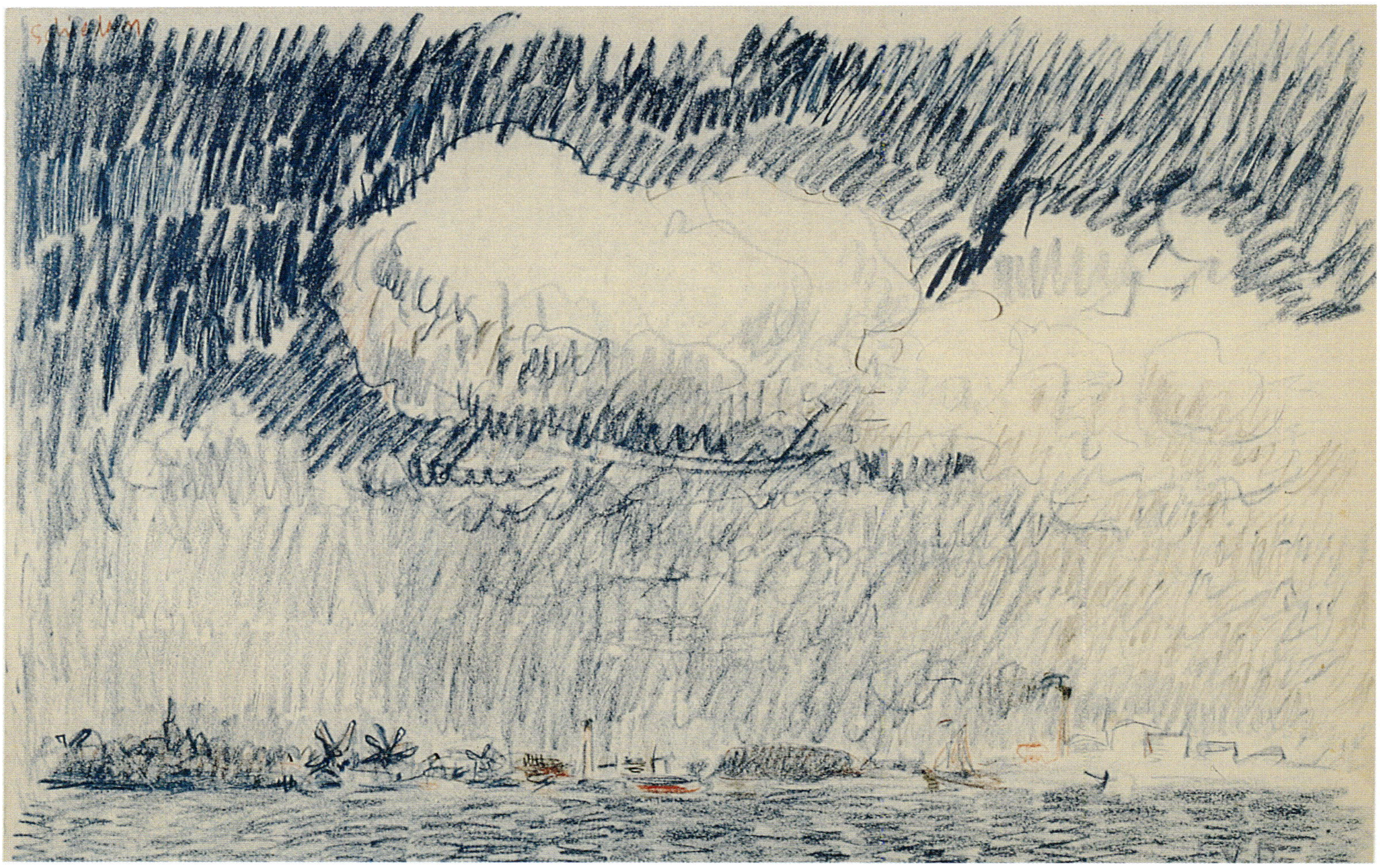

119. *De Maas à Schiedam*, 1907

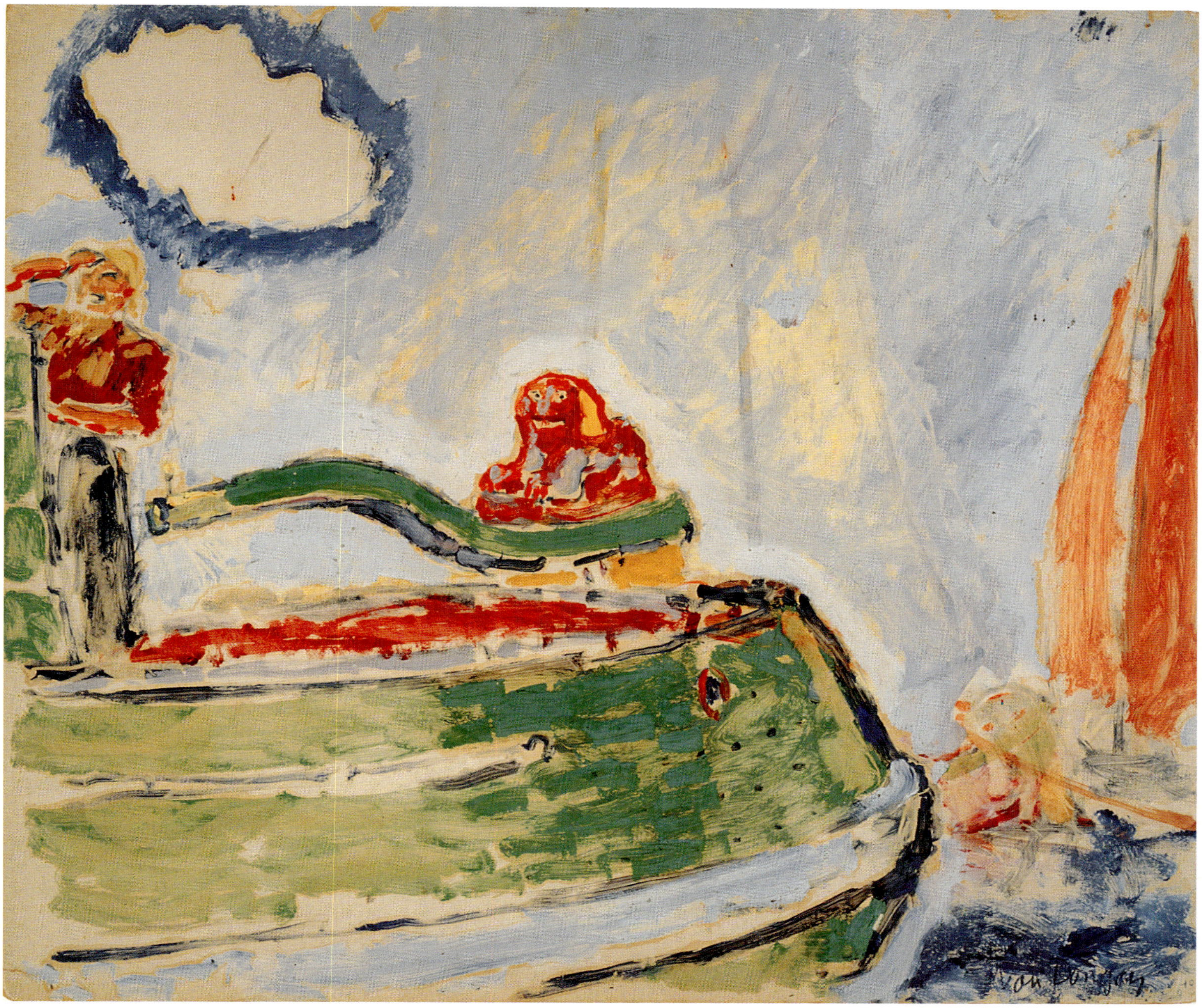

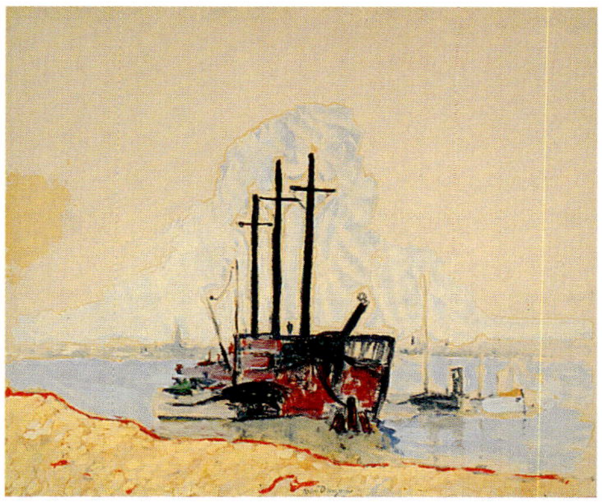

A three-master, 1907
Oil on cardboard, 600 x 725 mm
Boijmans van Beuningen Museum, Rotterdam

120. *Stern of a barge*, 1907

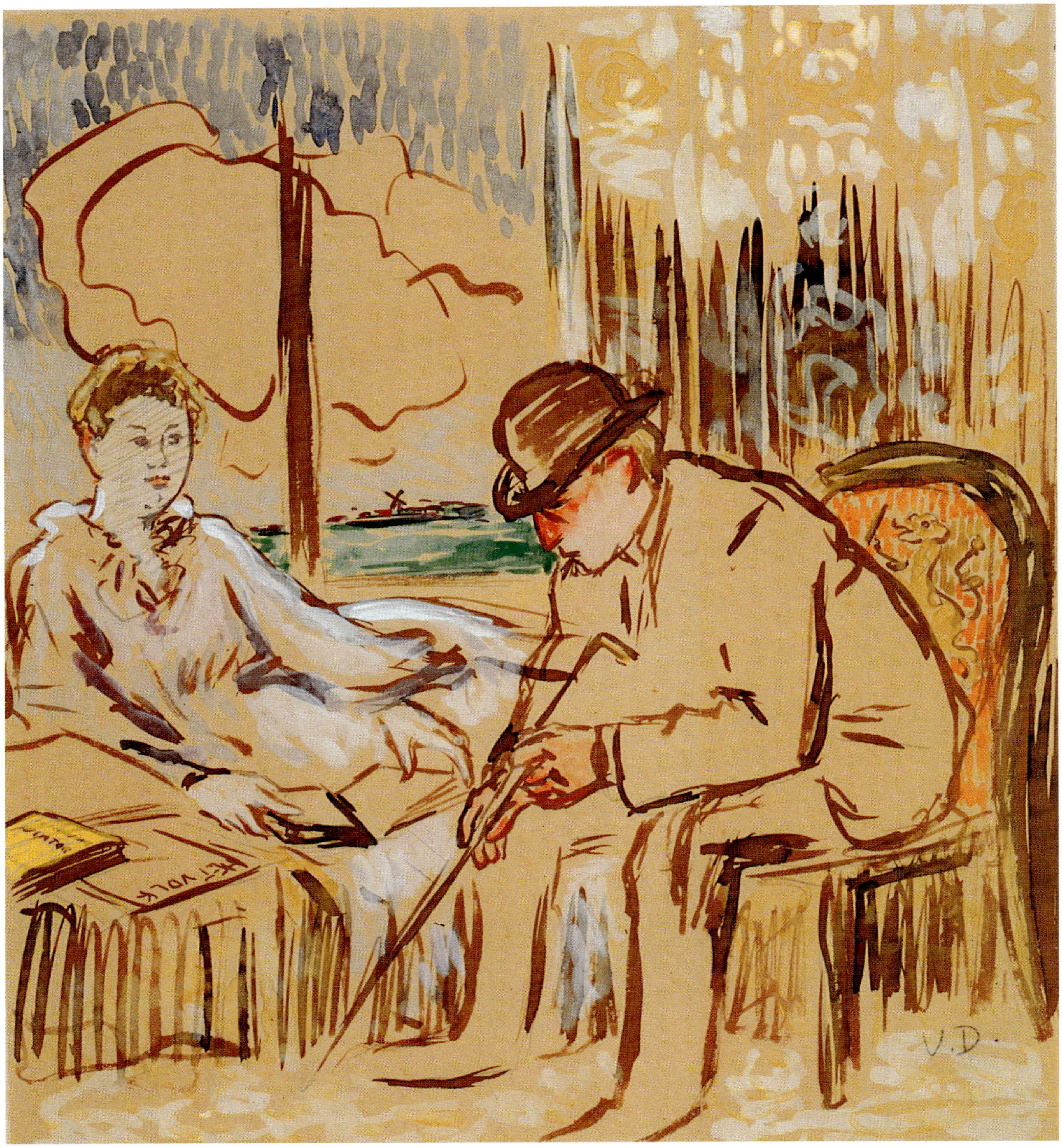

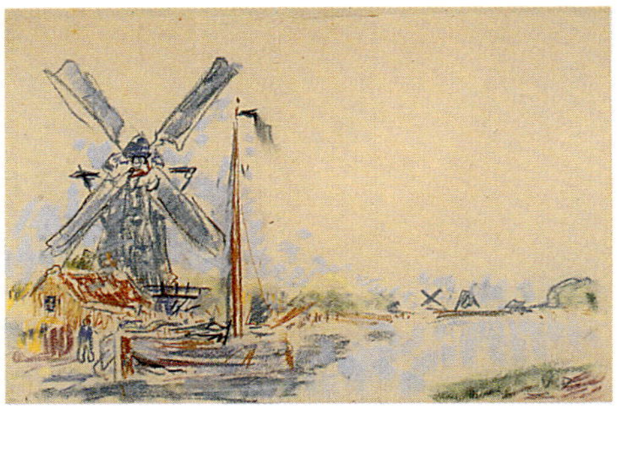

Sailing boat and mill, 1907, or verso *On the boat*
Coloured chalk, 539 x 338 mm

122. *Queen Wilhelmina and Prince consort*, 1907

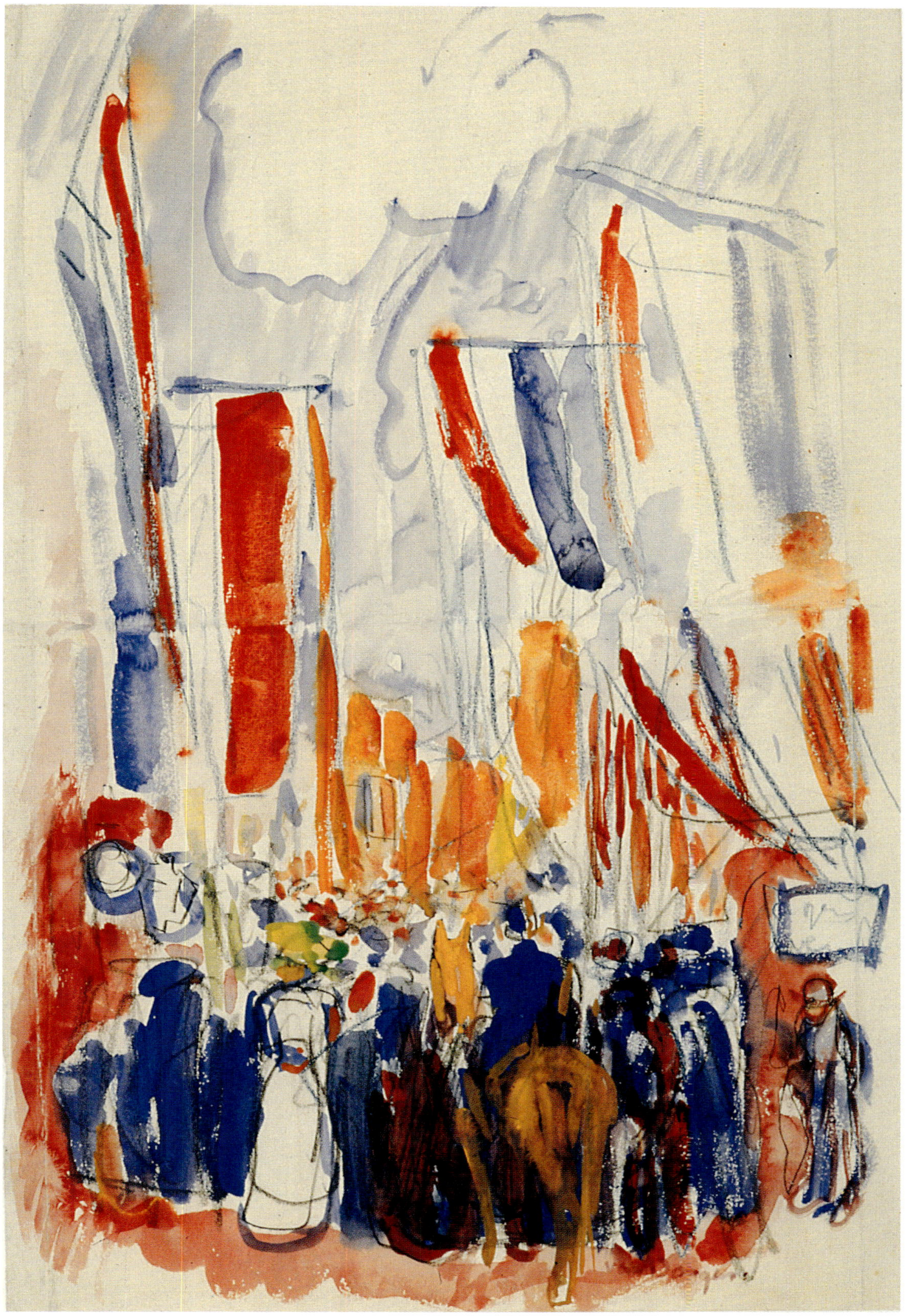

121. *Une fête en Hollande*, 1907

123. *Liverpool Light House*, 1907
Oil on canvas
100 x 81 cm
Signed upper left: *van Dongen*; right centre: *LIVERPOOL/[L]IGHT HOUSE*

PROVENANCE:
Bernheim-Jeune, Paris, 26 August 1907, purchased from the artist (Inv. 16.188; Bernheim-Jeune Archives); Galerie Max Moos, Geneva, 1918; Commandant Cormouls, Paris, 1953 (according to exhibition 1959 Nice, no. 3); Pierre M. Bloch, Paris; auction Paris, Palais Galliera (E. Ader), *Collection Pierre M. Bloch. Tableaux modernes, aquarelles, dessins...*, 12 March 1964, no. 36; Marlborough Fine Art, London, 1964; Fridart Stichting, 1967

EXHIBITIONS:
1908 Paris, Salon d'Automne, no. 580; 1908 Paris, Bernheim-Jeune, no. 40 (as: *Rotterdam*; 1905-1907); 1911 Paris, Bernheim-Jeune, no. 1; 1911 Geneva, no. 316; 1953 Paris, Galerie de Berri; 1962 Paris, no. 123 (fig.); 1964 London, no. 7; 1967 Paris, no. 47; 1975 Ontario, no. 24 (fig.); 1976 New York, p. 66 (fig.); 1982 Southampton, (no catalogue); 1989 Rotterdam, no. 13 (fig.); 1990 Paris, p. 71 (fig.); 1995 Sydney 1996, no. 40 (fig.)

LITERATURE:
Chaumeil 1967, p. 316, fig. 21; Loosjes-Terpstra 1987, p. 30, fig. 31

COLLECTION:
Fridart Foundation

The attractive canvas *Liverpool Light House* was painted by Van Dongen in 1907, encouraged by his visit to the Netherlands that year; the painting was probably begun in Rotterdam and finished in Paris. Its title is taken from a dance-hall of that name which was to be found near the corner of Zandstraat, part of the Rotterdam night-life scene. It may be the place that Brusse described – without mentioning the name – in one of his articles about the red-light area, typifying it as the 'largest and most celebrated dance show' surrounded by people 'on the look-out for partners'. On a drawing from 1901 which may represent the same street corner (with the seventeenth-century facade built facing the side street) Van Dongen gave us a glimpse of the 'social' exchange, the expectant couples and women eager for a client, and placed these, as in the later painted version, against a brightly lit window. (fig.) For the painting *Liverpool Light House*, Van Dongen highlighted a similar rendezvous – 'a long-legged hussar haggling with a girl about the price' and put it more daringly in the foreground. The hussar he painted as a dark silhouette, somewhat from below, which gives the figure a self-assured and imposing look. For the vista towards Zandstraat to the left, the artist seems to have used an earlier drawing of this street. (cat. 15) The way the street lighting is rendered in this depiction with coloured oil lamps must set the scene earlier since the oil lamps were replaced by modern gas lights in 1900. This brighter light made the colours brilliant as can be seen in the painting *Liverpool Light House*, of which the palette is entirely attuned to the red-white-blue coloured Dutch or French flag (depending on the order in which the colours are seen). Various renderings of the scene have been preserved, including a brush drawing in ink, which is regarded as a preliminary study for the painting. (fig.) It is more likely that the ink sketch was made after the painting *Liverpool Light House* and served as a composition sketch for an alternative painted version of this scene, auctioned in 1986.[2] This canvas, which according to notes on the back should be called *De Huzaar-Rotterdam*, was referred to by Chaumeil in his study as an entry to the Salon des Indépendants of 1904, but on the basis of the colours, the orange and pink blended tones, and other characteristics it might be more in tune with the 1950s.

The painting dated 1907 – the canvas exhibited here – appears to have been sold surprisingly quickly after Van Dongen's return to Paris, bought by Félix Fénéon for the Bernheim-Jeune gallery: in the art gallery archives 26 August 1907 is mentioned as the sale date. It was not until October 1908 that it was first publicly exhibited at the Salon d'Automne, after which the canvas could be seen at Van Dongen's solo exhibition at Bernheim-Jeune's in 1908. For the first event Bernheim-Jeune distributed a postcard of the painting, which shows that it was seen as an important and representative work.

1.
M.J. Brusse, 'Polder-herinneringen van een oud-politiecommandant in de Zandstraat', *Nieuwe Rotterdamsche Courant*, 22 March 1933.

2.
Auction London, Christie's, *Impressionist, expressionist and modern paintings...*, 23 June 1986, no. 34; Chaumeil 1967, p. 78, fig. 10.

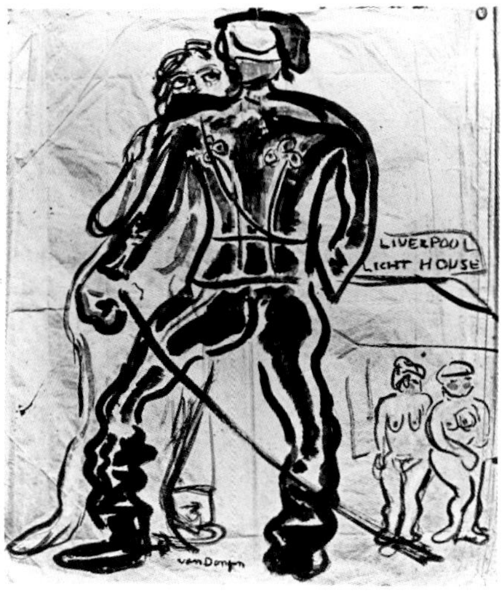

Liverpool Light House, possibly c. 1950
Brush in black ink, body colour, 700 x 585 mm

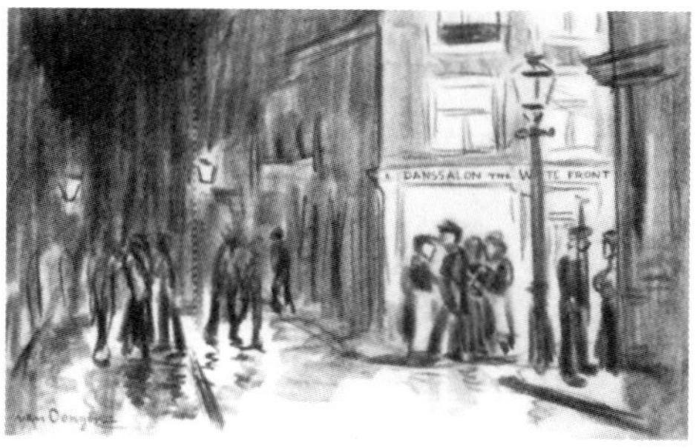

Dance-hall: The white front, 1901
Black chalk, 280 x 452 mm

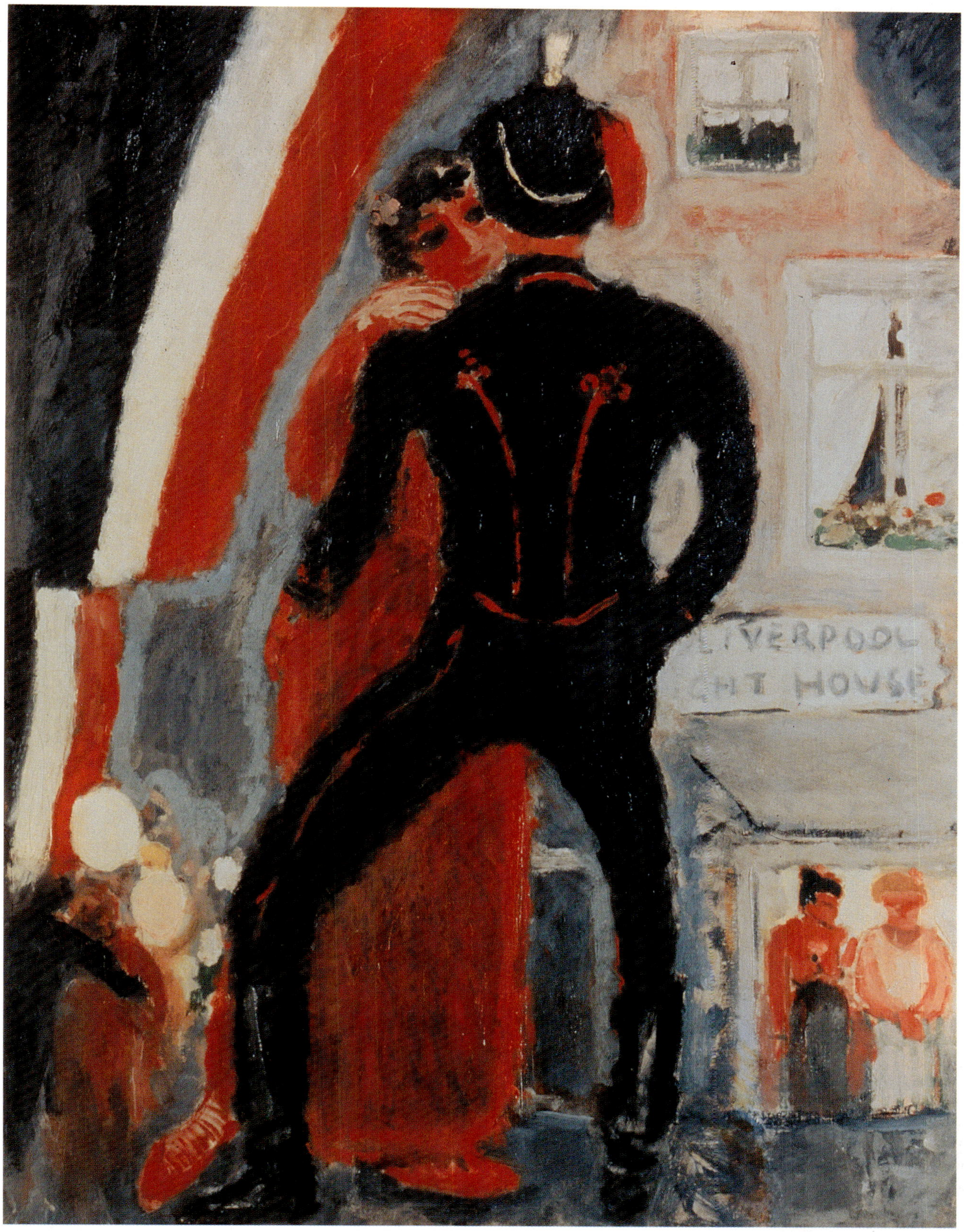

123. *Liverpool Light House*, 1907

124. *De zanger Modjesko* (The singer Modiesko), 1907
Watercolour, gouache
630 x 465 mm
Signed lower right in black chalk: *van Dongen*
PROVENANCE:
Private collection, Neuilly-sur-Seine; private collection
EXHIBITIONS:
1969 Marseilles, no 31; 1977 Tokyo, no. 53 (fig.)
LITERATURE:
Parinaud 1969 (fig.)
COLLECTION:
Private collection

1.
Cachin 1971, p. 83.
2.
W. 'Circus-Variété Pfläging in Rotterdam' (Reopening of Pläging's Circus after restoration), *Wereldkroniek*, 12 (1905/1906), p. 294 A. Moyne, *Le Courrier Français*, no. 34, 24 August 1905, p. 3.
3.
Auction Paris, Drouot (A. Bellier, J. Hessel), *Tableaux modernes*, 28 February 1930, no. 98.

The first time Van Dongen exhibited a portrait of the singer Modiesko was at an exhibition entitled *Portraits d'Hommes* organized by the Bernheim-Jeune gallery in December 1907. The canvas in question is probably the painted portrait which is at present to be found in the collection of the Museum of Modern Art in New York. (fig.) The 1907 exhibition pre-dates (*datum ante quem*) the painting and therefore also the studies that preceded it, like *The singer Modiesko*. The painted version was also to be seen later at Van Dongen's important solo exhibition at Bernheim-Jeune's in December 1908 and afterwards was acquired by the artist Paul Signac.[1] In the foreword which the Leblond brothers published in the catalogue accompanying the exhibition, the singer was called an 'acteur hollandais'. That may have been a mistake: the transvestite singer was of Rumanian origin; the portrait was in fact painted on the basis of studies made in Rotterdam in 1907. This is also indicated by a portrait by Ludovic-Rodo Pissarro made in the same period and annotated on the reverse side 'Rotterdam 1907'. It is also clear from a report in a Dutch periodical, the *Wereldkroniek*, that Modiesko performed in Rotterdam at that time. In this report it was announced that the actor, nicknamed 'the black Patti', who in the summer of 1905 still sang for a chic public in the Paris music-hall Olympia, was contracted for the winter season of 1905-06 by the Rotterdam Circus-Variété Pfläging: 'a bass singer with a beautiful soprano voice who sings duets with himself.' The contract must have been renewed the following year. A photograph of him in a periodical shows Modiesko in the same evening wear as in the rendering by Van Dongen already mentioned.

The water-coloured drawing titled *The singer Modiesko* appears to have been made just before the painting; the actor in the drawing has almost the same facial expression and pose as in the painting; the colour scheme, the bright green and red, saffron and ochre (the colour of the theatre light) is similar too. The drawing, which is fluently sketched and shows the singer's robe in its entirety, is probably one of the most successful studies that Van Dongen ever made of Modiesko's performance. At an exhibition in Bern in 1950, two other sheets on this subject were shown and a further sketch is also known to exist, entitled *Modiesko soprano singer*. (fig.) This was originally to be found in the collection of Daniel-Henry Kahnweiler and, after having been exhibited in Germany in the twenties, was auctioned in 1930 in Paris.[3] The painted portrait of Modiesko was to be seen for the first time after a great many years at the retrospective exhibition devoted to Van Dongen's work in 1949, and subsequently at an exhibition which the Paris gallery de Berri organized in 1953 to show the artist's Fauvist work. As a result of the last-mentioned exhibition, the canvas was bought by the Perls Gallery in New York, after which it was donated by the collector couple Peter A. Rübel to the museum in New York.

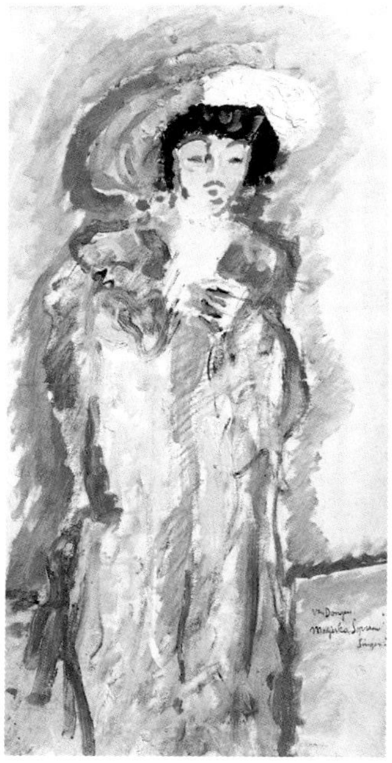

Modiesko soprano singer, 1907
Watercolour, body colour, 640 x 480 mm

Modiesko soprano singer, 1907
Oil on canvas, 100 x 81 cm
The Museum of Modern Art, New York

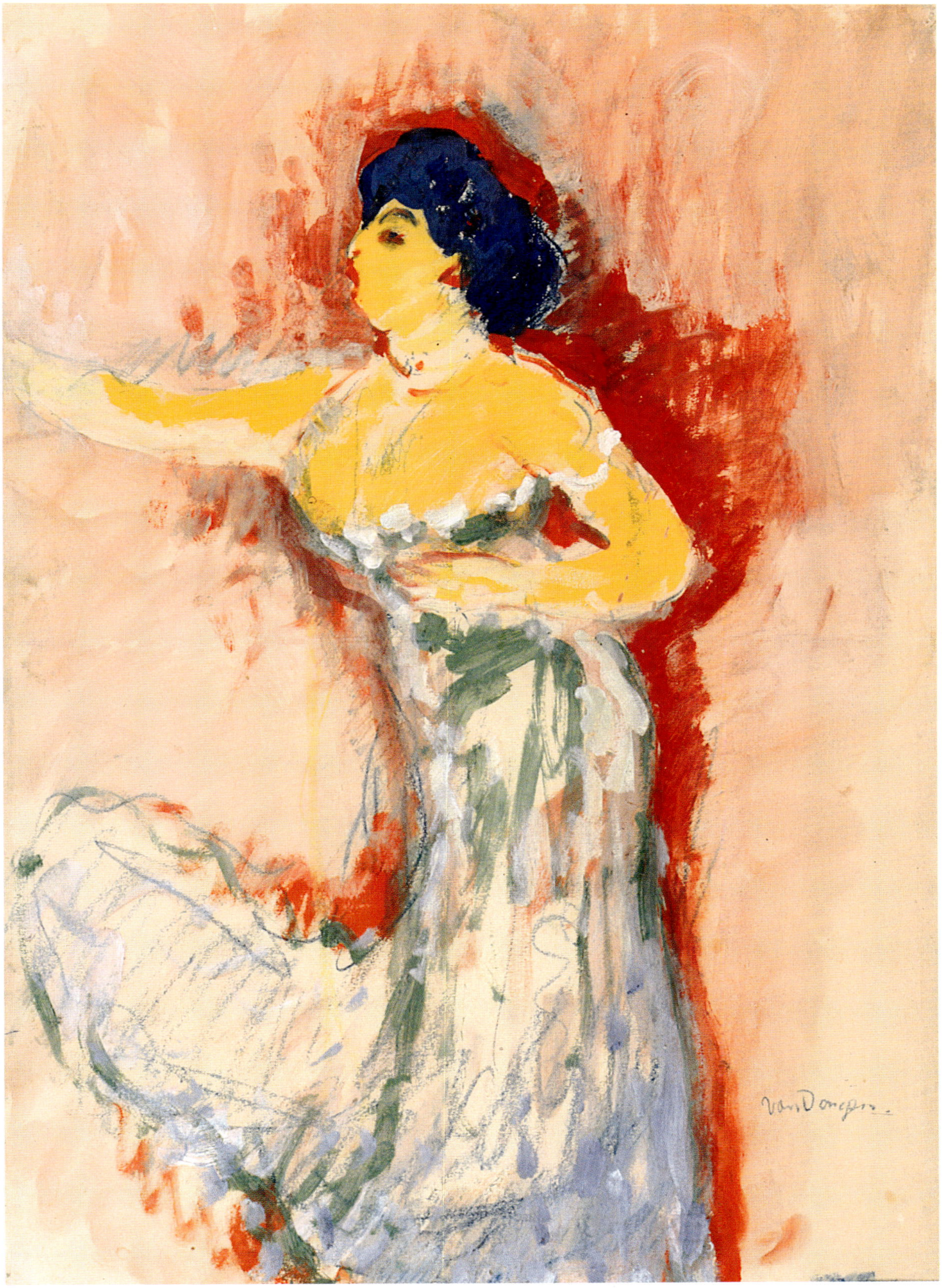

124. *The singer Modiesko*, 1907

125. *Portret van de kunstcriticus en verzamelaar Charles Malpel*
(Portrait of the art critic and collector Charles Malpel), c. 1907
Brush with black ink, white gouache
490 x 410 mm
Signed centre right in brush with black ink: *V.D.*
PROVENANCE:
Charles Malpel (1874-1926), Toulouse, c. 1907;
private collection
EXHIBITIONS:
1990 Paris, p. 128 (fig.); 1990 Toulouse, no. 115 (fig.)
COLLECTION:
Private collection

126. *Studie voor een portret van mevrouw Marie Malpel*
(Study for a portrait of Madame Marie Malpel), c. 1907
Black and coloured chalk
650 x 500 mm
Unsigned
PROVENANCE:
Charles Malpel (1874-1926), Toulouse c. 1907; private collection
EXHIBITIONS:
1990 Toulouse, no. 117 (fig.)
COLLECTION:
Private collection

Around 1907, Van Dongen made several portraits of the couple Charles and Marie Malpel. Charles Malpel was a lawyer and worked at the law courts in Toulouse. After inheriting his father's country estate, he was active as a wine grower. In addition to this he was an assiduous collector of modern art and built up an important collection between about 1900 and 1914.[1] As he was a collector, Malpel seems to have reacted quickly to new developments in terms of new purchases. As well as less famous names, he acquired work by the artists Toulouse-Lautrec, Signac and Picasso, besides Fauvist works by Matisse, Derain, Van Dongen, Vlaminck, Dufy, Chabaud and Valtat, André Lhote and Roger de la Fresnaye. Malpel signed a contract with the artist Chagall when he had established himself as an art dealer in Paris in 1913; it was a contract giving Malpel sole rights to sell Chagall's work. From 1907 onwards, Malpel published articles on current exhibitions and artists he appreciated in the newspaper the *Télégramme de Toulouse*, of which the most important were published in book form in 1910. From 1907 to 1910 he organized exhibitions of contemporary art in the editing offices of this paper.[2] This series of exhibitions opened with a homage dedicated to Henri de Toulouse-Lautrec who had died in 1901. The following exhibition in January 1908 was of the work of Kees Van Dongen. Malpel's articles, the exhibitions he organized and his collection – in as much as this can be reconstrued – clearly show his artistic preferences. One of the artists he was specially interested in was Kees van Dongen, whom he considered to be a painter of his times par excellence. With his 'pinceau instinctif' he thought Van Dongen had captured the essence of modern life – the dance-halls, electric light, the funfairs – as nobody else had done before him. Malpel possessed quite a few of Van Dongen's works including *View of Paris* and *Mademoiselle Léda*, the painting that is known under the title *La ballerina borgne*. (fig. pp. 58, 70)

The two sketched portraits by Van Dongen of Charles and Marie Malpel exhibited here can, on stylistic grounds, be dated to shortly before or after 1907. The style of drawing whereby a contour or a head of hair is indicated by shading, in zig-zag lines, was used by Van Dongen from 1907. The drawing of Mrs Malpel is a preliminary study for a painted portrait, formerly known under the title *Femme au chapeau*; the canvas was recently recognized as being of Mrs Malpel during the preparations for an exhibition in Toulouse, and it is one of the three painted portraits that Van Dongen made of her.[3] (fig.) These likenesses of Charles and Marie Malpel along with the collector's purchases and praise of Van Dongen's virtues in the articles he wrote about him, show just how much he appreciated the artist and date the contact he had with him to the period between 1907 and 1910.

1. P. Duchein, 'Hommage à Charles Malpel', *Bulletin du Musée Ingres*, no. 20, December 1966, pp. 25-42.
2. Ch. Malpel, *Notes sur l'art d'aujourd'hui et peut-être de demain*, 2 vols, Paris 1910, exhib.cat. 1990 Toulouse, p. 9.
3. Exhib.cat. 1990 Toulouse, nos 114, 117; exhib.cat. 1990 Paris, pp. 118-119, 121, 128.

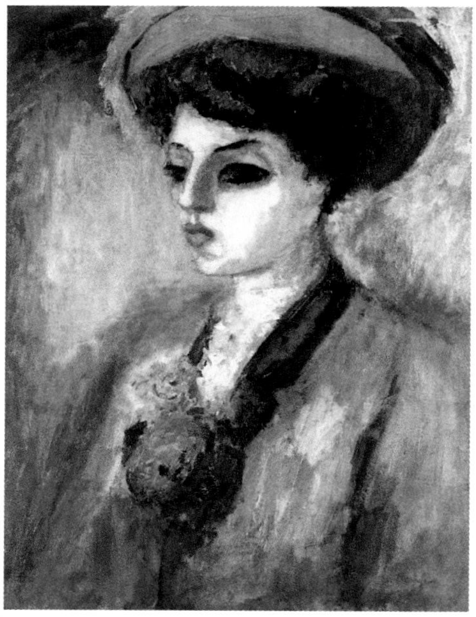

Portrait of Madame Malpel, 1907
Oil on canvas, 92 x 73 cm
Samir Traboulsi, Paris

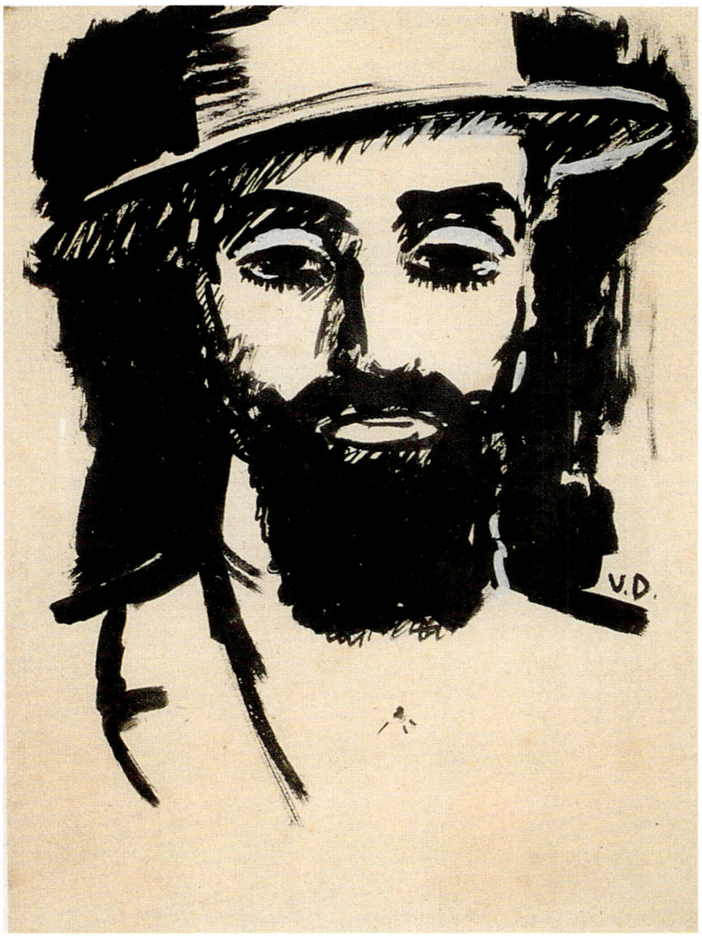

125. *Portrait of the art critic and collector Charles Malpel*, c. 1907

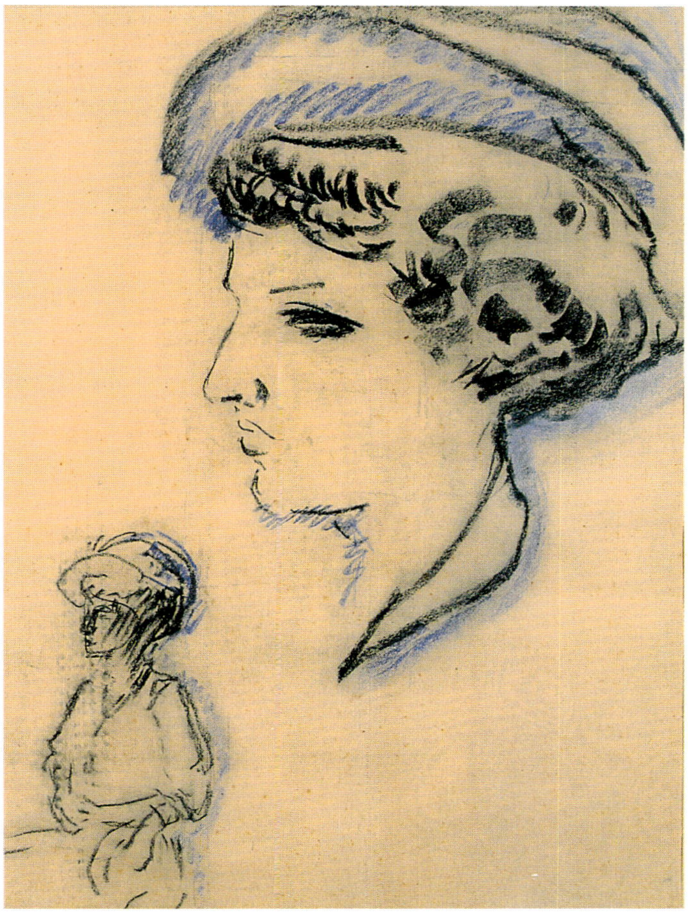

126. *Study for a portrait of Madame Marie Malpel*, c. 1907

127. *Le maillot blanc* (The white leotard), c. 1908
Oil on canvas
81 x 54 cm
Signed lower right: *van Dongen.*
PROVENANCE:
Bernheim-Jeune, Paris, 6 October 1908, bought from the artist (Inv. 16.777, Bernheim-Jeune Archives); Jacques Chalom, Paris, 1962; Leonard Hutton Galleries, New York, 1965; private collection, 1969; auction Enghien (Champin, Lombrail, Gautier), 24 November 1987, no. 20; auction Enghien (Champin, Lombrail, Gautier), 21 June 1990, no. 9; auction London, Sotheby's, *Impressionist and modern paintings...*, 2 December 1992, no. 122 (fig.); Kunsthandel Borzo, 's-Hertogenbosch, 1993; Sara Lee/DE, Utrecht, 1993
EXHIBITIONS:
1908 Paris, Kahnweiler, no. 13; 1908 Dresden, E. Richter, (?); 1908 Paris, Bernheim-Jeune, no. 58; 1908 Munich, Thannhauser, no. 19 (fig.); 1911 Paris, Bernheim-Jeune, no. 4; 1962 Asnières, no. 11 (fig.); 1965 New York, no. 6 (fig.); 1969 Marseilles, no. 11; 1972 Paris, no. 9
LITERATURE:
Kyriazi 1971, fig. 33; Werner 1965, p. 20 (fig.)
COLLECTION:
Sara Lee/DE Collection, Utrecht

128. *Tableau vivant* (Tableau), c. 1908
Pen and brush with brown ink, watercolour, blue chalk
149 x 112 mm
Unsigned; lower centre annotated in pen with brown ink: *TABLEAU VIVANT.*
PROVENANCE:
Auction Paris, Palais Galliéra (M. and Ph. Rheims, R.G. Laurin), *Tableaux anciens, tableaux modernes*, 28 June 1962, no. 186; private collection
COLLECTION:
Private collection

129. *Artistin* (Artiste), c. 1908
Oil on canvas
100 x 81 cm
Unsigned
PROVENANCE:
D.-H. Kahnweiler, Paris (according to Keller 1954); Kunsthalle Bremen, 1947 (bequest of Helene and Arnold Blome)
LITERATURE:
Keller 1954, p. 106; Gerkens 1973, pp. 92-93 (fig.); Kreul 1994, no. 308
COLLECTION:
Kunsthalle Bremen, Inv. 517-1947/21

130. *Portrait de Fernande Olivier* (Portrait of Fernande Olivier) 1905/1908
Oil on canvas
100 x 81 cm
Signed lower left: *van Dongen*
PROVENANCE:
Galerie de Berri, Paris; Galerie Bourdon, Paris (according to exhib.cat. 1987 Paris); André Fried, Paris (according to exhib.cat. 1959 Nice and 1964 Lyons); Jean Forges, Paris
EXHIBITIONS:
1949 Paris, no. 24; 1949 Rotterdam, no. 13; 1953 Paris, de Berri; 1959 Shaffhausen, no. 78; 1959 Nice, no. 13; 1962 Paris, no. 121 (fig.); 1964 Lyons, no. 13; 1987 Paris; 1989 Rotterdam, no. 6 (fig.); 1990 Paris, p. 106 (fig.)
LITERATURE:
Chaumeil 1967, fig. 47; Crespelle 1962, fig. 68; Giry 1981, p. 121, fig. 50; Richardson 1991, pp. 376-377
COLLECTION:
Samir Traboulsi Collection

131. *Femme à la toilette* (Woman making her toilet), c. 1908
Oil on canvas
100 x 60 cm
Signed lower right: *van Dongen* (partially painted over)
PROVENANCE:
Daniel Tzanck, Paris; auction Paris, Drouot (R.-G. Boisgirard), *Tableaux modernes, aquarelles, dessins...*, 23 May 1949, no. 105 (fig.); auction Versailles, Palais des Congrès (J.-P. Chapelle et al.), *Tableaux modernes et du XIXe siècle*, 26 November 1978, no. 42; Galerie Taménaga, Tokyo, 1990; Kanetaka Watanabe, Japan, 1990
EXHIBITIONS:
1990 New York, no. 2 (fig.)
COLLECTION:
Dr K. Watanabe collection

132. *Portrait de Rita* (Portrait of Rita), c. 1910
Black and coloured chalk, pastel
655 x 505 mm
Signed lower right in black chalk: *van Dongen.*; annotated in orange chalk: *RITA*
Artist's handwriting on reverse of cardboard on which drawing is mounted: *Kees van Dongen/6, rue Saulnier/Paris (9ième)*
PROVENANCE:
Auction London, Sotheby's, *Impressionist and modern drawings...*, 1 December 1982, no. 182 (fig.); art dealers' Schröder and Leisewitz, Bremen, 1982; private collection
EXHIBITIONS:
1918 Paris, no. 19 (?)
COLLECTION:
Private collection

133. *Buikdanseres* (Belly dancer), c. 1910
Oil on paper
875 x 680 mm
Signed lower centre in blue chalk: *vanDongen.*
Special features: the sheet is made up of four joined pieces of paper; blind-stamped watermark on three of the pieces: - *ANC^{NE} MANUF^{RE} CANSON & MONTGOLFIER-VIDALON-FILS-ANNONAY-B CRAYON-*
PROVENANCE:
Boymans Museum, Rotterdam, 1936 (gift of the artist; letter from Kees van Dongen to D. Hannema, 7 December 1936, GA Rotterdam)
EXHIBITIONS:
1989 Rotterdam, (ex. catalogue)
LITERATURE:
Van Gelder 1958 p. 81, fig. 215; Hannema 1937, p. 10; Hannema 1973, p. 48; Boymans Museum Annual Report 1937, p. 7
COLLECTION:
Boijmans Van Beuningen Museum, Rotterdam, Inv. KvD 27

134. *La chaloupée* (The swaying dance), c. 1911
Brush with black ink, gouache
650 x 620 mm
Signed lower left in pen and brush with black ink: *Van Dongen*
PROVENANCE:
Richard Anacréon (1907-1992), Juan-les-Pins, Spéracèdes, c. 1960; Musée d'Art Moderne Richard Anacréon, Granville, 1990 (gift of Richard Anacréon)
EXHIBITIONS:
1992 Granville, p. 30 (fig.)
COLLECTION:
Musée d'Art Moderne Richard Anacréon, Granville, Inv. RA 1975:75.1.171

135. *Le doigt sur la joue* (The finger on the cheek), 1911
Oil on canvas
65 x 54 cm
Signed lower right: *van Dongen*
Annotated and signed on reverse of lining canvas: *no 2/Le doigt sur la joue/Van Dongen* (Ebbinge Wubben, 1963); on reverse of frame a black-printed label marked in pen with black ink: *19031 R 1911/K.van Dongen/Le doigt sur la joue/Odd*; a black-printed label: 2nd *POST-IMPRESSIONIST EXHIBITION/Grafton Galleries, Oct.-Dec.1911*; marked in pen with black ink: *Van Dongen/Le doigt sur la joue (19031)/MM.*[Bernheim Jeune]; on the stretcher in blue chalk: *19031 R/1911*
PROVENANCE:
Galerie Bernheim-Jeune, Paris, 1911 (Inv. nr 19031); Grafton Galleries, London, 1911; Jacob de Graaff (1873-1947), London-Beaussiet, 1912 (letter from the Grafton Galleries to J. de Graaff, 31 October 1912, documentation in the Boijmans Van Beuningen Museum, Rotterdam); his wife, Louise de Graaff-Bachiene (1870-1963), Beausiet, 1947; Boijmans Van Beuningen Museum, Rotterdam, 1949 (gift of L. de Graaff-Bachiene)
EXHIBITIONS:
1911 Paris, Indépendants, no. 1877; 1911 Paris, Bernheim-Jeune (December) no. 1; 1912 Brussels, La Libre Esthétique, no. 251; 1912 London, Grafton Galleries, no. 52 (fig.); 1964 Florence, no. 47; 1967 Paris, no. 73 (fig.); 1969 Mechelen, no. 118 (fig.); 1971 Tucson, no. 59 (fig.); 1979 Amsterdam, no. 99; 1981 Utrecht, no. 58; 1981 Munich, no. 254 (fig.); 1989 Rotterdam, no. 31 (fig.); 1990 Paris, p. 154 (fig.); 1992 Heino, no. 17 (fig.)
LITERATURE:
Ebbinge Wubben 1950, pp. 38-39, 43 (fig.); Ebbinge Wubben 1963, p. 41; Ebbinge Wubben 1972, no. 88 (fig.); Loosjes-Terpstra 1987, p. 237, note 7; Sutton 1971, illus. 7
COLLECTION:
Boijmans Van Beuningen Museum, Rotterdam, Inv. St.78

136. *La mobilisation* (Mobilization), c. 1911
Oil on paper
640 x 492 mm
Signed lower right in pen with black ink: *van Dongen.*
Annotated and signed on the back in black chalk: *La mobilisation/van Dongen*
Special features: blind-stamped watermark at the left edge of the sheet: *B. CRAYON ANC^{NE} MANUF^{RE} CANSON & MONT-GOLFIER VIDALON-LES-ANNO*
PROVENANCE:
Auction London, Sotheby's, Wilkinson & Hodge, *Modern etchings and drawings*, 30-32 May 1922, no. 249 (?) (as 'The departure', acquired by Artz); art dealers' A.T.A. Artz, London, 1922 or Grafton Galleries, London (in De Graaff-Bachiene Archives, Hannema-De Stuers Foundation, Heino, various notes about this by Dirk Hannema); Jacob de Graaff (1873-1947) and Louise de Graaff-Bachiene (1870-1963), London-Beaussiet, c. 1922; Hannema-de Stuers Foundation, Heino, 1963 (gift of L. de Graaff-Bachiene)
EXHIBITIONS:
1992 Heino-Gent, no. 18 (fig.)
LITERATURE:
Hannema 1971, no. 599 (fig.)
COLLECTION:
Hannema-De Stuers Foundation, Het Nijenhuis Castle, Heino

1.
Letter from Dolly van Dongen to E. Hild, 13 June 1985, Musée de l'Annonciade, Saint-Tropez.
2.
Olivier 1988, pp. 218-221, p. 228.
3.
Postcard K. van Dongen to G. van Dongen, sent from North Africa, postmarked 12 August 1909, private collection.

After his return from the Netherlands in August 1907, Van Dongen found a new apartment in Montmartre at 35 rue Lamarck. At the end of 1907 he moved house once again, to 6 rue Saulnier where he lived until 1912. The move heralded a new period in Van Dongen's work. In these years Van Dongen painted the series inspired by actresses who performed for the travelling funfairs or places of entertainment like the Folies-Bergère, as well as the portrayal of a woman making her toilet, and very possibly the impressive Fauvist nudes with Fernande Olivier for a model. Several of these works were shown by Van Dongen in 1908 at Kahnweiler's and Bernheim-Jeune's. On a few of the paintings, like *Le maillot blanc* and *Artistin*, a revue artiste is shown in a tight-fitting leotard. They are probably actresses from the so-called 'revues à maillot'. This was a favourite number in music-halls and theatres of the time, whereby the artistes performed in figure-clinging leotards. (fig.) In a letter of 1985 Dolly van Dongen was convinced that the paintings of Fernande Olivier were created in the studio on rue Lamarck, therefore at the end of 1907 or the beginning of 1908.[1] It is a dating which seems quite likely on stylistic grounds too, for they show the same zig-zag contour as the other works which can definitely be dated to 1907-08. (fig.) The portraits may have been painted in the months when Fernande and Picasso drifted apart and Fernande was living temporarily at another address. Sometime during the spring of 1908 she is said to have returned to the Bateau-Lavoir.[2] In 1908 Van Dongen's first paintings of the revue artist Nini were created, portrayed in the small pen drawing *Tableau vivant*. After this, around 1909-10, the different versions of the dancing Anita are assumed to have followed, paintings which are known under titles like *Danseuse indienne* or *La belle Fatima et sa troupe* and which Van Dongen sent into exhibitions from 1909 onwards. (fig.) The works show the following style change which was partially inspired by his contacts with Die Brücke artists in 1908 and 1909 and his journeys to Morocco and Spain, where he was not only working in June 1910 but, it would appear from a postcard to Guus, already in the summer of 1909.[3]

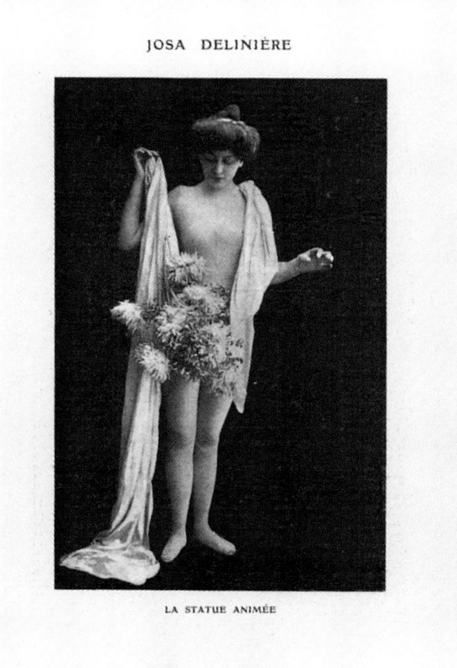

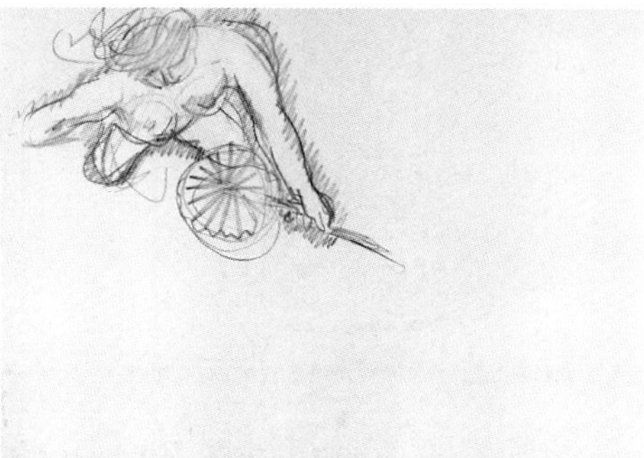

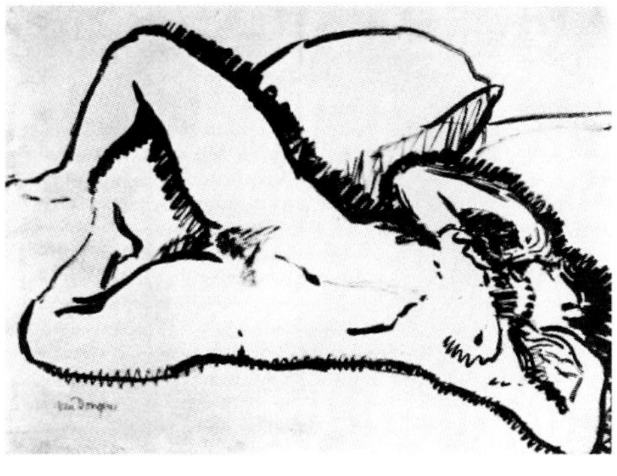

La statue animée, photo in *Les coulisses Parisiennes*, 1902
Rondel Collection, Bibliothèque de l'Arsenal, Paris

Woman with Japanese fan, verso *Dordrecht*, 1907
Black chalk, 489 x 340 mm
Museum Boijmans Van Beuningen, Rotterdam

Nude, c. 1907-08
Brush with black ink, size unknown

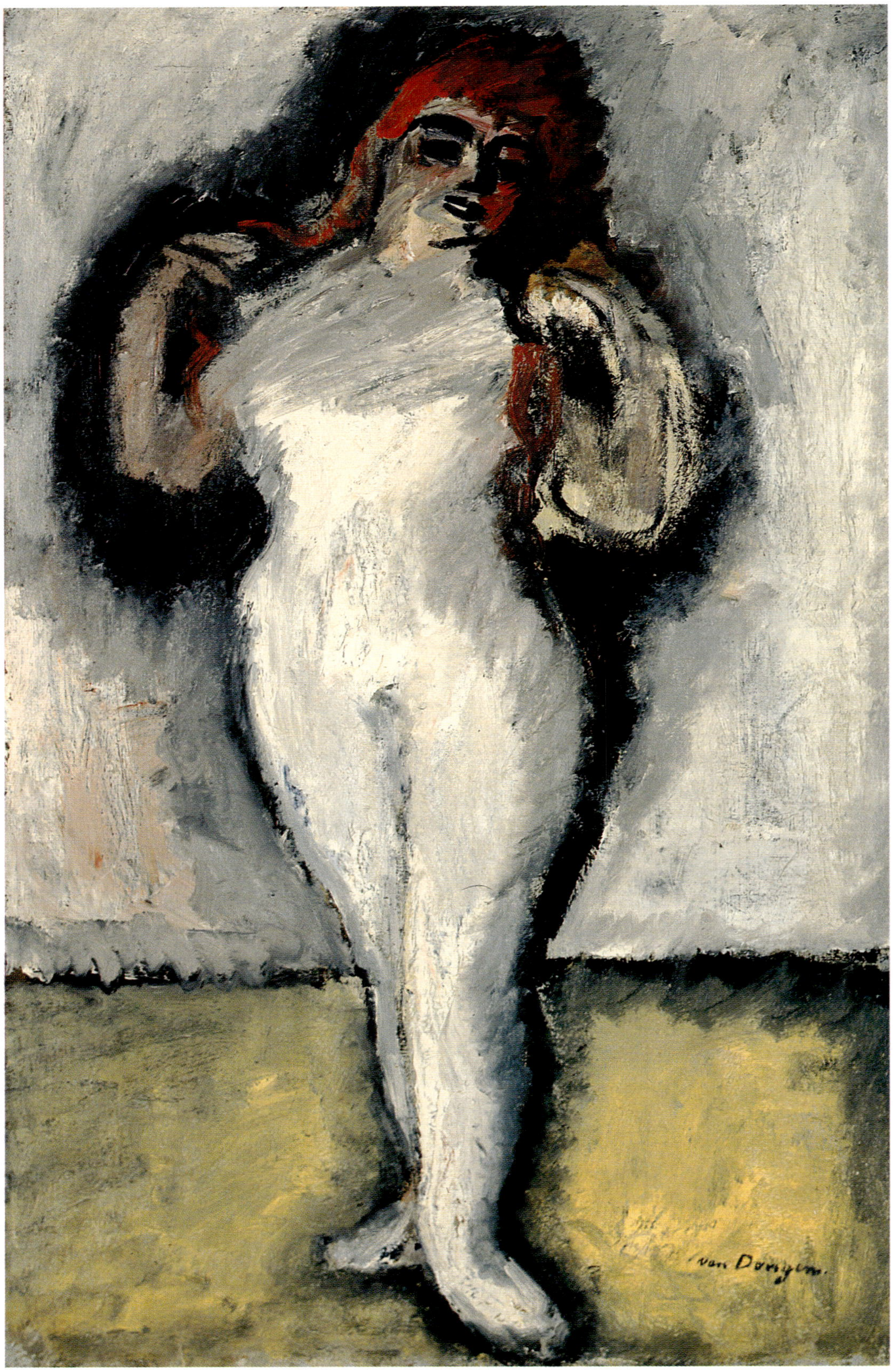

127. *Le maillot blanc*, c. 1908

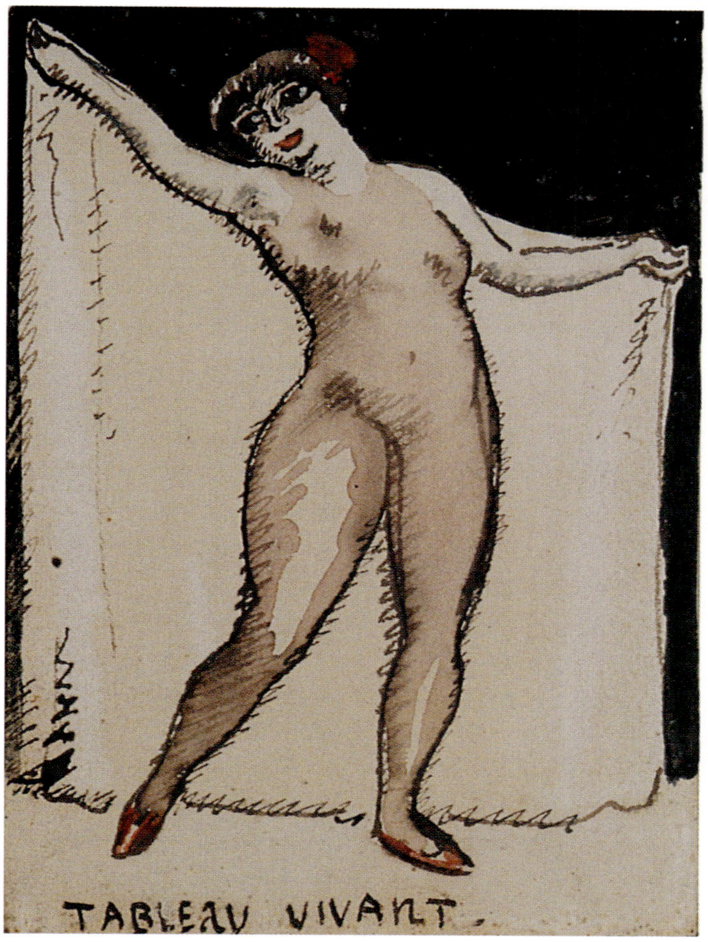

128. *Tableau vivant*, c. 1908

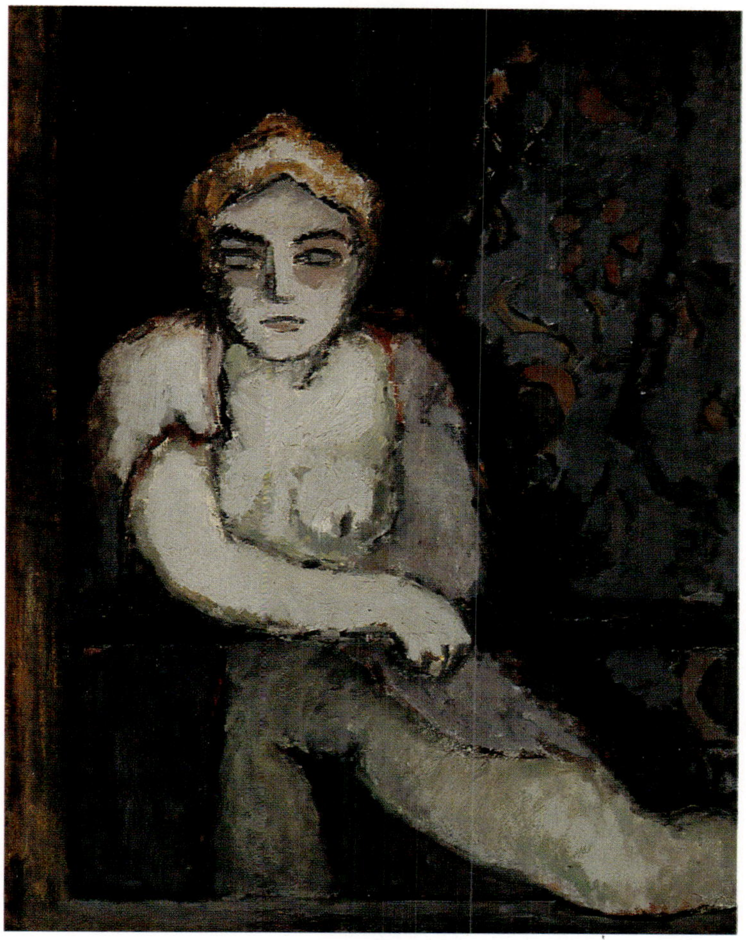

129. *Artiste*, c. 1908

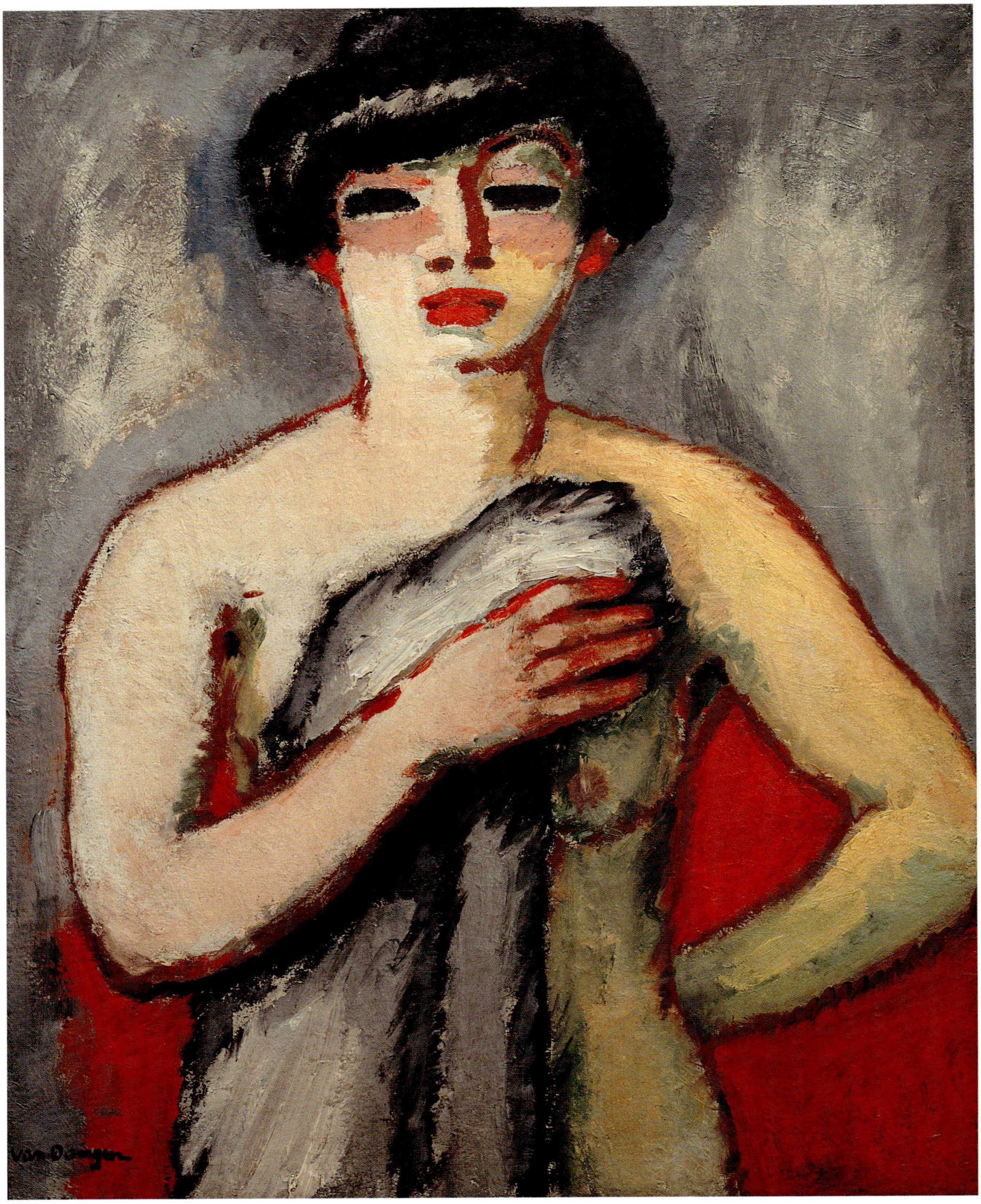

130. *Portrait de Fernande Olivier*, 1905/1908

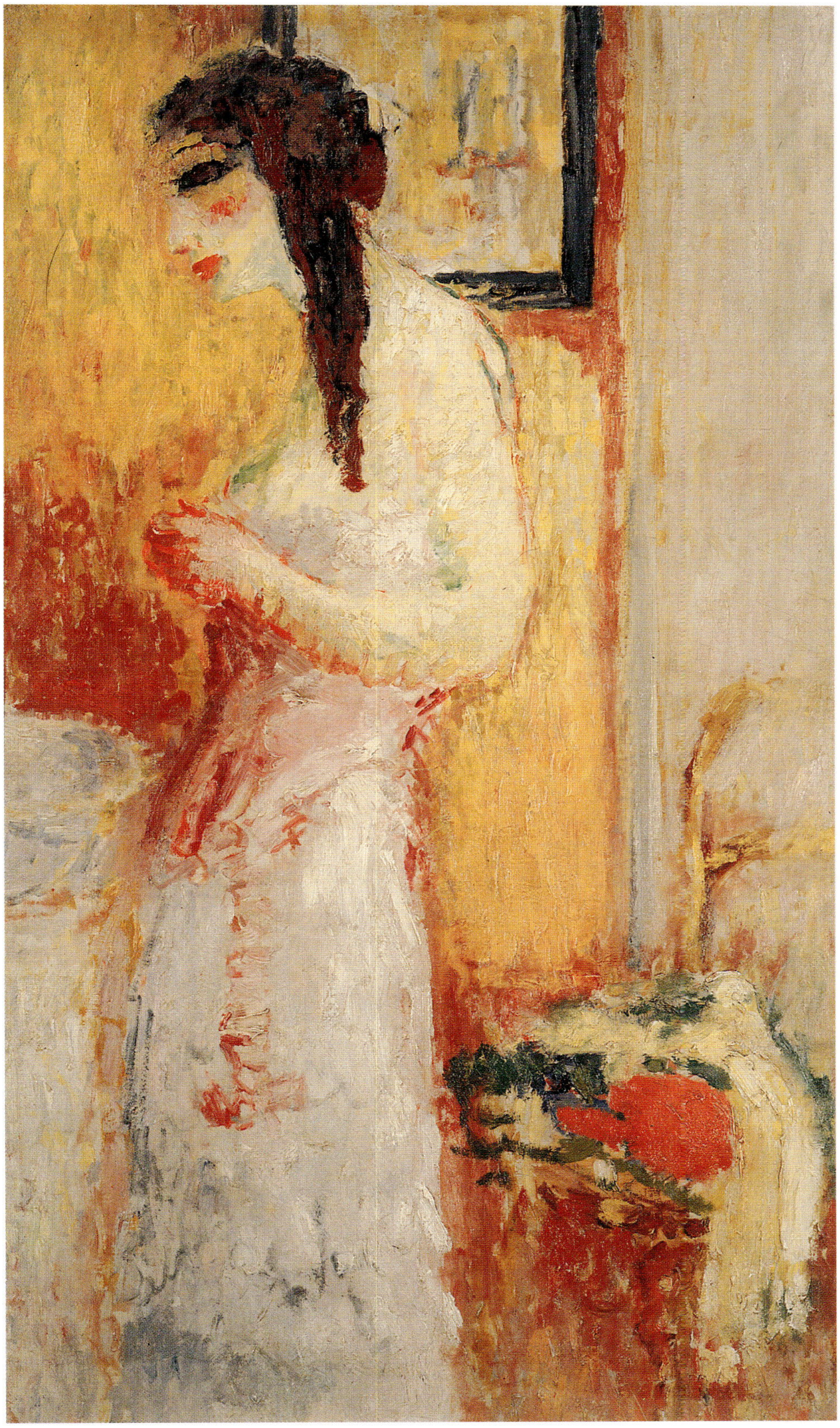

131. *Femme à la toilette*, c. 1908

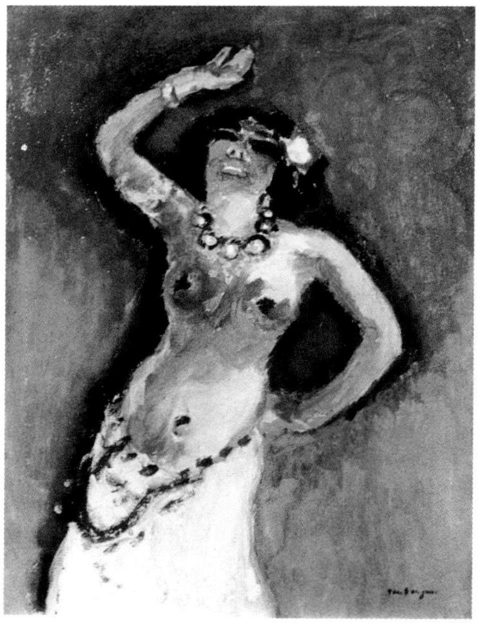

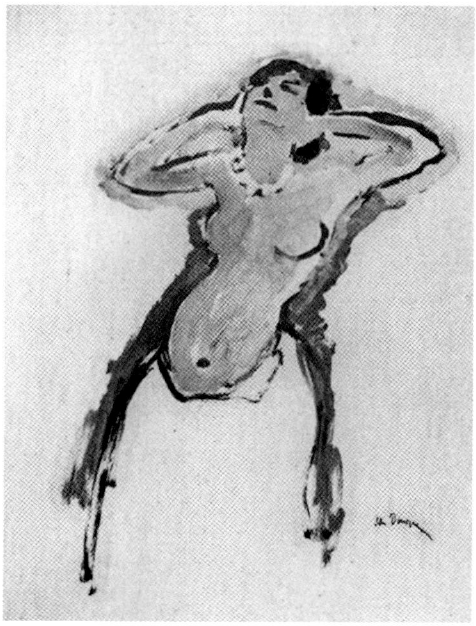

Danseuse bohémienne, c. 1909-10
Oil on canvas, 65,5 x 50 cm

Dancer, c. 1909-10
Oil on canvas, 62 x 48 cm

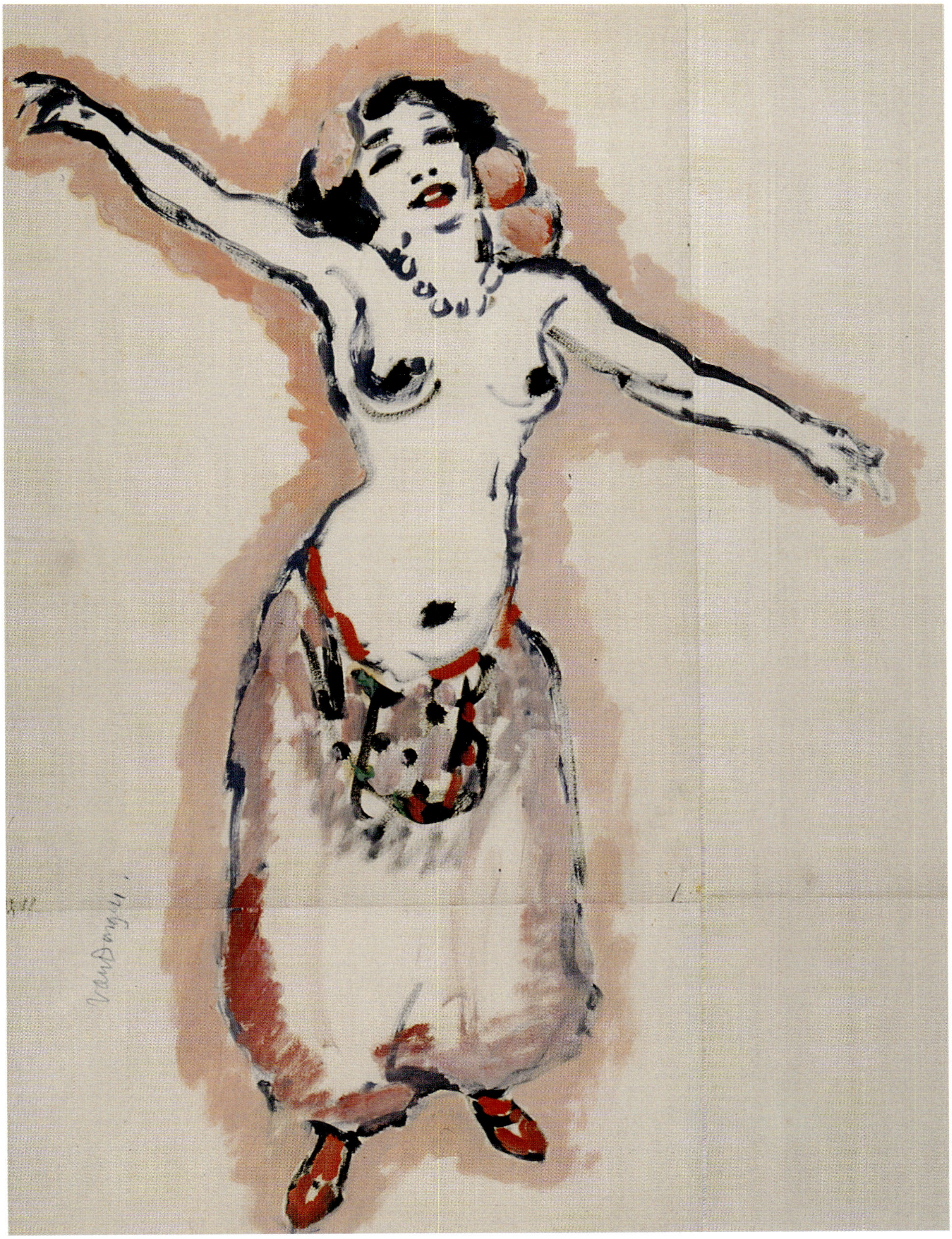

133. *Belly dancer*, c. 1910

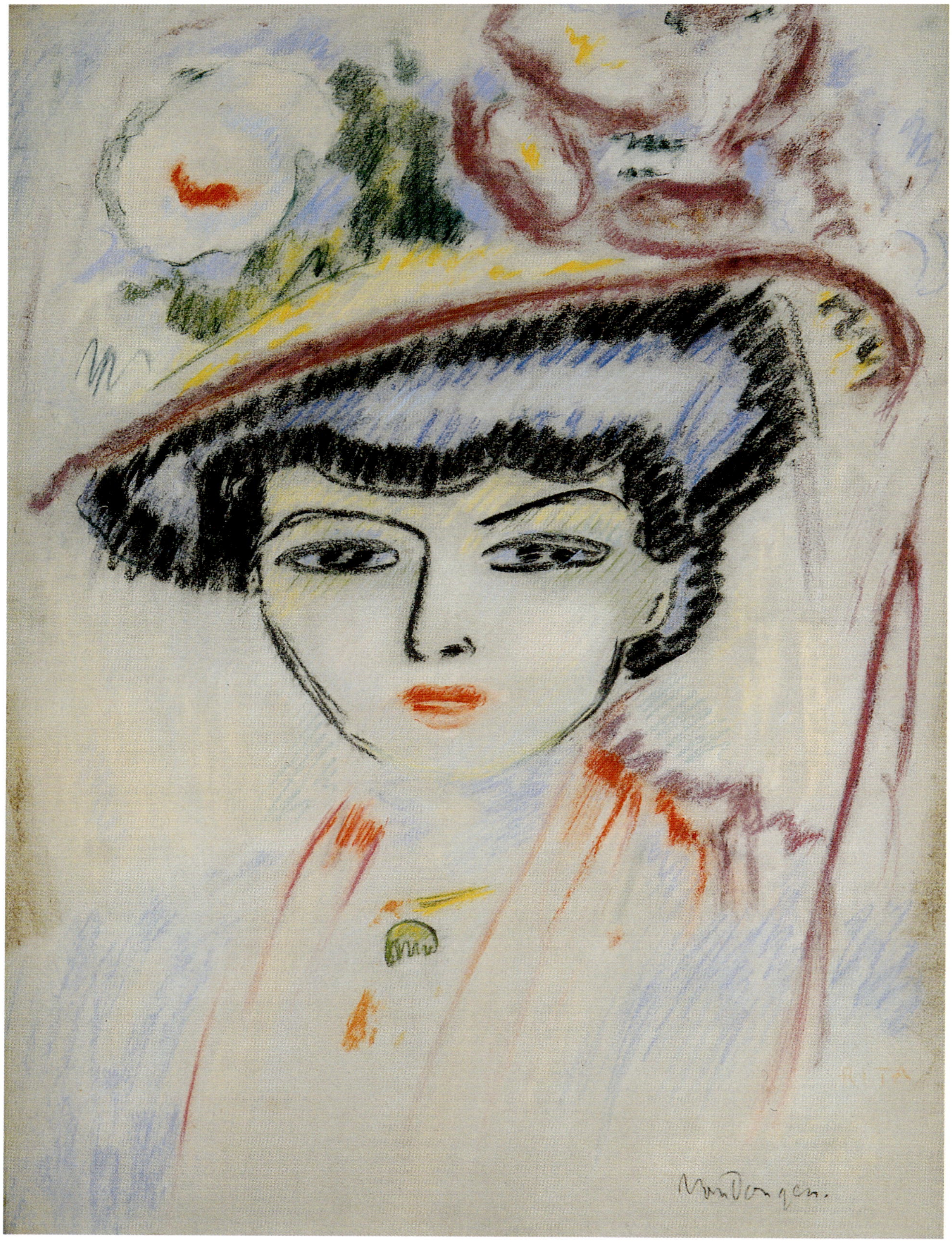

132. *Portrait de Rita*, c. 1910

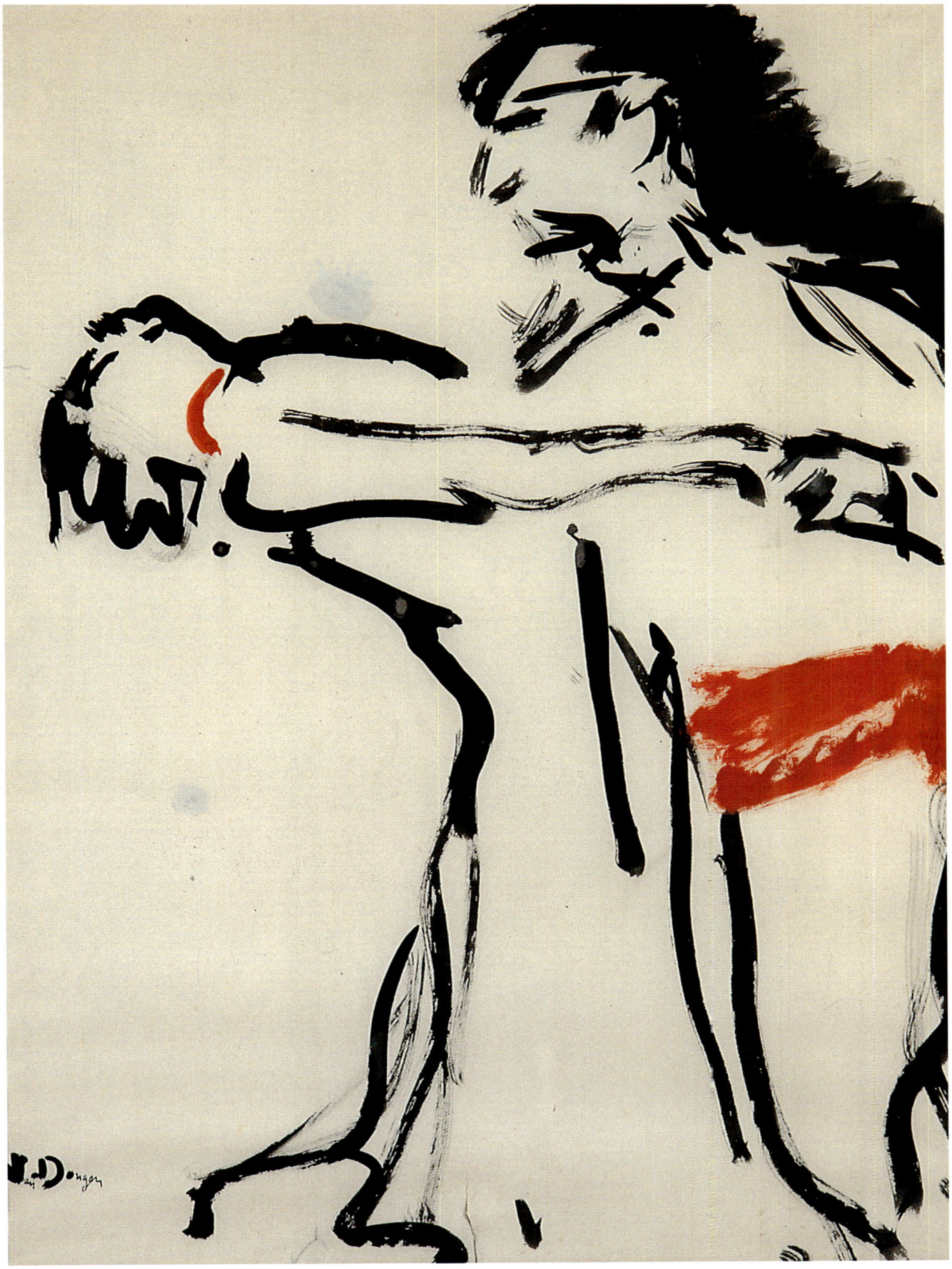

134. *La chaloupée*, c. 1911

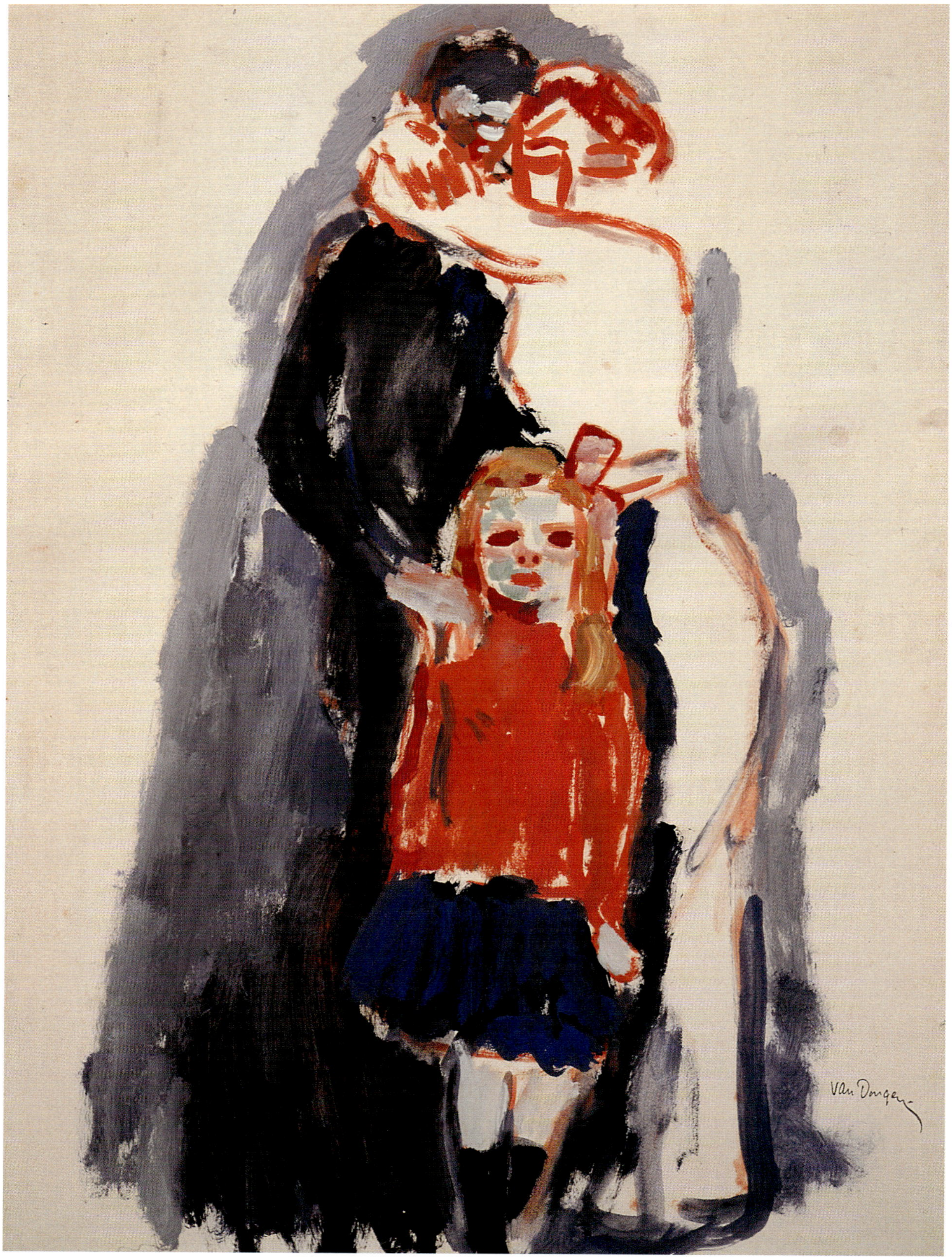

136. *La mobilisation*, c. 1911

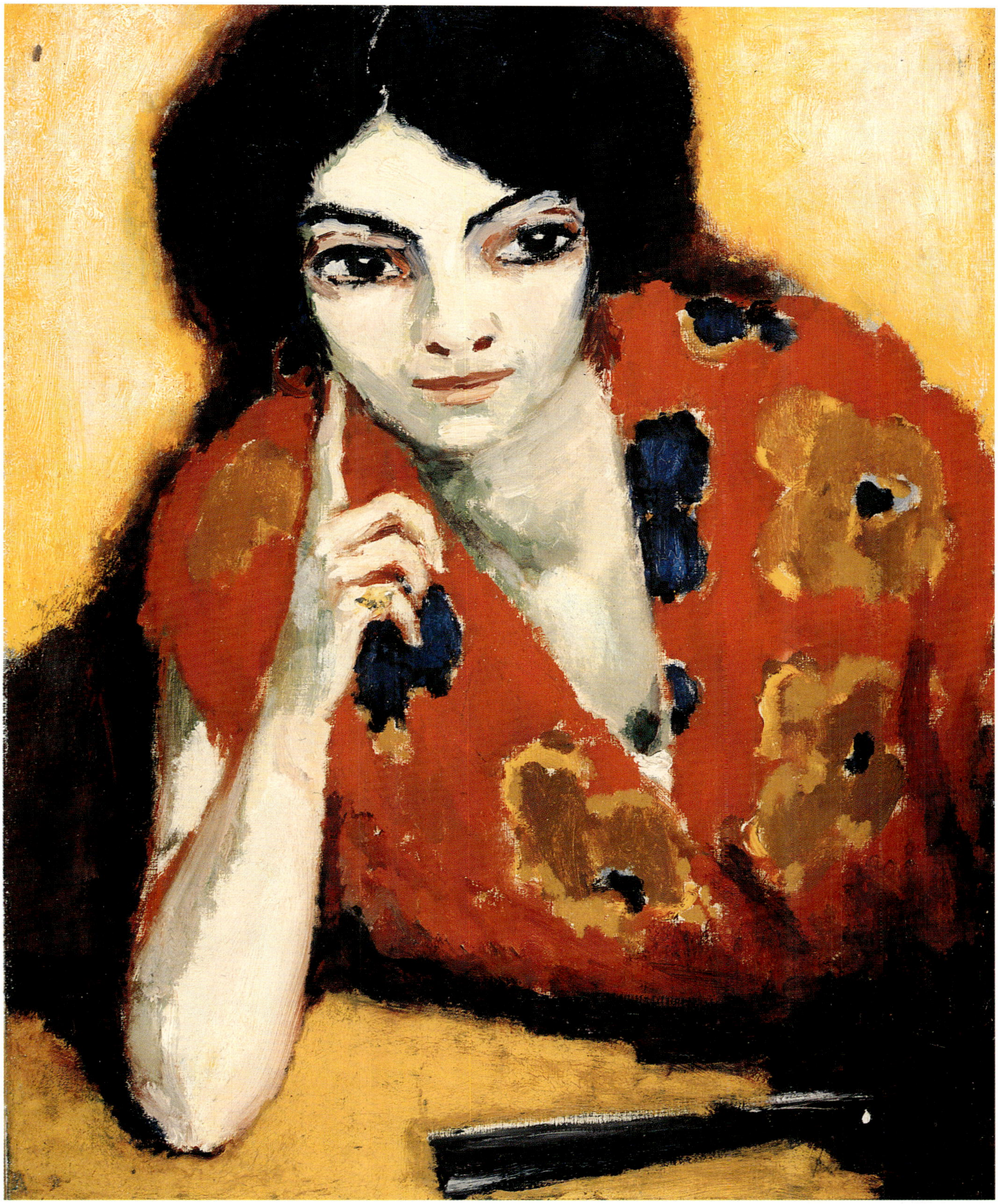

135. *Le doigt sur la joue*, 1911

Artistic Milieu

1. Siebe J. ten Cate (Sneek 1858-1908 Paris)
Rue d'Alsace (Besneeuwde straat – Snowy street), 1891
Pen with black ink, grey wash, white gouache
325 x 403 mm
Signed and dated lower left in pen with black ink: *ten Cate/91*
Special features: blind-stamped watermark at left edge: *[A]NNONAY MONTGOLFIER A ST MAR[TIN]*;
remains of border line above and below
PROVENANCE:
Mrs. Destree Vermeulen; Vereeniging tot het vormen van eene Openbare Verzameling van Hedendaagsche Kunst te Amsterdam (Society for the Formation of a Public Collection of Contemporary Art in Amsterdam), February 1944; Stedelijk Museum Amsterdam, 1962 (gift of the Vereeniging tot het vormen van eene Openbare Verzameling van Hedendaagsche Kunst te Amsterdam)
LITERATURE:
Amsterdam (Stedelijk Museum catalogue) 1948, no. 104
COLLECTION:
Stedelijk Museum, Amsterdam, Inv. A 21903

2. Siebe J. ten Cate (Sneek 1858-1908 Paris)
Après le bal (After the ball), 1900
Pastel on paper on canvas
335 x 240 mm
Signed lower centre in black chalk: *ten Cate/1900*
PROVENANCE:
Auction Berne, Galerie Dobiaschofsky, 9/10 May-6/7 June 1969, no. 65 (fig); auction Düsseldorf, Kunsthaus Peter Karbstein, 62. *Kunstauktion*, 29 February 1996, no. 131 (fig.); Kunsthandel Loutron, Amsterdam 1996; N.T. Scheeres, Amsterdam, 1996
COLLECTION:
N.T. Scheeres, Amsterdam

1.
C. Snabilié, 'Siebe ten Cate', *De Amsterdammer*, no. 1509, 27 May 1906, p. 7; R., 'Siebe ten Cate', *Nieuws van den Dag*, 15 December 1908.

2.
B. de Montgolfier et al, *Les catalogues d'art et d'histoire du Musée Carnavalet III. Pastels du Musée Carnavalet*, in *Bulletin du Musée Carnavalet*, 35 (1982), nos 1-2, pp. 16-23.

3.
S. (Ch. Snabilié), 'Fransche brieven', *Het Vaderland*, 18 February 1905.

4.
Anonymous cutting, April 1892, RKD The Hague; *Catalogus van schilderijen, pastels en gouaches door S.J. ten Cate*, Rotterdam (Art Club) April-May 1892, no. 64; *Marius Bauer, Siebe ten Cate, Philippe Zilcken*, The Hague (Pulchri Studio), October-November 1892, no. 75; see also Bulée (Ch. Snabilié), 'Siebe ten Cate', *Elsevier's Geïllustreerd Maandschrift*, 8 (1898), vol. 16, p. 487; Paris auction, Drouot (Hervé et al.), 19 January 1990, no. 61.

5.
C.L. ten Cate, *Genealogie van de Friese takken der (van oorsprong Doopsgezinde familie ten C(K)ate uit Borne*, Utrecht 1985, pp. 396-397.

Siebe J. ten Cate (Sneek 1858-1908 Paris)

The artist Siebe ten Cate, born in Sneek in 1858, is little known in the Netherlands. Having completed his artist's training at a number of schools in the Netherlands and Belgium, he left for Paris in 1883 where he became friends with Van Dongen at the end of the 1890s. (fig.) Ten Cate specialized in harbour scenes and cityscapes, mainly making a name for himself as an artist in France. [1] In order to be able to record cities other than just Paris he travelled throughout France – particularly in Normandy and Brittany – and the Netherlands, as well as other European countries. He sold his late-Impressionist cityscapes – a style similar to Pissarro – through famous Parisian art dealers such as Vollard, Goupil, Durand-Ruel and Bernheim-Jeune. Most of the works ended up in French collections; the Musée Carnavalet acquired ten pastel drawings and a canvas by him in 1900 from the Galerie des Peintres de Paris.[2] Ten Cate had regular exhibitions in Paris, some of which were with Durand-Ruel in 1891 and 1895, and Bernheim-Jeune in 1900 and 1901; from 1903 he was also represented at the Salon d'Automne. During his travels he retained his contacts with the Netherlands. He sent his work to the Exhibitions of Living Masters and exhibited with the Amsterdam dealers Van Wisselingh; in 1892 there was a Ten Cate exhibition in Rotterdam, The Hague and Amsterdam respectively. However, his name is not mentioned in books surveying nineteenth-century Dutch painting; on his death people regretted that he had been so little known in Holland. Only a few pieces ended up in Dutch public collections, such as the pen drawing *Rue d'Alsace* in the Stedelijk Museum Collection in Amsterdam.

Ten Cate preferred to paint his city or harbour scenes at twilight or dusk or under the grey light of the winter sky when buildings become reduced to blocks and passers-by stand out against them as dark silhouettes. Judging from his exhibitions and a few sales details, the public always liked Ten Cate's melancholic cityscapes and particularly his snow scenes. The writer Snabilié, who Ten Cate knew well, wrote in one of his 'Letters from Paris' that no sooner had it snowed heavily in the Netherlands and he had been informed of this by his family, than he picked up his 'travel bag and the paintbox that always stood ready' to journey to the north to paint 'the snow under a sombre winter sky.'[3] The drawing *Rue d'Alsace* from 1891, a street in a suburb of Paris near the Gare de l'Est, is an attractive early example of one such snow scene. The sheet is sober in technique. The light grey ink wash is thinly spread, over which have been added a few accents scratched with a pen and some sturdy, bristly strokes of white body colour to suggest snow that had already been pushed to the side of the road. By leaving parts of the originally light grey paper – though now faded to light brown – untouched, Ten Cate allowed it to become part of the image. The drawing is related, or identical to a picture (two more versions are known) that was exhibited in 1892 at the Rotterdam Art Club and later in The Hague Pulchri Studio. A pen drawing with the same title appears in the catalogue and was described by a critic as a wide street with snow: a heavy louring sky hangs over the street, everything seems covered with a leaden hue...in the distance a fiacre drives off, yellow and black; a piece of metropolitan loneliness..., summarized the reviewer.[4] It is a mood that dominates many of Ten Cate's city scenes. His tonal depictions, which are also reminiscent of the Dutch Hague School – Ten Cate took extra lessons from Anton Mauve – rarely produce a cheerful street scene. The figures in the surrounding buildings are shown as insignificant forms moving in indeterminate directions; they are almost always alone. A similar mood also dominates the beautiful pastel *Après le bal* in which a woman (possibly a demimondaine) in evening dress is drawn standing beside a waiting carriage. In the background and beside her stand various men in top hats, though none of them seems to be her partner; although she appears to be the centre of attention – even the newspaper vendor is looking towards her – she is leaving the ball alone. The picture has been inspired by the work of Steinlen who depicted in a similar way the loneliness of the big city, the spots of light in the night and dark silhouettes. Ten Cate died in 1908 from a heart attack; he was found dead in the street one night – it was said in the snow.[5] His pastels and drawings deserve a great deal more attention than they have hitherto received.

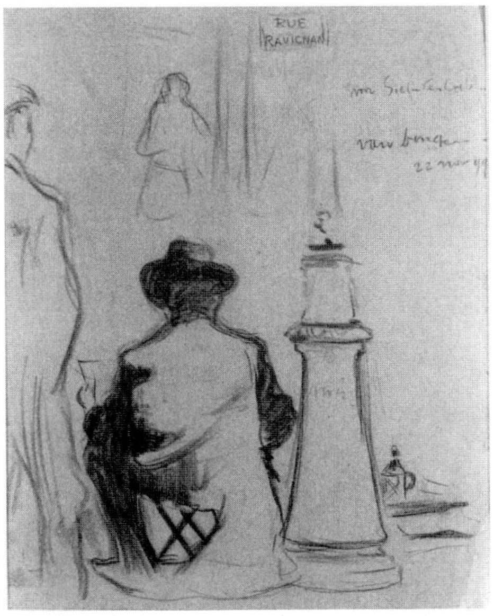

Kees van Dongen
Siebe ten Cate, Rue Ravignan, 1899
Black chalk, 260 x 220 mm

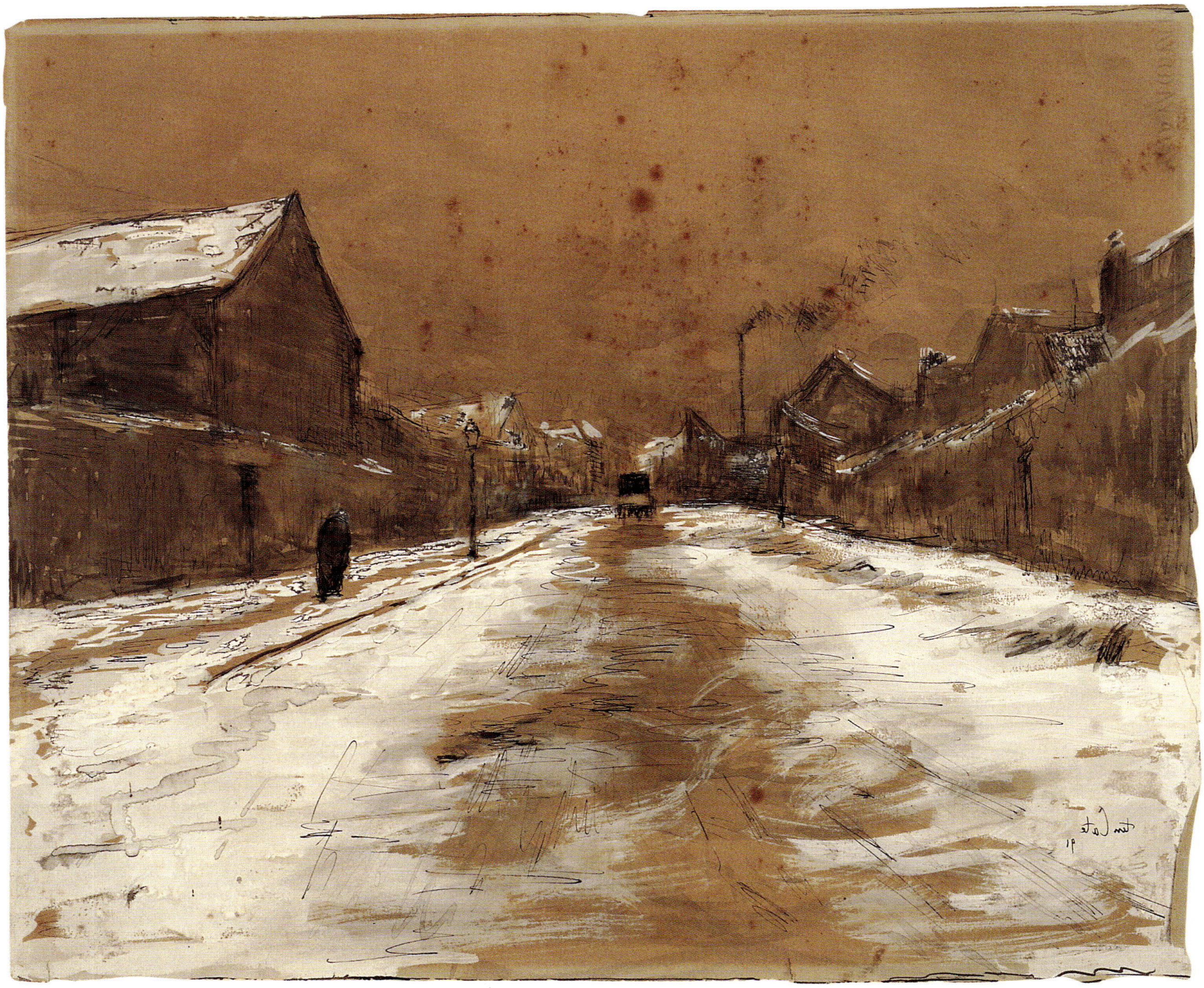

1. Siebe J. ten Cate, *Rue d'Alsace* (Snowy street), 1891

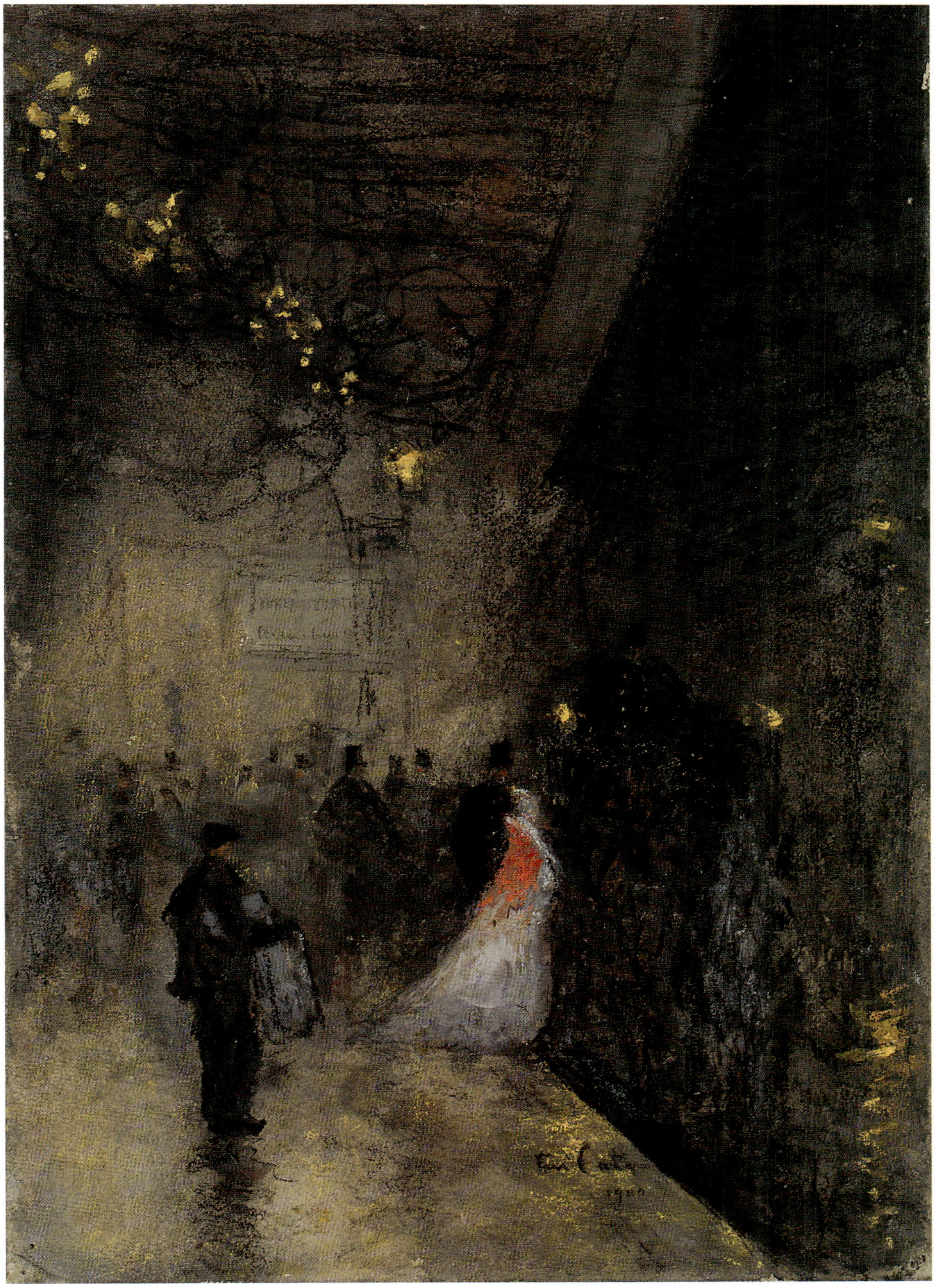

2. Siebe J. ten Cate, *Après le bal*, 1900

Théophile-Alexandre Steinlen (Lausanne 1859-1923 Paris)

Théophile-Alexandre Steinlen, who was Swiss by birth, went to Paris in 1881 where he took up residence in Montmartre. Many artists were attracted to the bohemian atmosphere of this district at the time and this part of Paris developed into an important social and entertainment centre. Steinlen's arrival in Paris coincided with the liberalization of press laws which greatly assisted the rise of the illustrated magazine. In Paris, Steinlen initially worked as a fabric designer in a drawing studio. In the evenings he would frequent the *café-chantant* Le Chat Noir with his compatriot Rudolphe Salis who helped him win his first commission to design a poster. From 1882, Salis published a paper *Le Chat Noir*, for which Steinlen, introduced by the artist Adolphe Willette, drew his first illustrations in 1883. After Salis had moved to larger premises, the room at Le Chat Noir was taken over by the singer Aristide Bruant, who had previously worked for Salis. Here Bruant founded his bar Le Mirliton and asked Steinlen to become the chief illustrator for the publication of the same name, *Le Mirliton*. Under the stimulating influence of this friendship and Bruant's songs, which told of life in Montmartre, Steinlen developed the realistic and socially engaged style of drawing which was to gain him a prominent position in the art of illustration in his day.

In the 1890s, as well as for Bruant, Steinlen also drew illustrations for the revolutionary paper *Le Chambard Socialiste* and from 1891 to 1900 for the daily *Gil Blas illustré*. In these years Steinlen drew almost all the cover designs for this colour supplement which came out once a week with the daily newspaper *Gil Blas* – a total of almost 700 drawings. If Steinlen's illustrations for the *Chambard Socialiste* had an obvious left-wing tone, for *Gil Blas* he drew more general social subjects, for which his sources were the literary contributions published in the magazine. The drawing *Ballade d'hiver* from 1896 illustrated a prose poem by Gustave Coquiot about the persevering insistence of prostitutes soliciting in the winter cold: 'Chaud, chaud, il fait chaud dans nos galetas!.' The coarse black chalk lines, accentuated in ink, and the extreme foreshortening forcefully portray the lot of these women and the gloom of the winter night. The colourful depiction *Sortie du théâtre* in black chalk and pastel, was published in 1896, as was the cover of the *Gils Blas illustré*. (fig.) Again this is a scene from Parisian night life, though this one is of two smart, upper-class, married women who in a moment of weakness, fall in love with another man – at least this is how the scene was described by the writer Maurice Leblanc in the same number. The drawings tell us about Steinlen's way of working: they are almost all the same size as the illustrations in *Gil Blas* and were barely reduced in printing. Both images were composed in black chalk and printed according to the artist's instructions in two support colours on the cover. The drawing *Sortie de théâtre* was richly coloured in by Steinlen – after it had been returned by the publisher – and sold as a separate sheet. He did this with most of the illustrations made for *Gil Blas*.[2]

The black chalk drawing, *Les pauvres gens*, also an evening scene in the winter cold, was drawn by Steinlen for the first number of *L'Assiette au Beurre*, which appeared on 4 April 1901. The illustration takes up two pages and has been printed full-size, whereby the expressive effect of the black chalk has been retained. The distressing poverty, accentuated by the old woman's question 'are the prisons perhaps heated?', did not miss its artistic impact. The drawing *L'hiver* in the number on prostitution that Kees van Dongen drew for *L'Assiette au Beurre*, for which *Sur un banc* perhaps served as a study, (fig.) appears to have been modelled on this. Siebe ten Cate's winter scene of a lonely tramp on a bench (fig.) is related to Steinlen's work.

3. Théophile-Alexandre Steinlen (Lausanne 1859-1923 Paris)
Ballade d'hiver (Winter ballad), 1896
Black chalk, brush with black ink, white gouache
325 x 260 mm
Signed lower right in brush with black ink: *Steinlen*
Drawing for *Ballade d'hiver*, cover of *Gil Blas illustré*, 6 (1896), 15 March, no. 11
PROVENANCE:
Auction London, Sotheby's, *Impressionist and modern drawings and watercolours*, 3 December 1986, no. 409 (fig.); auction London, Sotheby's, *Impressionist and modern art...*, 26 October 1994, no. 283 (fig.); Kunsthandel Loutron, Amsterdam 1994; N.T. Scheeres, Amsterdam, 1994
LITERATURE:
Cate 1982, pp. 87-88
COLLECTION:
N.T. Scheeres, Amsterdam

4. Théophile-Alexandre Steinlen (Lausanne 1859-1923 Paris)
Les pauvres gens (Poor people), 1901
Blue and black chalk, watercolour
270 x 450 mm
Signed lower right in black chalk: *Steinlen*; annotated under the drawing in black chalk: *"...les prisons, est-ce que c'est chauffé?-"*
Drawing for *Hiver* (Winter), illustration in *L'Assiette au Beurre*, 1 (1901), 4 April, no. 1, pp. 4-5
PROVENANCE:
Musée Petit Palais, Geneva, 1959 (purchased from private collection)
EXHIBITIONS:
Retrospective Théophile-Alexandre Steinlen, Charleroi (Palais des Beaux-Arts); Lausanne (Musée Cantonal des Beaux-Arts), 1971; Basle (Kunsthalle), 1970-1971, no. 19. *Steinlen 1859-1923*, Moscow (Pushkin Museum); St Petersburg (Hermitage), 1977, p. 80 (fig.). *Théophile-Alexandre Steinlen, 1859-1923*, Berlin (Staatliche Kunsthalle); Hamburg (Ernst Barlach Haus), 1978 (fig.). *Théophile-Alexandre Steinlen, 1859-1923*, Warsaw (National Museums); Wroclaw; Bytom; Torun, 1978, p. 73 (fig.). *Th.-A. Steinlen*, Geneva (Petit Palais), 1979-1980. *Théophile-Alexandre Steinlen*, Turin (Musée d'Art Moderne), 1980, no. 144 (fig.). *Steinlen*, Oberhausen (Staatliche Kunsthalle), 1983-1984 (fig.). *Steinlen*, South African National Gallery; Johannesburg Art Gallery; The Consultancy; Durban Art Gallery, 1985, p. 31 (fig.). *Le bel héritage Th.A. Steinlen. Rétrospective 1885-1922*, Montreuil (Musée de l'Histoire Vivante), 1987, no. 313bis (fig.). *Steinlen*, Salzburg (Rupertinum), 1990 (fig.) *Steinlen*, Bilbao (Fine Arts Museum), 1991 (fig.). *Théophile-Alexandre Steinlen (1859-1923)*, Cork (Crawford Municipal Art Gallery); Dublin (Hugh Lane Municipal Gallery), 1993, p. 23. *Théophile-Alexandre Steinlen 1859-1923. Oeuvres du Musée du Petit Palais de Genève*, Toulouse (Musée Paul Dupuy), 1993, no. 55 (fig.) *La famille vue par les peintres – de Bazille à Picasso*, Geneva (Musée du Petit Palais), 1994 (fig.). *Steinlen-Paris um 1900*, Pfäffikon (Seedamm Kulturzentrum), 1995, p. 28
COLLECTION:
Petit Palais, Musée d'art Moderne, Geneva, Inv. 2095

1. S. Gill, 'Steinlen's Prints: Social Imagery in Late 19th-century Graphic Art', *The Print Collector's Newsletter*, 10 (1979), March-April, pp. 8-12; Cate 1982; Gill 1982.
2. M.J. Brusse, 'Over de prentkunst van Steinlen', *De Gids*, 68 (1904), vol. 2, p. 508. For other examples from the collection of Henri Beraldi, see also exhib.cat., *Théophile-Alexandre Steinlen. 20 drawings for Gil Blas illustré 1892-1895*, The Hague (Art Dealers Ivo Bouwman); London (Stoppenbach & Delestre) 1995.

5. Théophile-Alexandre Steinlen (Lausanne 1859-1923 Paris)
Sortie du théâtre (On leaving the theatre), 1896
Black chalk, brush with black ink, coloured chalk
Signed lower right in brush with black ink: *Steinlen*
335 x 265 mm
Drawing for *Deux honnêtes femmes* (Two gentlewomen), cover *Gil Blas illustré*, 6 (1896), 8 May, no. 19

EXHIBITIONS:

Steinlen 1859-1923, Moscow (Pushkin-Museum); St. Petersburg (Hermitage), 1977, p. 58 (fig.). *Théophile Alexandre Steinlen, 1859-1923*, Berlin (Staatliche Kunsthalle); Hamburg (Ernst Barlach Haus), 1978, p. 93 (fig.). *Théophile-Alexandre Steinlen, 1859-1923*, Warsaw (Musées Nationaux), Wroclaw; Bytom; Torun, 1978. *Th.-A. Steinlen*, Geneva (Petit Palais), 1979-1980. *Théophile-Alexandre Steinlen*, Turin (Musée d'Art Moderne), 1980, no. 142 (fig.). *Théophile-Alexandre Steinlen*, New Jersey (Rutgers University Art Gallery), 1982-1983, no. 194 (fig.). *Steinlen*, Oberhausen (Staatliche Kunst Halle), 1983-1984 (fig.). *Steinlen*, Osaka (Museum Daimaru); Tokyo (Shibuya Parca part I); Kamakura (Museum of Modern Art), 1985, no. 51 (fig.). *Le bel héritage. Steinlen retrospective 1885-1922*, Montreuil (Musée de l'Histoire Vivante), 1987, no. 208 (fig.). *Steinlen*, Salzburg (Rupertinum), 1990 (fig.). *Steinlen*, Bilbao (Musée des Beaux-Arts), 1991 (fig.). *Théophile-Alexandre Steinlen (1859-1923)*, Cork (Crawford Municipal Art Gallery); Dublin (Hugh Lane Municipal Gallery), 1993, p. 2 (fig.), p. 23. *Théophile-Alexandre Steinlen 1859-1923. Oeuvres du Musée du Petit Palais de Genève*, Toulouse (Musée Paul Dupuy), 1993, no. 34 (fig.). *La Famille vue par les peintres-de Bazille à Picasso*, Geneva (Musée du Petit Palais) 1994 (fig.). *Steinlen-Paris um 1900*, Pfäffikon (Seedamm Kulturzentrum), 1995, cover. *Montmartre vivant – de Toulouse Lautrec à Utrillo*, Geneva (Musée du Petit Palais), 1996, p. 21.

COLLECTION:

Petit Palais, Musée d'art Moderne, Geneva, Inv. 3941

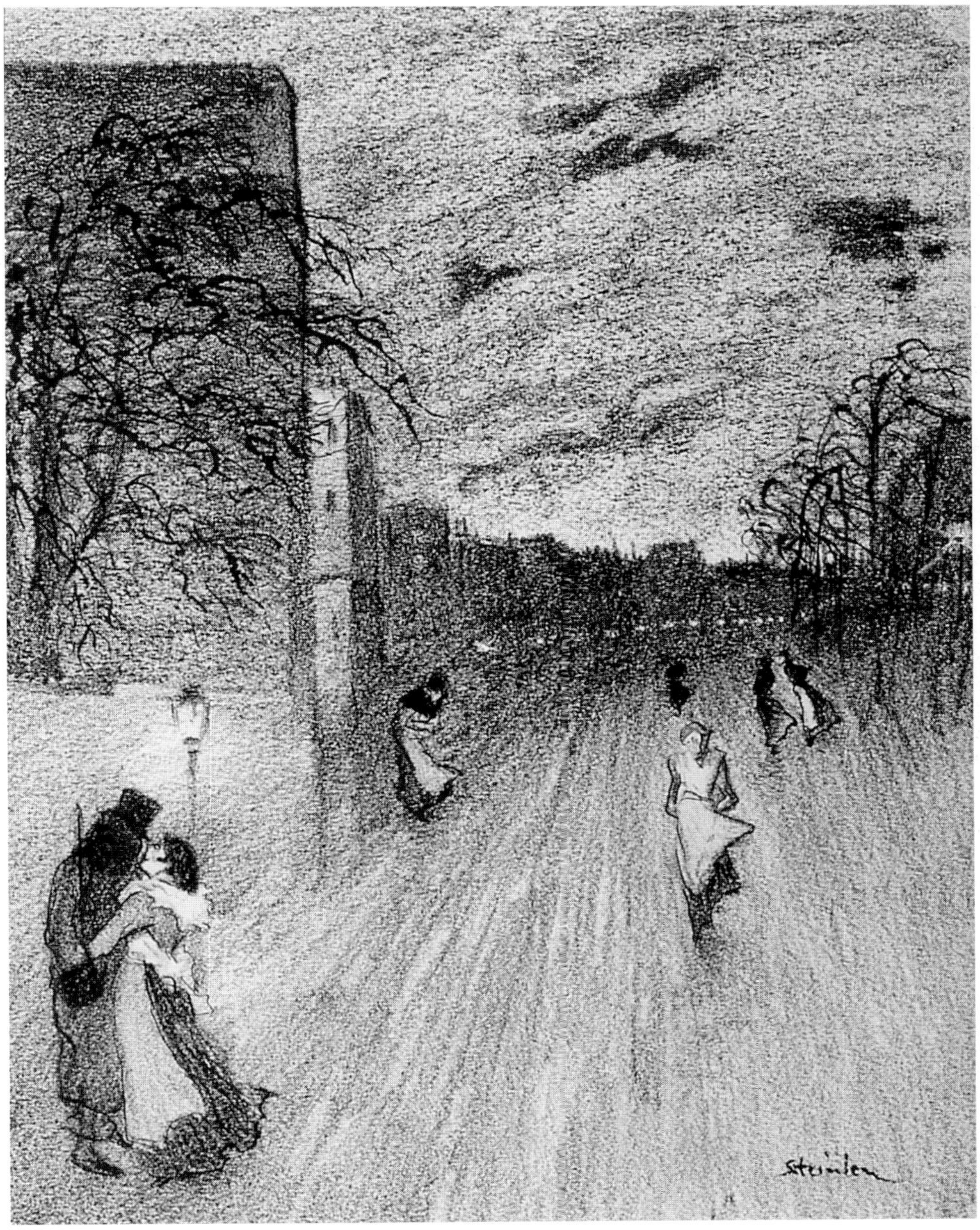

3. Théophile-Alexandre Steinlen, *Ballade d'hiver*, 1896

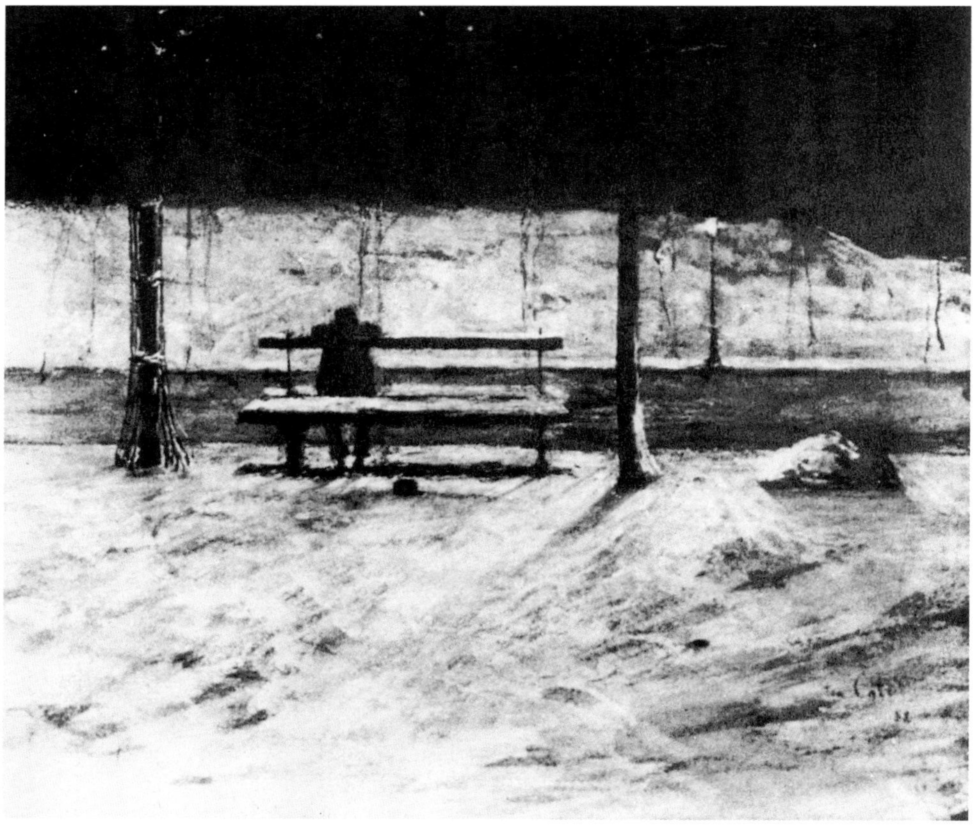

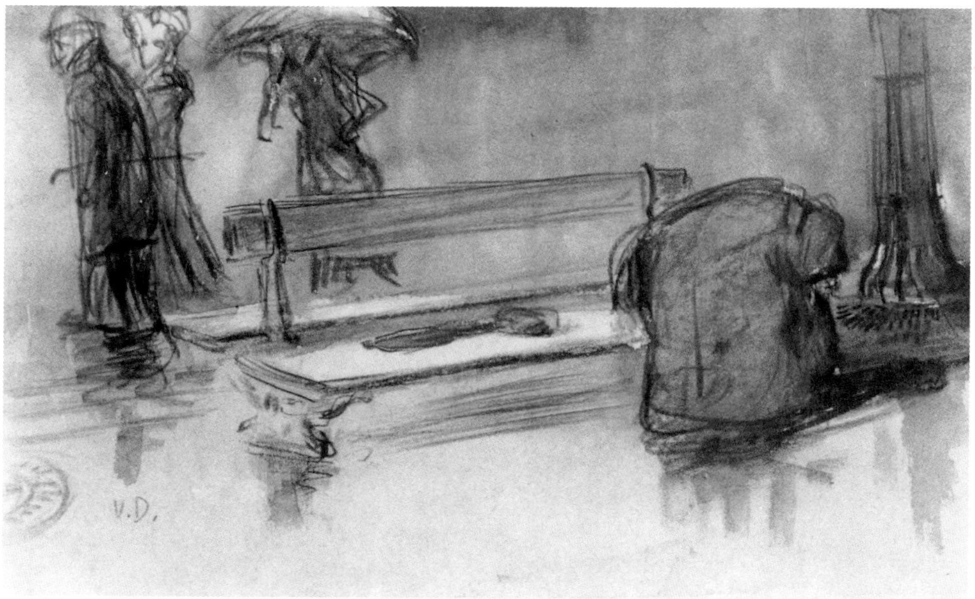

Siebe ten Cate, *Vagabond sur le banc en hiver*, 1888
Pastel, gouache, 380 x 460 mm

Kees van Dongen, *Sur un banc*, 1901
Black chalk, watercolour, 230 x 380 mm

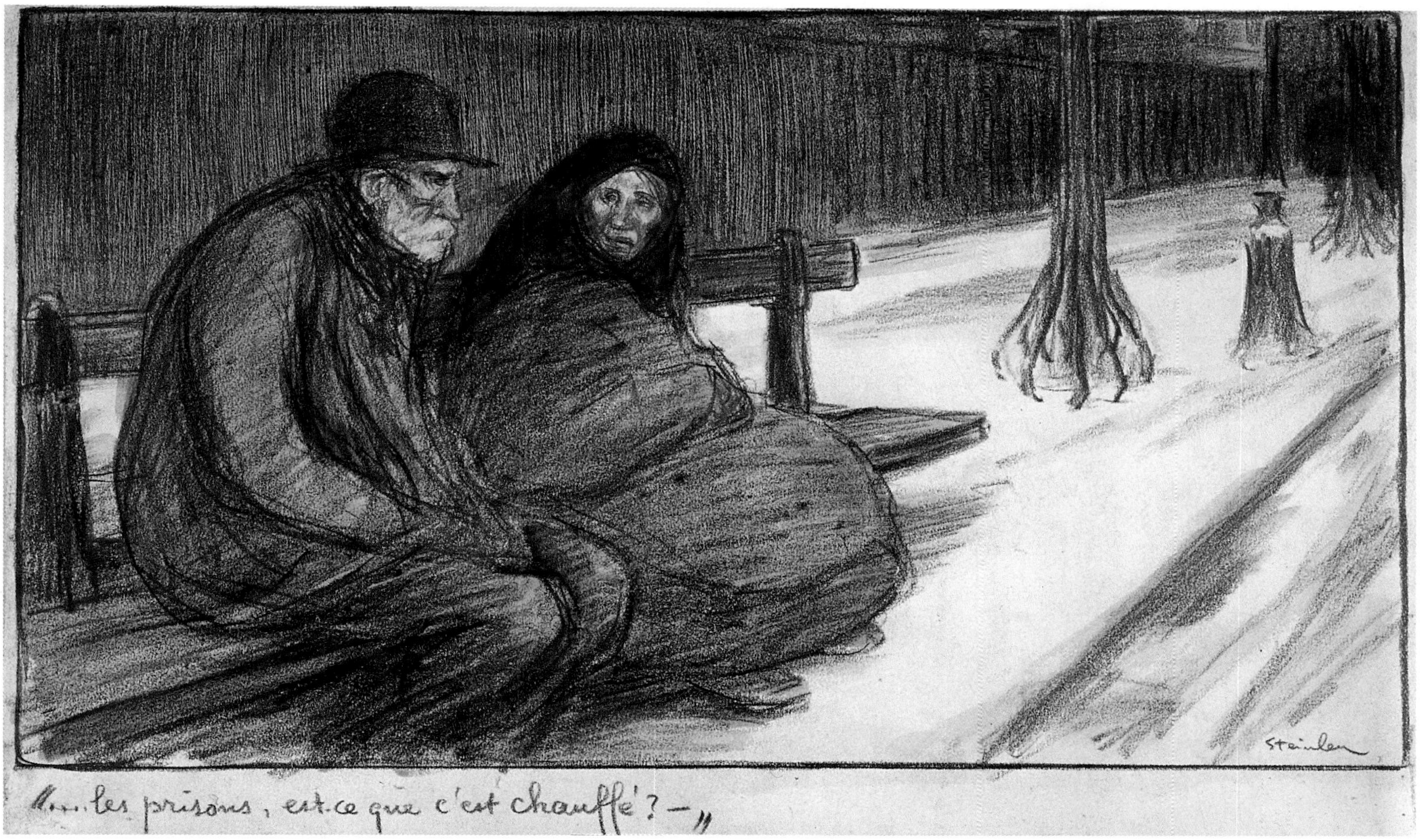

4. Théophile-Alexandre Steinlen, *Les pauvres gens*, 1901

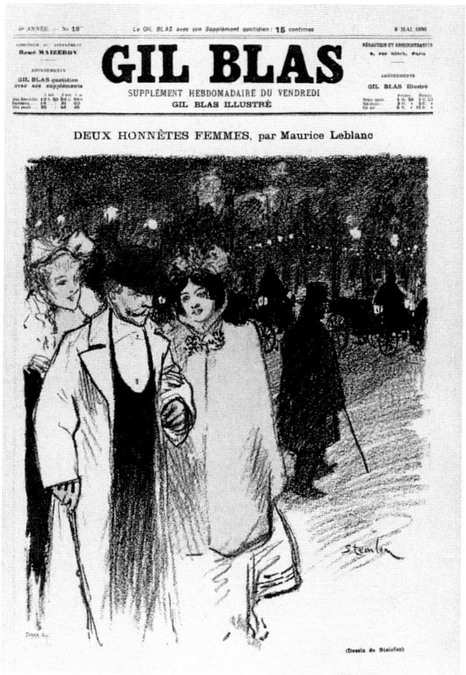

Th.A. Steinlen
Deux honnêtes femmes, 1896
Cover for *Gil Blas illustré*, no. 19, 8 May 1896

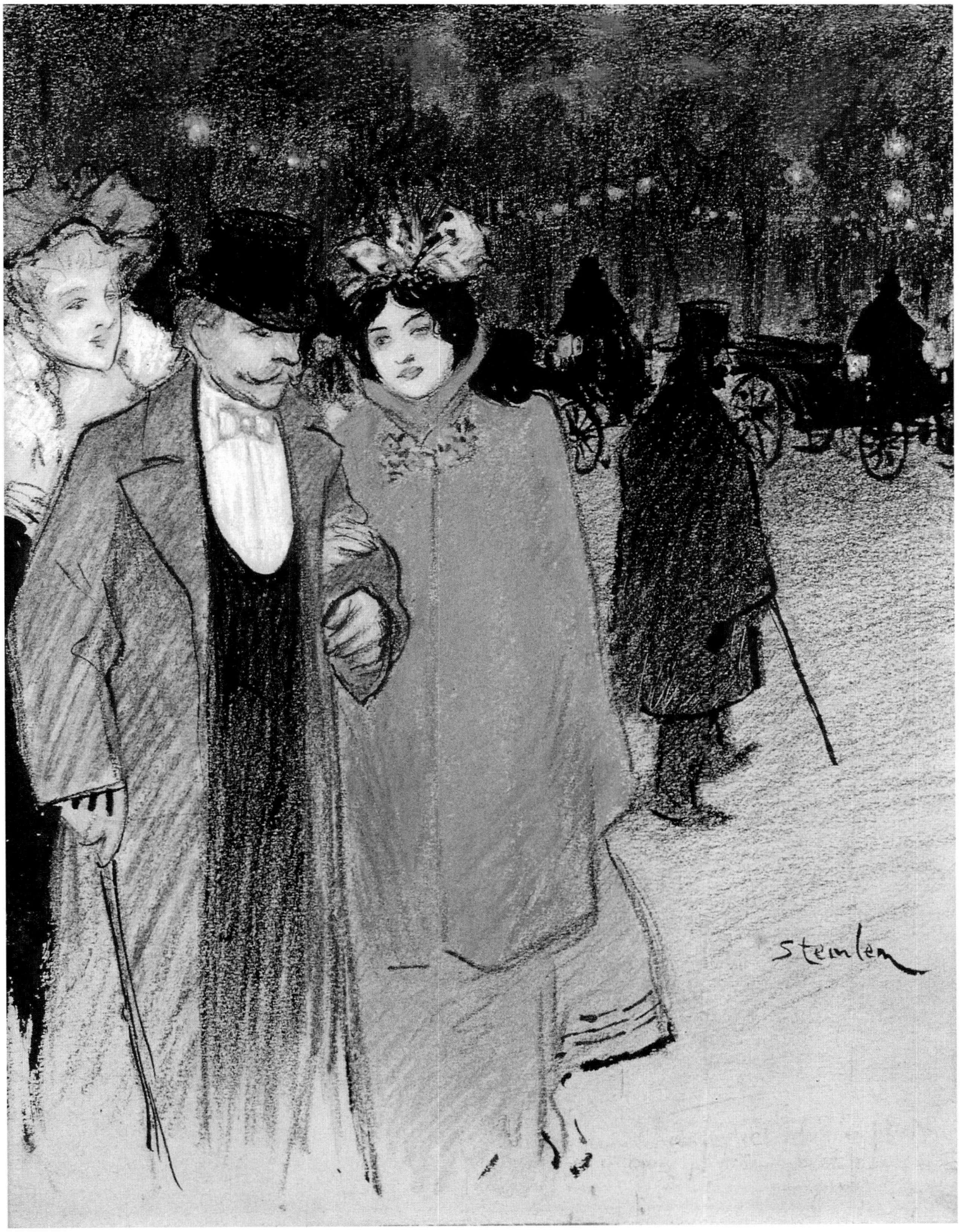

5. Théophile-Alexandre Steinlen, *Sortie du théâtre*, 1896

6.

Martinus Schildt (Rotterdam 1867-1921 Rotterdam)
Oude vrouw (Old woman), c. 1900
Watercolour over pencil sketch, black chalk
346 x 493 mm
Signed lower left in brown watercolour: *M. Schildt.*

PROVENANCE:
J.P. van der Schilden (1851-1925); Boymans Museum, Rotterdam, 1921 (gift of J.P. van der Schilden)

LITERATURE:
Wolf 1901, p. 158 (fig.); Hannema 1922, p. 3; Hannema 1927, no. 836

COLLECTION:
Boijmans Van Beuningen Museum, Rotterdam, Inv. M.S. I

1.
Prize for *Washer women* at the Exhibition of Living Masters in Amsterdam in 1899, the canvas he then submitted to the World Exhibition in Paris; the Rotterdam Academy Prize for the painting *Contentment* in 1895.

2.
Wolf 1901, p. 158.

Martinus Schildt (Rotterdam 1867-1921 Rotterdam)

Not many facts are know about the artists who were working in Rotterdam in the nineteenth and early twentieth century. Even today, little art-historical attention is paid to them, certainly when compared with the number of publications dedicated to their colleagues who were working in Amsterdam or The Hague. To a certain extent this is justified. Talented artists like Kees van Dongen or later, Willem de Kooning, left the city early on. Those who remained behind like Martinus Schildt or Johan Mastenbroek – who were friends of Van Dongen's – made a name for themselves in their own time but are not what we now consider to be important masters. Schildt, for instance, had international success at the Paris World Exhibition in 1900 with a truly Dutch painting: two women busily washing, standing in front of large wash tubs enveloped in steam. The canvas won him a silver medal. The following year he submitted it for a large international exhibition in Munich where it won gold and was acquired for the Neue Pinakothek.

Martinus Schildt trained as a lithographer and varnisher. Between 1880 and 1886 he went to evening classes at the Rotterdam Art Academy. In the years 1893-97 he received a royal scholarship which enabled him to fully concentrate on his art. He exhibited at the Exhibitions of Living Masters, was a member of various Dutch artists' societies and also won a number of prizes for paintings submitted to exhibitions in the Netherlands. Schildt had a preference for poverty-stricken interiors – modelled on seventeenth-century examples – and old, wrinkled, working-class characters in worn-out clothes. He journeyed to rural areas in Drenthe in the east and Brabant in the south in search of this atmosphere, where he found 'interesting spots' such as the shabby interior of a polder worker's house with a 'curious little bedstead with an old, faded curtain in front which makes it look so attractive.' With similar attention he made a study of the head of an old woman which, according to the same reviewer, typified 'the patient suffering of an old woman.' This is highly questionable. The watercolour *Old woman* is skilfully executed and the quality of it stands out from the rest of his work, but the head would sooner appear to be have been painted for the sake of the tone and character – as grey and wrinkled as a worn-out rag – rather than for the sentiments involved. The social element recorded by Van Gogh in Drenthe and Brabant is missing from Schildt's work. This might also explain why Schildt, after a promising beginning, never developed and remained merely technically able: he appears not to have had the artistic insight or desire for something more. Perhaps he too should have left the Netherlands.

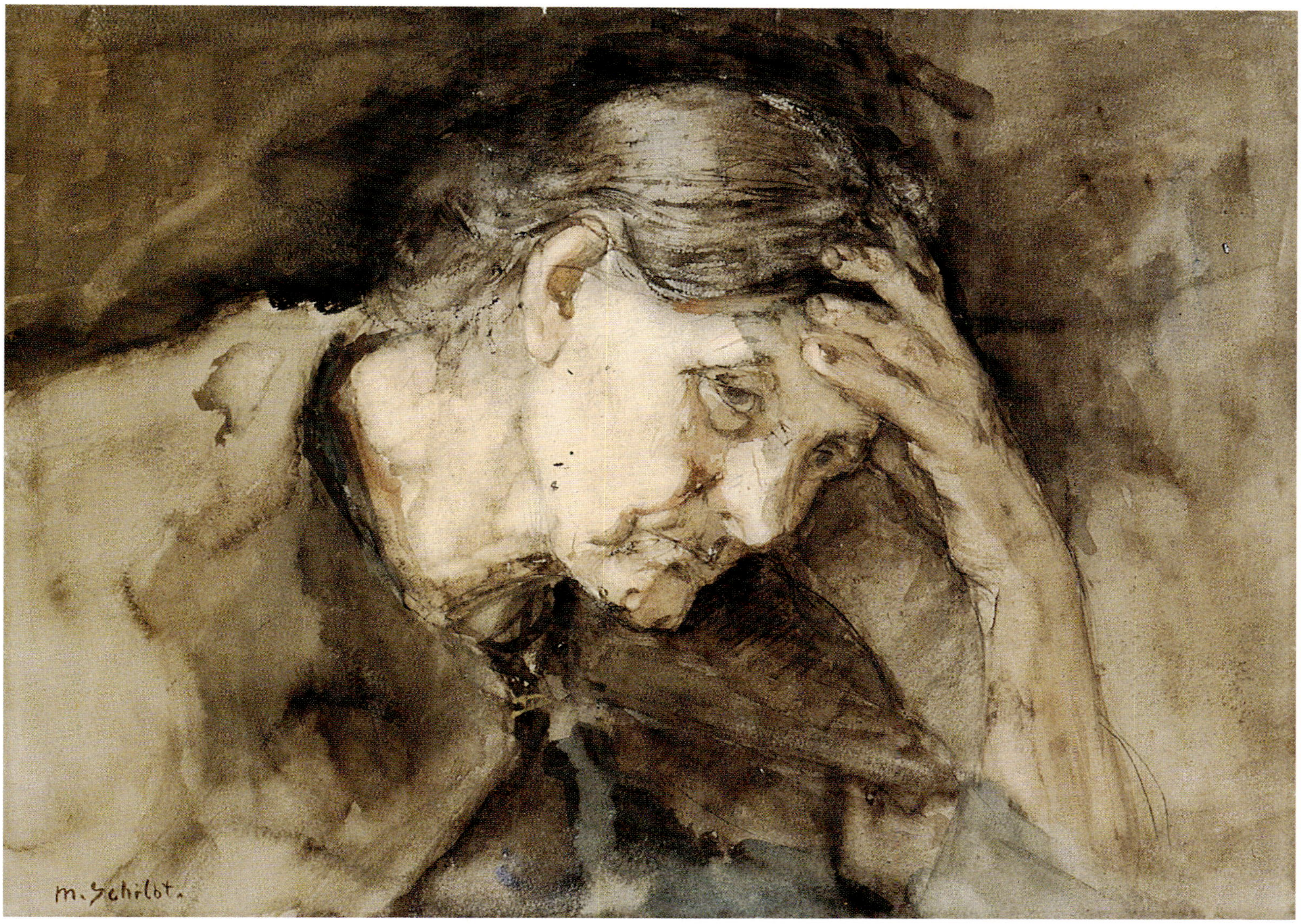

6. Martinus Schildt, *Old woman*, ca. 1900

7. Pablo Picasso (Malaga 1881- 1973 Antibes)
Femme assise à la terrasse d'un café (Woman sitting at a café terrace), 1901
Oil on paper on panel
49 x 33 cm/53 x 35 cm
Signed upper left: *Picasso*; and annotated: *a Sabartès* (?)

PROVENANCE:
D.G. van Beuningen (1877-1955), Rotterdam, 1935; Boymans Museum, Rotterdam, 1935 (gift of D.G. van Beuningen)

EXHIBITIONS:
Picasso. Festival de Lyon-Charbonnières, Lyons (Musée de Lyon), 1953, no. 6. *Picasso, peintures 1900-1955*, Paris (Musée des Arts Décoratifs), 1955, no. 3 (fig.). *Picasso 1900-1955*, Munich (Haus der Kunst); Cologne (Rheinisches Museum Köln-Deutz); Hamburg, 1955-1956, no. 6. *Musées d'art vivants*, Liège (Musée des Beaux-Arts), 1964, no. 53 (fig.). *Schilderkunst uit La belle époque*, Laren (Singer Museum), 1964, no. 56 (fig.). *Picasso*, Amsterdam (Stedelijk Museum), 1967, no. 1 (fig.). *Picasso-udstillingen*, Humblebaek, Louisiana, 1968, no. 3. *Der junge Picasso*, Berne (Kunstmuseum), 1984, no. 122 *Impressionisme: een schone kijk. De stroming en de aanloop*, Rotterdam (Boijmans Van Beuningen Museum), 1992, no. 90 (fig.). *Boijmans modern art masterpiece exhibition*, Tokyo (Isetan Museum of Art), 1995; Kochi (The Museum of Art); Matsue (Shimane Prefectural Museum); Osaka (Daimaru Museum, Umeda), 1995-96, no. 49 (fig.).

LITERATURE:
Daix 1966, p. 165, no. V.14; Ebbinge Wubben 1963, no. 1688; Ebbinge Wubben 1972, no. 232 (fig.); Boymans Museum Annual Report 1935, p. 20 (fig.); P. Cabanne, *Le roman des grands collectionneurs*, Paris, 1961, p. 75

COLLECTION:
Boijmans Van Beuningen Museum, Rotterdam, Inv. 1688

Henri de Toulouse-Lautrec (Albi 1864-1901 Château de Malromé) Pablo Picasso (Malaga 1881-1973 Antibes)

Kees van Dongen was always sparing with details about his relationships with other artists and their possible influences on his work. In later interviews Van Dongen usually gave evasive answers in reply to questions about artists he had identified himself with at the beginning of his career. The only people he sometimes named were Matisse, Picasso and Maurice de Vlaminck. A few times he referred to artists like Renoir, Degas and Toulouse-Lautrec as famous artists he had admired from a distance. [1] However, he hardly ever spoke of their work, as though he were not informed enough about it. In connection with a portrait of La Goulue from 1903 – the period when she performed as a belly dancer at travelling circuses where Van Dongen worked as a handyman – he claimed that he had rolled up Toulouse-Lautrec posters without realizing what they were.[2] Van Dongen was probably referring here to two large paintings Lautrec had made for La Goulue's circus tent in 1895, one of which referred to her early days of glory as a can-can dancer at the Moulin Rouge.[3]

It is true that Henri de Toulouse-Lautrec exhibited very little during the last few years of his life, but Van Dongen would certainly have been familiar with some of his work, such as the large canvas of the interior of the Moulin Rouge with the dancing Valentin le Désossé, that hung in the foyer of the dance hall. Furthermore, he would not have missed the homage paid to Lautrec on his death in September 1901. Ten works by Toulouse-Lautrec were on show at the Salon des Indépendants of 1902 and in May of that year there was an important retrospective at Durand-Ruel where 200 of the artist's pieces, including the famous *Elles* album were exhibited. According to Dortu's oeuvre catalogue, the red-chalk drawing *Sleeping woman* was also included. This drawing served as a preparatory study for the litho *Le sommeil* that Toulouse-Lautrec made shortly after the *Elles* album in 1896 which was also published by August Pelletin. The *Elles* album, which comprises eleven lithos, shows women making their toilet, lying in bed, in the company of a male admirer or another woman, a 'madam' or mother who is caring for her prostitute daughter. The series has always been seen as a record of daily life in one of the brothels visited by Toulouse-Lautrec, though nowadays it is thought that the lithos were based on drawings made from the model by the artist in his studio.[4] This is also true of the beautiful *Sleeping woman* in the Boijmans Van Beuningen Collection. Seeing the group *Elles* at Durand-Ruel, and the drawings associated with it, would have inspired Van Dongen to make such studies as *Sieste* (1902) and the intimate sheets made in 1903 about 'woman'.

Another exhibition that wouldn't have escaped Van Dongen's notice was that of Picasso in June-July 1901 at Galerie Vollard. This was the main reason for Picasso's second visit to the French capital where he had been once before in 1900 for the World Exhibition.[5] His friend Manach, who promoted his interests, had arranged the exhibition for him at Vollard's. Picasso arrived in the middle of May and the opening was planned for 24 June. Picasso took a number of canvases with him from Barcelona, but most of the work was painted in the remaining couple of weeks he spent in Paris. This added up to a total of 64 paintings, pastels and watercolours, alongside a number of unknown drawings. The scenes painted by Picasso are mainly concerned with Parisian social life and entertainment – prostitutes, absinthe drinkers, theatre artistes – as well as various portraits and cityscapes. *Femme assise à la terrasse d'un café* from 1901, in oil on paper and mounted on panel, was very probably made shortly after the exhibition. It is painted with loose marks in a style inspired by Toulouse-Lautrec. The model

1.
Anonymous, 'A lively link to *Les Fauves*', *Life*, 28 March 1960, p. 45; Chapsal 1963, p. 45.

2.
Note A.B. Loosjes-Terpstra, 12 October 1954, Loosjes-Terpstra archive.

3.
Frèches 1991, pp. 270-277 for La Goulue.

4.
Frèches 1991, pp. 436-453: *Elles*; pp. 454-455: *Le sommeil*; on a visits to a brothels by Lautrec, idem, pp. 406-411.

5.
Richardson 1991, pp. 193-207.

8. Henri de Toulouse Lautrec,
(Albi 1864-1901 Château de Malromé)
Slapende vrouw (Sleeping woman), c. 1896
Red chalk on blue laid paper
377 x 480 mm
Signed lower right in red chalk: *HTLautrec*
Special features: watermark ED&Cie in brackets

PROVENANCE:
F. Koenigs (L1023a), Haarlem, 1929; D.G. van Beuningen (1877-1955), Rotterdam, 1940; Gift of D.G. van Beuningen to the Boijmans Museum Foundation; Boijmans Van Beuningen Museum, Rotterdam

EXHIBITIONS:
Salon annuel, Brussels (La Libre Esthétique/Musée Moderne), 1902, no. 292. *Henri de Toulouse-Lautrec*, Paris (Galeries Durand-Ruel), 1902, no. 134. *Fransche meesters uit de XIXe eeuw, teekeningen, aquarellen, pastels*, Amsterdam (Paul Cassirer), 1938, no. 78. *Tekeningen van Fransche meesters 1800-1900*, Amsterdam (Stedelijk Museum), 1946, no. 181. *Toulouse-Lautrec*, Brussels (Paleis voor Schone Kunsten/Palais des Beaux-Arts); Amsterdam (Stedelijk Museum), 1947, no. 109 (fig.). *Le dessin français de Fouquet à Cézanne*, Paris (Musée du Louvre); Brussels (Palais des Beaux-Arts); Rotterdam (Museum Boijmans), 1949-1950, no. 214 (fig.). *Dessins du XVe au XIXe siècle, Musée Boijmans de Rotterdam*, Paris (Bibliothèque Nationale), 1952, no. 148 (fig.). *Le dessin de Toulouse-Lautrec aux cubistes*, Paris (Musée d'Art Moderne), 1954, no. 206. *Il disegno francese da Fouquet a Toulouse-Lautrec*, Rome (Palazzo di Venezia); Milan (Palazzo Reale), 1959-60, no. 206 (fig.). *Le dessin français dans les collections Hollandaises*, Paris (Institut Néerlandais); Amsterdam (Rijksmuseum), 1964. *Henri de Toulouse-Lautrec*, Vienna (Österreichisches Museum für angewandte Kunst), 1966, no. 61. *Henri de Toulouse-Lautrec*, Stockholm (National Museum) 1967-1968, no. 129 (fig.). *Lautrec; 'Elles'*, Albi (Musée d'Albi), 1976, no. 48 (fig.) *Nineteenth-century French drawings from the Museum Boijmans Van Beuningen*, Baltimore (The Baltimore Museum of Art), Los Angeles (Los Angeles County Museum of Art); Forth Worth (Kimbell Art Museum), 1986-1987, no. 95 (fig.). *Van Pisanello tot Cézanne. Keuze uit de verzameling tekeningen in het Museum Boijmans Van Beuningen, Rotterdam*, Rotterdam (Boijmans Van Beuningen Museum), 1990, no. 121 (fig.)

LITERATURE:
F. Daulte, *Le dessin français de Manet à Cézanne*, Lausanne 1954, no. 39 (fig.); M.G. Dortu, *Toulouse-Lautrec et son oeuvre*, vol. 6, New York 1971, no. D 4.100 (fig.); M.G. Dortu, J.A. Meric (eds.), *Henri de Toulouse-Lautrec: Dormeuses*, Paris 1976, no. 3; E. Haverkamp Begemann, *Vijf eeuwen tekenkunst*, Rotterdam 1957, no. 86 (fig.); Hoetink, 1968, no. 251 (fig.); A. Mongan, *Great drawings of all time, French thirteenth century to 1919*, Moskowitz (ed.), New York 1962, part 3, no. 835; R. Thompson *Toulouse-Lautrec*, London, 1977, fig. 63

COLLECTION:
Boijmans Van Beuningen Museum, Rotterdam, Inv. F II 1160

who posed for the painting was probably the actress Rose Demay whom Picasso also drew for an album commissioned by Gustave Coquiot, the author of the foreword in the catalogue of the Vollard exhibition. She also appears in a number of drawings by Picasso that were published in French magazines in 1902: *Le Journal pour Tous* and – seen together with the singer Polaire, with whom Picasso had a brief affair – in an edition of *Gil Blas illustré*. (fig.) Both drawings appeared in July, a couple of months after Picasso had returned to Barcelona. Perhaps he gave the painting *Femme assise à la terrasse d'un café* to his friend Jaime Sabartès who remained behind in Paris. The only partially legible inscription in the upper left corner of the canvas 'a Sabartès' may suggest this.

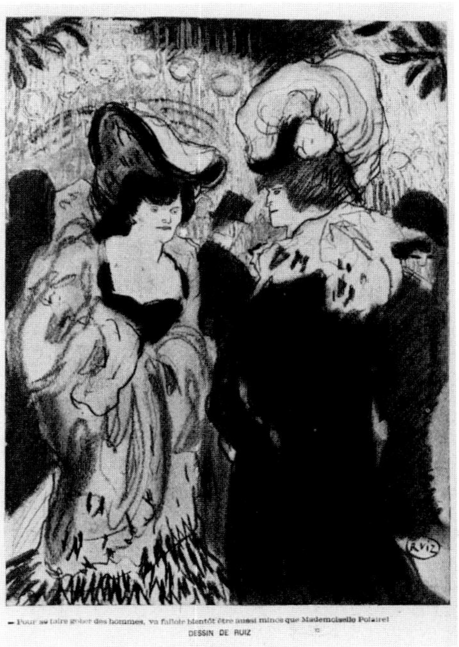

Pour se faire gober des hommes..., 1902
Illustration in *Gils Blas illustré*, no. 30, 25 July 1902

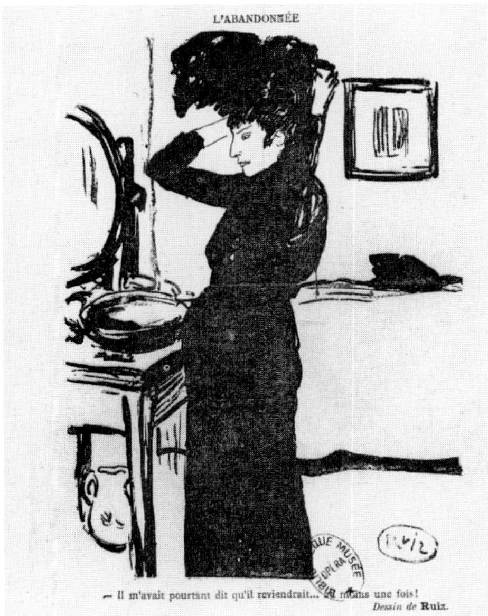

L'Abandonnée, 1902
Illustration in *Le Journal pour Tous*, no. 29, 17 July 1902, p. 3

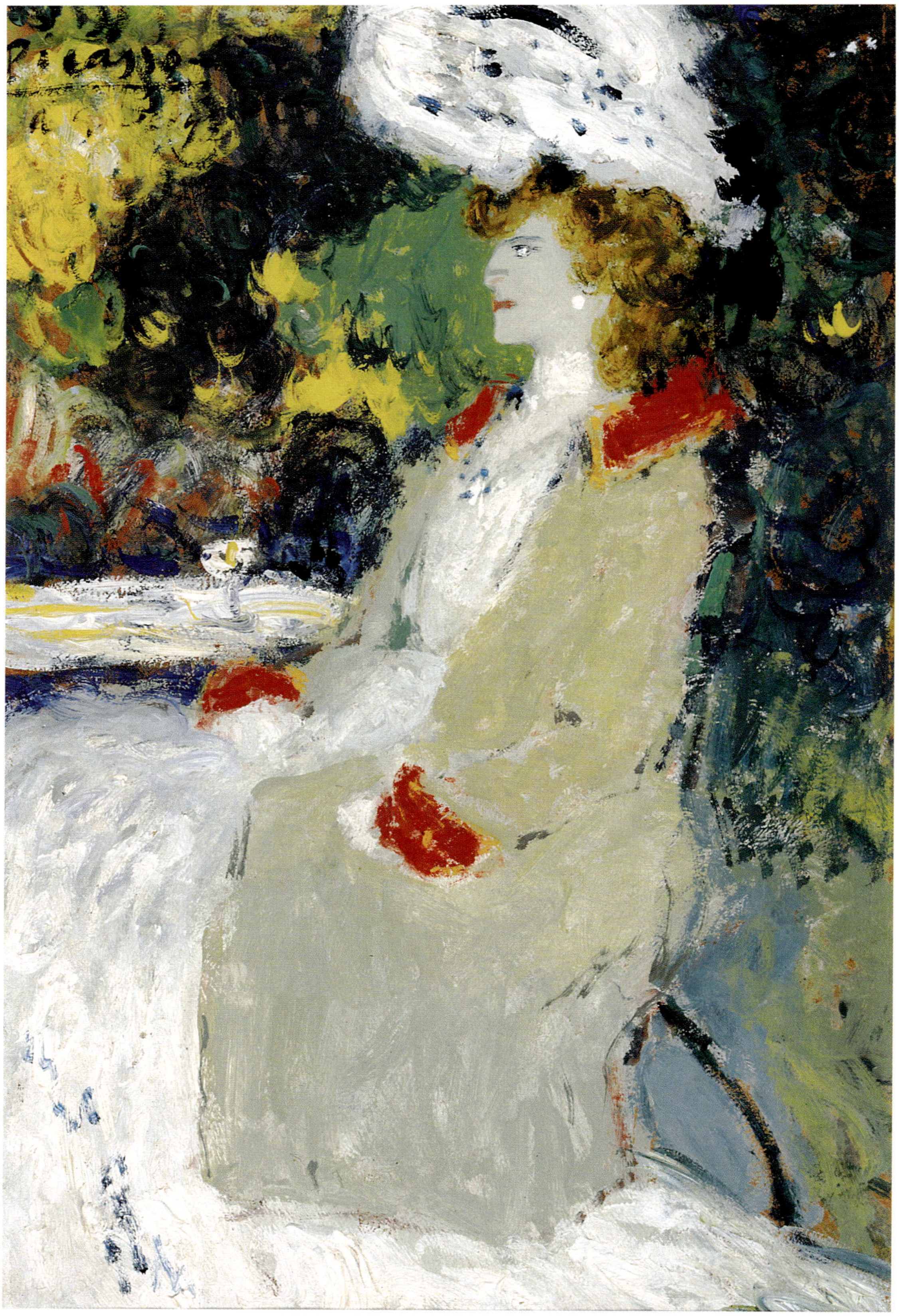

7. Pablo Picasso, *Femme assise à la terrasse d'un café*, 1901

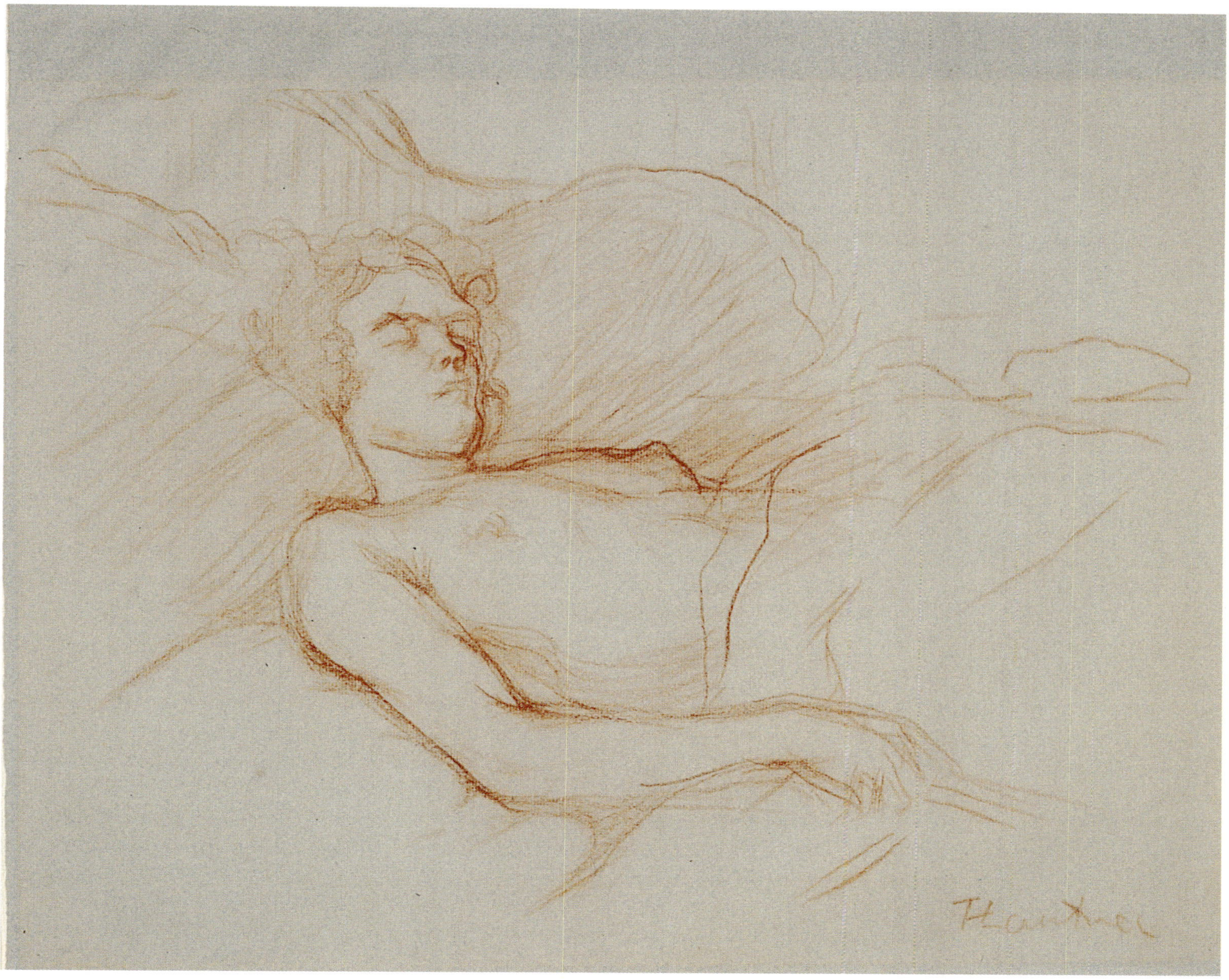

8. Henri de Toulouse-Lautrec, *Sleeping woman*, ca. 1896

9. J.C.W. Cossaar (Amsterdam 1874-1966 The Hague)
Kolenkar (Coal cart), c. 1904
Blue chalk, pencil, watercolour
499 x 644 mm
Signed lower right in pencil: *J. Cossaar*
Note lower centre in pencil: *66 x 53 PP FK 10 59,8 x 46,5*
Special features: pencil border
PROVENANCE:
Maur na Cossaar (1916-), daughter of the artist, 1966; Boijmans Van Beuningen Museum, Rotterdam, 1995
LITERATURE:
Hopmans 1992, p. 42 (fig.)
COLLECTION:
Boijmans Van Beuningen Museum, Rotterdam, MB 1995/T3

J.C.W. Cossaar (Amsterdam 1874-1966 The Hague)

The artist Ko Cossaar was a friend of Van Dongen's from the beginning of the century. During a stay in Paris in 1901 Cossaar spent time with him and they drew the same subjects together. [1] Two drawings by Cossaar refer to this friendship – one is a drawing from 1904 of Van Dongen on the beach in Normandy, and the other a portrait from 1909. (fig.)

Ko Cossaar is better known as an artist in England than in the Netherlands. After training in industrial design and attending evening classes at the Rijksacademie in Amsterdam, he went to study for a time with a decorative painter. In 1901 Cossaar, together with the artist Marius Bauer, painted the sets for tableaux-vivants that were performed in March at the Amsterdam City Theatre to celebrate the marriage of Queen Wilhelmina. It was perhaps on this occasion that Cossaar first came into contact with Van Dongen. Following the success of these decorative paintings, in 1901 and 1902 Cossaar was awarded a grant by the artists' society Arti et Amicitiae to continue his studies abroad. Cossaar used this money to go to Paris and London. In London he had some success with his busy city scenes of traffic in the streets. In March 1903 he was given a contract by the London art dealer the Goupil Gallery in which he was offered a fixed salary in return for all the paintings and watercolours he produced in a year. The success of the sales of his work through Goupil over several years was one of the reasons Cossaar worked almost exclusively in London until 1909 (in 1907 he spent a few months in Rotterdam) and why Cossaar's early work was predominantly distributed in Britain. In the course of 1909 Cossaar left London and moved to France – where he met Van Dongen in Paris – and then travelled back to the Netherlands where he took up residence in The Hague with his family.

The drawing *Coal cart* in pencil and watercolour – Cossaar's favourite drawing materials – was probably made during his stay in Paris in 1904. He undoubtedly drew this scene having in mind Van Dongen's series of Parisian work horses. Besides this, the way in which he has sketched in the facade in the background and the woman in the doorway, is strongly reminiscent of Van Dongen's early Zandstraat pictures. Cossaar's familiarity with his friend's oeuvre is also illustrated by the fact that the drawing *Les chevaux de Paris* (cat. 22) was originally in Cossaar's own collection. The stylistic similarities between both artists' early drawings, but most particularly Cossaar's choice of comparable urban street scenes and representations of the Rotterdam harbours, led to a considerable amount of his early work – that which had not been taken by Goupil and remained in the artist's studio until after his death – being sold as early Rotterdam work by Kees van Dongen.

1. Hopmans 1992.

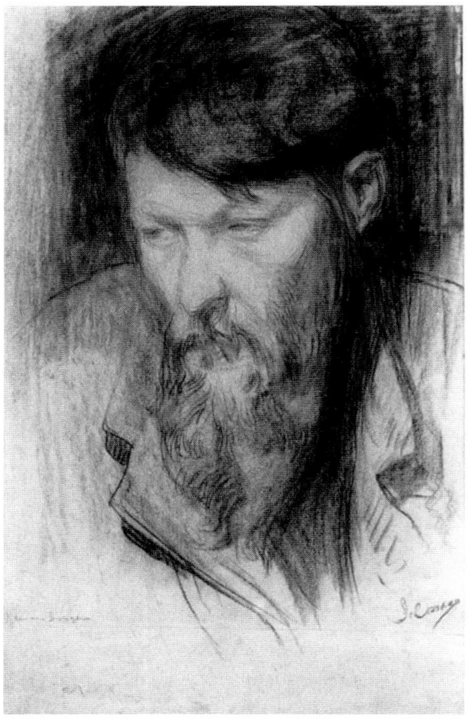

J.C.W. Cossaar, *Portrait of Kees van Dongen*, c. 1909
Black chalk on light-grey paper, 495 x 320 mm
Jacqueline Boucher Collection, Le Havre

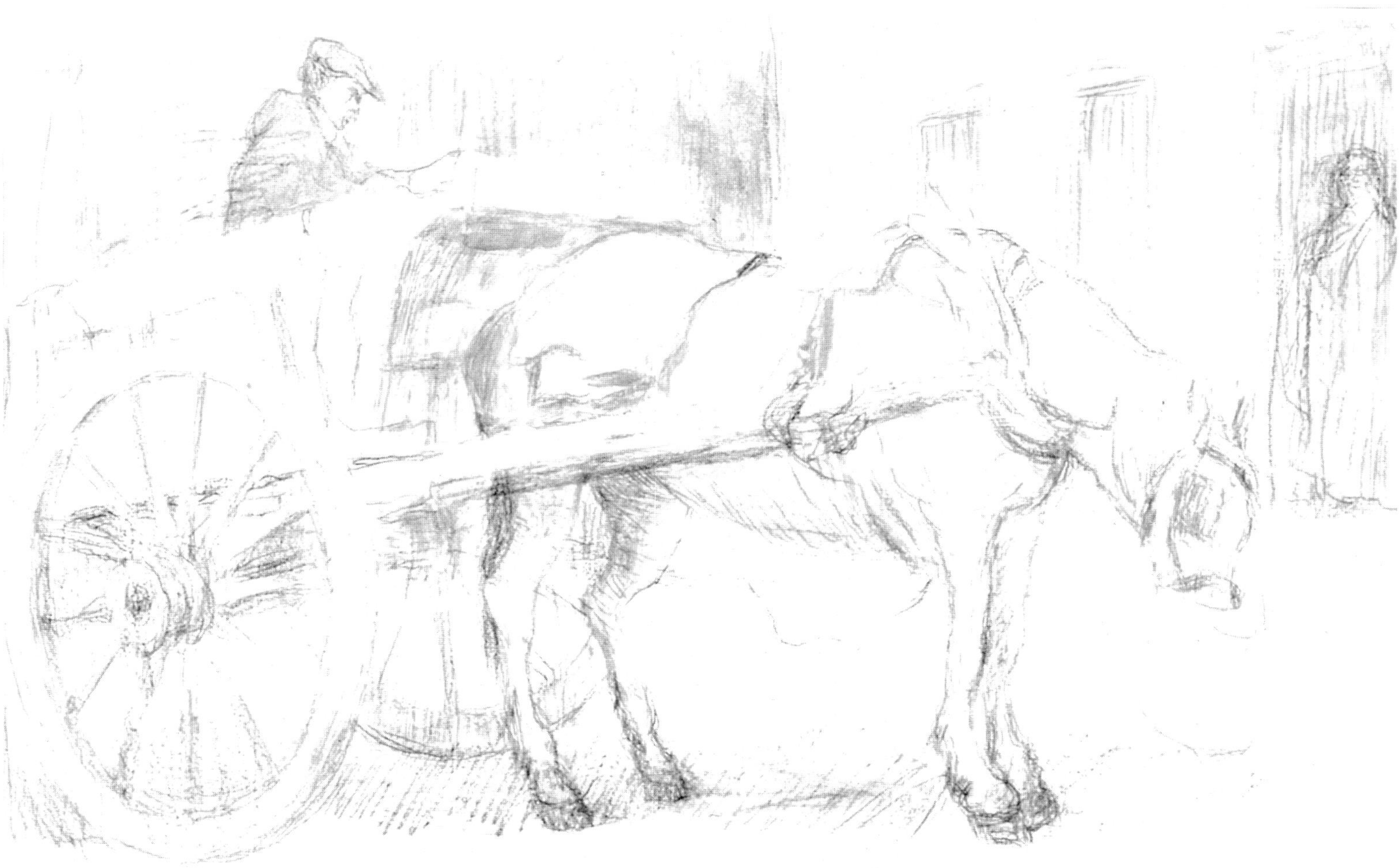

9. J.C.W. Cossaar, *Coal cart*, c. 1904

10. Albert Marquet (Bordeaux 1875-1947 Paris)
Dans la rue (In the street), c. 1904
Brush in black ink
218 x 165 mm
Signed lower left in brush with black ink: *a.m.*
On reverse: *Vrouwenbuste* (Bust of a woman) and
Kind van opzij (Child in profile), black chalk
PROVENANCE:
Marcelle Marquet, wife of the artist, Paris;
Musée des Beaux-Arts de Lyon, Lyons 1963
EXHIBITIONS:
Marquet, Lyons (Musée des Beaux-Arts de Lyon), 1962, no. 95.
De Géricault à Léger, Lyons (Musée des Beaux-Arts de Lyon), 1989, no. 119 (fig.).
COLLECTION:
Musée des Beaux-Arts de Lyon, Lyons, Inv. 1963-18

11 Albert Marquet (Bordeaux 1875-1947 Paris)
Passantes et cheval attelé (Passers-by and harnessed horse), c. 1904
Brush with black ink
172 x 214 mm
Signed lower right in brush with black ink: *a.m.*; note on reverse of cardboard on which drawing is mounted in pen with black ink: *167 XV B page d'album VII/Marseille 16*; in pencil: *7*; customs stamp
PROVENANCE:
Marcelle Marquet, wife of the artist; Musée National d'Art Moderne, Centre Georges Pompidou, Paris, 1959 (gift of M. Marquet)
EXHIBITIONS:
Från Bonnard till våra dagar. Akvarell, gouache, teckning, skulptur från Musée National d'Art Moderne, Paris, Stockholm (Riksförbundet för Bildande Konst), 1963; Louisiana 1964, no. 91.
LITERATURE:
Dorival 1960, pp. 282-83 (fig.)
COLLECTION:
Musée National d'Art Moderne, Centre Georges Pompidou, Paris, Inv. AM 2036 D

12. Albert Marquet (Bordeaux 1875-1947 Paris)
Joueurs de cartes au café (Card players in a café), c. 1904
Brush in black ink
180 x 285 mm
Signed lower left in brush with black ink: *marquet*
Note by Marcelle Marquet on back of original frame:
Joueurs de cartes au café/vers 1904
Special features: the drawing is mounted on cardboard
PROVENANCE:
Marcelle Marquet, wife of the artist; Boijmans Van Beuningen Museum, Rotterdam, 1956 (gift of M. Marquet)
EXHIBITIONS:
Les Fauves, New York (Museum of Modern Art); Minneapolis (Minneapolis Institute of Arts); San Francisco (San Francisco Museum of Art); Toronto (Art Gallery of Toronto), 1952-53, no. 86. *Marquet*, Rotterdam (Boijmans Van Beuningen Museum); Arnhem (Gemeentemuseum), 1955-56, no. 12 (drawings).
LITERATURE:
Petit de Beauverger 1955, p. 79 (fig.); Jourdain, 1959, p. 9
COLLECTION:
Boijmans Van Beuningen Museum, Rotterdam, Inv. MB 1955/T5

13. André Derain (Chatou 1880-1954 Garches)
A la terrasse (On the terrace), c. 1904
Pen and brush with black ink
232 x 308 mm
Studio stamp lower right: *ATELIER/André DERAIN* (L 668a)
PROVENANCE:
Studio of the artist; Galerie Paul Vallotton, Lausanne; Stoppenbach & Delestre, London
EXHIBITIONS:
Nineteenth and twentieth century French drawings and watercolours. Summer exhibition, London (Stoppenbach & Delestre), 1989, no. 24 (fig.). *André Derain. Drawings & Watercolours 1900-1906* London (Stoppenbach & Delestre), 1991, no. 12 (fig.).
COLLECTION:
Private collection
Courtesy Stoppenbach & Delestre, London

Albert Marquet (Bordeaux 1875-1947 Paris) André Derain (Chatou 1880-1954 Garches)

The two swift ink drawings by Marquet were undoubtedly made in the open air and were originally in a sketchbook. With a few quick brush strokes Marquet described the outline of a figure on the paper, then, with loose, exploratory marks and sweeps of the brush, he worked out the desired effect of movement. The last remains of the ink on the drying brush were wonderfully used to render the fabric of a skirt, an arm swinging forward or a figure walking in the distance. These two drawings are stylistically related, being almost the same size, and the light, cream-coloured paper used for both drawings is similar. Both sheets were probably drawn in 1904. The drawing in the Musée National d'Art Moderne in Paris, *Passantes et cheval attelé* has been dated to 1916 from an inscription on the reverse: *page d'album VII/Marseille 16*. However, this date is definitely too late since Marquet's drawings from this period are far more angular and linear.

Albert Marquet was born in Bordeaux and went to Paris in 1890 at the age of fifteen to train as a technical draughtsman and designer at the Ecole Nationale des Arts Décoratifs. [1] The increase in the industrial manufacturing of all kinds of products had led to an increased demand for technical draughtsmen.[2] As well as Marquet, artists like Henri Manguin and Henri Matisse also attended a part of this course; Manguin was a pupil there for the academic year 1891-92 and Matisse started the evening classes in October 1892.[3]

Albert Marquet attended this industrial design course for six years, going to both the day and evening classes. Beginning in May 1895 – his last year at the school – he worked in the studio of the artist Gustave Moreau. In doing this he followed Matisse's example who, a few months earlier, had managed to secure a place as a pupil there. In November of the same year, Manguin also gained a place in Moreau's studio.[4] In the meantime, their ambitions seem to have become wholly directed towards becoming independent artists. From 1894, Marquet competed on a number of occasions for a place in the drawing class at the Ecole des Beaux Arts, the 'Ecole proprement dite' – so-called to distinguish it from the studios affiliated with the school – and in July 1897 was accepted as a pupil, though he only attended this course for a year or two. However, Marquet spent longer at Moreau's studio. He left the studio at the same time as Matisse and Manguin, shortly after Moreau's death, in April 1898.[5] The artists regularly bumped into each other in the period that followed. In 1898-99, for instance, Marquet and Matisse both drew at the Académie Camillo, where the painter Eugène Carrière was a tutor and Jean Puy and André Derain sometimes visited. Marquet, Matisse and Manguin also worked with them in Jean Biette's studio after 1900, and, with the exception of Derain who was doing his military service between 1901-04, they all went on to Henri Manguin's studio in the rue Boursault.[6]

Direct and rapid sketching from life – Delacroix said one should be easily able to draw a man falling from the fourth floor of a building – was rather different to what is usually supposed. It was not an anti-academic practice and even less so was it reserved for the more liberal studios like Moreau's. The importance of quickly recording outside scenes on paper was especially propagated by Horace Lecoq de Boisbaudran around 1860.[7] This drawing teacher was director of the Ecole Impériale, later the Ecole des Arts Décoratifs, from 1866. Lecoq made sure that the 'dessin de mémoire' – practising the immediate depiction of a seen object – was included in the syllabus, alongside copying and life drawing. His views became generally accepted during the nineteenth cen-

14. Henri Matisse (Le Cateau-Cambrésis 1869-1954 Nice)
Marquet peignant un nu (Marquet painting a nude)
Albert Marquet in the studio of Henri Manguin,
61 rue Boursault, Paris, 1904-1905
Oil on paper
310 x 240 mm
Signed lower right in black chalk: *H.M.*

PROVENANCE:
Henri Manguin (1874-1949), Paris, c. 1905-1907; Musées Nationaux, 1957 (purchased from the wife of Henri Manguin); Musée National d'Art Moderne, Paris, 1957

EXHIBITIONS:
Les Fauves, Tokyo (Magasins Takashimaya); Osaka (Magasins Takashimaya); Fukuoka (Magasin Iwataya), 1965, no. 50.
Le fauvisme français et les débuts de l'expressionisme allemand, Paris (Musée National d'Art Moderne); Munich (Haus der Kunst), Hamburg (Kunsthalle), 1966, no. 91 (fig.). *Les salons d'Automne de Paris. Exposition des maîtres français*, Warsaw (Palais Zachenta); Katowice (Musée Municipal), 1973, p. 151. *Manguin parmi les fauves*, Martigny (Fondation Pierre Gianadda), 1983, no. 51.

LITERATURE:
Bock 1981 p. 79, fig. 42; Diehl 1954, p. 16; Dorival 1957, pp. 115-120 (fig.); Dorival 1961, p. 37; Elderfield 1976, pp. 33-34 (fig.) p. 151, note 7; Hild 1981; Monod-Fontaine 1980; Monod-Fontaine 1980, no. 5 (fig.); Monod-Fontaine 1989, p. 30, no. 6 (fig.)

COLLECTION:
Musée National d'Art Moderne, Centre Georges Pompidou, Paris, Inv. AM 3490 P

tury. And so, by around 1900, sketching from life in the street – *hors d'atelier* – to train the memory and exercise the hand was regularly practised not only at the Ecole des Arts Décoratifs, but also in the Ecole des Beaux-Arts and the so-called 'open' studios. Nous cherchions à dessiner la silhouette des passants, à discipliner notre trait. Nous nous efforcions de découvrir très rapidement ce qu'il ya a de caractéristique dans un geste, une attitude, is how Matisse later in an interview described this approach of making quick, outdoor sketches – something he often did together with Marquet both during their time at Moreau's studio and in the years that followed.[8]

Few of these street sketches by Matisse have survived, most of them having apparently been lost during a studio-cleaning session in 1936. A few examples can be found in the Musée National d'Art Moderne in Paris: ink sketches of carriages in the street, harnessed horses and a couple of sheets depicting performing actresses, from which it appears that the *spectacle de la vie* was also recorded by the artist in theatres and cafes. Apart from being the most talented in this approach to drawing, Marquet was probably the most productive, and quite a large number of street scenes by him are known. The Musée des Beaux-Arts in Bordeaux has a representative group of forty sketches of this sort in its collection and many other museums possess a few early drawings by Marquet. Most of these seem to have been drawn in brush and ink and it wouldn't be unreasonable to look to Japanese drawing as the source of this technique, which is what Matisse did in 1943: 'Lorsque je vois Hokusaï je pense à notre Marquet – et vice versa.'[9] In Paris at around the turn of the century, there were plenty of opportunities to become acquainted with Japanese art and Marquet and Matisse would also have able to find out more about Hokusai from Edmond de Goncourt's views on the artist and biographical background published in 1896.[10] Artists like Bonnard and Van Gogh had already done this earlier. In 1888, in the year he drew the landscape of the south of France with a reed pen, Vincent van Gogh wrote to his brother admiring the simplicity of feeling in the work of the Japanese masters from which, in his view, the rapid drawing technique developed – an approach he also tried in Arles: 'by allowing the pen a life of its own.'[11] The swift brush technique used by Marquet and Matisse, the open, interrupted or elliptical contours, allowing the brush strokes to speak, and the suggestive use of black and white areas, are elements that are consciously modelled on Japanese drawing.

Marquet became reasonably well-known early on with these swift ink drawings, 'movement and character sketches in one.' As a result, the writer Charles-Louis Philippe in 1904 asked Marquet to illustrate the second edition of his novel of city life *Bubu de Montparnasse*. Marquet worked on this during the summer of 1904, though in the end the drawings were rejected. An article written by Philippe about Marquet in 1908 shows that the writer felt the drawings competed too much with his words.[12] As a result the drawings were exhibited by Marquet, along with seven other paintings, at the Salon d'Automne of 1904; this is apparent from the Salon catalogue which lists '26 dessins non en carté, illustrations pour Bubu' as well as 26 mounted drawings 'en carté'. Around ten of these drawings were printed and discussed in Philippe's article on Marquet in *La Grand Revue* in 1908. (fig.) From this it is clear that some of Marquet's brush sketches in museums at Bordeaux, Lyons and Paris belong to the Bubu series or were studies for it. The sheet in the Boijmans Van Beuningen Museum Collection, *Joueurs de cartes au café*, can also be related to this series.

The drawings in the Salon d'Automne of 1904 can scarcely have escaped the attention of André Derain who would have just been released from military service in September 1904. He must have paid Marquet's drawings a great deal of attention. During his years in the army, Derain had illustrated two books by Maurice de Vlaminck and had made several attempts to have illustrations published in newspapers such as *Le Rire* and *Le Sourire*.[13] Derain's 'Fauvist' sketch in the collection of the Musée Nationale d'Art Moderne in Paris dating from this period, contains a number of painted sketches that strongly resemble Marquet's Bubu illustrations.[14] (fig.) Derain's sheet *A la terrasse* can also be compared to Marquet in its use of stripes and dots and an even, dextrous handling of a brush with split hairs. Derain would also have been influenced in this way of working by his admiration for Van Gogh's reed pen drawings.

After the summer of 1904, work continued for Marquet, Matisse, Manguin and Puy in Manguin's studio in rue Boursault; Derain had enrolled at the Académie Jullian. This period of working together resulted in a series of pieces from the same model, made in 1904-5, in which the painters depicted each other in the background of their pictures. A lovely example of this is the oil study *Marquet peignant un nu* that Matisse painted in Neo-Impressionist influenced colours. He had been experimenting with this technique since the summer of 1904. Matisse encouraged his colleagues to follow his example in the months that followed. Around 1905, a period which Jean Puy called 'époque de l'émulation', an important new movement in painting developed. This became known as Fauvism, which Van Dongen was soon to join.[15]

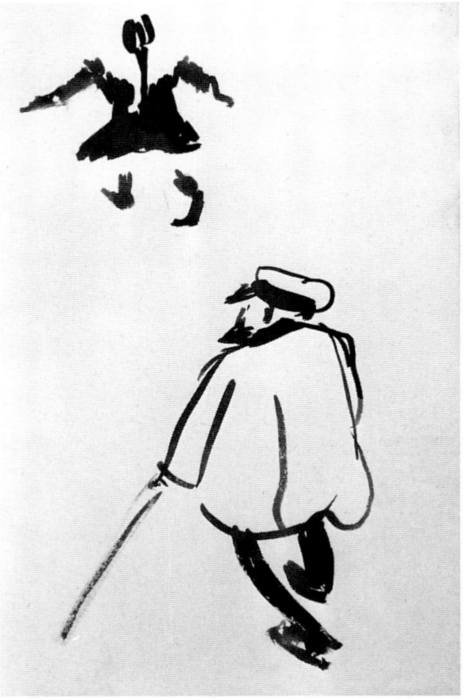

André Derain, *Street Scene*, c. 1904
Brush with black ink, 313 x 210 mm
Page from a sketchbook, 1903-1906
Musée National d'Art Moderne, Paris

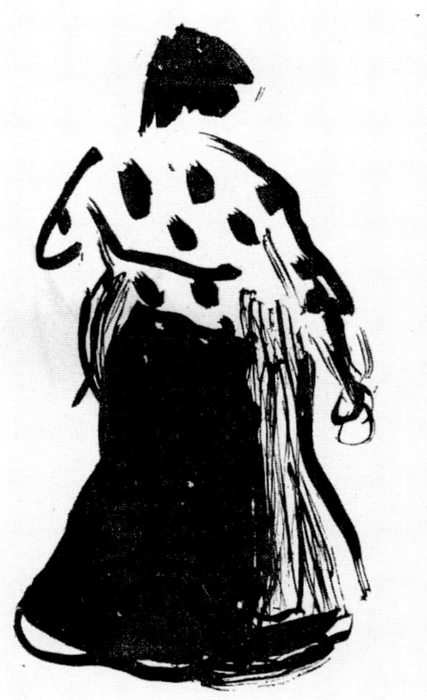

Albert Marquet
Illustration in C.L. Philippe, 'Dix dessins d'Albert Marquet',
la Grande Revue, 1908, vol. 51, p.736

1.
Marquet 1951, p. 20

2.
Cowart 1972, pp. 67-8

3.
Cowart 1972, pp. 62-6, on the training of these artists.

4.
Cowart 1972, pp. 95-6 for Moreau; on competing for a place at the Ecole des Beaux-Arts, pp. 65, 95-7, 158; for Matisse at Moreau's, March 1895, p. 65; Manguin, p. 66. It is not clear whether Marquet took up a place after taking the exam for the second time on 21 May 1898. For Matisse as a pupil on this course (1895-6) see Cowart 1972, pp. 65, 94.

5.
Cowart 1972, pp. 157-9.

6.
L. Vauxcelles, *Gils Blas*, 4 May 1904: Matisse, Marquet and Manguin copying in the Louvre. On the Academie Camillo, Cowart 1972, pp. 160-4; other famous pupils at this school: Pierre Laprade, Jean Biette, Auguste Chabaud. Jean Puy, 'Souvenirs', *Le Point*, July 1939. On work in Biette's studio's: Cowart 1972, pp. 160, 164-5, p. 183, note 32; and Manguin: Cowart 1972, pp. 170, 221-2; Monod-Fontaine 1980, p. 29.

7.
On Lecoq de Boisbaudran, Cowart 1972, pp. 40-3; Boime 1971, p. 181.

8.
Matisse in 1925, interview with J. Guenne, see Fourcade 1992, p. 81.

9.
For this statement by Matisse see A. Rouveyre, G. Besson, 'Marquet, dessins', *Le Point*, December 1943.

10.
E. de Goncourt, *Hokusaï*, Paris 1896.

11.
Van Uitert 1977, p. 26; letter from Van Gogh to his brother Theo, February 1888. See also Pickvance 1990, pp. 217-18.

12.
Consulted the publication from 1958, Charles-Louis Philippe, *Bubu de Montparnasse*, Paris 1958; first edition 1901. See Marquet 1951, pp. 22, 28-29; Cowart 1972, pp. 174 and 185, note 53; Ch.L. Philippe, 'Dix dessins d'Albert Marquet', *La Grand Revue*, 1908, vol. 51, pp. 731-741. On the importance of these drawings see also Salmon 1912, pp. 10-11; Carco 1953, p. 86.
For work on this in the summer of 1904, Freeman 1990, p. 62; on the letter from the publisher to Marquet about the rejection (7 September 1904), idem, p. 64.

13.
Dagen 1992, pp. 11-12; Derain made illustrations for Vlaminck's *D'un lit dans l'autre* and *Tout pur ça*, both published in 1902.

14.
Dorival 1969; Parke-Taylor 1980; Dagen 1984.

15.
Quoted from E. Hild, exhib.cat., *3 Nus fauves peints dans l'atelier de Manguin*, Saint-Tropez (Musée de l'Annonciade) summer 1981.

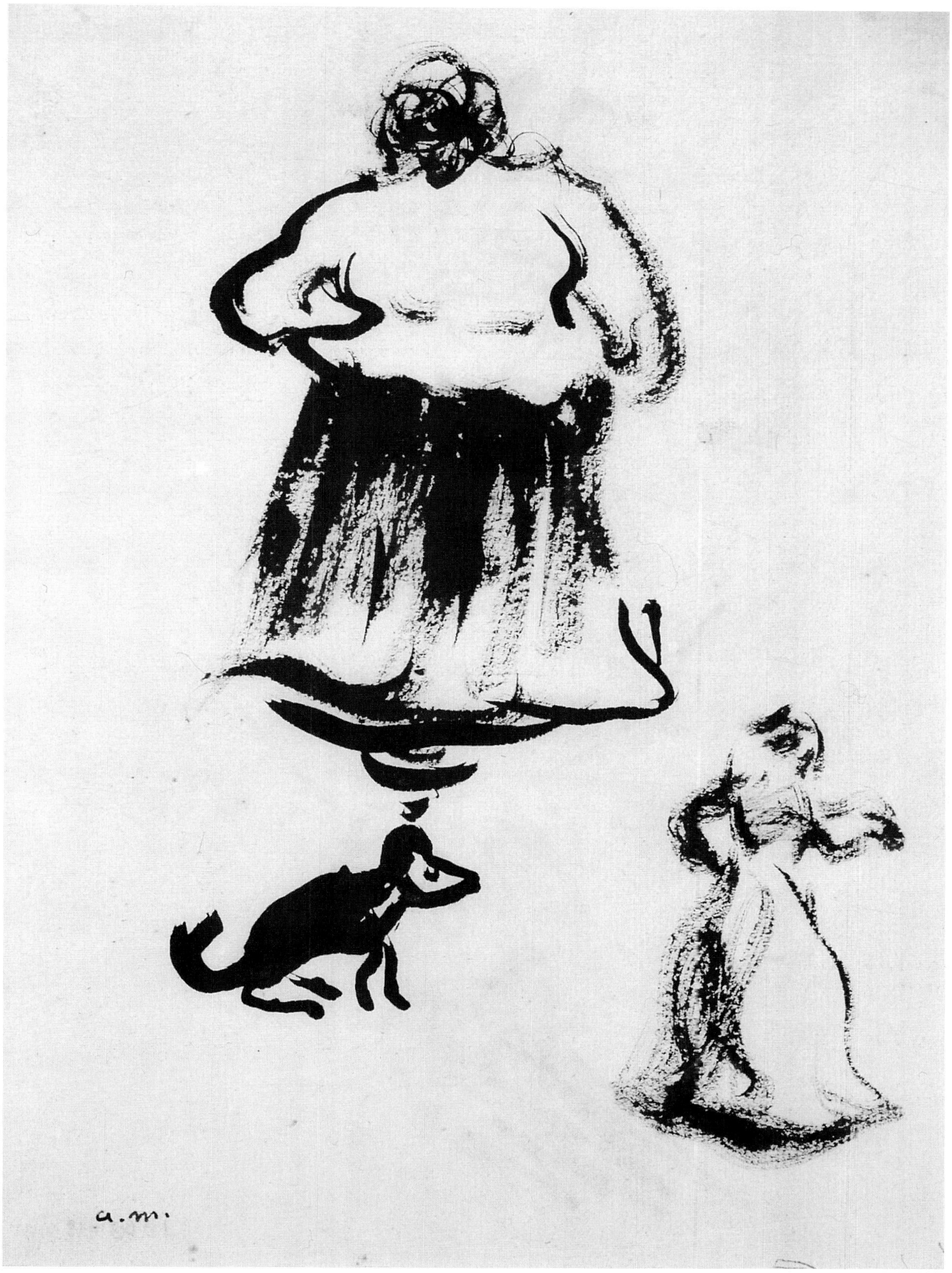

10. Albert Marquet, *Dans la rue*, c. 1904

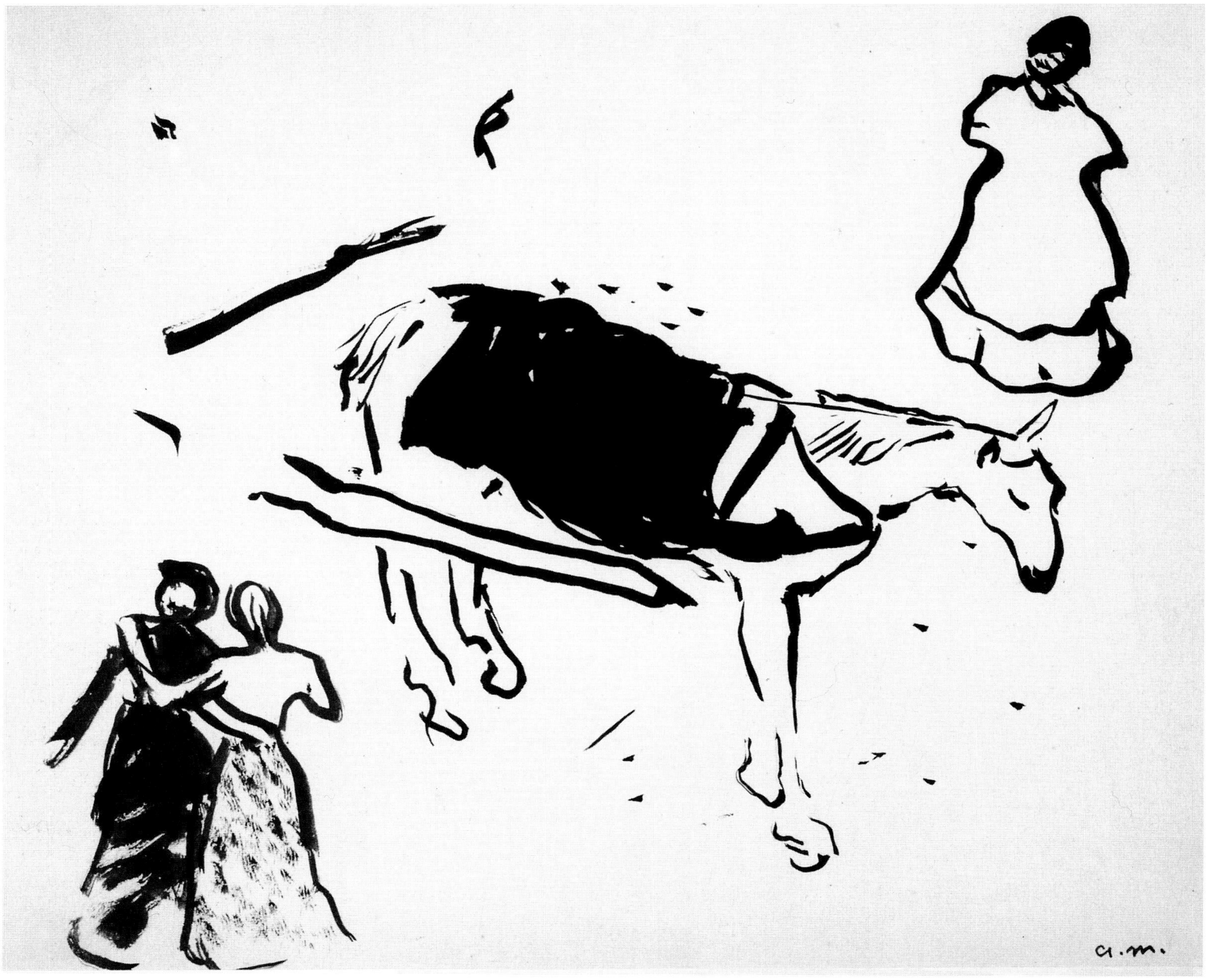

11. Albert Marquet, *Passantes et cheval attelé*, c. 1904

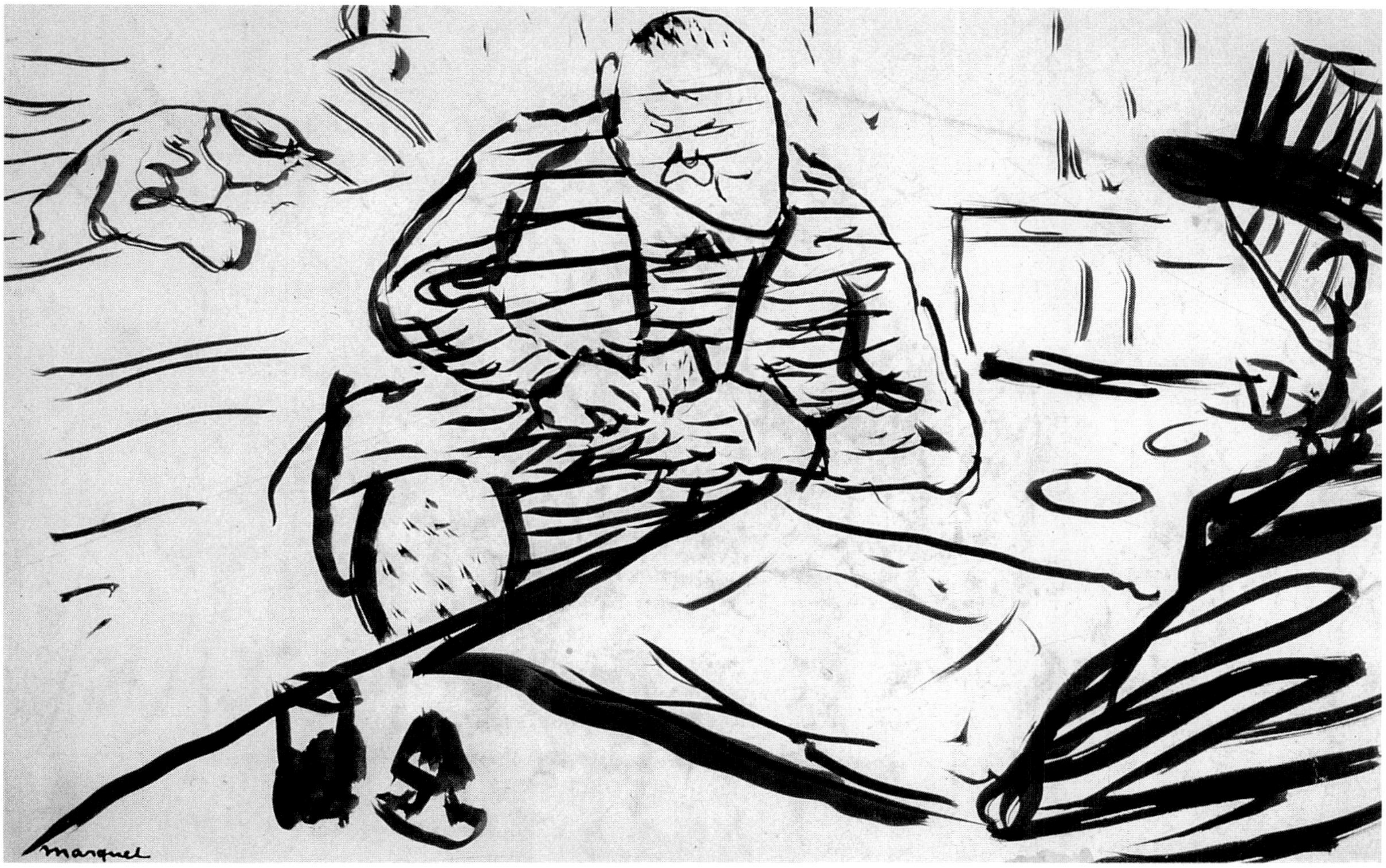

12. Albert Marquet, *Joueurs de cartes au café*, c. 1904

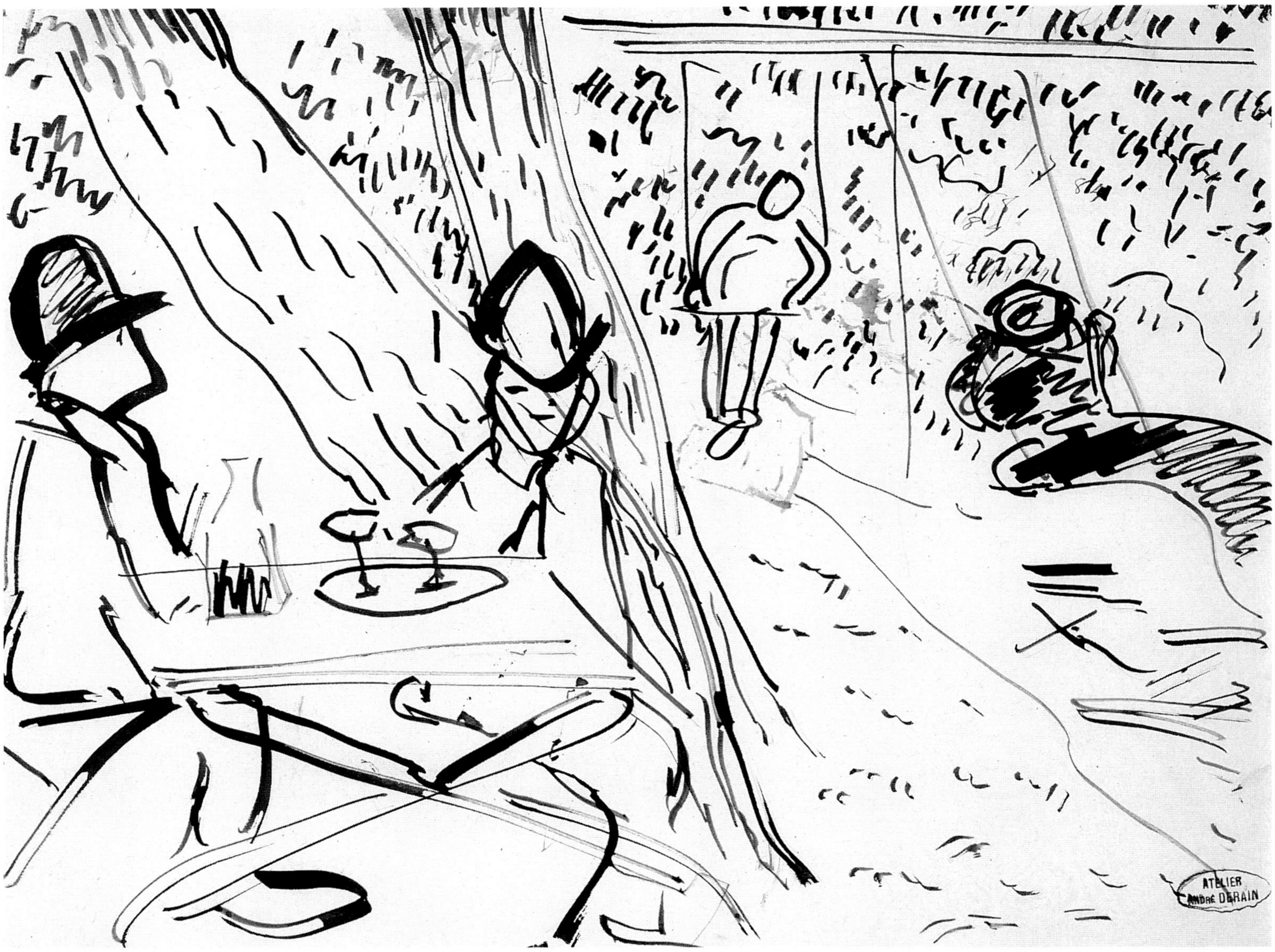

13. André Derain, *A la terrasse*, c. 1904

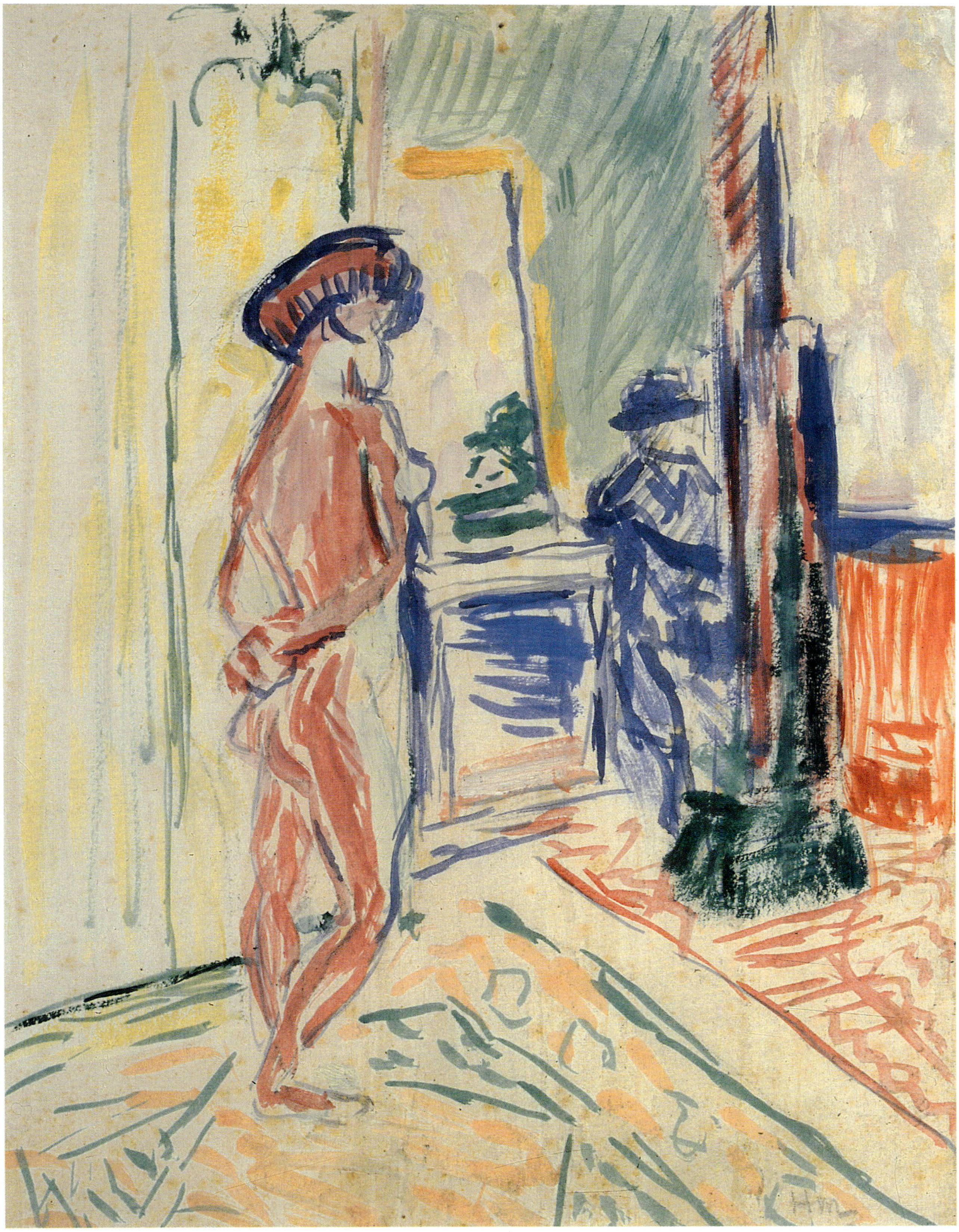

14. Henri Matisse, *Marquet peignant un nu*,
Albert Marquet in Henri Manguin's studio,
61 rue Boursault, Paris, 1904-1905

15. Albert Marquet (Bordeaux 1875-1947 Paris)
Pont Neuf au soleil (The Pont Neuf in sunshine), 1906
Oil on canvas
73 x 92 cm
Signed lower left: *marquet*
Signed and dated in brush with black on reverse of canvas, before lining in 1977: *Pont neuf au soleil/1906/MM*

PROVENANCE:
Marcelle Marquet, wife of the artist; Boijmans Van Beuningen Museum, Rotterdam, 1956 (gift of M. Marquet)

EXHIBITIONS:
Albert Marquet 1875-1947, Zürich (Kunsthaus), 1948, no. 38. *Albert Marquet*, Paris (Musée d'Art Moderne), 1948, no. 13; Algiers (Musée National des Beaux-Arts), 1949, no. 12. *Autour de 1900*, Paris (Galerie Charpentier), 1950, no. 117 (fig.). *Albert Marquet*, Copenhagen (Statens Museum for Kunst), 1950, no. 12. *Albert Marquet*, Tel Aviv (Musée de Tel Aviv); Oslo (Maison des Arts); Jerusalem (Musée de Bezalel), 1951, no. 12. *Paintings by Albert Marquet*, London (Galerie Wildenstein), no. 8; New York (Galerie Wildenstein), 1952, no. 18. *Exposition Marquet*, Vevey (Musée Jenisch), 1953, no. 19. *Marquet*, Paris (Maison de la Pensée Française), 1953, no. 17. *Marquet*, Rotterdam (Boijmans Van Beuningen Museum); Arnhem (Gemeentemuseum), 1955-56, no. 21. *Schilderkunst uit La belle époque*, Laren (Singer Museum), 1964, no. 46 (fig.). *Albert Marquet*, Hamburg (Kunstverein), 1964-1965, no. 21 (fig.). *Fauvisme in de Europese kunst*, Mechelen (Cultureel Centrum), 1969, no. 67. *Albert Marquet 1875-1947*, Bordeaux (Galerie des Beaux-Arts); 1975, Paris (Orangerie des Tuileries), 1975-1976. *The Fauve landscape*, Los Angeles (County Museum of Art), 1990, no. 329 (fig.).

LITERATURE:
Marquet 1953, p. 58, no. 11; Ebbinge Wubben 1963, no. 2411; Ebbinge Wubben 1972, p. 252 (fig.)

COLLECTION:
Boijmans Van Beuningen Museum, Rotterdam, Inv. 2411

From the inscription on the reverse of the canvas, the painting *Pont Neuf au soleil* by Marquet can dated as being from 1906. It shows a view of Paris's Pont-Neuf, the bridge at the western end of the Ile de la Cité that joins the two banks of the Seine. In the background the contours of a number of imposing buildings stand out – buildings that still determine the silhouette of Paris today. On the left is the dome of the Institut de France, on the right one of the Louvre's wings and behind the more distant Pont des Arts we can see the elongated outline of the Grand Palais. In the foreground, against the dark mass of the trees on the right, the statue of Henri IV on horseback can just about be distinguished. Although the title would suggest that this view of the Pont-Neuf was painted in full daylight, it appears rather to have been painted at the end of the day in the light of the late afternoon. This is indicated by the long shadows, the lit street lamps and the almost black, somewhat bent figures. Marquet laid out the canvas as a composition of silhouettes, whereby he harmonized the dark trees behind the statue with the frayed edges of the omnibus in the foreground.

Unlike the drawings which were made at some suitable spot somewhere in the street, for his paintings Marquet chose a high vantage point. [1] From about 1902-03, he started to paint the city from these raised positions as a compilation of blocks using broad brushstrokes, in between which he used a few dark strokes to position figures and vehicles. The first city scenes are quite rigid, but in time the architecture and traffic began to form more of a whole. Canvases that were made from 1905 on, partly through the influence of Matisse's work, were painted in looser dabs using a more colourful palette. Marquet seems to have had a preference for diagonal, tapering composition lines, a direction that was often determined by the representation of one of the banks of the Seine. These diagonals, together with the water of the river, the wave of the tree tops and the constantly shifting figures and vehicles, brought about the effect of movement Marquet was looking for – a 'panta rhei'. It is possible to deduce from the perspective and light the place where Marquet stood and the time of day when he made the painting.

This painterly development had a positive effect on the sales of his work. In 1905 Berthe Weill announced that as far as she was concerned in commercial terms Marquet was number two on the list; at the beginning of March of that year the art dealer Vollard negotiated the purchase of six canvases with Marquet.[2] This financial success enabled Marquet to travel. In 1905 he left for the Côte d'Azur where he visited Henri Manguin in Saint-Tropez and, sometimes in the company of the painter Camoin, travelled the coast from Marseilles to Menton. This was followed in 1906 by a stay on the Normandy coast with Raoul Dufy.[3] During his travels, Marquet painted Fauvist pictures of harbours and holiday-makers on the beach in bright colours with swift strokes of the brush. After his first contract in 1905, these paintings brought him a favourable contract with the art dealer Druet in December 1906. This financial leeway enabled Marquet to move house in Paris. In the spring of 1905 he moved from eccentric Auteuil to a studio on the banks of the Seine, 25 quai des Grands Augustins and at the end of 1906 to 29 Place Dauphine.[4] He quite probably painted *Pont Neuf au soleil* – a winter scene – from this apartment. The painting must have escaped Druet's eye – who according to the contract had first refusal on all Marquet's work – and as a result remained in the artist's private collection for a long time, until it was acquired by Boijmans Van Beuningen Museum for the first exhibition of Marquet's work in the Netherlands.

1. Jourdain 1959, pp. 76-77.
2. Freeman 1990, pp. 67-68; letter from A. Vollard to Marquet, 7 March 1905; B. Weill in *Pan! Dans l'oeil!*, Paris 1933, p. 115; the painter Camoin was at the top of her list.
3. Freeman 1990, pp. 69-73, p. 76.
4. Freeman 1990, pp. 67,99.

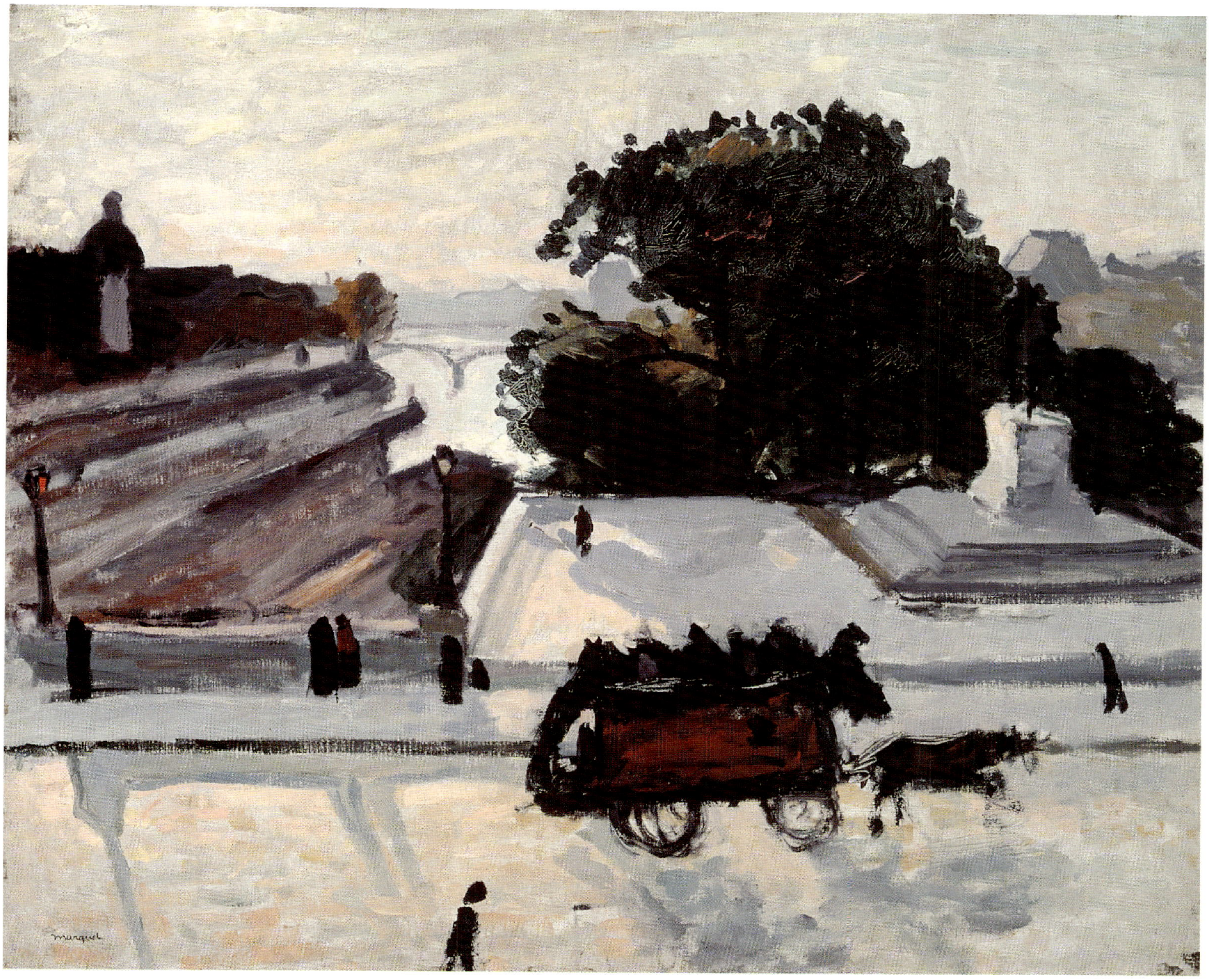

15. Albert Marquet, *Pont Neuf au soleil*, 1906

Paul Signac (Paris 1863-1935 Paris)

16. Paul Signac (Paris 1863-1935 Paris)
Les fumées (Columns of smoke), 1906
Charcoal, brush with black ink, grey wash
7 0 x 886 mm
Signed lower right: *P. Signac*; lower left in blue chalk: 9
Special features: remains of pencil border left and lower centre
In blue chalk on reverse of cardboard on which drawing is mounted: 15; on back of former frame a note in blue chalk: *Les Fumées Rotterdam/n° 23*; a black-printed label: *Exposition Paul Signac/19 au 30 Mai 1930/Collection/Galerie Bernheim Jeune et Cie/Faubourg St-Honoré, 83-PARIS*; marked in pen with black ink: *Les Fumées-Rotterdam 1906/Lévy Gaston*; black-printed label: *M.M. BERNHEIM-JEUNE/83, RUE DU FAUBOURG ST-HONORE PARIS-8e/EXPOSITION/Appartenant à*; marked in pen with black ink: *Signac*; in red ink: *X/M. Gaston Levy/1930*

PROVENANCE:
Gaston Levy, Paris, 1930; auction Paris, Galliera (M. and Ph. Reims), *Tableaux modernes*, 30 November 1961, no. 72 (fig.); Galerie Artina, Paris, September 1971; Jeffrey Alan Levitt, Baltimore; the State of Maryland; auction New York, Christie's, *Impressionist and modern drawings...*, 13 May 1987, no. 108 (fig.); Kunsthandel J. van Waning, Rotterdam, 1987; Boijmans Van Beuningen Museum, Rotterdam, 1987 (with the assistance of the Boijmans Van Beuningen Museum Foundation)

EXHIBITIONS:
Paul Signac, Paris (Galerie Bernheim-Jeune), 1930, no. 23
Stockholm (?); Rotterdam (Boijmans Van Beuningen Museum), 1988. *Impressionisme: een schone kijk. De stroming en de aanloop*, Rotterdam (Boijmans Van Beuningen Museum), 1992, no. 118.

COLLECTION:
Boijmans Van Beuningen Museum, Rotterdam, Inv. 1987/115

This monumental pen and ink drawing *Les fumées* – depicting the busy traffic on the river Maas in Rotterdam – served the painter Paul Signac as a preliminary drawing for a painting (fig.) of the same name which was exhibited in January 1907 at Bernheim-Jeune in Paris. [1] This is one of the works which resulted from a visit Signac and his wife paid to the Dutch port in April and probably November 1906. If the great number of studies that Signac made there and the series of paintings which resulted from the trip are anything to go by, they must have stayed there several weeks. On show at the Bernheim-Jeune exhibition of 1907, in addition to the painting *Les fumées*, were six other paintings and eighteen watercolours with the Maas as their principal motif, all depicting the river or the riverbanks of Rotterdam and nearby places like Overschie or Maasluis.[2] In combination with the many black chalk and watercolour studies known from later exhibitions, and one painting of the Maas at Rotterdam – presumed to have been painted some time in 1907 after the exhibition (which is also part of the Boijmans van Beuningen Collection (fig.) – they present a picture of an extremely industrious Signac and a very purposeful stay in the city.[3]

This was not the only journey Signac made in this period, nor was it the first time he had been to the Netherlands. From 1892 onwards he made an annual trip to his house in Saint-Tropez, travelled to London in 1898, to Venice in the winter of 1903 and the early part of 1904 and spent some time in Marseilles and Genoa in 1905. Earlier, in 1896, Signac went on a sailing trip to the far North.[4] The outcome of these journeys was a series of harbour views, each with a specific town as their subject. In 1906, the port of Rotterdam would also appear to have been carefully scrutinized, especially if compared to the ports of Venice or Marseilles. Signac's rendering of the latter was described by the press at the time as 'des paysages de noble style composées avec le souci de décor.'[5]

This system of travelling for work purposes and consequently devoting your time to one subject or technique is known to have played an important role at the inception of Fauvism. Signac's annual residence in Saint-Tropez sparked off a number of Fauvist journeys to the Mediterranean coast.[6] It can also be seen as a link in the chain joining the Neo-Impressionist Signac with the Impressionists. Signac's selection of the Dutch port of Rotterdam as a workplace is comparable to Claude Monet's earlier visits to North London in 1899-1901. The superb views of the Thames which resulted – painted by Monet at intervals between 1899-1904 – were first exhibited in 1904 in Paris by the art dealer Durand-Ruel.[7] This exhibition inspired the art dealer Vollard to coax André Derain to go to London at the end of 1905.[8] Monet's example must undoubtedly have challenged Signac too. The exhibition of his Rotterdam river Maas views summoned up, at least as far as the critics were concerned, a direct comparison with Monet's London impressions – but in terms of contrast. 'Elle me fait pas oublier cependant la Tamise de M. Claude Monet', was a critic's reaction to the exhibition of the above-mentioned Rotterdam harbour view (fig.) at the Salon des Indépendants of 1907, 'mais c'est autre chose, c'est une autre lumière', which was followed by a comparison between the reconstructed Neo-Impressionist method of analyzing light and colour and the submissive recording of impressions in Impressionism.[9]

It was Kees van Dongen who had recommended Rotterdam to Signac, as reported by the writer and journalist M.J. Brusse in his recollections of Signac in 1935: 'Kees van Dongen had sent me from Paris – at that time still very bohemian in the Impasse Girardon on the Butte – a warm-hearted letter about his friend Paul Signac whose eyes had been scorched by the unequivocal burning rays of the sun in the East...He had devised a cure for this fanatical luminist, to take place round about November – in Rotterdam – a place which still sent shivers down Van Dongen's spine when he recalled

1.
Exhib.cat., *Paul Signac*, Paris (Bernheim-Jeune) 21 January-2 February 1907 (foreword by Paul Adam), no. 1, *Les fumées*. The painting was auctioned in Paris, Drouot (A. Bellier), *Tableaux modernes...formant la collection Léon Pédron*, 2 June 1926, no. 58, under the title *Le port de Rotterdam*; exhib.cat., *Les maîtres de l'art indépendant*, Paris (Petit Palais), no. 86 (announcement M. Ferretti di Castelferretto). On the exhibition P. Jamot, 'Exposition Paul Signac (Galerie Bernheim)', *La Chronique des Arts et de la Curiosité*, 26 January 1907, p. 28.

2.
The exhibition had a total of 80 works: 40 paintings, 40 works on papier. The remaining Maas views exhibited were: 2. *La Meuse*, fig. in Cachin 1971, p. 97; 3. *Le Moulin*; 4. *Le Remorqueur*, fig. in Cachin 1971, p. 96; 5. *A la Remorque*, fig. in De Forges 1963, no. 69 (previously the Maximilien Luce Collection); 6. *Le Canal*, Kröller-Müller Museum Collection, Otterlo, Inv. no. 717-24; 7. *Les Moulins*.

3.
For *Rotterdam. The Port* (1907), Boijmans Van Beuningen Museum Rotterdam: Ebbinge Wubben 1963, St.96; Haverkamp-Begemann 1953, pp. 26-27; Van Heemstra 1992, no. 120; Sillevis 1990, p. 200; Wardwell Lee 1988, p. 156. De Forges 1963, no. 70: on the reverse of the stretcher, inscribed and signed: *Rotterdam. Le port. 1907. P. Signac*. For other studies of Rotterdam: Cousturier 1922, p. 41; exhib.cat., *Signac*, London (Marlborough) 1954, nos 25-26; exhib.cat., *Peintres français en Hollande*, Paris (Institut Néerlandais) 1961, nos 83-87; exhib.cat., *Dessins français du Metropolitan Museum of Art New York, de David à Picasso*, Paris (Musée du Louvre) 1973-1974, no. 89; exhib.cat., *Signac*, New York (Metropolitan Museum) 1977, nos 7 and 11; exhib.cat., *Dessins et estampes de la collection George et Adèle Besson*, Besançon (Musée des Beaux-Arts et d'Archéologie), 1985-1986, no. 182, and auctions.

4.
Cachin 1971, pp. 72, 84-86; Rewald 1949-1953, III, pp. 31-32; Ferretti-Bocquillon 1992, p. 66.

his youth in Delfshaven, with all the mud running past the houses and the boulders oozing feculence under the storm-frayed autumn skies. This would act as a balm and sooth the battered retina of the hunter of light. And he asked me if I would help him get started.'[10]

Brusse noted the arrival of the painter in this report dated November 1906. But a letter has also been preserved which Signac wrote from Rotterdam, dated 23 April 1906, which included the comment 'Changement de décor!'[11] In all probability, the journey was prepared in advance by an exploratory trip. A second stay must certainly have been in November, as Brusse's lively recollections of certain details would seem to support. Brusse arranged a room for Signac on one of the highest floors at the front of the Rotterdam Victoria hotel on the Willemsplein, with a view of the river Maas.[12] A location which is once again a reminder of Monet, who painted the Thames from the top floor of the Savoy hotel. Having arrived at his hotel, Brusse relates, Signac began 'sketching on the balcony straight away using watercolours, in an elated mood – even though his hands were half-frozen.' At the end of the day he was subsequently to find him 'in despair'. The floor of his hotel room was 'completely submerged under countless rejected sketches'. Signac is said to have admitted 'to being unable to make anything worthwhile of the subject'. 'Accustomed to the clear, stable luminosity of the southern sky' the reporter continues, 'he could not capture our typical Dutch skies with the ever-changing effect of fading light and cloud cover.'[13] Signac would no doubt have had this sort of difficulty at the beginning. In a postcard showing a view of the Maas he wrote: 'De ma fenêtre! Quel ballet tournoyant! Suis enthousiaste, mais deconcerté – Amitiés.'[14]

It would seem that Brusse had subsequently helped Signac, wherever necessary, in performing the task he had set himself: 'to paint the Maas and the harbours in that chill, muddy, fading twilight and in capturing the gleam of the soaking wet November with its fleeting snow storms. When Signac had positioned his easel closer to the edge of the quayside at the entrance of the Leuvenhaven and found himself in danger of ending up in the water due to the surge of curious spectators, it was Brusse who is said to have obtained a covered barge for him. This fact corresponds with the various sketches by Signac that still exist of ships on the water seen from close by. Otherwise the report of the naturalist writer-journalist Brusse – a great admirer of Amsterdam Impressionism – should be read with great wariness. His praise for Signac's perseverance, which 'commanded respect for his struggling on despite chilblains and hands swollen by the winter cold, sometimes in rough seas in that appalling spectrum of splashing, turbulent greyness and dense sea mist' would seem to have indicated that in his view the Divisionistic analysis of the so typical Dutch tonal light was an impossible task – especially in the autumn. The end of Brusse's report does not therefore come as a surprise. After Signac had spent 'a few weeks, poring over the subject with great difficulty day and night, yet steadily plodding on' eventually progressing to 'a large painting of the Maas in front of the city – which, as a conclusion to his impressions, would soon be finished', a street urchin is said to have thrown a cobblestone straight through the canvas whereupon the artist left post-haste for Paris. Despite the pointed irony here, this ending would seem to be partially based on the truth: in an announcement of his return to friends, Signac describes himself as 'vaincu par la meuse' and 'lapidé par les gosses de Maasluis.'[15]

Brusse's Recollection is mainly of documentary interest. It demonstrates the purposefulness of Signac's journey and the studious efforts on the part of the painter, who had become engrossed in the atmosphere of an industrious city and the character of its inhabitants. Brusse writes that he explained 'all sorts of things' to him which had a bearing on 'the most puissant port' and that he also took him on trips to 'the markets, the wharfs, the inner harbours, the streets of the inner city, not forgetting the Zandstraat neighbourhood, 'the blood-red amorous sinful heart of the world port.'[16] Signac

5.
O. Maus, 'Le salon des Indépendants', *L'Art Moderne*, 6 May 1906, pp. 141-142; quoted in De Forges 1963, p. 74.

6.
Freeman 1990.

7.
Série de vues de la Tamise à Londres (1900 à 1904), Paris (Galeries Durand-Ruel), 9 May-4 June 1904. On this series: House 1987, pp. 75-88; Callen 1973, pp. 33-38.

8.
Callen 1973, pp. 71-74; Freeman 1990; Marquet 1994-1, pp. 140-144; Dagen 1994-1, p. 171, note 1. Dagen points out that only one stay of Derain's in London can be proven between January and March 1906. No details are known of another trip by Derain to London – in the literature usually placed in the autumn of 1905. It highly questionable whether this actually took place.

9.
A. Pératé, 'Les salons de 1907 (premier article)', *Gazette des Beaux-Arts*, 49 (1907), vol. 37, pp. 357-358; quoted in De Forges 1963, p. 79. Exhib.cat., *Salon des Indépendants*, Paris (Grandes Serres), 20 March-30 April 1907, no. 4538, as: *Rotterdam*.

10.
See Brusse 1935; this memorial article appeared after Signac's death in the *Nieuwe Rotterdamsche Courant*. Anonymous, 'Paul Signac', *Nieuwe Rotterdamsche Courant*, 18 August 1935, quoted as Signac 1935.

11.
Freeman 1990, p. 87, letter from Signac to Henri Manguin, note 125.

12.
Brusse 1935 in front of the Victoria Hotel.

13.
Brusse 1935; Signac 1935.

14.
Lespinasse 1988, p. 385.

15.
Cousturier 1922, p. 41.

16.
Brusse 1935; Brusse 1917, p. 6. Signac also visited the Rijksmuseum and Stedelijk Museum in Amsterdam.

17.
Ferretti-Bocquillon 1992, pp. 62, 64, 86; Bock 1981, p. 61. Citaat in Rewald 1949-1953, II, p. 282 (15 September 1898); see also Besson 1947, p. 76 (September 1902).

18.
Signac 1899 (ed. 1939), pp. 73-74; Cachin 1971, pp. 73-76; Bock 1981, pp. 61-62. Measurements of the painting *Rotterdam. The Port*, 870 x 1140 mm; preparatory drawing 87 x 114 cm (auction Paris, Drouot, 2 June 1926, no. 56). Measurements of the painting *Les fumées*, 75 x 92 cm; preparatory drawing 710 x 886 mm.

19.
Kellermann 1992, p. LI.

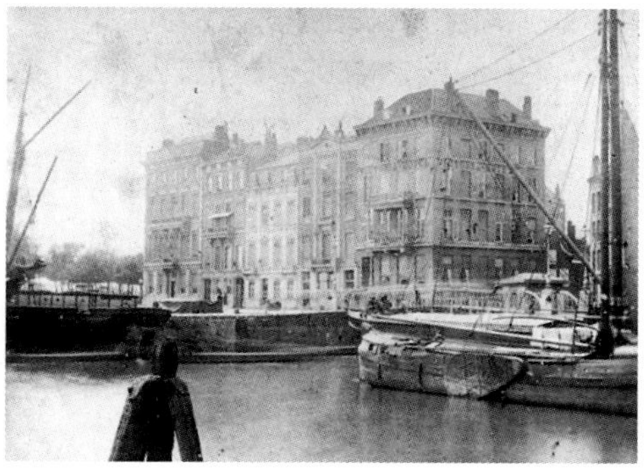

Hotel Victoria, c. 1890
Municipal Archives, Rotterdam

did not however return to Paris with painted impressions of the river Maas, but with a portfolio of black chalk and watercolour studies. These sketches 'on the motif', also called by Signac 'renseignements' or 'documents', were intended for use as documentation material, 'on doit se documenter et non copier.'[17] It was only afterwards, in his Paris studio, that the series of paintings depicting the Rotterdam port were made.

The chalk studies and the colourful watercolours made in Rotterdam aided Signac in his painting, in his translation of the Neo-Impressionist palette of pure colours and also in his search for the most suitable complementary contrast. The pen and ink drawing *Les fumées*, which at a first glance would seem to be far removed from Signac's painted impression, was also a part of this creative process. The composition in blacks and greys, almost the same size as the painting, was put together from different studies made on the spot, and in this way created the abstraction that Signac was looking for.[18] It is 'the line' in Signac's canvases which consist ostensibly of 'colour'. The preparatory drawing in pen and ink on cardboard, served as a compositional aid when painting in his well-known chequered marks. Vestiges of this studio practice are perhaps traceable to the few blobs of paint on the drawing. Thus the condensed image can still, without any difficulty, be located as depicting the Leuvenhaven. The pontoon and the group of tugboats to the left, with the old, later demolished, level-crossing behind it form one perspective (fig.); the silhouette of the harbour-sheds, industrial buildings and the steeple of the church on the Stieltjesplein, a second. (fig.)

In the drawing *Les fumées*, Signac stylized the wisps of smoke of the steam tugboats, the factory chimneys, and a train, which together with the ribbons of clouds and the waves of the river water formed one decorative pattern, a composition of arabesques, which suggest movement and activity. What is so exquisite about this abstraction is the fact that Signac's beautiful passionate hand was maintained. Ultimately, it was this effect that André Derain admired at the exhibition at Bernheim-Jeune in 1907, far more than the balanced colour compositions in oils: 'Par contre il en a fait des croquis sur le catalogue qui sont des chefs d'oeuvre.'[19] (fig.)

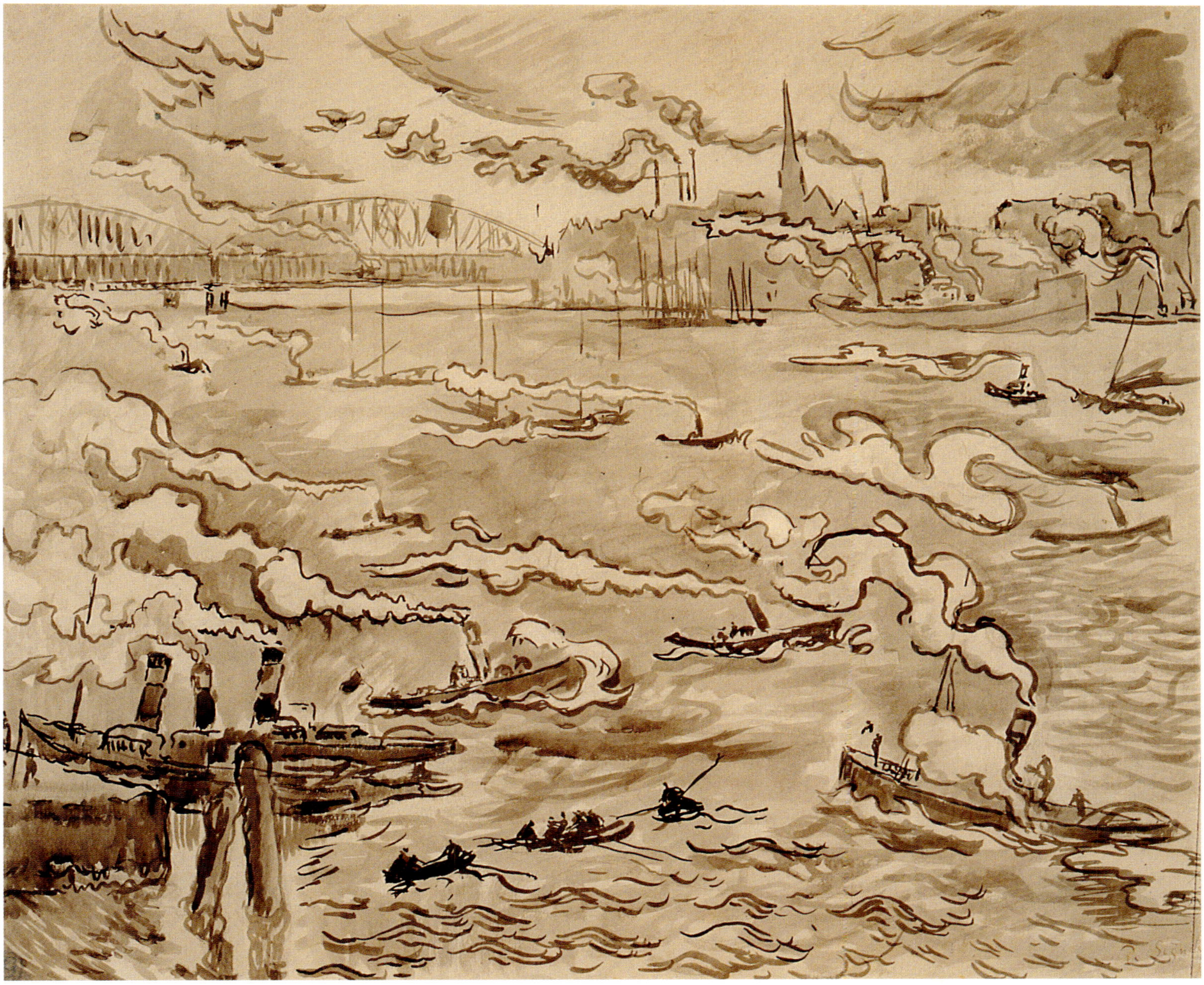

16. Paul Signac, *Les fumées*, 1906

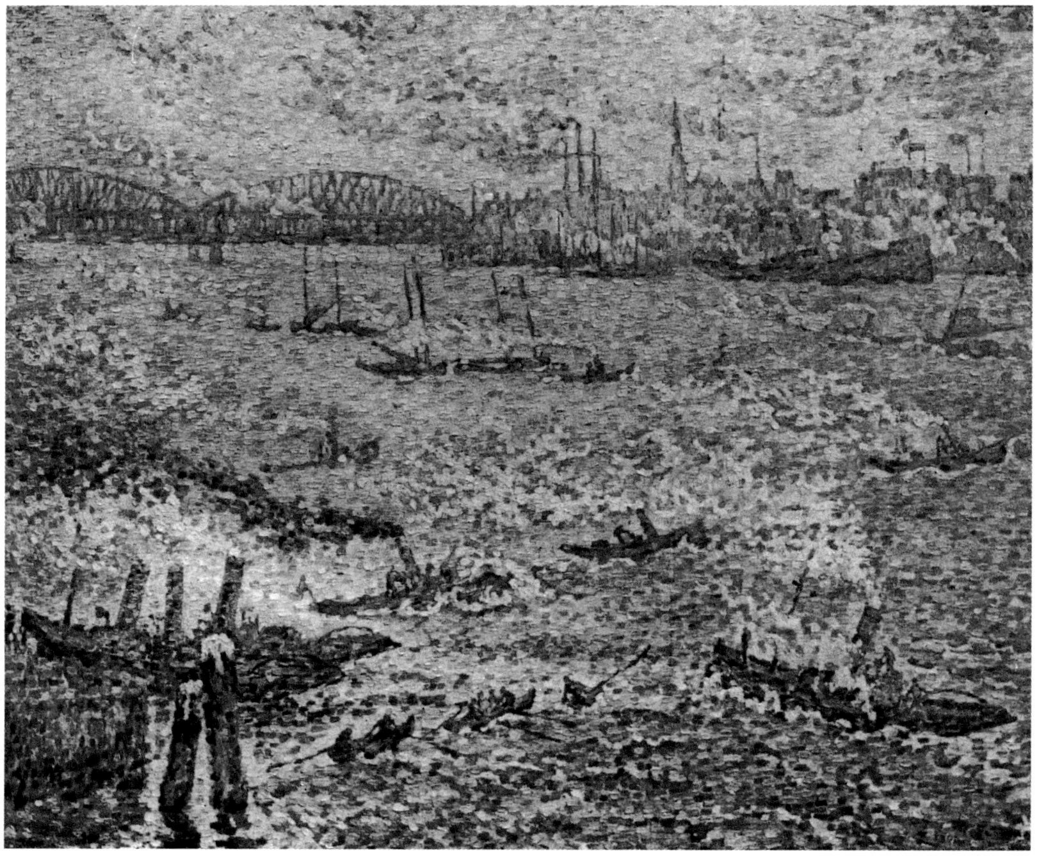

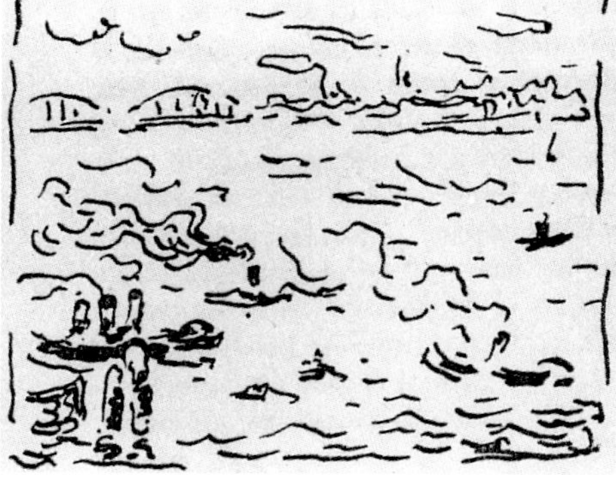

Paul Signac
Les fumées, 1906
Oil on canvas, 75 x 92 cm

Paul Signac, *Les fumées*,
fig. 1 in exhib.cat., *Paul Signac*, Paris (Bernheim-Jeune) 1907

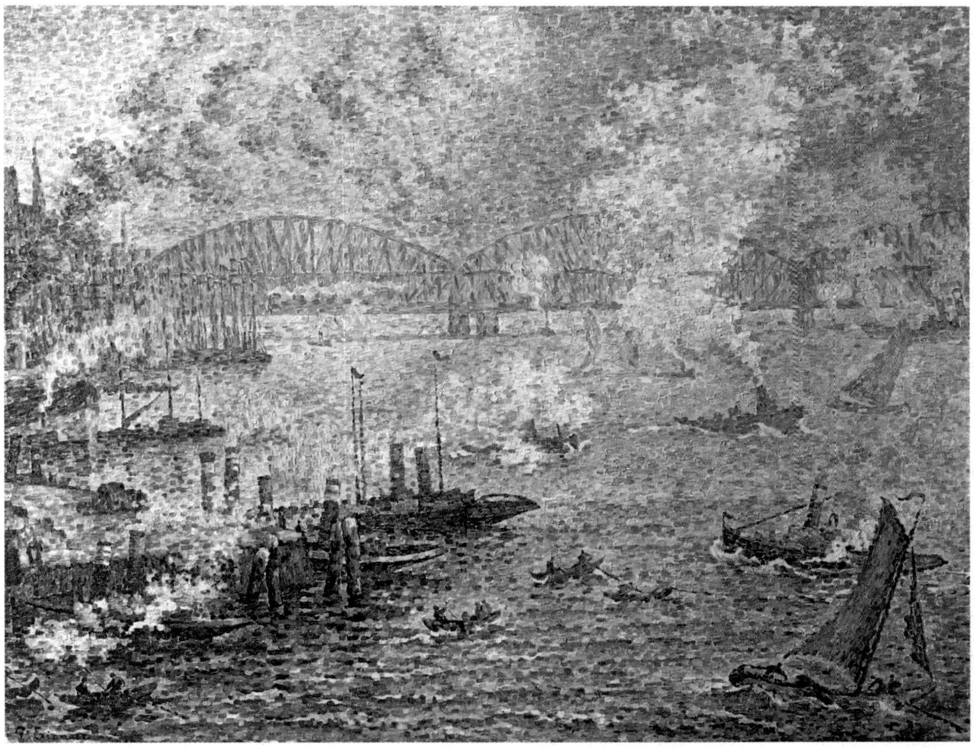

Paul Signac, *Rotterdam. The port,* 1907
Oil on canvas, 87 x 114 cm
Boijmans Van Beuningen Museum, Rotterdam

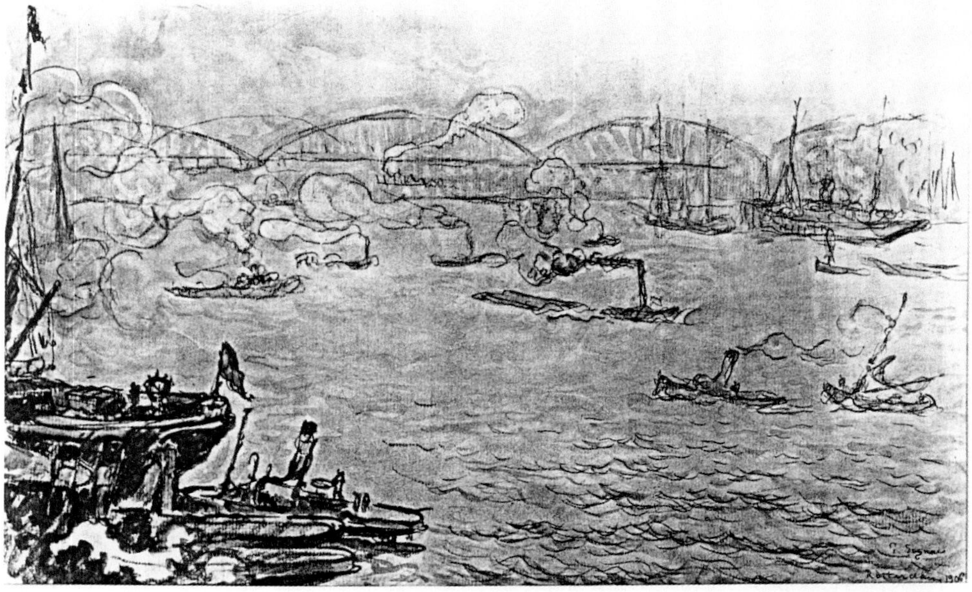

Paul Signac, *Les fumées*, 1906
Black chalk, watercolour, 265 x 433 mm

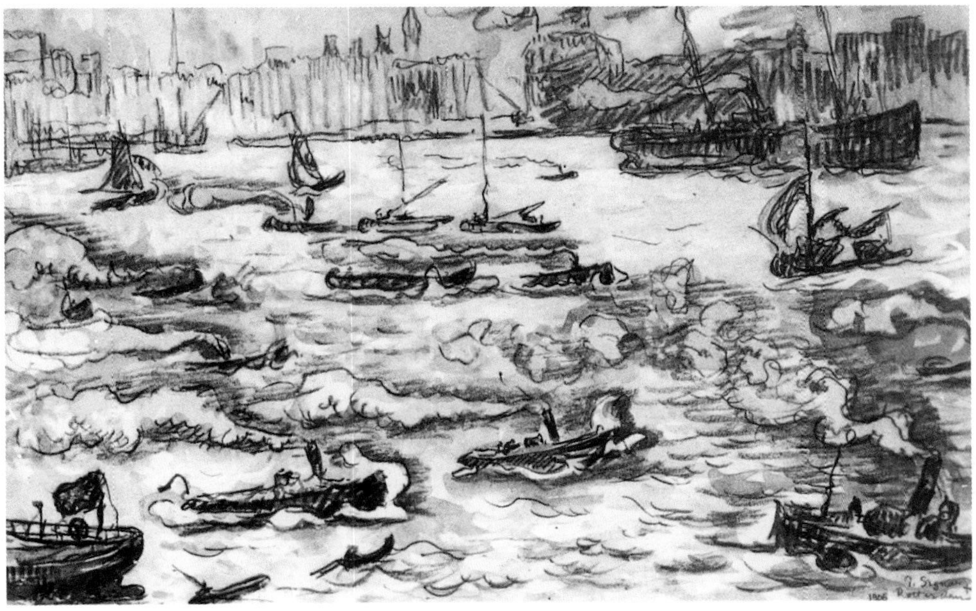

Paul Signac, *Rotterdam*, 1906
Black chalk, watercolour, gouache, 269 x 446 mm

17. Paul Signac (Paris 1863-1935 Paris)
La Calanque (The Calanque), 1906
Pencil, brush with black ink, watercolour
278 x 438 mm
Unsigned
EXHIBITIONS:
Signac & Saint-Tropez 1892-1913, Saint-Tropez (Musée de l'Annonciade); Reims (Musée des Beaux-Arts), 1992, no. 39 (fig.)
COLLECTION:
Private collection

In outdoor watercolour studies like *La Calanque*, Signac tried to capture his experience of nature as directly as possible using line and colour. The artist Camille Pissarro had drawn his attention to this technique back in 1888, as a much quicker way of rendering nature than, for example, sketching in oils: 'Je vous recommande l'aquarelle, c'est précieux, très pratique, on peut arriver en quelques minutes à prendre des notes impossibles autrement, la fluidité d'un ciel, certaines transparences, un tas de petits renseignements qu'un lent travail ne peut donner, c'est si fugitif les effets!.'[1] In the years that followed 1895 these studies became more important to Signac. Around about this period he left Pointillism and George Seurat's idea of optical colour-mixing and moved on to painting in large chequered marks. Through these larger marks, and the interplay between them, Signac tried to achieve an effect whereby the pure colours stand out. Also, he was more interested than he had previously been in incorporating his personal observations into his paintings. From then on he made more expressive use of the colour relations and the marks of paint, together with the composition, though he still largely leaned on the colour theories and principles of Neo-Impressionism. 'Nous sortons de la dure période d'analyse pour entrer dans celle de la création personelle et varié', was the way he summarized his new insights in his journal dated September 1895.[2] The watercolour studies served as *documents*, with the aid of which the impressions of colour registered could be transposed into more balanced, painted colour compositions.

The entries in his journal reveal the great importance Signac attached to these watercolour studies. It appears that while painting the canvas *Saint-Tropez. Le phare* (1895), a view of the harbour at sunset, he regularly returned to his subject in the evenings to refresh his colour impressions on the spot: *pris tous les soirs de nombreux renseignements pour mon* Soleil couchant.[3] During the preparation for another painting, a rendition of stormy skies, *Saint-Tropez. L'orage* (1895), he even used preparatory studies he had lithographed so that he could note down his impressions more rapidly.[4] The importance which Signac attributed to his watercolour sketches is also demonstrated by the fact that at his first solo exhibition at Gallery Bing in Paris in 1902, he exhibited no less than 100 watercolours – in addition to twenty paintings and oil studies. At following exhibitions there was a more even balance between the different media.

Countless examples of these quickly-drawn outdoor studies of Signac's have been preserved: drawings in pencil or black chalk, showing swift sweeps of the brush in the style of Jongkind, or a more structured approach using pen and ink filled in with watercolour, inspired by Van Gogh's style.[6] Signac allowed himself more freedom in these watercolours than in his paintings. This can be seen in the study *La Calanque* (fig.) of 1906, a mass of rocks, overgrown by fir trees, along the coast near Saint-Tropez which he rendered in various warm shades of orange, red, violet and yellow, using casual strokes that run into one another, unconcerned with theories on colour contrast. In this case, the freedom filtered through to the painting: the canvas *La Calanque* is painted with an equally warm-coloured palette, full of half-tones, with lively paint marks running in different directions which are not complemented in a systematic way.[7] The canvas ended up in Anna Boch's collection, one of the few people to have bought a Van Gogh from the artist when he was still alive.[8]

Many people appreciated Signac's watercolour studies more than his paintings.[9] Watercolour, pen and ink studies like *La Calanque*, in which both colour and line determine the picture, offered Fauvist painters Henri Matisse and Kees van Dongen a point of reference for paintings like *Le bonheur de vivre* and *La jarretière* (cat. 116) of around 1906, in which the figures represented are surrounded by firm contour lines. A solution which, for Signac, was a step too far.[10]

1.
Letter 30 August 1888, quoted in Cachin 1971, p. 73; Ferretti-Boquillon 1992, p. 85.
2.
Ferretti-Boquillon 1992, pp. 64, 86. For this drawing see, 1 September 1895, Rewald 1949-1953, I, p. 126. See also Bock 1981, pp. 61-62.
3.
Diary note 12 June 1895, quoted in Ferretti-Boquillion 1992, p. 64; see Rewald 1949-1953, I, p. 125.
4.
Ferretti-Boquillon 1992, pp. 62, 95.
5.
Exposition d'oeuvres de Paul Signac, Paris (Galerie Bing), June 1902; here Signac exhibited 100 watercolours as well as 9 paintings, 12 oil studies and 2 pastel drawings; see De Forges 1963, p. 98. At Bernheim-Jeune in 1907, 40 paintings and 40 watercolours.
6.
For Signac's interest in Jongkind: P. Signac, *Jongkind*, Paris 1927; Signac's admiration of Van Gogh in Hammacher 1962. See also Ferretti-Boquillon 1992, pp. 85-87.
7.
Ferretti-Boquillon 1992, pp. 82, 107.
8.
Ferretti-Boquillon 1992, p. 82. For the painting by Van Gogh, De la Faille 1970, no. 495. See further M. Bailey, *Apollo*, March 1996, pp. 20-21.
9.
Cachin 1971, pp. 77-84. According to Jean Puy, Matisse is supposed to have been completely *emballé* by Signac's exhibition at Druet's, December 1904; Cachin 1971, p. 79.
10.
Letter from Signac to Charles Angrand, 14 January 1906. See Barr 1951, p. 82; Bock 1981, p. 124, note 64; Flam 1993, pp. 226-235; see also cat. 116.

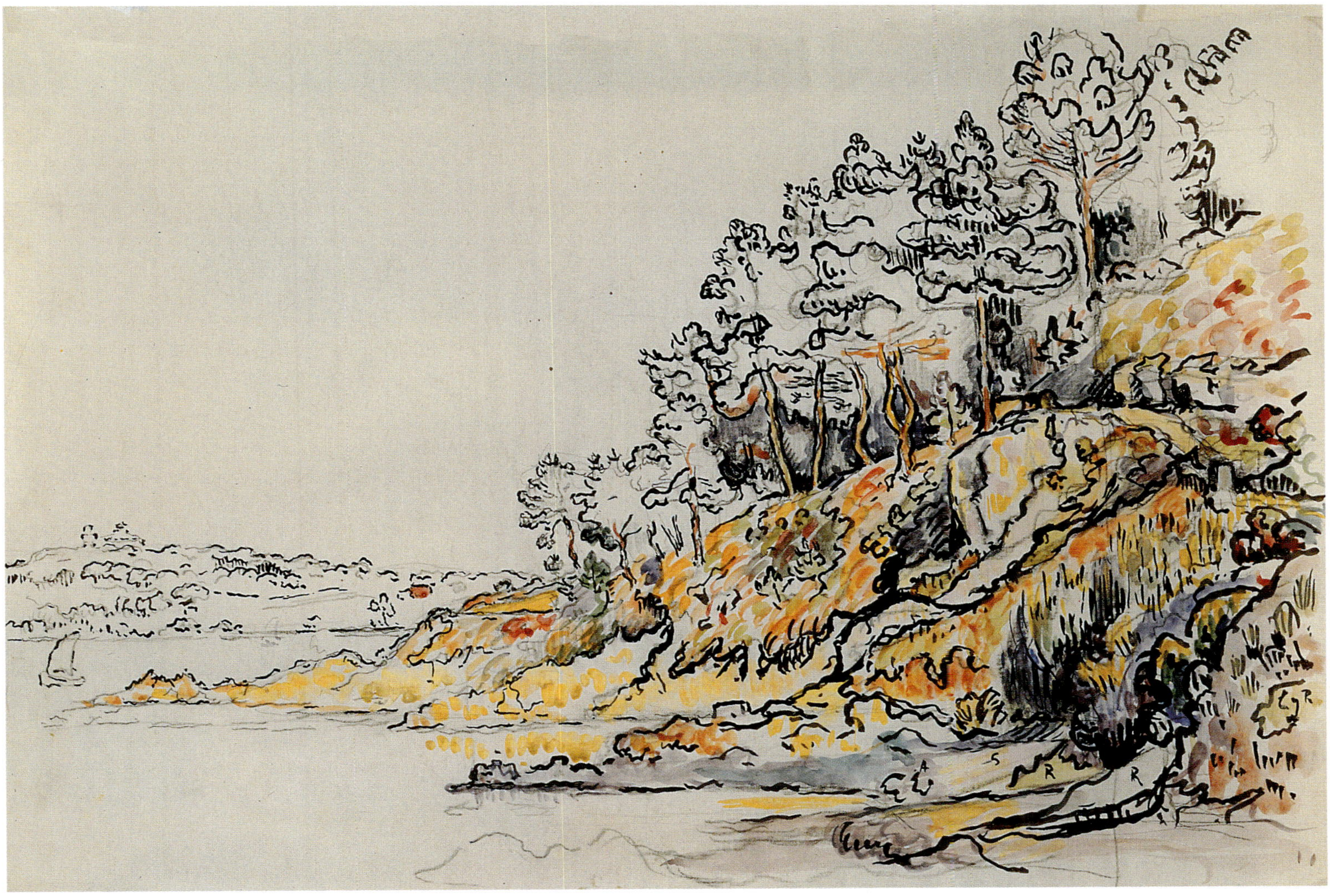

17. Paul Signac, *La Calanque*, 1906

18. Henri Matisse (Le Cateau-Cambrésis 1869-1954 Nice)
Le port de Collioure (The port of Collioure), 1905
Pen with black ink
274 x 445 mm
Signed lower right in black chalk: *H.M.*
On verso: stamp Galerie Ketterer Stuttgart, no. 848
PROVENANCE:
Private collection, 1931 (purchased from Henri Matisse); Frank Perls, Beverly Hills, c. 1970; auction Berne, Kornfeld & Klipstein, 9 June 1976, no. 636 (fig.); Lionel Pregger, 1981; Galerie Dina Vierny, Paris, 1982; Galerie Rosengart, Lucerne, 1982; Fondation Pierre Gianadda, Martigny, 1989
EXHIBITIONS:
Matisse, Paris (Galerie Dina Vierny), 1982, p. 45 (fig.)
COLLECTION:
Fondation Pierre Gianadda, Martigny, Switzerland

19. André Derain (LeChatou 1880-1954 Garches)
Collioure, 1905
Watercolour
320 x 235 mm
Lower right studio stamp: *ATELIER/André DERAIN* (L 668a)
PROVENANCE:
Artist's studio; Galerie Romanet, Paris, 1963; private collection
EXHIBITIONS:
Deux cents aquarelles et dessins de Renoir à Picasso, Paris (Galerie Romanet), 1963, no. 22 (illus.). *Le début du siècle aux Indépendants. 'Ni jury ni récompenses'*, Paris (Grand Palais), 1967, no. 24.
COLLECTION:
Private collection

20. Henri Matisse (Le Cateau-Cambrésis 1869-1954 Nice)
Grand nu (Large nude), 1906
Brush in ink
535 x 455 mm
Lower right artist's stamp: *HM*
PROVENANCE:
Artist's legacy; private collection
COLLECTION:
Private collection

Henri Matisse
(Le Cateau-Cambrésis 1869-1954 Nice)
André Derain
(Chatou 1880-1954 Garches)

In the years 1905-07, Matisse on several occasions spent periods of a few months in the French fishing village of Collioure on the Mediterranean coast near the border with Spain. He drew the harbour scene *Le port de Collioure* during his first visit in 1905 from a point somewhere on the edge of the village on the southern side of the bay.[1] The loosely sketched lines in the background depict the spit of land that encloses the northern side of the harbour. Encouraged by Matisse, André Derain also came to spend some time there in the summer of 1905. His watercolour entitled *Collioure* shows the bay seen from the north with the foothills of the Pyrenees in the background. The creative competition between the two artists led to works being made in Collioure which created an enormous uproar at the Salon d'Automne of 1905. The question is what role did the drawings and watercolours by Matisse and Derain play in the development of the new style of Fauvist painting.

Matisse stayed in Collioure from May to September of 1905. He managed to rent a work space in the building of the local train station with a view looking out over the sea; a little later Derain also found a studio in this building.[2] The idea of spending the summer months somewhere on the Mediterranean coast instead of in Paris was obviously a result of an earlier occasion when Matisse stayed with Signac in Saint-Tropez.[3] During this summer of 1904 Matisse's painting methods changed considerably. Influenced by the views of his host and the southern light, in Saint-Tropez he painted in a Neo-Impressionist palette of pure colour which he applied to the canvas in loose dabs. That he found this way of working disappointing, and that his artistic communication with Signac was sometimes awkward, is apparent from various 'lettres désolées' Matisse wrote to Manguin and Marquet from Saint-Tropez.[4] Yet he must have considered the stay worthwhile; it provided him with the impetus for a new direction in his work. Once back in Paris in the autumn of 1904, based on the studies he'd made in the summer, Matisse began work on the large, Neo-Impressionist canvas *Luxe, calme et volupté* – a group of figures on the beach – which he exhibited at the Salon des Indépendants of 1905. What was innovative in Matisse's work was that, unlike his immediate example of Signac, he spread the dabs of colour out on the canvas leaving white spaces in between which increased the brightness, or the strength of the light in his image whereby the colours worked far more strongly together. This led to a sort of duel between the colours, a vibration of colour: 'il préfère...demander au pointillisme plus de vibrations, de luminosité', observed the obviously well-informed critic, Louis Vauxcelles, about Matisse's new approach.[5] In 1905, the results he had achieved led him to once again decide to spend the summer on a southern piece of coast to continue his Neo-Impressionist experiments.[6]

On 25 June 1905, after he had been in Collioure for about a month, Matisse wrote a postcard to the young André Derain persuading him to come and join him there: 'je ne saurais trop insister pour vous persuader qu'un séjour ici vous est absolument nécessaire pour votre travail. Vous y seriez dans les conditions les plus avantageuses et vous tirerez des bénéfices péuniaires sur le travail que vous y ferez.'[7] Derain arrived at the beginning of July and stayed two months. Derain wrote enthusiastically of the 'blond, dorée' southern light there in the first letter he sent to Maurice de Vlaminck in mid July. Not much later, on 28 July, Derain told Vlaminck what he had already gained from the trip: first, the discovery of a new idea of light, that shadow doesn't exist, that the world is full of colour; and second, that he had all but eradicated the work he had earlier done on

1.
For a comparable drawing, Flam 1986, p. 126, fig. 115. See also Schneider 1984, pp. 204-220.
2.
Freeman 1990, pp. 68-69; Monod-Fontaine 1993, pp. 66-68; Marquet 1994, pp. 112-116.
3.
Bock 1981, pp. 63-67; Flam 1986, pp. 110-112. Matisse left for Saint-Tropez on 11 July: Schneider 1984, p. 135, note 36.
4.
Monod-Fontaine, 1993, pp. 63-64. The name 'lettres désolées' comes from Marquet in a letter to Manguin, 8 August 1904; Freeman 1990, pp. 63-64, note 16 and 18. Bock 1981, pp. 66, 139-140, note 9, puts in perspective the argument that was supposed to have taken place between Matisse and Signac.
5.
Louis Vauxcelles, 'Le Salon d'Automne', *Gil Blas*, 17 October 1905. Vauxcelles earlier praised the painting *Tulipes perroquets II*, *Gil Blas*, 14 June 1905: exhibition A. Prath & P. Maynier, Paris. He wrote about it to Matisse 27 June 1905. See Fourcade 1993, p. 142, no. 9; Monod-Fontaine 1993, pp. 66-67. On luminosity, Flam 1986, p. 124; Flam 1994, p. 40.
6.
Amélie Matisse may possibly have made a reconnaisance visit to Collioure in October 1904, Freeman 1990, p. 64.
7.
Monod-Fontaine 1993, p. 67; Marquet 1994, p. 116, note 8.

the division of colour – something Matisse, observed Derain, was still persisting with. But Derain allowed himself to be entirely led by colour: 'Je me suis laissé aller à la couleur pour la couleur.'[8]

The two artists were extremely productive. Self-aware, Derain wrote on 5 August – a couple of weeks before his return to Paris – J'aurai, pour mon retour, trente toiles de faites, vingt dessins et une cinquantaine de croquis. Matisse informs us of his achievements in a letter from 4 September: c'est-à-dire quarante aquarelles, une centaine de dessins et quinze toiles.[9] The results were exhibited in the famous Salon d'Automne of 1905 in Paris where the 'orgy of pure colour' chiefly provoked distaste and resistance. Matisse exhibited a total of ten pieces including paintings, drawings and watercolours, all of which, though perhaps with a few exceptions, had been made during his stay at Collioure or shortly afterwards. Among these was the drawing *Le pêcheur* (fig.) and the paintings *La fenêtre ouverte* and *Femme au chapeau* (fig.), a portrait of his wife with a fan and wearing an extravagant hat which was painted in exuberant colours and became the centre of attention at the Salon. At the end of the Salon, the painting was bought by the American collectors Gertrude Stein and her brother Leo.[10] Derain's contribution to the Salon comprised five canvases and four pastel drawings, probably all works made, or started in Collioure. Among these was the beautiful canvas, almost entirely painted in primary colours, *Le séchage des voiles* (fig.), which came into the possession of the Russian collector Ivan Morosov during the Salon. Derain also met the art dealer Vollard who decided to buy everything Derain had made up to that point.[11] The financial benefits Matisse had predicted, had become a fact.

This first success led to more success for Matisse. Like the year before, in the winter of 1905-06 using the studies he had made in the summer, he worked on a large canvas which was intended to encompass his latest views on painting. The result of this, *Le bonheur de vivre*, once again a pastoral scene, was the only piece he submitted to the Indépendants of 1906. During this exhibition Leo Stein, realizing that this was possibly 'the most important painting of our time', bought the work. It can now be found in the Barnes Foundation in Merion.[12]

New journeys followed these sales and contacts. Derain worked in London for the first few months of 1906 and in the summer he went to l'Estaque near Marseilles. Here he stayed, with a short break in Paris for the Salon d'Automne, until the end of the year. After a short trip to Algeria in May, Matisse spent the summer months of 1906, and later on the winter season, in Collioure. The human figure is the main subject in Matisse's work from 1906. In Collioure, in the mornings he drew his wife nude in the wooded countryside and, he wrote, liberated himself from every established method, by working directly from nature. During this year, Matisse was also in contact with the sculptor Aristide Maillol (who was staying at Banyuls-sur-Mer in the south) and worked on a number of sculptures, again with the human figure as the subject. A third summer season in Collioure followed in 1907.[13]

Clearly, Matisse and Derain's stays on the coast were highly productive. The strikingly self-aware letters quoted above, in which both artists told their friends about a number of works they had made in 1905 also inform us of their artistic views: they indicate the importance that drawings or preparatory studies had for them. From the letters it is apparent that Matisse, unlike Derain, made considerably more preparatory studies than finished paintings (140 drawings compared to 15 paintings). It is also characteristic of Matisse that he first mentioned the works on paper, referring to the drawings and watercolours separately, whereas Derain, in his letter, spoke first of the paintings, a total of thirty (in contrast to 70 works on paper). Derain painted twice as many canvases in Collioure as Matisse, even though he wasn't there for as long. These facts correspond well with the picture we have of both their ways of working. The importance Matisse placed on his drawings is comparable to that of Signac. However, Matisse, unlike Signac, drew a clear distinction between the uses for the watercolours (research

8.
Freeman 1990, p. 73: 8 July 1905 Derain was in Collioure. Letter, about mid July, Dagen 1994-1, p. 159; letter 28 July, idem, p. 161: 'J'ai donc deux grands points, sur lesquels mon voyage m'aura beaucoup servi. 1° Une nouvelle conception de la lumière qui consiste en ceci: la négation de l'ombre. Ici, les lumières sont très fortes, les ombres très claires. L'ombre est tout un monde de clarté et de luminosité qui s'oppose à la lumière du soleil: ce qu'on apelle des reflets. 2° Savoir, dans le voisinage du travail de Matisse, extirper tout ce que la division du ton avait dans la peau. Il continue, mais moi, j'en suis complètement revenu et je ne l'emploie presque plus'. Marquet 1994-1, pp. 114, 116, note 18: the much talked-about visit to Georges-Daniel de Monfreid probably never took place.

9.
Letter from Derain to Vlaminck, Dagen 1994-1, p. 166; letter from Matisse to Signac, Monod-Fontaine, 1993, p. 69.

10.
Flam 1986, pp. 140-43, fig. 133. Schneider 1984, p. 188.

11.
Marquet 1994, p. 114, no. 22; Freeman 1990, p. 251, fig. 266. Pushkin Museum Collection, Moscow. For Vollard: Marquet 1994, p. 437, *reçu* purchase dated 23 November 1905.

12.
Flam 1993, p. 235; Monod-Fontaine 1993, p. 74.

13.
For Derain see: Marquet 1994, p. 438; Dagen 1994-1, pp. 177-179; Monod-Fontaine 1993, p. 76. For Matisse: Freeman 1990, pp. 92-94, note 145; Monod-Fontaine 1993, pp. 76-78. Manguin was in Collioure from 12 July tot 14 August.

14.
Schneider 1984, p. 216, quoted from: Duthuit 1962, p. 198. For Matisse's 'spatial' drawing style in 1905, Cowart 1972, pp. 229-231.

15.
Cowart 1972, p. 229; Elderfield 1984, p. 30. For the maximum effect of this technique, Jean Puy 1939, p. 22, quoted in Elderfield 1984, p. 30.

16.
Dauberville 1995, vol. 1, pp. 428-429, no. 78: the drawing by Matisse was bought by Berheim-Jeune on 10 July 1919. In this catalogue the drawing is placed after *Nu vu de dos*, thus dated about 1907. A date sometime in 1906 is more likely.

17.
Cachin 1971, p. 79; Cowart 1972, p. 161.

18.
Schneider 1984, pp. 98, 264; Fourcade 1993, p. 420.

19.
Monod-Fontaine 1993, p. 68. Article in *L'Occident*, July 1904, pp. 17-30; concerns an interview by Emile Bernard with Cézanne. See also Cachin 1995, p. 564.

20.
Geldzahler 1962, p. 503: a Provence landscape given to Matisse by John Russell 1897, F 1427, Philadelphia Museum of Art Collection, Inv.no. 62-229-1. Monod-Fontaine 1990, pp. 253-54: a portrait of Patience Escalier, F 1461, provenance Ambroise Vollard and before that Emile Bernard. The third drawing, *Oogsters* (Harvesters), is F 1491, National Gallery of Art Collection, Washington, same provenance as F 1461. I thank Martha Op de Coul, RKD The Hague, for this information. *Salon des Indépendants, Exposition rétrospective Vincent van Gogh (1853-1890)*, Paris (Grandes serres) 24 March-30 April 1905, nos 29 (F 1461), 30 (F 1491), 31 (F 1427).

21.
Dagen 1994-1, p. 75, letter about March 1902.

22.
Marquet 1994, pp. 112-114.

into colour) and drawing. This is apparent from a note from 1905 in a sketchbook he used in Collioure: 'Employer le dessin pour indiquer l'expression des objets les uns par les autres...Employer la couleur pour son intensité lumineuse, dans ses diverses combinaisons, accords, et non pour définir les objets...' (...use drawing to indicate the expression of the objects in relation to one another...use colour for its luminous intensity, in its various combinations and harmonies, and not for defining objects).[14]

In the pen drawing *Le port de Collioure*, the definition of the relationships between objects seems to have been particularly important. The sketched ripples in the water serve to indicate the space between the drawing's foreground and background (the coast and the peninsula behind). The vertical lines of the ships' masts offer a firm hold: the rolling, horizontal (water) lines are contrasted with the ships' masts which help to determine the distance. With the few lines (ropes) that run from the group of fishing boats and the coastline to the figure in the foreground, another spatial effect is created. The attention Matisse paid to the depiction of space is also expressed in the drawing *Le pêcheur* (fig.) in which the lines in the water, together with the curve of the coastline on the right, depict the distance between the rocks in the foreground and the foothills of the mountains in the distance.[15] This linear suggestion of space is increased by the attention Matisse paid to the depiction of light. In *Le port de Collioure*, for example, this light is wonderfully represented by alternate white areas and marked, hatched shaded areas. Judging by the shadows, the sun was shining from the right suggesting that this sheet was made in the calm of early morning. The whole atmosphere of the drawing, the smooth water, the unrigged ships is also reminiscent of this time.

Matisse's choice of materials for these drawings – pen and black ink – was not accidental. The contrast between the white paper and black-ink lines is striking, as are the effects between the white and darker parts of his drawing. In this aspect the work is related to the strong, expressive use of colour he searched for in his Neo-Impressionist paintings. A few pen drawings from 1906, in which the more strongly applied lines increased the contrast between the light and dark areas even more, also bear witness to this. In *Entrée du Port* (fig.) there is a complete absence of tonal range.[16] The small sketches in the upper margin of this sheet illustrate how Matisse gave form to this contrast. Here a sailing ship has been sketched three times. Firstly as a graphic symbol, a simple triangle, then more realistically, using perspective, with a billowing sail and finally in a version in which the ship has been translated into light and dark areas. Matisse has drawn a line around this last sketch, as if to indicate that this was the best way to draw it. When comparing the drawings *Le port de Collioure* and *Entrée du port* it becomes clear that Matisse's way of working in 1905 was still exploratory and descriptive, and that he developed a more expressive drawing style in 1906.

From Signac we know that, in Saint-Tropez, Matisse had drawn directly from the subject with a plumb line to hand. The painter Jean Puy described how Matisse, during a drawing session at the Academie Camillo, by measuring and calculating, determined the position of the model he wanted to draw and in this way set out the main lines for his composition.[17] Also apparent from surviving letters is the extent to which this exploratory way of drawing – which completely conformed with the academic tradition – and the research into the liberation of colour, maintained an artistic hold on the ever-experimenting Matisse. In response to Signac's purchase of the previously mentioned canvas *Luxe, calme et volupté* (winter 1904-05), Matisse wrote to him on 14 July 1905: 'Avez-vous trouvé, dans mon tableau des Baigneuses [Luxe, calm et volupté], un accord parfait entre le caractère du dessin de la peinture? Selon moi, ils me paraissent totalement différents l'un de l'autre et même absolument contradictoires.'[18] Considering the conclusion that Matisse reached after this – that the Divisionist, or Neo-Impressionist technique destroys drawing whereas it is precisely in line that the strength of drawing lies – it would seem that the seed of rejection of Neo-Impressionism had already been sown. Matisse found further support for his artistic development in the work of Paul

Cézanne. In the same letter from July 1905 Matisse asks Signac to copy from an article a statement by Cézanne on the use of line and colour ('les deux plastiques') for him. Signac sent this to Matisse on 14 August: 'Le dessin et la couleur ne sont point distincts...Quand couleur est à sa richesse, la forme est à sa plénitude. Les contrastes et les rapports de ton: voilà le secret du dessin et du modelé.'[19] Matisse enquired about this comment by Cézanne because, dissatisfied with earlier solutions, he was looking for possibilities to link line and colour together, something that he only later, in the autumn of 1905 and then in 1906, appears to have achieved. In *Fenêtre ouverte* (1905) or *Le bonheur du vivre* (1906) his strong lines are combined with alternating large, closed and open, painted areas of colour. These canvases are also built up of contrasting areas of colour. In terms of effect and intensity of light, the drawings from 1906 can be measured against this Fauvist high-point in oil paint.The most impressive example of Matisse's drawing is perhaps *Nude in a Folding Chair* (fig.), for which the drawing entitled *Grand nu* would seem to have been a study or preparatory sketch. Finally, Matisse found an example for his specific way of drawing – the frenetic short strokes or strongly applied lines – in Van Gogh. Matisse had three drawings from Arles in his possession. He lent the drawings to the Van Gogh retrospective at the Salon des Indépendents in the spring of 1905.[20] This exhibition increased the interest Matisse already had for Van Gogh's drawings. In a single sheet made in Collioure, *Madame Matisse dans les oliviers* (fig.), he was influenced by both the artistic signature and the composition of the drawing *Haystacks* (fig.) by Van Gogh which he had in his possession.

This Van Gogh retrospective was perhaps even more significant for Derain than for the more cautious Matisse. Van Gogh's name crops up more than once in early letters from Derain to Maurice de Vlaminck, often with the name of Cézanne. And so the earlier exhibition of Van Gogh's work organized by Bernheim-Jeune in March 1901 was referred to several times by Derain: 'Il ya bientôt un an que nous avons vu Van Gogh et, vraiment, son souvenir me hante sans cesse.'[21] It was at this exhibition at Bernheim-Jeune that Matisse met Vlaminck and the latter expressed his enthusiasm for Van Gogh as the most important painter of the time. In the years that followed Van Gogh's work influenced the way both Vlaminck and Derain were to develop. This is clearly visible in Derain's work from early 1905. The pen drawings and *Séchage des voiles* that Derain made at Collioure – probably in the first few weeks of his stay there – are a direct result of this. The drawing *Vue de Collioure* (fig.) for example, which offers a view of the fishing harbour, is – in terms of technique – doubtless related to Van Gogh. It is also striking that in this sheet Derain strives towards a stark contrast between light and dark.

Despite recent attention for this artist, it is still far from clear how the work Derain made in Collioure should be ordered chronologically. An introduction to the places where he painted, seems more or less possible: first, the bay on the edge of the village; second, from the balcony of a friend's house which he rented with Matisse; and third, locations further up in the village and in the immediate area.[22] He appears to have worked with a restricted palette of pure colour to begin with. These are the colours Derain observed on his arrival in a letter to Vlaminck, 'des poteries rouge, voiles blanches, des barques multicolores'. The canvases that he made later on in Collioure are painted in a wider range of colours and mixed tones. The colourful watercolour titled *Collioure* would therefore have been made at the beginning of his stay rather than at the end, and in terms of approach can be compared to the painting *Séchage des voiles* with which he had so much success at the Salon.

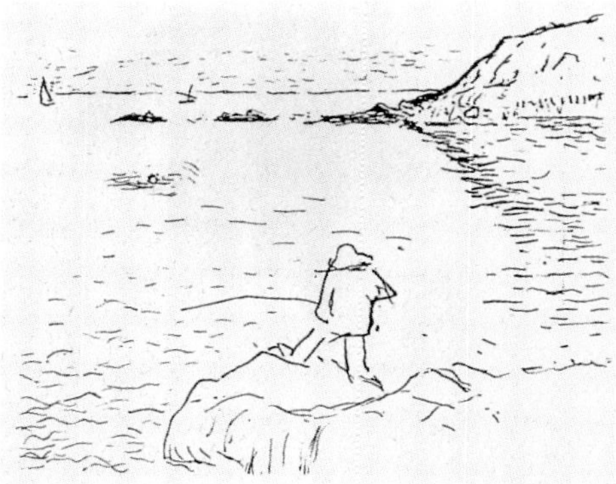

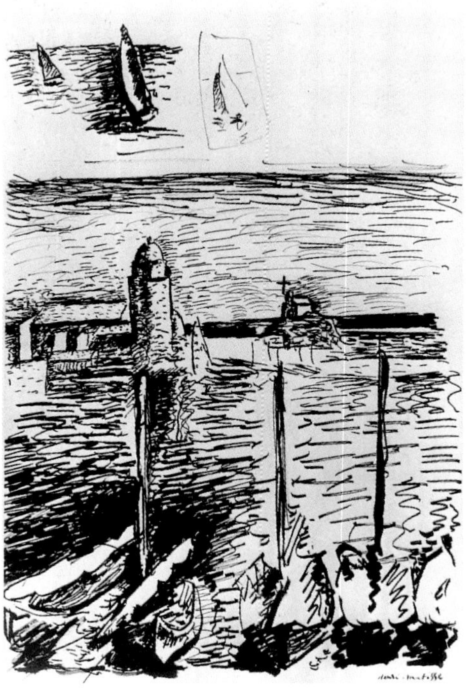

Henri Matisse, *Le pêcheur*, 1905
Pen and ink, 310 x 500 mm
Pushkin Museum, Moscow

Henri Matisse, *Entrée du port*, 1906
Pen and ink, 300 x 200 mm

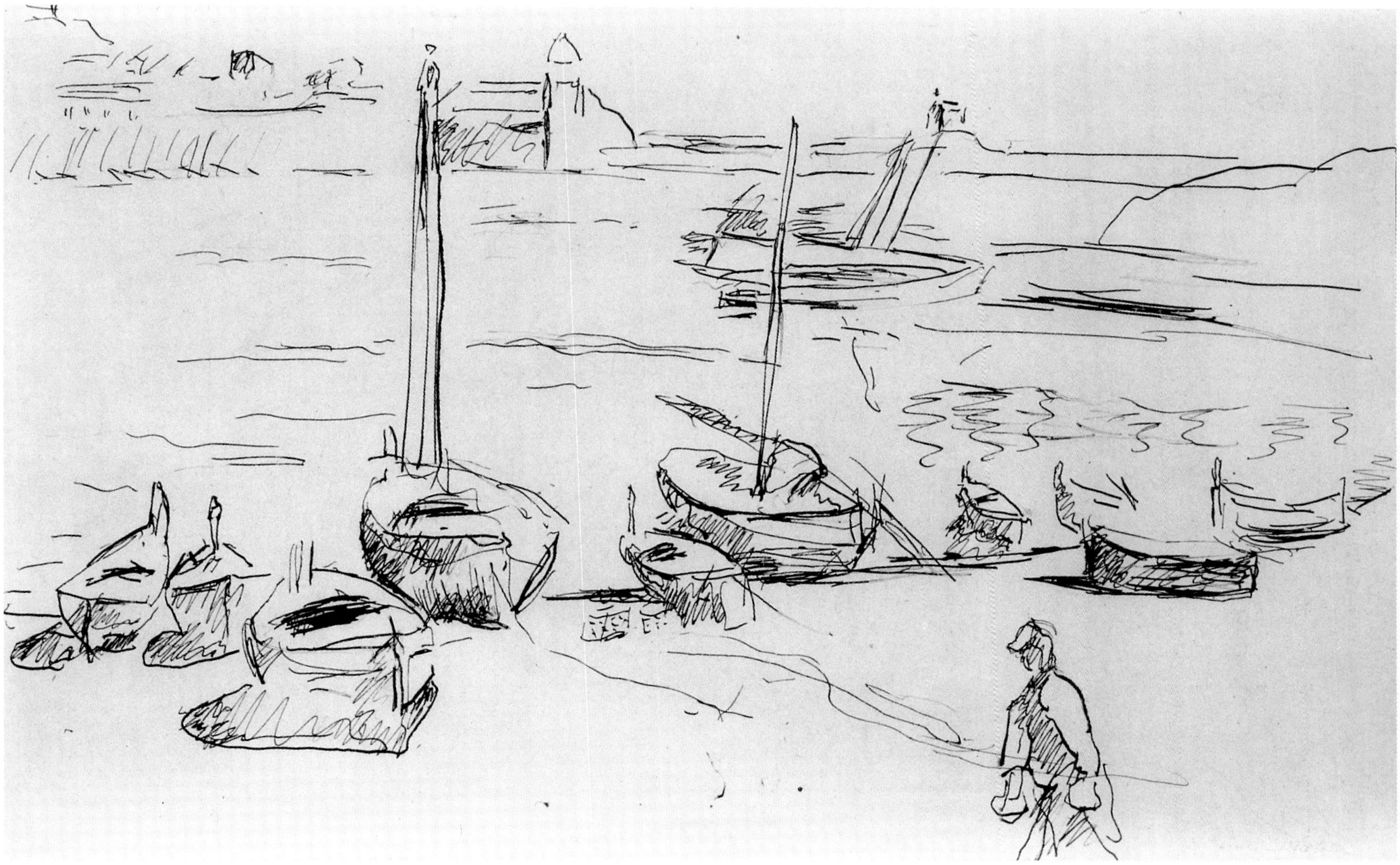

18. Henri Matisse, *Le port de Collioure*, 1905

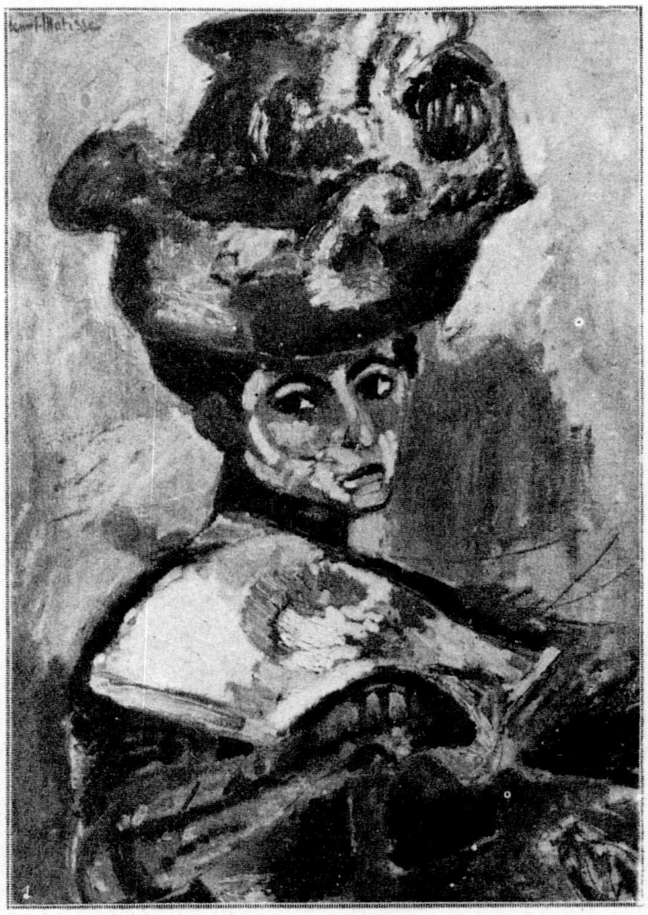

HENRI MATISSE. — Femme au chapeau.

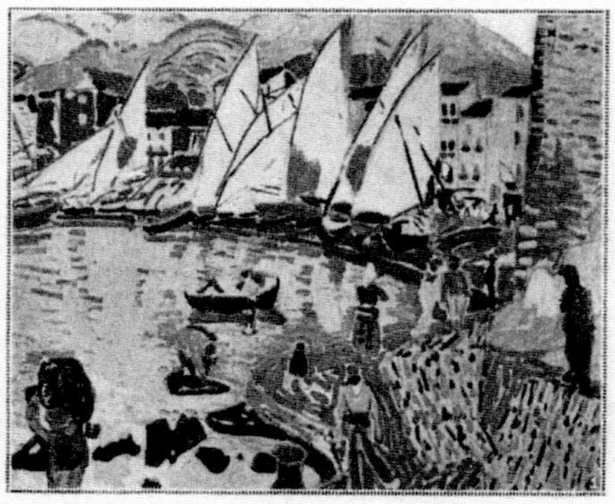

ANDRÉ DERAIN. — Le séchage des voiles.

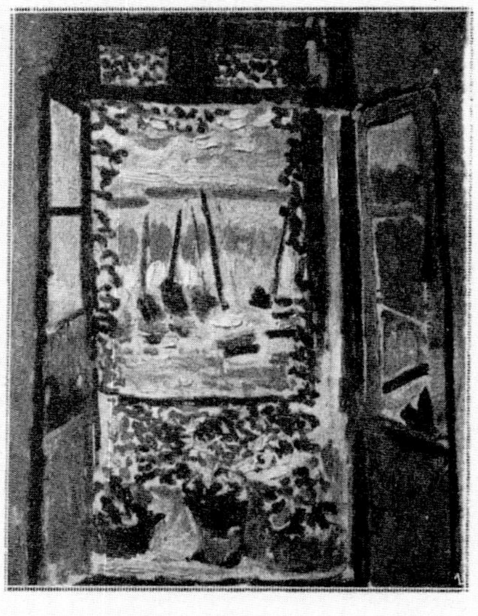

HENRI MATISSE. — Fenêtre ouverte.

Photo in 'Le Salon d'Automne', *L'Illustration*, no. 3271, 4 November 1905, p. 295

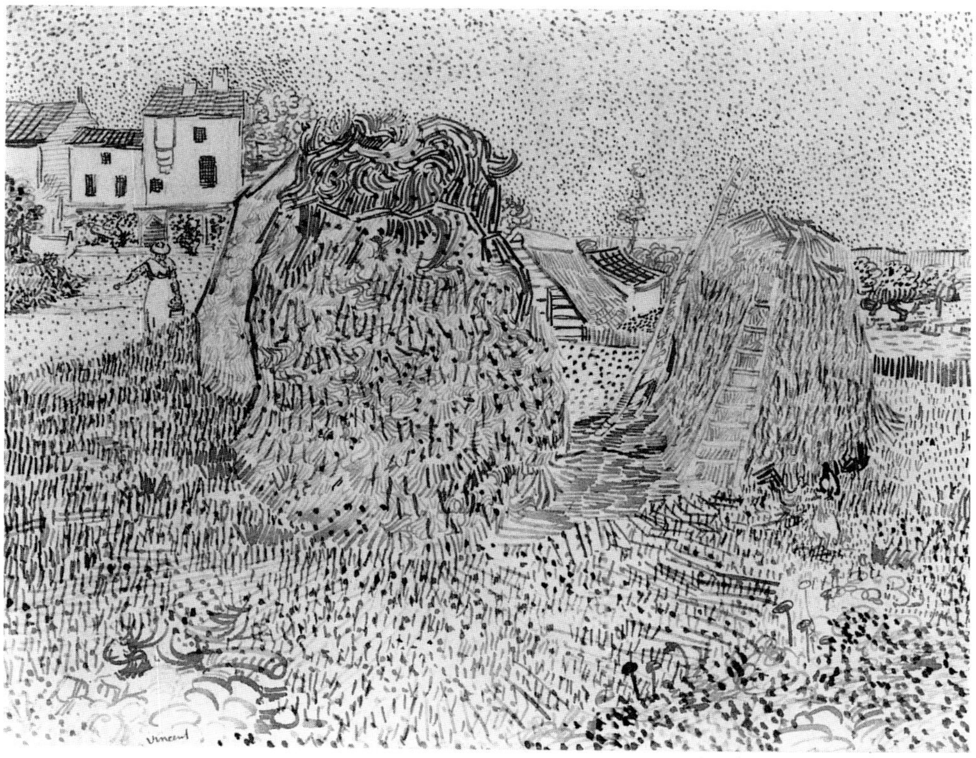

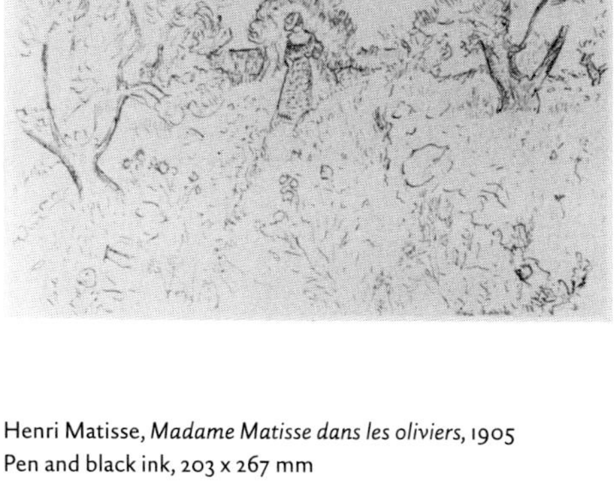

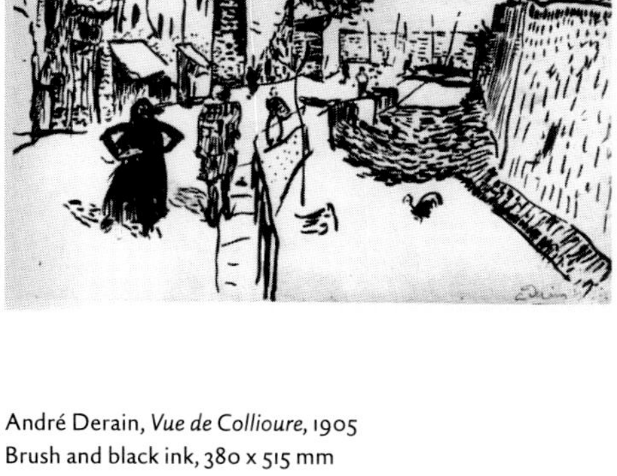

Henri Matisse, *Madame Matisse dans les oliviers*, 1905
Pen and black ink, 203 x 267 mm

André Derain, *Vue de Collioure*, 1905
Brush and black ink, 380 x 515 mm

Vincent van Gogh, *Haystacks*, 1888
Pencil, quill and reed pen in brown ink, 240 x 310 mm
The Philadelphia Museum of Art, Philadelphia

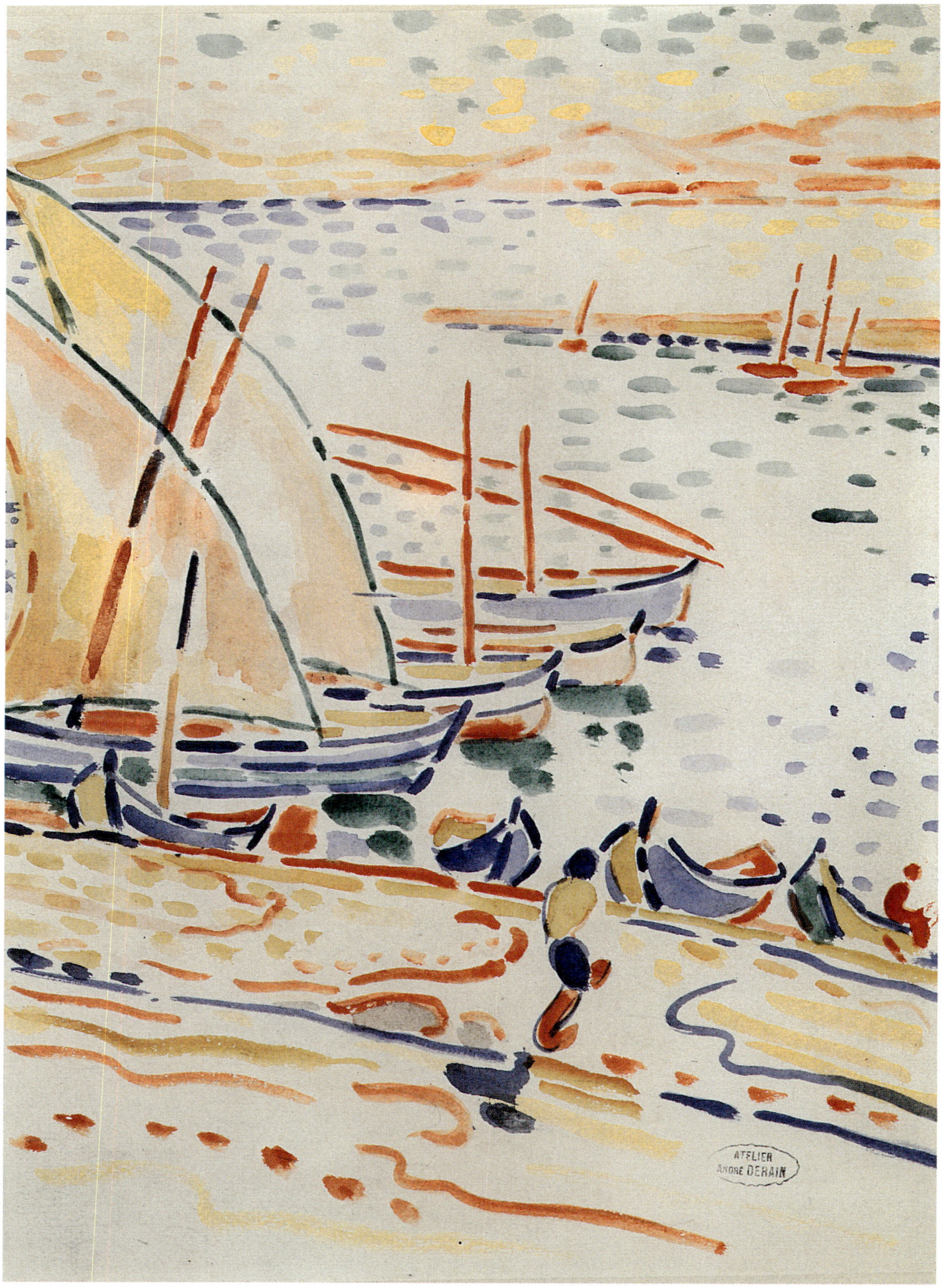

19. André Derain, *Vue de Collioure*, 1905

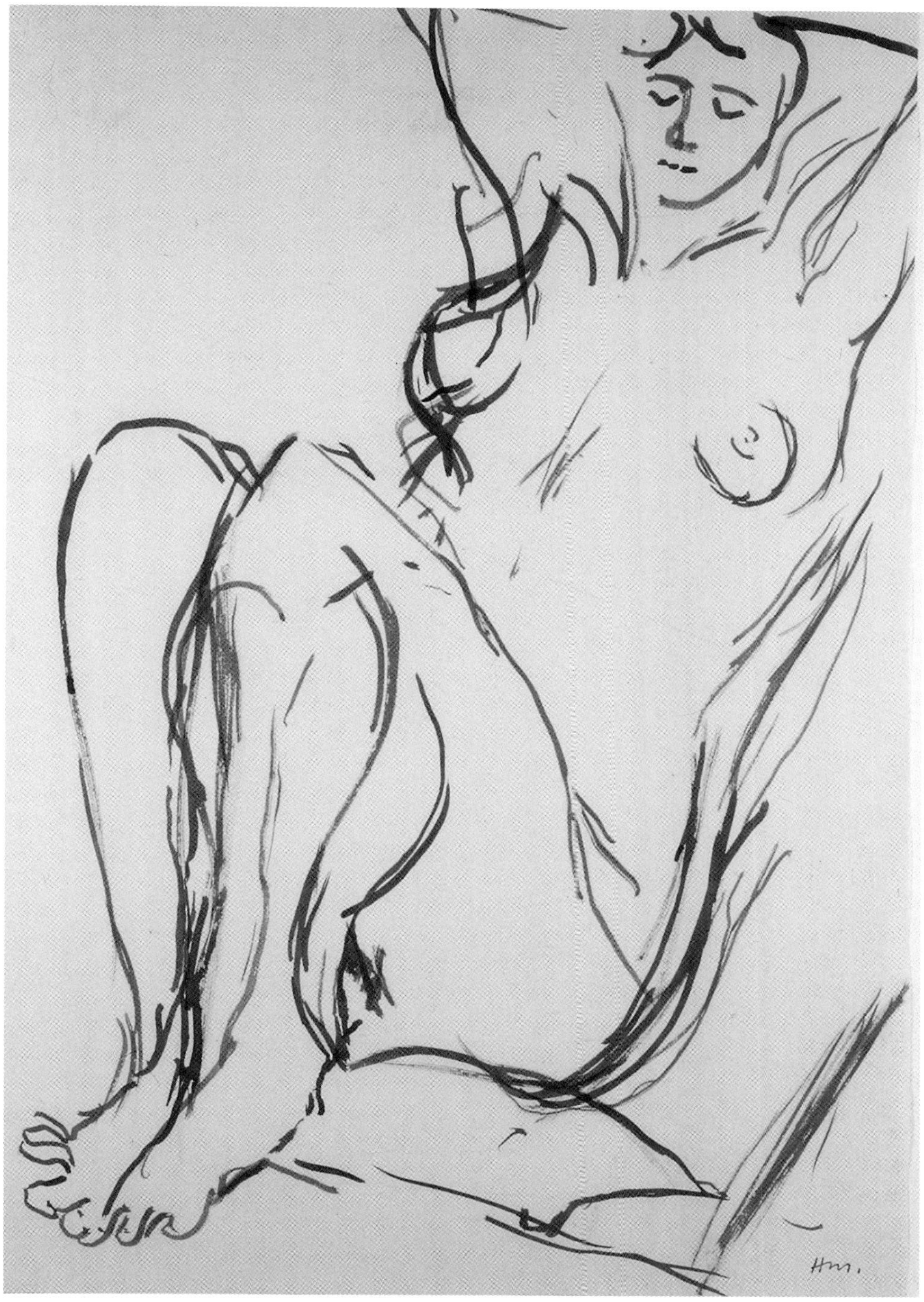

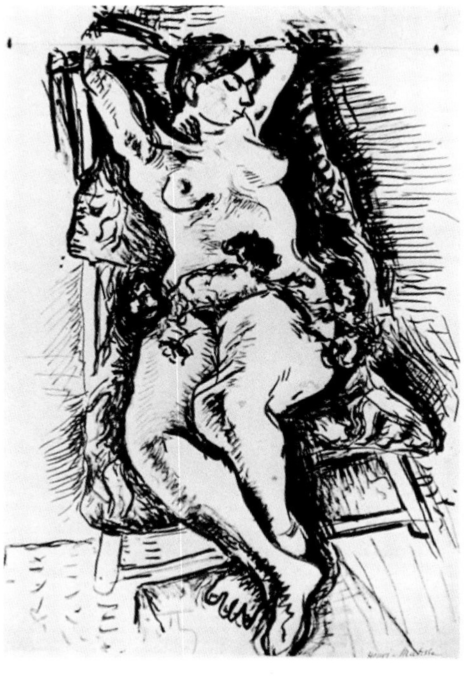

Henri Matisse, *Nude in a folding chair*, 1906
Brush and black ink, 657 x 467 mm
The Art Institute of Chicago, Chicago

20. Henri Matisse, *Grand nu*, 1906

21. Otto van Rees (Freiburg 1884-1957 Utrecht)
Boerenerf (Farm at Fleury), 1905
Pastel chalk on grey-green paper
251 x 363 mm
On back studio stamp: *VR* (in ligature) */van Rees*
Special features: pinholes in upper left and lower right corners
PROVENANCE:
Magdalena Kuitenbrouwer-van Rees, daughter of the artist (1910-1990); private collection
EXHIBITIONS:
Otto van Rees 1884-1957, Amsterdam (Stedelijk Museum), 1960-1961, no. 12
LITERATURE:
Henkels 1975, p. 12
COLLECTION:
Private collection

1.
Loosjes-Terpstra 1987, pp. 17-19; Henkels 1975, pp. 20-25, 75-76. Postcard from O. van Rees from Domburg to his mother, postmarked 25 June 1904: 'Always walk on my own in the evenings, spending a great deal of time with Toorop'; legacy Otto van Rees.
2.
Heyting 1994, pp. 59-77; 85-89; Hopmans 1989, pp. 48-49.
3.
Vrede, 8 (1905), no. 11 (28 January). Ludovic-Rodo Pissaro (Paris 1878-1952 Paris).

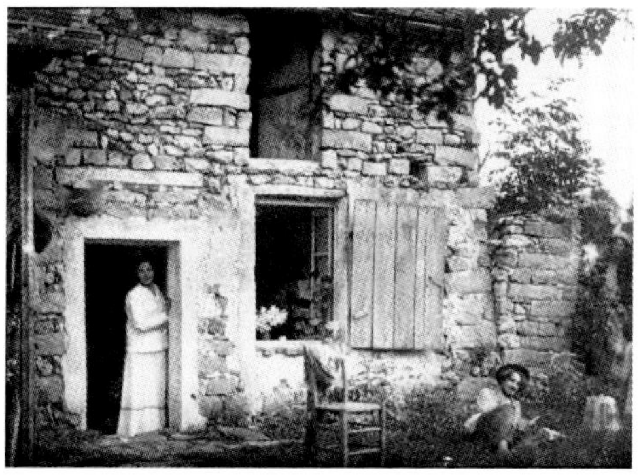

The farm at Fleury-en-Bière; Guus van Dongen, Otto van Rees, Kees van Dongen, 1905
Photograph Otto van Rees legacy

Otto van Rees (Freiburg 1884-1957 Utrecht)

The Dutch painter Otto van Rees went to Paris in October 1904, at the age of twenty, where he spent some time drawing and painting from the model in the studio founded by Eugène Carrière in Montmartre, the Academie Carrière. Prior to this, in the Netherlands, he had received drawing lessons from the painter Herman Heijenbrock and in the summer of 1904 he had worked on the coast in Domburg under the guidance of Jan Toorop. It was on the advice of this artist – who at the time himself painted in a pointillist, Neo-Impressionist style – that Van Rees went to Paris to further develop himself.[1]

Otto van Rees probably quite consciously chose not to have an academic education. His father, Jacob van Rees, was a confirmed follower of the Christo-Anarchist ideas of Leo Tolstoy. To further propagate his views, he had moved to Blaricum in 1900 – a village in the rural Gooi region (not far from Amsterdam) – where he founded an agrarian commune. The painter Otto van Rees held the same views as his father: he lived in Blaricum from 1902-04 in a simple house on the edge of the village where he painted and drew simple, 'real' subjects and the landscape of the surrounding countryside.[2] In December 1904 in Paris he entered into a common-law marriage with the painter Adya Dutilh who had followed him from Holland.[3]

Having first lived with the Dutch journalist Tom Schilperoort, in 1905 on Picasso's invitation Van Rees and Adya moved to a studio flat in the Bateau Lavoir. Together with Kees van Dongen – whom he may possibly have met earlier through Schilperoort and whose wife Guus had given birth to their daughter Guusje (Dolly) in April – Otto and Adya van Rees-Dutilh spent the summer months of 1905 in a rented farm at Fleury-en-Bière. The families sometimes worked from the same subjects in the fields surrounding the village; Van Dongen also went to Paris and Neuilly from time to time to paint merry-go-rounds at the summer fairs.

The landscapes painted by Van Dongen in Fleury and his harvest scenes are the first drawings he made using pastel chalks. It is possible that Otto van Rees introduced him to this drawing material; Van Rees had probably worked with this medium the year before in Domburg on Toorop's instigation. Otto van Rees's fine, carefully built-up pastel drawing *Farm at Fleury* from 1905 perfectly illustrates his drawing style of that time: the sheet is dotted and striped in loose marks but follows the local colour and not the Neo-Impressionist palette from which he had adopted the marks he used. In this respect, Van Dongen was more developed as an artist. His Fleury drawings, apart from a loose style and more relaxed composition, were also more experimental in their use of colour: various pastels by him are drawn in complimentary colours. (cat. 108, 112) In Fleury, Van Dongen applied an expressive way of working which had already been set out in 1905, and was inspired by Neo-Impressionism – among other things in a painting style that used rough, block-like marks. Following this example, and influenced by the Fauvist work exhibited at the next Paris Salon d'Automne, Otto van Rees painted landscapes in lighter and more pronounced colours with intensely Pointillist skies, first in 1905 and in Anzio in Italy in 1906 and 1907. After staying a few months in the Netherlands, the couple returned to establish themselves in Paris in 1908. Adya dedicated herself to embroidery; Otto painted in a stylized, decorative manner until about 1910. Until that time they continued to have regular contact with the Van Dongens. Hereafter their paths separated and, via a geometric style and Cubism, Van Rees developed into a Dadaist in Zurich in 1915.

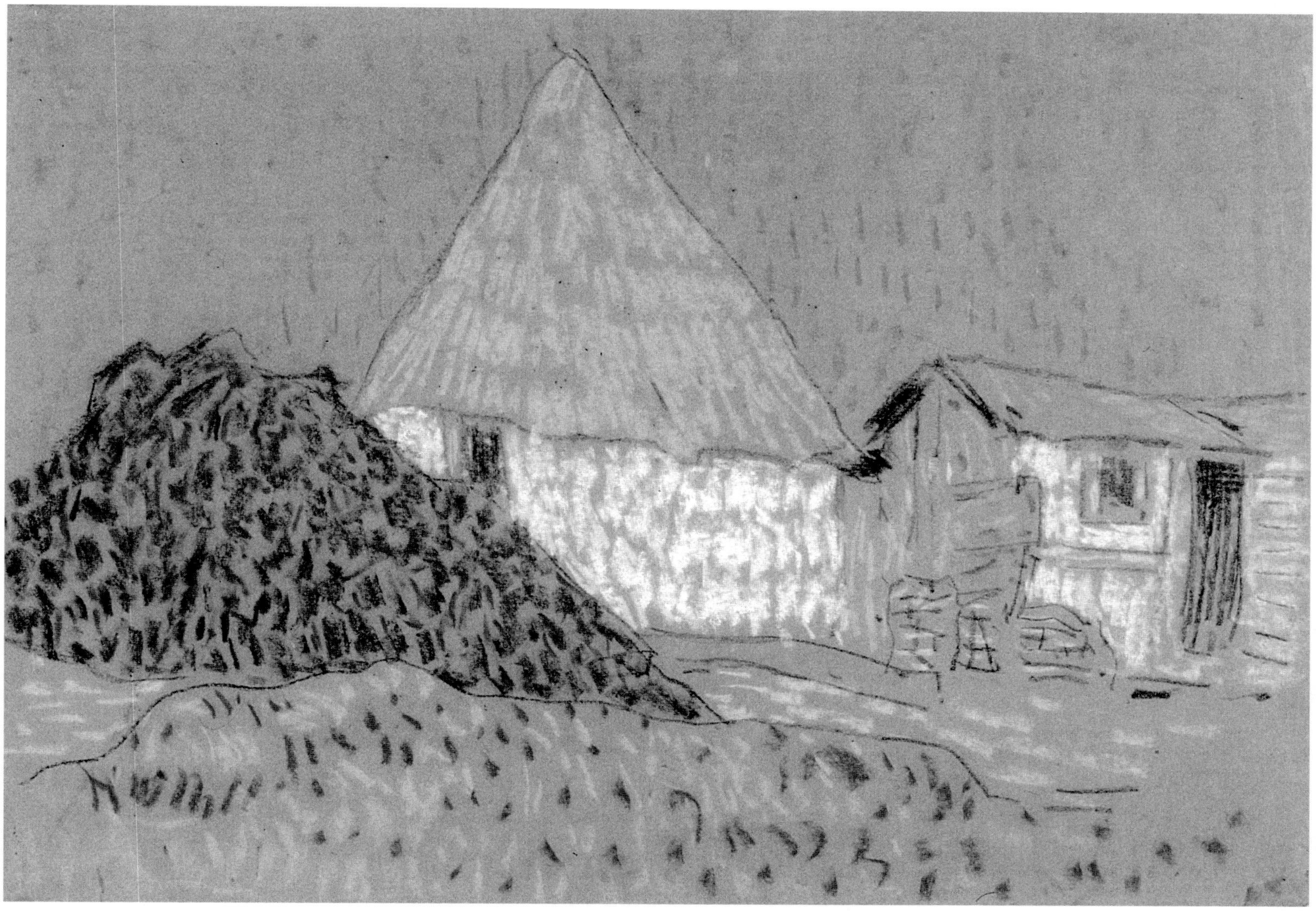

21. Otto van Rees, *Farm at Fleury*, 1905

22. Ludovic-Rodo Pissarro (Paris 1878-1952 Paris)
Le chanteur Modjesko (The singer Modiesko), 1907
Oil on canvas
55 x 46 cm
Signed on back of canvas in grey: *Ludovic Rodo*; signed on stretcher in ballpoint pen: *LUDOVIC RODO*; and annotated in blue chalk: *Le Chanteur Modjesko-Rotterdam 1907*; a grey stamp: *SHERATON WAREHOUSE INC/614 WEST 49th STREET/NEW YORK 19, N.Y.*; a blank label marked in ballpoint pen: *90*; note in white chalk: *von caave*

PROVENANCE:
Auction London, Sotheby's, *Impressionist and modern paintings, drawings...*, 3-4 June 1968, no. 158; John Nicholas Streep (-1973), New York; auction Amsterdam, Sotheby's, *Algemene veiling. Schilderijen, aquarellen...*, 21-22 February 1989, no. 489

COLLECTION:
J. Vandewalle, Antwerp

Ludovic-Rodo Pissarro (Paris 1878-1952 Paris)

Ludovic-Rodo Pissarro was the fourth son of the famous Impressionist painter Camille Pissarro. Like his three brothers, Luciën, Manzana and Paul-Emile, he followed in his father's footsteps. In order to distinguish himself from the rest of his family he signed his work using his given name, Ludovic-Rodo. In 1898 he rented a studio in Montmartre with his brother Manzana, who was a few years older, and chose his subjects from the surrounding neighbourhood. Evening entertainment in dance halls as the Bal Tabarin, the merry-go-rounds at the travelling fairs, the prostitutes and the artistes in the *café-chantants* particularly attracted his attention. Ludovic-Rodo drew and painted around 1907-10 in a Fauvist, though sometimes rather caricatural style. With the painter Maximilien Luce, he visited the Netherlands in May and June of 1907 where they spent a few months with Kees van Dongen. Letters from Luce and Charles Angrand and a postcard from Kees van Dongen to Paul Signac, sent 2 June 1907 in which he comments that Luce is constantly drunk (*il est toujours saoul)*, bear witness to this. This comment is typical of Van Dongen. From the catalogue of the drawings and paintings of Luce, Ludovic-Rodo's sketchbooks in the Camille Pissarro Museum in Pontoise and the work that Kees van Dongen made, it is quite clear that they were also highly productive. Perhaps the artistic intentions of Luce were more serious than those of Ludovic-Rodo by whom there are more sketches known from the trip than finished paintings.

The sketchbooks and a few comments from Ludovic-Rodo to his brother Luciën in England, together with the letters from Maximilien Luce to Charles Angrand, paint a picture of this stay: the artists visited the most important Dutch museums, including the Mauritshuis in The Hague and the Rijksmuseum in Amsterdam, and worked a lot from the ships on the river Maas, the working harbours in Rotterdam and Delfshaven, and the polder landscape in the immediate surroundings. More so than Luce, Ludovic-Rodo also recorded in lively sketches Rotterdam nightlife in the Zandstraat district. It is striking that these provide us with a far more direct record of the erotic pleasure of the cafes than the studies we know by Van Dongen. (fig.) Even the Rumanian transvestite singer Modiesko, who performed in the Rotterdam variety theatre Pfläging, was captured by Ludovic-Rodo in a more brutal and sensual way than by Van Dongen. Judging from a photographic portrait of the performer from 1905 (fig.) we could conclude that Van Dongen's depictions were closer to reality and were painted more for the sake of expressive colour. The portrait of the singer by Ludovic-Rodo, however, really forces the character of the actor upon us; it is provocative. The banality and somewhat flat, undetailed style is most appropriate. This is one of Ludovic-Rodo's best pieces.

1.
A few details in J. Bailly-Herzberg, exhib.cat., *Manzana Pissarro*, Paris (Galerie Dario Boccara) 1973.

2.
Letter from K. van Dongen to P. Signac, Archives Signac, Paris.

3.
Letters from Ludovic-Rodo Pissarro to Luciën Pissarro, Pissarro Archive, Ashmolean Museum Oxford.
P. Cazeau, *Maximilien Luce*, Lausanne 1982, pp. 153-155; J. Bouin-Luce, D. Bazetoux, *Maximilien Luce. Catalogue de l'oeuvre peint*, Paris 1986, vol. 2, pp. 359-375.
Letter from Luce to Charles Angrand, c. 1907, The Getty Centre, Santa Monica.

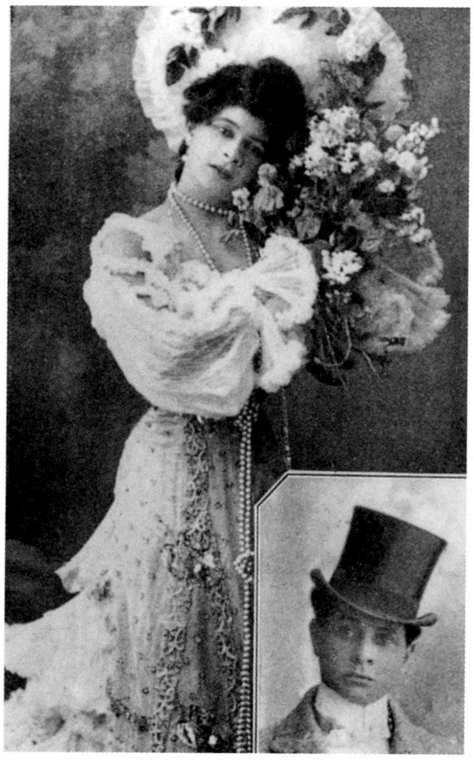

Modiesko, The baritone-soprano, c. 1905
Photograph in *Wereldkroniek*, 12 (1905/06), p. 294

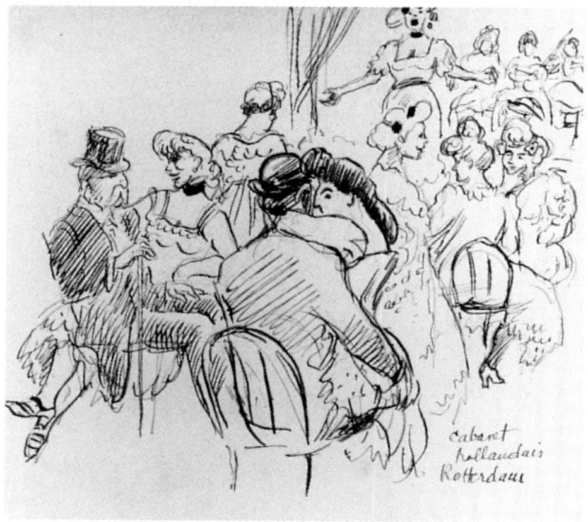

Ludovic-Rodo Pissarro
Cabaret hollandais Rotterdam, 1908
Sheet from a sketchbook 1908, after a sketch from 1907
Musée de Pontoise, Pontoise

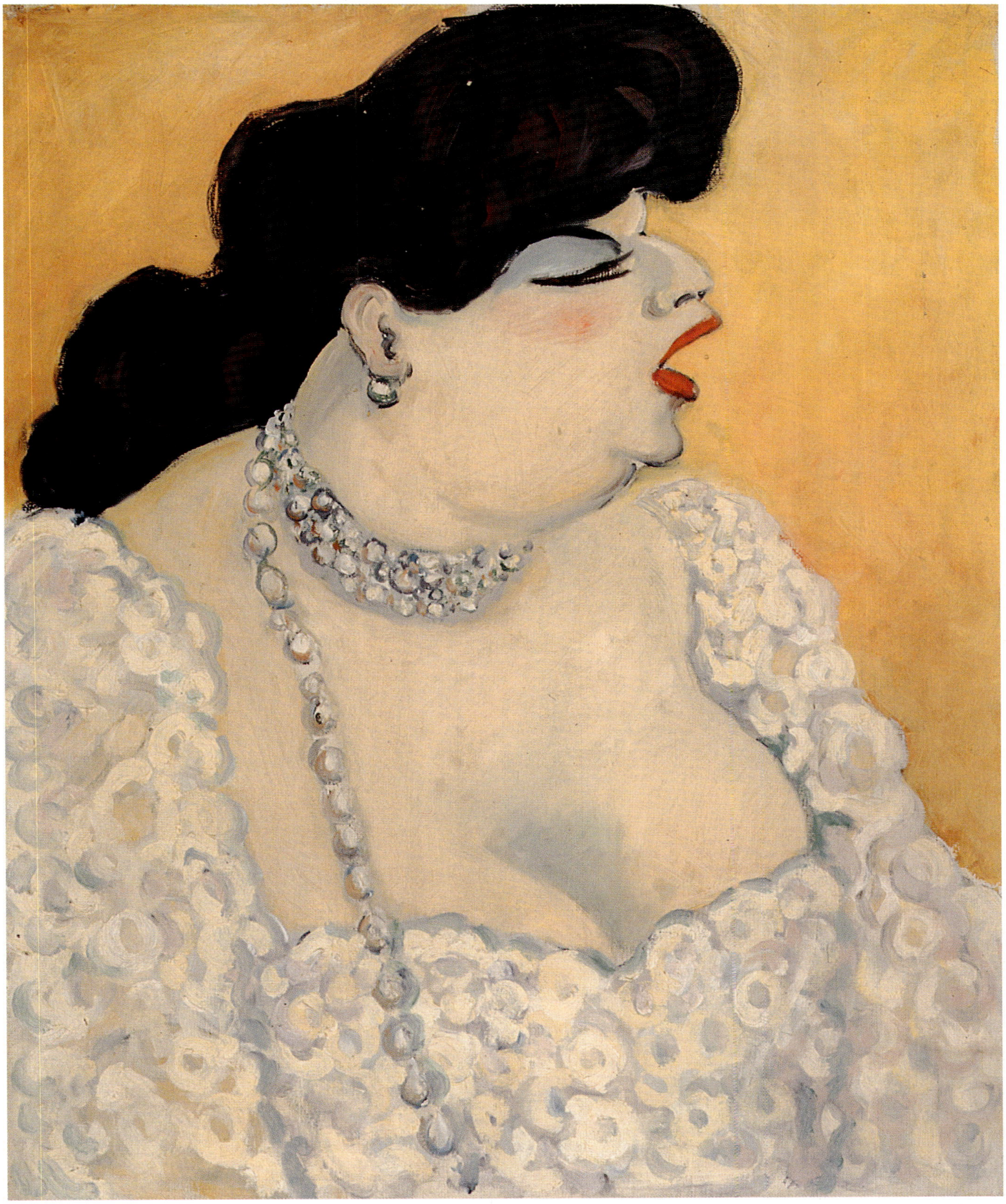

22. Ludovic-Rodo Pissarro, *Le chanteur Modjesko*, 1907

Explanatory note

In the catalogue, exhibitions are categorized under date and place (1895 Amsterdam); titles of books and articles under author and date (Hopmans 1989). The bibliography contains additional relevant literature. Articles or sources referring to specific subjects that are mentioned in the main text and amplified in the notes do not appear again in the bibliography. The exhibition *The Van Dongen Nobody Knows. Early and Fauvist Drawings 1895-1912* covers the period up to about 1914 and I have tried to present a complete picture of the exhibitions of Van Dongen's work held during these years. After 1914 only solo exhibitions are listed, as well as the shows that are referred to in the catalogue text. For the others the reader is referred to Gordon 1974, Clement 1994 (pp. 45-141, 475-99) and the list compiled by Christian Briend which appears in the exhibition catalogue *Van Dongen, Le peintre* (1990 Paris). The latter provided a starting point for the list published in this catalogue. Additions to Briend's list of exhibitions are marked with an asterisk. Exhibitions that were not held such as the one in Galerie Flechtheim (1908 Düsseldorf) have been omitted without further comment.

The provenance of a sizeable number of works was established through extensive research into auctions. In many cases this led us to the first owner. The following auction lists were consulted: Van Eijk van Voorthuizen 1946; Fage 1941-47; Hyslop 1968; Lang 1918-29; Lugt 1987; Mayer 1963; Spar 1948-55; and an anonymous list, Auction 1940-43. Collections of cuttings from auction catalogues also offered useful information, in particular the collection of illustrative documentation in the Netherlands Institute for Art History in The Hague (the RKD), and the archives of the Witt Library in London. No auction indexes are available for the years 1929 to 1941 and this period has therefore not been systematically researched. Some information about these years is offered by Bénézit 1950; this has details concerning the prices of Van Dongen's work, listed under the auctions where they were sold. Supplementary data for the 1930s was sought in information about former auctions found in auction catalogues, and in picture archives. Most of the auction catalogues were consulted at The Hague's RKD, famed for its large collection in this area. In Paris research was carried out at Drouot Documentation. Photographic archives and documentation were also provided by the various museums engaged in this project. The documentation concerning Van Dongen in the Bibliothèque Nationale and the Bibliothèque d'Art et d'Archéologie in Paris was also consulted.

The works included in this catalogue and exhibition are identified by auction labels and provenance as well as by labels of art dealers and exhibitions. It appeared that false labels were in circulation for the solo exhibitions of Van Dongen's work held in Galerie Charpentier, Paris, in 1942 and 1949. When this was discovered, the labels on the relevant works included in the exhibition were carefully examined. The extraordinary degree of cooperation shown by art dealers and archivists was essential for this research into provenance and authenticity. In preparing this catalogue the archives of the following art dealers were consulted: Bernheim-Jeune (Paris);

Kunsthandel M.L. de Boer (Amsterdam); Galerie Brame & Lorenceau (Paris); Kunsthandel Buffa (Amsterdam); Paul Cassirer (Berlin); Galerie Kahnweiler (Paris); Galerie Max Moos (Geneva); Galerie Pétridès (Paris); Roland, Browse & Delbanco (London); Galerie Paul Vallotton (Lausanne); E.J. van Wisselingh & Co. (Amsterdam); also documentation from Van Dongen's daughter, the late Dolly van Dongen, from Ron Manheim, Rudolf Engers and Werner J. Schweiger; and several exhibition archives including that of the Boijmans Van Beuningen Museum Rotterdam, the Musée d'Art moderne de la Ville de Paris and the Musée de l'Annonciade in Saint-Tropez. Additional information was also offered by the Rotterdam Kunstkring where Van Dongen held an important retrospective in June 1906; this offer helped to identify some of his work. Based on this research a considerable number of works by Van Dongen received a new title – the original one given by the artist himself – or new dating. Sources used for this research included reviews of exhibitions – culled from newspapers and journals, or press cuttings from the RKD in The Hague, and correspondence from the period. All this data has combined to present a clear overview of Van Dongen's early work as an artist. The works are arranged in the catalogue according to this new chronology. When a fact could not be verified it is stated where the reference occurs.

The catalogue uses the following abbreviations:

AHKB Koninklijke Musea voor Schone Kunsten:
the archives for contemporary art in Belgium
in the Royal Museums for Fine Arts, Brussels

RKK Archive:
The Archives of the Rotterdam Kunstkring (Art Circle)

GA Amsterdam:
The Archives of the City of Amsterdam

GA Rotterdam:
The Archives of the City of Rotterdam

HKK The Hague:
The Hague Kunstkring (Art Circle, The Hague)

IISG Amsterdam:
The International Institute for Social History, Amsterdam

NLMD The Hague:
The Netherlands Museum of Literature and Documentation Centre, The Hague

RKD The Hague:
Netherlands Institute for Art History

Exhibitions

1895 Amsterdam*
Tentoonstelling van levende meesters, Amsterdam (Stedelijk Museum), 14 September-, 1895 (2 nos)

1897 Paris*
Quinzième exposition des peintres impressionistes et symbolistes, Paris (Galerie Le Barc de Boutteville), 1 December-, 1897 (2 nos, 1 ex. catalogue)

1900 Paris*
Exposition internationale universelle de 1900. Groupe II. Oeuvres d'art (Classe 8, gravure et lithographie), Paris (Grand Palais), 15 April-15 October (1 no.)

1901 Paris
Salon de la Société Nationale des Beaux-Arts (11th), Paris (Grand Palais), 22 April-30 June 1901 (1 no.)

1901 Rotterdam*
Tentoonstelling ter gelegenheid van het 50-jarig bestaan. Werk der leerlingen, oudleerlingen en leden, Rotterdam (Academie van Beeldende Kunsten en Technische Wetenschappen), 6-21 July 1901 (2 nos, 1 ex. catalogue)

1903 Paris
Salon de la Société Nationale des Beaux-Arts (13th), Paris (Grand Palais), 16 April-30 June 1903 (1 no.)

1904 Paris
Salon des Indépendants (20th), Paris (Grandes Serres), 21 February-24 March 1904 (6 nos)

1904 Paris
Salon d'Automne (2nd), Paris (Petit Palais), 15 October-15 November 1904 (2 nos)

1904 Paris
Kees van Dongen, Paris (Galerie Vollard), 15-25 November 1904 (125 nos)

1905 Paris
Exposition de peintures et dessins par MM. Carré, Delannoy, Deltombe, Torent, Van Dongen, Paris (Galerie Berthe Weill), 16 January-15 February 1905 (21 nos)

1905 Paris
Exposition de dessins, aquarelles & peintures par mm. Beaufrère, Boudin, Dufy, Lautrec, Van Dongen, Paris (Galerie Berthe Weill), 25 February-25 March 1905 (10 nos)

1905 Paris
Salon des Indépendants (21st), Paris (Grandes Serres), 24 March-30 April 1905 (7 nos)

1905 Paris
Salon d'Automne (3rd), Paris (Grand Palais), 18 October-25 November 1905 (2 nos)

1905 Paris
Kees van Dongen. Une saison, Paris (Galerie E. Druet), 23 October-11 November 1905 (19 nos)

1905 Paris*
Untitled, Paris (A. Prath & P. Maynier, Librairie ancienne et moderne), 1-31 December 1905 (4 nos)

1906 The Hague*
Tentoonstelling van zwart en wit, The Hague (Haagsche Kunstkring), 1-14 February 1906 (1 no.)

1906 Paris
Salon des Indépendants (22nd), Paris (Serres de la Ville), 20 March-30 April 1906 (8 nos)

1906 Rotterdam
Schilder- en teekenwerk van Kees van Dongen (Parijs), Rotterdam (Rotterdamsche Kunstkring), 24 May-17 June 1906; Zwolle*, (V.V.V./Sociëteit De Harmonie) 24-28 June 1906 (73 nos)

1906 Paris
Salon d'Automne (4th), Paris (Grand Palais), 6 October-15 November 1906 (3 nos)

1906 Paris*
Camoin, Derain, Manguin, Marquet, Matisse, Puy, Van Dongen, Paris (Galerie Berthe Weill), November 1906 (no catalogue)

1907 Toulouse*
Union Artistique de Toulouse. Exposition de 1907, Toulouse, 15 March-, 1907 (3 nos)

1907 Amsterdam
Aquarellen en teekeningen moderne meesters, en een collectie teekeningen van Kees van Dongen, Amsterdam (Kunsthandel C.M. van Gogh), July-August 1907 (47 nos)

1907 Amsterdam*
Stedelijke tentoonstelling van kunstwerken van levende meesters (Vierjaarlijksche), Amsterdam (Stedelijk Museum), 7 September-, 1907 (1 no.)

1907 Rotterdam*
Werk van Rotterdamsche schilders en beeldhouwers. Eerste groep, Rotterdam (Rotterdamsche Kunstkring), 23 October-10 November 1907 (3 nos)

1907 Paris*
Camoin, Derain, Manguin, Marquet, Henri Matisse, Kees van Dongen, Vlaminck, Paris (Berthe Weill), 2 November-, 1907 (no catalogue)

1907 Paris
Portraits d'hommes, Paris (Bernheim-Jeune), 16 December 1907-4 January 1908 (2 nos)

1908 Toulouse*
L'Art au Télégramme. Kees van Dongen, A. Guénot, Toulouse (Hôtel du Télégramme), 1-11 January 1908 (64 nos)

1908 Paris
Exposition d'oeuvres de Kees van Dongen, Paris (Galerie Kahnweiler), 2-28 March 1908 (30 nos)

1908 Toulouse*
Union Artistique de Toulouse. Exposition de 1908, Toulouse, 15 March-, 1908 (6 nos)

1908 Paris
Salon des Indépendants (24th), Paris (Serres du Cours), 20 March-2 May 1908 (6 nos)

1908 Berlin
Berliner Secession (15th), Berlin (Ausstellungshaus am Kurfürstendamm), spring (2 nos)

1908 Moscow
Gulden Vlies (1st), Moskow (Galerie Trétiakov), 18 April-24 May 1908 (4 nos)

1908 Toulouse*
L'Art au Télégramme, Toulouse (Hôtel du Télégramme), 1-10 May 1908 (1 no.)

1908 Le Havre*
Cercle de l'Art Moderne (3me exposition), Le Havre (Hôtel de Ville du Havre), June 1908 (4 nos)

1908 Dresden*
Gemälde, Zeichnungen und Graphik von Amiet, Heckel, Kirchner, Pechstein, Schmidt-Rotluff, Giacometti, Nölken. Vertretern der modernsten Richtung in Frankreich, Dresden (Kunstsalon Emil Richter), 1-23 September 1908 (2 nos, no catalogue)

1908 Paris
Salon d'Automne (6th), Paris (Grand Palais), 1 October-8 November 1908 (4 nos)

1908 Paris
Van Dongen, Paris (Bernheim-Jeune), 25 November-8 December 1908 (88 nos)

1908 Paris*
La Comédie Humaine, Paris (Georges Petit), December 1908 (4 nos)

1908 Paris
Exposition d'aquarelles et dessins, Paris (Galerie Druet), 21 December 1908-16 January 1909 (no catalogue)

1909 Moscow
Gulden Vlies (2nd), Moscow (Galerie Trétiakov), 24 January-28 February 1909

1909 Paris
Salon des Indépendants (25th), Paris (Jardin des Tuileries), 25 March-2 May 1909 (2 nos)

1909 Interlaken*
Internationale Ausstellung, Interlaken,
August-September 1909 (no catalogue)

1909 Paris
Salon d'Automne (7th), Paris (Grand Palais),
1 October-8 November 1909 (8 nos)

1909 Odessa
Salon 2. International Art Exhibition, Odessa,
17 December 1909-6 February 1910;
Kiev, 25 February-27 March 1910 (4 nos)

1910 Prague
Manes. Les Indépendants (31st), Prague,
February-March 1910 (14 nos)

1910 Berlin
Berliner Secession (20th), Berlin (Ausstellungshaus am
Kurfürstendamm), spring 1910 (1 no.)

1910 Elberfeld*
Gustave Courbet und die Entwicklung der modernen französischen Malerei, Elberfeld (Städtischen Museum Elberfeld),
March-April 1910 (no catalogue)

1910 Paris
Artistes Indépendants (26th), Paris (Cours-la-Reine),
18 March-1 May 1910 (2 nos)

1910 Budapest
Internationale tentoonstelling van impressionisten, Budapest
(Müvészház), April-May 1910 (2 nos)

1910 Paris
Exposition de dessins, aquarelles & peintures par mm. Csaba, Derain, Girieud, Mathan, Rouault, Van Dongen, Paris
(Galerie B. Weill), 28 April-28 May 1910 (no catalogue)

1910 St Petersburg
Salon 2. International Art Exhibition, St Petersburg,
2 May-7 June 1910; Riga, 25 June-20 July 1910 (4 nos)

1910 Paris
Nus, Paris (Bernheim-Jeune), 17-28 May 1910 (1 no.)

1910 Düsseldorf
Ausstellung des Sonderbundes Westdeutscher Kunstfreunde und Künstler (3rd), Düsseldorf (Städtische Kunstpalast),
10 July-9 October 1910 (1 no.)

1910 Munich
Neue Künstlervereinigung, München E.V., II. Ausstellung. Turnus 1910, Munich (Moderne Galerie Thannhauser),
1-14 September 1910 (2 nos)

1910 Paris
Salon d'Automne (8th), Paris (Grand Palais),
1 October-8 November 1910 (2 nos)

1910 Paris*
Tentoonstelling van het Russisch Kunst- en Literatuurgenootschap, Paris (Impasse Ronsin),
November 1910 (no catalogue)

1910 Paris
La Faune, Paris (Bernheim-Jeune),
19-30 December 1910 (1 no.)

1911 Berlin
Neue Künstler-Vereinigung München. VI. Ausstellung, Berlin
(Paul Cassirer), January-February 1911 (1 no.)

1911 Berlin
Berliner Secession (22nd), Berlin (Ausstellungshaus am
Kurfürstendam), spring 1911 (2 nos)

1911 Paris
Salon des Indépendants (27th), Paris (Quai d'Orsay),
21 April-13 June 1911 (5 nos)

1911 Amsterdam*
Jaarlijksche tentoonstelling van kunstwerken der vereeniging St. Lucas (21st), Amsterdam (Stedelijk Museum),
30 April-11 June 1911 (18 nos)

1911 Düsseldorf
Sonderbund Westdeutscher Kunstfreunde und Künstler (4th),
Düsseldorf (Städtische Kunsthalle),
20 May-2 July 1911 (2 nos)

1911 Paris
Van Dongen, Paris (Bernheim-Jeune), 6-24 June 1911 (36 nos)

1911 Amsterdam
Moderne Kunst Kring. Internationale tentoonstelling van moderne kunst, Amsterdam (Stedelijk Museum),
6 October-5 November 1911 (3 nos)

1911 Paris
Oeuvres nouvelles de Van Dongen, Paris (Bernheim-Jeune),
4-16 December 1911 (29 nos)

1912 Moscow
Knave of Diamonds (2nd), Moscow (Galerie Trétiakov),
January (2 nos)

1912 Brussels
La Libre Esthétique (19th), Brussels (Koninklijk Museum
voor Schone Kunsten), 9 March-14 April 1912 (7 nos)

1912 Paris
Salon de Mai, Paris (Ateliers Quai Rive-Neuve),
1-15 May 1912 (2 nos)

1912 Cologne
Sonderbund Westdeutscher Kunstfreunde und Künstler (5th),
Cologne (Städtische Ausstellungshalle am Aachener Tor),
25 May-30 September 1912 (1 no.)

1912 Hagen
Moderne Kunst: Plastik, Malerei, Graphik, Hagen
(Museum Folkwang), July 1912 (1 no.)

1912 Barmen*
Kollektionen von Kees van Dongen, Franz Marc, Carl Caspér, Adolf Erbslöh, Alexander Kanoldt, Barmen (Der Kunstverein
Barmen), October 1912 (no catalogue, 31 nos)

1912 Munich
Neue Kunst.Erste Gesamt-Ausstellung, Munich (Hans Goltz),
October 1912 (4 nos)

1912 Paris
Salon d'Automne (10th), Paris (Grand Palais),
1 October-8 November 1912 (2 nos)

1912 London
Second Post-Impressionist Exhibition, London
(Grafton Galleries), 5 October-31 December 1912 (4 nos)

1912 Amsterdam
Moderne Kunst Kring (2nd), Amsterdam (Stedelijk Museum)
6 October-7 November 1912 (1 no.)

1912 Brussels
Kees van Dongen, Brussels (Galerie Giroux),
20 October-5 November 1912 (60 nos)

1912 Barmen*
Sammlung Werner Dücker, Düsseldorf (Der Kunstverein
Barmen), December 1912-January 1913 (no catalogue, 1 no.)

1913 Düsseldorf*
Eröffnungs-Ausstellung, Düsseldorf
(Galerie Alfred Flechtheim), 1913 (1 no.)

1913 Vienna
Die Neue Kunst, Vienna (Galerie Miethke),
January-February 1913 (1 no.)

1913 Paris
Van Dongen, Paris (Bernheim-Jeune),
27 January-8 February 1913 (37 nos)

1913 Rome
Secessione, Ie Internazionale, Rome, March-June 1913 (3 nos)

1913 Paris
Salon des Indépendants (29th), Paris (Quai d'Orsay),
19 March-18 May 1913 (2 nos)

1913 Berlin
Berliner Secession (26th), Berlin (Austellungshaus am
Kurfürstendamm), spring 1913 (1 no.)

1913 Munich*
Kees van Dongen, Munich (Moderne Galerie Thannhauser),
May-June 1913 (no catalogue)

1913 Munich
11e Gesamtausstellung, Munich (Hans Goltz),
August-September 1913 (1 no.)

1913 Budapest
De grote meesters van de 19e eeuw, Budapest (Ernst-Museum),
autumn 1913 (2 nos)

1913 Berlin
Erste Ausstellung, Berlin (Neue Galerie),
October-November 1913 (3 nos)

1913 Amsterdam
Moderne Kunst Kring, Amsterdam (Stedelijk Museum),
7 November- 8 December 1913 (1 no.)

1913 Paris
Salon d'Automne (11th), Paris (Grand Palais),
15 November 1913-5 January 1914 (3 nos)

1913 Frankfurt
Untitled, Frankfurt (Goldschmidt), December 1913 (2 nos)

1914 Lausanne
Kees van Dongen, Aloys Hugonnet, Lausanne
(Galerie Paul Vallotton), 19 January-14 February 1914

1914 Paris
Salon des Indépendants (30th), Paris (Champ de Mars),
1 March-30 April 1914 (3 nos)

1914 Lyons*
Exposition Internationale 1914, Lyons (Beaux-Arts),
1 May-1 November 1914 (2 nos)

1914 Rotterdam
Werken van Franse en Belgische kunstenaars, Rotterdam
(Rotterdamsche Kunstkring), 3-31 May 1914 (4 nos)

1914 Amsterdam
De Onafhankelijken. 3rd Internationale jury-vrije tentoonstelling, Amsterdam (Tentoonstellingsgebouw
Amstelveensche weg), May-June 1914 (8 nos)

1914 Prague
Vý'stava S.V.U. Manes (46th), Prague, May-June 1914 (3 nos)

1914 Munich
Neue Kunst Sommerschau 1914, Munich (Hans Goltz),
summer 1914

1917 Paris
Van Dongen, Paris (Galerie d'Antin),
9-31 March 1917 (50 nos)

1918 Paris
Oeuvres de Van Dongen, Paris (Galerie Paul Guillaume),
March 1918 (25 nos)

1918 Geneva
Exposition d'art français, Geneva (Galerie Moos),
December 1918

1918 Paris*
Exposition des oeuvres de Van Dongen, Paris (Galerie Devambez), December 1918 (57 nos)

1919 Berlin
Kees van Dongen, Berlin (Paul Cassirer), June-July 1919 (27 nos)

1919 Hamburg*
Kees van Dongen, Hamburg (Galerie Commeter), August 1919 (26 nos)

1919 Düsseldorf
Kees van Dongen. Frauen, Düsseldorf (Galerie Alfred Flechtheim), 5-18 October 1919 (29 nos)

1920 Haarlem*
Van Dongen, Haarlem (Kunsthandel J.H. de Bois), February 1920 (13 nos)

1920 The Hague*
Kees van Dongen, The Hague (Kunsthandel Walrecht), July 1920

1920 Paris*
Deauville 1920, Paris (artist's studio), 30 October-10 November 1920 (25 nos)

1921 Paris
Van Dongen, Paris (Bernheim Jeune), 1-9 March 1921 (43 nos)

1922 Hanover
48. Sonderausstellung Meisterwerke Deutscher Kunst aus Hannoverschem Privatbesitz; Kees van Dongen, H.F. Bieling, Gerlwh, Hanover (Kestner-Gesellschaft E.V.), 5 February-1 March 1922 (56 nos)

1923 Paris
Van Dongen. Portraits, peintures, dessins, Paris (artist's studio), 16 November-16 December 1923 (29 nos)

1923 Paris*
Kees van Dongen, Paris (Galerie du Centaure), 17 November-2 December 1923 (27 nos)

1924 Paris*
Paris par Van Dongen, Paris (artist's studio), 15 November-15 December 1924 (24 nos)

1925 Paris*
Van Dongen, Paris (artist's studio), 15 November-15 December 1925 (81 nos)

1926 Paris*
Van Dongen. Aquarelles, dessins, Paris (Quatre chemins), 11-30 June 1926

1927 Brussels*
Kees van Dongen, Brussels (Galerie Le Centaure), 5-16 February 1927 (32 nos)

1927 Amsterdam
Kees van Dongen, Amsterdam (Stedelijk Museum), 9 April-8 May 1927 (35 nos)

1927 Rotterdam
Kees van Dongen, Rotterdam (Rotterdamsche Kunstkring), 14 May-6 June 1927 (35 nos)

1927 The Hague*
Kees van Dongen, The Hague (Pulchri Studio), 11 June-10 July 1927 (35 nos)

1927 Amsterdam*
Kees van Dongen, Amsterdam (Frans Buffa & Zonen), 28 November-12 December 1927

1929 London*
Watercolours by Kees van Dongen, London (St George's Gallery), May-June 1929 (47 nos)

1931 Paris
30 ans de peinture, Paris (artist's studio), 4-31 May 1931 (64 nos)

1931 Brussels*
Kees van Dongen, Brussels (Galerie Le Centaure), 21 November-2 December 1931 (30 nos)

1931 Amsterdam
Nieuwe werken door Kees van Dongen, Amsterdam (Frans Buffa & Zonen), 12 December 1931-10 January 1932 (30 nos)

1935 Amsterdam
Nieuwe werken door Kees van Dongen, Amsterdam (Frans Buffa & zonen), 4-27 March 1935 (29 nos); Rotterdam (Rotterdam Kunstkring) 1935; The Hague (Koninklijke Kunstzaal Kleykamp) 1935

1936 Paris
Donation Emanuele Sarmiento, Paris (Petit Palais), 1936 (1 no.)

1937 Rotterdam*
Aanwinsten van Kees van Dongen, W.B. Tholen, Dirk Nijland en Aristide Maillol, Rotterdam (Museum Boijmans), 1937

1937 Eindhoven
Van Dongen 1877-1937, Eindhoven (Stedelijk Van Abbemuseum), 1937 (70 nos)

1937 Paris*
Van Dongen, Paris (Galerie de l'Elysée), March 1937 (28 nos)

1937 New York
Paintings by Van Dongen, New York (René Gimpel Gallery), 31 March-5 May 1937 (55 nos)

1937 Brussels
Van Dongen, Brussels (Palais des Beaux-Arts), 17 April-2 May 1937 (48 nos)

1938 Paris
Exposition Van Dongen, Paris (Galerie Borghese), 1938 (39 nos)

1938 Utrecht*
Werken van Kees van Dongen, Utrecht (Genootschap Kunstliefde, Kunstzalen Nobelstraat), 1938 (17 nos)

1938 The Hague*
Tentoonstelling van werken door Kees van Dongen, The Hague (Gebr. Koch), 10 May-3 June 1938 (21 nos)

1938 London
Exhibition of works by Van Dongen, London (Rosenberg & Helft), 17 October-16 November 1938 (24 nos)

1939 Rotterdam
Van Dongen, Rotterdam (Gebr. Koch), 24 June-31 July 1939 (21 nos)

1939 Amsterdam*
Van Dongen. Teekeningen, aquarellen, lithografieën, Amsterdam (Kunsthandel Buffa), December 1939 (43 nos); Rotterdam (Gebroeders Koch), 1940

1940 Rotterdam
Tentoonstelling van schilderijen, beeldhouwwerken en grafiek van Rotterdamsche beeldende kunstenaars, Rotterdam (Museum Boymans), 27 April-27 May 1940 (9 nos)

1942 Paris
Van Dongen. Cinquante ans de peinture, Paris (Galerie Charpentier), 1942 (248 nos)

1943 Bordeaux
Van Dongen, Bordeaux (Musée de Bordeaux), 11 December 1943-3 January 1944 (163 nos)

1947 Eindhoven*
Moderne meesters, Eindhoven (Stedelijk Van Abbemuseum), 10 December 1947-9 February 1948

1949 Middelburg*
Schilderijen van de Nederlandse kunstenaar Kees van Dongen, Middelburg (Kunstmuseum), 1949 (34 nos)

1949 Paris
Van Dongen, Paris (Galerie Charpentier), March 1949 (240 nos)

1949 Arles*
Dessins et aquarelles du XXe siècle, Arles (Musée Réattu), 15 April-31 August 1949 (1 no.)

1949 Rotterdam
Tentoonstelling Kees van Dongen werken van 1894 tot 1949, Rotterdam (Museum Boymans), 28 May-10 July 1949 (100 nos); Utrecht* (Genootschap Kunstliefde), 7-28 August 1949

1949 Amsterdam
Kees van Dongen, Amsterdam (Kunstzaal De Moderne Boekhandel), 31 August-24 September 1949 (30 nos)

1950 Berne
Les Fauves und die Zeitgenossen, Berne (Kunsthalle), 29 April-29 May 1950 (9 nos)

1952 Paris
Van Dongen, Paris (Galerie Paul Pétridès), 28 February-15 March 1952 (30 nos)

1952 Rennes
Le Fauvisme, Rennes (Musée de Rennes), 28 April-25 May 1952 (4 nos)

1952 London
Kees van Dongen, London (Ohana Gallery), 19 May-8 June 1952 (38 nos)

1952 Albi*
Toulouse-Lautrec à Picasso, Albi (Musée d'Albi), 5 July-30 September 1952 (12 nos)

1952 Geneva*
Exposition Van Dongen, Geneva (Galerie Motte), October 1952 (32 nos)

1953 Paris*
Collection Carle Dreyfus léguée aux Musées nationaux et au Musée des Arts Décoratifs, Paris (Musée du Louvre), 1953

1953 Paris
Van Dongen, époque fauve, Paris (Galerie de Berri), 15 October-15 November 1953 (20 nos)

1953 New York
Recent paintings by Kees van Dongen, New York (Wildenstein), 9 December 1953-16 January 1954 (28 nos)

1954 Paris*
Le dessin de Toulouse-Lautrec aux cubistes, Paris (Musée national d'art moderne), 1954 (1 no.)

1957 Amsterdam*
Isaac Israels, Jan Sluyters en anderen, Amsterdam (Kunsthandel M.L. de Boer), 1957 (no catalogue)

1957 Roermond*
Bloemlezing uit een Roermondse collectie, Roermond (Gemeentelijk Museum Roermond), 1957

1957 Pau*
Maîtres modernes. Choix de dessins, aquarelles, gouaches, Pau (Musée des Beaux-Arts), 21 June-1 September 1957 (1 no.)

1957 Rotterdam*
Rotterdam in teken- en prentkunst, Rotterdam (Boijmans Van Beuningen Museum), 22 June-28 July 1957

1958 Berlin*
Schätze der Weltkultur von der Sowjetunion gerettet, Berlin (Staatliche Museen zu Berlin, National-Galerie/Pergamon-Museum), 1958 (2 nos)

1958 Essen*
Brücke 1905-1913, eine Künstlergemeinschaft des Expressionismus, Essen (Folkwang Museum), 12 October-14 December 1958 (2 nos)

1958 Luxemburg*
Du Néo-Impressionisme à nos jours. Aquarelles, gouaches, dessins du Musée national d'art moderne de Paris, Luxemburg (Musée de l'Etat), 15 November-14 December 1958 (1 no.)

1959 Nice
Van Dongen, Nice (Galerie des Ponchettes), 1959 (112 nos)

1959 Basle*
Ausstelling June-August 1959, Basle (Galerie Beyerler), June-August 1959 (3 nos)

1959 Schaffhausen
Triumph der Farbe. Die Europäischen Fauves, Schaffhausen (Museum zu Allerheiligen); Berlin (Nationalgalerie), 5 July-13 September 1959 (5 nos)

1959 Geneva
Van Dongen, Geneva (Musée Rath), 30 October-29 November 1959 (126 nos)

1959 Villeneuve sur Lot*
Le dessin français de Signac aux abstraits, Villeneuve sur Lot, etc. (travelling exhibition organized by the Service Educatif de la Direction des Musées de France), 1959-1960

1960 Amsterdam*
Het landschap 19e en 20e eeuw, Amsterdam (Kunsthandel M.L. de Boer), 26 March-23 April 1960 (1 no.)

1960 Albi
Van Dongen, Albi (Musée Toulouse-Lautrec), 1-30 April 1960 (106 nos)

1962 Asnières
Hommage à Van Dongen, Asnières (Salon d'Asnières), 1962 (15 nos)

1962 Breda*
Nederlandse aquarellen en gouaches van 1850 tot heden, Breda (Cultureel Centrum De Beyerd), 26 January-4 March 1962 (4 nos)

1962 Manchester*
Loan exhibition of modern pictures from the collection of Sir Robert Adeane, Manchester (Whitworth Art Gallery, University of Manchester), 15 August-15 September; Nottingham (Department of Fine Art, University of Nottingham, University Art Gallery), 2 October-28 October; Norwich (Castle Museum), 3 November-25 November 1962 (2 nos)

1962 Mexico*
100 años de dibujo francés, 1850-1950, Mexico (Universidad Nacional Autónoma de México, Museo de Ciencias y Arte), 20 October-30 November 1962 (1 no.)

1962 Paris
Les Fauves, Paris (Galerie Charpentier), 1962 (14 nos)

1963 Stockholm*
Från Bonnard till våra dagar. Akvarell, gouache, teckning, skulptur från Musée national d'art moderne, Paris, Stockholm (Riksförbundet för Bildande Konst), 1963; Louisiana, 1964 (1 no.)

1963 Paris
Les dessins de Van Dongen, Paris (Galerie Bellechasse), June-November 1963 (48 nos)

1964 Florence
L'espressionismo. Pittura, scultura, architettura, Florence (Palazzo Strozzi), May-June 1964 (3 nos)

1964 Lyons
Van Dongen, Lyons (Musée de Lyon), June-October 1964; Charleroi (Palais des Beaux-Arts), 1964; Rotterdam (Boijmans Van Beuningen Museum), 1964 (86 nos)

1964 London*
Aspects of Twentieth Century Art, London (Marlborough Fine Art), 16 July-31 August 1964 (1 no.)

1965 New York
A comprehensive exhibition of painting 1900 to 1925 by Van Dongen, New York (Leonard Hutton Galleries), 16 November-18 December 1965 (35 nos)

1967 London*
Drawings of importance from 1860 to 1960, London (Roland, Browse & Delbanco), 5 May-10 June 1967 (1 no.)

1967 Paris
Van Dongen, Paris (Musée national d'art moderne), 13 October-26 November 1967; Rotterdam (Boijmans Van Beuningen Museum), 8 December 1967-28 January 1968 (164 nos)

1969 Charleroi
Utrillo et les peintres de Montmartre, Charleroi (Palais des Beaux-Arts), 11 January-16 February 1969 (7 nos)

1969 Marseilles
Hommage à Van Dongen, Marseilles (Musée Cantini), June-September 1969 (94 nos)

1970 London*
Drawings of importance of the 19th and 20th century, London (Roland, Browse & Delbanco), 5 June-1 August 1970 (1 no.)

1971 Tucson
Cornelis Theodorus Marie Van Dongen 1877-1968, Tucson (The University of Arizona Museum of Art); Kansas City (Nelson Gallery-Atkins Museum), 1971 (110 nos)

1971 Lausanne
Hommage à Van Dongen, Lausanne (Galerie Paul Vallotton), 9-18 September 1971 (29 nos)

1972 Paris
Salon d'Automne 1972. Grandes Oeuvres Russes des collections françaises. Van Dongen, Paris (Grand Palais), 31 October-27 November 1972 (42 nos)

1973 Brussels*
De private verzamelingen, Brussels (Galerie Govaerts), 1973 (2 nos)

1973 Paris*
Quelques signatures rares, Paris (Galerie Félix Vercel), 11 April-30 May 1973 (2 nos)

1974 Paris*
Dessins du musée d'art moderne, Paris (Musée national d'art moderne), 1974-1975

1975 Dartmouth*
Works on paper. Nineteenth and twentieth century drawings and watercolors from the Dartmouth College Collection, Dartmouth (Carpenter Art Galleries, Carpenter Hall), 30 May-21 September 1975 (1 no.)

1975 Lausanne
Le nu dans l'école de Paris, Lausanne (Galerie Paul Valloton), 29 May-21 June 1975

1975 Toronto
The Fauves, Toronto (Art Gallery of Ontario), 11 April-11 May 1975 (3 nos)

1976 New York
Fauvism. The 'Wild Beasts' and its affinities, New York (The Museum of Modern Art), 26 March-1 June; San Francisco (San Francisco Museum of Modern Art), 29 June-15 August; Fort Worth (The Kimbell Art Museum), 11 September-31 October 1976 (6 nos)

1976 Paris*
La donation Germaine Henry, Robert Thomas. Peintures, sculptures et objets d'art, Paris (Musée d'Art moderne de la Ville de Paris), 1976 (2 nos)

1976 Montrouge
21st Salon de Montrouge. Art Contemporain, Montrouge, 3 May-2 June 1976 (76 nos)

1976 Geneva
Van Dongen 1877-1968, Genève (Musée de l'Athénée), 15 July-15 October 1976 (59 nos)

1977 Nice*
Hommage à Kees van Dongen, Nice (Musée des Beaux-Arts Jules Chéret), January-, 1977 (23 nos)

1977 Tokyo*
Le Bateau-Lavoir, Tokyo (Nihonbashi Mitsukoshi), 12-24 April 1977; Osaka (Mitsukoshi), 3-15 May 1977 (12 nos)

1978 Tokyo*
Van Dongen, Tokyo (Tokyo Shimbun; Galerie de Isetan, Shinjuku), 2-13 March 1978 (82 nos)

1978 Isère
Hommage à Kees van Dongen 1877-1968, Isère (Fondation Rey-Pieferd), 25 March-11 June 1978 (30 nos)

1978 Paris
Donation Picasso. La collection personnelle de Picasso, Paris (Musée du Louvre), May-, 1978 (1 no.)

1979 Amsterdam*
Nederlandse schilderkunst 1815-1914, Amsterdam (Rijksmuseum Vincent van Gogh), 8-28 March 1979; Tokyo (Oderkyn Grand Gallery); Sapporo; Hiroshima; Nagoya (2 nos)

1979 Cannes
Retrospective de Van Dongen 1877-1968, Cannes (Galerie Robin), 4 April-5 May 1979 (no catalogue)

1981 Nice
Kees van Dongen (1877-1968). Aquarelles et dessins, Nice (Musée des Beaux-Arts Jules Chéret), summer 1981 (35 nos)

1981 Utrecht*
Van Gogh tot Cobra. Nederlandse schilderkunst 1880-1950, Stuttgart (Würtembergsche Kunstverein), 1980; Utrecht (Centraal Museum), 1981; Bonn (Landesmuseum), 1981 (3 nos)

1982 Saint-Antoine*
7ème Festival des arts plastiques de la musique et de la poésie, Saint-Antoine (Le Monastère Saint-Antoine l'Abbaye; Musée Départemental Jean Vinay), 1982 (no catalogue)

1982 Southampton
Sounds of color, Southampton (Southampton Art Gallery), 1982; Nottingham (Castle Museum), 1984; (travelling exhibition organized by The Arts Council, London) (no catalogue)

1983 Munich*
Alexej Jawlensky 1864-1941, Munich (Städtische Galerie im Lenbachhaus), 23 February-17 April 1983; Baden-Baden (Staatliche Kunsthalle), 1 May-26 June 1983 (1 no.)

1983 Paris
94th Exposition Société des Artistes Indépendants. Montmartre, les ateliers du génie, Paris (Grand Palais), 8-27 March 1983; Tokio (Isetan), 28 April-17 May 1983; Miyasaki (Musée Miyasaki), 22 May-26 June 1983; Kumanoto (Musée de Kumanoto), 7 July-7 August 1983; Nagoya (Musée de Nagoya), 25 August-6 September 1983; Hyogo (Musée de Hyogo), 10 September-16 October 1983 (16 nos)

1984 Paris*
Donation Louise et Michel Leiris. Collection Kahnweiler-Leiris, Paris (Musée national d'art moderne, Centre Georges Pompidou), 22 November 1984-28 January 1985 (1 no.)

1984 Wuppertal*
Der westdeutsche Impuls 1900-1914. Kunst und Umweltgestaltung im Industriegebiet. Stadtentwicklung, Sammlungen, Ausstellungen, Wuppertal (Von der Heydt-Museum), 23 March-20 May 1984 (1 no.)

1985 Saint-Tropez
Kees van Dongen 1877-1968, Saint-Tropez (Musée de l'Annonciade), 6 July-30 September; Toulouse (Réfectoire des Jacobins), October-November 1985 (39 nos)

1986 The Hague*
Impressionisten en postimpressionisten, The Hague (Kunsthandel Ivo Bouwman), 1986 (no catalogue)

1987 Paris*
Feminissima, Paris (Galerie Artcurial), Paris 1987

1988 Deurne*
Van Alma tot Zadkine. Particulier bezit uit de regio Deurne, Deurne (Museum De Wieger), 1988 (1 no.)

1988 London*
French 19th and 20th century paintings and watercolours. Summer exhibition, London (Stoppenbach & Delestre), 1988

1988 Lausanne
Maîtres suisses et français des XIXe et XXe siècles, Lausanne (Galerie Paul Vallotton), 17 March-23 April 1988 (1 no.)

1989 London*
Boudin to Picasso. An exhibition of impressionist and modern drawings and watercolours, London (Frost & Reed LTD), 1989

1989 London*
Nineteenth and twentieth century french drawings and watercolours. Summer exhibition, London (Stoppenbach & Delestre), summer 1989 (1 no.)

1989 Lyons*
De Géricault à Léger. Dessins français des XIXe et XXe siècles dans les collections du Musée des Beaux-Arts de Lyon, Lyons (Musée des Beaux-Arts de Lyon), 18 May-3 September 1989 (2 nos)

1989 Rotterdam
Kees van Dongen, Rotterdam (Boijmans Van Beuningen Museum), 17 December 1989-11 February 1990 (53 nos)

1989 Saitama*
Collection Kahnweiler-Leiris, Saitama (Musée d'Art Moderne de la Préfecture Saitama), 1989; Funabashi (Funabashi Art Forum), 1989-1990; Shizuoka (Musée d'Art de l'Arrondissement de Meguro); Osaka (Musée Daimaru, Iméda), 1990

1990 New York*
Exposition Kees van Dongen, New York (Galerie Taménaga), May 1990 (20 nos)

1990 Paris
Van Dongen, le peintre 1877-1968, Paris (Musée d'Art moderne de la Ville de Paris), 22 March-17 June 1990 (134 nos)

1990 Osaka*
Utrillo et les artistes de Montmartre, Osaka (Musée d'Art Kintetsu), 22 June-4 July 1990; Kyoto (Musée d'Art de Daimaru, Kyoto), 4-8 October 1990; Tokyo (Musée d'Art de Daimaru), 18-30 October 1990 (1 no.)

1990 Toulouse*
1900 Toulouse et l'art moderne, Toulouse (Musée Paul Dupuy), 3 December 1990-2 April 1991 (8 nos)

1991 Boston*
Pleasures of Paris: Daumier to Picasso, Boston (Museum of Fine Arts), 5 June-1 September; New York (IBM Gallery of Science and Art), 15 October-28 December 1991 (1 no.)

1992 Rotterdam*
Impressionisme: een schone kijk. De stroming en de aanloop, Rotterdam (Boijmans Van Beuningen Museum), 19 September-29 November 1992 (1 no.)

1992 Granville*
Autour du Fauvisme, Granville (Musée Richard Anacréon), December 1992-September 1993 (2 nos)

1994 Düsseldorf*
Die Sammlung Kahnweiler. Von Gris, Braque, Léger und Klee bis Picasso, Düsseldorf (Kunstmuseum), 3 December 1994-19 March 1995 (4 nos)

1994 Norwich*
The Adeane collection, Norwich (Norwich Castle Museum), 19 March-21 August 1994 (folder, 2 nos)

1995 New York*
Center stage. Entertainment in American and European art, New York (Hirschl & Adler Galleries), 20 April-2 June 1995 (1 no.)

1995 Tokyo*
Boymans modern art masterpiece exhibition, Tokyo (Isetan Museum of Art), 19 October-28 November 1995; Kochi (The Museum of Art, Kochi), 16 December 1995-21 January 1996; Matsue (Shimane Prefectural Museum), 26 January-18 February 1996; Osaka (Daimaru Museum, Umeda), 28 February-18 March 1996 (1 no.)

1995 Sydney*
Fauves, Sydney (The Art Gallery of New South Wales), 8 December 1995-18 February 1996; Melbourne (National Gallery of Victoria), 29 February-13 May 1996 (6 nos)

1996 Rotterdam*
De onbekende Van Dongen. Vroege en fauvistische tekeningen 1895-1912 (The Van Dongen Nobody Knows. Early and Fauvist drawings 1895-1912), Rotterdam (Boijmans Van Beuningen Museum), 2 November 1996-5 January 1997; Lyons (Musée des Beaux-Arts de Lyon), 23 January-6 April 1997; Paris (Institut Néerlandais), 17 April-8 June 1997 (136 nos)

Bibliography

Academy 1914
Anonymous, *Het onderwijs aan de academie voor beeldende kunsten en technische wetenschappen te Rotterdam in 1913*, Rotterdam 1914

Academy 1935
Anonymous, *Het gebouw van de academie voor beeldende kunsten en technische wetenschappen te Rotterdam van 1 mei 1873 tot 1 september 1935*, Rotterdam 1935

Academy Annual Reports 1882-1898
Verslagen van de Academie van Beeldende Kunsten en Technische Wetenschappen, Rotterdam 1882-1898

Van Adrichem 1989
J. van Adrichem, 'Kees van Dongen: vroege jaren in Rotterdam en Parijs', pp. 6-33, in exhib.cat., *Kees van Dongen*, Rotterdam (Boijmans Van Beuningen Museum) 1989-1990

Amsterdam 1948
Mus.cat., *De verzameling van de vereeniging tot het vormen van eene openbare Verzameling van Hedendaagsche Kunst te Amsterdam*, Amsterdam (Stedelijk Museum) 1948

Andral 1994
J.L. Andral, 'Derain en plein Midi', pp. 67-74, in Marquet 1994

Apollinaire 1925
G. Apollinaire, *Il y a*, Paris 1925

Apollinaire 1960
G. Apollinaire, *Chroniques d'art 1902-1918*, Paris 1960

Apollo 1962
Anonymous, 'Pictures from the Adeane collection', *Apollo*, 76 (1962), November, p. 722

Assouline 1988
P. Assouline, *L'homme de l'art. D.H. Kahnweiler 1884-1979*, Paris 1988

Auction 1940-1943
Anonymous, *Les ventes de tableaux, aquarelles, gouaches, dessins, miniatures à l'Hôtel Drouot*, Paris (l'Archipel) 1940-1943

Aust 1984
G. Aust et al., *Der westdeutsche Impuls 1900-1914. Kunst und Umweltgestaltung im Industriegebiet. Stadtentwicklung, Sammlungen, Ausstellungen*, Wuppertal (Von der Heydt-Museum) 1984

Bailly-Herzberg 1985
J. Bailly-Herzberg, *Dictionnaire de l'estampe en France 1830-1950*, Paris 1985

Barr 1951
A.H. Barr jr, *Matisse, his art and his public*, New York 1951

Bayard 1900
E. Bayard, *La caricature et les caricaturistes*, Paris 1900

Bazin 1933
G. Bazin, 'Van Dongen', *L'Amour de l'art*, 14 (1933), no. 5, pp. 125-128, in Huyghe 1935

Bel 1993
J. Bel, *Nederlandse literatuur in het fin de siècle. Een receptiehistorisch overzicht van het proza tussen 1885-1900*, Amsterdam 1993

Bellanger 1972
Cl. Bellanger, J. Godechot, P. Guiral, F. Terrou, *Histoire générale de la presse française*, vol. 3, Paris 1972

Bénézit 1955
E. Bénézit, *Dictionnaire critique et documentaire*, Paris 1955

Benjamin 1987
R. Benjamin, *Matisse's 'Notes of a painter'. Criticism, theory, and context, 1891-1908*, Ann Arbor 1987

Benjamin 1990
R. Benjamin, 'Fauves in the landscape of criticism. Metaphor and scandal at the Salon', pp. 241-266, in Freeman 1990

Van Berge-Gerbaud 1994
M. van Berge-Gerbaud, H. Buijs (eds.), *Morceaux choisis parmi les acquisitions de la Collection Frits Lugt realisées sous le directorat de Carlos van Hasselt 1970-1994*, Paris 1994

Bergsma 1994
R. Bergsma, P. Hefting (eds.), exhib.cat., *George Hendrik Breitner 1857-1923. Schilderijen, tekeningen, foto's*, Amsterdam (Stedelijk Museum) 1994

Besnard-Bernadac 1985
M.L. Besnard-Bernadac et al., mus.cat., *Musée Picasso. Catalogue sommaire des collections*, Paris (Musée Picasso) 1985

Besson 1947
G. Besson (ed.), 'Fragments du journal de Paul Signac', *Arts de France*, 1947, nos 11-12, pp. 97-102; nos 17-18, pp. 75-82

Besson 1967
G. Besson, 'Lettre à une provinciale. Van Dongen et cie', *Les lettres françaises*, no. 1204, 18 October 1967, p. 27

Bionda 1991
R. Bionda, C. Blotkamp (ed.), exhib.cat., *De schilders van Tachtig. Nederlandse schilderkunst 1880-1895*, Amsterdam (Rijksmuseum Vincent van Gogh) 1991; Glasgow (The Burrell Collection) 1990-1991

Blotkamp 1978
C. Blotkamp et al., exhib.cat., *Kunstenaren der idee. Symbolistische tendenzen in Nederland, ca. 1880-1930*, The Hague (Haags Gemeentemuseum) 1978

Bock 1981
C.C. Bock, *Henri Matisse and Neo-impressionism 1898-1908*, Michigan 1981

Boime 1971
The Academy and French painting in the nineteenth century, New York 1971

De Bodt 1995
S. de Bodt, M. Sellink, exhib.cat., *Nederlandse tekeningen uit de negentiende eeuw 2*, Rotterdam (Boijmans Van Beuningen Museum) 1995

Boijmans Museum Annual Report 1921
D. Hannema, *Verslag omtrent den toestand en de aanwinsten van het Museum Boijmans over het jaar 1921*, Rotterdam 1922

Boijmans Museum Annual Report 1935
D. Hannema, *Verslag omtrent den toestand en de aanwinsten van het Museum Boijmans over het jaar 1935*, Rotterdam 1936

Boijmans Museum Annual Report 1936
D. Hannema, *Verslag omtrent den toestand en de aanwinsten van het Museum Boijmans over het jaar 1936*, Rotterdam 1937

Boijmans Museum Annual Report 1937
D. Hannema, *Verslag omtrent den toestand en de aanwinsten van het Museum Boijmans over het jaar 1937*, Rotterdam 1938

Boyer 1988
P.E. Boyer, 'The artist as illustrator in fin-de-siècle', pp. 113-169, in Cate 1988

Brachlianoff 1989
D. Brachlianoff, exhib.cat., *De Géricault à Léger. Dessins français des XIXe et XXe siècles dans les collections du Musée des Beaux-Arts de Lyon*, Lyons (Musée des Beaux-Arts) 1989

Breunig 1960
L.C. Breunig, *Chroniques d'art 1902-1918*, Paris 1960

Brodskaya 1987
N. Brodskaya, *Van Dongen*, Leningrad 1987

Browse 1978
L. Browse, *Forain. The painter 1852-1931*, London 1978

Brücke-Archiv 1970
'Die Schenkungen Erich Heckels an das Brücke-Museum 1966-1969', *Brücke-Archiv* 1970, no. 4, pp. 40-51

Bruinier 1993
S. Bruinier, *En al die onaangenaamheden omdat je geen man bent. Brieven van een jonge schilderes rond 1900*, Amsterdam, Antwerp 1993

Brusse 1899
Van af- tot aanmonsteren. Het leven van den zeeman aan den wal, n.p., n.d. (1899)

Brusse 1901
Godsdienst in de Zandstraat. Het nachtwerk van Jeruël, Amsterdam 1901

Brusse 1904
M.J. Brusse, 'Over de prentkunst van Steinlen', De Gids, 68 (1904), vol. 2, pp. 488-510

Brusse 1907
In de nachtbuurt, Rotterdam 1907 (enlarged edition of Brusse 1901)

Brusse 1912
M.J. Brusse, *Het rosse leven en sterven van de Zandstraat. (De Rotterdamsche 'polder' gesloopt)*, Rotterdam (W.L. & J. Brusse) 1912

Brusse 1917
M.J. Brusse, *Het rosse leven en sterven van de Zandstraat. De Rotterdamsche 'polder' gesloopt*, Rotterdam (W.L. & J. Brusse) 1917 (2nd enlarged edition)

Brusse 1921
M.J. Brusse, *Rotterdamsche zedeprenten*, Rotterdam 1921

Brusse 1927
M.J. Brusse, 'Jeugdherinneringen', I, II, III, *Nieuwe Rotterdamsche Courant*, 10, 15, 20 April 1927

Brusse 1935
M.J. Brusse, 'Herinnering aan Paul Signac', *Nieuwe Rotterdamsche Courant*, 24 August 1935

Brusse 1935-1936
W.L. Brusse, *J.H. Speenhoff*, 1935-1936 (unpublished; private collection)

Brusse 1936
W.L. Brusse, *Kees van Dongen (Jeugdherinneringen)*, 1936 (unpublished; private collection)

Bulée 1900
Bulée (Ch. Snabilié), *Een greep uit het Parijsche leven*, Amsterdam (E.L.E. van Dantzig) 1900

Byvanck 1892
W.G.C. Byvanck, *Parijs 1891. Notities van W.G.C. Byvanck*, Leiden 1892

Cachin 1971
F. Cachin, *Paul Signac*, Paris 1971

Cachin 1995
F. Cachin, J.J. Rishel et al., exhib.cat., *Cézanne*, Paris (Galeries nationales du Grand Palais) 1995-1996; London (Tate Gallery) 1996; Philadelphia (Philadelphia Museum of Art) 1996

Caillaud 1985
D. Caillaud, exhib.cat., *Les grands boulevards*, Paris (Musée Carnavalet) 1985

Caizergues 1992
P. Caizergues, H. Seckel (eds.), *Picasso-Apollinaire. Correspondance*, Paris 1992

Callen 1973
A. Callen, exhib.cat., *The Impressionists in London*, London (Hayward Gallery) 1973

Carco 1921
F. Carco, *Les humoristes*, Paris 1921

Carco 1927
F. Carco, *De Montmartre au quartier latin*, Paris 1927

Carco 1953
F. Carco, *L'ami des peintres*, Paris 1953 (1944)

Cate 1982
Ph.D. Cate, S. Gill, exhib.cat., *Théophile-Alexandre Steinlen*, New Jersey (Rutgers University Art Gallery) 1982

Cate 1988
Ph.D. Cate (ed.), *The graphic arts and French society 1871-1914*, New Brunswick, London 1988

Chapsal 1963
M. Chapsal, 'Entretien Kees van Dongen', *L'Express*, 27 June 1963 (Numéro spécial), pp. 45-47

Charensol 1924
G. Charensol, 'Chez Van Dongen', *Paris-Journal*, 11 January 1924, p. 4

Chaumeil 1952
L. Chaumeil, 'Van Dongen chez les fauves', *Le Peintre*, 9 (1952), no. 42, pp. 9-10

Chaumeil 1961
L. Chaumeil, 'Van Dongen et le fauvisme', *Art de France*, 1 (1961), pp. 386-389

Chaumeil 1967
L. Chaumeil, *Van Dongen. L'homme et artiste, la vie et l'oeuvre*, Geneva 1967

Clement 1994
R.T. Clement, *Les fauves. A sourcebook*, London 1994

Cocheret 1948
Ch.A. Cocheret, 'Vroeger en vandaag', *Delftsche Poort*, 1 (1948), no. 11, p. 5

Cocheret 1951
Ch.A. Cocheret, W.F. Lichtenauer (eds.), *Bekende Rotterdammers door hun stadgenoten beschreven*, Rotterdam 1951

Cocheret 1955
Ch.A. Cocheret, *Openbare vermakelijkheden*, Rotterdam 1955

Cohen 1908
A. Cohen, 'Tentoonstelling Kees van Dongen', *De Telegraaf*, 6 December 1908, pp. 63-65, in Nord 1981

Cohen 1929
A. Cohen, *Uitingen van een reactionair (1896-1926)*, Baarn 1929

Cohen 1961
A. Cohen, *Van anarchist tot monarchist*, 2 vols, Amsterdam 1961 (1936)

Cohen 1967
A. Cohen, *In Opstand*, Amsterdam 1967 (1932)

Cohen 1996
A. Cohen, *Brieven 1888-1961: verzorgd door Ronald Spoor*, Amsterdam 1996

Coquiot 1914
G. Coquiot, *Cubistes, futuristes, passéistes*, Paris 1914

Coquiot 1921
G. Coquiot, *Les Indépendants 1884-1920*, Paris 1921

Des Courières 1925-I
E. des Courières, *Van Dongen*, Paris 1925

Des Courières 1925-II
E. des Courières, 'Van Dongen', *l'Art Vivant*, 30 March 1925, no. 6, pp. 5-7

Cousturier 1922
L. Cousturier, *Paul Signac*, Paris 1922

Cowart 1972
W.J. Cowart, *"Ecoliers" to "Fauves", Matisse, Marquet, and Manguin drawings: 1890-1906*, diss. Baltimore (The John Hopkins University) 1972

De Crauzat 1913
E. de Crauzat, *L'Oeuvre gravé et lithographié de Steinlen*, Paris 1913

Dagen 1984
Ph. Dagen, 'L'exemple égyptien: Matisse, Derain et Picasso entre fauvisme et cubisme (1905-1908)', *Bulletin de la Société de l'Histoire de l'Art Français*, 1984, pp. 289-302

Dagen 1986
Ph. Dagen, *La peinture en 1905: l'enquête sur les tendances actuelles des arts plastiques de Charles Morice*, Paris 1986

Dagen 1992
Ph. Dagen, *André Derain dessins inconnus 1901-1954*, Orléans 1992

Dagen 1994-I
Ph. Dagen (ed.), *André Derain. Lettres à Vlaminck, suivies de la correspondance de guerre*, Paris 1994

Dagen 1994-II
Ph. Dagen (ed.), *Collection pour ou contre. Le fauvisme, textes de peintres, d'écrivains et de journalistes*, Paris 1994

Daix 1966
P. Daix, G. Boudaille, J. Rosselet, *Picasso 1900-1906. Catalogue raisonné de l'oeuvre peint*, Paris 1966

Daix 1971
P. Daix, 'Quand Picasso dessinait pour la presse parisienne', *Les lettres françaises*, 3 March 1971, pp. 24-25

Van Dalen 1985
M. van Dalen, *Interview met Dolly van Dongen* (film), 1985

Dardel 1987
A. Dardel, exhib.cat., *Les Temps Nouveaux. Un hebdomadaire anarchiste et la propagande par l'image*, Paris (Musée d'Orsay) 1987-1988

Dauberville 1995
G.P. and M. Dauberville, *Matisse. Henri Matisse chez Bernheim-Jeune*, 2 vols, Paris 1995

Décaudin 1960
M. Décaudin, *La crise des valeurs symbolistes*, Toulouse 1960

Décaudin 1970
M. Décaudin, 'Apollinaire et les peintres en 1906 d'après quelques notes inédites', *Gazette des Beaux-Arts*, 112 (1970), vol. 75, pp. 117-122

Denis 1912
M. Denis, *Théories 1890-1910. Du symbolisme et de Gauguin vers un nouvel ordre classique*, Paris 1912

Denis 1920
M. Denis, *Théories 1890-1910*, Paris 1920

Van Deputte 1994
J. van Deputte, exhib.cat., *Le Salon des Cent: 1894-1900. Affiches d'artistes*, Paris (Musée Carnavalet) 1994

Derain 1991
A. Derain, exhib.cat., *André Derain. Drawings & watercolours 1900-1906*, London (Stoppenbach & Delestre) 1991

Devroye 1984
A. Devroye, *L'Oeuvre de Kees van Dongen jusqu'en 1920*, Paris (Thèse de l'Ecole du Louvre) 1984

Diehl 1954
G. Diehl, *Henri Matisse*, Paris 1954

Diehl 1968
G. Diehl, *Van Dongen*, Paris 1968

Dixmier 1974
Elisabeth & Michel Dixmier, *L'Assiette au Beurre. Revue satirique illustrée 1901-1912*, Paris 1974

Domela Nieuwenhuis 1904
F. Domela Nieuwenhuis, *Gedenkboek opgedragen aan F. Domela Nieuwenhuis. Eerlijk strijder voor de rechten van den arbeider, krachtig figuur in den strijd tegen onrecht...als herinnering aan de oprichting van 'Recht voor Allen' deze hulde*, Amsterdam 1904

Domela Nieuwenhuis 1910
F. Domela Nieuwenhuis, *Van christen tot anarchist. Gedenkschriften*, 2 vols, Amsterdam 1910

Van Dongen 1927
K. van Dongen, *La vie de Rembrandt*, Paris 1927

Van Dongen 1960
Anonymous, 'A lively link to 'Les Fauves'. Hobos, madmen, masters by Kees van Dongen', *Life. International*, 28 March 1960, pp. 43-48

Donkersloot 1994
P. Donkersloot, exhib.cat., *Otto van Rees 1884-1957. 40 opere dalle collezioni in Ticino*, Ascona (Museo comunale d'arte moderna) 1994

Dorgelès 1947
R. Dorgelès, *Bouquet de bohème*, Paris 1947

Dorgelès 1962
R. Dorgelès, 'Les souvenirs de Roland Dorgelès: Max Jacob, Picasso, Charles Dullin et leurs amis', *Figaro Littéraire*, 29 December 1962

Dorgelès 1963
R. Dorgelès, *Au beau temps de la butte*, Paris 1963

Dorival 1957
B. Dorival, 'Nouvelles oeuvres de Matisse et Marquet au musée national d'art moderne', *La Revue des Arts. Musées de France*, 7 (1957), no. 3, pp. 115-120

Dorival 1960
B. Dorival, 'La vie des musées, nouvelles acquisitions', *La Revue des Arts. Musées de France*, 10 (1960), no. 6, pp. 279-283

Dorival 1961
B. Dorival, *L'école de Paris au Musée national d'art moderne*, Paris 1961

Dorival 1969
B. Dorival, 'Un album de Derain au Musée national d'art moderne, *La Revue du Louvre*, 19 (1969), pp. 257-268

Dorn 1990
R. Dorn et al., exhib.cat., *Vincent van Gogh en de moderne kunst 1890-1914*, Essen (Museum Folkwang); Amsterdam (Rijksmuseum Vincent van Gogh) 1990

Dreesmann 1951
Verzameling Amsterdam W.J.R. Dreesmann, vol. 3, Amsterdam 1951

Druart
Dictionnaire Druart [notes], Cabinet des Estampes, Bibliothèque Nationale, Paris

Ducatel 1976
P. Ducatel, *Histoire de la IIIe république. La Belle Epoque 1891-1910*, vol. 3, Paris 1976

Dunlop 1972
I. Dunlop, *The shock of the new. Seven historic exhibitions of modern art*, London 1972

Dupont 1947
W.F. Dupont, *Pieter Dupont. Een Nederlandsch graveur. Zijn leven en werken*, Oisterwijk 1947

Duthuit 1949
G. Duthuit, *Les Fauves*, Geneva 1949

Duthuit 1962
G. Duthuit, *Le feu des signes*, Geneva 1962

Ebbinge Wubben 1950
J. C. Ebbinge Wubben, 'De schenking De Graaff aan de stichting Museum Boymans', *Bulletin Museum Boymans Rotterdam*, 1 (1937/1950), no. 2-3, pp. 38-39, 43

Ebbinge Wubben 1963
J.C. Ebbinge Wubben, mus.cat., *Catalogus schilderijen na 1800*, Rotterdam (Boijmans Van Beuningen Museum) 1963

Ebbinge Wubbe 1972
J.C. Ebbinge Wubben, mus.cat., *Kunst van de 20^e eeuw*, Rotterdam (Boijmans Van Beuningen Museum) 1972

Van Eijk van Voorthuijsen 1946
J.J.B. van Eijk van Voorthuijsen, *World collectors Annuary*, Voorburg 1946

Elderfield 1976
J. Elderfield, exhib.cat., *The 'wild beasts' fauvism and its affinities*, New York (The Museum of Modern Art); San Francisco (Museum of Modern Art); Fort Worth (The Kimbell Art Museum) 1976

Elderfield 1984
J. Elderfield, *The drawings of Henri Matisse*, London 1984

Engers 1949
R. Engers, 'Kees van Dongen', *De Ramlehraket*, 4 (1949), no. 4, pp. 2-4

Ertel 1967
K.F. Ertel, 'Kees van Dongen, anlässlich seines 90. Geburtstages', *Die Kunst und das schöne Heim*, 79 (1967), no. 8, pp. 367-371

Escholier 1936
Cl. Escholier, 'La donation Sarmiento', *Bulletin des Musées de France*, 8 (1936), pp. 60-61

Ewers-Schultz 1996
I. Ewers-Schultz, exhib.cat., *Aufbruch zur Farbe. Luministische Malerei in Holland und Deutschland*, Ahlen (Kunst-Museum); Neuss (Clemens-Sels-Museum); Bonn (August Macke Haus) 1996

Van Faassen 1993
S. van Faassen, H. Oldewarris, K. Thomassen, *W.L. & J. Brusse's uitgeversmaatschappij 1903-1965*, Rotterdam 1993

Fage 1941-1947
A. Fage, *Annuaire général des ventes publiques en France*, Paris 1941-1943, subsequently idem, *Les ventes publiques en France. Tableaux, peintures, aquarelles, pastels, gouaches ...*, Paris 1943-1947

De la Faille 1970
J.B. de la Faille, *The works of Vincent van Gogh. His paintings and his drawings* (revised and enlarged edition) Amsterdam 1970

Faust 1925
L. Faust, 'Uit de grenzen gegroeide nederlanders. Kees van Dongen', *Het Leven*, 1925, pp. 64-65

Fegdal 1925
Ch. Fegdal, *Ateliers d'artistes*, Paris 1925

Fels 1959
F. Fels, 'La caricature française de 1789 à nos jours', *Le Crapouillot*, 1959, no. 44, pp. 53-72

Ferretti-Bocquillon 1992
M. Ferretti-Bocquillon, J.P. Monery, exhib.cat., *Signac & Saint-Tropez 1892-1913*, Saint-Tropez (Musée de l'Annonciade) 1992; Rheims (Musée des Beaux-Arts) 1992

Ferrier 1992
J.L. Ferrier, *Les Fauves. La règne de la couleur*, Paris 1992

Fields 1984
B.S. Fields, *Jean-François Raffaelli (1850-1924). The naturalist artist*, Ann Arbor 1984

Fierens 1926
P. Fierens, 'Van Dongen', *Art et Décoration*, vol. 49, January 1926, pp. 23-32

Fierens 1927
P. Fierens, *Van Dongen*, Paris 1927
(previously published in part in Fierens 1926)

Flam 1984
J.D. Flam, 'Matisse and the Fauves', pp. 211-239, in Rubin 1984

Flam 1986
J.D. Flam, *Matisse. The man and his art 1869-1918*, London 1986

Flam 1993
J.D. Flam, 'Henri Matisse, Le bonheur de vivre (The joy of life)', pp. 226-293, in Wattenmaker 1993

Flam 1994
J.D. Flam, 'La difficulté d'être André Derain', pp. 37-49, in Marquet 1994

Flament 1923
A. Flament, 'Van Dongen le surprenant', *La Revue de Paris*, 30 (1923), vol. 4, pp. 452-455

De Forges 1963
M.Th. de Forges, exhib.cat., *Paul Signac*, Paris (Musée du Louvre) 1963

Fourcade 1992
D. Fourcade (ed.), *Henri Matisse. Ecrits et propos sur l'art*, Paris 1992 (1972)

Fourcade 1993
D. Fourcade, I. Monod-Fontaine et al., exhib.cat., *Henri Matisse 1904-1917*, Paris (Musée national d'art moderne, Centre Georges Pompidou) 1993

Frèches 1991
C. Frèches et al., exhib.cat., *Toulouse-Lautrec*, London (Hayward Gallery) 1991; Paris (Galeries nationales du Grand Palais) 1992

Freeman 1990
J. Freeman et al., exhib.cat., *The fauve landscape*, Los Angeles (Los Angeles County Museum of Art) 1990; New York (The Metropolitan Museum of Art) 1991; London (Royal Academy of Arts) 1991

Freeman 1995
J. Freeman, exhib.cat., *Fauves*, Sydney (The Art Gallery of New South Wales) 1995-1996; Melbourne (National Gallery of Victoria) 1996

Gassier 1983
P. Gassier, exhib.cat., *Manquin parmi les fauves*, Martigny (Fondation Pierre Gianadda) 1983

Van Gelder 1958
J.G. van Gelder, *Prenten en tekeningen* (*De schoonheid van ons land*, vol. 15), Amsterdam 1958

Geldzahler 1962
H. Geldzahler, 'Two early Matisse drawings', *Gazette des Beaux-Arts*, 104 (1962), vol. 60, pp. 497-505

Georges-Michel 1942
M. Georges-Michel, *Peintres et sculpteurs que j'ai connus*, New York 1942

Georges-Michel 1926
M. Georges-Michel, 'Kiki, peintre mondain', *Le Quotidien*, 7 February 1926, p. 2

Georges-Michel 1954
M. Georges-Michel, *De Renoir à Picasso. Les peintres que j'ai connu*, Paris 1954

Georges-Michel 1967
M. Georges-Michel, 'Van Dongen venu à Paris pour trois jours peint chez nous depuis 70 ans', *L'Aurore*, 5 April 1967

Gerards 1989
I. Gerards, E. van Uitert, 'Jan Toorop. Een fabuleuze bevattelijkheid: het symbolistische scheppen', *Jong Holland*, 5 (1989), no. 1, pp. 2-17

Gerards 1994
I. Gerards, E. van Uitert, *In de lijn van Jan Toorop. Symbolisme in de kunst*, The Hague 1994

Gerkens 1973
G. Gerkens, U. Heiderich (with foreword by G. Busch), mus.cat., *Katalog der Gemälde des 19. und 20. Jahrhunderts in der Kunsthalle Bremen*, 2 vols, Bremen 1973

Gill 1982
S. Gill, *Théophile Steinlen: a study of his graphic art, 1881-1900*, diss. New York (The City University) 1982

Giraudy 1971
P. Giraudy, 'Correspondance Henri Matisse-Charles Camoin', *Revue de l'Art*, 12 (1971), pp. 7-34

Giry 1968
M. Giry, 'Le Salon d'Automne de 1905', *L'Information de l'Histoire de l'Art*, 13 (1968), pp. 16-25

Giry 1970
M. Giry, 'Le salon des Indépendants de 1905', *L'Information de l'Histoire de l'Art*, 15 (1970), pp. 110-114

Giry 1981
M. Giry, *Le fauvisme: ses origines, son évolution*, Neuchâtel 1981

Giry 1990
M. Giry, 'Van Gogh en de fauvisten', pp. 220-245, in Dorn 1990

Gobin 1960
M. Gobin, *L'art expressif au XIXe siècle français*, Paris 1960

Gombrich 1971
E.H. Gombrich, 'Psycho-analysis and the history of art', pp. 30-44, in idem, *Meditations on a hobby horse and other essays on the theory of art*, London, New York 1971

Gordon 1974
D.E. Gordon, *Modern art exhibitions 1900-1916*, 2 vols, Munich 1974

De Graaf 1938
J. de Graaf, *Le réveil littéraire en Hollande et le naturalisme français 1880-1900*, Amsterdam, Paris 1938

Gsell 1925
P. Gsell, 'Le peintre des névroses élégantes', *La Renaissance*, 8 (1925), February, pp. 63-74

Guth 1949
P. Guth, 'Van Dongen', *La Revue de Paris*, 56 (1949), vol. 1, pp. 132-140 (also published in *Le Peuple*, 22 February 1951; in *Echo-Soir*, 27 July 1957; in Guth 1957)

Guth 1957
P. Guth, A. Siegfried (foreword), *Eloge de Van Dongen*, Paris 1957

Haas 1969
A. de Haas, 'Kees van Dongen, 1877-1968, portrettist van een tijdvak', *Rotterdams Jaarboekje*, 7 (1969), pp. 161-168

Haas 1971
A. de Haas, *'t Was anders. Leven en levenskring van de heer J.H. Speenhoff dichter-zanger 1869-1945*, Rotterdam, The Hague 1971

Halperin 1970
J.U. Halperin (ed.), *Oeuvres plus que complètes*, 2 vols, Geneva 1970

Halperin 1988
J.U. Halperin, *Félix Fénéon. Aesthete & anarchist in Fin-de-siècle Paris*, New Haven, London 1988

Hammacher 1962
A.M. Hammacher, 'Van Gogh's relationship with Signac', pp. 90-97, in exhib.cat., *Van Gogh's life in his drawings. Van Gogh's relationship with Signac*, London (Marlborough Fine Art) 1962

Hannema 1922
D. Hannema, *Verslag omtrent den toestand en de aanwinsten van het Museum Boijmans over het jaar 1921*, Rotterdam 1922

Hannema 1927
D. Hannema, *Catalogus der schilderijen, teekeningen en beeldhouwwerken tentoongesteld in het Museum Boymans te Rotterdam*, Rotterdam 1927

Hannema 1937
D. Hannema, 'Teekeningen en aquarellen van Kees van Dongen', *Bulletin Museum Boymans*, 1 (1937), p. 10

Hannema 1967
D. Hannema, *Beschrijvende catalogus van de schilderijen, beeldhouwwerken, aquarellen en tekeningen, behorende tot de verzameling van de Stichting Hannema-De Stuers Fundatie*, Rotterdam 1967

Hannema 1971
D. Hannema, *Supplement 1971 van de Catalogus schilderijen, beeldhouwwerken, aquarellen en tekeningen, behorend tot de verzameling van de Stichting Hannema-de Stuers Fundatie*, Rotterdam 1971

Hannema 1973
D. Hannema, *Flitsen uit mijn leven als verzamelaar en museumdirecteur*, Rotterdam 1973

Harithas 1965
J. Harithas, F.M. Hinkhouse (foreword), mus.cat., *Paintings, drawings and sculptures in the Phoenix Art Museum Collection*, Phoenix (Phoenix Art Museum) 1965

Harris 1993
N. Harris, 'William Preston Harrison: The disappointed collector', *Archives of American Art Journal*, 33 (1993), no. 3, pp. 13-28

Harrison 1993
C. Harrison et al., *Primitivism, cubism, abstraction. The early twentieth century*, New Haven, London 1993

Haskell 1987
F. Haskell, *Past and present in art and taste. Selected essays*, New Haven, London 1987

Haverkamp Begemann 1953
E. Haverkamp Begemann, 'De haven van Rotterdam door Paul Signac', *Bulletin Museum Boymans*, 4 (1953), pp. 26-27

Van Heemstra 1992
G. van Heemstra, 'De haven van Rotterdam', p. 180 in: P. de Jonge et al., exhib.cat., *Een schone kijk. De stroming en de aanloop*, Rotterdam (Boijmans Van Beuningen Museum) 1992

Hefting 1970
P. Hefting, *G.H. Breitner in zijn Haagse tijd*, Utrecht 1970

Hefting 1978
V. Hefting, exhib.cat., *J.Th. Toorop. De jaren 1885-1910*, Otterlo (Rijksmuseum Kröller-Müller) 1978

Hefting 1989
V. Hefting, *Jan Toorop. Een kennismaking*, Amsterdam 1989

Heijbroek 1985
J.F.Heijbroek, A.A.M. Vis, *Verlaine in Nederland. Het bezoek van 1892 in woord en beeld*, Amsterdam 1985

Heijbroek 1987
J.F. Heijbroek, 'Een onbekend portret van Fritz Mannheimer door Kees van Dongen', *Bulletin van het Rijksmuseum*, 35 (1987), no. 4, pp. 329-333

Heijbroek 1991
J.F. Heijbroek, 'Het Rijksmuseum voor moderne kunst van Willem Steenhoff. Werkelijkheid of utopie?', *Bulletin van het Rijksmuseum*, 39 (1991), no. 2, pp. 163-255

Henkels 1975
H. Henkels et al., exhib.cat, *Otto en Adya van Rees. Leven en werk tot 1934*, Utrecht (Centraal Museum); The Hague (Haags Gemeentemuseum) 1975

Henkels 1993
H. Henkels, 'Cézanne en Van Gogh in het Rijksmuseum voor Moderne Kunst in Amsterdam: de collectie van Cornelis Hoogendijk (1866-1911)', *Bulletin van het Rijksmuseum*, 41 (1993), no. 3-4, pp. 155-287

Herbert 1960
R.L. and E.W. Herbert, 'Artists and anarchism: unpublished letters of Pissarro, Signac and others', I, II, *Burlington Magazine*, 102 (1960), pp. 473-482, pp. 517-522

Herbert 1961
E.W. Herbert, *The artist and social reform. France and Belgium, 1885-1898*, New York 1961

Herbert 1988
R.L. Herbert, *Impressionism. Art, leisure, and Parisian society*, New Haven, London 1988

Herbert 1992
J.D. Herbert, *Fauve paintings. The making of cultural politics*, New Haven, London, 1992

Hergott 1992
F. Hergott et al., exhib.cat., *Rouault. Première période 1903-1920*, Paris (Musée national d'art moderne, Centre Georges Pompidou) 1992

Van Heugten 1996
S. van Heugten, mus.cat., *Vincent van Gogh tekeningen. Vroege jaren 1880-1883*, Amsterdam (Van Gogh Museum) 1996

Heyting 1994
Lien Heyting, *De wereld in een dorp. Schilders, schrijvers en wereldverbeteraars in Laren en Blaricum 1880-1920*, Amsterdam 1994

Hiekisch-Picard 1986
S. Hiekisch-Picard, 'Künstlerische Tendenzen der französischen satirischen Illustration um 1900', pp. 18-26, and catalogue section pp. 34-215, in Langemeyer 1986

Hild 1981
E. Hild, exhib.cat., *3 Nus fauves, peints dans l'atelier Manguin*, Saint-Tropez (Musée de l'Annonciade) 1981

Hoetink 1968
H. Hoetink, *Franse tekeningen uit de 19e eeuw. Catalogus van de verzameling in het Museum Boymans-van Beuningen*, Rotterdam 1968

Hoog 1963
M. Hoog, 'La direction des Beaux-arts et les fauves. 1903-1905', *Art de France*, 3 (1963), pp. 363-366

Hoog 1971
M. Hoog, 'Repères pour Van Dongen', *Revue de l'Art*, 1971, no. 12, pp. 93-97

Hoog 1991
M. Hoog, exhib.cat., *Un certain Derain*, Paris (Musée de l'Orangerie) 1991-1992

Hopmans 1989
A. Hopmans, exhib.cat., *Kunst is spiegeling. Kees Verwey, een studie naar zijn oeuvre*, Dordrecht (Dordrechts Museum) 1989

Hopmans 1991
A. Hopmans, exhib.cat., *Jan Sluijters 1881-1957. Aquarellen en tekeningen*, 's-Hertogenbosch (Noordbrabants Museum) 1991

Hopmans 1992
A. Hopmans, 'Cossaar uit de schaduw', *Jong Holland*, 8 (1992), no. 4, pp. 35-47

Hopmans 1993
A. Hopmans, 'Het electrische licht als artistieke bron', *Kunstschrift*, 37 (1993), no. 1, pp. 26-33

De la Horbe 1978
A. de la Horbe, *Mémoires d'outre-tubes*, Paris 1978

House 1987
J. House, 'London in the art of Monet and Pissarro', pp. 75-88 in exhib.cat., *The image of London. Views by travellers and emigrés 1550-1920*, London (Barbican Art Gallery) 1987

Hulton 1977
P. Hulton (intro.), mus.cat., *100 oeuvres nouvelles 1974-1976*, Paris (Musée national d'art moderne, Centre Georges Pompidou) 1977

Huyghe 1935
R. Huyghe, G. Bazin, *Histoire de l'art contemporain. La peinture*, Paris 1935

Hyslop 1968
D. Hyslop (ed.), *The Art Sales Index*, Weybridge 1968

Isaacson 1982
J. Isaacson, 'Impressionism and journalistic illustration', *Arts Magazine*, 56 (1982), no. 10, pp. 95-115

Israëls 1900
H. Louis Israëls, *Nederlandsche gids op de Parijsche tentoonstelling in 1900* (with illustrations by Kees van Dongen and street plans by J.D. Looyen), Amsterdam 1900

Ives 1989
C. Ives, H. Giambruni, S.M. Newman, exhib.cat., *Pierre Bonnard. The graphic art*, New York (The Metropolitan Museum of Art) 1989

Jackson 1960
A.B. Jackson, *La Revue Blanche (1889-1903). Origine, influence, bibliographie*, Paris 1960

Jourdain 1926
F. Jourdain, *Le Salon d'Automne*, Paris 1926

Jourdain 1953
F. Jourdain, *Sans remords ni rancune*, Paris 1953

Jourdain 1959
F. Jourdain, *Albert Marquet*, Paris 1959

Joosten 1980
J.M. Joosten, *De Brieven van Johan Thorn Prikker aan Henri Borel en anderen 1892-1904. Met ter inleiding fragmenten uit het dagboek van Henri Borel 1890-1892*, Nieuwkoop 1980

Kahnweiler 1982
D.H. Kahnweiler, *Mes galeries et mes peintres. Entretiens avec Francis Crémieux*, Paris 1982

Kalb 1991
D. Kalb, S. Kingma, *Balans en perspectief van de Nederlandse cultuurgeschiedenis. Fragmenten van vermaak, macht en plezier in moderniserend Nederland*, Amsterdam, Atlanta 1991

Van Kalmthout 1990
Ton van Kalmthout, 'Tempels aan de muzen gewijd. Multidisciplinaire kunstkringen in Nederland tussen 1880 en 1914', *De Negentiende Eeuw*, 14 (1990), no. 1, pp. 95-110

Kelk 1967
F. Kelk, 'Kees van Dongen over Kees van Dongen', *Revue*, 9 September 1967, pp. 24-28

Keller 1954
G. Busch, H. Keller, mus.cat, *Handbuch der Kunsthalle Bremen*, Bremen 1954

Kellermann 1992
M. Kellermann, *André Derain. Catalogue raisonné de l'oeuvre peint*, Paris 1992

Van de Kerckhove 1993
F. van de Kerckhove et al., exhib.cat., *Henry van de Velde in de collecties van de Koninklijke Bibliotheek Albert I*, Brussels (Koninklijke Bibliotheek Albert I) 1993

Kleijn 1873
F.J. Kleijn, *Beschrijving en geschiedenis van Delfshaven benevens die van Schoonderlo en het slot Spange*, Delfshaven 1873

Klein 1990
J. Klein, 'New lessons from the School of Poitou. Derain and Vlaminck in the Paris Suburbs', pp. 123-148, in Freeman 1990

Knoester 1988
J. Knoester, exhib.cat., *P.C. de Moor. 1866-1953*, Assen (Drents Museum); Zutphen (Stedelijk Museum); Eindhoven (Museum Kempenland) 1988-1989

Komen 1995
K. Komen, *Picasso in Holland. Parijs-Schoorl 1905*, Schoorl 1995

Koomen 1927
P. Koomen, 'Kees van Dongen', *Weekblad van Rotterdam*, May 1927, incorporated in Koomen 1949

Koomen 1936
P. Koomen, 'P. Cornelis de Moor 1866-1936', *Nieuwe Rotterdamsche Courant*, 27 May 1936

Koomen 1949
P. Koomen, *In het zand gefixeerd. Beschouwingen over Nederlandsche beeldende kunstenaars*, The Hague 1949

Kreul 1994
A. Kreul, mus.cat., *Kunsthalle Bremen. Verzeichnis sämtlicher Gemälde*, Wiesbaden 1994

Kropotkin 1897
P. Kropotkin, *De anarchie. Philosophie en ideaal*, The Hague (I.I. Samson) n.d. [1897]

Kyriazi 1971
J. Melas Kyriazi, *Van Dongen et le fauvisme*, Paris, Lausanne 1971

Lang 1918-1929
L.M. Lang, *Annuaire des ventes de tableaux, dessins, aquarelles, pastels, gouaches, miniatures. Guide du marchand de l'amateur*, Paris 1918-1929

Langemeyer 1986
G. Langemeyer (ed.), exhib.cat., *Bilderwelten II. Satirische Illustrationen im Frankreich der Jahrhundertwende. Aus der Sammlung von Kritter*, Dortmund (Museum für Kunst und Kulturgeschichte) 1986

O'Laoghaire 1992
N. O'Laoghaire, *The influence of Van Gogh on Matisse, Derain and Vlaminck 1898-1908*, diss. Toronto (University of Toronto) 1992

Lapidoth 1894
F. Lapidoth, *Fransche teekenaars*, The Hague (1894)

Léal 1991
B. Léal et al., exhib.cat., *Picasso jeunesse et genèse. Dessins 1893-1905*, Paris (Musée Picasso) 1991, Nantes (Musée des Beaux-Arts) 1992

De Leeuw 1977
R. de Leeuw et al., exhib.cat., *Haagse Kunstkring: werk verzameld*, The Hague (Pulchri Studio) 1977

Leighten 1989
P. Leighten, *Re-Ordering the universe. Picasso and Anarchism, 1897-1914*, Princeton 1989

Leighten 1990
P. Leighten, 'The white peril and l'art nègre: Picasso, primitivism, and anticolonialism', *The Art Bulletin*, 72 (1990), pp. 609-630

Lemaitre 1962
H. Lemaitre (ed.), *Curiosités esthétiques. L'art romantique et autres oeuvres critiques de Baudelaire*, Paris 1962

Lespinasse 1988
F. Lespinasse, *Charles Angrand. Correspondances 1883-1926*, Rouen 1988

Lethève 1961
J. Lethève, *La caricature et la presse sous la IIIe République*, Paris 1961

Level 1959
A. Level, *Souvenirs d'un collectionneur*, Paris 1959

Leymarie 1987
J. Leymarie, *Le Fauvisme*, Geneva 1987

Loosjes-Terpstra 1987
A.B. Loosjes-Terpstra, *Moderne kunst in Nederland 1900-1914*, Utrecht 1987 (1959)
Lugt 1921
F. Lugt, *Les marques de collections de dessins & d'estampes*, Amsterdam 1921; *Supplément*, The Hague 1956

Lugt 1987
F. Lugt, *Répertoire des catalogues de ventes publiques intéressant l'art ou la curiosité...Quatrième période 1901-1925*, vol. 4, Paris (Fondation Custodia) 1987

Maas 1951
F.A. Maas, *Honderd jaar Academie voor beeldende kunsten en technische wetenschappen*, Rotterdam 1951

Maitron 1951
J. Maitron, *Histoire du mouvement et anarchiste en France (1886-1914)*, Paris 1951

Malpel 1910
C. Malpel, *Notes sur l'art d'aujourd'hui et peut-être de demain*, 2 vols, Paris, Toulouse 1910

Marius 1903
G.H. Marius, *De Hollandsche schilderkunst in de negentiende eeuw*, The Hague 1903

Marquet 1951
M. Marquet, *Marquet*, Paris 1951

Marquet 1953
M. Marquet, F. Daulte, *Marquet*, Lausanne 1953

Marquet 1975
F. Marquet, exhib.cat., *Albert Marquet 1875-1947*, Bordeaux (Galerie des Beaux-Arts) 1975; Paris (Orangerie des Tuileries) 1975-1976

Marquet 1994
F. Marquet, M. Simon, J. Munck et al., exhib.cat., *André Derain. Le peintre du 'trouble moderne'*, Paris (Musée d'Art moderne de la Ville de Paris) 1994-1995

Maus 1926
M.O. Maus, *Trente années de lutte pour l'art 1884-1914*, Brussels 1926

Mayer 1963
E. Mayer, *The international yearbook of sales/ Annuaire international des ventes*, New York, Paris 1963

McMullen 1960
R. McMullen, 'Van Dongen remembers', *Réalités*, no. 115, June, 1960, pp. 64-73

Meder 1923
J. Meder, *Die Handzeichnung. Ihr Technik und Entwicklung*, Vienna 1923 (2nd ed.)

Le Men 1993
S. Le Men, exhib.cat., *Les Français peints par eux-mêmes. Panorama social du XIXe siècle*, Paris (Musée d'Orsay) 1993

Van der Meulen 1901
R. van der Meulen, *Brinkman's catalogus der boeken, plaat- en kaartwerken die sedert 1891 tot en met 1900 in Nederland zijn uitgegeven of herdrukt*, Leiden 1901

Van der Meulen 1912
R. van der Meulen, *Brinkman's catalogus der boeken, plaat- en kaartwerken die gedurende 1901 tot en met 1910 in Nederland zijn uitgegeven of herdrukt*, Leiden 1912

Meyers 1993
J. Meyers, *Domela, een hemel op aarde. Leven en streven van Ferdinand Domela Nieuwenhuis*, Amsterdam 1993

Millman 1993
I. Millman, exhib.cat., *Georges de Feure 1868-1943*, Amsterdam (Rijksmuseum Vincent van Gogh) 1993

Moeller 1990
M.M. Moeller, 'Van Gogh en de receptie in Duitsland voor 1914', pp. 278-343, in Dorn 1990

Molinard 1995
S. Molinard, exhib.cat., *Passions privées. Collections particulières d'art moderne et contemporain en France*, Paris (Musée d'Art moderne de la Ville de Paris) 1995

Monod-Fontaine 1980
I. Monod-Fontaine, *Matisse. Oeuvres de Henri Matisse (1869-1954)*, Paris (Musée national d'art moderne, Centre Georges Pompidou) 1980

Monod-Fontaine 1984-I
I. Monod-Fontaine, A. Angliviel de la Baumelle, Cl. Laugier et al., *Donation Louise et Michel Leiris. Collection Kahnweiler-Leiris*, Paris (Musée national d'art moderne, Centre Georges Pompidou) 1984

Monod-Fontaine 1984-II
I. Monod-Fontaine, Cl. Laugier et al., exhib.cat., *Daniel-Henry Kahnweiler. Marchand, éditeur, écrivain*, Paris (Musée national d'art moderne, Centre Georges Pompidou) 1984

Monod-Fontaine 1989
I. Monod-Fontaine, A. Baldassari, Cl. Laugier, mus.cat., *Matisse. Collection du Musée national d'art moderne*, Paris (Musée national d'art moderne, Centre Georges Pompidou) 1989

Monod-Fontaine 1990
I. Monod-Fontaine, 'Henri Matisse', pp. 249-254, in Dorn 1990

Monod-Fontaine 1993
I. Monod-Fontaine, C. Laugier, 'Elements de chronologie (1904-1918)', pp. 61-126, in Fourcade 1993

Morin 1913
L. Morin, *Le dessin humoristique*, Paris 1913

Mornand 1950
P. Mornand, J.R. Thomé, R. Cogniat (intro.), *Vingt artistes du livre*, Paris 1950

Negri 1990
R. Negri, S. Venturi, *Van Dongen et les fauves*, Paris 1990

Nevejan 1983
G. Nevejan, *Le portrait féminin dans l'oeuvre de Kees van Dongen* (Mémoire de maîtrise, Université de Paris-Sorbonne, Institut d'Art et d'Archéologie) Paris 1983

Niehaus 1942
K. Niehaus, *Levende Nederlandsche kunst*, Amsterdam n.d. (1942)

Nord 1981
M. Nord (ed.), *Alexander Cohen. Uiterst rechts. Journalistiek werk 1906-1920*, Amsterdam 1981

NRC 1937
Anonymous, 'Kees van Dongen. Bij zijn zestigsten verjaardag', *Nieuwe Rotterdamsche Courant*, 26 January 1937

Oberlé 1956
J. Oberlé, *La vie d'artiste*, Paris 1956

Oberthur 1984
M. Oberthur, *Cafes and cabarets of Montmartre*, Salt Lake City 1984

Oberthur 1994
M. Oberthur, exhib.cat., *Montmartre en liesse 1880-1900*, Paris (Musée Carnavalet) 1994

Olivier 1933
F. Olivier, *Picasso et ses amis*, Paris 1933

Olivier 1988
F. Olivier, *Souvenirs intimes*, Paris 1988

Ollinger-Zinque 1993
G. Ollinger-Zinque et al., exhib.cat., *Les XX. La Libre Esthétique*, Brussels (Koninklijke Musea voor Schone Kunsten van België) 1993

Oppler 1976
E.C. Oppler, *Fauvism reexamined*, New York, London 1976

Orwicz 1994
M.R. Orwicz (ed.), *Art criticism and its institutions in nineteenth-century France*, Manchester, New York 1994

Oxenaar 1968
R.W.D. Oxenaar, mus.cat., *Tekeningen uit de 19de en 20ste eeuw*, Otterlo (Rijksmuseum Kröller-Müller) 1968

Paap 1936
W.A. Paap, *Vincent Haman*, Amsterdam 1936

Parinaud 1969
A. Parinaud, 'Van Dongen, un féroce et joyeux éclat de rire', *La Galerie des Arts*, 15 February 1969, no. 65 (supplement)

Parke-Taylor 1980
M. Parke-Taylor, 'Copies de l'album fauve', *Cahiers du Musée national d'art moderne*, 5 (1980), pp. 363-377

Perruchot 1958
H. Perruchot, 'Quand le dessin frappe à la porte. Van Dongen', *Les Nouvelles Littéraires*, 7 August 1958, pp. 1 and 4

Perry 1993
G. Perry, 'The decorated and the "culte de la vie": Matisse and Fauvism', pp. 46-85, in Harrison 1993

Peters 1987
H.A. Peters et al., exhib.cat., *Alfred Flechtheim. Sammler, Kunsthändler. Verleger*, Düsseldorf (Kunstmuseum Düsseldorf) 1987

Peters 1994
H.A. Peters et al., exhib.cat. *Die Sammlung Kahnweiler. Von Gris, Braque, Léger und Klee bis Picasso*, Düsseldorf (Kunstmuseum) 1994

Petit de Beauverger 1955
Baron Petit de Beauverger, 'Albert Marquet (openingsrede)', *Bulletin Museum Boymans*, 6 (1955), pp. 74-81

Philippe 1901
Charles-Louis Philippe, *Bubu de Montparnasse*, Paris 1901

Philippe 1908
Ch.L. Philippe, 'Dix dessins d'Albert Marquet', *La Grande Revue*, 12 (1908), pp. 731-741

Pickvance 1990
R. Pickvance, 'Arles', pp. 217-239, in Van der Wolk 1990

Pingeot 1986
A. Pingeot et al., mus.cat., *Catalogue sommaire illustré des sculptures* (Musée d'Orsay) 1986

Polak 1955
B. Polak, *Het fin-de-siècle in de Nederlandse schilderkunst. De symbolistische beweging 1890-1900*, The Hague 1955

Puy 1907
M. Puy, 'Les Fauves', *La Phalange*, 2 (1907), pp. 450-459

Py 1987
Ch. Py, C. Ferenczi, *La fête foraine d'autrefois, les années 1900*, Paris 1987

Van der Pyl 1931
F. van der Pyl, *Peintres de mon époque*, Paris 1931

Ragon 1972
M. Ragon, *Les maîtres du dessin satirique*, Paris 1972

Ratsma 1979
P. Ratsma, *Rotterdam getekend*, Rotterdam 1979

Raynal 1927
M. Raynal, *Anthologie de la peinture en France de 1906 à nos jours*, Paris 1927

Rearick 1985
Ch. Rearick, *Pleasures of the Belle Epoque. Entertainment & festivity in turn of the century France*, New Haven, London, 1985

Reff 1971
Th. Reff, 'Harlequins, saltimbanques, clowns, and fools', *Art Forum*, 9 (1971), no. 10, pp. 30-43

Reinhardt 1977
G. Reinhardt, 'Die frühe "Brücke". Beiträge zur Geschichte und zum Werk der Dresdner Künstlergruppe "Brücke" der Jahre 1905 bis 1908', *Brücke-Archiv*, 1977/78, no. 9/10, pp. 6-215

Rewald 1949-1953
J. Rewald (ed.), 'Extraits du journal inédit de Paul Signac, I. 1894-1895; II, 1897-1898; III. 1898-1899', *Gazette des Beaux-Arts*, in respectively: 91 (1949), vol. 36, pp. 97-128; 94 (1952), vol. 39, pp. 265-284; 95 (1953), vol. 42, pp. 27-57

Richardson 1991
J. Richardson, *A life of Picasso: 1881-1906*, New York 1991

Roëll 1920
W.F.A. Roëll, 'Kees van Dongen', *Op de Hoogte*, 17 (1920), September, pp. 188-190

Romanet 1963
Exhib.cat., *200 aquarelles et dessins de Renoir à Picasso*, Paris (Galerie Romanet) 1963

Romer 1979
H. Romer, *Delven in Delfshaven. Beknopte geschiedenis van een Rotterdams stadskwartier*, The Hague 1979

Romer 1981
H. Romer, *Rotterdam rondom een eeuwwisseling 1890-1910*, Zaltbommel 1981

Rubin 1984
W. Rubin, exhib.cat., *Primitivism in 20th century art. Affinity of the Tribal and the Modern*, 2 vols, New York (The Museum of Modern Art) 1984

Rummens 1994
M. Rummens, 'Van Goghs expressieve onhandigheid', *Jong Holland*, 10 (1994), no. 4, pp. 27-39

Saint-Georges de Bouhélier 1946
Saint-Georges de Bouhélier, *Le printemps d'une génération*, Paris 1946

Salmon 1912
A. Salmon, *La jeune peinture française*, Paris 1912

Salmon 1945
A. Salmon, *L'air de la butte*, Paris 1945

Salmon 1953
A. Salmon, *Van Dongen*, Paris 1953

Salmon 1955
A. Salmon, *Souvenirs sans fin. Première époque (1903-1908)*, Paris 1955

Salmon 1956
A. Salmon, *Souvenirs sans fin. Deuxième époque (1908-1920)*, Paris 1956

Salmon 1961
A. Salmon, *Souvenirs sans fin. Troisième époque (1920-1940)*, Paris 1961

Scharten 1905
C. Scharten, 'Kees van Dongen', *De Amsterdammer*, no. 1461, 25 June 1905, p. 7

Scheffer 1981
H.J. Scheffer, *In vorm gegoten. Het Rotterdamsch Nieuwsblad in de negentiende eeuw*, The Hague 1981

Scheffer 1987
H.J. Scheffer, 'De Ware Jacob, tijd en plaats', *Rotterdams Jaarboekje*, 5 (1987), 9th series, pp. 233-239

Scherphuis 1991
A. Scherphuis, 'De zes zonen Brusse over hun vader (en die van Boefje)', *Vrij Nederland*, 16 November 1991, pp. 40-49

Scheen 1969
P.A. Scheen, *Lexicon Nederlandse beeldende kunstenaars 1750-1950*, 2 vols, The Hague 1969

Schilperoort 1905
T. Schilperoort, 'Kees van Dongen', *Op de Hoogte*, 2 (1905), pp. 735-739

Schilperoort 1909
T. Schilperoort, 'Oud-Delfshaven', *Buiten*, 10 July 1909, no. 328, pp. 328-330

Schneider 1984
P. Schneider, *Matisse*, Paris 1984

Schultze 1994
J. Schultze et al., exhib.cat., *Paris Belle Epoque 1880-1914*, Essen (Villa Hügel/Kulturstiftung Ruhr) 1994

Seigel 1986
J. Seigel, *Bohemian Paris. Culture, politics, and the boundaries of bourgeois life 1830-1930*, New York 1986

Sennet 1976
R. Sennet, *The fall of public man*, Cambridge, London, Melbourne 1976

Shapiro 1976
T. Shapiro, *Painters and politics. The European avant-garde and society, 1900-1925*, New York, Oxford, Amsterdam, 1976

Shapiro 1981
B. Stern Shapiro, Anne E. Havinga et al., exhib.cat., *Pleasures of Paris: Daumier to Picasso*, Boston (Museum of Fine Arts) 1981

Shiff 1984
R. Shiff, *Cézanne and the end of Impressionism. A study of the theory, technique, and critical evaluation of Modern art*, Chicago, London 1984

Signac 1899
P. Signac, *D'Eugène Delacroix au néo-impressionisme*, Paris 1899 (4th ed. 1939)

Signac 1904
Exhib.cat., *Paul Signac. Venise, Hollande, Paris, Provence*, Paris (Galerie Druet) 13-31 December 1904 (with foreword by Félix Fénéon)

Signac 1907
Exhib.cat., *Paul Signac*, Paris (Galerie Bernheim-Jeune) 21 January-2 February 1907 (with foreword by Paul Adam)

Signac 1927
P. Signac, *Jongkind*, Paris 1927

Signac 1935
Anonymous, 'Paul Signac', *Nieuwe Rotterdamsche Courant*, 18 August 1935

Sillevis 1990
J. Sillevis et al., exhib.cat., *Een feest van kleur. Postimpressionisten uit particulier bezit*, 's-Hertogenbosch (Noordbrabants Museum) 1990

Simon 1994
M. Simon, 'Collioure', pp. 112-116, in Marquet 1994

Spar 1948-1955
F. Spar, *L'annuaire des collectionneurs. Répertoire des prix des tableaux, peintures vendu à l'Hôtel Drouot et la province*, Paris 1948-1955

Speenhoff 1939
J.H. Speenhoff, 'Herinneringen (Kees van Dongen)', *Groot-Nederland*, 37 (1939), vol. 1, pp. 333-344

Speenhoff 1943
J.H. Speenhoff, *Daar komen de schutters! Herinneringen van J.H. Speenhof*, The Hague 1943

Springer 1979
A. Springer, 'Terrorism and anarchy: late 19th-century images of a political phenomenon in France', *Art Journal*, summer 1979 pp. 261-266

Starobinski 1970
J. Starobinski *Portrait de l'artiste en saltimbanque*, Geneva 1970

Stuyvesant 1896
P.A. Stuyvesant, 'Over Rotterdam', *Woord en Beeld*, 1 (1896), pp. 59-65

Sutton 1971
D. Sutton, 'A diamond as big as the Ritz', *Apollo* 38 (1971), no. 1, pp. 36-43

Teychiné Stakenburg 1985
A.J. Teychiné Stakenburg (ed.), *Uit de kunst. 75 jaar Rotterdamsche Kunst Kring*, Rotterdam 1985

Thorson 1979
V. Thorson (ed.), *Great drawings of all time. The twentieth century*, 2 vols, Redding 1979

Van Uitert 1977
E. van Uitert, *Vincent van Gogh. Tekeningen*, Keulen, Bentveld-Aerdenhout 1977

Valotaire 1926
M. Valotaire, 'An interview with Kees van Dongen', *Drawing and Design*, 1 (1926), no. 3, pp. 83-86

Vauxelles 1958
L. Vauxelles, *Le Fauvisme*, Geneva 1958

Van Veen 1900
A. van Veen, 'P. Cornelis de Moor. Een beschouwing', *Elsevier's Geïllustreerd Maandschrift*, 10 (1900), vol. 20, pp. 97-116

Van Veen 1906
A. van Veen, 'Rotterdamsche kunstkring', *Algemeen Handelsblad*, 13 June 1906, p. 7

Venema 1978
A. Venema, 'Nederlandse schilders in Parijs, 1900-1914', *De Engelbewaarder*, Christmas annual 1978, pp. 151-206

Venema 1980
A. Venema, *Nederlandse schilders in Parijs 1900-1940*, Baarn 1980

Verheul 1926
J. Verheul, *Vijf en zeventig jarig bestaan van de academie van Beeldende Kunsten en Technische Wetenschappen te Rotterdam*, Rotterdam 1926

Veth 1905
C. Veth, 'Illustreerkunst hier te lande en elders', *De Kroniek*, 11 (1905), no. 535, pp. 92-93

Veth 1905
J. Veth, *Hollandsche teekenaars van dezen tijd*, Amsterdam 1905

Veth 1920
C. Veth, *De politieke prent in Nederland*, Leiden 1920

Veth 1921
C. Veth, *Geschiedenis van de Nederlandsche caricatuur en van de scherts in de Nederlandsche beeldende kunst*, Leiden 1921

Veth 1941
C. Veth, *Een eeuw Nederlandsche caricatuur*, Amsterdam 1941

Veth 1950
C. Veth, *Oude meesters der illustratie*, Alkmaar 1950

Visser 1913
J.C. Visser, 'De Rotterdamsche Kunstkring: een terugblik na twintig jaren', pp. 7-23, in *Gedenkboek Rotterdamsche Kunstkring 1893-1913*, Rotterdam 1913

De Vlaminck 1929
M. de Vlaminck, *Tournant dangereux. Souvenirs de ma vie*, Paris 1929

De Vlaminck 1943
M. de Vlaminck, *Portraits avant décès*, Paris 1943

Vollard 1957
A. Vollard, *Souvenirs d'un marchand de tableaux*, Paris 1957 (1938)

De Vos 1976
H. de Vos, *Geschiedenis van het socialisme in Nederland in het kader van zijn tijd*, vol. 1, Baarn 1976

De Vrankrijker 1950
A.C.J. de Vrankrijker, *Het wervende woord. Geschiedenis der socialistische week- en dagbladpers in Nederland*, Amsterdam 1950

De Vrankrijker 1972
A.C.J. de Vrankrijker, *Onze anarchisten en utopisten rond 1900*, Bussum 1972

Van Vree 1991
F. van Vree, 'De verlokkingen van de Zandstraat. Vertier aan de zelfkant van een stedelijke samenleving', pp. 25-42, in Kalb 1991

De Vries 1990
J. de Vries, *Gemeenschap en wereld-ik, geheel op de wijze der kunst. Nederlandse kunstkritiek en moderne kunst circa 1900-1920. Albert Verwey, Albert Plasschaert, Just Havelaar, Theo van Doesburg*, diss. Amsterdam (University of Amsterdam) 1990

Wagner 1985
A. Wagner, *Isaac Israels*, Venlo 1985

Ward 1994
M. Ward, 'From art criticism to art news: journalistic reviewing in late-nineteenth-century France', pp. 162-179, in Orwicz 1994

Wardwell Lee 1988
E. Wardwell Lee et al., exhib.cat., *Neo-impressionisten. Seurat tot Struycken*, Amsterdam (Rijksmuseum Vincent van Gogh) 1988

Warnod 1925
A. Warnod, *Les berceaux de la jeune peinture. Montmartre-Montparnasse*, Paris 1925

Warnod 1947
A. Warnod, *Ceux de la Butte*, Paris 1947

Warnod 1955
A. Warnod, *Fils de Montmartre. Souvenirs*, Paris 1955

Warnod 1965
A. Warnod, *Les peintres mes amis*, Paris 1965

Warnod 1986
J. Warnod, *Le bateau-lavoir*, Paris 1986

Wattenmaker 1993
R.J. Wattenmaker et al., *Great French paintings from the Barnes foundation. Impressionist, Post-impressionist, and Early Modern*, Boston, Toronto, London 1993

Week in beeld 1949
Anonymous, 'Kees van Dongens eerste liefde', *Week in beeld*, 2 July 1949, p.1 and pp. 14-15

Weisberg 1986
G.P. Weisberg, *Art Nouveau Bing. Paris style 1900*, Paris 1986

Welsh-Ovcharov 1988
B. Welsh-Ovcharov, exhib.cat., *Emile Bernard 1868-1941. The theme of bordellos and prostitutes in turn-of-the-century French art*, New Brunswick (The Jane Voorhees Zimmerli Art Museum) 1988

Werner 1965
A. Werner 'Van Dongen', *Arts Magazine*, 40 (1965), December, p. 20

Wiessing 1960
H.P.L. Wiessing, *Bewegend portret. Levensherinneringen*, Amsterdam 1960

Winkel 1986
H. Winkel, *De Ware Jacob. Spotblad uit het begin van de twintigste eeuw*, Amsterdam, Zutphen 1986

Wolf 1901
N.H. Wolf, 'Martinus Schildt', *Elsevier's Geïllustreerd Maandschrift*, 11 (1901), vol. 21, pp. 155-164

Wolfe 1994
J. Wolfe, 'Van Wim tot Bill de Kooning. Zeven decennia thematiek en vorm', *Jong Holland*, 10 (1994), no. 1, pp. 6-28

Van der Wolk 1990
J. van der Wolk, R. Pickvance, E.B.F. Fey, exhib.cat., *Vincent van Gogh. Tekeningen*, Otterlo (Rijksmusuem Kröller-Müller) 1990

Wouters 1988
F. Wouters et al., exhib.cat., *Jan Striening 1827-1903. Teekenmeester in Deventer en Rotterdam*, Zwolle 1988

Youngna 1980
K. Youngna, *The early works of Georges Braque, Raoul Dufy and Othon Friesz: the Le Havre group of fauvist painters*, diss. Ohio (The Ohio State University) 1980

Zeldin 1973
Th. Zeldin, *France 1849-1945. Ambition, love and politics*, vol. 1, Oxford 1973

Our special thanks go to the private collectors and public institutions who have kindly lent their valuable works for this exhibition. Many of the lenders wish to remain anonymous, but those we may name are.

Collection Frits Lugt, Institut Neérlandais, Paris
Fondation Pierre Gianadda, Martigny
Gemeentearchief Amsterdam, Amsterdam
Hannema de Stuers Fundatie, Heino
Hood Museum of Art, Hanover
Koninklijke Bibliotheek, The Hague
Kunsthalle Bremen, Bremen
Musée d'Art moderne de la Ville de Paris, Paris
Musée Toulouse-Lautrec et Galerie d'Art Moderne, Albi
Musée d'Art Moderne Richard Anacréon, Granville
Musée Léon Dierx, Saint-Denis (La Réunion)
Musée national d'art moderne/Centre de Création Industrielle, Centre Georges Pompidou, Paris
Musée Picasso, Paris
Nederlands Letterkundig Museum en Documentatiecentrum, The Hague
Norfolk Museum, Norfolk
Petit Palais, Musée d'Art Moderne, Geneva
Phoenix Art Museum, Phoenix
Rijksmuseum, Rijksprentenkabinet, Amsterdam
Société des lecteurs de Jean Paulhan et Librairie Giraud-Badin, Paris
Staatliche Museen zu Berlin, Kupferstichkabinett, Berlin
Stedelijk Museum, Amsterdam
Universiteitsbibliotheek Amsterdam, Amsterdam

Richard Benaïm
Mr and Mrs Carroll L. Cartwright
Fridart Foundation
La Galerie, Paris
Alain Lesieutre
Mrs Teresa Longyear and Mr David Bull
Françoise Marquet
Mrs Jane B. and Mr Leonard S. Meranus
Pierre Monart
Mr and Mrs Irving Moskovitz
Sara Lee/DE nv
N.T. Scheeres
Samir Traboulsi
Jacques Vandewalle
Kaneta Watanabe
Mr and Mrs Irwin and Margo Winkler

We are extremely grateful to the following people and establishments for their cooperation.

David Acton
(Worcester Art Museum)
Maryam Ansari-Rodari, Paris
Arthephot, Paris
Hubert Baya
(Rijksmuseum, Amsterdam)
Denise Bazetoux, Paris
Willem van Beek
(Library Stedelijk Museum, Amsterdam)
Jeanine Bailly-Herzberg, Paris
Anita Beloubek-Hammer
(Staatliche Museen zu Berlin, Kupferstichkabinett, Berlin)
Huguette Berès, Paris
Maître Philippe Bismuth, Paris
Carel Blotkamp
(Free University, Amsterdam)
Th.M. de Boer
(Kunsthandel M.L. de Boer, Amsterdam)
P.A. Boot
Jacqueline Boucher
Claude Bouret
(Bibliothèque Nationale, Estampes, Paris)
Ivo Bouwman
(Kunsthandel Ivo Bouwman, The Hague)
Dominique Brachlianoff, Dominique Dumas, Laurence Tilliard
(Musée des Beaux-Arts de Lyon)
Sylvie Brame
(Brame & Lorenceau, Paris)
Maître Francis Briest, Paris
Anthony Brown
(Connaught Brown, London)
Lillian Browse, Gustave Delbanco
(formerly Roland, Browse & Delbanco, London)
Ytzen Brusse
Margh van der Burgh, Pieter Ratsma, Mieke van Balen
(Gemeentelijke Archiefdienst Rotterdam)
Hans Buijs
(Fondation Custodia, Paris)
Françoise Cachin
Stefan Campo
(BVBA Stefan Campo, Antwerp)
Margaret Cergerès
(Etude Loudmer, Paris)
François Cheval
Françoise Cohen
(Musée des Beaux-Arts, Le Havre)
Marie-Cécille Comerre
(Drouot Documentation, Paris)
Crane Kalman Gallery, London
Magdalena Dabrowski
(The Museum of Modern Art, New York)
Louis Damen
(Paper conservator, Boijmans Van Beuningen Museum, Rotterdam)
Guy-Patrice en Michel Dauberville
(Bernheim-Jeune, Paris)
Liza Daum
(Bibliothèque Historique de la Ville de Paris)
Thierry Devynck
(Bibliothèque Forney, Paris)
Pim Donkersloot
Randi Doorman
Roland Dorn
(Cassirer-Archiv)
A.C.R. Dreesmann
Marina Ducrey
(Galerie Paul Vallotton SA, Lausanne)
Paul Duchein
Claude Duthuit
J.C. Ebbinge Wubbe
Adrian Biddell Kate Garmeson, Danielle Enoch
(Sotheby's London)
Rudi Ekkart, Jan Teeuwisse, Martha Op de Coul, Goos Dullaert
(Rijksbureau voor Kunsthistorische Documentatie, The Hague)
Rudolf Engers, Amsterdam
Matthijs Erdman
(Christie's London)
Carla Esser
Marina Ferrett -Bocquillon
Jean Forneris
(Musée des Beaux-Arts, Nice)
Judi Freeman
(Portland Museum of Art)
Galerie Félix Vercel, Paris
Galerie Gilbert & Paul Pétridès, Paris
Galerie Taménaga, Paris, Tokyo
Galleria Pieter Coray, Lugano
Galleria Annunciata, Milan
Françoise Garcia
(Musée et Galerie des Beaux-Arts de Bordeaux)
Mr and Mrs Gard-Kickert
Hans Geissler, Nachlass Erich Heckel
Gerlach Art Shipping, Amsterdam
The Getty Center for the History of Art and Humanities, Santa Monica
Léonard Gianadda
(Fondation Pierre Gianadda, Martigny)
Xavier Girard
(Musée Matisse, Cimiez)
Peter van der Graaf
Agnes C.M. Grondman
(Hannema-de Stuers Fundatie, Heino)
Wanda de Guébriant
(Archives Matisse, Paris)
Colin Harrison
(Ashmolean Museum of Art, Oxford)
Carlos van Hasselt
Mallory Hathaway, Laurel Beckett
(Sotheby's New York)
Catherine Heesterbeek
(Library, Koninklijke Musea voor Schone Kunsten, Brussels)
Herbert Henkels
Lien Heyting

Jetske Homan van der Heide
(Christie's Amsterdam)
Sjraar van Heugten, Fred Leeman, Louis van Tilborgh
(Van Gogh Museum, Amsterdam)
Michel Hoog, Paris
Mrs. Leonard Hutton
(Leonard Hutton Galleries)
Frans Jacobs
(Galerie K, Amsterdam)
A.M. de Jong-Hug
(E.J. van Wisselingh & Co, Naarden)
Mariette Josephus-Jitta, Tineke Groen
(Haags Gemeentemuseum, Prentenkabinet, The Hague)
Assia Kantor-Gukoyskaya
(Hermitage, St.Petersburg)
Fabrice van de Kerckhove
(Archives & Musée de la Littérature,
Koninklijke Musea voor Schone Kunsten, Brussels)
Gillian M. Kinloch, Adams Well
Joanna Kleiverda
Koninklijke Bibliotheek, The Hague
Michiaki Koshikawa
(The National Museum of Western Art, Tokyo)
Mevr. Kronenburg
(Library Wallraf-Richartz Museum, Cologne)
Irène Kuitenbrouwer Lesparre
Sunhild Kufferath
(Gallery Schröder und Leisewitz, Bremen)
Ellen Melas Kyriazi
Willem Laanstra, Amsterdam
Mary Lapides
(Christie's New York)
Quentin Laurens
(Galerie Louise Leiris, Paris)
Françoise Lechien
(Musée David et Alice van Buuren)
Pierre Lévy
Leendert van Lier
William S. Liebermann
(The Metropolitan Museum of Art, New York)
Maître Guy Loudmer, Paris
Michel Maket, Paris
Ron Manheim
Marlborough Fine Art, London
Maxwell Galleries LTD, San Francisco
Rainer Michael Mason
(Musée d'Art et d'Histoire, Geneva)
Kurt Meissner, Zürich
Piet Moget
(Lieu d'art contemporain, Hameau du Lac, Sigean)
Pierre Monart
Jean-Paul Monery
(Musée de l'Annonciade, Saint-Tropez)
Isabelle Monod-Fontaine, Didier Schulman, Evelyne Pomey,
Nathalie Leleu
(Musée national d'art moderne/Centre de Création
Industrielle, Centre Georges Pompidou, Paris)
Kazuto Morita
(Galerie Taménaga, Paris)
Jean-Pierre Moueix
Jacqueline Munck, Miriam Simon
(Musée d'Art moderne de la Ville de Paris)
Musée des Beaux-Arts et d'Archéologie, Besançon
Musée de Grenoble
National Art Library, Victoria & Albert Museum, London
Nederlands Letterkundig Museum en Documentatie-
centrum, The Hague
A.G. Nevill
(Frost & Reed, London)
Michiel Nijhoff
(Library Boijmans Van Beuningen Museum Rotterdam)
Kelly Pask
(Hood Museum of Art, Hanover)
Jacqueline Paulhan
Jean Penent
(Musée Paul Dupuy, Toulouse)
Photographie Giraudon, Paris
Ronald Pickvance
Jurrie Poot
(Stedelijk Museum, Amsterdam)
Louis Putman, Amsterdam
Joop van Roosmalen, Tilburg
Marc Rosen Fine Art, New York
Paul J. van Rosmalen
(Kunsthandel Borzo, 's-Hertogenbosch)
Peter Schatborn, Ger Luyten, Freek Heijbroek
(Rijksmuseum, Rijksprentenkabinet, Amsterdam)
Oscar Scheps, Danielle Hodel
(Petit Palais, Musée d'Art Moderne, Geneva)
Manuel Schmit
(Galerie Schmit, Paris)
Kitty Schreurs Fine Art BV
Werner J. Schweiger, Vienna
Schweizerisches Institut für Kunstwissenschaft, Zürich
David E. Scraze
(The Fitzwilliam Museum, Cambridge)
Service de Documentation de la Conservation
du Musée d'Orsay, Paris
Rob Sneep
(Sotheby's Amsterdam)
Ronald Spoor
Robert Stoppenbach
(Stoppenbach & Delestre, London)
Marguerite Tuyn
Evert van Uitert
(University of Amsterdam)
Monique Vatinel
(Musée Camille Pissarro, Pontoise)
Jacoba Vautier, Geneva
Françoise Viatte
(Musée du Louvre, Département des Arts Graphiques, Paris)
Dingenus van de Vrie, Peter van der Stel, Fred van der Wiel,
Tjibbe Spruit
(Print workshop and technicians, Boijmans Van Beuningen
Museum, Rotterdam)
Anita Vriends, Monique Hageman
(Library Van Gogh Museum, Amsterdam)
Anna Wagner
Jeanine Warnod
Jean Watelet
Pierre Wicart
Suzanne Vincent
Hans van der Windt
Witt Library, London
Zentralinstitut für Kunstgeschichte, Munich
Els van Zoest

Photo credits

Cat.
refers to the catalogue numbers for works by Kees van Dongen
Cat.am
refers to the catalogue numbers for works from his artistic milieu
Fig.
refers to the supporting illustrations (passim)

Frontispiece photo, fig. 1 p. 10, from De Telegraaf, 26 January 1952
Agence Photographique de la Réunion des Musées Nationaux, Paris: cat. 111
Ali-Elai Camerarts Inc., New York: cat. 21
Archief Rotterdams Dagblad, Rotterdam: fig. 17
The Art Institute of Chicago, Chicago: fig. A p. 303
Artephoto, Paris: cat. 33, cat.am 19
Artic Photodesign, The Hague: cat. 102
A. Basset, Lyons: cat. 50, 84, 85; cat.am 10; fig. B p. 146
Bibliothèque de l'Arsenal, Paris: fig. A p. 243
Bibliothèque Forney, Paris: fig. 12, 35, 36; fig. B p. 96, fig. A p. 147, fig. A p. 159, fig. A p. 172, fig. A p. 174, fig. A p. 185
Bibliothèque National, Paris: figs 32, 34, 39; fig. A p. 96, fig. A p. 152, figs A and B, p. 184, fig. A p. 225
Bibliothèque de l'Opéra, Paris: fig. C p. 156, fig. A p. 269
Brücke-Museum, Berlin: cat. 71, fig. A p. 156
Collection Frits Lugt, Institut Néerlandais, Paris: cat. 17
Author's collection: figs 3, 10, 13, 14, 19, 27, 44, 45, 46, 52, 53, 55, 58; fig. A p. 114, fig. A p. 206, figs A,B and D p. 212, fig. A p. 257, fig. A p. 300
Constance B. and Carroll L. Cartwright: cat. 26
Prudence Cumming Associates, London: cat.am 13
Edimadia, Paris: fig. 49
Fridart Foundation: cat. 123
La Galerie, Paris: cat. 44
Gemeentelijke Archiefdienst Rotterdam: fig. 16; fig. C p. 114, fig. A p. 285
Historisch-topografische Atlas, GA Amsterdam: cat. 64
Hood Museum of Art, Hanover: cat. 96
Leonard Hutton Galleries, New York: fig. B p. 114
J. Hyde, Paris: cat. 113
IMEC, Paris: cat. 113
IISG, Amsterdam: fig. 37
Koninklijke Bibliotheek, The Hague: figs 11, 15, 18, 24, 25, 26; fig. C p. 108, figs A and B p. 123, fig. C p. 212, fig. A p. 236, fig. A p. 264, figs A,B p. 269, fig. B p. 276
Kunsthalle Bremen, Bremen: cat. 129
Kunsthandel Borzo, 's-Hertogenbosch: cat. 127
Theresa Longyear and David Bull, Washington: cat. 57
Musée Besançon, Troyes: fig. 54
Musée Richard Anacréon, Granville: cat. 134
Musée Léon Dierx, Saint-Denis (La Réunion): cat. 23, 98
Musée Toulouse-Lautrec et Galerie d'Art Moderne, Albi: cat. 70, 76
Ph. Migeat, Paris: cat. 1, 72, 95; cat.am 11, cat.am 14; fig. 2; fig. A p. 276
Legacy of Otto van Rees: fig. D p. 214
NLMD, The Hague: cat. 110
Norfolk Museum, Norfolk: cat. 77, 78
Private collections: cat. 4, 9, 13, 14, 22, 35, 39, 40, 41, 42, 43, 45, 46, 47, 48, 49, 51, 52, 53, 55, 56, 66, 74, 75, 79, 83, 87, 90, 99, 101, 112, 116, 131; cat.am 17; fig. 30, 47, 48, 51, 56; A p. 134
Private collection, with thanks to Stefan Campo, Antwerp: cat. 69
Petit Palais, Musée d'Art Moderne, Geneva: cat.am 4, cat.am 5
Philadelphia Museum of Art, Philadelphia: fig. A p. 301
Phoenix Art Museum, Phoenix: cat. 27
Photothèque des Musées de la Ville de Paris: cat. 3, 37, 80
H. Preisig, Martigny: cat.am 18
Netherlands Office for Fine Art, The Hague: fig. 1; fig. A p. 86, A-B p. 208
N.T. Scheeres, Amsterdam: cat.am 2
Schröder und Leisewitz, Bremen: cat. 133
Seventh Square, Pascal Faligot, Paris: cat. 89
Sotheby's London: cat. 25; fig. 4, 5, 6, 21; fig. C p. 123, fig. A p. 151
Sotheby's New York: cat. 107
Staatliche Museen zu Berlin, Preussischer Kulturbesitz, Kupferstichkabinett, Berlin: cat. 54, 81, 82
Stedelijk Museum Amsterdam: cat.am 1
Stichting Rijksmuseum Amsterdam: cat. 16, 18, 19, 28, 29, 30; fig. A-D p. 116, fig. A p. 118
Studio Tom Haartsen, Oudekerk aan de IJssel: cat. 2, 5, 6, 7, 8, 10, 11, 12, 15, 20, 24, 31, 32, 34, 36, 38, 58, 59, 60, 61, 62, 63, 65, 67, 68, 73, 88, 91, 92, 93, 94, 97, 100, 103, 105, 106, 108, 109, 114, 115, 118, 119, 120, 121, 122, 124, 125, 126, 132, 135; cat.am 3, am 6 am 7, am 8, am 9, am 12, am 15, am 16, am 20 (copyright H. Matisse), am 21, am 22; fig. 6, 8, 9, 10, 20, 22, 23, 28, 29, 31, 38, 40, 41, 43, 50, 57; fig. A p. 90, A p. 91, B p. 96, A and C p. 102, A and B p. 108, A-D p. 132, A p. 133, A p. 164, A-D p. 166, A-D p. 167, E (copyright H. Matisse) p. 208, C p. 314 A p. 233, A p. 234, B p. 243, A p. 272, A p. 289
Samir Traboulsi, Paris: fig. A p. 240
Valéry Wallace, Paris: cat. 128
Foto Westerink, Zwolle: cat 136, fig. 7

Catalogue editor and exhibition curator
Anita Hopmans

Exhibition organization
Anita Hopmans
Maartje de Haan
Christian Briend
Manfred Sellink

Secretarial support
Anke Smit
Mariëtte van der Waal

English translation
Wendie Shaffer
Michèle Hendricks
Annabel Howland
Kate Williams

Design
Gracia Lebbink

Typesetting
Holger Schoorl

Printing
Snoeck-Ducaju & Zoon nv, Gent

Production supervision
Jan van Cappellen

Print numbers
English edition: 1200

ISBN 90-6918-170-3

Corporate Members of
the Boijmans Van Beuningen Museum:

ABN AMRO Bank N.V.
CALDIC
Internatio-Müller NV
DURA BOUW ROTTERDAM B.V.
Rollins Hudig Hall Nederland
Koninklijke Nedlloyd N.V.
Unilever
Loyens & Volkmaars
Koninklijke Econosto N.V.
Koninklijke Pakhoed N.V.
MeesPierson N.V.
Gimbrère en Dohmen Software B.V.
Hollandsche Beton Maatschappij bv
Generale Bank Nederland N.V.
Moret Ernst & Young
Nauta Dutilh
Siemens Nederland N.V.
PTT Telecom District Rotterdam
Bakker Beheer Barendrecht BV
Mobil Oil B.V.
Nationale Nederlanden
Van der Vorm Vastgoed B.V.
Heineken Nederland B.V.
Glaxo Wellcome B.V.
HAL Investments B.V.
KPMG Accountants Belastingadviseurs Consultants
EOE-Optiebeurs
SGS Nederland B.V.
Stichting Organisatie van Effectenhandelaren te Rotterdam
Hagé International B.V.
Parc Makelaars
Nidera Handelscompagnie b.v.
Automobielbedrijf J. van Dijk & Dochters b.v.
KOEN VISSER GROEP
Stad Rotterdam Verzekeringen
Gebrs. Coster Beheer B.V.
Croon Elektrotechniek B.V.
Van Dijk Delft B.V.